T0335478

Ontologies and Big Data Considerations for Effective Intelligence

Joan Lu
University of Huddersfield, UK

Qiang Xu
University of Huddersfield, UK

A volume in the Advances in Information Quality and Management (AIQM) Book Series

www.igi-global.com

Published in the United States of America by
   IGI Global
   Information Science Reference (an imprint of IGI Global)
   701 E. Chocolate Avenue
   Hershey PA, USA 17033
   Tel: 717-533-8845
   Fax: 717-533-8661
   E-mail: cust@igi-global.com
   Web site: http://www.igi-global.com

                       Library of Congress Cataloging-in-Publication Data
Names: Lu, Zhongyu, 1955- editor. | Xu, Qiang, 1963- editor.
Title: Ontologies and big data considerations for effective intelligence /
   Joan Lu and Qiang Xu, editors.
Description: Hershey, PA : Information Science Reference, [2017] | Includes
   bibliographical references and index.
Identifiers: LCCN 2016052556| ISBN 9781522520580 (H/C) | ISBN 9781522520597
   (eISBN)
Subjects: LCSH: Data mining. | Big data. | Ontologies (Information retrieval)
Classification: LCC QA76.9.D343 O58 2017 | DDC 006.3/12--dc23 LC record available at https://lccn.loc.gov/2016052556

This book is published in the IGI Global book series Advances in Information Quality and Management (AIQM) (ISSN:
2331-7701; eISSN: 2331-771X)

British Cataloguing in Publication Data
A Cataloguing in Publication record for this book is available from the British Library.

All work contributed to this book is new, previously-unpublished material. The views expressed in this book are those of the
authors, but not necessarily of the publisher.

For electronic access to this publication, please contact: eresources@igi-global.com.

Advances in Information Quality and Management (AIQM) Book Series

Siddhartha Bhattacharyya
RCC Institute of Information Technology, India

ISSN:2331-7701
EISSN:2331-771X

MISSION

Acquiring and managing quality information is essential to an organization's success and profitability. Innovation in information technology provides managers, researchers, and practitioners with the tools and techniques needed to create and adapt new policies, strategies, and solutions for information management.

The **Advances in Information Quality and Management (AIQM) Book Series** provides emerging research principals in knowledge society for the advancement of future technological development. This series aims to increase available research publications and emphasize the global response within the discipline and allow for audiences to benefit from the comprehensive collection of this knowledge.

COVERAGE

- E-Collaboration
- Application of IT to Operation
- Human and Societal Issue
- IT Management in Public Organizations
- Knowledge Management
- Decision Support and Group Decision Support Systems
- Supply Chain Management
- Emerging Technologies Management
- Mobile Commerce
- Web services and technologies

IGI Global is currently accepting manuscripts for publication within this series. To submit a proposal for a volume in this series, please contact our Acquisition Editors at Acquisitions@igi-global.com or visit: http://www.igi-global.com/publish/.

Titles in this Series

For a list of additional titles in this series, please visit: www.igi-global.com

Handbook of Research on Information Architecture and Management in Modern Organizations
George Leal Jamil (Informações em Rede, Brazil) José Poças Rascão (Polytechnic Institute of Setúbal, Portugal)
Fernanda Ribeiro (Porto University, Portugal) and Armando Malheiro da Silva (Porto University, Portugal)
Information Science Reference • copyright 2016 • 625pp • H/C (ISBN: 9781466686373) • US $325.00 (our price)

Inventive Approaches for Technology Integration and Information Resources Management
Mehdi Khosrow-Pour (Information Resources Management Association, USA)
Information Science Reference • copyright 2014 • 315pp • H/C (ISBN: 9781466662568) • US $205.00 (our price)

Quality Innovation Knowledge, Theory, and Practices
Latif Al-Hakim (University of Southern Queensland, Australia) and Chen Jin (Zhejiang University, China)
Information Science Reference • copyright 2014 • 640pp • H/C (ISBN: 9781466647695) • US $245.00 (our price)

Rethinking the Conceptual Base for New Practical Applications in Information Value and Quality
George Leal Jamil (FUMEC University, Brazil) Armando Malheiro (Universidade do Porto, Portugal) and Fernanda
Ribeiro (Universidade do Porto, Portugal)
Information Science Reference • copyright 2014 • 345pp • H/C (ISBN: 9781466645622) • US $175.00 (our price)

Cases on Electronic Records and Resource Management Implementation in Diverse Environments
Janice Krueger (Clarion University of Pennsylvania, USA)
Information Science Reference • copyright 2014 • 467pp • H/C (ISBN: 9781466644663) • US $175.00 (our price)

www.igi-global.com

701 E. Chocolate Ave., Hershey, PA 17033
Order online at www.igi-global.com or call 717-533-8845 x100
To place a standing order for titles released in this series, contact: cust@igi-global.com
Mon-Fri 8:00 am - 5:00 pm (est) or fax 24 hours a day 717-533-8661

Table of Contents

Detailed Table of Contents

Section 1

Chapter 1

Carson K.-S. Leung, University of Manitoba, Canada
Christopher L. Carmichael, University of Manitoba, Canada
Patrick Johnstone, University of Manitoba, Canada
Roy Ruokun Xing, University of Manitoba, Canada
David Sonny Hung-Cheung Yuen, University of Manitoba, Canada

High volumes of a wide variety of data can be easily generated at a high velocity in many real-life applications. Implicitly embedded in these big data is previously unknown and potentially useful knowledge such as frequently occurring sets of items, merchandise, or events. Different algorithms have been proposed for either retrieving information about the data or mining the data to find frequent sets, which are usually presented in a lengthy textual list. As "a picture is worth a thousand words", the use of visual representations can enhance user understanding of the inherent relationships among the mined frequent sets. However, many of the existing visualizers were not designed to visualize these mined frequent sets. This book chapter presents an interactive next-generation visual analytic system. The system enables the management, visualization, and advanced analysis of the original big data and the frequent sets mined from the data.

Chapter 2

Robab Saadatdoost, Islamic Azad University, Parand Branch, Iran
Alex Tze Hiang Sim, Universiti Teknologi Malaysia, Malaysia
Hosein Jafarkarimi, Islamic Azad University, Damavand Branch, Iran
Jee Mei Hee, Universiti Teknologi Malaysia, Malaysia

This project presents the patterns and relations between attributes of Iran Higher Education data gained from the use of data mining techniques to discover knowledge and use them in decision making system of IHE. Large dataset of IHE is difficult to analysis and display, since they are significant for decision making in IHE. This study utilized the famous data mining software, Weka and SOM to mine and visualize

IHE data. In order to discover worthwhile patterns, we used clustering techniques and visualized the results. The selected dataset includes data of five medical university of Tehran as a small data set and Ministry of Science - Research and Technology's universities as a larger data set. Knowledge discovery and visualization are necessary for analyzing of these datasets. Our analysis reveals some knowledge in higher education aspect related to program of study, degree in each program, learning style, study mode and other IHE attributes. This study helps to IHE to discover knowledge in a visualize way; our results can be focused more by experts in higher education field to assess and evaluate more.

Chapter 3

Grace L. Samson, University of Huddersfield, UK
Joan Lu, University of Huddersfield, UK
Mistura M. Usman, University of Abuja, Nigeria
Qiang Xu, University of Huddersfield, UK

Spatial databases maintain space information which is appropriate for applications where there is need to monitor the position of an object or event over space. Spatial databases describe the fundamental representation of the object of a dataset that comes from spatial or geographic entities. A spatial database supports aspects of space and offers spatial data types in its data model and query language. The spatial or geographic referencing attributes of the objects in a spatial database permits them to be positioned within a two (2) dimensional or three (3) dimensional space. This chapter looks into the fundamentals of spatial databases and describes their basic component, operations and architecture. The study focuses on the data models, query Language, query processing, indexes and query optimization of a spatial databases that approves spatial databases as a necessary tool for data storage and retrieval for multidimensional data of high dimensional spaces.

Chapter 4

Reda Mohamed Hamou, University of Saïda, Algeria
Abdelmalek Amine, University of Saïda, Algeria
Moulay Tahar, University of Saïda, Algeria

Spam is now of phenomenal proportions since it represents a high percentage of total emails exchanged on the Internet. In the fight against spam, we are using this article to develop a hybrid algorithm based primarily on the probabilistic model in this case, Naïve Bayes, for weighting the terms of the matrix term -category and second place used an algorithm of unsupervised learning (K-means) to filter two classes, namely spam and ham (legitimate email). To determine the sensitive parameters that make up the classifications we are interested in studying the content of the messages by using a representation of messages using the n-gram words and characters independent of languages (because a message may be received in any language) to later decide what representation to use to get a good classification. We have chosen several metrics as evaluation to validate our results.

Chapter 5

Baramee Navanopparatskul, Chulalongkorn University, Thailand
Sukree Sinthupinyo, Chulalongkorn University, Thailand
Pirongrong Ramasoota, Chulalongkorn University, Thailand

Following the enactment of computer crime law in Thailand, online service providers are compelled to control illegal content including content that is deemed harmful or problematic. This situation leads to self-censorship of intermediaries, often resulting in overblocking to avoid violating the law. Such filtering flaw both infringes users' freedom of expression and impedes the business of OSPs in Thailand. The Innovative Retrieval System (IRS) is thus developed to investigate intermediary censorship in online discussion forum, Pantip.com, as a case study of social media. The result shows that there is no consistency of censorship pattern on the website at all. The censorship criteria depend on type of content in each forum. Overblocking is also high, over 70% of removed content, due to intimidation of governmental agencies, lawsuits from business organizations, and fear of intermediary liability. Website administrator admitted that he would cut off some users to avoid business troubles.

Chapter 6

Natalia Danilova, City University London, UK
David Stupples, City University London, UK

A semantic Web-based search method is introduced that automates the correlation of topic-related content for discovery of hitherto unknown intelligence from disparate and widely diverse Web-sources. This method is in contrast to traditional search methods that are constrained to specific or narrowly defined topics. The method is based on algorithms from Natural Language Processing combined with techniques adapted from grounded theory and Dempster-Shafer theory to significantly enhance the discovery of related Web-sourced intelligence. This paper describes the development of the method by showing the integration of the mathematical models used. Real-world worked examples demonstrate the effectiveness of the method with supporting performance analysis, showing that the quality of the extracted content is significantly enhanced comparing to the traditional Web-search approaches.

Chapter 7

Faisal Tawfiq Ammari, University of Huddersfield, UK
Joan Lu, University of Huddersfield, UK

The eXtensible Markup Language (XML) has been widely adopted in many financial institutions in their daily transactions. This adoption was due to the flexible nature of XML providing a common syntax for systems messaging in general and in financial messaging in specific. Excessive use of XML in financial transactions messaging created an aligned interest in security protocols integrated into XML solutions in order to protect exchanged XML messages in an efficient yet powerful mechanism. However, financial institutions (i.e. banks) perform large volume of transactions on daily basis which require securing XML messages on large scale. Securing large volume of messages will result performance and resource issues. Therefore, an approach is needed to secure specified portions of an XML document, syntax and processing rules for representing secured parts. In this research we have developed a smart approach for securing financial XML transactions using effective and intelligent fuzzy classification techniques. Our approach defines the process of classifying XML content using a set of fuzzy variables. Upon fuzzy classification phase, a unique value is assigned to a defined attribute named "Importance Level". Assigned value indicates the data sensitivity for each XML tag. The research also defines the process of securing classified financial XML message content by performing element-wise XML encryption on selected parts defined in fuzzy classification phase. Element-wise encryption is performed using symmetric encryption using AES algorithm with different key sizes. Key size of 128-bit is being used on tags classified with "Medium" importance level; a key size of 256-bit is being used on tags classified with "High" importance level. An implementation has been performed on a real-life environment using online banking system in Jordan Ahli Bank one of the leading banks in Jordan to demonstrate its flexibility, feasibility, and efficiency. Our experimental results of the system verified tangible enhancements in encryption efficiency, processing-time reduction, and resulting XML message sizes. Finally, our proposed system was designed, developed, and evaluated using a live data extracted from an internet banking service in one of the leading banks in Jordan. The results obtained from our experiments are promising, showing that our model can provide an effective yet resilient support for financial systems to secure exchanged financial XML messages.

Chapter 8

  Yousef E. Rabadi, University of Huddersfield, UK
  Joan Lu, University of Huddersfield, UK

TCP and UDP communication protocols are the most widely used transport methods for carrying out XML data messages between different services. XML data security is always a big concern especially when using internet cloud. Common XML encryption techniques encrypt part of private sections of the XML file as an entire block of text and apply these techniques directly on them. Man-in-the-Middle and Cryptanalysts can generate statistical information, tap, sniff, hack, inject and abuse XML data messages. The purpose of this study is to introduce architecture of new approach of exchanging XML data files between different Services in order to minimize the risk of any alteration, data loss, data abuse, data misuse of XML critical business data information during transmission; by implementing a vertical partitioning on XML files. Another aim is to create a virtual environment within internet cloud prior to data transmission in order to utilise the communication method and rise up the transmission performance along with resources utilisation and spreads the partitioned XML file (shredded) through several paths within multi agents that form a multipath virtual network. Virtualisation in cloud network infrastructure to take advantage of its scalability, operational efficiency, and control of data flow are considered in this architecture. A customized UDP Protocol in addition to a pack of modules in RIDX adds a reliable (Lossless) and Multicast data transmission to all nodes in a virtual cloud network. A comparative study has been made to measure the performance of the Real-time Interactive Data Exchange system (RIDX) using RIDX UDP protocol against standard TCP protocol. Starting from 4 nodes up to 10 nodes in the domain, the results showed an enhanced performance using RIDX architecture over the standard TCP protocol.

Ad targeting has been receiving more and more attention in the online publishing world, where advertisers want their ads to be seen by potential consumers at the right time. This chapter aims to address the major challenges with user queries in the context of behavioral targeting advertising by proposing a user intent representation strategy and a query enhancement mechanism. The authors focus on investigating the intent based user classification performance and the effectiveness of user segmentation under a topic model that helps explore semantic relation between user queries in behavioral targeting. In addition, the authors propose an alternative to define user's search intent for the evaluation purpose, in the case that the dataset is sanitized.

Section 2

Ontology has been a subject of many studies carried out in artificial intelligence (AI) and information system communities. Ontology has become an important component of the semantic web, covering a variety of knowledge domains. Although building domain ontologies still remains a big challenge with regard to its designing and implementation, there are still many areas that need to create ontologies. Information Science (IS) is one of these areas that need a unified ontology model to facilitate information access among the heterogeneous data resources and share a common understanding of the domain knowledge. The objective of this study is to develop a generic model of ontology that serves as a foundation of knowledge modelling for applications and aggregation with other ontologies to facilitate information exchanging between different systems. This model will be a metadata for a knowledge base system to be used in different purposes of interest, such as education applications to support educational needs for teachers and students and information system developers, and enhancing the index tool in libraries to facilitate access to information collections. The findings of the research revealed that overall feedback from the IS community has been positive and that the model met the ontology quality criteria. It was appropriate to provide consistency and clear understanding of the subject area. OIS ontology unifies information science, which is composed of library science, computer science and archival science, by creating the theoretical base useful for further practical systems. Developing ontology of information science (OIS) is not an easy task, due to the complex nature of the field. It needs to be integrated with other ontologies such as social science, cognitive science, philosophy, law management and mathematics, to provide a basic knowledge for the semantic web and also to leverage information retrieval.

Chapter 11

The literature review gives the background to the research process, which consisted of three main aspects to find out the theoretical background essential to this project. These aspects were: ontological engineering, Information Science, and Communities of Practice within knowledge management. The following sections provide an overview of key literature relevant to this project. Firstly, however, the background starts with some basic definitions to establish what is meant by ontology and what the significance of creating ontology is. The survey will come back to the three key aspects of this study and review literature on these; firstly, ontology.

Chapter 12

In the previous chapter we have discussed the main fields related to the research: ontological engineering, knowledge management, and Virtual communities of practice. As stated before, our concern is representing domain knowledge by creating OIS ontology. After reviewing the ontology literature to find an appropriate theoretical perspective focusing on the content-related variables for theoretical model construction, we found that theories can help to define formal ontological properties that contribute to characterising the concepts. Meanwhile, ontologists nowadays have a choice of formal frameworks which derive from formal logic, algebra, category theory, set theory and Mereotopology. However, to gain a better understand of OIS ontology development and its role in semantic web, the framework is established to describe the main theoretical base. The theoretical base of our framework is based on ontology theoretic.

Chapter 13

This chapter presents the development of OIS ontology and the main elements that formalised in OWL-DL. The OIS ontology followed Methontology as a general framework of methodology. The main result will be introduced, namely, the modelling design of OIS ontology which follows the description of the activities involved in designing the OIS ontology model. The OIS ontology model identifies the terms and definitions in the IS domain. Also, designing the ontocop system and how it can be a useful platform for supporting and assessing the OIS ontology. It starts by introducing OIS designing methodology. At the end of this chapter we will discuss how this tool will help to develop the OIS ontology to be modelled in a comprehensive and consistent manner.

Ontology development is meaningful and useful for both users and IR; therefore, it needs to be evaluated. In this chapter, we are going to test and evaluate the results produced in the research, which is the development of the OIS ontology life cycle. It describes the testing and validation which was applied to the whole model from the initial implementation to ensure consistency of modelled knowledge. The evaluation objective was to collect feedback on OIS ontology by using our evaluation system. The Ontocop system is a platform that has been implemented to get feedback from the IS community. The feedback is assessing and eliciting further details that support the ontology development. The evaluation and discussion will be at two levels based on Gòmez-Pérez's view.

Chapter 15

This study is concluded in this chapter. The research problem and questions derived from it are answered. In addition, the achievements and the limitations of this study are discussed. The research started with identifying the problem. To achieve these objectives, the OIS was designed and developed. Feedback and evaluation from the domain's experts has led to constant improvement in the ontology's development. The current version of the OIS ontology is presented in this research. At the end of this chapter, possible research leads for the future are suggested. The study aimed at the creation of OIS ontology of Information Science domain to visualise its knowledge, in order to be integrated with other ontologies to be applied for a specific application. The resulting ontology covers three main areas of domain knowledge: library science, archival science and computing science. The vocabularies of these branches are formalised in class hierarchy with relations which are interconnecting concepts from all these areas, in order to define a sufficient model of the Information Science domain.

Preface

OVERVIEW

Information retrieval is a classical topic. Most existing books in the area are textbooks, which go back to 1963's *Natural Language and Computer* (Garvin, 1963). A number of books were published in 1990s. The books were mainly focused on document engineering, as addressed in *Text-Based Intelligent Systems: Current Research and Practice in Information Extraction and Retrieval* (Jacobs, 1992), *Lexical Acquisition: Exploiting On-Line Resources to Build a Lexicon* (Zernik, 1991), and *From Documentation to Information Science: The Beginnings and Early Development of the American Documentation Institute* (Farkas-Conn, 1990), and rarely extended to interdisciplinary and multiple disciplinary collaborations.

In 2008, a book titled *An Introduction to Information Retrieval* by Christopher D. Manning, Prabhakar Raghavan, and Hinrich Schütze was published. The book introduced some theories and technology, such as Web, Internet, and XML into the topic area. However, the focus of the book is still on the publishing area.

In 2010, Stefan Büttcher, Charles L. A. Clarke, and Gordon V. Cormack published a book titled *Information Retrieval: Implementing and Evaluating Search Engines*. This textbook provided detailed materials for the students at both theoretic and practical levels mainly in the search engines that were used in IR.

In 1999 a textbook titled *Modern Information Retrieval* by Ricardo Baeza-Yates and Berthier Ribeiro-Neto was published by Anderson Wesley Longman. This chapter-based book was written by leading researchers, each chapter for one topic in the subject area. However, powerful environments like distributed systems (e.g. Grid, Cloud, etc.) for IR were still in laboratory-based investigations at that time, or were not developed at all. Thus, this knowledge introduced in this book certainly needs to be updated.

Likewise, in 2015, Springer published a research-based book titled *Advances in Information Retrieval* (Hanbury, Kazai, Rauber, & Fuhr, 2015). This book is the conference proceedings that revealed there is no systematically serious research approach as the contents are a collection of short papers. Table 1 shows a summery for the requested information, although they are not completely presented.

In the light of above, Information Retrieval (IR) is experiencing a challenge moving forward from traditional technology to emerging technologies. Today's IR needs the support from Web services, distributed systems (e.g. Cloud storage), security measures, big data science, including static text message passing and dynamic imaging processing, dynamic data streaming, and data visualization. Single technology, single topic and discipline are insufficient to cope with the fast increase of data/document exchanging and transferring speed and volume, variety of resources, and maintaining the quality of data.

Table 1. Published books on information retrieval

Titles	Authors	Publisher	Price	Year	Pages
Natural Language and the Computer	Paul L. Garvin	McGraw-Hill	Not found	1963	420
Text-Based Intelligent Systems: Current Research and Practice in Information Extraction and Retrieval	Paul S. Jacobs	Lawrence Erlbaum Associates	£61.6	1992	300
From Documentation to Information Science: The Beginnings and Early Development of the American Documentation Institute	Irene S. Farkas-Conn	Greenwood Press	£74 (Amazon)	1990	248
Lexical Acquisition: Exploiting On-Line Resources to Build a Lexicon	Uri Zernik	Lawrence Erlbaum Associates	Hardcover, £95 Paper cover, £51.59 (Amazon)	1991	216
Modern Information Retrieval	Ricardo Baeza-Yates and Berthier Ribeiro-Neto	Addison Wesley Longman	£24.99 (Amazon)	1999	544
Introduction to Information Retrieval	Christopher D. Manning, Prabhakar Raghavan, and Hinrich Schütze	Cambridge University Press	£39.99 (Amazon)	2008	506
Information Retrieval: Implementing and Evaluating Search Engines	Stefan Büttcher, Charles L. A. Clarke, and Gordon V. Cormack	MIT Press	£44.95 (Amazon)	2010	632
Advances in Information Retrieval	Hanbury, Kazai, Rauber, and Fuhr	37th European Conference on IR Research, ECIR 2015, Vienna, Austria, March 29 - April 2, 2015. Proceedings, Series: Lecture Notes in Computer Science, Vol. 9022, Subseries: Information Systems and Applications, incl. Internet/Web, and HCI	£74	2015	894

HOW THE TOPIC FITS INTO TODAY'S WORLD

The proposed book integrates emerging technologies into the IR domain. The organisation of the book is a research-based structure that differs from other existing textbooks and from chapter-based short paper collections. The topics are uniquely presented in retrieval and extraction, such as ontology, e-reading, particularly related to the education for the children, XML security, a sensitive topic in modern document retrieval, data transferring in distributed systems, image processing, which involves large data process and is always debated in the latest research topic of big data science, and the contributions of distributed systems to IR. Each section is a complete piece of research consisting of several chapters. Researchers, students, professors, lecturers, and professionals at different levels can benefit from the materials provided in the book. The authors of this book are from international communities from countries in Europe (the UK), the Middle East (Jordan, Libya), and the Far East (China) that may provide a good marketing opportunity to promote the book in the near future.

THE TARGET AUDIENCE

Immediate audiences for this book are from the area of information retrieval around world. The book targets the readers who are interested in the latest theories, methods, technologies, and tools for IR in interdisciplinary and multidisciplinary research and applications; researchers who are working in higher education, industrial companies, and professional bodies can also benefit from the book; professors, lectures, and teachers from a wide range of subject areas can benefit from the book if they are interested in IR. The book can be an inspiration for research initiatives, reading material for educators and students, and a library collection for this fast-developing subject area with emerging cutting-edge technologies.

THE IMPORTANCE OF EACH OF THE CHAPTER

This book is organized in 2 sections with 15 chapters. Section 1 is about "Big Data Consideration and Data Technologies." Section 2 is about "A Generic Model of Ontology to Visualize Information Science Domain (OIS)." The importance of each chapter will be introduced as follows.

Chapter 1 presents an investigation into interactive visual analytics of big data. High volumes of a wide variety of data can be easily generated at a high velocity in many real-life applications. Implicitly embedded in these big data is previously unknown and potentially useful knowledge such as frequently occurring sets of items, merchandise, or events. Different algorithms have been proposed for either retrieving information about the data or mining the data to find frequent sets, which are usually presented in a lengthy textual list. As "a picture is worth a thousand words", the use of visual representations can enhance user understanding of the inherent relationships among the mined frequent sets. However, many of the existing visualizers were not designed to visualize these mined frequent sets. This book chapter presents an interactive next-generation visual analytic system. The system enables the management, visualization, and advanced analysis of the original data and the frequent sets mined from the data.

Chapter 2 presents a research into Knowledge Discovery for Large Databases in Education Institutes. This project presents the patterns and relations between attributes of Iran Higher Education (Iran Higher Education) data gained from the use of data mining techniques to discover knowledge and use them in decision making system of IHE. Large dataset of IHE is difficult to analysis and display, since they are significant for decision making in IHE. This study utilized the famous data mining software, Weka and SOM to mine and visualize IHE data. In order to discover worthwhile patterns, we used clustering techniques and visualized the results. The selected dataset includes data of five medical university of Tehran as a small data set and Ministry of Science - Research and Technology's universities as a larger data set. Knowledge discovery and visualization are necessary for analyzing of these datasets. Our analysis reveals some knowledge in higher education aspect related to program of study, degree in each program, learning style, study mode and other IHE attributes. This study helps to IHE to discover knowledge in a visualize way; our results can be focused more by experts in higher education field to assess and evaluate more.

Chapter 3 brings an overview in spatial databases. Spatial databases maintain space information which is appropriate for applications where there is need to monitor the position of an object or event over space. Spatial databases describe the fundamental representation of the object of a dataset that comes from spatial or geographic entities. A spatial database supports aspects of space and offers spatial data types in its data model and query language. The spatial or geographic referencing attributes of the objects in a spatial database permits them to be positioned within a two (2) dimensional or three (3) dimensional space. This chapter looks into the fundamentals of spatial databases and describes their basic component, operations and architecture. The study focuses on the data models, query Language, query processing, indexes and query optimization of a spatial databases that approves spatial databases as a necessary tool for data storage and retrieval for multidimensional data of high dimensional spaces.

Chapter 4 discusses the impact of the mode of data representation for the result quality of the detection and filtering of spam. Spam is now seized of the Internet in phenomenal proportions since it high represents a percentage of total emails exchanged on the Internet. In the fight against spam, we are interested in this article to develop a hybrid algorithm based primarily on the probabilistic model in this case Naïve Bayes for weighting the terms of the matrix term -category and second place used an algorithm of unsupervised learning (K-means) to filter two classes namely spam and ham. To determine the sensitive parameters that improve the classifications we are interested in studying the content of the messages by using a representation of messages by the n-gram words and characters independent of languages (because a message may be received in any language) to later decide what representation opt to get a good classification. We have chosen several metrics evaluation to validate our results.

Chapter 5 demonstrates a research work in innovation of retrieval system to investigate censorship online social media. Provision of intermediary liability in computer crime law in Thailand has induced online service providers to control illegal content including content that is deemed harmful or problematic excessively. The constructed Innovative Retrieval System (IRS) had investigated four forums in the most popular social media forum in Thailand, Pantip.com, and found that excessive censorship or overclocking in the website is prevalent. There is no consistency of censorship pattern among forums. The censorship criteria depend mostly on type of content in each forum and the judgment of website administrator. The result of IRS investigation also found that overclocking rate in each forum is quite high. Over 70% of all content removed were not illegal. They were all removed because online service providers are fear of three factors: intimidation of governmental agencies, threat of lawsuits from business organizations, and fear of intermediary liability. Even if such censorship flaw both infringes users' freedom of expression and impedes the social media business, website administrator *admitted that it would worth it to cut off some users to avoid troubles*. Therefore, government interference and intermediary liability provision in computer crime law are likely to be main obstacles threatening not only ingenious communication of the public, but also Internet business, innovation, and economic growth. The investment and growth in the Internet industry in Thailand would be deterred as long as these obstacles remain.

Chapter 6 researches into semantic approach to web-based discovery of unknowns to enhance intelligence gathering. A semantic Web-based search method is introduced that automates the correlation of topic-related content for discovery of hitherto unknown intelligence from disparate and widely diverse Web-sources. This method is in contrast to traditional search methods that are constrained to specific or narrowly defined topics. The method is based on algorithms from Natural Language Processing combined with techniques adapted from grounded theory and Dempster-Shafer theory to significantly enhance the discovery of related Web-sourced intelligence. This paper describes the development of the method by showing the integration of the mathematical models used. Real-world worked examples demonstrate the effectiveness of the method with supporting performance analysis, showing that the quality of the extracted content is significantly enhanced comparing to the traditional Web-search approaches.

Chapter 7 presents the research that defines the process of securing classified financial XML message content by performing element-wise XML encryption on selected parts defined in fuzzy classification phase. Element-wise encryption is performed using symmetric encryption using AES algorithm with different key sizes. Key size of 128-bit is being used on tags classified with "Medium" importance level; a key size of 256-bit is being used on tags classified with "High" importance level. An implementation has been performed on a real-life environment using online banking system in Jordan Ahli Bank one of the leading banks in Jordan to demonstrate its flexibility, feasibility, and efficiency. Our experimental results of the system verified tangible enhancements in encryption efficiency, processing-time reduction, and resulting XML message sizes. Finally, our proposed system was designed, developed, and evaluated using a live data extracted from an internet banking service in one of the leading banks in Jordan. The results obtained from our experiments are promising, showing that our model can provide an effective yet resilient support for financial systems to secure exchanged financial XML messages.

Chapter 8 discusses about building a secured XML Real-Time interactive data exchange architecture. TCP and UDP communication protocols are the most widely used transport methods for carrying out XML data messages between different services. XML data security is always a big concern especially when using internet cloud. Common XML encryption techniques encrypt part of private sections of the XML file as an entire block of text and apply these techniques directly on them. Man-in-the-Middle and Cryptanalysts can generate statistical information, tap, sniff, hack, inject and abuse XML data messages. The purpose of this study is to introduce architecture of new approach of exchanging XML data files between different Services in order to minimize the risk of any alteration, data loss, data abuse, data misuse of XML critical business data information during transmission; by implementing a vertical partitioning on XML files. Another aim is to create a virtual environment within internet cloud prior to data transmission in order to utilise the communication method and rise up the transmission performance along with resources utilisation and spreads the partitioned XML file (shredded) through several paths within multi agents that form a multipath virtual network. Virtualisation in cloud network infrastructure to take advantage of its scalability, operational efficiency, and control of data flow are considered in this architecture. A customized UDP Protocol in addition to a pack of modules in RIDX adds a reliable (Lossless) and Multicast data transmission to all nodes in a virtual cloud network. A comparative study has been made to measure the performance of the Real-time Interactive Data Exchange system (RIDX) using RIDX UDP protocol against standard TCP protocol. Starting from 4 nodes up to 10 nodes in the domain, the results showed an enhanced performance using RIDX architecture over the standard TCP protocol.

Chapter 9 investigates user query enhancement for behavioral targeting. Ad targeting has been receiving more and more attention in the online publishing world, where advertisers want their ads to be seen by potential consumers at the right time. This chapter aims to address the major challenges with user queries in the context of behavioral targeting advertising by proposing a user intent representation strategy and a query enhancement mechanism. The authors focus on investigating the intent based user classification performance and the effectiveness of user segmentation under a topic model that helps explore semantic relation between user queries in behavioral targeting. In addition, the authors propose an alternative to define user's search intent for the evaluation purpose, in the case that the dataset is sanitized.

Section 2 includes six chapters that provide the following contributions to the present state of the art on ontology construction, a new model of Information Science ontology OIS. The model has defined 706 concepts which will be widely used in Information Science applications. It provides the standard definitions for domain terms used in annotation databases for the domain terms and avoids the consistency problems caused by various ontologies that have the potential of development by different groups and institutions in the IS domain area. A framework for analyzing IS knowledge to obtain a classification based on facet classification is explored. The ontology modelling approach is based on top-down and bottom-up. The top-down begins with an abstract of the domain view while the bottom-up method starts with description of the domain to gain a hierarchal taxonomy. An Ontocop system to support the developing process as specific virtual community of IS is also explored.

CONCLUSION

This book opens a set of discussions into today's information retrieval paradigm. The concepts and the state-of-the-art technology in the information retrieval and approaches are addressed. It covers:

1. Contributions of key technologies in IR (i.e., spatial data mining, ontology, big data analytic tool, spatial data mining, XML security, distributed systems, web mining, text mining, etc.);
2. Contributions of key application areas to IR (i.e., multimedia, social media, e-banking, information science, etc.); and
3. New challenges in the research into retrieval efficiency, accuracy, and correctness for a wide range of disciplines.

REFERENCES

Baeza-Yates, R., & Ribeiro-Neto, B. (1999). *Modern information retrieval*. Reading, MA: Addison Wesley Longman.

Büttcher, S., Clarke, C. L. A., & Cormack, G. V. (2010). *Information retrieval: Implementing and evaluating search engines*. Cambridge, MA: MIT Press.

Farkas-Conn, I. S. (1990). *From documentation to information science: The beginnings and early development of the American Documentation Institute*. Westport, CT: Greenwood Press.

Garvin, P. L. (1963). *Natural language and the computer*. New York: McGraw-Hill.

Hanbury, A., Kazai, G., Rauber, A., & Fuhr, N. (Eds.). (2015). *Proceedings of the advances in information retrieval, 37th European conference on IR research*. Vienna, Austria: Springer.

Jacobs, P. S. (1992). *Text-based intelligent systems: Current research and practice in information extraction and retrieval*. Hoboken, NJ: Lawrence Erlbaum Associates.

Manning, C. D., Raghavan, P., & Schütze, H. (2008). *Introduction to information retrieval*. Cambridge, UK: Cambridge University Press.

Zernik, U. (1991). *Lexical acquisition: Exploiting on-line resources to build a lexicon*. Hoboken, NJ: Lawrence Erlbaum Associates.

Acknowledgment

Special thanks are sent to reviewers and editorial review board, with their critical feedback and vigorous review, the book is able to be introduced to this challenging area. Huge thanks send to the IGI global team, especially to Ms. Maria Rohde and Ms. Lindsay Johnson, for their strong support, help, guidance and patience.

Section 1

Chapter 1
Interactive Visual Analytics of Big Data

Carson K.-S. Leung
University of Manitoba, Canada

Patrick Johnstone
University of Manitoba, Canada

Christopher L. Carmichael
University of Manitoba, Canada

Roy Ruokun Xing
University of Manitoba, Canada

David Sonny Hung-Cheung Yuen
University of Manitoba, Canada

ABSTRACT

High volumes of a wide variety of data can be easily generated at a high velocity in many real-life applications. Implicitly embedded in these big data is previously unknown and potentially useful knowledge such as frequently occurring sets of items, merchandise, or events. Different algorithms have been proposed for either retrieving information about the data or mining the data to find frequent sets, which are usually presented in a lengthy textual list. As "a picture is worth a thousand words", the use of visual representations can enhance user understanding of the inherent relationships among the mined frequent sets. However, many of the existing visualizers were not designed to visualize these mined frequent sets. This book chapter presents an interactive next-generation visual analytic system. The system enables the management, visualization, and advanced analysis of the original big data and the frequent sets mined from the data.

INTRODUCTION

With advances in technology, high volumes of a wide variety of data can be generated easily. These include:

1. Structured data in relational or transactional databases,
2. Semi-structured data in text documents or the World Wide Web, and
3. Unstructured data in social media or networks.

DOI: 10.4018/978-1-5225-2058-0.ch001

This leads us into the new era of big data (Keim et al., 2013; Zhang et al., 2013; Leung, 2014; Leung & Jiang, 2015). Intuitively, *big data* are interesting high-velocity, high-value, and/or high-variety data with volumes beyond the ability of commonly-used software to capture, manage, and process within a tolerable elapsed time. Hence, new forms of processing data are needed to enable enhanced decision making, insight, knowledge discovery, and process optimization. Moreover, embedded within these data is potentially useful knowledge that professionals, researchers, students, and practitioners want to discover. This calls for both

1. *Information retrieval* (Meng & Lu, 2013; Cuzzocrea et al., 2015), which returns explicit and highly relevant information or resources about data, and
2. *Data mining* (Frawley et al., 1991), which discovers implicit, previously unknown and potentially useful knowledge from data.

A common data mining task is *frequent set mining* (Agrawal et al., 1993), which analyzes the data to find frequently occurring sets of items (e.g., frequently collocated events, frequently purchased bundles of merchandise products) . These frequent sets serve as building blocks for many other data mining tasks such as the mining of association rules, correlation, sequences, episodes, emerging patterns, web access patterns, maximal patterns, closed frequent sets, constrained patterns, weighted patterns, and social patterns (Pasquier et al., 1999; Pei et al., 2000; Lakshmanan et al., 2003; Leung et al., 2007; Kumar et al., 2012; Leung et al., 2012; Fariha et al., 2015; Leung et al., 2016). Moreover, these frequently occurring sets of items can be used in mining tasks like classification (Al-Rajab & Lu, 2016) such as *associative classification* (Liu, 2009). Frequent sets can also answer many questions that help users make important decisions for real-life applications in different domains such as health care, bioinformatics, social science, as well as business. For example, knowing the sets of frequently purchased merchandise helps store managers make intelligent business decisions like item shelving, finding the sets of popular elective courses helps students select the combination of courses they wish to take, and discovering the sets of frequently occurring patterns in genes helps professionals and researchers get a better understanding of certain biomedical or social behaviours of human beings.

Frequent set mining has drawn the attention of many researchers as it has played important roles in many data mining tasks and has contributed to various real-life applications. Since the introduction of the frequent set mining problem (Agrawal et al., 1993), numerous algorithms (Han et al., 2007; Cheng & Han, 2009; Leung et al., 2014; Jiang & Leung, 2015) have been proposed to mine frequent sets from databases. Most of these algorithms return the mining results in textual forms such as a very long unsorted list of frequent sets of items. Presenting a large number of frequent sets in such a conventional lengthy list does not lead to ease of understanding. Consequently, users may not easily discover the useful knowledge that is embedded in the databases.

As "a picture is worth a thousand words", a visual representation matches the power of the human visual and cognitive system. Hence, having a visual representation of the frequent sets makes it easier for users (e.g., professionals, researchers, students, practitioners) to view and analyze the mining results when compared to presenting a lengthy textual list of frequent sets of items. This leads to *visual analytics*, which is the science of analytical reasoning supported by interactive visual interfaces (Thomas & Cook, 2005; Keim et al., 2008; Keim et al., 2009a; Keim et al., 2009b; Heimerl et al., 2016). Since numerous frequent set mining algorithms (which analyze large volumes of data to find frequent sets of items) have been proposed, what we need are interactive systems for *visualizing* the mining results so that we can take advantage of both worlds (i.e., combine advanced data analysis with visualization).

Many existing visualization systems were built to visualize data or the mining results (i.e., the input or output of the knowledge discovery process, respectively). Existing visualization systems for the latter mostly show the knowledge discovered for other data mining tasks—such as groups of similar objects (for clustering), decision trees (for classification), and rules (for association rule mining)—rather than frequently occurring sets of items (for frequent set mining). In the current book chapter, we present an interactive visual analytic system (iVAS) for effective management, advanced analysis, and interactive visualization of big data—from which frequent sets of items can be mined.

This book chapter is an expansion of our journal article about visual analytics of databases to be analyzed and the corresponding analysis results (Leung et al., 2013). Here, we enhance and update the research found in the journal article, and incorporate recent developments and literature. In addition, new materials in the current book chapter include

1.   Visual analytics of *big data*, and
2.   Its application to big unstructured data—namely, social media and network data.

The remainder of this book chapter is organized as follows. We first provide background and literature review on relevant data mining, frequent set mining, and visualization techniques. Then, we focus on our iVAS. We explain how it represents information about data (e.g., database transactions) and knowledge discovered from the data (e.g., mined frequent sets) as horizontal lines in a two-dimensional space, detail its interactive features for conducting visual analytics, and illustrate how iVAS can be applied to various real-life applications. We also discuss our future research directions on iVAS, and summarize the key features of iVAS in the conclusion.

BACKGROUND

Several visualization systems have been developed over the past two decades. In this section, we review

1.   Systems for visualizing information (e.g., data),
2.   Systems for visualizing knowledge (e.g., results of data mining tasks other than frequent set mining),
3.   Systems that were built to visualize association rules but can be used for visualizing frequent sets, as well as,
4.   Systems that were designed specifically to visualize frequent sets.

Data visualization systems provide features to arrange and display information or data in various forms. Examples include Spotfire (Ahlberg, 1996), VisDB (Keim & Kriegel, 1996), independence diagrams (Berchtold et al., 1998), Polaris (Stolte et al., 2002), rExtractor (Anderson & Hong, 2013), and Protael (Sedova et al., 2016). Among them, VisDB provides users with pixel-oriented techniques, parallel coordinates, and stick figures for exploring large volumes of data. Polaris provides a visual interface to help users formulate complex queries against a multi-dimensional data cube. rExtractor visually extracts structured data from web queries. Protael provides users with protein data visualization library for visualizing biological sequences. However, the majority of these systems are not connected to any data mining engine, let alone were they designed to display the mining results. In contrast, our proposed iVAS allows users to visualize and analyze the data as well as the mining results (in the form of frequent sets of items).

In addition to the systems that were designed to visualize data, there are also systems that were designed to visualize knowledge discovered as the results of various data mining tasks like classification, clustering, and anomaly detection. For example, Ankerst et al. (1999) proposed a visual framework, which allows users to participate in the building of decision trees. Zhu et al. (2013) produced a mixed-norm regularizer for mulit-view multi-label visual classification. Koren and Harel (2003) designed a visualization method for cluster analysis and validation. Schreck et al. (2008) used interactive Kohonen Maps to perform visual cluster analysis on trajectory data. Dietrich et al. (2013) exploited visual appearance to cluster rogue software. Akoglu et al. (2012) presented OPAvion to visualize and detect anomalies from large graphs. Note that all these systems visualize the results of classification, clustering, or anomaly detection. Conversely, our proposed iVAS visualizes the results of another data mining task—namely, frequent set mining.

Besides visualizing the results of the data mining tasks of classification and clustering, some systems were built for visualizing association rules (Yang, 2009). For example, AViz (Han & Cercone, 2000) discretizes numeric attributes and visualizes the mined two-dimensional association rules as a collection of two-dimensional planes in a three-dimensional space. ARVis (Blanchard et al., 2007) uses a rule-focusing methodology, which is an interactive methodology for the visual post-processing of association rules, to perform constraint-based association rule mining. Each of the mined rules is represented by an object consisting of a sphere perched on top of a cone. Liu et al. (2013) used different colors to represent association rules that contain (or do not contain) a specific user-selected domain item in their AssocExplorer system. Note that all these systems focus on visualizing the results of association rule mining. They are not intended for frequent set visualization.

Some other systems, although were built for visualizing association rules, can be used for visualizing frequent sets. For instance, Yang (2005) designed a system mainly to visualize association rules in a two-dimensional space consisting of many vertical axes. Such a system can also be used to visualize frequent sets. In his system, all domain items are sorted according to their frequencies and are evenly distributed along each vertical axis. A frequent set consisting of k items (also known as a k-itemset) is then represented by a curve that extends from one vertical axis to another connecting k such axes. The thickness of the curve indicates the frequency of the frequent set. However, such a representation suffers from the following problems:

1. The use of thickness only shows the *relative* (but not the *exact*) frequency of the frequent set. Comparing the thickness of curves is not easy.
2. Domain items are sorted and *evenly* distributed along the axes.

So, users only know some items are more frequent than the others but cannot get a sense of how these items are related to each other in terms of their exact frequencies (e.g., whether item a is twice as frequent as, or just slightly more frequent than, item b). As a preview, our iVAS does not suffer from these problems.

In addition, some researchers built systems for the purpose of visualizing frequent sets. For example, Munzer et al. (2005) presented the PowerSetViewer (PSV), which was specifically designed to visualize frequent sets. The PSV provides users with guaranteed visibility of frequent sets in the sense that the pixel representing a frequent set is guaranteed to be visible by highlighting such a pixel. However, multiple frequent sets mined from large databases may be represented by the same highlighted pixel.

Over the past few years, a frequent itemset visualizer (FIsViz) was proposed (Leung et al., 2008a). It aims to visualize frequent sets. FIsViz represents each frequent set by a polyline (which is a continuous line composed of one or more line segments) in a two-dimensional space. The location of the polyline explicitly indicates the exact frequency of the frequent set. While FIsViz enables users to visualize the mining results (i.e., frequent sets) for many real-life applications, users may require some effort to be able to clearly visualize frequent sets when the number of frequent sets is huge. The problem is caused by the use of polylines for representing frequent sets because the polylines can be bent and/or can cross over each other. Bothorel et al. (2013) visualized frequent sets with nested circular graph layout. However, like FIsViz, polylines in the nested circular graphs for representing frequent sets are bundled and crossed over each other. Consequently, one may encounter some difficulties in distinguishing one polyline (representing a frequent set) from another.

To deal with this problem, both WiFIsViz (Leung et al., 2008b) and FpViz (Leung & Carmichael, 2009) were developed. Between them, WiFIsViz uses two half-screens to visualize the mined frequent sets. Specifically, the left half-screen gives the frequency information of the frequent sets, and the right half-screen shows the relationships among the frequent sets. In contrast, FpViz uses a full-screen to visualize the mined frequent sets. As a preview, our iVAS, on the other hand, can be used for visualizing not only the mined frequent sets (the output of the knowledge discovery process) but also the database transactions (the input of the knowledge discovery process).

Moreover, two additional visualizers—namely, FpMapViz (Leung et al. 2011) and RadialViz (Leung & Jiang, 2012)—were designed to visualize frequent sets with an emphasis on showing the relationships (in particular, prefix/extension relationships) among the frequent sets. For instance, given two frequent sets $\{a, b, c\}$ and $\{a, b, c, d\}$, the two visualizers show that $\{a, b, c\}$ is a prefix of $\{a, b, c, d\}$ and that $\{a, b, c, d\}$ is an extension of $\{a, b, c\}$. Inspired by the tree map representation of hierarchical information, FpMapViz represents frequent sets as squares in a hierarchical fashion so that extensions of a frequent set are embedded within squares representing the prefixes of that frequent set. The colour of the square representing a frequent set indicates the frequency range of that frequent set. Similarly, RadialViz also visualizes frequent sets but in a radial layout. Since such a representation of frequent sets is orientation free, the legibility of the represented frequent sets is not be impacted by the orientation. Moreover, RadialViz also represents frequent sets in a hierarchical fashion so that extensions of a frequent set are embedded within sectors representing the prefixes of that frequent set. The frequency of a frequent set is represented by the radius of the sector representing that frequent set. Like WiFIsViz and FpViz, both FpMapViz and RadialViz are designed to visualize only the mined frequent sets. In contrast, our proposed iVAS can be used for visualizing not only the mined frequent sets but also the database transactions.

INTERACTIVE VISUAL ANALYTICS

In this book chapter, we present our *interactive visual analytic system* (*iVAS*), which helps users analyze the databases for finding frequent sets of items (which are also known as *frequent itemsets*). The system visually presents each transaction in the database (the input of the knowledge discovery process) and each frequent set of items in the mining results (the output of the knowledge discovery process) as a horizontal line in a two-dimensional space. By doing so, our iVAS reduces unnecessary bends and avoids crossover of lines. Moreover, iVAS is also equipped with interactive features and analytical capabilities so that users can easily perceive, relate, and make conclusions in the knowledge discovery process. Furthermore, iVAS follows both

1.   The visual information seeking mantra (Shneiderman, 1996), which states "Overview first, zoom and filter, then details on demand", and
2.   The visual analytics mantra (Keim et al., 2006), which states "Analyze first; show the important; zoom, filter and analyze further; details on demand".

To elaborate, iVAS shows an overview of the transaction database so that users can gain insight about the distribution of items in the database, allows users to express their interests and *filter* out the uninteresting data, and finally provides users with interactive features to *zoom in* and *zoom out* examining the *details* of the interesting data at different resolutions. Afterwards, iVAS further *analyzes* the data automatically to *show the important* knowledge in the form of frequent sets of items. It also allows users to express their interests and *filter* out the uninteresting sets; it provides users with interactive features to *zoom in* and *zoom out* exploring and *analyzing further* the interesting frequent sets at different resolutions so that users can obtain more *details* on the discovered knowledge (i.e., the mined frequent sets)

Visual Analytics on Information or Data

- **"Overview First":** Recall that the visual information seeking mantra stated "Overview first, zoom and filter, details on demand". Hence, given a database of n transactions, our interactive visual analytic system (iVAS) first provides users with an overview so that they can gain some insight about the distribution of data. Specifically, our iVAS displays the contents of the transaction database in a two-dimensional space. The x-axis shows the domain items, and the y-axis shows the transaction IDs. A transaction containing k items is then represented by k circles, and these circles are linked by a horizontal line. With this representation, users can easily spot the presence or absence of some domain items in each database transaction. For instance, the presence of a circle at (x, t_y)-location implies that transaction t_y contains item x. Conversely, the absence of a circle from (x', t_y)-location implies that transaction $t_{y'}$ does not contain item x'.

As an illustrative example, let us consider a database containing five domain items a, b, c, d and e. Suppose the first transaction t_1 of the database contains four items a, b, c and e. Then, iVAS represents t_1 by a horizontal line connecting four circles that are located at $(a, t_1), (b, t_1), (c, t_1)$ and (e, t_1). Similarly, suppose the next three transactions t_2, t_3 and t_4 of the database contain two items b & e, one item b, and three items b, c & e, respectively. Figure 1 shows how iVAS represents these four transactions. From the figure, one can easily observe the following:

- The contents (i.e., items) of each transactions (e.g., $t_1 = \{a, b, c, e\}$ contains fours items a, b, c and e);
- The presence of some particular items (e.g., item a is present in transaction t_1);
- The frequentness of some particular items (e.g., item b occurs very frequently); and
- The absence of some particular items (e.g., item d is absent from all four transactions).

Figure 1. Visual analytics of databases by iVAS

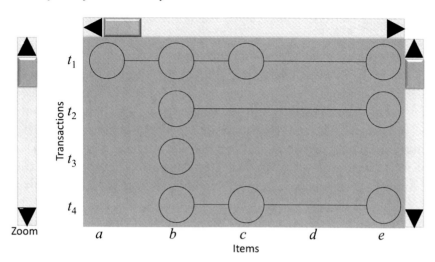

Our iVAS tries to fit all the horizontal lines onto a single screen to give an overview. Such a visual representation helps users gain some insight about the data distribution. For a real-life example, a restaurant manager may reveal the uniform data distribution for the restaurant transactions, in which the eaters often ordered similar menu items throughout the years. As another example, a store manager may reveal the skewed data distribution for the retail transactions, in which the customers often bought ski jackets & snow boots in the winter and swimwear & sunscreen in the summer. To draw an analogy, the overview gives users a "world map" showing the overall distribution of domain items in the database transactions.

- **"Zoom and Filter":** While the "world map" shows the overall distribution, the users may also request to zoom in to get a "street map" for obtaining more detailed information. In response to this request, our iVAS provides users with a *resolution slider*, which enables users to zoom in or zoom out from certain regions of the screen. When zooming out, users see an overview of the data on one screen; when zooming in, users get the details about the data split onto multiple screen spaces.

Recall that, when displaying the contents of the transaction database, the *x*-axis of iVAS shows the domain items and the *y*-axis shows the transaction IDs. Thus, to allow users to view the information across multiple screen spaces, iVAS also provides users with

1. A *vertical scrollbar* for visualizing different transactions, and
2. A *horizontal scrollbar* for visualizing different domain items.

With the zoom-in view, users can obtain more details about the data in the database.

With this zoom-in view or with the overview (i.e., the zoom-out view), iVAS allows users to interactively select some domain items and/or transactions of interest. For example, users can draw a box in the overview to enclose those items and/or transactions in some dense regions of the screen (e.g., a region representing the transactions that took place in the summer) for further analysis. By doing so, iVAS filters out the items and/or transactions that are uninteresting to users. For a real-life example, a store manager, who wants to run a promotional campaign for sunscreen, can specify that he wants to explore only those transactions taking place in the months of July & August and containing any brand of sunscreen for further analysis.

Alternatively, users can click on the domain items (on the *x*-axis) and/or the transaction IDs (on the *y*-axis) shown in the zoom-in view to interactively select some specific items and/or transactions. Like the aforementioned box-drawing interactive technique, iVAS filters out the items and/or transactions that are uninteresting to users. Unlike the box-drawing interactive technique (with it the box enclose consecutive transactions and/or items), users have the flexibility to click and select some individual or non-consecutive transactions and/or items. For a real-life example, with iVAS, a store manager can specify that he wants to explore only those transactions taking place in the weekdays (but not weekends) in the month of August and containing a specific brand of sunscreen for further analysis.

- **"Details on Demand":** In addition, our iVAS also provides users with details on demand, which consists of techniques that provide more details whenever users request them. The key idea is that, when users hover the mouse over a horizontal line or a circle, iVAS shows the contents (i.e., items within the transaction represented by circles on that line). For instance, when users hover the mouse over the first horizontal line in Figure 1 representing a transaction that contains four items, iVAS displays the details of the transaction by showing its contents: $t_1 = \{a, b, c, e\}$.

Visual Analytics on Knowledge or Mined Frequent Sets

- **"Analyze First":** Once the users gained an insight about the distribution of data in the transaction database and selected interesting data from the overview or the zoom-in view, the users can then request iVAS to start the frequent set mining process to analyze the selected data for finding frequent sets of items. The results of this mining process—i.e., frequent sets of items—are displayed by our iVAS in a two-dimensional space. The *x*-axis shows the domain items, and the *y*-axis shows the frequency. A frequent set of items consisting of *k* items (also known as a frequent *k*-itemset) is then represented by *k* nodes, and these nodes are linked by a horizontal line. For example, a frequent 2-itemset $\{a, b\}$ is represented by a horizontal line connecting two nodes representing items *a* and *b*. This representation enables users to easily visualize frequent sets and their frequencies.
- **"Show the Important" Frequent Sets by Using Intuitive Glyph Icons:** Note that, when visualizing database transactions, the *y*-axis shows the transaction ID so that each *y*-position shows one transaction. Here, when visualizing frequent sets, it is not uncommon that more than one frequent set may have the same frequency.

A naïve representation is to have a band showing several frequent sets of the same frequency. However, such a representation would require a large amount of vertical space that may go beyond a single screen. In order to give users an overview of all the mined frequent sets on a single screen, a compressed representation is needed.

One way to reduce the amount of required vertical space is to combine the related frequent sets that have the same frequency. More specifically, if two sets X and Y having the same frequency such that X is a prefix of Y, then our iVAS combines the horizontal lines representing X and Y (i.e., reduces the number of horizontal lines from two to one). When using this compression technique, a potential problem is how can users tell whether the resulting single horizontal line represents

1. Both X and Y, or
2. Just Y?

Recall that, when visualizing database transactions, iVAS represents a transaction consisting of k items by a horizontal line linking k circles. Hence, it may seem logical to adapt such a representation and use circles to represent nodes/items. As such, any frequent k-itemset would be represented by a horizontal line linking k nodes, where each node would be represented by a circle. With this representation, a way to solve the aforementioned potential problem of distinguishing X and Y from just Y is to fill the last circle representing the last item in a frequent k-itemset. In other words, let X be a j-itemset and Y be a k-itemset such that $X \subset Y$ (where $j < k$). If X and Y have the same frequency, then X and Y are represented by a single horizontal line connecting k circles with the jth and the kth circles filled (and the remaining $k-2$ circles are unfilled). On the surface, the use of filled/unfilled circles solves the problem so that (experienced) users could tell whether a single horizontal line represents:

1. Both X and Y, or
2. Just Y. However, the use of filled/unfilled circles may not be too intuitive for all users. For instance, those who less frequently use the system may wonder why some circles are filled but some are not.

Hence, iVAS uses a more meaningful and *intuitive glyph icons* to represent the first item, the last item, and all other $k-2$ intermediate items with a frequent k-itemset. Specifically, to make good use of visual clues, iVAS logically represents a k-itemset by a horizontal line connecting a left-triangle (which indicates the first item according to some ordering R of domain items), $k-2$ circles (which indicate the $k-2$ intermediate items), and a right-triangle (which indicates the last item). For $k=2$, the item pair (i.e., 2-itemset) is represented by a horizontal line connecting a left-triangle and a right-triangle. For $k=1$, the singleton item (i.e., 1-itemset) is represented by a diamond (formed by putting a left-triangle and a right-triangle together). With the intuitive glyph icons, users can easier spot the number of itemsets embedded in a single horizontal line by counting the number of right-triangles.

For example, Figure 2 shows two frequent sets $X = \{b, c\}$ and $Y = \{b, c, d\}$ both having the same frequency of 40%. As X is a 2-itemset, it is represented by a horizontal line connecting a left-triangle for item b and a right-triangle for item c. As Y is a 3-itemset, it is represented by a horizontal line connecting a left-triangle for item b, a circle for item c and a right-triangle for item d. Since $X \subset Y$, iVAS represents these two sets by a horizontal line with two right-triangles indicating that c & d are the last items of the respective sets. Figure 2 also shows a 1-itemset $\{c\}$, which is represented by a diamond symbol.

To a further extent, this compression technique is not confined to combining two horizontal lines (representing two frequent sets that have the same frequency and are related by the prefix relationship) but multiple horizontal lines (representing several sets that have the same frequency and are related by the prefix relationship).

- **"Show the Important" Frequent Sets by Using "Forks":** The above consider situations where frequent sets have the same frequency and have a prefix/extension relationship. There are other situations where two sets X and Y have the same frequency but just share a common prefix such that $X \not\subset Y$. In these situations, our iVAS is unable to reduce the number of horizontal lines, but it can reduce the number of *nodes* (especially, left-triangles and circles). To elaborate, let X be a j-itemset and Y be a k-itemset such that X and Y share a common prefix consisting of h items

Figure 2. Visual analytics of some mined frequent sets by iVAS

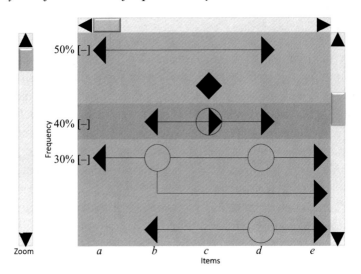

(where $h < j, k$). If X and Y have the same frequency, then X and Y are represented by a "fork": A horizontal line connecting j nodes and another horizontal line (which connects the last k–h items of Y) "branching" from the hth node of the first line. Here, to improve the legibility of graphs and to preserve graph aesthetics, iVAS reduces the number of edge crossings by using an orthogonality mechanism that limits edge crossings to a minimum. Specifically, bends for the "branch" occur only at 0° or 90° angles. This minimizes crossings, facilitating legibility and visual comprehension. Again, the compression technique can be applied to multiple sets sharing some common prefix and the same frequency.

For example, Figure 2 shows two frequent sets X = {a, b, d, e} and Y = {a, b, e} having the same frequency of 30%. Then, X is represented by a horizontal line connecting a left-triangle for item a, two circles for items b & d and a right-triangle for item e; Y is represented by a horizontal line connecting a left-triangle for item a, a circle for item b and a right-triangle for item e. Since X and Y share the common prefix {a, b}, our iVAS represents X and Y by a "fork" consisting of the horizontal line for X and another line containing the right-triangle for item e "branching" from the circle for item b.

- **"Show the Important" Frequent Sets by Applying Projection:** The use of "forks" help compress the representation of frequent sets and thus reduce the number of horizontal lines as well as the number of nodes displayed. However, for a large number of frequent sets, further reduction in the number of horizontal lines is needed so that the final results can all fit onto a single screen for the overview. To do so, our iVAS projects all p horizontal lines representing multiple ($\geq p$) frequent sets having the same frequency onto a single line (regardless whether or not they share any common prefix). The resulting horizontal line is a single line without any "branches", and it connects all the nodes that can be found in the p horizontal lines. Consequently, a horizontal line connecting these nodes represents a "virtual" set (i.e., does not represent a real set). To distinguish such a "virtual" set from the real one, iVAS uses a *dashed* horizontal line to represent the "virtual" set (the projection result) and uses a *solid* horizontal line to represent a real set.

For example, Figure 2 shows three frequent sets {*a, b, d, e*}, {*a, b, e*} and {*b, d, e*} having the same frequency of 30%. Our iVAS projects the horizontal lines representing these three frequent sets onto a single horizontal line connecting four nodes representing items *a, b, d* & *e* in Figure 3. The nodes for items *a, d*, and *e* in the resulting horizontal line are represented by a left-triangle, a circle, and a right-triangle, respectively. It is interesting to note that the node for item *b* is represented by both a circle (because *b* is an intermediate item in sets {*a, b, d, e*} and {*a, b, e*}) and a left-triangle (because *b* is the first item within set {*b, d, e*}). Moreover, in Figure 3, the solid horizontal line for frequency 40% represents two real sets {*b, c*} and {*b, c, d*}. The dashed horizontal line for frequency 50% does not represent a real set {*a, c, d*}; it represents the result of projecting two sets onto a single line.

- **"Show the Important" Closed Frequent Sets:** Although the projection technique reduces the amount of required vertical space, our iVAS provides users with an alternative option of showing the important *closed* frequent sets. A frequent set X is *closed* if there does not exist any proper superset of X having the same frequency as X. Recall that, if two sets X and Y have the same frequency such that X is a prefix of Y, then iVAS combines the horizontal lines representing X and Y when showing the important frequent sets. Our iVAS does so by putting two right-triangles representing the last items within X and Y. When X is a prefix of Y and both have the same frequency, then X is not a closed set (as Y is a proper superset X and has the same frequency as X). So, with the option of showing closed frequent sets, iVAS does not need to show the horizontal line for X. This reduces the number of horizontal lines that need to be shown (i.e., reduces the number of frequent sets that need to be visualized).

The above illustrates a special case of a subset/superset relationship between two sets X and Y—specifically, X is a prefix of Y (e.g., X = {*b, c*} and Y = {*b, c, d*}). However, there are situations in which the two sets X and Y have the same frequency such that X is a subset (but not a prefix) of Y. For example, X = {*b, d, e*} and Y = {*a, b, d, e*}. In these situations, unless the aforementioned projection technique is applied, two horizontal lines need to be shown as the corresponding two sets do not share a common prefix. With the option of showing closed frequent sets, iVAS does not need to show the horizontal line for X (as it is a subset of Y and has the same frequency as Y). This reduces the number of horizontal lines that need to be shown (i.e., reduces the number of sets that need to be visualized).

Figure 3. Our iVAS applies projection to show the important frequent sets

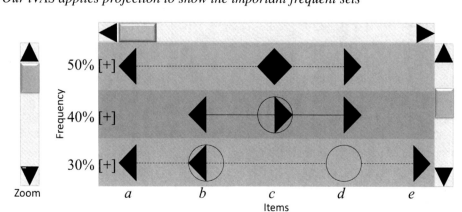

Not only do we reduce the amount of required vertical space, another benefit of showing closed sets is that we also reduce the computation for the mining process. Specifically, instead of using the usual frequent set mining algorithms such as Apriori (Agrawal & Srikant, 1994) or FP-growth (Han et al., 2000), iVAS uses closed frequent set mining algorithms such as CHARM (Zaki & Hsiao, 2005) and MPFCI (Tong et al., 2012) when users select the option of showing the important closed frequent sets.

- **"Zoom, Filter, and Analyze Further":** As our iVAS tries to squeeze all the horizontal lines and fit them onto a single screen, users sometimes need to zoom in to get more detailed information. Hence, iVAS provides users with a *resolution slider*, which enables users to zoom in/out on certain regions of the screen. When zooming out, users get a big picture on one screen; when zooming in, users get the details split onto multiple screen spaces. To allow users to view the information across multiple screen spaces, iVAS provides users with
  - A *vertical scrollbar* for visualizing sets having different frequency values, and
  - A *horizontal scrollbar* for visualizing different domain items within some sets. With the zoom-in view, users can obtain more details about the frequent sets mined from the database.

Our iVAS provides users with interactive features to select some frequent sets of interest and to filter out those uninteresting sets based on the domain items within the sets and/or the frequency values of the sets. To perform the selection, users can draw a box to enclose interesting frequent sets in some regions of the screen (e.g., a region representing sets with very high frequency) for further analysis. Users can also click on the items (on the *x*-axis) and/or the frequency values (on the *y*-axis) to interactively select those interesting sets. By doing so, iVAS filters out the frequent sets that are uninteresting to users. For example, a store manager, who wants to run a promotional campaign for very frequently purchased collections of winter clothing, can specify that he wants to explore only and analyze further those frequent sets having frequency ≥ 80% and containing a specific brand of winter clothing.

In addition to allowing users to select interesting frequent sets (and filter out other uninteresting frequent sets) based on the domain items and/or frequency, iVAS also provides users with the flexibility to select frequent sets of certain cardinality (e.g., only show frequent 2-itemsets, 5-itemsets, and 11-itemsets) by imposing some *cardinality constraints*. This reduces the number of frequent sets shown, and thus enables users to focus on those interesting frequent sets. For a real-life application, a sport promoter could use iVAS to visualize popular teams of 2 players for tennis tournaments. Similarly, another sport promoter could also use iVAS to visualize popular teams of 5 or 11 players for the games of basketball or soccer.

Recall that, in order to fit all frequent sets in the overview, iVAS projects all the horizontal lines representing frequent sets having the same frequency onto a single line. To reveal the details (i.e., the sets embedded within such a dashed line), iVAS allows users to interactively expand the line by clicking the [+] button. Once the line is expanded, users can view all horizontal lines representing real sets having such frequency. For example, by clicking the [+] buttons of all three lines shown in Figure 3 (representing the result of projecting sets of three distinct frequency values onto three different lines), users get Figure 2 (representing the mined frequent sets before projection). Conversely, clicking the [−] buttons in Figure 2 projects the sets that have the same frequency value onto a single line, which results in Figure 3.

Note that a benefit of using the intuitive glyph icons in iVAS is that users can easily read off important and useful information from the compressed representation without clicking the [+] buttons to expand the horizontal lines. Let us elaborate in the following cases:

- Given only a diamond symbol, iVAS shows a 1-itemset, and such a 1-itemset is the only frequent set at that frequency.
- Given a solid horizontal line with only one left-triangle and one right-triangle, iVAS shows a 2-itemset, and such a 2-itemset is the only frequent set at that frequency.
- Given a solid horizontal line with only one left-triangle and one right-triangle, together with some circles, iVAS shows a k-itemset (where $k \geq 3$), and such a k-itemset is the only frequent set at that frequency.
- Given a solid horizontal line with only one left-triangle but multiple right-triangles, together with no or some circles, iVAS shows at least two frequent sets having the same frequency, and the frequent sets are related in the sense that one is a prefix of another (e.g., $\{b, c\}$ and $\{b, c, d\}$ in Figure 3).
- Given a dashed horizontal line with only multiple left-triangles but one right-triangle, together with no or some circles, iVAS shows at least two frequent sets having the same frequency, and the frequent sets are related in the sense that they share a common suffix (e.g., $\{a, b, d, e\}$ and $\{b, d, e\}$ in Figure 3).
- **"Details on Demand":** Besides providing an overview and allowing users to zoom & filter, our iVAS also provides users with details on demand. When users hover the mouse over a horizontal line or a node, iVAS shows the contents (i.e., items within that frequent sets represented by nodes on that line).

SAMPLE APPLICATIONS OF iVAS

In this section, we illustrate how our proposed iVAS visualizes and analyzes information (data) and knowledge (the mined frequent sets) in some sample applications.

Application 1: Visual Analytics of Cellular Phone Call Records

The first application is to apply our proposed iVAS to the VAST 2008 Mini-challenge (Grinstein et al., 2008) for the visual analytics of cellular phone call records that were collected over a period of 10 days in June 2006. The goal of this mini-challenge is to apply the visual analytic approach to help users (e.g., investigators) understand this collection of phone call records and get some idea about the network of a specific caller (Caller 200 whose name is Ferdinando Catalano).

Given this collection of $n = 9,834$ cellular phone call records made by $m \approx 400$ unique cellular phone callers (each caller can be uniquely identified by a caller ID), our proposed iVAS first gives a single-screen overview showing these phone call records in a two-dimensional space. The x-axis shows the caller IDs, and the y-axis shows the phone call record IDs. Each record consists of two callers (Callers X and Y such that X called Y), which are represented by two circles. The circles are linked by a horizontal line. Then, users (e.g., investigators) can use the resolution slider of iVAS to change the display resolution so that they can zoom in to a certain region of the screen and get more details on that region. As information is scattered across multiple screen spaces, users can use the vertical scrollbar to visualize different phone call records and the horizontal scrollbar to visualize different callers. Finally, with prior knowledge that Caller 200 named Ferdinando Catalano is the caller of interest, the users interactively select Caller 200 by clicking the x-label for caller ID = 200. By doing so, iVAS highlights all 47 phone call records related to this caller (i.e., all 23 outgoing phone calls made by Caller 200 and all 24 incoming calls received by Caller 200), sends them for further analysis (e.g., data mining), and ignores the remaining $9,834 - 47 = 9,787$ records.

The previous paragraph described how iVAS visualizes and analyzes the database of $n = 9,834$ cellular phone call records. Specifically, it gave an overview of all records in the database, zoomed in and filtered out all records other than those related to Caller 200, and provided users with details—in response to users' demand—about the 23 outgoing & 24 incoming = 47 phone call records related to Caller 200. The next steps are to

1.   Apply the frequent set mining process to these 47 phone call records, and
2.   Visualize and analyze the mining results.

Specifically, iVAS gives an overview of the mining results in a two-dimensional space. Similar to the overview of the phone call records, the *x*-axis of the overview of the mining results also shows the caller IDs. Unlike the *y*-axis of the overview of the phone call records (which shows the record IDs), the *y*-axis of the overview of the mining results shows the frequencies. Here, the important mining results are shown in the form of frequent 2-itemsets only, which are indicated by five horizontal lines. It is interesting to observe that there is no horizontal line involving three or more nodes (callers). This means that Caller 200 did not use any 3-way calls or multi-party conference calls.

Among the five horizontal lines, four are solid lines indicating four real frequent sets. Each of these lines connects two nodes (i.e., left triangle and right triangle) representing the caller who made the phone call and the caller who received the call. The following are some observations (see Figure 4):

*   One of the horizontal lines represents the frequent set {Caller 5, Caller 200} with a frequency value of 14, which means that Callers 5 and 200 communicated with each other in 14 phone calls.
*   Another frequent set is {Caller 1, Caller 200} with a frequency value of 9.
*   The third horizontal line shown by iVAS is a dashed one with a frequency value of 8, which indicates that more than one frequent set has a frequency of 8. Horizontal lines representing multiple frequent sets are projected onto this single dashed line. By interactively clicking the [+] button, iVAS expands the dashed line and reveals to users the details that the two mined frequent sets {Caller 2, Caller 200} and {Caller 3, Caller 200} both have the same frequency value of 8.
*   The other two frequent sets—namely, {Caller 137, Caller 200} and {Caller 97, Caller 200}—have frequency values of 5 and 3, respectively.

For this VAST 2008 Mini-challenge on cellular phone call records, users were also given prior information as follows:

Close relatives and associates that Ferdinando Catalano would be calling include David Vidro, Juan Vidro, Jorge Vidro and Estaban Catalano. Ferdinando would call his brother, Estaban, most frequently. David Vidro coordinates most activities.

Based on this prior information and the six mined frequent sets displayed by iVAS, users can induce that Caller 5 is highly likely to be Estaban Catalano (brother of Ferdinando—Caller 200) because these two callers communicated most frequently. Users can also induce that the next three frequent callers (in

Figure 4. Our iVAS applies visual analytics to cellular phone call records

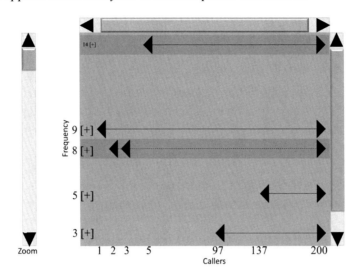

terms of communication with Caller 200)—namely, Callers 1, 2 and 3—are likely to be David Vidro, Juan Vidro and Jorge Vidro. In other words, by using iVAS, users can reveal the social network of Ferdinando Catalano (Caller 200).

As data mining is supposed to be an exploratory and iterative process, users can make use of iVAS to further discover more useful knowledge. For example, if users not only select records related to Caller 200 from the overview of phone call records but also select all 9,834 records related to every caller for the frequent set mining process, then users can visualize more frequent sets. Among them, the 1-itemset {Caller 1} has the highest frequency of 313, which means that Caller 1 communicated 313 times (with 54 distinct callers): He made 24 calls (to 15 callers) and received 289 calls (from 51 callers). Based on this result and the prior information that David Vidro coordinated most activities, users can induce that Caller 1 is highly likely to be David Vidro.

As another example, let us consider a case where, after clicking Caller ID = 200 (which selects and highlights all the records related to Caller 200) from the overview of phone call records, users further refine their selection by drawing a box to select only the incoming calls received by Caller 200 (and ignore the outgoing calls made by Caller 200). The mining results on these 24 incoming calls, shown by iVAS, provide users with more details: Caller 200 received seven calls from Caller 5, six calls from Caller 1, five from Caller 3, four from Caller 2, and one call each from Callers 97 as well as 137. Alternatively, users can draw a box to refine their selection so that only those outgoing calls made by Caller 200 are sent to the data mining process. As such, iVAS analyzes these 23 outgoing calls and visualizes the results that Caller 200 called Caller 5 seven times, Callers 2 and 137 four times each, Callers 1 and 3 three times each, and Caller 97 twice.

In addition to selecting phone call records based on the direction of calls (e.g., selecting only the incoming calls or only the outgoing calls), users can also select the records based on the day (e.g., can select only the records for some specific date). For example, users can draw a box to select only those records captured on Day 1. Then, iVAS provides more details about Day 1: Callers 1, 2, 3 and 5 called Caller 200, who also returned calls to Callers 1 and 5. Similarly, users can also draw a box to select the records captured on each of the nine subsequent days for further analysis, and iVAS then returns the following details:

- On Day 2, Callers 1, 2, 3 and 5 communicated both ways with Caller 200, who also called Caller 137 but did not receive any phone calls from Caller 137.
- For the next five days (Days 3-7), Caller 200 continued to communicate with some of Callers 1, 2, 3 and 5.
- On Day 8, Caller 200 did not communicate with anyone.
- On Days 9 and 10, communication patterns between Caller 200 and others were changed. Specifically, Caller 200 no longer communicated with his usual callers (e.g., Callers 1, 2, 3 and 5). Instead, he communicated with a new caller (e.g., he called Caller 97 twice on Day 9 and received a call from Caller 97 on Day 10).

To summarize, the detailed information provided by our iVAS helps users (e.g., investigators) visualize and analyze the *temporal behaviour* of these callers and their social network.

Application 2: Visual Analytics of Social Media and Network Data

The emergence of social networking sites and web-based communities has led to the existence of high volumes of social media data. For instance, as of the end of March 2016,

1. Facebook had 1.65 billion monthly active users making friend connections,
2. Twitter reached 310 million monthly active users generating tweets, and
3. LinkedIn also passed 433 million registered members.

Embedded in these social data are rich sets of meaningful knowledge about the social networks. The second application is to apply our proposed iVAS to these social networks consisting of large collections of social media data like audios, videos, posts, and tweets on social networking sites. Specifically, each social entity and its egocentric network can be considered as a transaction. Each transaction consists of a set of social networking pages followed by such a social entity. Then, iVAS allows users (say, social analysts) to get an insight from the overview showing the distribution of social networking pages and to select those pages of interest. After applying *social media mining and social network analysis* (Siau et al., 2010; Leung et al., 2013b; Schreck & Keim, 2013; Leung et al., 2014; Leung & Jiang, 2015; Leung et al., 2016a, Leung et al., 2016b), iVAS helps users visualize the mined associations in the form of interesting patterns such as "following" patterns that reveal popular or frequently followed social networking pages. This mined knowledge help users get a deep understanding of the social networks being analyzed and allow them to make appropriate friend or page recommendation.

Application 3: Visual Analytics of Text Documents and Web Data

The third application is to apply our proposed iVAS to text databases consisting of large collections of documents from various sources like digital libraries, e-mail messages, news articles, references, research papers, and textbooks (Alencar et al., 2012; Qi, 2013). Specifically, each document in the text database can be considered as a transaction. Each transaction consists of a set of keywords found in the text document. Then, iVAS allows users (say, readers of some text documents) to get an insight from the overview showing the distribution of keywords and to select those keywords and/or documents of interest. After applying the text mining technique (specifically, keyword-based association analysis), iVAS helps users visualize the mined associations in the form of terms/phrases that comprise sets of frequently occurring consecutive or closely located keywords. Among the mined keyword-based associations, some can be compound associations (e.g., domain-dependent terms or phrases like {"data", "mining"}, {"information", "retrieval"}, {"knowledge", "discovery"}) while others can be non-compound associations (e.g., {"balance", "charges", "invoice", "tax", "total"}). The mined keyword-based associations help users get a deep understanding of the text documents.

In addition, text is also available on the Web. So, another application is to apply iVAS to visualize and analyze web data. Note that the World Wide Web can be considered as a huge widely distributed global information service center for advertisements, consumer information, e-commerce, education, financial management, government, news, and other services. It also contains a rich collection of hyperlink information as well as web page access and usage information. When users (say, web service providers) apply iVAS to conduct visual analytics on the web log data that contain web page access and usage information, each transaction consists of the web pages visited by web surfers in a single session. Then, iVAS allows users to get an insight from the overview showing the distribution of web pages and select those pages of interest. After applying the web mining technique (specifically, web usage mining), iVAS helps users visualize the mined web access patterns that consist of sets of frequently visited web pages. This helps users discover web access patterns, allows users to identify potential clients, and thus enables users to enhance the quality of services provided to the web surfers.

Moreover, iVAS can also be applied to visualize and analyze webpage layout or semantic structure for useful knowledge about web contents. Furthermore, iVAS can be applicable to visualizing and analyzing hyperlink structure, as well as to show the important knowledge about web linkage structures for further analysis.

Application 4: Visual Analytics of Student Enrolment Databases

The fourth application is to apply our proposed iVAS to another domain—namely, a student enrolment database. Here, each transaction in the database represents a collection of courses taken by a university student in an academic term. In a term, a student can take at least one course and at most six courses concurrently. Given such an enrolment database, iVAS shows an overview of the data distribution of student enrolment. This gives users (e.g., administrators, course instructors, etc.) an insight about the data distribution.

In the overview, the *x*-axis shows the course IDs, and the *y*-axis shows student IDs. Each transaction is denoted by either a circle (representing a student taking a single course) or a horizontal line connecting at least two and at most six circles (representing a student taking at least two and at most six courses). When users adjust the resolution slider to zoom in, they can get more details and/or can select and focus on only computer science courses. By vertically counting the number of circles for each course ID, users can obtain the exact number of students enrolled in each course. Even without precise counting, users can get an insight about the popularity of a course by observing whether there are many or just a few circles along the "vertical axis" for that course. If there are any courses of interest, users can select those courses by clicking their course IDs or by drawing a box enclosing those enrolment records of interest. Similarly, if there are any students of interest, users can select those students by clicking their student IDs or by drawing a box enclosing those enrolment records of interest. These enrolment records are then passed to the mining process for further analysis.

Once the frequent sets are found from the selected enrolment records, iVAS displays them in a two-dimensional space. The *x*-axis shows the course IDs, and the *y*-axis shows the frequency of the frequent sets. Each set is denoted by either a diamond symbol (representing a popular course) or a horizontal line connecting a left-triangle and a right-triangle with 0-4 additional circles in between the two triangles (representing a set of 2 to 6 popular courses taken concurrently by students). With the general view of the frequent sets (the output of the data mining process), users can automatically obtain the exact count of the students enrolled in a course without manually counting the number of circles along the "vertical axis" for that course in the overview of the enrolment records (the input of the data mining process).

For an enrolment database, it is not unusual that several combinations have the same frequency so that their corresponding horizontal lines are projected onto a single dashed one in the overview. To obtain the details, users need to expand such a line by clicking the [+] buttons. In such an expanded view, users (e.g., administrators, course instructors, etc.) can get answers to many questions. Answers to these questions help users make intelligent administrative decisions. The following are some samples:

1. *Which course is the most popular (i.e., 1-itemset with the highest frequency)?*

Using the student enrolment data that we collected last academic term, we observed that CS 438 is the most popular course. Based on this information about the popularity of CS 438, users (e.g., administrators) may consider offering an extra section of CS 438 if resource permits.

2. *Which combinations of courses are popular (i.e., frequent k-itemset)?*

We observed that {CS 435, CS 438, CS 458} is the most popular combination of courses (i.e., *k*-itemset with the highest frequency). Based on this information, when users schedule for exams, the users are suggested to avoid scheduling the exam dates for CS 435, CS 438 and CS 458 on the same day. In other words, the users may want to spread out the exam dates for these three courses so as to reduce the chance of exam hardship. Similar suggestions can be applied to other popular combinations of courses such as {CS 215, CS 301} and {CS 438, CS 455}.

3. *Which combination of courses is the least popular (i.e., k-itemset with the lowest frequency)?*

We also observed that CS 430 is the least popular course. Based on this information, if users need to reduce the offerings of courses, they may consider reducing the number of section or cancelling CS 430 as it is the least popular course.

For this database, iVAS first gives an overview of the enrolment information. For instance, there are horizontal lines connecting 2-6 circles (each of which indicates that a student took 2 to 6 courses in an academic term) and there are also some independent circles (each of which indicates that a student took only 1 course in an academic term). Moreover, iVAS also applies a data mining algorithm—specifically, a frequent set mining algorithm—to find 421 frequent sets of popular courses. The contents of these sets were represented by a total of 421 horizontal lines. Some of them are represented by diamonds (each of which indicates a popular course), and some of them are represented by horizontal lines connecting triangles and circles (each of which indicates a combination of popular courses). Recall that iVAS provides users with an option of showing the important knowledge in the form of closed frequent sets. When users pick this option, iVAS applies a closed set mining algorithm instead. Consequently, it saves computation and returns only 107 closed sets (vs. 421 frequent sets). There closed sets are represented by iVAS in 107 horizontal lines. When projecting these horizontal lines, we observe 3 solid lines and 17 expandable dashed lines. This means that, among 107 closed sets,

1. 3 of them have unique frequencies, and
2. Some of the remaining $107 - 3 = 104$ closed sets share the same frequencies (one of the 17 frequency values).

FUTURE RESEARCH DIRECTIONS

So far, we have presented our interactive visual analytic system—iVAS—for exploratory or visual data mining. We have shown how iVAS uses cardinality constraints to display only those frequent sets that satisfy the user cardinality constraint (i.e., those frequent sets consisting of k items, where k is a single value or a range of values specified by the user). By imposing cardinality constraints, iVAS reduces the number of frequent sets to be visualized and analyzed, thus reducing the amount of computation. Besides the cardinality constraints, there are other constraints. Hence, a future research direction is to adapt *constraint-based mining techniques* (Bonchi, 2009; Leung, 2009; Cuzzocrea et al., 2014) for constrained visual analytics. By doing so, users could focus the mining on certain subsets of the databases and/or frequent sets by freely specifying some constraints to express their interest. The resulting visual analytics technique could then push the constraints into the mining process so that the technique could discover all and only those frequent sets that satisfy the user-specified constraints (e.g., constrained frequent sets) directly—without having a post-processing step to examine and/or visualize all frequent sets and distinguish those that satisfy the constraints from those that do not.

Moreover, iVAS currently visualizes and analyzes the transactions in traditional *static* databases as well as the frequent sets mined from these databases containing *precise* data such that the presence of an item in a transaction or the absence of an item from a transaction is definitely known. Due to advances in technology, large volumes of *data streams* (Gaber et al., 2005; Leung et al., 2013a; Cuzzocrea et al., 2015) can be easily generated at a rapid rate. In many real-life applications, technologies for visualizing and analyzing these *dynamic* streams of data are needed. Moreover, as we are living in an uncertain world, there are situations (e.g., laboratory test results, medical diagnosis, etc.), in which we need to handle *uncertain data* (Leung et al., 2008c; Aggarwal & Yu, 2009; Leung & Tanbeer, 2013; Ahmed et al., 2016). In these situations, the presence of an item in a transaction is *uncertain*. One can only express the likelihood of the occurrence of such an item or event, but one cannot guarantee the absolute presence or absence of such an item or event. As future work, we plan to extend our iVAS to visualize and analyze these *streams of uncertain data* as soon as they arrive.

CONCLUSION

Many frequent set mining algorithms return the data analysis results in the form of a textual list of frequently occurring sets of items. This lengthy list can be difficult for the human user to comprehend. As suggested by the adage "a picture is worth a thousand words", it is desirable to use visualization techniques. This book chapter presents an *interactive visual analytic system* (*iVAS*) for effective next-generation visual analytics of

1. Information (e.g., transactions in data), and
2. Knowledge (e.g., the frequent sets of items mined from these transactional data).

We also demonstrated the practicability of iVAS in several real-life applications. For both the input (i.e., information) and the output (i.e., knowledge) of the mining process, iVAS provides users with interactive visual analytics of the original data and the mined frequent sets. By following both the visual information seeking and visual analytics mantras, iVAS gives the user an overview, manages and analyzes the data, shows the important knowledge, allows the user to zoom in on the information of interest, filters out uninteresting information so that the remainder can be analyzed further, and provides the user with details on demand. Such a system facilitates next-generation information retrieval and knowledge resources management by providing interactive visual analytics in the era of big data.

REFERENCES

Aggarwal, C. C., & Yu, P. S. (2009). A survey of uncertain data algorithms and applications. *IEEE Transactions on Knowledge and Data Engineering, 21*(5), 609–623. doi:10.1109/TKDE.2008.190

Agrawal, R., Imieliński, T., & Swami, A. N. (1993). Mining association rules between sets of items in large databases. In P. Buneman, & S. Jajodia (Eds.), *Proceedings of the 1993 ACM SIGMOD International Conference on Management of Data* (pp. 207-216). New York: ACM. doi:10.1145/170035.170072

Agrawal, R., & Srikank, R. (1994). Fast algorithms for mining association rules in large databases. In J.B. Bocca, M. Jarke, & C. Zaniolo (Eds.), *Proceedings of the 20th International Conference on Very Large Data Bases* (pp. 487-499). San Francisco, CA: Morgan Kaufmann.

Ahlberg, C. (1996). Spotfire: An information exploration environment. *SIGMOD Record, 25*(4), 25–29. doi:10.1145/245882.245893

Ahmed, A. U., Ahmed, C. F., Samiullah, M., Adnan, N., & Leung, C. K.-S. (2016). Mining interesting patterns from uncertain databases. *Information Sciences, 354*, 60–85. doi:10.1016/j.ins.2016.03.007

Akoglu, L., Chau, D. H., Kang, U., Koutra, D., & Faloutsos, C. (2012). OPAvion: mining and visualization in large graphs. In K.S. Candan, Y. Chen, R.T. Snodgrass, L. Gravano, & A. Fuxman (Eds.), *Proceedings of the 2012 ACM SIGMOD International Conference on Management of Data* (pp.717-720). New York: ACM. doi:10.1145/2213836.2213941

Al-Rajab, M. M., & Lu, J. (2016). A study on the most common algorithms implemented for cancer gene search and classifications. *International Journal of Data Mining and Bioinformatics, 14*(2), 159–176. doi:10.1504/IJDMB.2016.074685

Alencar, A. B., de Oliveira, M. C. F., & Paulovich, F. V. (2012). Seeing beyond reading: A survey on visual text analytics. *WIREs Data Mining and Knowledge Discovery, 2*(6), 476–492. doi:10.1002/widm.1071

Anderson, N., & Hong, J. (2013). Visually extracting data records from query result pages. In Y. Ishikawa, J. Li, W. Wang, R. Zhang, & W. Zhang (Eds.), *Proceedings of the 15th Asia-Pacific Web Conference* (LNCS), (vol. 7808, pp. 392-403). Heidelberg, Germany: Springer. doi:10.1007/978-3-642-37401-2_40

Ankerst, M., Elsen, C., Ester, M., & Kriegel, H.-P. (1999). Visual classification: an interactive approach to decision tree construction. In U. Fayyad, S. Chaudhuri, & D. Madigan (Eds.), *Proceedings of the Fifth ACM SIGKDD International Conference on Knowledge Discovery and Data Mining* (pp. 392-396). New York: ACM. doi:10.1145/312129.312298

Berchtold, S., Jagadish, H. V., & Ross, K. A. (1998). Independence diagrams: a technique for visual data mining. In R. Agrawal, P.E. Stolorz, & G. Piatetsky-Shapiro (Eds.), *Proceedings of the Fourth International Conference on Knowledge Discovery and Data Mining* (pp. 139-143). Menlo Park, CA: AAAI Press.

Blanchard, J., Guillet, F., & Briand, H. (2007). Interactive visual exploration of association rules with rule-focusing methodology. *Knowledge and Information Systems*, *13*(1), 43–75. doi:10.1007/s10115-006-0046-2

Bonchi, F. (2009). Constraint-based pattern discovery. In J. Wang (Ed.), *Encyclopedia of data warehousing and mining* (2nd ed.; pp. 313–319). Hershey, PA: IGI Global. doi:10.4018/978-1-60566-010-3.ch050

Bothorel, G., Serrurier, M., & Hurter, C. (2013). Visualization of frequent itemsets with nested circular layout and bundling algorithm. In G. Bebis, R. Boyle, B. Parvin, D. Koracin, B. Li, F. Porikli, V. Zordan, J. Klosowski, S. Coquillart, X. Luo, M. Chen, & D. Gotz (Eds.), *Proceedings of the 9th International Symposium on Visual Computing* (LNCS), (vol. 8034, pp. 396-405). Heidelberg, Germany: Springer. doi:10.1007/978-3-642-41939-3_38

Cheng, H., & Han, J. (2009). Frequent itemsets and association rules. In L. Liu & M. T. Özsu (Eds.), *Encyclopedia of database systems* (pp. 1184–1187). New York: Springer.

Cuzzocrea, A., Jiang, F., Leung, C.K., Liu, D., Peddle, A., & Tanbeer, S.K. (2015). Mining popular patterns: a novel mining problem and its application to static transactional databases and dynamic data streams. *LNCS Transactions on Large-Scale Data- and Knowledge-Centered Systems (TLDKS) XXI* (LNCS), (vol. 9260, pp. 115-139). Springer. doi:10.1007/978-3-662-47804-2_6

Cuzzocrea, A., Lee, W., & Leung, C. K.-S. (2015). High-recall information retrieval from linked big data. In S.I. Ahamed, C.K. Chang, W. Chu, I. Crnkovic, P.-A. Hsiung, G. Huang, & J. Yang (Eds.), *Proceedings of the 39th IEEE International Computer Software and Applications Conference* (Vol. 2, pp. 712-717). Los Alamitos, CA: IEEE Computer Society. doi:10.1109/COMPSAC.2015.152

Cuzzocrea, A., Leung, C. K., & MacKinnon, R. K. (2014). Mining constrained frequent itemsets from distributed uncertain data. *Future Generation Computer Systems*, *37*, 117–126. doi:10.1016/j.future.2013.10.026

Dietrich, C. J., Rossow, C., & Pohlmann, N. (2013). Exploiting visual appearance to cluster and detect rogue software. In S.Y. Shin, & J.C. Maldonado (Eds.), *Proceedings of the 28th Annual ACM Symposium on Applied Computing* (pp. 1776-1783). New York: ACM. doi:10.1145/2480362.2480697

Fariha, A., Ahmed, C. F., Leung, C. K.-S., Samiullah, M., Pervin, S., & Cao, L. (2015). A new framework for mining frequent interaction patterns from meeting databases. *Engineering Applications of Artificial Intelligence*, *45*, 103–118. doi:10.1016/j.engappai.2015.06.019

Frawley, W. J., Piatetsky-Shapiro, G., & Matheus, C. J. (1991). Knowledge discovery in databases: an overview. In G. Piatetsky-Shapiro & W. J. Frawley (Eds.), *Knowledge discovery in databases* (pp. 1–30). Cambridge, MA: The MIT Press.

Gaber, M. M., Zaslavsky, A., & Krishnaswamy, S. (2005). Mining data streams: A review. *SIGMOD Record, 34*(2), 18–26. doi:10.1145/1083784.1083789

Grinstein, G., Plaisant, C., Laskowski, S., O'Connell, T., Scholtz, J., & Whiting, M. (2008). VAST 2008 Challenge: introducing mini-challenges. In D. Ebert, & T. Ertl (Eds.), *Proceedings of the 2008 IEEE Symposium on Visual Analytics Science and Technology* (pp. 195-196). Piscataway, NJ: IEEE. doi:10.1109/VAST.2008.4677383

Han, J., & Cercone, N. (2000). AViz: A visualization system for discovering numeric association rules. In T. Terano, H. Liu, & A.L.P. Chen (Eds.), *Proceedings of the Fourth Pacific-Asia Conference on Knowledge Discovery and Data Mining* (LNAI), (vol. 1805, pp. 269-280). Heidelberg, Germany: Springer. doi:10.1007/3-540-45571-X_33

Han, J., Cheng, H., Xin, D., & Yan, X. (2007). Frequent pattern mining: Current status and future directions. *Data Mining and Knowledge Discovery, 15*(1), 55–86. doi:10.1007/s10618-006-0059-1

Heimerl, F., Han, Q., Koch, S., & Ertl, T. (2016). CiteRivers: Visual analytics of citation patterns. *IEEE Transactions on Visualization and Computer Graphics, 22*(1), 190–199. doi:10.1109/TVCG.2015.2467621 PMID:26529699

Jiang, F., & Leung, C. K.-S. (2015). A data analytic algorithm for managing, querying, and processing uncertain big data in cloud environments. *Algorithms, 8*(4), 1175–1194. doi:10.3390/a8041175

Keim, D. A., & Kriegel, H.-P. (1996). Visualization techniques for mining large databases: A comparison. *IEEE Transactions on Knowledge and Data Engineering, 8*(6), 923–938. doi:10.1109/69.553159

Keim, D. A., Mansmann, F., Schneidewind, J., Thomas, J., & Ziegler, H. (2008). Visual analytics: scope and challenges. In S.J. Simoff, M.H. Böhlen, & A. Mazeika (Eds.), Visual Data Mining: Theory, Techniques and Tools for Visual Analytics (LNCS), (vol. 4404, pp. 76-90). Heidelberg, Germany: Springer. doi:10.1007/978-3-540-71080-6_6

Keim, D. A., Mansmann, F., Schneidewind, J., & Ziegler, H. (2006). Challenges in visual data analysis. In E. Banissi, R.A. Burkhard, A. Ursyn, J.J. Zhang, M. Bannatyne, C. Maple, A.J. Cowell, G.Y. Tian, & M. Hou (Eds.), *Proceedings of the 10th IEEE International Conference on Information Visualisation* (pp. 9-16). Los Alamitos, CA: IEEE Computer Society. doi:10.1109/IV.2006.31

Keim, D. A., Mansmann, F., Stoffel, A., & Ziegler, H. (2009a). Visual analytics. In L. Liu & M. T. Özsu (Eds.), *Encyclopedia of database systems* (pp. 3341–3346). New York: Springer.

Keim, D. A., Mansmann, F., & Thomas, J. (2009b). Visual analytics: How much visualization and how much analytics? *SIGKDD Explorations, 11*(2), 5–8. doi:10.1145/1809400.1809403

Keim, D. A., Qu, H., & Ma, K.-L. (2013). Big-data visualization. *IEEE Computer Graphics and Applications, 33*(4), 20–21. doi:10.1109/MCG.2013.54 PMID:24921095

Koren, Y., & Harel, D. (2003). A two-way visualization method for clustered data. In L. Getoor, T.E. Senator, P. Domingos, & C. Faloutsos (Eds.), *Proceedings of the Ninth ACM SIGKDD International Conference on Knowledge Discovery and Data Mining* (pp. 589-594). New York: ACM. doi:10.1145/956750.956824

Kumar, A., Kumar, S., & Saxena, S. (2012). An efficient approach for incremental association rule mining through histogram matching technique. *International Journal of Information Retrieval Research*, 2(2), 29–42. doi:10.4018/ijirr.2012040103

Lakshmanan, L. V. S., Leung, C. K.-S., & Ng, R. T. (2003). Efficient dynamic mining of constrained frequent sets. *ACM Transactions on Database Systems*, 28(4), 337–389. doi:10.1145/958942.958944

Leung, C. K.-S. (2009). Constraint-based association rule mining. In J. Wang (Ed.), *Encyclopedia of data warehousing and mining* (2nd ed.; pp. 307–312). Hershey, PA: IGI Global. doi:10.4018/978-1-60566-010-3.ch049

Leung, C. K.-S. (2014). Big data mining and analytics. In J. Wang (Ed.), *Encyclopedia of data business analytics and optimization*. Hershey, PA: IGI Global. doi:10.4018/978-1-4666-5202-6.ch030

Leung, C. K.-S., & Carmichael, C. L. (2009). FpViz: A visualizer for frequent pattern mining. In K. Puolamäki (Ed.), *Proceedings of the ACM SIGKDD Workshop on Visual Analytics and Knowledge Discovery: Integrating Automated Analysis with Interactive Exploration* (pp. 30-39). New York: ACM. doi:10.1145/1562849.1562853

Leung, C. K.-S., & Carmichael, C. L. (2011). iVAS: An interactive visual analytics system for frequent set mining. In Q. Zhang, R. Segall, & M. Cao (Eds.), Visual analytics and interactive technologies: Data text, and web mining (pp. 213-231). Hershey, PA: IGI Global. doi:10.4018/978-1-60960-102-7.ch013

Leung, C.K.-S., Cuzzocrea, A., & Jiang, F. (2013a). Discovering frequent patterns from uncertain data streams with time-fading and landmark models. *LNCS Transactions on Large-Scale Data- and Knowledge-Centered Systems*, 8, 174-196. doi:10.1007/978-3-642-37574-3_8

Leung, C. K.-S., Irani, P. P., & Carmichael, C. L. (2008a). FIsViz: a frequent itemset visualizer. In T. Washio, E. Suzuki, K.M. Ting, & A. Inokuchi (Eds.), *Proceedings of the 12th Pacific-Asia Conference on Knowledge Discovery and Data Mining* (LNAI), (vol. 5012, pp. 644-652). Heidelberg, Germany: Springer. doi:10.1007/978-3-540-68125-0_60

Leung, C. K.-S., Irani, P. P., & Carmichael, C. L. (2008b). WiFIsViz: effective visualization of frequent itemsets. In F. Giannotti, D. Gunopulos, F. Turini, C. Zaniolo, N. Ramakrishnan, & X. Wu (Eds.), *Proceedings of the Eighth IEEE International Conference on Data Mining* (pp. 875-880). Los Alamitos, CA: IEEE Computer Society. doi:10.1109/ICDM.2008.93

Leung, C. K.-S., & Jiang, F. (2012). RadialViz: An orientation-free frequent pattern visualizer. In P.-N. Tan, S. Chawla, C.K. Ho, & J. Bailey (Eds.), *Proceedings of 16th Pacific-Asia Conference on Knowledge Discovery and Data Mining* (LNAI), (vol. 7302, pp. 322-334). Heidelberg, Germany: Springer. doi:10.1007/978-3-642-30220-6_27

Leung, C. K.-S., & Jiang, F. (2015) Big data analytics of social networks for the discovery of "following" patterns. In S. Madria & T. Hara (Eds.), *Proceedings of 17th International Conference on Big Data Analytics and Knowledge Discovery* (LNCS), (vol. 9263, pp. 123-135). Heidelberg, Germany: Springer. doi:10.1007/978-3-319-22729-0_10

Leung, C. K.-S., Jiang, F., & Irani, P. P. (2011). FpMapViz: a space-filling visualization for frequent patterns. In M. Spiliopoulou, H. Wang, D.J. Cook, J. Pei, W. Wang, O.R. Zaïane, & X. Wu (Eds.), *Workshop Proceedings of 2011 IEEE 11th International Conference on Data Mining* (pp. 804-811). Los Alamitos, CA: IEEE Computer Society. doi:10.1109/ICDMW.2011.86

Leung, C. K.-S., Jiang, F., Pazdor, A. G. M., & Peddle, A. M. (2016a). Parallel social network mining for interesting following patterns. *Concurrency and Computation*, *28*(15), 3994–4012. doi:10.1002/cpe.3773

Leung, C. K.-S., Jiang, F., Sun, L., & Wang, Y. (2012). A constrained frequent pattern mining system for handling aggregate constraints. In B.C. Desai, J. Pokorný, & J. Bernardino (Eds.), *Proceedings of the 16th International Database Engineering & Applications Symposium* (pp. 14-23). New York: ACM. doi:10.1145/2351476.2351479

Leung, C. K.-S., Khan, Q. I., Li, Z., & Hoque, T. (2007). CanTree: A canonical-order tree for incremental frequent-pattern mining. *Knowledge and Information Systems*, *11*(3), 287–311. doi:10.1007/s10115-006-0032-8

Leung, C. K.-S., MacKinnon, R. K., & Tanbeer, S. K. (2014). Fast algorithms for frequent itemset mining from uncertain data. In R. Kumar, H. Toivonen, J. Pei, J.Z. Huang, & X. Wu (Eds.), *Proceedings of the 14th IEEE International Conference on Data Mining* (pp. 893-898). Los Alamitos, CA: IEEE Computer Society. doi:10.1109/ICDM.2014.146

Leung, C. K.-S., Mateo, M. A. F., & Brajczuk, D. A. (2008c). A tree-based approach for frequent pattern mining from uncertain data. In T. Washio, E. Suzuki, K.M. Ting, & A. Inokuchi (Eds.), *Proceedings of the 12th Pacific-Asia Conference on Knowledge Discovery and Data Mining* (*LNAI 5012*, pp. 653-661). Heidelberg, Germany: Springer. doi:10.1007/978-3-540-68125-0_61

Leung, C. K.-S., Medina, I. J. M., & Tanbeer, S. K. (2013b). Analyzing social networks to mine important friends. In G. Xu & L. Li (Eds.), *Social media mining and social network analysis: Emerging research* (pp. 90–104). Hershey, PA: IGI Global. doi:10.4018/978-1-4666-2806-9.ch006

Leung, C. K.-S., & Tanbeer, S. K. (2013). PUF-tree: a compact tree structure for frequent pattern mining of uncertain data. In J. Pei, V.S. Tseng, L. Cao, H. Motoda, & G. Xu (Eds.), *Proceedings of the 17th Pacific-Asia Conference on Knowledge Discovery and Data Mining* (LNAI), (vol. 7818, pp. 13-25). Heidelberg, Germany: Springer. doi:10.1007/978-3-642-37453-1_2

Leung, C. K.-S., Tanbeer, S. K., & Cameron, J. J. (2014). Interactive discovery of influential friends from social networks. *Social Network Analysis and Mining*, *4*(1), 154. doi:10.1007/s13278-014-0154-z

Leung, C. K.-S., Tanbeer, S. K., Cuzzocrea, A., Braun, P., & MacKinnon, R. K. (2016b). Interactive mining of diverse social entities. *International Journal of Knowledge-based and Intelligent Engineering Systems*, *20*(2), 97–111. doi:10.3233/KES-160332

Liu, B. (2009). Classification by association rule analysis. In L. Liu & M. T. Özsu (Eds.), *Encyclopedia of database systems* (pp. 335–340). New York: Springer.

Liu, G., Suchitra, A., Zhang, H., Feng, M., Ng, S.-K., & Wong, L. (2013). AssocExplorer: an association rule visualization system for exploratory data analysis. In Q. Yang, D. Agarwal, & J. Pei (Eds.), *Proceedings of the 18th ACM SIGKDD International Conference on Knowledge Discovery and Data Mining* (pp. 1536-1539). New York: ACM Press. doi:10.1145/2339530.2339774

Meng, Z., & Lu, J. (2013). Integrating technical advance in mobile devices to enhance the information retrieval in mobile learning. *International Journal of Information Retrieval Research, 3*(3), 1–25. doi:10.4018/ijirr.2013070101

Munzer, T., Kong, Q., Ng, R. T., Lee, J., Klawe, J., Radulovic, D., & Leung, C. K.-S. (2005). *Visual mining of power sets with large alphabets (Tech. rep. UBC CS TR-2005-25)*. Vancouver, BC, Canada: The University of British Columbia.

Pasquier, N., Bastide, Y., Taouil, R., & Lakhal, L. (1999). Discovering frequent closed itemsets for association rules. In C. Beeri & P. Buneman (Eds.), *Proceedings of the Seventh International Conference on Database Theory* (LNCS), (vol. 1540, pp. 398-416). Heidelberg, Germany: Springer. doi:10.1007/3-540-49257-7_25

Pei, J., Han, J., Mortazavi-Asl, B., & Zhu, H. (2000). Mining access patterns efficiently from web logs. In T. Terano, H. Liu, & A.L.P. Chen (Eds.), *Proceedings of the Fourth Pacific-Asia Conference on Knowledge Discovery and Data Mining* (LNAI), (vol. 1805, pp. 396-407). Heidelberg, Germany: Springer. doi:10.1007/3-540-45571-X_47

Qi, Y. (2013). Text mining in bioinformatics: Research and application. *International Journal of Information Retrieval Research, 3*(2), 30–39. doi:10.4018/ijirr.2013040102

Schreck, T., Bernard, J., Tekušová, T., & Kohlhammer, J. (2008). Visual cluster analysis of trajectory data with interactive Kohonen Maps. In D. Ebert, & T. Ertl (Eds.), *Proceedings of the 2008 IEEE Symposium on Visual Analytics Science and Technology* (pp. 3-10). Piscataway, NJ: IEEE. doi:10.1109/VAST.2008.4677350

Schreck, T., & Keim, D. (2013). Visual analysis of social media data. *IEEE Computer, 46*(5), 68–75. doi:10.1109/MC.2012.430

Sedova, M., Jaroszewski, L., & Godzik, A. (2016). Protael: Protein data visualization library for the web. *Bioinformatics (Oxford, England), 32*(4), 602–604. doi:10.1093/bioinformatics/btv605 PMID:26515826

Shneiderman, B. (1996). The eyes have it: A task by data type taxonomy for information visualizations. In *Proceedings of the 1996 IEEE Symposium on Visual Languages* (pp. 336-343). Los Alamitos, CA: IEEE Computer Society. doi:10.1109/VL.1996.545307

Siau, K., Nah, F. F.-H., Mennecke, B. E., & Schiller, S. Z. (2010). Co-creation and collaboration in a virtual world: A 3D visualization design project in second life. *Journal of Database Management, 21*(4), 1–13. doi:10.4018/jdm.2010100101

Stolte, C., Tang, D., & Hanrahan, P. (2002). Query, analysis, and visualization of hierarchically structured data using Polaris. In D. Hand, D. Keim, & R. Ng (Eds.), *Proceedings of the Eighth ACM SIGKDD International Conference on Knowledge Discovery and Data Mining* (pp. 112-122). New York: ACM. doi:10.1145/775047.775064

Thomas, J. J., & Cook, K. A. (Eds.). (2005). *Illuminating the path: the research and development agenda for visual analytics*. Los Alamitos, CA: IEEE Computer Society.

Tong, Y., Chen, L., & Ding, B. (2012). Discovering threshold-based frequent closed itemsets over probabilistic data. In A. Kementsietsidis, M. Antonio, & V. Salles (Eds.), *Proceedings of the IEEE 28th International Conference on Data Engineering* (pp. 270-281). Los Alamitos, CA: IEEE Computer Society. doi:10.1109/ICDE.2012.51

Yang, L. (2005). Pruning and visualizing generalized association rules in parallel coordinates. *IEEE Transactions on Knowledge and Data Engineering, 17*(1), 60–70. doi:10.1109/TKDE.2005.14

Yang, L. (2009). Visual association rules. In L. Liu & M. T. Özsu (Eds.), *Encyclopedia of Database Systems* (pp. 3346–3352). New York: Springer.

Zaki, M. J., & Hsiao, C.-J. (2005). Efficient algorithms for mining closed itemsets and their lattice structure. *IEEE Transactions on Knowledge and Data Engineering, 17*(4), 462–478. doi:10.1109/TKDE.2005.60

Zhang, L., Stoffel, A., Behrisch, M., Mittelstädt, S., Schreck, T., Pompl, R., & Keim, D. et al. (2013). Visual analytics for the big data era - a comparative review of state-of-the-art commercial systems. In G. Santucci, & M. Ward (Eds.), *Proceedings of the 2012 IEEE Conference on Visual Analytics Science and Technology* (pp.173-182). Los Alamitos, CA: IEEE Computer Society.

Zhu, X., Huang, Z., & Wu, X. (2013). Multi-view visual classification via a mixed-norm regularizer. In J. Pei, V.S. Tseng, L. Cao, H. Motoda, & G. Xu (Eds.), *Proceedings of the 17th Pacific-Asia Conference on Knowledge Discovery and Data Mining* (LNAI), (vol. 7818, pp. 520-531). Heidelberg, Germany: Springer. doi:10.1007/978-3-642-37453-1_43

KEY TERMS AND DEFINITIONS

Big Data: Big data are high-velocity streams of a wide variety of valuable data with volumes beyond the ability of commonly-used software to capture, manage, and process within a tolerable elapsed time. These big data necessitate new forms of processing to deliver high veracity (and low vulnerability) and to enable enhanced decision making, insight, knowledge discovery, and process optimization.

Data Mining: Data mining discovers implicit, previously unknown, and potentially useful knowledge from data.

Frequent Set: A frequent set is a set of items having frequency exceeds or equals the use-specified minimum threshold.

Frequent Set Mining: Frequent set mining aims to discover implicit, previously unknown, and potentially useful knowledge in the form of sets of frequently co-occurring items.

Information Retrieval: Information retrieval returns explicit and highly relevant information or resources about data.

Itemset: An itemset is a set of items.

Visual Analytics: Visual analytics is the science of analytical reasoning supported by interactive visual interfaces; it is also the new enabling and accessible analytics reasoning interactions supported by the combination of automated and visual analysis.

Chapter 2
Knowledge Discovery for Large Databases in Education Institutes

Robab Saadatdoost
Islamic Azad University, Parand Branch, Iran

Hosein Jafarkarimi
Islamic Azad University, Damavand Branch, Iran

Alex Tze Hiang Sim
Universiti Teknologi Malaysia, Malaysia

Jee Mei Hee
Universiti Teknologi Malaysia, Malaysia

ABSTRACT

This project presents the patterns and relations between attributes of Iran Higher Education data gained from the use of data mining techniques to discover knowledge and use them in decision making system of IHE. Large dataset of IHE is difficult to analysis and display, since they are significant for decision making in IHE. This study utilized the famous data mining software, Weka and SOM to mine and visualize IHE data. In order to discover worthwhile patterns, we used clustering techniques and visualized the results. The selected dataset includes data of five medical university of Tehran as a small data set and Ministry of Science - Research and Technology's universities as a larger data set. Knowledge discovery and visualization are necessary for analyzing of these datasets. Our analysis reveals some knowledge in higher education aspect related to program of study, degree in each program, learning style, study mode and other IHE attributes. This study helps to IHE to discover knowledge in a visualize way; our results can be focused more by experts in higher education field to assess and evaluate more.

INTRODUCTION

Describe the general perspective of the chapter. End by specifically stating the objectives of the chapter.

Nowadays each organization deals with some data about their area and during time it increases, one of these organizations that includes big volume of data is higher education institute that has always held much data about universities, students and teachers. Thus, it is possible for us to discover some worthwhile relations or patterns that can be useful for making decision. For examples, planning the future development of a university and identifying the cluster of students who required more attentions. Management

DOI: 10.4018/978-1-5225-2058-0.ch002

faces many challenges particularly in planning and for this purpose it needs some facts extracted from data. In our rapidly changing world, every year we accumulate data and add it to our data sets so after several years we will have a massive databank, in this environment every year our data volume increases so we need some tools to analysis this data for extracting some valuable outcome from it. Data mining has many techniques that can apply and facilitate analyzing of data.

Data mining has many definitions and almost all of them point to the discovery of patterns, and the analysis of some relations between variables in data. It does not limit to collecting and managing data; it also includes analysis. In this study, we intend to use historical data as the basis of discovering hidden relations. We intend to perform data mining techniques to discover knowledge. There are some examples, such as:

- Mining of statistical data of one university to discover successful students (Venus Shokorniaz & Akbari, 2008).
- Mining on students and discovering groups of students those are available from the data and their relations (Yghini, Akbari, & Sharifi, 2008).

In this project, we applied data mining techniques on data related to Iran Higher Education Institute to discover some relations and patterns that are useful in decision making system of higher education.

We have chosen this topic because of government and management of universities need to plan before an event occurrence. We face huge data and need to analysis them to reach some knowledge. For this purpose, we need some techniques that data mining helps us on this way, data mining has two common techniques that are classification and clustering. In this project we study about these techniques and choose one of them in our project.

Clustering is a data mining technique that is a division of data elements into groups of similar objects without advance knowledge of the group definitions. In addition, it is a tool for data analysis, which solves classification problems. In clustering, there are strong associations between members of each group and according to the type of clustering; Clustering algorithms have 4 types: exclusive, overlapping, Hierarchical, and Probabilistic. We may find some associations between different groups. Some of these associations are strong and some of them are weak. For example exclusive algorithm has weak association and overlapping has strong (Berkhin, 2006). Clustering is a discovery tool that may discover associations and patterns in data which is not previously obvious. In short: clustering attempts to find some groups of elements, based on some similarities (Ong, 2000). One of the cluster analyses is SOM (self-organizing method) that is one of the most important algorithms in data visualization and exploration. Visualization transforms from the invisible to the visible (Alhoniemi et al., 2002, 2003). SOM is a particular type of neural network used in clustering. It maps high dimensional input onto two dimensional.

Classification is a data mining technique that predicts data elements' group, for example we can predict the weather of a day will be sunny, rainy or cloudy. In classification we have predefined classes that classification is a task to assign instances to these classes opposite of clustering that we don't have knowledge about group definitions. In clustering we cluster elements based on their attribute on the contrary in classifying we classify elements into groups by recognizing pattern.

Our concern in this study is finding a way to discover exciting knowledge for universities management to achieve an appropriate plan to improve society. Each society can be affected by higher education; its economic, political and scientific improvement can be resulted by advanced higher education, when we develop our programs and management part in universities so its output will be successful graduated students that can be helpful in every part of one society.

The main problem is the volume of data that we have in higher education and government needs to analysis and discover fast and correct knowledge from them. "How we can discover it?" is our significant question. Our endeavour was proposing a methodology to discover knowledge that reveals some patterns and relations between data. We have huge databases about universities but most of time we cannot use them efficiently because we don't have appropriate pattern for our executive system whereas we have data to this purpose.

We encounter many challenges in higher education such as allocating budget to universities in start of new semester without delay, accepting accurate number of students for every semester, finding ways for effective teaching. In this study our intension is discover some findings that help us in this way to improve higher education decisions and policies.

Objectives of this study are:

- To study for an appropriate data mining approach suitable for analysing Higher Education Institute of Iran.
- To analyse data on medical universities to discover patterns usable for managerial decision making.
- To generalise steps for discovery on larger number of universities.
- To suggest an appropriate software for the analyses of this research.

Knowledge discovery is necessary for most of our plantings. Nowadays planning for higher education has significant impact on developing of one society, successful planning needs to analysis some huge and historical data that is available in higher education institutes; most of the time there is not any correct and precise analysis whereas this analysis can be helpful for managers, researchers to plan, report and discover some knowledge.

The other importance of this project is collection of data with large volume that relate to many universities during many years so it has high probability to discover some exciting knowledge. This study can be used in every university, because it faces much data about students, teachers, staff and financial resources and most of the time, this data includes information and worthwhile patterns.

The methodology that will be suggested is helpful for higher education institute in collecting data and to discover some knowledge for improving management decisions. Furthermore, it can be useful for researchers that study and research about higher education. This knowledge leads us to development in technical, scientific and economic aspects according to type of data that we will analyse.

Background

Provide broad definitions and discussions of the topic and incorporate views of others (literature review) into the discussion to support, refute, or demonstrate your position on the topic.

Data mining (DM) contains some algorithms aimed at discovering patterns and relations from raw data (Aldana, 2000). It was introduced in 1990 and its goal is extracting useful knowledge that helps human to understand better. Data mining origins from three disciplines: statistics, artificial intelligence (AI) and machine learning. Statistics contains some concepts like cluster analysis standard deviation and standard variance (Aldana, 2000). It is foundation of data mining and helps us to study data and its relationships.AI is based on heuristic, heuristic is a way of finding something or an idea hidden in a program for example its functions are used in measuring how far a node is from a goal (Aldana, 2000). AI endeavour is applying human-thought-like processing to statistical problems; it needs high computer processing power (Aldana, 2000). The third discipline is machine learning. It merges statistics and AI, its price is lower than AI so it is an evolution of AI, it uses both of AI and heuristics and statistical analysis (Aldana, 2000). Machine learning use statistics for concepts and AI algorithms to achieve its objectives (Aldana, 2000). Data mining is best defined as the integration of historical and new development in statistics, AI and machine learning (Aldana, 2000). All of these techniques are used to study data and discover hidden rules and patterns within (Aldana, 2000).

Definition

At first we need to know about some terminologies. According to Russell Ackoff human mind can be classified to 5 groups: data, information, knowledge, understanding and wisdom (Bellinger, Castro, & Mills, 2010):

- Data is raw and it does not have meaning of itself.
- Information is data that have given meaning by some relations.
- Knowledge is collection of information and its purpose is to be useful.
- Understanding is the process by which we can produce and discover new knowledge from past knowledge.
- Wisdom is a human state. It gives us understanding about which there has been no understanding, it is a process by which we can judge between true and false.

There is diagram that is described by Ackoff (Bellinger et al., 2010) (Figure 1). It represents the transitions from data, to information, to knowledge, and finally to wisdom and understanding supports the transition from each level to the next (Bellinger et al., 2010).

Figure 1. Transition from data to wisdom

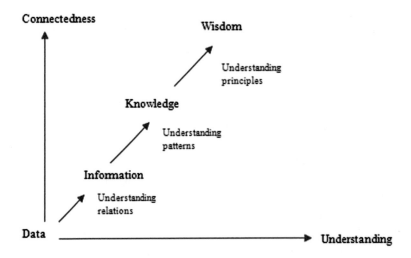

Data mining is a new technology to process information; it has gained some important outcomes in higher education. It extracts knowledge that hidden in the data. Data mining combines machine learning, statistics, database technology and some other subjects (Fangjun, 2010). In the recent years data mining had a rapid growth in research issues and applied in various backgrounds such as industry, agriculture, knowledge management, finance and so on (Fangjun, 2010). Before rapid growth of database volumes, it is possible for users to manually extract knowledge from data, but due to large volumes of datasets we have to use knowledge discovery in database which is related to data mining and helps to automatic extraction of meaningful, unknown patterns or rules and useful information from data. Data mining has gained much attention in database communities because of its wide usages (Tsai & Chen, 2001) .Nowadays we collect large volume of data, so for understanding the real value of data we need a solution, this solution can be knowledge discovery that is a process which analysis large data sets for discovering hidden patterns (Famili, 2009). Knowledge discovery is the process of applying many techniques like statistical, machine learning and the others to databases (Saraee & Theodoulidis, 1995). All of these results are crucial for management of higher education to make the best decision and strategy according to hidden rules in the large volumes of historical datasets.

Knowledge Discovery Process

In this project we faced three terminologies: data mining, knowledge discovery and knowledge discovery in data bases. Data mining (DM) is one of the steps of knowledge discovery process and it is a synonym for knowledge discovery (KD) (Cios, pedrycz, swiniarski, & kurgan 2007). Knowledge discovery process (KDP) is called knowledge discovery in database (KDD) that extract new knowledge from massive datasets (Cios et al., 2007).

KDP includes many steps, one of these steps is DM. knowledge discovery attempts to cover the entire extraction process including storing, accessing data, how to use efficient algorithms to analysis huge volume of data and how to visualize the results. (Cios et al., 2007) There are different KDPs; all of them have common characteristic and it is the definition of inputs and outputs (Cios et al., 2007). The inputs consist of database, image, video, XML, HTML and so on (Cios et al., 2007). The output is a new knowledge showed in various formats like rules, classification model, patterns, statistical analysis, etc (Cios et al., 2007).

KDD process has some steps mentioned below (Fayyad & Uthurusamy, 1996):

- Data selection.
- Pre-processing.
- Transform.
- Data mining.
- Validate.

In data selection step a sample dataset is selected, in the pre-processing step the irrelevant records and null fields and repetitive records are eliminated, this step helps us to increase quality of information that we want to discover (Fayyad & Uthurusamy, 1996). After pre-processing we have new variable in the transformation step, this step help increase validity of model in data mining step (Fayyad & Uthurusamy, 1996). In data mining step DM algorithms is applied (Fayyad & Uthurusamy, 1996). We need validity step to evaluate discovered information for its validity and usefulness, after validation our result is knowledge (Fayyad & Uthurusamy, 1996). These steps are shown in Figure 2 (Fayyad & Uthurusamy, 1996).

Figure 2. KDD process steps

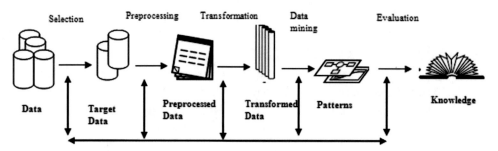

Advantages of Knowledge Discovery

The goal of Knowledge discovery in database (KDD) is "turn data into knowledge" so its advantages relate to this knowledge that is extracted from massive datasets (Fangjun, 2010). Therefore, we need to focus on knowledge, knowledge extracting during knowledge discovery is hidden knowledge that people do not know and it will be useful.

By knowledge discovery we can categorize our databank to some meaningful categories and study about them and make decision for them, for example one knowledge discovery doing in higher education is apply data mining to Students' Choosing Teachers, benefit of this discovery is finding 4 categories of students that choose teacher in different ways (Fangjun, 2010).We can study about each category and via them solve some problems in university, change some rules and make better decision for future. Knowledge extracted from mining a financial database could revise business practice. Knowledge from medical databank can publish in a medical journal (Pazzani, 2000).

With KDD models, country's competitiveness factors can be predicted (Zanakis & Becerra-Fernandez, 2005). In each country there are many databanks with large volume of data, apply data mining and knowledge discovery techniques on them can reveal many patterns to be in top in economic, social issues and so on. KDD was applied on countries datasets including economic, stock market performance/risk and regulatory efficiencies variables for predicting country investment risk (Becerra-Fernandez, Zanakis, & Walczak, 2002).

Data Mining Techniques

There are many techniques in data mining; these techniques help people with new power to analysis the massive databases (Al-Noukari & Al-Hussan, 2008). Data mining processes discover exciting and hidden relations and patterns for other usages like decision making for management (Al-Noukari & Al-Hussan, 2008).

There are some tasks that we can do with data mining. The below list shows the most popular of them (LAROSE, 2005):

- Description.
- Estimation.
- Prediction.
- Classification.

- Clustering.
- Association.

Description: Sometimes researchers' attempt is finding ways to describe patterns and relations within data. Transparency is an important feature in data mining models. Some data mining methods are more suitable for a transparent explanation such as decision tree (LAROSE, 2005).

Estimation: Estimation is like classification but its target variable is numeric (LAROSE, 2005).

Prediction: It is like estimation and classification but its results relates to the future. Any methods that are be used in classification and estimation may be used in prediction (LAROSE, 2005).

Classification: There is a target that is divided into some categories. In classification there are predefined classes and we learn to assign instances to these classes. Classification is a supervised task because Classes are predefined and we use training or learning set of objects to make a classifier for classification (Witten & Frank, 2005a).

Clustering: It makes groups from records. A cluster is a collection of data elements that are similar to each other and different from elements of other cluster. Clustering is different from classification; in clustering we don't have any target variable (LAROSE, 2005). There is not any estimation, prediction on the value of target variables (LAROSE, 2005). Clustering seeks to cluster data into clusters with maximum similarity between elements of each cluster and minimum similarity between elements of two different clusters. Clustering is an unsupervised task because classes are unknown and it wants to discover them from data, clustering can be used for exploratory data analysis and visualize data, with clustering we can discover instances that are similar to each other (LAROSE, 2005).

Association: This task of data mining is used for finding relationship between two or more attributes (LAROSE, 2005). Association tries to find rules between attributes. These rules can be vital in predict some significant events (LAROSE, 2005).

In this project, we used clustering technique, clustering is the most important unsupervised learning technique and try to find a structure in a collection of unlabeled data and organize elements into groups (Lam, 2007). The major reasons to select clustering technique are its simplification, pattern detection, unsupervised learning process and usefulness of it in data concept construction (Lam, 2007). Our intention in this study is reaching from massive data without any knowledge to exciting knowledge so we chose clustering that cluster elements without any predefined classes (Lam, 2007).

Machine Learning Software

Machine learning, statistic and databases are three areas that their tools are combined using data mining (Mannila, 1996). There is close relation between data mining, machine learning and statistic; their goal is finding or relation from data. The core of data mining is formed from machine learning methods (Mannila, 1996). The technical basis of data mining is provided by machine learning (Witten & Frank, 2005b). We use machine learning to extract knowledge from data in datasets, this knowledge is used for many purposes, and data mining is an application of machine learning. In data mining we use techniques like decision trees, etc (Witten & Frank, 2005b). There are many machine learning tools and techniques that are used in data mining (Witten & Frank, 2005b). Data mining is a practical, not a theoretical sense (Witten & Frank, 2005b).

Machine learning focus is on automatically learning to detect hidden and complex patterns and make decision based on data. There are many software suites but we select four of them to describe:

- Orange.
- RapidMiner.
- Matlab (SOM toolbox).
- Weka.

Orange is a data mining tool and it is like one of Weka parts (knowledge flow). Its strength is having many different tools for visualization of data. Although it can compute basic statistical functions but it has weakness in statistical part (Jakulin, 2010). Some of Orange features are:

- Visual programming.
- Visualization.
- Integration and data analytics.
- Large toolbox.
- Scripting interface.

Orange is an open source tool for analysis and data visualization (Jakulin, 2010).

RapidMiner is software for machine learning and data mining experiments (Mitchell, 1997). The initial version has been developed by artificial intelligence unit of university of Dortmund since 2001 (Mitchell, 1997). It includes data pre-processing and visualization. It can be used with text mining, multimedia mining, and data stream mining and so on (Mitchell, 1997). RapidMiner is useful in many business areas like banking, production, IT industry and universities (Mitchell, 1997). It is written with java programming language and so it can be run in any operating system (Mitchell, 1997).

SOM (self-organizing map) is a toolbox in Matlab package; Matlab has many toolboxes for various machine learning areas. SOM is a method that provide low dimensional grid that can be developed to visualize and explore properties of the data (Vesanto & Alhoniemi, 2000). This toolbox direction is powerful visualization functions (Vesanto, Himberg, Alhoniemi, & Parhankangas, 1999). The SOM is a significant tool for visualization, cluster extraction and exploratory step of data mining. It contains neurons (map units) that are arranged in a regular and one or two dimensional grid (Himberg, 1999).

Weka (Waikato Environment for Knowledge Analysis) is popular software for machine learning written in java and developed by university of Waikato, New Zealand (Witten & Frank, 2005b). Weka is free software, it includes tools for data pre-processing, classification, clustering, association rules and visualization. It is open source software (Witten & Frank, 2005b). Weka has graphical user interface for easy access to all functions (Witten & Frank, 2005b). The original version of Weka was non java and it was used as a tool for analysing agricultural data, but java based version is used in various domains like educational and research. Weka has some main features such as (Mark Hall 2010):

- 49 data pre-processing tool.
- 76 classification algorithms.
- 8 clustering techniques.
- 10 algorithms for attribute selection.
- 3 algorithms for association rules.
- 3 user interfaces (The Explorer, The Experimenter, The KnowledgeFlow).

The Weka was a project that funded by New Zealand government since 1993 (Mark Hall 2010). This project aims to develop machine learning techniques (Mark Hall 2010). Table 1 shows Weka history's timeline (Mark Hall 2010).

Figure 3 illustrates download history for Weka (Mark Hall 2010).

Each of machine learning software suits has some advantages and some disadvantages, all of them have their own users because of many factors, in this project we use Weka because of some features. Weka has some powerful attributes (Holmes, Donkin, & Witten, 1994):

- It is free software.
- It is portable due to its full implementation with java programming language and it can run in any platform.
- It includes a complete collection of data pre-processing and modelling techniques.
- Due to graphical interface it can be used by inexpert people.

Table 1. Weka timeline

Late 1992	Funding was done by Ian Witten.
1993	Interface and infrastructure developed • Weka acronym introduced by Geoff Holmes • Weka's file format(ARFF) was created by Andrew Donkin
1994	First internal release user interface and learning algorithms written mostly in C.
1996	First public release V 2.1
July 1997	Weka 2.2
Early 1997	Rewrite Weka in java
May 1998	Weka 2.3
Mid 1999	Weka 3(100% java)

Figure 3. Download histories for Weka

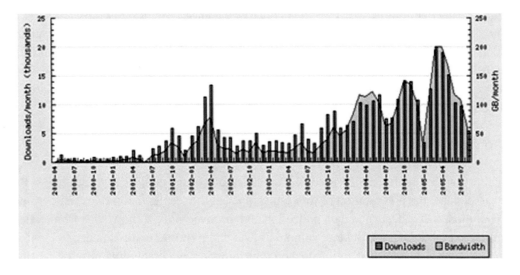

Weka has various parts, it contains (Holmes et al., 1994):

- Pre-processing.
- Classification.
- Clustering.
- Association.
- Attribute selection.
- Visualization.

Pre-processing: A pre-processor is a program that process input file to convert it to output that is useful in another program (Mitchell, 1997).

Classification: It is a supervised machine learning procedure; each example is a pair consisting of an input object and a desired output. Items are grouped based on quantitative information on one or more characteristics of items and previously labelled items (Mitchell, 1997).

Clustering: It is a discovery tool that may discover associations and patterns in data which is not previously obvious. In short: clustering attempts to find some groups of elements, based on some similarity (Ong, 2000). Clustering is an unsupervised machine learning procedure. Clustering has some algorithms like:

- **EM:** It clusters using expectation maximization. In this algorithm we can choose number of clusters or the algorithm can choose it using cross-validation (Witten & Frank, 2005a).
- **Cobweb:** It implements the Cobweb and Classit clustering algorithms; Cobweb for nominal attributes and Classit for numeric attributes (Witten & Frank, 2005a).
- **FarthestFirst:** It uses FarthestFirst traversal algorithm (Witten & Frank, 2005a).
- **MakeDensitybasedclusterer:** A metaclusterer that enclose a clustering algorithm to cause it return a probability density and distribution (Witten & Frank, 2005a).
- **SimpleKMeans:** It uses K-means; we have to choose the number of clusters. It is one of the simplest unsupervised learning algorithms.

Association: Association rules can predict any attribute not just class (Witten & Frank, 2005a). It can discover interesting relations between variables in large databases (Witten & Frank, 2005a).

Attribute selection: It helps to select a subset of relevant features for building powerful models (Mitchell, 1997). Performance of learning models will increase by removing irrelevant attribute from data (Mitchell, 1997).

Visualization: It is a way to visualize data; it shows scatter plots for all attribute pairs (Tan, Steinbach, & Kumar, 2006).

Data and Data Visualization

Data visualization techniques can be used in knowledge discovery process at three stages: to conduct discovery, to conduct the presentation of the results, present the results themselves (Hilderman, Liangchun, & Hamilton, 1997). Data and data collection and discover hidden knowledge from collected data are connected to each other, due to large volume of data and its complexity, it is needed to use data visualization techniques. Data visualization convert data into more understanding form of data to discover hidden knowledge from data (Ghanbari, 2007). Human being always looks for shapes, patterns, trends, structures and relationships in data (Ghanbari, 2007). Data visualization is a term to summarize data and give an overview of large and complex datasets (Ghanbari, 2007). In this project higher education data with large size of dataset and containing worthwhile patterns and relations needs to be visualized for the purpose of knowledge discovery.

Use of Data Mining Tools in Higher Education Institute and Others

There are many areas that data mining techniques can apply on data to analysis and discover knowledge, various tools can be used in this process. More recently, knowledge discovery in database (KDD) and data mining (DM) is known as new generation techniques which aid the human to discover valuable information automatically.

Higher education records contain valuable information about students and so on. Many researchers have been done to analysis this information and some models have been suggested and implemented.

Delavari and Beikzadeh (2004) model describes how DM can be used in higher education system to improve productivity of traditional processes in higher education, they present a guideline for decision making system (N. Delavari & Beikzadeh, 2004). Potawat et al. (2003) for finding various relations between attributes and the student status have used rough set theory as a classification approach to analysis student data. Delavari et al. (2005) is known as a roadmap for the application of DM in higher education system (N Delavari, Beikzadeh, & Amnuaisuk, 2005). Mierle et al. (2005) model is used to discover all knowledge about student behaviour in writing the code of assignment, their endeavour was because of finding some statistical patterns, rules and predicators that can be used to enhance student's performance in writing the code (Mierle, K., Roweis, & Wilson, 2005). As a part of Guruler (2005) study, MUSKUP (Mugla University Student Knowledge Discovery Unit Program) is developed as a system that integrates the knowledge discovery function with the database management system (DBMS) (Guruler, Istanbullu, & Karahasan, 2010).

In MUSKUP case study their goals are:

- Set up KDD process.
- Have a single program to access to all tasks via it.
- Access to SQL Server by programming techniques.

MUSKUP user interface contains three parts:

- Data base connection (connect, table manage).
- Data preparation (clean, transform, research (data analysing)).
- Model development (create model, split, validate).

School of information technology Jiangxi University of finance and economics did a survey on students' reasons for choosing teacher. They randomly select 286 students who register in year 2004 and 2005 in every course from Jiangxi University (Fangjun, 2010). They did a questionnaire methodology and collected data. It included many factors like teachers' professional title, age, classes delaying, home work assignment, classroom discipline, and effect of roommate and so on (Fangjun, 2010). They used the data mining software SPSS to mine the factors that have effect on students' selecting teachers. They did K-Mean cluster analysis and divided students into 5 groups. They called cluster 1 as knowledge-seeking, cluster 2 as reasoning, cluster 3 as emotional and cluster 4 as indifferent (Fangjun, 2010). The first cluster contains students that seek teachers with high academic level and best teaching methods (Fangjun, 2010). The second group thinks the academic level of teachers and their experience are not very important and it is enough that they have their teaching tools (Fangjun, 2010). Students in group 3 believe in academic background of teachers and prefer handsome teachers that studied overseas, the season and classmate can affect these students idea (Fangjun, 2010). The last group is indifferent, none of these factors like academic level, appearance, and classmate and so on cannot influence them (Fangjun, 2010). Therefore by using SPSS they could divide students and discover significant factor which are effective in choosing teacher (Fangjun, 2010).

The other research team used knowledge discovery based on academic data analysis. Their endeavour is discovering knowledge about academic achievement success and failure, student retention and student desertion (Salazar, Gosalbez, Bosch, Miralles, & Vergara, 2004). They used historical data and after filtering of missing data, their final records reach 22969 (Salazar et al., 2004). They used c-mean algorithm and obtained some clusters and after using c4.5 algorithm they generated a set of decisions like:

- In the first study of academic study students' performance is poor.
- The majority of students that enter university with higher age than usual may desert at any level of study.
- The students that enter the university with lowest ages have high probabilities to gain good academic performance.

After doing knowledge discovery, they evaluated findings by university experts. In the last stage of project, they proposed some strategies to improve academic processes (Salazar et al., 2004).

There is another similar case study about uncovering hidden information within students' data using data mining techniques. This data belongs to Sebha University in Libya. Clustering was used to group elements according to similarities; neural network, logistic regression and decision tree were used to predictive analysis and choose one of them as the best one (Siraj & Abdoulha, 2009). In this research, they used CRISP–DM methodology that is made from six phases (Siraj & Abdoulha, 2009): business methodology, data understanding, data preparation, modelling, evaluation and deployment (Siraj & Abdoulha, 2009). Business understanding cannot be achieved until data studying; data understanding involves data collection and some activities to understand data (Siraj & Abdoulha, 2009). Dataset includes 8510 instances from 1998 to 2006. There are 38 attributes, after pre-processing the instance number is reduced to 6830 (Siraj & Abdoulha, 2009).

At the first they made frequency table and identified relationships between attributes (Siraj & Abdoulha, 2009). Also clustering is applied to dataset to find similarities between attributes, after that predictive model is run and comparison between these models leads them to choose the best model (Siraj & Abdoulha, 2009). After these steps, some results are found such as distribution of student population in several branches of Sebha University, from this funding they can consider why students in some locations are low. The cross tabulation is done for finding relations between attributes such as faculty chart with respect to gender (Siraj & Abdoulha, 2009). This shows the majority of population is female but in detail according program, the ratio is different for example for law, engineering programs is seen more male than female students (Siraj & Abdoulha, 2009). The other analysis is funding relations between gender and student status like: enrol, move, quit and completed the study. It is observed that the percentage of female that completed their study in science, arts and medicine are more than male and male percentage that completed their study in sport and law are higher than female (Siraj & Abdoulha, 2009). The other result is more male in comparison with female have been expelled. After cross tabulation the clustering using Kohonen network is applied and three clusters is detected (Siraj & Abdoulha, 2009). Cluster 0 and 1 faculties are different from cluster 2 (Siraj & Abdoulha, 2009). Sport, accounting and agronomy programs are seen in cluster 0 and 1. More percentages of students that are resident in university belong to cluster 0. For prediction, three techniques are used. This study helps university planners to choose suitable and effective plans for university.

Geospatial data due to large size of dataset, complexity and some unknown and hidden patterns is difficult to analyse (Koua, 2005). Neural network is one solution for analysing this data, self-organizing map is often recommended as a solution for exploratory analysis of data (Koua, 2005). SOM is used to reduce complexity and facilitate the knowledge discovery (Koua, 2005). In this case Geo – Information science community can use some approaches such as visualization that is helpful in finding relations and patterns (Koua, 2005). They used SOM for exploring geospatial data and they can discover patterns and structure from this dataset. Some visual representations are explored: clusters using U-Matrix (Unified Distance Matrix), projection, visualization of component planes and their relations (Koua, 2005).

The other case study that in which SOM is used for musical artist recommendation, the Amazon reviews for the artists from Amazon web service and stores in the text form that these documents are basic information for SOM, these documents were organized and then similar documents were located nearby (Vembu & Baumann, 2004). Thus this task was done to explore similarities between various artist reviews to provide similar artists for recommendation service (Vembu & Baumann, 2004). They presented results from 400 musical artists and validate them using another common recommendation service that is Echocloud (Vembu & Baumann, 2004).

Higher Education Institute and Higher Education Attributes

Table 2 shows the descriptions of some attributes in higher education.

Institute for research and planning in higher education (IRPHE) affiliated to higher education ministry and constituted for improving planning in higher education. The major goals of this institute are:

- Help to the higher education ministry in planning.
- Make more improvement in research and innovation in the sciences related to higher education.
- Strategy and decision making for higher education.
- Cooperation in planning for improving of human resources in Iran.

In Table 3 we list down some requirements for higher education institute in Iran:

METHODOLOGY

This research consists of 6 phases and some steps for validation of methodology and knowledge discovery; to facilitate collecting data for higher education we need to have a data collection plan; IHE (Iran Higher Education) has a system for this purpose. At first it needs to define required attributes and their appropriate and predefined values. For these attributes it is needed to design a proper database. After

Table 2. Attributes description

Year	This is the first year that students enrol in university. (Julian year = solar year + 621)
University	This is the name of university.
Province	It is province that university is located.
City	It is city that university is located.
Type	This is type of degree: continuous and discontinuous • Continuous relates to programs that pass in continuous years and does not have any stop. • Discontinuous relates to program that passes step by step, as a case in point, one student first passes certificate degree then starts bachelor degree.
Woman	This field shows the number of females that study in particular program.
Man	This field shows the number of males that study in particular program.
Sum	This field shows the number of students that study in particular program.
Dependency	This field specifies affiliation of university to special ministry.
Learning style	• Face to face: This is one style of education which learning process is done by attending in physical classes. • Mixed: In this style some parts of learning process is done by audio, video and electronic media and other parts by face to face manner. • Non face to face: This style of education is done without attending in physical class and it is just by audio, video and electronic media.
Study mode	Study mode is a term for type of constituting of programs. It has 4 types: • Daily: student can attend in class without tuition fee and in face to face learning style. • Overnight: student can study with tuition fee and in face to face learning style. • Pervasive: This type relates to Payamnoor University and like that and don't have entrance exam and students after passing some course in the first semester according some rules can continue their study. • Equivalent: it involves someone that cannot to finish its course or someone that enter university without exam. • Podmany: This type relates to Science University – Applied and this university has some special rules for entrance and sometimes has separate exam for admission. • Free: it does not have any official degree but maybe has a degree affiliated to an organization. • Electronic: learning is done by virtual classes and electronic media. This is new term and does not exist in our data.
Degree	Educational process that student after passing some courses can graduate in special degree. • Certificate: This degree takes 2 years and it is lowest academic degree in Iran. • Bachelor: This degree takes 4 years; students can study in this one after high school or after certificate period. • Master: It is after bachelor degree and takes 2 years. • MD display: It takes 6 years and relates to medical and agricultural programs. In other words, it is medical profession. • PhD: The highest degree that starts after master or MD display degree.
Study field	Collection of programs that are similar is titled a study field. 6 study fields are defined for programs: • Agricultural -veterinary • Art • Basic Sciences • Engineering Sciences • Humanities • Medical
Program	Each Program has special course material and runs according particular layout in various degrees.

initial steps, one training step is needed to train universities' staff about the concept of attributes and their values. After training, user interface is provided for universities to collect data. Finally, all data are collected in a unique database. We received selected data from IRPHE institute. Phase 1 and 2 are done by IRPHE institute:

Table 3. Requirements

Requirements
Uncover areas in each university that have opportunity to help universities to compete with other universities.
Identify the degrees of related to each program for assessing constituting of new degree for some programs.
Know about the launching year of new study mode, study type, learning style to research more about them and effective reasons for creating them.
Detect the gaps during several years for each program in order to study and research more about them.
Discover study modes related to each degree with the purpose of study about effective factors.
Get the number of students in each degree in each program.
Group data into some clusters with similar degree and more similarities.
Discover some knowledge about female and male population in each program, degree and so on.
Discover which of study fields is major one and has high density and find the effective factors.
Meet the reasons of high increase in the number of students in the latest years.
Look for the major learning style and assess it for its advantages in order to increase rank of each university.
Cluster data into groups according to year of study based on similarity.
Find distribution of universities in the different provinces.
Discover a group with a great increase in the number of student in the recent years.
Discover universities with the greatest number of students in the recent years that cause to growth in the quantity.

Phase 1 – Make a User Interface: This phase is a basement for collecting data; at first IRPHE should define attributes and some standard values for each attribute then they must make required database and tables and specify relations between them. After making database they need user interface to connect database to collect data.

Phase 2 – Data Collection: For data collection from various places, IRPHE has to train someone that are responsible for preparing data about attributes and their values, after training, user interface should be provided for users to use it for collecting data, after collecting data by them this institute must collect all data in a unique database.

Phase 3 – Pre-Processing: In this phase data has to be prepared according to format that is useful for software that we use. We have to make ARFF file for using by Weka.

Phase 4 – Filtering and Data Visualizing: In this phase filtering can be applied on data and then we can visualize data in visualizing part of software.

Phase 5 – Apply Techniques on Data to Discover Knowledge: We need to select the best technique to apply on our data, after applying results must be visualized.

Phase 6 – Analysis Findings: This phase relates perception of data and how to extract some knowledge and patterns to improve management in higher education. Some knowledge was found that certainly will be useful for university and government in decision making. We can recommend according to our findings about way of collecting data, dispersal of one program in a country and so on.

The description of phases illustrated in the steps shown in Figure 5.

The proposed methodology is validated according to standard data mining methodology like CRISP-DM consisting six phase: business methodology, data understanding, data preparation, modelling, evaluation and deployment (Siraj & Abdoulha, 2009). Furthermore it can be supported by knowledge discovery process steps: data selection, pre-processing, transform, data mining, validate (Fayyad & Uthurusamy,

Figure 4. Methodology (The overview) *Figure 5. Methodology (The details)*

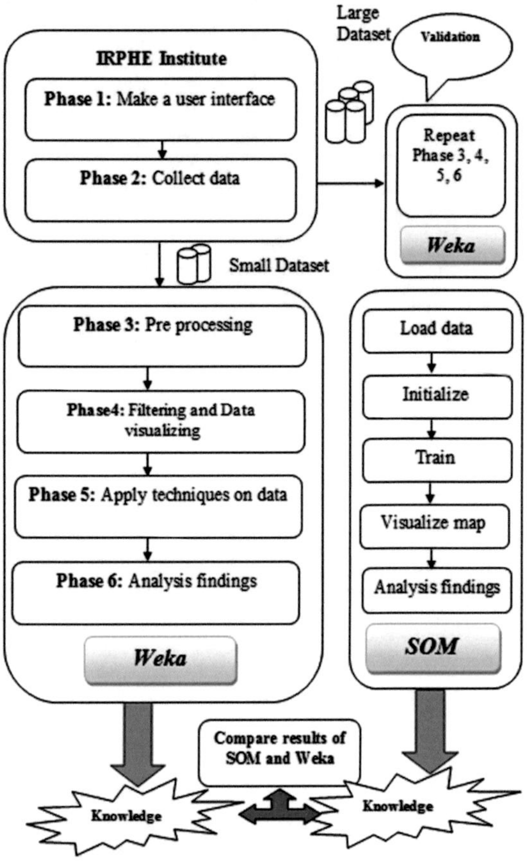

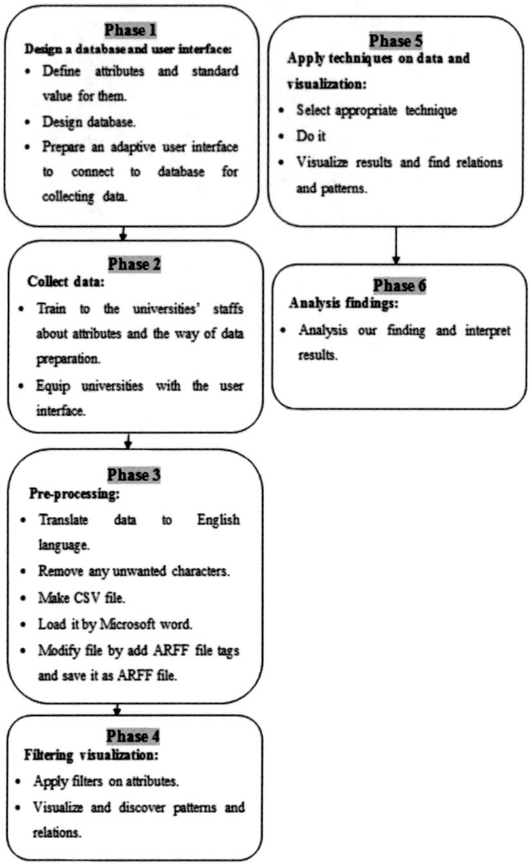

1996). Specification of proposed methodology in this study is its utility in higher education institute that has communication with so many universities, in this methodology we considered all problems that may we have in such institutes. One of these problems is unfamiliarity of staffs that are responsible to collect data and send it to this institute. The other issue is preparing input file from data in Persian language that is considered in pre-processing phase, Persian alphabetic were not readable in visualizing part to counter, we proposed to translate the data. For this purpose, we used Google translator.

DATA ANALYSIS AND FINDINGS

As mentioned before, our scope is divided in to small and large ones to reach an appropriate methodology, so in this chapter our focus is on the smaller dataset that is medical universities of Tehran province. Our findings are identified based on chapter 3 and it will be discussed about knowledge discovery by data mining techniques in Weka. Our findings can be found through two ways, one way is visualizing our data in visualize section of Weka, in this way we do not use any technique but in the other way our results have discovered by applying clustering technique.

Visualize Each Attribute

In the pre-processing part of Weka we can see some simple visualization of selected attribute; it illustrates count number of each value of attributes, in other words it prepares a table and a graph for each attribute to show attribute's name, type, missing percentage, distinct number and unique percentage as a header of table and lists values of each attribute in the table with the count number of each value. The related graph shows table content as a graph.

In Figure 6 selected attribute is university; the count of each value of attribute is obvious through table and visualizing graph, for example it shows that Tehran University of medical sciences has the greatest number of records in our data bank; the lowest number in our data bank is related to Blood transfusion institute with 12 records.

By Figure 8, we can see overall status of each attribute, the chosen attribute will also be used as the class attribute when a filter applied, in the above figure we presented degree that students study by the university class, this class divided degree into various universities with different colours, this graph presents that the proportion of Tehran University of medical sciences in PhD and Master degree is made the majority of that degree, the other outstanding observation is high proportion of shaheed Beheshti University of medical sciences in bachelor degree. Institute Pastor Iran contains just PhD and master degree, Blood Transfusion institute also contains Master and certificate degree. Have attention to this fact that these graphs show just the count of records and not number of students. We can visualize all of them in a separate page and in an overall perspective like this figure:

Figure 6. Visualize the selected attribute

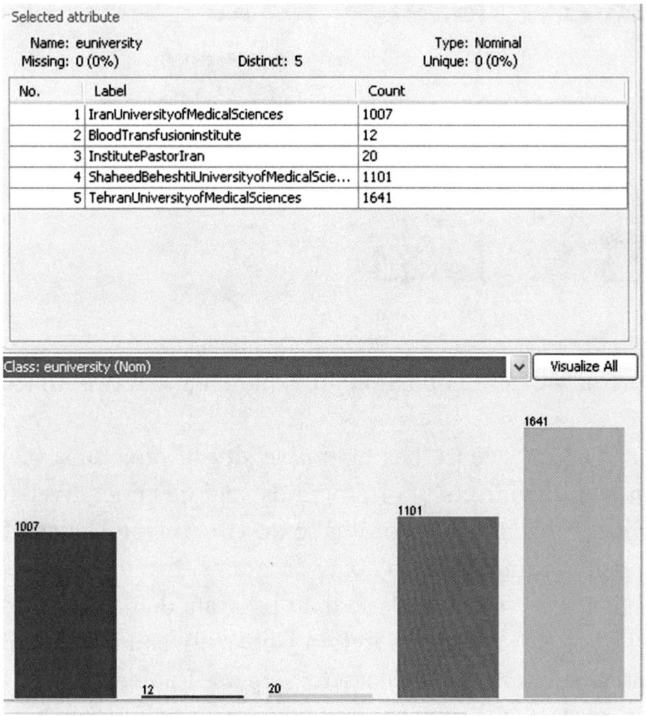

Figure 7. Degree by university class

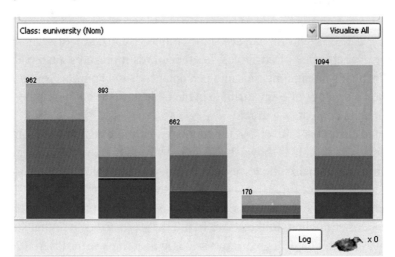

Figure 8. Visualize all attributes

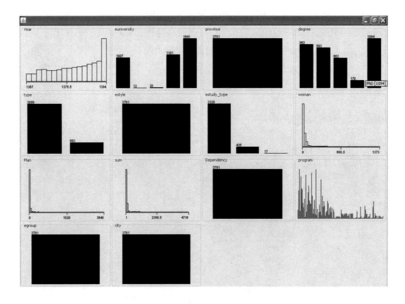

In the visualizing part of Weka, it is possible to explore data in two dimensional(X, Y) plots like Figure 9.

Tehran University of medical science has high diversity of programs, blood transfusion institute and institute pastor Iran have low diversity of programs, and this high diversity in Tehran University is because of size of university and oldness of it (Figure 10). Tehran University of medical science is the oldest medical university in Iran so it has many programs. Institute Pastor Iran and blood transfusion institute were established to special goals so their program domains are limited thus some special programs. It is seen that there are some areas in Iran University and Shaheed Beheshti University that have capability to add new programs like: Thoracic Surgery, Radiology Oral and Maxillofacial, Oral Diseases, Engineering improvements.

Figure 9. Visualizing section of Weka

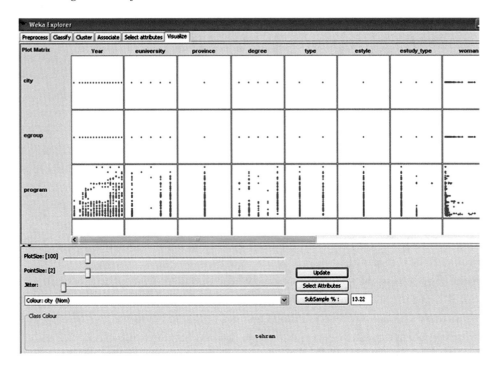

Figure 10. University – program

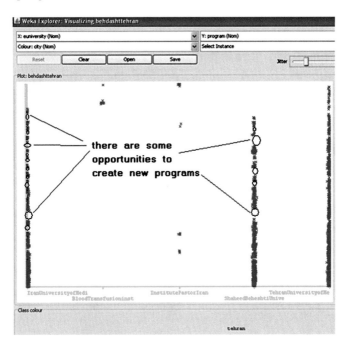

In Institute Pastor Iran and Blood transfusion institute, there are low programs but we have some limitations to add new programs because they are for some special programs.

Almost all of programs has been taught in PhD level and it shows MDdisplay that is a medical profession degree (is lower than PhD level and students after finishing this level start their PhD course) relates to some programs like medical, pharmacy, dentistry and so on. It is seen that some programs' degree is certificate however we do not have BA or MA degree for them so it can be useful for medical ministry to create a committee to asses these programs weather they can be taught in high degree or not. Certainly this decision can help to improvement in medical aspect.

According to the plot (Figure 68) in the appendix, from 1367 to 1374, we had just daily study mode, nowadays because of our needs and limited capacity for daily study; they added 2 other types. For facilitating study, it must be assessed new type like virtual learning in medical universities, there is an issue that virtual courses due to low direct communication between students and lecturers maybe are not appropriate solution for medical programs that have many practical programs, but in our rapidly growing world by using new technologies, it can be possible by adding some simulation and advanced software that have simulated the real world.

Based on the Figure 69 in the appendix, we discovered that there was not any discontinuous program from 1367 to 1381, due to constituting of new programs during last years, this type is added. For example, in the past years there was not any discontinuous nursing program but nowadays we have discontinuous type for nursing in PhD and master degree, one of the reasons for this event can be difficulty of entering exam for continuous programs like PhD of nursing. So for making it easy, they divided these programs to several levels, these levels are bachelor, master and PhD degrees.

Figure 11. Degree – program

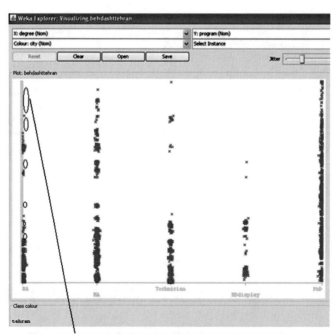

There are some programs that be taught in Master degree but there is not bachelor degree for them and so on for other degrees.

Figure 12. University - Degree

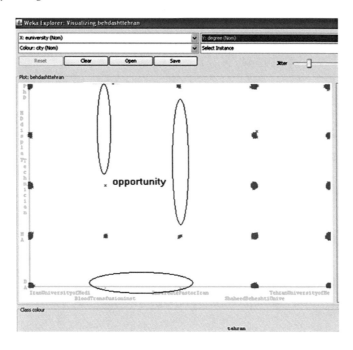

Tehran University of Medical Sciences, Iran University of Medical Sciences and shaheed Beheshti university of Medical sciences have all variety of degrees but Institute pastor Iran has PhD and master degrees and blood transfusion institute has master and certificate degrees. The significant factor that causes this division is because of program type in each university, the university history and vision and mission of each university has effect on this. The indicated areas in the figure 4.6 can be an opportunity for universities, for example there is a big opportunity for Blood transfusion institute for establishing PhD courses.

From the plot in the appendix (Figure 70) can be found that Tehran University of Medical Sciences and Shaheed Beheshti university of Medical sciences have all types of study mode, Iran University of Medical Sciences has daily and overnight study mode, Institute pastor Iran has just daily, and blood transfusion institute has daily and equivalent. This diversity origin from each university's programs, goals, policies. Overnight study mode helps to increase capacity of university for some programs and make profit from economical aspect so Blood transfusion institute and institute Pastor Iran should be assessed to add overnight study mode to their study mode to accept more applicants and increase university budget.

The plot (Figure 13) shows existence of programs during several years, for example these programs: haematological, transfusions of blood, biological products were not existed before 1374. During 1367, 1369 it can be seen that there was the lowest domain for programs and we have much improvement in medical aspect after 18 years, it can be because of global improvement in medical aspects and our improvement along with it. In this graph a big gap is discovered that is needed to pay attention and asses for finding interesting results for example Dental children, Orthodontics, Nerve Disease, General Surgery are discontinuous during several years.

Figure 13. Program – Year

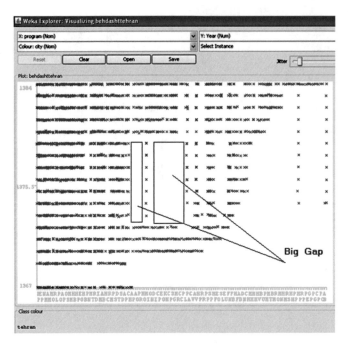

According to the appendix it is observed (Figure 71) that all degrees have daily study mode, during 18 years MD display degree never has constituted overnight, certificate degree also never belongs to equivalent study mode.

SimpleKMeans Clustering Technique

After visualizing data, we used clustering technique to detect some groups with some differences that helped us to discover some interesting results. We used SimpleKMeans; it is one of the simplest unsupervised learning algorithms, this technique has some inputs like number of clusters, seed number and other inputs, in this project we tried various K to find the best K. The default value for K is 2.

Test 1: We tried K equals 2.

With this initialization, SSE (sum of squared errors)[1] will be 8333, we found the below results, these results show Cluster centroids.

Table 4. Test 1 with K=2

K	displayStdDevs	DontReplace MissingValue	PreserveInstancesOrder	Seed
2	true	false	true	10

Cluster 0:

- University = Shaheed Beheshti University of Medical Sciences
- Degree = BA
- Type = Continuous
- Study mode = Daily
- Woman= 83.1865
- Man= 67.8135
- Sum= 151
- Program = Laboratory science

Cluster 1:

- University = Tehran University of Medical Sciences
- Degree = PhD
- Type = Continuous
- Study mode = Daily
- Woman = 34.6285
- Man = 46.7647
- Sum = 81.3932
- Program = Occupational health

The number of records in full data are 3781; 1609 of records belongs to cluster 0 and remain (2172 records) are members of cluster 1. This does not mean cluster 1 has higher number of students than cluster 0, from the above results it is clear that cluster 0 with Sum= 151 has greater number of students than cluster 1 with Sum = 81.3932.

Figure 14. Degree – Sum of students

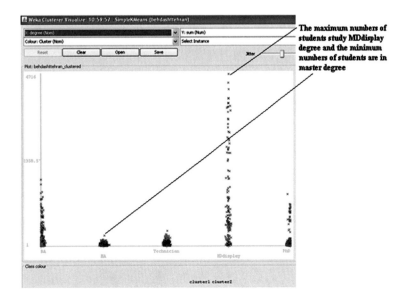

This plot (Figure 14) shows that maximum numbers of students' study MDdisplay degree and minimum numbers of students are in master degree. The most of instances in BA degree are blue and it shows the previous fact: maximum numbers of records in cluster 0 are BA degree. The most of PhD degree instances are red colour that presents maximum numbers of records in cluster 1 belong to PhD degree.

From the plot in the appendix (Figure 72) we discovered this fact that the greater percentages of programs are PhD degree and the lowest percentages are MDdisplay. In other words, for most of programs, we just have PhD degree to study. For example, Biological Products program is taught in PhD level, in this plot we can discover some results but it needs professional experts to do that because medical programs and their level are so complex such as Infectious Diseases program that is just taught in PhD level because it is for students that graduated in medical program in MDdisplay and this program does not have BA, MA or MDdisplay degree.

According to the plot in the appendix (Figure 73) with program as X axis and sum as a Y axis, we can find that most of students' study in Medical program, it displays that medical program has high capacity for accept applicants in this program, the other fact is that capacity of programs varies according to demands of customers. Some of the most common programs with the great number of students listed here: Medical, nursing, pharmacy, dentistry, laboratory science.

The plot in the appendix (Figure 74) presents information on number of students during several years, from 1367 to 1384, as it is seen we have decrease in the last year in province Tehran, this is maybe due to increase in other province and the other reason can be interest of new generation to non-medical programs rather than the past. The other observation is the highest number of students in 1370. But this statistic is about 5 years ago and nowadays we have increase in the number of students.

As can be seen in Figure 15, Tehran University of Medical Sciences has greater number of students than others; the most popular colour in this university is red and belongs to second cluster. Blood Transfusion institute has the lowest number of students between the five universities. As mentioned before the greatest number of Tehran University of Medical Sciences is because of oldness of this university and

Figure 15. University – Sum of students

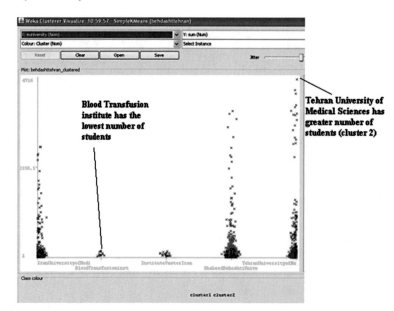

Table 5. Test 2 with K=5

K	displayStdDevs	DontReplace MissingValue	PreserveInstancesOrder	Seed
5	true	false	true	100

the lowest number of students in Blood Transfusion institute occurred because it has made for special programs and its size is small and of course its students are limited.

The other k that we tried is K=5 because we have 5 universities, with these features:

Test 2: We tried K equals 5.

With this initialization, SSE (sum of squared errors) will be 6636.5549.

From this plot (Figure 16) it can be found each university's programs and related cluster, for example it can be seen that transfusion of blood affairs (in cluster 3) just be taught in Blood Transfusion institute and it is needed some assessment on requests for this program and universities capability for satisfy applicants. Medical Biotechnology is the other program that is available in Institute Pastor Iran, Iran University of Medical Sciences and Tehran University of Medical Sciences.

According to this plot (Figure 17) we can name cluster 1 and 5 as a cluster with PhD and MA degree, cluster 2 and 4 as BA, cluster 3 as certificate. Cluster1 covers many programs and cluster 2 includes low variety of programs.

It is seen in Figure 18 that cluster 2 has made the most of instances of overnight study mode in 3 universities, Iran, Tehran and Shaheed that Shaheed university has the maximum number of students

Figure 16. University – Program

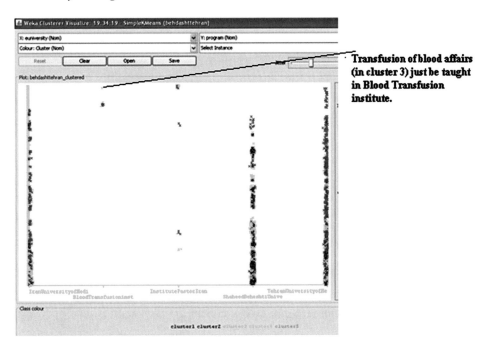

Transfusion of blood affairs (in cluster 3) just be taught in Blood Transfusion institute.

Figure 17. Cluster – Program- Degree

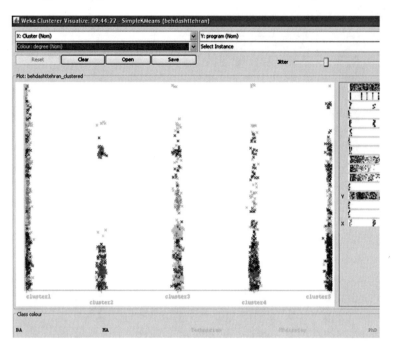

Figure 18. University – Study mode

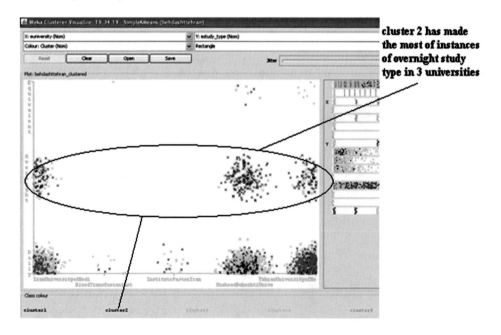

that study in this study mode. Like this, equivalent study mode members are in blood, Shaheed and Tehran universities, cluster 2 has made the maximum of this study mode, so for improving this study mode or omitting it from universities, we can assess cluster 2's universities, and special programs to achieve proper response.

From the plots in the appendix (Figure 75, Figure 76) is found that Tehran University of Medical Sciences has the greatest female students between other universities. The most of female students in Iran University of Medical Science are members of cluster 4, in Blood Transfusion institute are members of cluster 5, in Institute Pastor Iran, the majority of female belong to cluster 3 and 4 and in Shaheed Beheshti university of medical science belongs to cluster 3 and in Tehran university of medical science relates to cluster 5. So cluster 3, 4, 5 have made the majority of female students.

According to the plots in the appendix (Figure 77, Figure 78), Tehran University of Medical Sciences has the greatest male students between other universities. The most of male students in Iran University of Medical Science are members of cluster 4, in Blood Transfusion institute are members of cluster 5, in Institute Pastor Iran, the majority of female belong to cluster 4 and in Shaheed Beheshti University of medical science belongs to cluster 3 and in Tehran University of medical science relates to cluster 5. The findings are like what we find about female students.

From Figure 19 and Figure 20 we can discover Table 6.

Figure 19. Cluster – University – Degree

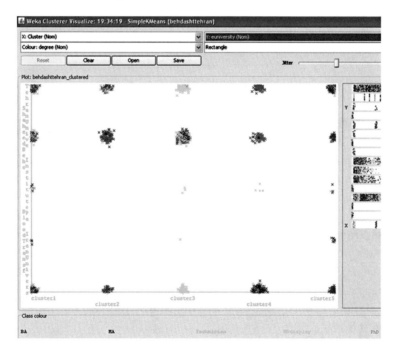

Table 6. Table of most common degree

Cluster	University	The Most Common Degree
1	All universities	PhD
2	Tehran, Iran, Shaheed Beheshti	BA
3	All universities	MDdisplay
4	Tehran, Iran, Shaheed Beheshti, Pastor	MDdisplay
5	All universities	MDdisplay

Figure 20. Cluster – Sum of students - Degree

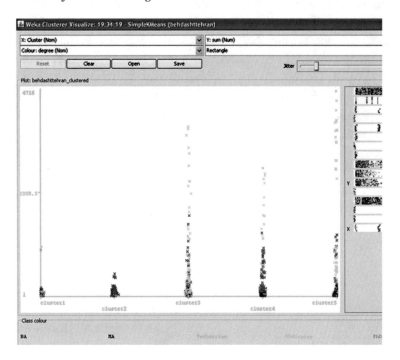

This table determines members of each cluster and the most common degree with the high number of students in each cluster. For example, cluster 1 includes students from all five universities and most of its students' study in PhD degree.

The plot shown in Figure 21 illustrates Table 7.

This table determines members of each cluster and the most common type with the high number of students in each cluster. It shows that all of the students with discontinuous type are the member of cluster 1.

The Figure 22 and Table 8 present information on each cluster's study mode and the most common of them in each cluster, except cluster 2, the clusters' common study mode is daily, so for any research on overnight study mode, it will be effective and efficiency to focus on cluster 2 records.

According to the experts' experience, we tested K that got from EM technique because it chooses the best number of clusters automatically by cross-validating[2]; EM generated K=13 for our dataset so in this project we tried it.

Table 7. Table of most common type

Cluster	University	The Most Common Type
1	All universities	Discontinuous
2	Tehran, Iran, Shaheed Beheshti	Continuous
3	All universities	Continuous
4	Tehran, Iran, Shaheed Beheshti, Pastor	Continuous
5	All universities	Continuous

Figure 21. Cluster – Sum of students – Type

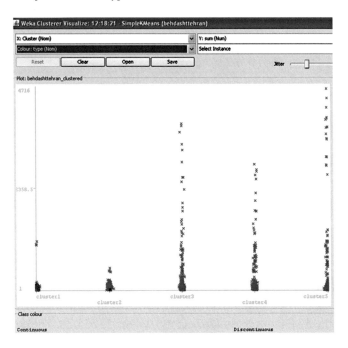

Figure 22. Cluster – Sum of students – Study mode

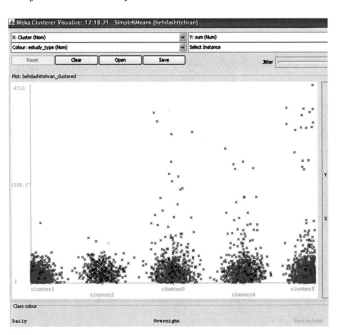

Table 8. Table of most common study mode

Cluster	Study type	The Most Common Study Mode
1	Daily, Over night	Daily
2	Daily, Overnight, Equivalent	Over night
3	Daily, Overnight, Equivalent	Daily
4	Daily, Over night	Daily
5	Daily, Overnight, Equivalent	Daily

Table 9. Test 3 with K=13

K	displayStdDevs	DontReplace MissingValue	PreserveInstancesOrder	Seed
13	true	false	true	20

Test 3: We tried K equals 13.

With this initialization, SSE (sum of squared errors) will be 5558.022. The details of cluster centroids can be found in the Appendix. The majority of clusters relate to Iran University of Medical Sciences, Shaheed Beheshti University of Medical Sciences and Tehran University of Medical Sciences so about the other universities that are small one, we make clear their belonging clusters according to Figure 23.

As can be seen, Blood transfusion institute is member of cluster 3, 5, 7, 9 and Institute Pastor Iran relates to cluster 4, 5, 6, 7, and 12.

For having an effective division, high K may be the best way because when we choose high K, our large universities like Tehran, Iran and Shaheed are divided in to some parts that need to be studied and focused separately. In my opinion we can try many Ks and discover some findings, it is not a most to choose one of them because each K can show some facts and we can use them in our decisions and future plans.

The plot shown in Figure 24 presents information on density of records during several years in each cluster, Table 10 shows the important years in each cluster.

Cluster 5 and 8 are important clusters due to their year domains, because high density of records in these two clusters during several years show some gaps. It will be useful for some researchers that want to study about these years, and they can choose one cluster and focus more on it to extract much knowledge. For example in cluster 8, it is seen high density from 1367 to 1373 and then it decreases suddenly in the last years (1380-1384), for cluster 5 density is low then after years it increases and then decreases, thus any decreases in the recent years should be focused.

From Figure 25, we can discover the ordering of clusters from the number of students aspect. Some densities are obvious but in some cases like number 8 that is greater than 9,10,11,12, there are some doubts, for solving this issue we can select instances like rectangle and choose some areas to make clear like Figure 26.

Figure 26 shows information on the number of students in proportion to degree as X axis and clusters as colour. The most popular colours in BA degree belong to cluster 1, 2, 10, and 13; and the most common colours in MA degree relate to cluster 3, 5, 7 and 9, for certificate degree we have cluster 10

Figure 23. University - Cluster

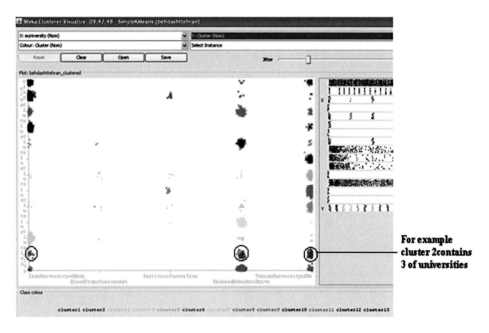

Figure 24. Cluster – Year

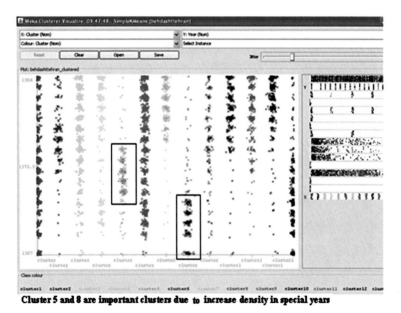

mostly and there are some mixed of all clusters for MDdisplay and cluster 4, 6, 12 for PhD degree. So we can use these findings in some decision making, for example by assessing cluster 1, 2, 10, 13 that contain the most students with BA degree, we can study about this whether for all programs in these clusters we can have MA degree in the related clusters or not.

Table 10. The important years in each cluster

Cluster 1	1367-1384
Cluster 2	1375-1384
Cluster 3	1367-1384
Cluster 4	1367-1384
Cluster 5	*1372-1377*
Cluster 6	1367-1384
Cluster 7	1378-1384
Cluster 8	*1367-1373*
Cluster 9	1367-1384
Cluster 10	1377-1384
Cluster 11	1375-1384
Cluster 12	1377-1384
Cluster 13	1367-1384

Figure 25. Cluster – Sum of students

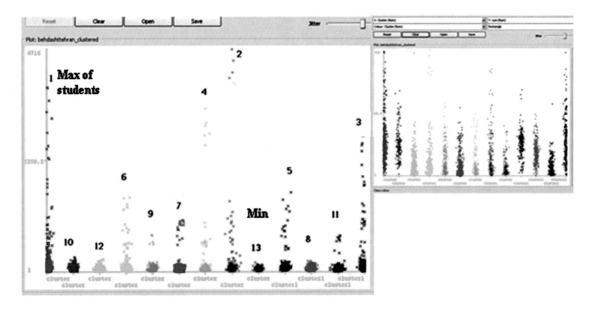

From the plot in appendix (Figure 79), Tehran University of Medical Sciences covers many programs and most of its instances are member of cluster 6, between these programs in Tehran University of Medical Sciences, immunology is the major program that is repeated in the most of records.

Summary of our findings by using Weka listed in Table 11.

For example, cluster 1 includes students from all five universities and most of its students' study in PhD degree. This cluster has effects on increasing of rank of universities so it must be considered.

Overnight study mode is a type that makes income for universities so cluster 1 should be focused to find knowledge such as which programs are taught in this type and like that.

Figure 26. Degree – Sum – Cluster

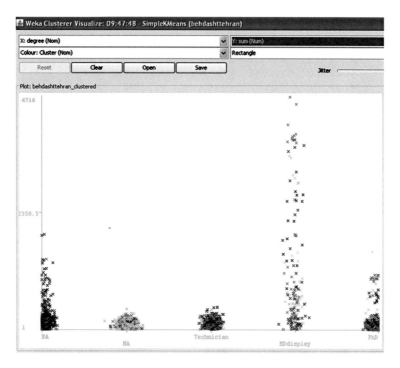

Table 11. Summary of findings

Method	Result
Visualizing two attributes (University - program)	There are some areas in Iran University and Shaheed Beheshti University that have capability to add new programs like: Thoracic Surgery, Radiology Oral and Maxillofacial, Oral Diseases, Engineering improvements. It helps them to compete with Tehran University of medical sciences that has these programs.
Visualizing two attributes (Degree - program)	It is seen that some programs are taught in certificate degree however we do not have BA or MA degree for them so it can be useful for medical ministry to create a committee to asses these programs weather they can be taught in high degree or not. Certainly this decision can help to improvement in medical aspect.
Visualizing two attributes (Study mode - Year)	From 1367 to 1374, we had just daily study mode but nowadays we have 3 study modes (daily, overnight and equivalent) so we can add new study mode like virtual learning that was effective in the Ministry of Science - Research and Technology.
Visualizing two attributes (Year - Type)	There was not any discontinuous program from 1367 to 1381 for example there was not any discontinuous nursing program but now we have it so we can do it for other programs to ease entering to university.
Visualizing two attributes (University – Degree)	There is a big opportunity for Blood transfusion institute for establishing PhD courses; it helps to increase rank of university.
Visualizing two attributes (Program - Year)	During 1367, 1369 it can be seen that there was the lowest domain for programs. Like these programs: haematological, transfusions of blood, biological products that were not taught before 1374. There are some gaps that show some programs are discontinuous during years. Dental children, Orthodontics, Nerve Disease, and General Surgery are discontinuous during several years. Assessing this event helps to discover some knowledge.
Visualizing two attributes (Study mode - Degree)	MD display degree that is in lower level than PhD never has constituted in overnight study mode. However, adding overnight study mode helps to increase income of university because it is not free course.
Clustering (Degree–Sum of students)	Maximum numbers of students' study MDdisplay degree and minimum numbers of students are in master degree. It shows the most of applicants for medical programs are interested to MDdisplay degree that contains medical, pharmacy programs and the lowest number for MA shows that capacity of university for this degree is low.

continued on following page

Table 11. Continued

Method	Result
Clustering (Degree - Program)	The greater percentages of programs are PhD degree and lowest percentages are MDdisplay because PhD is professional degree and after graduating in MDdisplay degree we can start many branches in PhD level.
Clustering (Program-Sum of students)	We can find that most of students' study in Medical program, it displays that medical program has high capacity for accept applicants in this program, the other fact is that capacity of programs varies according to demands of customers. Some of the most common programs with the great number of students listed here: Medical, nursing, pharmacy, dentistry, laboratory science.
Clustering (Year-Sum of students)	We have decrease in the last year in province Tehran, this is maybe due to increase in other province and the other reason can be interest of new generation to non-medical programs rather than the past.
Clustering (University– Sum of students)	Tehran University of Medical Sciences has greater number of students than others and Blood Transfusion institute has the lowest number of students between the five universities.
Clustering (University - Program)	Transfusion of blood affairs just is taught in Blood Transfusion institute. Medical Biotechnology is the other program that is available in Institute Pastor Iran, Iran University of Medical Sciences and Tehran University of Medical Sciences, so Shaheed Beheshti University needs to add Biotechnology program to its programs.
Clustering (Program-Degree)	In clustering with 5 clusters we can name cluster 1 and 5 as a cluster with PhD and MA degree, cluster 2 and 4 as BA, cluster 3 as certificate. Cluster1 covers many programs and cluster 2 includes low variety of programs. From these divisions we can focus to some clusters and it saves time and cost.
Clustering (University – Study mode)	Cluster 2 contains the most of instances with overnight study mode, so we can say cluster 2 helps to increase income of university. Shaheed University has the maximum number of students that study in this study mode.
Clustering(University – female students)	Tehran University of Medical Sciences has the greatest female and male students rather than others.
Clustering (University - Program)	Tehran University of Medical Sciences covers many programs and most of its instances are member of cluster 6 (between 13 clusters), between these programs in Tehran University of Medical Sciences, immunology is the major program that is repeated in the most of records. So cluster 6 contains programs with high diversity and can be useful for some researchers that want to study about programs.

Table 12. Table of most common degree

Cluster	University	The Most Common Degree
1	All universities	PhD
2	Tehran, Iran, Shaheed Beheshti	BA
3	All universities	MDdisplay
4	Tehran, Iran, Shaheed Beheshti, Pastor	MDdisplay
5	All universities	MDdisplay

Table 13. Table of most common study mode

Cluster	Study type	The Most Common Study Mode
1	Daily, Over night	Daily
2	Daily, Overnight, Equivalent	Over night
3	Daily, Overnight, Equivalent	Daily
4	Daily, Over night	Daily
5	Daily, Overnight, Equivalent	Daily

Table 14. Table of important clusters

Cluster 5	*1372-1377*
Cluster 8	*1367-1373*

Cluster 5 and 8 (between 13 clusters) are important clusters due to their year domains, it will be useful for some researchers that want to study about these years, and they can choose one cluster and focus on it, it helps to save time, cost and energy.

For more description, for example in cluster 8, it is seen high density from 1367 to 1373 and then it decreases suddenly in the last years (1380-1384), for cluster 5 density is low then after years it increases and then decreases, thus any decreases in the recent years should be focused.

SOM Toolbox

As mentioned before, in this chapter our focus is on the smaller dataset that is medical universities of Tehran province. Based on our objectives we used other visualizing tool to compare differences and similarities between data mining softwares. In this part we used SOM (self-organizing map) toolbox that is in Matlab package (2007). SOM is used for data pre-processing, initializing and training, visualizing and analysing features of data and SOMs like relations between variables, clusters and quality of SOM (Vesanto et al., 1999), SOM is suitable toolbox for data understanding and analysis.

According to these steps we analysed our data and extract some knowledge. The format of data that we use in this toolbox is .xls file that we convert it to that .dat file. The variables in the SOM should be numerical not nominal, the majority of our attributes in our dataset are nominal thus we applied code labelling on nominal attributes to use in SOM. Tables 15-18 show used code for nominal attributes.

As a beginning we used command window in Matlab and loaded file using the below command: SD=som_read_data('small.dat');

The 'small.dat' is our file name, by this command we loaded data and then we used it. There are some commands like **som_normalize() for** preprocessing, **som_make**() for creating, initializing and training a SOM using default parameters, **som_show() for** Showing visualizations of SOM like component planes,

Table 15. University code

University	
Name	**Code**
Blood Transfusion Institute	1
Institute Pastor Iran	2
Iran University of Medical Sciences	3
Shaheed Beheshti university of Medical sciences	4
Tehran University of Medical Sciences	5

Table 16. Degree code

Degree	
Name	**Code**
Certificate	0
Bachelor	1
Master	2
MDdisplay	3
PhD	4

Table 17. Type code

Type	
Name	**Code**
Continuous	1
Discontinuous	2

Table 18. Study mode code

Study Mode	
Name	**Code**
Daily	1
Equivalent	2
Overnight	3

Figure 27. Matlab _ SOM

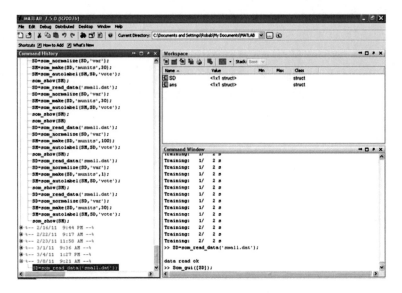

unified distance matrices as well as empty planes and fixed colour planes. In this study we used SOM initialization and training tool by typing this command in command window of Matlab:

Som_gui([SD]);

After evaluation of this command we can see the window (Figure 28), it contains some parts for loading of dataset, initializing and training of map. Each part has some default value and setting that we can change them. In this project we just changed map size in initializing part and tried various sizes to choose the best one.

Figure 28. Initialization and training

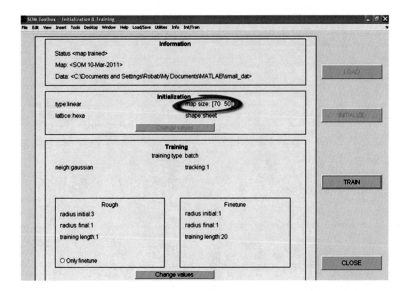

We selected [70, 50] as map size and trained it by using default values, after training we can visualize map through utilities tab in this window and see maps like the below figure:

Figure 29 shows U- Matrix and component planes of each attributes that are explained in the next parts.

In the U-Matrix we can see two regions that correspond to low and high value in the U-Matrix. In Figure 30 we separate two regions and titled them as cluster 1 and cluster 2.

According to U-Matrix and component planes we can describe each cluster properties like Table 19.

In cluster 1, the major codes are 3, 4, 5 that are related to Iran University of Medical Sciences, Shaheed Beheshti university of Medical sciences, Tehran University of Medical Sciences. The common code in cluster 2 is code 5 (Tehran University of Medical Sciences).

The cluster 1 contains all kinds of degree (0, 1, 2, 3, and 4): Certificate, Bachelor, Master, and MD-display, PhD. The major degree in cluster 2 is code 3 (MDdisplay degree). This degree in this cluster relate to Tehran University of Medical Sciences.

The cluster 1 includes all types of study (1, 2) continuous and discontinuous types. The cluster 2 contains just continuous type. This division shows that cluster 1 covers the recent years and new type of study (discontinuous).

All modes with 1, 2, and 3 codes and Daily, Equivalent, and Overnight values are seen in the cluster 1; the cluster 2 contains just code 1 with daily study mode.

The record with the highest number of students relates to cluster 2's records. It does not mean this cluster has the greatest number of students. It is obvious that cluster 1 has the greatest number of students due to its large region.

The cluster 1 covers all programs. According to the major colour, cluster 2 contains some special programs like medical mycology (78). The other codes like 77, 79, and 80 relate to medical library, medical physics and medical records.

Several years are covered by cluster 1. The significant years in the cluster 2 are between 1370, 1382.

Figure 38 presents correlation between university and year component planes. Via comparing these two planes, it is seen that movement from year 1367 to 1384 shows that students of Tehran medical

Figure 29. Visualizing of U-Matrix and component planes

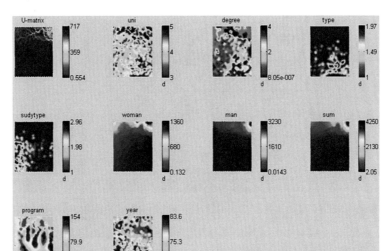

Figure 30. U-Matrix

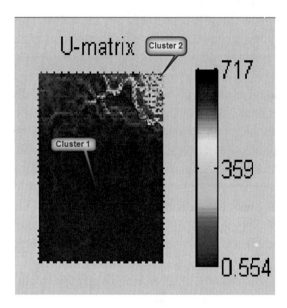

Table 19. University component plane

University	
Cluster 1	The major codes are 3, 4, 5 that are related to Iran University of Medical Sciences, Shaheed Beheshti university of Medical sciences, Tehran University of Medical Sciences.
Cluster 2	The common code is 5 (Tehran University of Medical Sciences).

Table 20. Degree component plane

Degree	
Cluster 1	This cluster contains all degrees (0,1,2,3,4) Certificate, Bachelor, Master, MDdisplay, PhD.
Cluster 2	The major degree is code 3 (MDdisplay).

Figure 31. University component plane

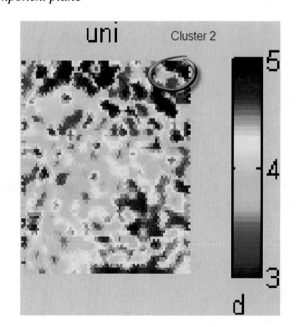

Figure 32. Degree component plane

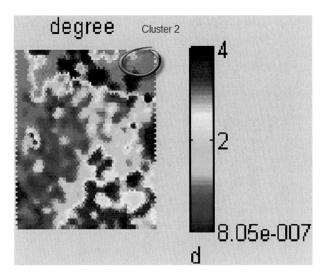

Table 22. Type component plane

Type	
Cluster 1	This cluster includes all types (1, 2) continuous and discontinuous.
Cluster 2	This cluster contains continuous type.

Table 23. Study mode component plane

Study Mode	
Cluster 1	This cluster includes all modes (1, 2, and 3): Daily, Equivalent, and Overnight.
Cluster 2	This cluster contains code 1(Daily) mode.

Figure 33. Type component plane

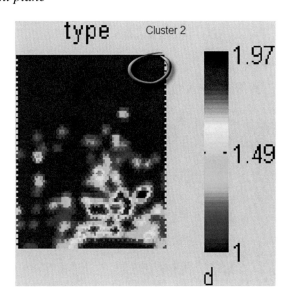

Figure 34. Study mode component plane

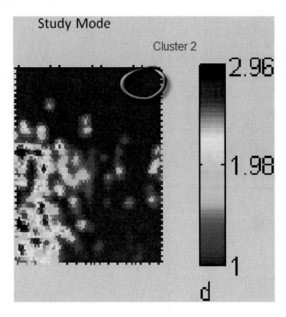

Table 24. Sum component plane

Sum
The record with the highest number of students relates to cluster 2's records. It does not mean this cluster has the greatest number of students.

Table 25. Program component plane

Program	
Cluster 1	This cluster covers all programs.
Cluster 2	According to major colour, cluster 2 contains some special programs like medical mycology (78). The other codes like 77, 79, and 80 relate to medical library, medical physics and medical records.

Figure 35. Sum component plane

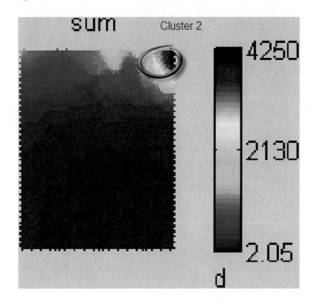

Figure 36. Program component plane

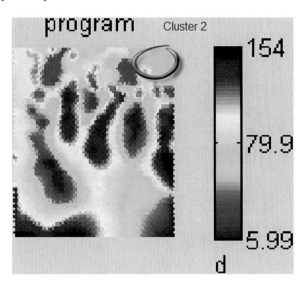

Table 26. Year component plane

Year	
Cluster 1	This cluster covers several years.
Cluster 2	The significant years in this cluster are between 1370, 1382.

Figure 37. Year component plane

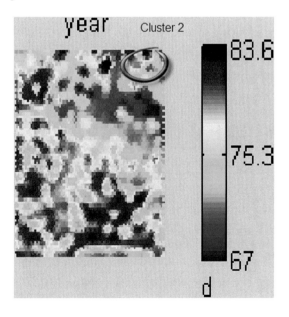

Figure 38. Relation between university and year

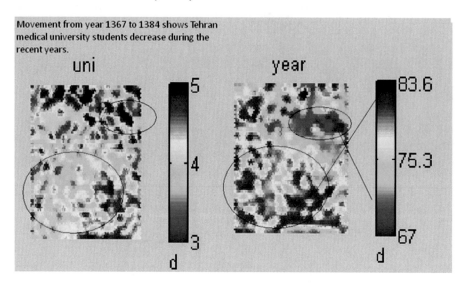

university has been decreased during the recent years. On the other hand small oval in the year plane almost is filled with blue colour and it presents this area relates to year in range of 1367 (old years), the large oval in the year plane with mostly red colour exposes years in the range of 1384 (recent years), according to these description and corresponding areas in university plane, it can be seen that small area in university plane contains high density of red colour (Tehran medical university) thus declining of red colour in the large oval in university plane shows students of Tehran medical university has been decreased during the recent years.

Figure 39 illustrates that high density of the latest years that is seen in year plane corresponds with MDdisplay and PhD degree in degree component plane. The dark blue in the degree plane relates to certificate degree and distribute during several years but the greatest number of students for certificate degree occurred between 1367 and 1375.

Figure 39. Relation between degree and year

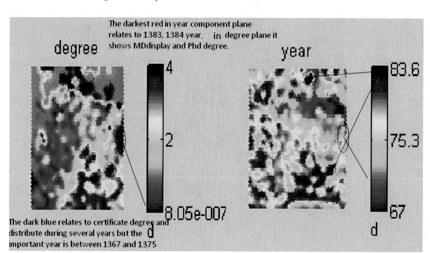

Figure 40. Relation between type and year

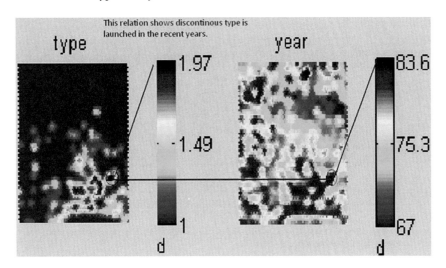

The relation between component planes in Figure 40 depicts that discontinuous type is launched in the recent years. Thus in the old years we just had continuous type. For more description it is seen that red colour in type plane corresponds with dark red in year plane hence it presents that discontinuous type of study is introduced in the recent years.

As stated by Figure 41, two modes of study (overnight and equivalent) are appeared in the recent years; it presents information about daily study mode that is distributed during several years and creates the maximum number of students. On the other hand, the rectangle in the study mode plane with red colour density and its relation with year plane describes this fact that overnight and equivalent modes are mostly belongs to the latest years.

It appears to be the case that Tehran University of Medical Science covers the majority of high degree like MDdisplay and PhD.

Figure 41. Relation between study mode and year

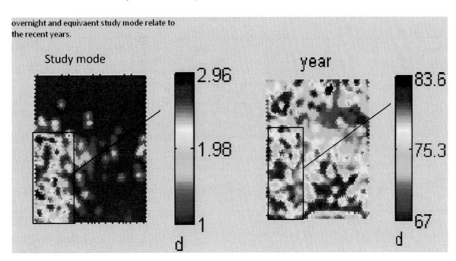

Figure 42. Relation between university and degree

According to the relation between these two component planes, we can extract that Tehran University of Medical Science covers the majority of high degree like MDdisplay and PhD.

The Comparison between Weka and SOM

Table 27 shows some of our findings by using Weka, our intension is compare them with SOM findings to assess whether we can extract them by SOM or not, based on our comparison it is understood that SOM cannot cover some facts, through SOM we cannot observe each instance description in the dataset so it is not possible to state facts exactly, in Weka we can click on each instance and observe values for all attributes like university, degree, type and so on. Only numeric data utilized in SOM algorithms so for our dataset with various nominal data it is not the best solution.

Table 27. The comparison between Weka and SOM results

Method	Result of Weka	Comparison
Visualizing two attributes (University - program)	There are some areas in Iran University and shaheed Beheshti University that have capability to add new programs like: Thoracic Surgery, Radiology Oral and Maxillofacial, Oral Diseases, Engineering improvements. It helps them to compete with Tehran University of medical sciences that has these programs.	It was not found through SOM analysis.
Visualizing two attributes (Degree - program)	It is seen that some programs are taught in certificate degree however we do not have BA or MA degree for them so it can be useful for medical ministry to create a committee to asses these programs weather they can be taught in high degree or not. Certainly this decision can help to improvement in medical aspect.	It was not found through SOM analysis.
Visualizing two attributes (Study mode - Year)	From 1367 to 1374, we had just daily study mode but nowadays we have 3 study modes (daily, overnight and equivalent) so we can add new study mode like virtual learning that was effective in the Ministry of Science - Research and Technology.	SOM: Two modes of study (overnight and equivalent) are appeared in the recent years; it presents information about daily study mode that is distributed during several years and creates the maximum number of students.
Visualizing two attributes (Year - Type)	There was not any discontinuous program from 1367 to 1381 for example there was not any discontinuous nursing program but now we have it so we can do it for other programs to ease entering to university.	SOM: The discontinuous type is launched in the recent years. Thus in the old years we just had continuous type.
Visualizing two attributes (University – Degree)	There is a big opportunity for Blood transfusion institute for establishing PhD courses; it helps to increase rank of university.	It was not found through SOM analysis.

continued on following page

Table 27. Continued

Method	Result of Weka	Comparison
Visualizing two attributes (Program - Year)	During 1367, 1369 it can be seen that there was the lowest domain for programs. Like these programs: haematological, transfusions of blood, biological products that were not taught before 1374. There are some gaps that show some programs are discontinuous during years. Dental children, Orthodontics, Nerve Disease, and General Surgery are discontinuous during several years. Assessing this event helps to discover some knowledge.	With SOM domain of program is obvious but we cannot detect exact program title like Weka.
Visualizing two attributes (Study mode - Degree)	MD display degree that is in lower level than PhD never has constituted in overnight study mode. However, adding overnight study mode helps to increase income of university because it is not free course.	It can be extracted from SOM.
Clustering (Degree–Sum of students)	Maximum numbers of students' study MDdisplay degree and minimum numbers of students are in master degree. It shows the most of applicants for medical programs are interested to MDdisplay degree that contains medical, pharmacy programs and the lowest number for MA shows that capacity of university for this degree is low.	We can find that maximum records relate to MDdisplay degree but about sum of records we cannot mention this fact through SOM.
Clustering (Degree - Program)	The greater percentages of programs are PhD degree and lowest percentages are MDdisplay because PhD is professional degree and after graduating in MDdisplay degree we can start many branches in PhD level.	It cannot be extracted exactly.
Clustering (Program-Sum of students)	We can find that most of students study in Medical program, it displays that medical program has high capacity for accept applicants in this program, the other fact is that capacity of programs varies according to demands of customers. Some of the most common programs with the great number of students listed here: Medical, nursing, pharmacy, dentistry, laboratory science.	It was not found through SOM analysis.
Clustering (Year-Sum of students)	We have decrease in the last year in province Tehran, this is maybe due to increase in other province and the other reason can be interest of new generation to non-medical programs rather than the past.	It was not found through SOM analysis.
Clustering (University–Sum of students)	Tehran University of Medical Sciences has greater number of students than others and Blood Transfusion institute has the lowest number of students between the five universities.	It cannot be extracted exactly.
Clustering (University - Program)	Transfusion of blood affairs just is taught in Blood Transfusion institute. Medical Biotechnology is the other program that is available in Institute Pastor Iran, Iran University of Medical Sciences and Tehran University of Medical Sciences, so Shaheed Beheshti University needs to add Biotechnology program to its programs.	It was not found through SOM analysis.
Clustering (Program-Degree)	In clustering with 5 clusters we can name cluster 1 and 5 as a cluster with PhD and MA degree, cluster 2 and 4 as BA, cluster 3 as certificate. Cluster1 covers many programs and cluster 2 includes low variety of programs. From these divisions we can focus to some clusters and it saves time and cost.	We can detect 2 clusters with SOM.
Clustering(University – Study mode)	Cluster 2 contains the most of instances with overnight study mode, so we can say cluster 2 helps to increase income of university. Shaheed University has the maximum number of students that study in this study mode.	We can detect 2 clusters with SOM.
Clustering(University – female students)	Tehran University of Medical Sciences has the greatest female and male students rather than others.	It is obvious that records with high quantity relates to Tehran University of Medical Sciences.
Clustering (University - Program)	Tehran University of Medical Sciences covers many programs and most of its instances are member of cluster 6 (between 13 clusters), between these programs in Tehran University of Medical Sciences, immunology is the major program that is repeated in the most of records. So cluster 6 contains programs with high diversity and can be useful for some researchers that want to study about programs.	We can find that Tehran University of Medical Sciences covers many programs.

Table 28. Clusters in the SOM analysis

Cluster 1	Cluster 2
Iran University of Medical Sciences, Shaheed Beheshti university of Medical sciences, Tehran University of Medical Sciences.	Tehran University of Medical Sciences
Certificate, Bachelor, Master, MDdisplay, PhD	MDdisplay
continuous and discontinuous	continuous
Daily, Equivalent, and Overnight	Daily
several years	between 1370, 1382

Table 28 shows clusters in the SOM analysis; we detected 2 clusters and determined their features:

The other knowledge that were extracted from SOM analysis; all of the below findings can be found through Weka:

1. It is seen that movement from year 1367 to 1384 shows students of Tehran medical university has been decreased during the recent years.
2. High density of the latest years that is seen in year plane corresponds with MDdisplay and PhD degree in degree component plane. The dark blue in the degree plane relates to certificate degree and distribute during several years but the greatest number of students for certificate degree occurred between 1367 and 1375.
3. The relation between component planes in the above figure depicts that discontinuous type is launched in the recent years. Thus in the old years we just had continuous type. For more description it is seen that red colour in type plane corresponds with dark red in year plane hence it presents that discontinuous type of study is introduced in the recent years.
4. Two modes of study (overnight and equivalent) are appeared in the recent years; it presents information about daily study mode that is distributed during several years and creates the maximum number of students.
5. It appears to be the case that Tehran University of Medical Science covers the majority of high degree like MDdisplay and PhD.

Table 29. Weka and SOM features

Tool	Data format	Data type	Utilities
WEKA	ARFF format	numeric <nominal-specification> string date [<date-format>]	Data pre-processing, classification, regression, clustering, association rules, and visualization
SOM	.xls, .dat, .data	The Toolbox can handle both numeric and categorical data, but only the former is utilized in the SOM algorithm.	pre-process data, initialize and train SOMs, visualize SOMs in various ways, and analyse the properties of the SOMs and data

According to this study and using Weka and SOM as data mining software, we found Weka more useful than SOM, Weka contains different parts to apply any techniques of data mining thus Weka is more complete than SOM as a data mining tool. One of the powerful features of SOM is visualizing of high dimensional data although it also can be used for data preparation, classification and modelling.

LARGE DATASET ANALYSIS AND FINDINGS

As mentioned before, to validate the proposed methodology in this project we repeated methodology's phases on large dataset, thus in this chapter our focus is on the larger dataset that is Ministry of Science - Research and Technology of Iran. Our findings can be found through two ways, one way is visualizing our data in visualize section of Weka, in this way we do not use any technique but in the other way our outcomes can be discovered by applying clustering technique.

Attribute Visualizing

This part is similar to small dataset and just dataset has changed. There are some figures that are listed in the following and show some knowledge about large dataset.

As we mentioned before, each program is divided to 6 study fields; Agricultural-veterinary, Art, Basic Sciences, Engineering Sciences, Humanities and Medical. A general overview shows that humanities study field is major study field in Iran universities; we zoom in the area and found that all universities in various cities with different geographical and financial situation show high density of humanities study field. This is mostly due to low level requirement of this study field's programs that are very easy to provide, for example these branches do not need professional lab and high budget to constitute, so every

Figure 43. Study mode – sum number of students

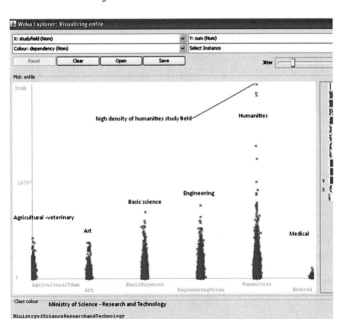

Figure 44. Study mode - city

Figure 45. Year – sum number of students

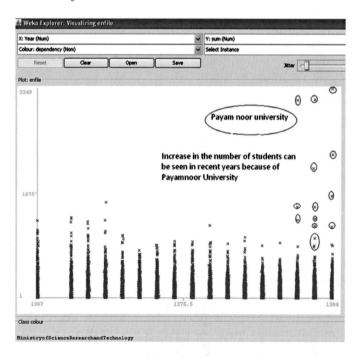

small university in everywhere can add these branches to their programs. The other reason can be high availability of lecturers for these programs.

Sharp increase in the number of students can be seen in recent years because of Payamnoor University, this university has many branches in Iran; we can find one of them in every city so it constitutes majority of students, in addition admission for this university is not very difficult and its ranking is low in comparison with other universities.

As can be seen in Figure 80, Figure 81 and Figure 82, the number of male is greater than female in the engineering study field, this is mostly due to culture of this country and their belief to some specific jobs based on gender but some increases during the last year's show that changes belief and find the capability of female in engineering fields. Nowadays many analyses are done to decrease discrimination like that.

The plot (Figure 46) shows high density of students in bachelor degree rather than others. There are many reasons for this; bachelor degree is the base for academic studies so majority of people are eager to have a basic academic degree so we can see high interest rate of people to study in bachelor degree and then move to the market and industry. Other reason can be low capacity of universities to post graduate degree so we observe many of students move to international universities for post graduate degree. Therefore, some policies and strategies must to apply to prevent this event like make facilities for post graduate students such as increase capacity of universities, decrease tuition fee, increase grant and so on.

Learning style of education is divided to 3 types; face to face and non-face to face and mixed (advanced research) which in our database we have face to face and mixed that high density belongs to face to face learning style and large numbers of mixed students relate to Payamnoor University and it shows this university prepares some facilities for students that cannot attend in face to face class (Figure 83, Figure 84).

Figure 46. Degree – sum number of students

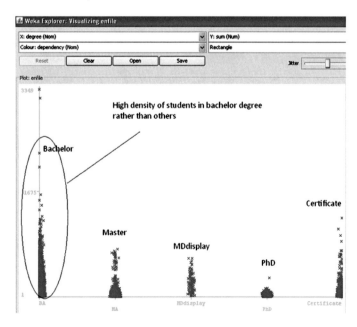

Figure 47. City – program

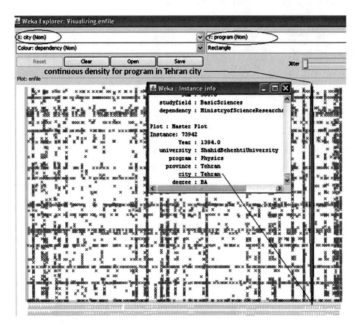

The plot (Figure 47) illustrates continuous density for program in Tehran city and it means all program are available in Tehran and it is due to it is capital of country and many of top and old universities exist in this city so it supports all programs. The plot shows continuous and linear density of programs in big cities like Tehran, Mashhad, Shiraz, and Isfahan.

Figure 48. Learning style – study mode

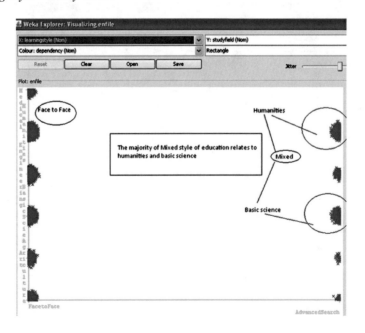

As can be seen in Figure 48, the majority of mixed learning style of education relates to humanities and basic science fields. It can be because of independency of these study fields to face to face classes.

Mixed learning style of study has launched from 1381, and it shows society needs to this style so our management can launch new style for studying that take less time for students for attending in class and in recent years we observe new style of non-face to face or virtual learning that has many customers.

According to Figure 50, students' data in these years: 1367 and 1369, relates to the limited cities: Tehran, Tabriz, Ardebil and Kermanshah. The most of records were filled with null city; this is occurred due to Iran war in these years thus these gaps in the plot shown in Figure 50 are related to data missing in city field.

The plot (Figure 51) illustrates that the major degree in the distribution of programs in all cities is related to Bachelor degree (blue colour).

SimpleKMeans Clustering Technique

After visualizing each attribute, our intension is using clustering technique to detect some groups with some differences that can help to find some interesting results. We used SimpleKMeans, it is one of the simplest unsupervised learning algorithms, this technique has some inputs like number of clusters, seed number and other inputs, and in this project we try various K to discover knowledge.

Figure 49. Year – learning style

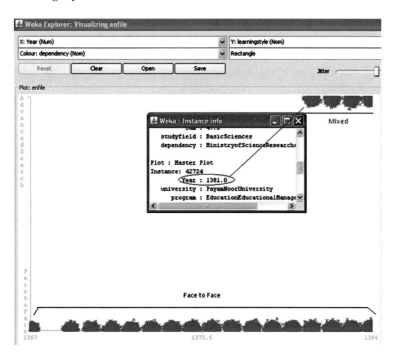

Figure 50. City - year

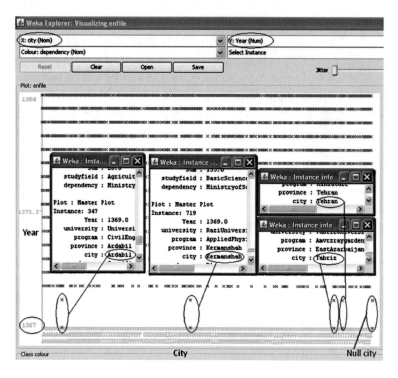

Figure 51. City – program – colour (degree)

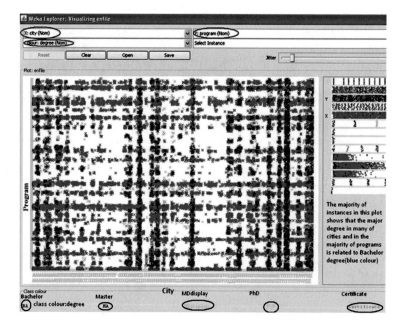

Table 30. Test 1 with K=3

K	displayStdDevs	DontReplace MissingValue	PreserveInstancesOrder	Seed
3	true	false	true	10

Figure 52. Cluster (K=3) – colour (year)

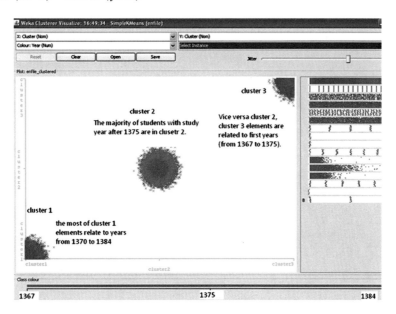

Test 1: We tried K equals 3.

Based on the Figure 52 with K equals 3 (Figure 85) our dataset groups to 3 clusters that most of cluster 1's elements relate to years from 1370 to 1384, the majority of students with study year after 1375 are in cluster 2 and vice versa cluster 2, cluster 3 elements are related to the first years (from 1367 to 1375). According to Figure 86, the common degree in all clusters is bachelor degree.

Total number of records is 77206. In the above plot (Figure 53), records are divided to 3 clusters and it shows that data from 1367 to 1374 are put in cluster 3, nearly the majority of 1375 to 1379's data is incorporated in cluster 1 and remain years almost are grouped to cluster 2.

From the plot (Figure 54) it is obvious that most of the instances are related to Payam Noor University. Cluster 2 includes the majority of instances with red colour. Experts can focus more on cluster 2, because it is a large group that contains Payam Noor University as one of the big universities in Iran. Quality of this university and its rank between Iran universities is low, its growth in recent years causes to increase of students but it does not mean quality of higher education has had growth like quantity growth.

The common study modes are daily and overnight modes. These two modes are popular between universities of Ministry of Science - Research and Technology. The daily mode quality is higher than other modes. The Podmany mode's density is concentrated on Science University Applied and Pervasive mode relates mostly to Payam Noor University.

Figure 53. Instance number – year – colour (cluster)

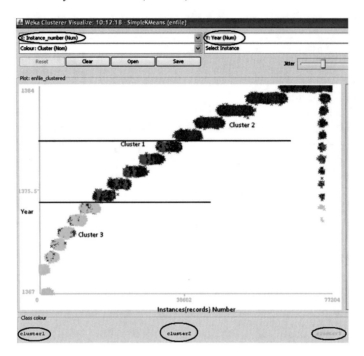

Figure 54. City – university – colour (cluster)

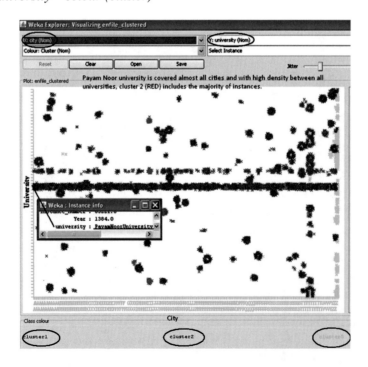

Figure 55. Study mode – university – colour (cluster)

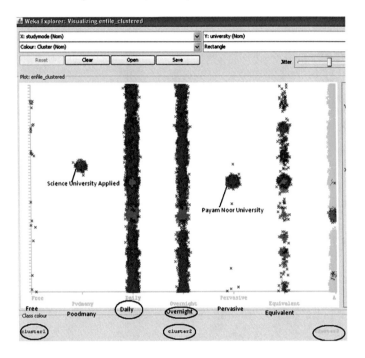

Figure 56. Year – province – colour (cluster)

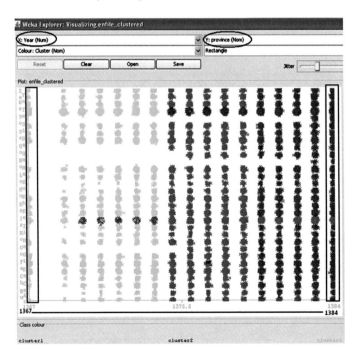

From 1367 to 1384 is seen that the distribution of universities in different provinces is increased. For example, in 1367 any data were not reported for Qazvin province. All of these gaps have capacity to discover knowledge by experts.

Focus on the type attribute in the above plot conduct us to launching year of discontinuous type in Iran higher education that is 1381. Cluster 3 contains just continuous type, the common type in cluster 1 is also continuous and just cluster 2 can be considered for the both of types.

High density can be seen for the mixed learning style in Payam Noor University (Figure 58), this style is constituted in some universities but major university for this style is Payamnoor.

As we can see in the Figure 87, the most common study field in all clusters is humanities field; cluster 3 contains the maximum of students.

Test 2: We tried K equals 5.

The Figure 88 shows that between 5 clusters, cluster 3 is the one that assigned majorly to students before year 1375.

Figure 59 illustrates that cluster 5 contains students with master degree; according to the previous paragraph it is obvious that cluster 3 that most of its elements are related to year before 1375 thus it is extracted great increase in the number of students with master degree in the recent years.

Table 31. Test 2 with K=5

K	displayStdDevs	DontReplace MissingValue	PreserveInstancesOrder	Seed
5	true	false	true	10

Figure 57. Year – type – colour (cluster)

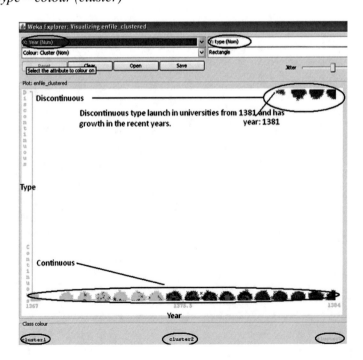

Figure 58. University – learning style – colour (cluster)

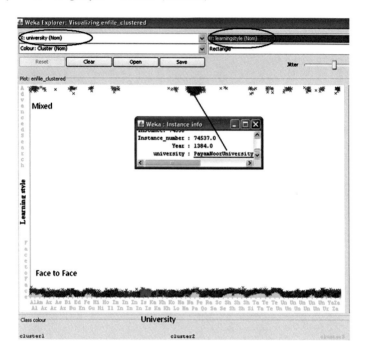

Figure 59. Cluster – cluster – colour (degree)

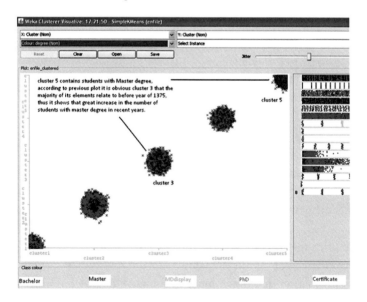

Figure 89 shows that cluster 2 involves the majority of mixed learning style, from this fact it is seen that Payam Noor University that is common university in this style belongs to cluster 2. Figure 90 presents information about cluster 3 (is mostly related to years before 1375) that shows Null values for study mode, this cluster can be modified by estimation ways to fill missing data thus this cluster creates low reliability in our analysis.

Figure 60. University – city – colour (cluster)

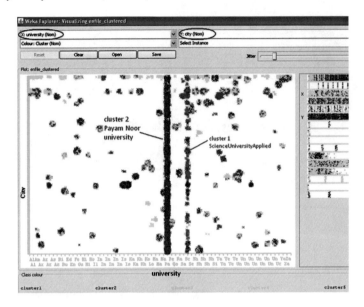

Table 32. Test 3 with K=13

K	displayStdDevs	DontReplace MissingValue	PreserveInstancesOrder	Seed
13	true	false	true	100

A general overview shows that Payam Noor University and Science Applied University make the greatest number of students in Iran. In the above plot (Figure 60) these universities are appeared in cluster 2 and cluster 1; cluster 2 has elevated density between other groups.

Test 3: We tried K equals 13.

In the plot (Figure 61) it is seen that some clusters like cluster 6, 9 and 12 contains very low universities.

As a result, by zooming on cluster 6 mentioned above we can find similarities between elements of each cluster, for example cluster 6 elements have similarity in bachelor degree and humanities and basic science study field.

Figure 63 shows the area that relates to Payam Noor University, it is obvious that the maximum of densities in this area are orange colour, consequently this university had growth in the recent years.

Figure 64 presents information that the number of female students has clear growth after 1375, it is seen orange colour density is more than blue colour density.

Test 4: We tried K equals 7.

Figure 65 shows that after 1375, there is a great growth in density of humanities and engineering field.

Figure 61. University – cluster – colour (cluster)

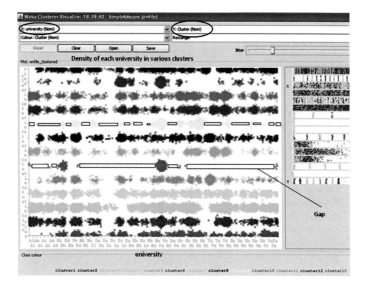

Figure 62. Degree – program – colour (study field)

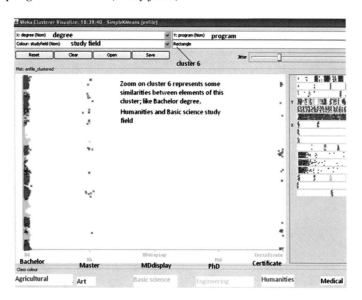

Table 33. Test 4 with K=7

K	displayStdDevs	DontReplace MissingValue	PreserveInstancesOrder	Seed
7	true	false	true	10

Figure 63. University – cluster – colour (year)

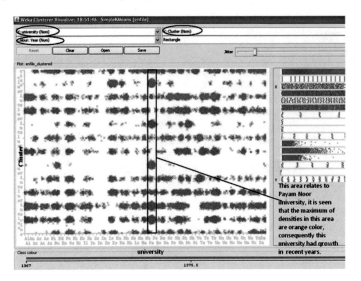

Figure 64. female students – cluster – colour (year)

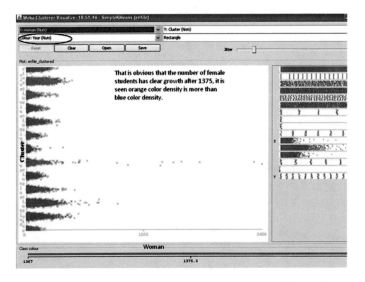

We can zoom on any value and find its status in each cluster; for example, in the above plot (Figure 66) we zoomed on the medical study field and found that cluster 2 has very low elements related to medical study field. Cluster 1, 3 and 7 make up the majority of medical study field.

Seven clusters are seen in the Figure 91 plot, we can focus on one of them and visualize each attribute in one group, and for example we focused on cluster 2 (Figure 92).

Cluster 2 in several years shows high density from 1367 to 1380. Bachelor degree has the greatest number of students in cluster 2. Cluster 2 does not have any student with mixed learning style. Humanities field has the highest density between other study fields (Figure 67).

Figure 93, Figure 94 and Figure 95 present information about cluster 2 as below:

Figure 65. Year – cluster – colour (study field)

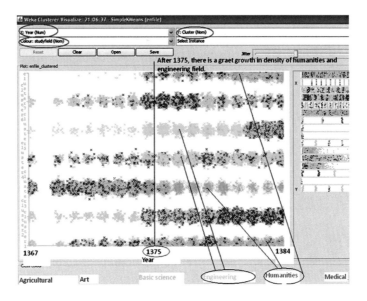

Figure 66. Cluster – program – colour (cluster)

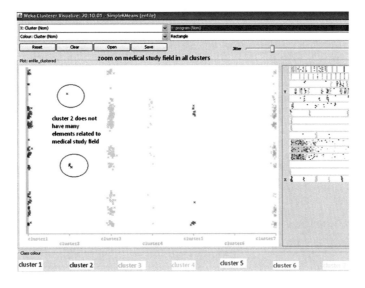

Bachelor degree has the greatest number of students in cluster 2; cluster 2 does not have any student with the mixed learning style; humanities field has the highest density between other study fields.

Summary of Findings

Summary of finding extracted from large dataset are shown in Table 34.

Figure 67. Instance number – cluster – colour (cluster)

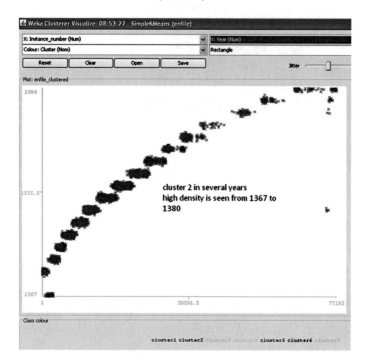

Table 34. Summary of findings (Large dataset)

Method	Result
Visualizing these attributes (study mode – sum number of students) (study mode - city)	A general overview shows that humanities study field is major study field in Iran universities; we zoom in the area and found that all universities in various cities with different geographical and financial situation show high density of humanities study field.
Visualizing two attributes (year – sum number of students)	Sharp increase in the number of students can be seen in recent years because of Payamnoor University, this university has many branches in Iran; we can find one of them in every city so it constitutes majority of students, in addition admission for this university is not very difficult and its ranking is low in comparison with other universities.
Visualizing (study field – female students), (study field –male students)	The number of male is greater than female in the engineering study field, this is mostly due to culture of this country and their belief to some specific jobs based on gender but some increases during the last year's show that changes belief and find the capability of female in engineering fields.
Visualizing (degree – sum number of students)	High density of students in bachelor degree rather than others.
Visualizing (learning style –sum number of students) (university - learning style)	High density belongs to face to face style and also large numbers of mixed students relate to Payamnoor University and it shows this university prepares some facilities for students that cannot attend in face to face class.
Visualizing (city – program)	The plot illustrates continuous density for program in Tehran city and it means all program are available in Tehran and it is due to it is capital of country and many of top and old universities exist in this city so it supports all programs. The plot shows continuous and linear density of programs in big cities like Tehran, Mashhad, Shiraz, and Isfahan.
Visualizing (learning style – study mode)	The majority of mixed style of education relates to humanities and basic science fields. It can be because of independency of these study fields to face to face classes.
Visualizing (year – learning style)	Mixed style of study has launched from 1381, and it shows society needs to this style so our management can launch new style for studying that take less time for students for attending in class and in recent years we observe new style of non-face to face or virtual learning that has many customers.

continued on following page

Table 34. Continued

Method	Result
Visualizing (city – year)	Students' data in these years: 1367 and 1369, relates to the limited cities: Tehran, Tabriz, Ardebil and Kermanshah. The most of records were filled with null city, this is occurred due to Iran war in these years thus these gaps in the below plot are related to data missing in city field.
Visualizing (city – program – colour (degree))	The plot illustrates that the major degree in the distribution of programs in all cities is related to Bachelor degree (blue colour).
Visualizing (cluster (K=3) – colour (year))	Based on the Figure 5.10 with K equals 3 (Figure A.18) our dataset groups to 3 clusters that most of cluster 1's elements relate to years from 1370 to 1384, the majority of students with study year after 1375 are in cluster 2 and vice versa cluster 2, cluster 3 elements are related to the first years (from 1367 to 1375). According to Figure A.19, the common degree in all clusters is bachelor degree.
Visualizing (instance number – year – colour (cluster))	Total number of records is 77206. In this plot (Figure 5.11), records are divided to 3 clusters and it shows that data from 1367 to 1374 are put in cluster 1, nearly the majority of 1375 to 1379's data is incorporated in cluster 2 and remain years almost are grouped to cluster 3.
Visualizing (city – university – colour (cluster))	From this plot (Figure 5.12) it is obvious that most of the instances are related to Payam Noor University. Cluster 2 includes the majority of instances with red colour. Experts can focus more on cluster 2, because it is a large group that contains Payam Noor University as one of the big universities in Iran. Quality of this university and its rank between Iran universities is low, its growth in recent years causes to increase of students but it does not mean quality of higher education has growth like quantity growth.
Visualizing (study mode – university – colour (cluster))	The common study modes are daily and overnight modes. These two modes are popular between universities of Ministry of Science - Research and Technology. The daily mode quality is higher than other modes. The Podmany mode's density is concentrated on Science University Applied and Pervasive mode relates mostly to Payam Noor University
Visualizing (year – province – colour (cluster))	From 1367 to 1384 is seen that the distribution of universities in different provinces is increased. For example in 1367 any data were not reported for Qazvin province. All of these gaps have capacity to discover knowledge by experts.
Visualizing (year – type – colour (cluster))	Focus on the type attribute in the below plot conduct us to launching year of discontinuous type in Iran higher education that is 1381. Cluster 3 contains just continuous type, the common type in cluster 1 is also continuous and just cluster 2 can be considered for the both of types.
Visualizing (university – learning style – colour (cluster))	High density can be seen for the mixed learning style in Payam Noor University, this style is constituted in some universities but major university for this style is Payam Noor University.
Visualizing (cluster – cluster – colour (degree))	The Figure illustrates that cluster 5 contains students with master degree; according to the Figure A.21 it is obvious that cluster 3 that most of its elements are related to year before 1375 thus it is extracted great increase in the number of students with master degree in the recent years.
Visualizing cluster – cluster – colour (learning style) cluster – cluster – colour (study mode)	The Figure A.22 shows that cluster 2 involves the majority of mixed learning style, from this fact it is seen that Payam Noor University that is common university in this style belongs to cluster 2. The presents information about cluster 3 (is mostly related to years before 1375) that shows Null values for study mode, this cluster can be modified by estimation ways to fill missing data thus this cluster creates low reliability in our analysis.
Visualizing university – city – colour (cluster)	A general overview shows that Payam Noor University and Science Applied University figure the greatest number of students in Iran. In the above plot (Figure 5.18) these universities are appeared in cluster 2 and cluster 1; cluster 2 has elevated density between other groups.
Visualizing university – cluster – colour (year)	This Figure shows the area that relates to Payam Noor University, it is obvious that the maximum of densities in this area are orange colour, consequently this university had growth in the recent years.
Visualizing (female students – cluster – colour (year))	This Figure presents information that the number of female students has clear growth after 1375, it is seen orange colour density is more than blue colour density.
Visualizing (cluster – program – colour (cluster))	We zoomed on the medical study field and found that cluster 2 has very low elements related to medical study field. Cluster 1, 3 and 7 make up the majority of medical study field.

CONCLUSION

Data mining is an interesting field that is essential for any organization to get benefits from collected data. Data is collected in databanks for more applications and is mined for finding of relations, patterns and exciting knowledge. There are many techniques and software suits that help us in this way but in higher education there are many challenges to discover knowledge from large organizations such as universities for finding some knowledge that is beneficial in decision making and planning in higher education so in this study we tried to use some of them and propose a suitable methodology.

In this section we summarize our findings extracted from small and large dataset related to Iran higher education, these discoveries make benefits for higher education management and researchers.

Small Dataset

- There are some areas in Iran University and Shaheed Beheshti University that have capability to add new programs like: Thoracic Surgery, Radiology Oral and Maxillofacial, Oral Diseases, Engineering improvements. It helps them to compete with Tehran University of medical sciences that has these programs.

- It is seen that some programs are taught in certificate degree however we do not have BA or MA degree for them so it can be useful for medical ministry to create a committee to asses these programs weather they can be taught in high degree or not. Certainly this decision can help to improvement in medical aspect.

- From 1367 to 1374, we had just daily study mode but nowadays we have 3 study modes (daily, overnight and equivalent) so we can add new study mode like virtual learning that was effective in the Ministry of Science - Research and Technology.

- There was not any discontinuous program from 1367 to 1381 for example there was not any discontinuous nursing program but now we have it so we can do it for other programs to ease entering to university.

- There is a big opportunity for Blood transfusion institute for establishing PhD courses; it helps to increase rank of university.

- During 1367, 1369 it can be seen that there was the lowest domain for programs. Like these programs: haematological, transfusions of blood, biological products that were not taught before 1374. There are some gaps that show some programs are discontinuous during years. Dental children, Orthodontics, Nerve Disease, and General Surgery are discontinuous during several years. Assessing this event helps to discover some knowledge.

- MD display degree that is in lower level than PhD never has constituted in overnight study mode. However, adding overnight study mode helps to increase income of university because it is not free course.

- Maximum numbers of students' study MDdisplay degree and minimum numbers of students are in master degree. It shows the most of applicants for medical programs are interested to MDdisplay degree that contains medical, pharmacy programs and the lowest number for MA shows that capacity of university for this degree is low.

- The greater percentages of programs are PhD degree and lowest percentages are MDdisplay because PhD is professional degree and after graduating in MDdisplay degree we can start many branches in PhD level.

- We can find that most of students' study in Medical program, it displays that medical program has high capacity for accept applicants in this program, the other fact is that capacity of programs varies according to demands of customers. Some of the most common programs with the great number of students listed here: Medical, nursing, pharmacy, dentistry, laboratory science.

- We have decrease in the last year in province Tehran, this is maybe due to increase in other province and the other reason can be interest of new generation to non-medical programs rather than the past.

- Tehran University of Medical Sciences has greater number of students than others and Blood Transfusion institute has the lowest number of students between the five universities.

- Transfusion of blood affairs just is taught in Blood Transfusion institute. Medical Biotechnology is the other program that is available in Institute Pastor Iran, Iran University of Medical Sciences and Tehran University of Medical Sciences, so Shaheed Beheshti University needs to add Biotechnology program to its programs.

- In clustering with 5 clusters we can name cluster 1 and 5 as a cluster with PhD and MA degree, cluster 2 and 4 as BA, cluster 3 as certificate. Cluster1 covers many programs and cluster 2 includes low variety of programs. From these divisions we can focus to some clusters and it saves time and cost.

- Cluster 2 contains the most of instances with overnight study mode, so we can say cluster 2 helps to increase income of university. Shaheed University has the maximum number of students that study in this study mode.

- Tehran University of Medical Sciences has the greatest female and male students rather than others.

- Tehran University of Medical Sciences covers many programs and most of its instances are member of cluster 6 (between 13 clusters), between these programs in Tehran University of Medical Sciences, immunology is the major program that is repeated in the most of records. So cluster 6 contains programs with high diversity and can be useful for some researchers that want to study about programs.

Large Dataset

- A general overview shows that humanities study field is major study field in Iran universities; we zoom in the area and found that all universities in various cities with different geographical and financial situation show high density of humanities study field.

- Sharp increase in the number of students can be seen in recent years because of Payamnoor University, this university has many branches in Iran; we can find one of them in every city so it constitutes majority of students, in addition admission for this university is not very difficult and its ranking is low in comparison with other universities.

- The number of male is greater than female in the engineering study field, this is mostly due to culture of this country and their belief to some specific jobs based on gender but some increases during the last year's show that changes belief and find the capability of female in engineering fields.

- High density of students in bachelor degree rather than others.

- High density belongs to face to face style and also large numbers of mixed students relate to Payam Noor University and it shows this university prepares some facilities for students that cannot attend in face to face class.

- The plot illustrates continuous density for program in Tehran city and it means all program are available in Tehran and it is due to it is capital of country and many of top and old universities exist in this city so it supports all programs. The plot shows continuous and linear density of programs in big cities like Tehran, Mashhad, Shiraz, and Isfahan.

- The majority of mixed style of education relates to humanities and basic science fields. It can be because of independency of these study fields to face to face classes.

- Mixed style of study has launched from 1381, and it shows society needs to this style so our management can launch new style for studying that take less time for students for attending in class and in recent years we observe new style of non-face to face or virtual learning that has many customers.

- Students' data in these years: 1367 and 1369, relates to the limited cities: Tehran, Tabriz, Ardebil and Kermanshah. The most of records were filled with null city, this is occurred due to Iran war in these years thus these gaps in the below plot are related to data missing in city field.

- The plot illustrates that the major degree in the distribution of programs in all cities is related to Bachelor degree (blue colour).

- Based on the Figure 5.10 with K equals 3 (Figure A.18) our dataset groups to 3 clusters that most of cluster 1's elements relate to years from 1370 to 1384, the majority of students with study year after 1375 are in cluster 2 and vice versa cluster 2, cluster 3 elements are related to the first years (from 1367 to 1375). According to Figure A.19, the common degree in all clusters is bachelor degree.

- Total number of records is 77206. In this plot (Figure 5.11), records are divided to 3 clusters and it shows that data from 1367 to 1374 are put in cluster 1, nearly the majority of 1375 to 1379's data is incorporated in cluster 2 and remain years almost are grouped to cluster 3.

- From this plot (Figure 5.12) it is obvious that most of the instances are related to Payam Noor University. Cluster 2 includes the majority of instances with red colour. Experts can focus more on cluster 2, because it is a large group that contains Payam Noor University as one of the big universities in Iran. Quality of this university and its rank between Iran universities is low, its growth in recent years causes to increase of students but it does not mean quality of higher education has growth like quantity growth.

- The common study modes are daily and overnight modes. These two modes are popular between universities of Ministry of Science - Research and Technology. The daily mode quality is higher than other modes. The Podmany mode's density is concentrated on Science University Applied and Pervasive mode relates mostly to Payam Noor University.

- From 1367 to 1384 is seen that the distribution of universities in different provinces is increased. For example, in 1367 any data were not reported for Qazvin province. All of these gaps have capacity to discover knowledge by experts.

- Focus on the type attribute in the below plot conduct us to launching year of discontinuous type in Iran higher education that is 1381. Cluster 3 contains just continuous type, the common type in cluster 1 is also continuous and just cluster 2 can be considered for the both of types.

- High density can be seen for the mixed learning style in Payam Noor University, this style is constituted in some universities but major university for this style is Payam Noor University.

- The Figure illustrates that cluster 5 contains students with master degree; according to the Figure A.21 it is obvious that cluster 3 that most of its elements are related to year before 1375 thus it is extracted great increase in the number of students with master degree in the recent years.

- The Figure A.22 shows that cluster 2 involves the majority of mixed learning style, from this fact it is seen that Payam Noor University that is common university in this style belongs to cluster 2. The presents information about cluster 3 (is mostly related to years before 1375) that shows Null values for study mode, this cluster can be modified by estimation ways to fill missing data thus this cluster creates low reliability in our analysis.

- A general overview shows that Payam Noor University and Science Applied University figure the greatest number of students in Iran. In the above plot (Figure 5.18) these universities are appeared in cluster 2 and cluster 1; cluster 2 has elevated density between other groups.

- This Figure shows the area that relates to Payam Noor University, it is obvious that the maximum of densities in this area are orange colour, consequently this university had growth in the recent years.

- This Figure presents information that the number of female students has clear growth after 1375, it is seen orange colour density is more than blue colour density.

- We zoomed on the medical study field and found that cluster 2 has very low elements related to medical study field. Cluster 1, 3 and 7 make up the majority of medical study field.

IRPHE Institute that is a responsible centre for higher education data, started to run web portal that can collect data via online from data centres of universities, this can bring improvement to higher education, and our recommendation to this system is incorporating new analysing tools to this significant data bank to discover knowledge and hidden patterns in very quick and visualizing way that is very important in our rapid growing world.

REFERENCES

Al-Noukari, M., & Al-Hussan, W. (2008). *Using Data Mining Techniques for Predicting Future Car market Demand; DCX Case Study.* Paper presented at the Information and Communication Technologies: From Theory to Applications, 2008. ICTTA 2008. 3rd International Conference on. doi:10.1109/ICTTA.2008.4530367

Aldana, W. A. (2000). *A Brief History of Data Mining*. Academic Press.

Alhoniemi, E., Himberg, J., Hollm´en, J., Laine, S., PasiLehtim¨aki, Raivio, K., . . . Vesanto, J. (2002). *SOM in data mining*. Academic Press.

Becerra-Fernandez, I., Zanakis, S. H., & Walczak, S. (2002). Knowledge discovery techniques for predicting country investment risk. *Computers & Industrial Engineering, 43*(4), 787–800. doi:10.1016/S0360-8352(02)00140-7

Bellinger, G., Castro, D., & Mills, A. (2010). *Data*. Information, Knowledge, and Wisdom.

Berkhin, P. (2006). *A Survey of Clustering Data Mining Techniques*. Academic Press.

Cios, K. J., Pedrycz, W., Swiniarski, R., & Kurgan, L. A. (2007). *Data Mining- A knowledge discovery approach*. Academic Press.

Delavari, N., & Beikzadeh, M. R. (2004). *A new model for using data mining in higher educational system*. Academic Press.

Delavari, N., Beikzadeh, M. R., & Amnuaisuk, S. (2005). *Application of enhanced analysis model for data mining processes in higher educational system*. Academic Press.

Famili, F. (2009). *Knowledge discovery and management in life sciences: Impacts and challenges*. Paper presented at the Data Mining and Optimization, 2009. DMO '09. 2nd Conference on.

Fangjun, W. (2010). *Apply Data Mining to Students' Choosing Teachers Under Complete Credit Hour*. Paper presented at the Education Technology and Computer Science (ETCS), 2010 Second International Workshop on.

Fayyad, U. M., & Uthurusamy, R. (1996). *Data mining and knowledge discovery in databases*. Academic Press.

Ghanbari, M. (2007). *Visualization Overview*. Paper presented at the System Theory, 2007. SSST '07. Thirty-Ninth Southeastern Symposium on.

Guruler, H., Istanbullu, A., & Karahasan, M. (2010). A new student performance analysing system using knowledge discovery in higher educational databases. *Computers & Education, 55*(1), 247–254. doi:10.1016/j.compedu.2010.01.010

Hilderman, R. J., Liangchun, L., & Hamilton, H. J. (1997). *Data visualization in the DB-Discover system*. Paper presented at the Tools with Artificial Intelligence, 1997. Proceedings., Ninth IEEE International Conference on.

Himberg, J. (1999). *SOM based cluster visualization and its application for false coloring*. Academic Press.

Holmes, G., Donkin, A., & Witten, I. H. (1994). *Weka: A machine learning workbench*. Academic Press.

Koua, E. L. (2005). *Using self-organizing maps for information visualization and knowledge discovery in complex geospatial datasets*. Seminar on Data and Information Management SS 2005 2D, 3D and High-dimensional Data and Information Visualization.

Lam, S. B. (2007). *Data mining with clustering and classification*. Academic Press.

Larose. (2005). Discovering knowledge in data. Academic Press.

Mannila, H. (1996). *Data mining: machine learning, statistics, and databases*. Paper presented at the Scientific and Statistical Database Systems, 1996. Proceedings., Eighth International Conference on.

Mierle, K., K., L., Roweis, S., & Wilson, G. (2005). *Mining student CVS repositories for performance indicators*. Academic Press.

Mitchell, T. M. (1997). *Machine Learning*. Academic Press.

Ong, C. S. (2000). *Knowledge discovery in databases: An information retrieval perspective*. Academic Press.

Pazzani, M. J. (2000). Knowledge discovery from data? *Intelligent Systems and their Applications, IEEE, 15*(2), 10-12.

Venus, S., & Akbari, A. H. A. (2008). *Mining of statistical data of one university to discover successful students.* Academic Press.

Salazar, A., Gosalbez, J., Bosch, I., Miralles, R., & Vergara, L. (2004). *A case study of knowledge discovery on academic achievement, student desertion and student retention.* Paper presented at the Information Technology: Research and Education, 2004. ITRE 2004. 2nd International Conference on.

Saraee, M. H., & Theodoulidis, B. (1995). *Knowledge discovery in temporal databases.* Paper presented at the Knowledge Discovery in Databases, IEE Colloquium on (Digest No. 1995/021 (A)).

Siraj, F., & Abdoulha, M. A. (2009). *Uncovering Hidden Information Within University's Student Enrollment Data Using Data Mining.* Paper presented at the Modelling & Simulation, 2009. AMS '09. Third Asia International Conference on. doi:10.1109/AMS.2009.117

Tan, S. (2006). Introduction to Data Mining. Academic Press.

Tsai, P. S. M., & Chen, C.-M. (2001). Discovering knowledge from large databases using prestored information. *Information Systems*, *26*(1), 1–14. doi:10.1016/S0306-4379(01)00006-0

Vembu, S., & Baumann, S. (2004). A Self-Organizing Map Based Knowledge Discovery for Music Recommendation Systems.*Computer Music Modeling and Retrieval Second International Symposium, CMMR 2004.*

Vesanto, J., & Alhoniemi, E. (2000). Clustering of the Self-Organizing Map. *IEEE Transactions on Neural Networks*, 11. PMID:18249787

Vesanto, J., Himberg, J., Alhoniemi, E., & Parhankangas, J. (1999). Self-organizing map in Matlab: the SOM Toolbox.*Proceedings of the Matlab DSP Conference 1999.*

Witten, I. H., & Frank, E. (2005a). *Data Mining: Practical Machine Learning Tools and Techniques.* Academic Press.

Witten, I. H., & Frank, E. (2005b). Data Mining: Practical machine learning tools and techniques (2nd ed.). Academic Press.

Yghini, M., Akbari, A., & Sharifi, M. (2008). *Mining on students and discovering groups of students those are available from the data and their relations.* Academic Press.

Zanakis, S. H., & Becerra-Fernandez, I. (2005). Competitiveness of nations: A knowledge discovery examination.*European Journal of Operational Research*, *166*(1), 185–211. doi:10.1016/j.ejor.2004.03.028

KEY TERMS AND DEFINITIONS

Classification: Classification is a data mining technique that predicts data elements' group, for example we can predict the weather of a day will be sunny, rainy or cloudy.

Clustering: Clustering is a data mining technique that is a division of data elements into groups of similar objects without advance knowledge of the group definitions.

Data Mining: It is a technology to process information; it extracts knowledge that hidden in the data.

Data Visualization Techniques: They can be used in knowledge discovery process at three stages: to conduct discovery, to conduct the presentation of the results, present the results themselves.

Knowledge Discovery Process: Knowledge discovery process is called knowledge discovery in database that extract new knowledge from massive datasets.

SOM: The SOM is a significant tool for visualization, cluster extraction and exploratory step of data mining.

Weka: Weka (Waikato Environment for Knowledge Analysis) is popular software for machine learning written in java and developed by university of Waikato, New Zealand.

ENDNOTES

[1]   For each instance in the cluster, summing the squared differences between each attribute value and corresponding one in the cluster centroids. These are summed up for each instance in the cluster and for all clusters.

[2]   In cross-validation, we decide on a fixed number of *folds,* or partitions of the data. Suppose we use four. Then the data is split into four approximately equal partitions and each in turn is used for testing and the remainder is used for training. That is, use two-thirds for training and two-third for testing and repeat the procedure four times so that, in the end, every instance has been used exactly once for testing.

APPENDIX

The Figures of Discoveries

Figure 68. Study mode – year

Figure 69. Year - type

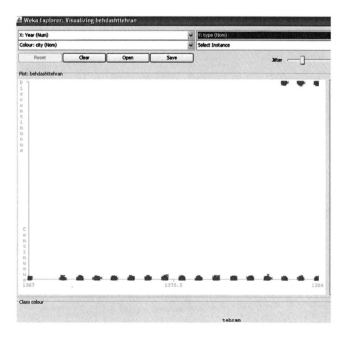

Figure 70. University – Study mode

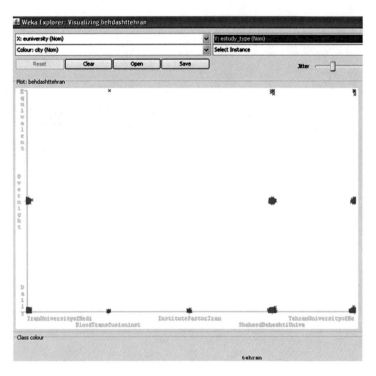

Figure 71. Study mode - degree

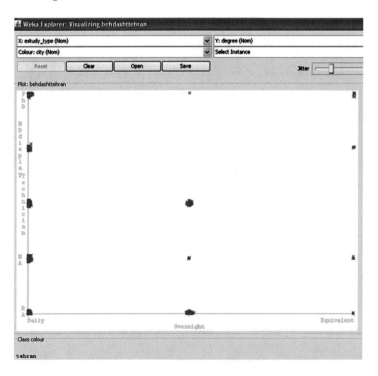

Figure 72. Degree – Program

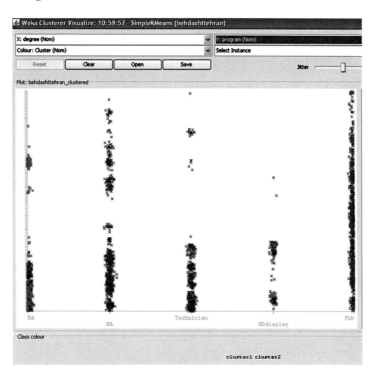

Figure 73. Program - Sum

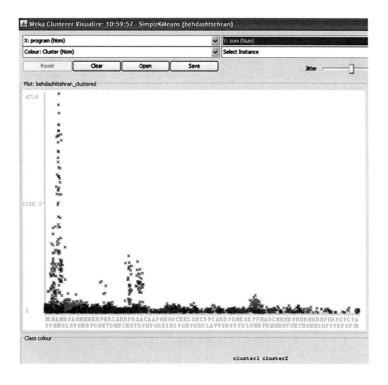

Figure 74. Year - Sum

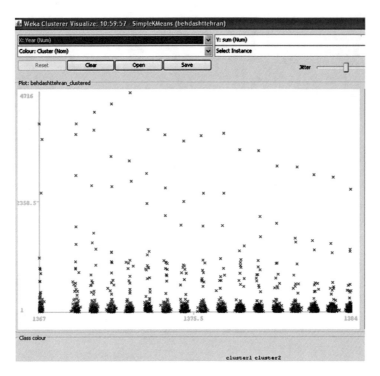

Figure 75. University – female students

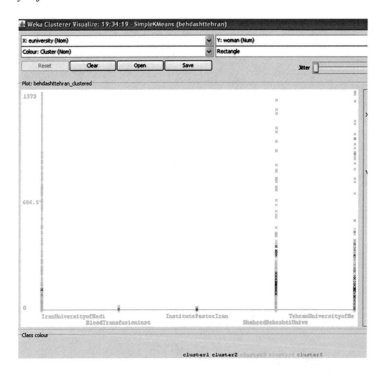

Figure 76. University – female students with jitter function

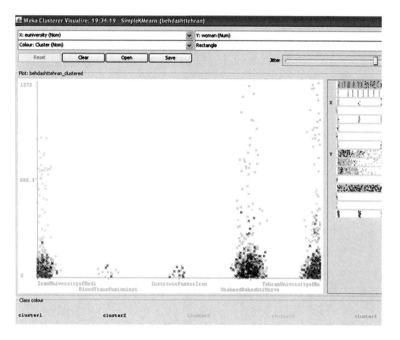

Figure 77. University –male students with jitter function

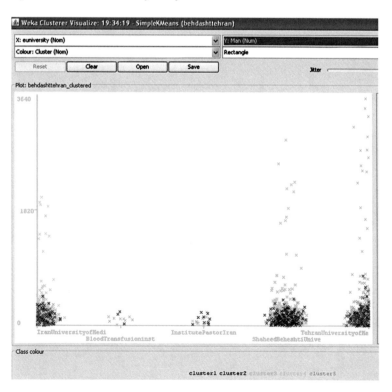

Figure 78. University –male students

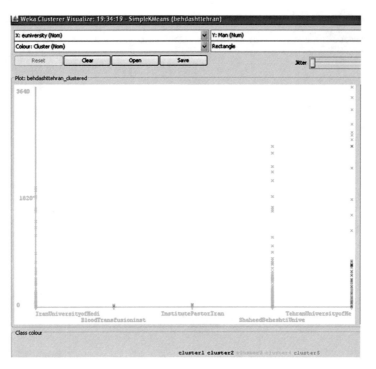

Figure 79. University –Program

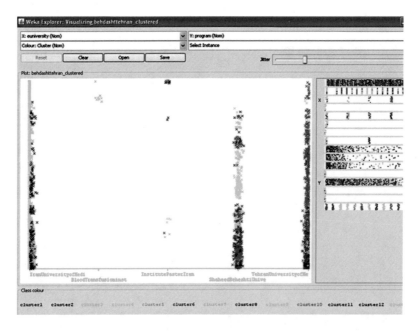

Figure 80. Study field – female students

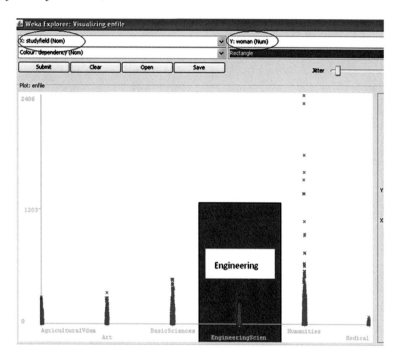

Figure 81. Study field – female students

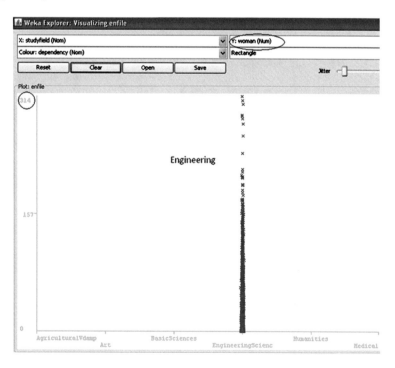

Figure 82. Study field –male students

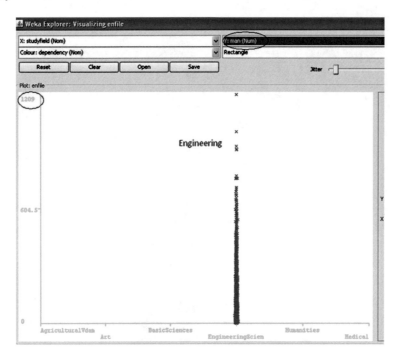

Figure 83. Learning style –sum number of students

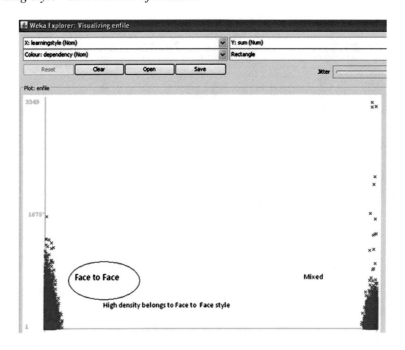

Figure 84. University - learning style

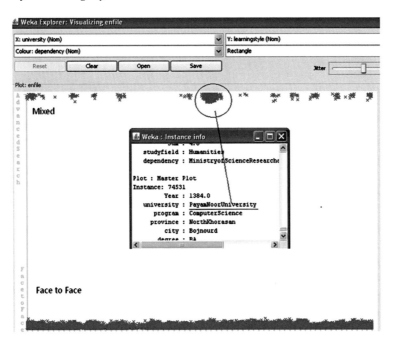

Figure 85. Clusters with K=3

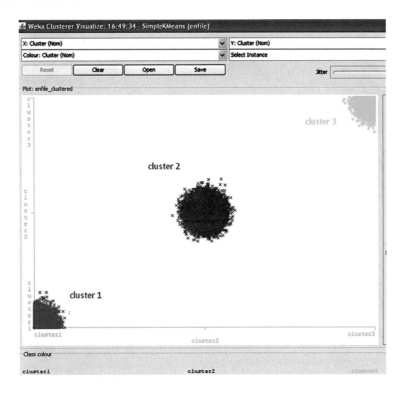

Figure 86. Clusters (K=3) – colour (degree)

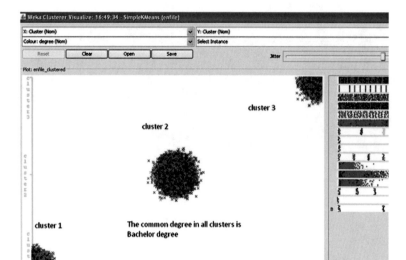

Figure 87. Cluster – sum – colour (study field)

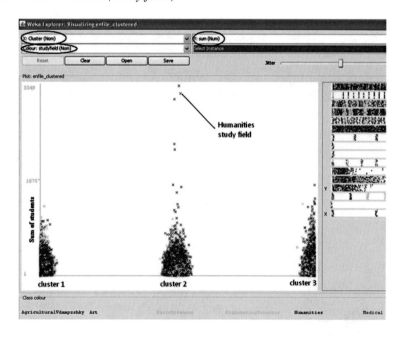

Figure 88. Cluster – cluster – colour (year)

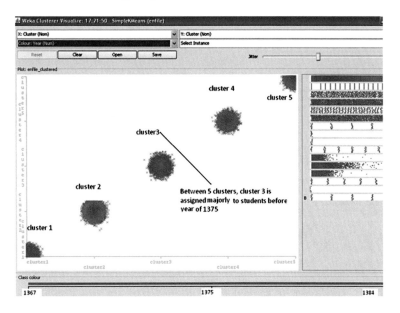

Figure 89. Cluster – cluster – colour (learning style)

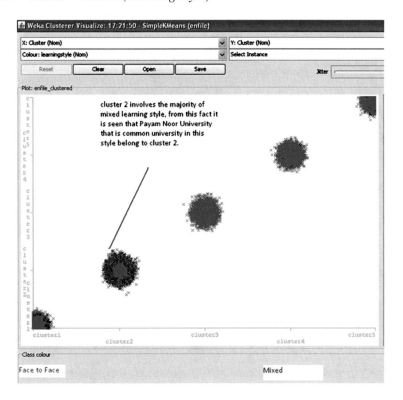

Figure 90. Cluster – cluster – colour (study mode)

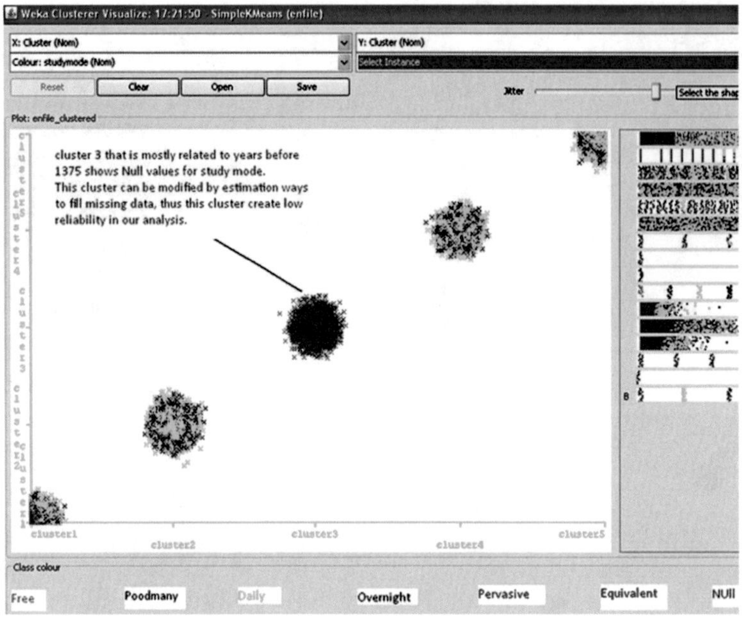

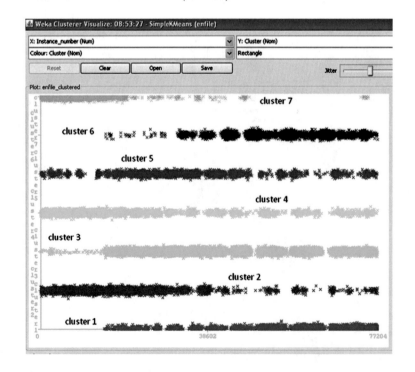

Figure 91. Instance number – cluster – colour (cluster)

Figure 92. Focus on cluster 2 (instance number – cluster – colour (cluster))

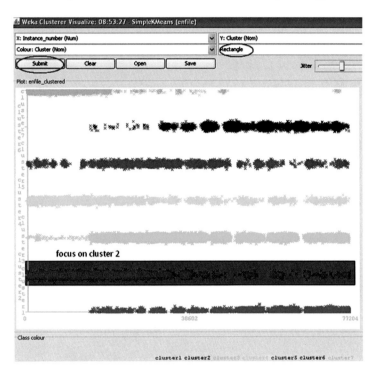

Figure 93. Degree – sum – colour (cluster)

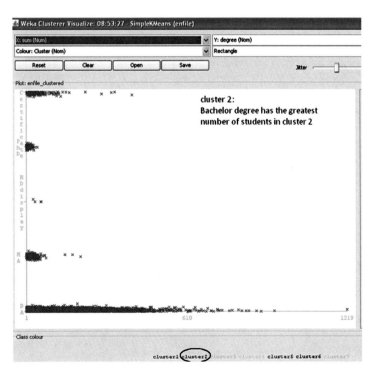

Figure 94. Sum – learning style - colour (cluster)

Figure 95. Sum –study field - colour (cluster)

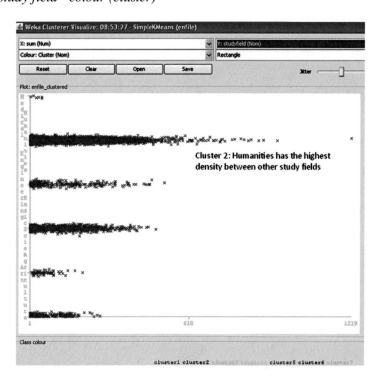

Chapter 3
Spatial Databases:
An Overview

Grace L. Samson
University of Huddersfield, UK

Mistura M. Usman
University of Abuja, Nigeria

Joan Lu
University of Huddersfield, UK

Qiang Xu
University of Huddersfield, UK

ABSTRACT

Spatial databases maintain space information which is appropriate for applications where there is need to monitor the position of an object or event over space. Spatial databases describe the fundamental representation of the object of a dataset that comes from spatial or geographic entities. A spatial database supports aspects of space and offers spatial data types in its data model and query language. The spatial or geographic referencing attributes of the objects in a spatial database permits them to be positioned within a two (2) dimensional or three (3) dimensional space. This chapter looks into the fundamentals of spatial databases and describes their basic component, operations and architecture. The study focuses on the data models, query Language, query processing, indexes and query optimization of a spatial databases that approves spatial databases as a necessary tool for data storage and retrieval for multidimensional data of high dimensional spaces.

INTRODUCTION

The extensive and increasing availability of collected data from geographical information system devices and technology has made it excessively difficult to manage these information using existing spatial database methods thus this has led to research advances in behavioural aspects of monitored subjects. Geographic information systems (GIS) can efficiently handle all the major tasks of information extraction (which include data input and data verification, storage and manipulation, output and presentation, data transformation and even interactions with the end users) from large datasets. This signifies that geographic information system are complete database management systems which can handle all the task mentioned above (Rigaux et al. 2003). Notwithstanding, based on the purpose of whatever application under a user's consideration, the objects in these (GIS) databases must be properly modelled for real

DOI: 10.4018/978-1-5225-2058-0.ch003

world data simplification (i.e. simplifying real world data so as to create an actual prototype of it) in other to enhance efficient performance of the database. To achieve this, data analyst constantly seek an appropriate data structure that efficiently stores the objects data in the database and allows for a better database management. Spatial databases maintain space information which is appropriate for applications where there is need to monitor the position of an object or event over space. Spatial databases describe the fundamental representation of the object of a dataset that comes from spatial or geographic entities. A spatial database supports aspects of space and offers spatial data types in its data model and query language. The spatial or geographic referencing attributes of the objects in a spatial database permits them to be positioned within a two (2) dimensional or three (3) dimensional space. A spatial database unlike the classical database do not only query data based on their attributes alone, they also have the capacity for querying data elements with respect to their locations. Spatial databases are built to compliment the classical database using some defined architecture (figure 2 a and b). This chapter looks into the fundamentals of spatial databases and describes their basic component, operations and architecture. Figure 1 shows a typical classical database system environment.

BACKGROUND

Spatial Database Management System Architecture

According to Ester et al. (1999), Spatial Database Systems (SDBS) are relational databases plus a concept of spatial location and spatial extension, and the explicit location and extension of objects define implicit relations of spatial neighbourhood. Ester et al. (1997), argued that the efficiency of many KDD algorithms for SDBS depends heavily on an efficient processing of these neighbourhood relationships since the neighbours of many objects have to be investigated in a single run of a KDD algorithm. The *DBMS architecture are frequently* employed in the construction of spatial databases. Nevertheless, while typical databases can understand various numeric and character types of data according to Shekhar (1999), additional functionality needs to be added for them to process spatial data types, these are typically called geometry or features. Figure 2 shows three basic architectures for designing a spatial database management system according to Güting (1994) are the layered and the dual architecture. In layered architecture

Figure 1. Diagram showing a typical environment of database management

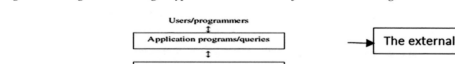

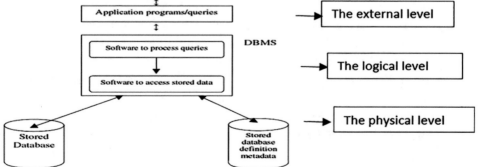

Figure 2. The diagram of spatial database architecture (a) the layered architecture (b) the dual architecture (Güting, 1994); (c) the integrated architecture in full detail

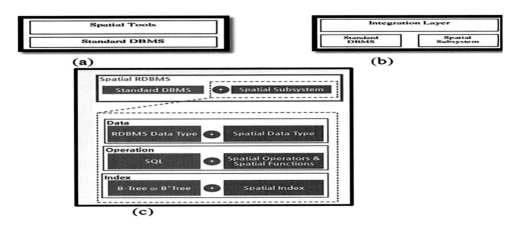

the database uses the standard DBMS and on top of the databases there is spatial tools as a top layer of it while in the dual architecture the top layer is the integration layer that will integrate between standard DBMS with spatial subsystem in bottom layer.

Spatial databases describe the fundamental representation of the object of a dataset that comes from spatial or geographic entities. The spatial or geographic referencing attributes of the objects permits them to be positioned within a two (2) dimensional or three (3) dimensional space. Basically, there are two fundamental aspects of a spatial database that needs to be modelled: the spatial component (where) and their attributes (what). These two factors determines the spatial data and attribute data that makes up the spatial database. Spatial data describes the location of the object of concern while attribute data tries to specify characteristics at that location (e.g. how much, when etc.). However representing these data in the form that the computer would understand requires grouping the data into layers according to the individual components with similar features (example layer could be waterlines, elevation, temperature, topography etc.). Nonetheless, the data properties of each layer (such as scale, projection, accuracy, and resolution) needs to be set by selecting appropriate properties for each of these layers. This is where the logical layer of spatial database management system (SDBMS) comes in. The logical layer Rigaux et al. (2003) carries the definition of *spatial database schema* which describes the structure of the information as managed by the application. It also carries the constraints to be respected by the data in the database. Defining the schema allows for further database operation (including data insert and delete) and database query using an appropriate spatial *query language*. In other words it is correct to state that the particular structures, constraints, and operations provided by the SDBMS depend wholly on the *logical data model as* supported by this SDBMS (Rigaux et al. 2003).

Data Representation in a Spatial Database:

The content of spatial data according to Densham and Goodchild (1989); Li et al., (2006), describes spatial objects' specific geographic orientation and spatial distribution in the real world. Spatial data also includes space entities attributes, the number, location, and their mutual relations. The data can be the value of point, height, road length, polygon area, building volume and the pixel gray. It can be the string of geographical name and annotation. It can also be graphics, images, multimedia, spatial relationships or other topologies. Spatial phenomenon is described using dimensional objects such as points, lines polygons or area, thus this complexity of spatial data and its intrinsic spatial relationships limits the usefulness of conventional data mining techniques for extracting spatial patterns. Figure 3 can be considered as a typical example of a spatial dataset. The picture is a Satellite Image of a County (the wards in Yorkshire and the Humber for the 2011 census) showing the County's boundary (the dashed white line), the Census block including name, area, population, Boundary (shown by dark line), and Water bodies (dark polygons) as obtained from Census (2011).

Given a d-dimensional space $\mathbb{R}^d$ with a Euclidean distance, assume the dimension of d is 2 in that Euclidean space, also assume that the space is a big rectangle with edges parallel to the axes of the coordinate system (see Figure 3), then with such space we obtain our spatial dataset. Therefore in other to store the data in spatial database table, we starts by creating a table with the item sets as obtained from the image using a classical relational database model.

If we bring out a single block of the census_area in its 2-dimensional space from Figure 3(c), we could get an information on each record. Figure 4 is a typical example of a single object as would be represented as a record on the database table

Traditional database (Shekhar and Chawla, 2003) do not support the boundary (polygon) data types as seen in our illustration above as such, there arise the need to create a separate relation using spatial data model and then mapping the new table into a classical database, thus demanding us to create additional tables that can store the spatial data types. For each of the rectangular block in the study area, the following are identified; *polygon, edge and point* and a separate table is created for it as shown in Figure 5.

Spatial Data Types

Unlike the classical relational database management system which store data as numbers, alphabets, alphanumeric or even symbols, spatial databases store data abstract data types (ADTs) such as points,

Figure 3. Example spatial dataset: 2 thematic map of Yorkshire County and the relational database tables describing them (Census 2011): (a) indicates the areas where actual census was conducted (b) shows the areas in Yorkshire where English is spoken as a major language (c) a relation representing the two spatial objects

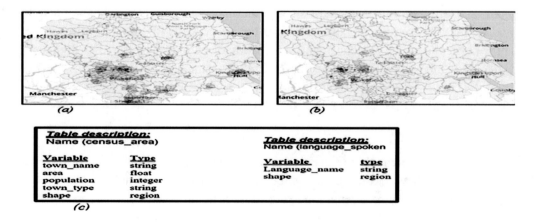

Figure 4. Representation of a single record the census_area database table

Table: Census_area

Town_id	Name	Population	Area	Boundary
132	Huddersfield	120000	1	((0,0), (0,1), (1,0), (1,1))
....	......			

Figure 5. Relational database table storing the spatial properties of the object

Table: New_census_area

Name	Area	Population	Boundary_id
35	1	2000	101

Table: Polygon

Boundary_id	Name_of_edge
101	A
101	B
101	C
101	D

Table: points

endpoint	x-coordinate	y-coordinate
1	0	0
2	0	1
3	1	1
4	1	0

Table: Edges

Name_of_edge	Endpoint
A	1
A	2
B	2
B	3
C	3
C	4
D	4
D	1

lines, polygons, coordinates (latitude and longitude coordinates which define a given location on the surface of the earth), topology or other data types that can be mapped (Samson et al, 2013; Ernest and Djaoen, 2015). The definition and implementation of spatial data types is the most fundamental issue in the development of a spatial database systems (Güting and Schneider, 1993). In Schneider (1999) it is shown that spatial data types are necessary to model geometry and to suitably represent geometric data in a database system. The basic data types according to the author includes: point, line and region and the more complex types are partitions and graphs including networks (roads, rivers etc.). In Güting and Schneider (1993) spatial data types (points, lines and regions) are described as elements of a spatial object which describes the objects attributes regardless of whether the database management system uses a relational, complex object, object-oriented or some other data model. Spatial database (made up of collection of both spatial and non-spatial data) is optimized so as to optimally store and cross-examine data objects located spatially. Compared with normal databases, which work only with numeric, character or calendar data, spatial databases offer additional functions that allow processing spatial data types (Velicanu & Olaru, 2010). According to (Ernest & Djaoen, 2015) spatial data types which generally describes the physical location and shape of geometric objects are classified into two types namely: geometry and geography data types. The geometry data types allows data to be stored using the x and y (Euclidean) coordinate system, using this method, the xy coordinates therefore positions the spatial object (points, polygon/region or lines) on a 2dimensional Euclidean space. The geography types of spatial data Ernest and Djaoen (2015) stores data based on round-earth coordinate system. In this case, the spatial object is stored using its latitude and longitude coordinate's value. More elucidation on spatial data types can be found in Samson et al., (2013: 2014), but for a simple example let us look at the illustration below.

Suppose the problem at hand is to find the nearest town to the centre of Yorkshire Counties (marked P) from the map in Figure 8, then we need to store the cities A through M in our database. By this we could store the cities as point locations by taking the values of their x and y coordinates. In doing this we create a table called Census_town and then follow the steps explained above. Figure 6 highlights different types of spatial objects and how they hey are represented and Figure 7 shows a general overview of the various spatial data types and how they are described as presented in Rigaux et al. (2003)

Figure 6. The different data types for representing spatial objects

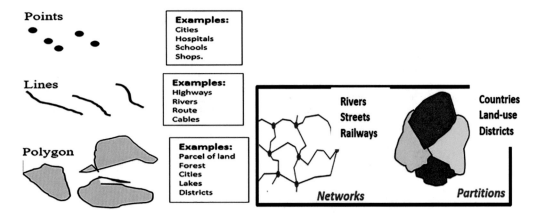

Figure 7. Methods for representing spatial data types (Rigaux et al., 2003)

Geometric Type	Representation	Description
point	(x, y)	Point in space
line	$((x_1, y_1), (x_2, y_2))$	An infinite straight line defined by two points
lseg	$((x_1, y_1), (x_2, y_2))$	A line segment defined by its two endpoints
box	$((x_1, y_1), (x_2, y_2))$	A rectangle (rectangular box)
path	$((x_1, y_1), \ldots)$	A *closed* polyline (closed path)
path	$[(x_1, y_1), \ldots]$	A polyline (open path)
polygon	$((x_1, y_1), \ldots)$	Polygon
circle	$< (x, y), r >$	A circle (with center and radius)

SPATIAL DATABASE MANAGEMENT SYSTEM

Point Data Types

Point data are completely characterized by their locations in a multidimensional space (Velicanu & Olaru, 2010). Point data types are basically used to represent a single object in a given location in a multidimensional space. In Samson et al, (2014) Points are shown to be efficient when modelling for example, cities, forests, or buildings and also ideal object of a thematic maps describing for instance land use/cover or the for the partitioning of a country into districts. A Point is the most important object type supported by the spatial data types -both geometry and geography- (Ernest and Djaoen, 2015) and they represent a singular position in space. The position of a point in space can be defined by using an X-coordinate and Y-coordinate value-pair based on a planar (geometry) coordinate system or on the latitude and longitude coordinates from a geographic coordinate system (Ernest and Djaoen, 2015). In vector spaces, points can also be used to store extracted features from data e.g. text. Raster data model are best expressed using points (which are used to store the raster image as pixels where each point represents a single atomic cell of the image) because the raster say something about all the point in the raster space, in this way the raster image can then be modelled as a single collection of spatially related objects. In general, Points are simple geometry of dimension zero and they are not bounded by areas either in length or in breath. For a better idea on how to analyse point patterns from a spatial dataset see Samson et al, (2014) and for better understanding of sampling point data see Samson et al, (2013).

To define a point A from the geometric point of view we refer to the values its xy coordinate in the plane. For instance in a 2 dimensional plane where x= 2 and y= 9,we write point A as A(2,9) for 3 dimsion A(x, y, z), for 4 dimensinsion A(x, y,m,z) etc. The Z coordinate refers to the height or elevation of a Point, and the M coordinate represents a measure value - which is a user-defined value- (Ernest and Djaoen, 2015). Figure 8 is a thematic map of the image in Figure 3, the map depicts the number of females (in percentage) usual residents aged 16 to 74 in professional occupations in towns A through M around the Yorkshire County. In this illustration, the towns has been modelled as point locations as such will be represented (stored) on the database using their individual xy coordinates.

Figure 8. Using point locations to represent the towns around the county

Storing Region Data Types

In the previous section we have used point representations to model the spatial objects. In this section we would model the objects using a rough geometric approximations of their spatial extent in addition to which most Objects also have location and boundary (Mamoulis, 2012). Figure 9 is another version of the image in Figure 8 where the spatial objects are modelled using geometric (rectangular) shapes, as such is said to be a vector representation in which case the extent of the spatial objects has significant effect on the result and performance of the query processing (Shekhar et al., 2011). Regions are abstract data types (ADT) that represents the geometric part of a spatial object.

In most cases representing objects with large areas (like lakes, forest etc) normally require solid shapes with a surface (an example is a two or three dimensional object). In essence these kinds of large area entities are fitted using polygons (mostly rectangles), the boundary of the regions are enclosed in polylines around the polygon

Converting a Region to Point Data

Representing the regions in Figure 10 with points is not a straightforward transformation, a procedure has to be applied that can execute the functions by converting the features on the map into a set of points. Notwithstanding, Candan and Sapino (2010) iterated the fact that this approach is particularly useful for measuring similarities and distances where it is assumed that there is only one point per feature, it cannot be used for instance to express topological relationships between regions. Towns represented with points **A** through **M** (in Figure 8 and 9) has been converted from large geometric areas (of 2-dimension) to smaller sized points (of zero-dimension). This conversion is justifiable because their extents (shapes) are not considered useful when considering their locations on the larger scale map. In other words the result of the queries that concerns the object's location on the map is not affected by reducing the shape of the object to a point because considering the space they cover in contrast to the space that contains them, the significance of the size of the their shape is inconsequential.

Figure 9. Using rectangles (minimum bounding rectangles) to enclose the regions before storage

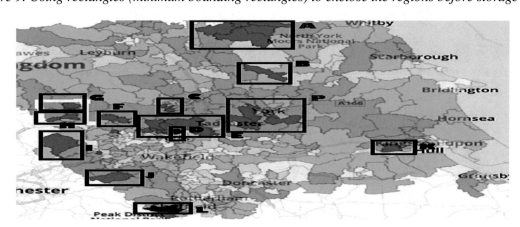

The basic steps to converting from polygon to point is itemised as follows:

1. Find a two dimensional bounding box (MBR) around the points by:
   a. Finding the convex hull for the set points or regions,
   b. Eliminating points that are redundant to the solution, and
   c. Enclose the polygon (convex) with the minimum bounding box that contains its m-number of vertices.
2. Estimate the centre (centroid) of the object (on the x-axis) using the MBRs. (This in most cases is used as the point that represents the object).

Minimum Box/Rectangle (MBB/MBR)

Minimum bounding box or minimum bounding rectangle/regions (MBR) is a paradigm for clustering points based on their similarity measure. Points which are closer to each other (in space) to a certain extent are always put together as objects in one cluster also known bucket (mostly rectangular in shape). Samet (2009) describes a bucket as a subspace (of an underlying space) which contains sorted spatial objects that has been grouped together in a natural way of arranging them based on their spatial order (also known as spatial occupancy). In Mamoulis (2012), constructing the MBR of a spatial object or objects is seen as a technique for handling spatial objects by approximating their geometric extent using the minimum bounding box that encloses the object's geometry minimally and more efficiently. This idea is an optimal filtering method of managing spatial databases by preserving objects' natural locality. When this spatial approximation is effectively (in terms of computational cost) achieved, then the objects are guaranteed to retain their exact original geometry. The study in Güting (1994) expresses MBRs as a generic approximation of the spatial data types (points, line, polygons) which links them to different spatial access methods and allows the spatial objects to be organised in a database which is stored on an external memory using certain size of buckets (MBR) as a match to the pages of the memory of the storage system (Dröge & Schek, 1993). Figure 10is the map of the administrative area of Britain as obtained from (GADM, 2009). We have used the map as a spatial dataset to like illustrate the various stages involved in converting regions to point data for spatial data analysis. The files were extracted from GADM version created 2009.

Convex Hull

The convex hull of a set of points *t* is the smallest convex polygon that encloses *t* (Rigaux et al, 2003) and computing the convex hull from that set of points which together makes up the convex polygon (in which all points vertices outward from the centre) with the minimum area that includes all these points is a way to represent the region occupied by the points (Asaeedi et al, 2013). Note that the points are convex because we have assumed that for any two of them say a and b, the line segment ab is totally within points a through b. Figure 11 is a sample dataset (a digitised map of one of the towns in Figure 10 a) with selected points picked from the towns boundary to another town, Therefore the points around the polygon in Figure 11 are the convex points of the spatial object (town). Thus if we call the set of all points p and if we choose C to be the convex points then the convex hull of p is the smallest convex polygon that encloses p. Note that the points that did not fall on the polygon are non-convex point and are insignificant in finding the convex hull of the object. For any subset of a plane coordinate system (say points, rectangle, simple polygons), the convex hull is the smallest convex set that contains that subset.

*Figure 10. Various stages involved in converting to point location: (a) map representing the study area (b) regions on the map represented by their convex hull (c) constructed MBR around the convex hull (d) centroid of regions using their MBR (e) expanded view of the area (in figure 10 d) around the point marked **d** (f) region fully represented using points*

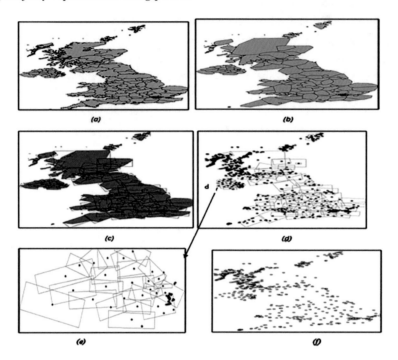

Figure 11. Digitized map of one of the towns in Figure 10 (a) showing its MBR (red rectangle)

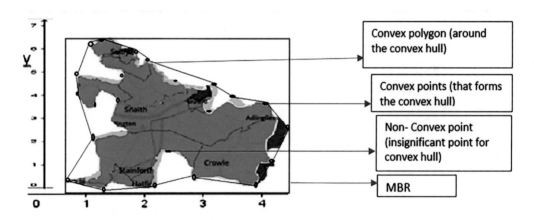

Algorithm for Finding the Convex Hull around a Polygon

```
Assuming all the points in
   p
are distinct
```

```
Let the space be of dimension 2
Then
{
Enter coordinates representing each point (2* P),
```
Set of all points = p Set of all convex points = C //Where $p = \left(a,b,c....r\right)$ Then

for all $p_i \in p, \left(i = 1....r\right)$ Find $\left\{s \mid s \le p \wedge p \in C\right\}$ Start with the s **value** that has the

smallest y-coordinate. Sort the points following a polar angle with s to get

simple (convex) polygon.

```
Consider points in anticlockwise order, and eliminate those that would create
a clockwise turn.
}
Return convex polygon
// sorted list of points t along the boundary (moving anticlockwise) with the
convex hull of S
```

Fitting the Rectangle

Assuming we have a set of points on a 2dimensional plane, we could compute the minimum bounding rectangle that encloses the points. It is only natural that the minimum bounding rectangle for the points be supported by the convex hull of the points (which is a convex polygon) and any points interior to the polygon have no influence on the bounding rectangle (Eberly, 2015). More so, it has also been established by Freeman and Shapira (1975) that the most important constraint to be met in fitting a minimum bounding box (mbb) is to ensure that at least one of the edges of the mbb coincides with some edges of the convex polygon.

Thus the simple algorithm below could be used to construct a minimum bounding box (mbb) around the convex polygon obtained above (section 3.2.1)

Algorithm for Finding the Minimum Bounding Box around a Convex Polygon

```
Given:
A set of convex points say p // the points constitutes the convex polygon
Produce:
The minimum bounding box for the set of points say q// the output points is
expected to be smaller than input points
Start:
// let V be the number of edges on the convex polygon
        For v = 1…V
        Draw a rectangle with vᵢ as the base (i.e. vᵢ is collinear with an edge
of the rectangle)
Calculate the area A of the rectangle
Repeat for all v
Display the rectangle with the smallest area as the minimum bounding box (mbb)
Other simpler method can be used by just finding the xmin,ymin,xmax,ymax val-
```

```
ues
Start
Get min x, max x
Get min y, max y
Using these bounds
        Draw the rectangle around the points
        // despite the fact that (Eberly, 2015) claimed that it is not neces-
sary, the rectangle produced using this method will be axis aligned (that is
being orthogonal with one or both of the axes)
```

Baum and Hanebeck (2010) describes axis-aligned rectangles as rectangles in any dimensional space which is represented with the extreme values (the minimum and maximum) on each axis, in addition, they also demonstrated how the time complexity (in applying certain number of steps) for computation can be calculated. Axis-aligned rectangles are very significant in SDMSs for objects with *extents* as we can see in the elucidation given by Samet (1995) for instance, in other to store such arbitrary object we need to represent them as n-dimensional rectangles for which each node in the storage structure (say tree) corresponds to the n-dimensional rectangles that holds the child but most importantly the main spatial objects which is stored in the leaf (node) of the tree are basically represented by the smallest axis-aligned rectangle that contains them. It is important to remember that the nodes we refer to here relates to the pages on a disk (computer memory)as such building the tree structure should put into consideration the fact that minimum number of disk pages needs to be visited for any query operation or the indexing structure is considered suboptimal

Finding the Centre (Centroid) of the Spatial Objects

After the rectangle is built, in then depending on the task at hand, the next thing we need to do is finding the centre of the rectangle and this will help us with further processing. In the study of plane geometry according to Bourne (2015), the centroid of area of geometric shapes or object in 2 dimension can generally be seen as the mass of that object (or shape). It is similar to the centre of mass of the object except for the fact that calculating the centroid Efunda (2016) involves only the geometrical shape of the solid. If we assume we want to calculate the centroid from the bounding rectangle, we can summarise the formula as in in equation 1.

Algorithm for Finding the Centroid of a Spatial Object

For a simple rectangle: $C_{x,y} = \left(\dfrac{x2 - x1, y2 - y1}{2} \right)$ $\hspace{2cm}$ (1)

Generally, this equation can be broken down into the sequence below.

i.   *Get the **x** and **y** coordinates of each vertex **v**, in any order*
ii. *For each $v_j \in V$ of the i_{th} coordinates (**i** =1,2... **d**) in a **d** dimensional space*
Compute centroid:

$$C_i = \left(\frac{dxi, dyi}{d} \right) \tag{2}$$

d is the number of dimension

iv.   *Return a set of coordinates i , (e.g. x, y for just xy coordinates)*

The formula described above is useful when we want to take the centroid from the bounding rectangle of the spatial object under consideration, but generally, if we want to get the centroid on an polygon based on the **j**-vertices then the formula below proves more useful.

Given any p points

*With masses **m**ⱼ at positions **x**ⱼ for all j-vertices*

Then centroid of that set of points is

$$\bar{x} = \left(\frac{\sum_{j=1}^{p} m_j x_j}{\sum_{j=1}^{p} m_j} \right) \tag{3}$$

Though Equation 3 is a general equation for finding the centroid of a polygon with m masses, the equation transforms to Equation 4 if all these masses are equal.

$$\bar{x} = \left(\frac{\sum_{j=1}^{p} x_j}{p} \right) \tag{4}$$

EXTENDING THE CLASSICAL RELATIONAL DATABASE FOR SPATIAL DATASET

Spatial Data Model

Developing a spatial database normally starts with developing a data model (which relates to the conceptual, logical and physical data modelling), that describes the contents of the database and their relationship (Singh & Singh, 2014). There are two common data models for modelling spatial information: field based models and object-based models (shekhar et al. 1999). Raster data structure (also known field based, space based or raster model) according to Gregory et al. (2009) is similar to placing a regular grid over a study region and representing the geographical feature found in each grid cell numerically. The model treats spatial information such as rainfall, altitude and temperature as a collection of spatial functions transforming space partition to an attribute domain. Raster are associated with image processing, dynamic modelling and image processing and are easily manipulated using map algebra (e.g. multiplying geographically corresponding cell values in two or more datasets). Spatial data can also be represented as continuous surfaces (e.g. elevation, temperature, precipitation, pollution, noise e.tc) using the grid or raster data Model in which a mesh of square cells is laid over the landscape and the value of the variable defined for each cell (Samson et al., 2014). The object based data model (which can also be called the vector, feature or entity based model) treats the information space as if it is populated by discrete, identifiable, spatially referenced entities. An implementation of a spatial data model in the context of Object-Relational databases consists of a set of spatial data types and the operations on those types. Vector data structure represents geographic objects with the basic elements points, lines and areas, also called polygons. From the description given by Gregory et al. (2009), vector data is based on recording point locations (zero dimensions) using x and y coordinates, stored within two columns of a database. By assigning each feature a unique ID, a relational database can be used to link location to an attribute table describing what is found there. Every element in a vector model is described mathematically and bases on points that are defined by Cartesian coordinates (Neuman et al. 2010).

Spatial Data Modelling Paradigm

Typically, database design process is often divided into three main task, namely: conceptual, logical and physical data modelling (Elmasri and Navathe 1989). In the conceptual modelling process, the objects (or entities) are represented as a spatial and non-spatial datasets, and their attributes and the relationships between them are identified (Akinyemi 2010). The conceptual model describes how a system is organized and how the system operates. The logical model produces a conceptual data model in terms data that will be computed. This stage according to Singh and Singh (2014) constructs (entity classes or object classes), operations (create relationships) and validity constraints (rules). At the stage of physical modelling, we produce the actual database design based on the requirements established at the logical modelling stage. Figure 12 shows the various stages involved in designing a spatial database and what they entail.

Figure 12. Stages in building a spatial database (Singh and Singh, 2014)

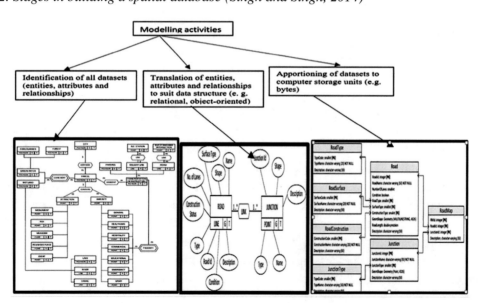

Choice of DBMS for Building Spatial Databases

Relational database technology is inadequate for managing spatial data (Mamoulis, 2012). That means it is quite tedious to build a spatial database directly using a classical database model, therefore the traditional system needs to be extended to handle spatial data types (abstract data type - ADT) in other words, relational databases should be equipped to manage and support spatial data types (or data models), spatial functions, and spatial indexes. Spatial database management system are software tools that can work with a classical DBMS but in addition, such a system would be able to supports a query language from which spatial data types are callable, possess efficient algorithms for processing spatial operations and provide rules for query optimization (Shekhar & Chawla, 2003).

In Ramakrishnan and Gehrke, (2003) two basic types of extended DBMS which are designed to handle the complexity associated with spatial data were described. The new extended systems are basically object oriented and therefore are able to provide support for database systems in terms of handling complex data types. The two object databases described are:

Object-Oriented Database Systems (OODBMS) and object relational database systems (ORDBMS) both of which are able to Support user defined (spatial) abstract data types like polygons, line, points coordinates and other complex types including; partitions and graphs (networks e.g. roads, rivers etc.). It is expected of an efficient spatial data management system to support spatial query operations and the same time support relational operations. Whereas object-oriented databases model real world entities (considering their behaviours, relationship) unambiguously (without the use of tables and keys) providing high computational power where users can implement functions and embed them into the database (Candan & Sapino, 2010), the object-relational counterpart which is an extension of the relational database features the functionalities that provides users the opportunity to model spatial databases by either extending existing relational models with object-oriented features or by adding a special row and table based data types into object-oriented databases (Stonebraker et al., 1990). According to Shekhar et al. (2011) spatial types and operations may be integrated into query languages such as SQL, which allows spatial querying to be combined with object-relational database management systems. Figure 13 is a clear conceptualization of both approaches that are described in this section.

The interesting thing about objects based modelling is that they allow users to define their own new data types, and complex objects like the ones in Figure 6 (the network and partitions data types), object based modelling also benefit from having functionalities that allow the user to define methods (in form

Figure 13. Object oriented paradigm for spatial databases

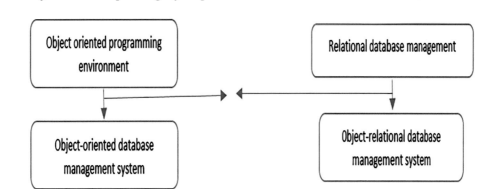

of codes which are used to define object's behaviour, properties and their state) and rules (that monitors events and validate them against certain constraints and the results of queries from such databases are held in containers (e.g. lists or sets)

```
Example Object-oriented database implementation
❖ Class Census_Town
Row (tuple) (town_code: integer, town_name: string, town_type: string, popula-
tion: integer, area: float, shape: region)
❖ Class Language_Spoken
Row (tuple) (language_name: string, shape: region)
Object-relational database implementation
❖ CREATE TABLE censusTown
(town_code integer,
town_name: string,
town_type: string,
population: integer,
area: float,
shape: region, Primary Key (town_code))
❖ CREATE TABLE languageSpoken
(language_code integer,
language_name: string,
town_name: string
shape: region, Primary Key (language_code),
Foreign Key (town_code) References Census_Town)
```

SPATIAL QUERY PROCESSING

Spatial database management deals with the storage, indexing, and querying of data with spatial features, such as location and geometric extent (Mamoulis 2012). Thus for a *spatial database* evaluations are frequently made between all structure with respect to *complexity*, query support, *data type support* and *application* (Patel and Garg 2012). According to Candan and Sapino, (2010) typical query could be any problem which is related to the spatial attributes of a given object, most data features (spatial or non-spatial) can be represented in the form of one (or more) of the four common base models: *strings, vectors, fuzzy/probabilistic logic-based* and *graphs/trees, representations*). In many spatial database applications, object extents could be ignored or approximated (using the filter and refine) in a case where the scale of the query is much larger than the scale of the objects thus, the filter-and-refine technique used in spatial query processing according to Shekhar et al (2011) plays a vital role in managing multidimensional-index structures. Figure 14 shows a typical example of a spatial query process were *w* is the query object. The diagram explains the basic steps of filtering and refining in a spatial query. In Figure 14b, the objects are filtered by finding their mbrs and the mbrs that intersects the query area are returned. At the stage of figure c, the rectangles that intersects the query window are evaluated (the evaluation is carried out based on the actual object) and the through this refinement process, rectangles

*Figure 14. Steps involved in querying rectangular objects (Mamoulis 2012): (a) is the region dataset with **w** as the query window, (b) is the approximated (refined) dataset (c) is the final refinement stage*

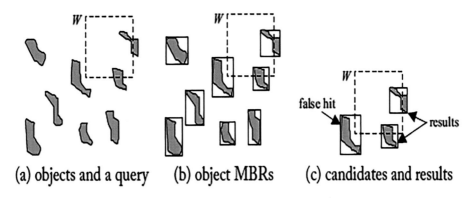

(a) objects and a query   (b) object MBRs   (c) candidates and results

which containing actual objects which do not have any topological relationship with the query window are recorded as false hits.

A simple example query is given below:

```
SELECT
town_name
language_name
FROM
censusTown c, languageSpoken l
WHERE
c. town_name = l. town_name
And c. population > 10,000,
And l.language_name = 'English'
```

The simple query above takes the relations censusTown and languageSpoken, censusTown stores the towns in Yorkshire County and languageSpoken stores the language prevalent in each town. The query basically checks the towns where English is the major language and the population if greater than 10,000. There are basically three types of queries according to Güting (1994) that arise over spatial (point) data namely: *spatial range queries, nearest neighbour queries,* and *spatial join queries.* For rectangle data one is normally faced with queries like *Intersection query* (e.g. find all rectangles that intersects a query rectangle) or *Containment query* (for example find all region/rectangles that are completely within a query rectangle (Güting, 1994). In point and window query which are important examples of spatial queries, we try to find the objects whose geometry contains a given point or overlaps a rectangle (Rigaux et al., 2003)

Range Queries

In range queries according to Papadias al. (2003) the range typically corresponds to a rectangular window (like the one in figure 15) or a circular area around a query point. In this case one of the attributes of the spatial object is identified as the range. For example find all primary schools that falls within

20miles of the University of Huddersfield. Range queries also known as similarity/distance threshold queries Candan and Sapino (2010), tries to find matches in a database that are within the threshold associated with a given distance or a similarity measure based query. In general, a typical question for a range query on point and spatial data would be: find all objects within a given range of another object. Basically, range queries –for region – search according to Samet (2006), identifies a set of data points whose specified keys have specific values or whose values are within given ranges.

Nearest Neighbour Queries

Nearest neighbour (similarity) searching or retrieval (Cazals et al., 2013), is a central computational problem with significant applications in many field of study. The similarity between the objects according to Jain et al. (1999); Jiawei (2001), is determined using distance measures over the numerous dimensions in the dataset. Nearest neighbour queries mostly answer distance based questions like find the nearest point/region to any given query point/region. The nearest neighbour to a point query is the point or object that is closest to that point/object in the Euclidean space. Figure 15 shows points G, H…..J around the point p and we are expected to find the nearest neighbour to P, this query will return J, but if the query is modified to find k-nearest neighbour (say k=2) then the output will be E, J.

In Mamoulis (2012), nearest neighbour search was described as; find the nearest object (the *k*-nearest objects) to a point *q* in the spatial relation when given a well-defined reference object *q* (*in other words the query* retrieves from a spatial relation *R*, the nearest object to a query object *q*). In most database applications with high-dimensional data nearest neighbour queries are very important (Berchtold et al. 1996) therefore the main concern for nearest neighbour search (if the database was indexed with a tree data structure) is CPU-time rate which is always higher because the search is required to sort all the nodes based on their min-max distance. Thus if the spatial relation is not indexed according to Mamoulis (2012), then there would be need for the nearest neighbour algorithm (for clustering, classification or any other purpose) to access all objects in the relation, in order to find the nearest neighbour to a query object *q*.Figure 16 gives an illustration of how to find nearest neighbour of an object in space by simple defining a criteria to approximate an optimal neighbour.

Figure 15. Different point locations with their distances to a central point p

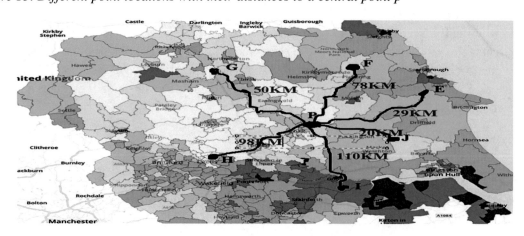

Figure 16. Example of how to approximate nearest neighbour search

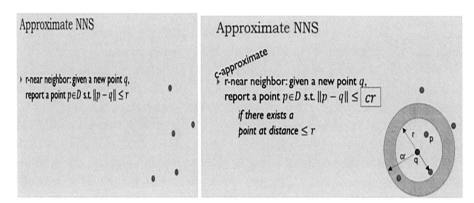

Basically, the problem of finding the nearest neighbours to an object in space in its general form according to Lifshits and Zhang (2009) can be defined as follows; Let U be a set of elements and let d be a distance function that maps each pair of elements from U to some positive real number (where d is a metric distance function, i.e., it satisfies the triangle inequality) although this need not always be the case.

Spatial Join

Spatial join operation combine two or more spatial datasets based on some certain spatial relationship. For instance, if we want to get the list of all hospitals around the towns in Huddersfield then we could set a query like:

```
SELECT
Name
FROM
Hospitals, Hudd_town
WHERE
Name_is_within (Hospitals.region, Hudd_town.region)
```

Spatial join is an important example of spatial query operation. According to (Rigaux et al., 2003), using spatial join operation one could answer the query: find a pair of object that satisfy some spatial relationships if given two different sets of spatial objects. As a simple example find the languages spoken in different cities in Yorkshire. To answer this query, we would need a thematic map of the cities in Yorkshire County and the language predominant in each city, then we join the two maps and display the each city and their language on a single map. It is important to note that intersection joins are useless for point datasets as such the accurate problem would be the e-distance join, which finds all pairs of objects (s,t) s$\in$S, t$\in$T within (Euclidean) distance e from each other of the e-distance join Rigaux et al., (2003).

Spatial Attributes

The data inputs of spatial database management are made up of two distinct types of attributes: non-spatial attributes and spatial attributes Shekhar et al (2011). Spatial attributes are used to define the spatial location and extent of spatial objects (Bolstad (2002). The spatial attributes of a spatial object most often include information related to spatial *longitude, latitude* and *elevation, shape, area* etc. and the relationships among these objects are often implicit, such as *overlap, intersect, behind..* (Ganguly and Steinhaeuser 2008). This is quite unlike that of non-spatial objects that are explicit in data inputs according to Agrawal and Srikant, (1994); Jain and Dubes, (1988). One feasible way to deal with implicit spatial relationships is to materialize the relationships into traditional data input columns and then apply classical data mining techniques - although the materialization may result in loss of information.

Components of a Spatial Database

Geographic objects such as rivers and roads are always related to the same geographic area and they are according to Rigaux et al. (2003) basically made up of the following components: (a) *Description* and (b) spatial components. (The spatial component are known as their spatial attribute or extent);

These components describes the size of the objects and their location, orientation and shape in 2-Dimensional or 3-Dimensional space. They also describe the objects by means of their *non-spatial* attributes. Whereas the *Description* component describes the object by setting out some *descriptive attributes (like the* name and the population of a city) which constitute the description of its alphanumeric attributes. The spatial component of a spatial object represents the geometry (location, shape etc.) and topology (relationships among spatial objects) (Rigaux et al., 2003).

Operations on Spatial Data

Spatial data objects can be grouped into themes. A theme is the geospatial information corresponding to a particular topic. The details of spatial datasets are gathered in a *theme.* A theme is similar to a relation as defined in the relational model. It has a schema and instances. Rivers, cities, andcountries are examples of themes. (Rigaux et al., 2003).

Operations on Themes

Ester et al. (1997) has claimed that for knowledge retrieval and discovery from spatial databases (which contains information on specific themes) that most algorithms will make use of neighbourhood relationships since that is the main difference between the classical database and its spatial counterpart. This phenomenon according to them can be proven by the fact that the behaviour and characteristics of a spatial object is influenced by certain neighbouring objects which may "cause" the existence of the spatial object as such, the attributes of its neighbours may have an influence on the object itself Ester et al. (1999). For instance, given the 2-themes in Figure 3: Yorkshire towns (with their attributes such *as name, capital, population,* and a geometric attribute say *boundary*), and Languages (expressing the distribution of main spoken languages or groups of similar languages). If we express the themes using the schema below:

- Towns (name, capital, population, *region*: **region**)
- Languages (name, *location*: **region**).

Then some of the common manipulations of these themes based on operations from the relational algebra, include: overlay, join (or intersection), union, selection, nearest neighbour, overlap, distance etc.
A simple example for join operation

- *Find all the town in Huddersfield where English language is spoken.*

Suggested Solution (Spatial Join)

```
SELECT
T.name
FROM
Towns T, Languages L
WHERE
name_is_within (Towns.region, Languages.region)
```

In Schneider (1997), most of the different operations that are applicable to spatial datasets have been enumerated including their return functions; these include topological relationships – example of a spatial predicates that returns boolean values - (e.g. intersect (overlap), meet (touch), equal, covered by, adjacent (neighbouring), outside etc.), directional relationships –also a spatial predicate - (e.g., north / south, left / right) and so on. Equally, Candan and Sapino, (2010) stated that spatial predicates and operations are broadly categorized into two based on whether the information of interest is a single *point* in space or has a spatial extent (e.g., a *line* or a *region*) and they established that the predicates and operators that are needed to be supported by the database management system depend on the underlying spatial data model and on the applications' needs. In summary, according to Ester et al. (1999) it is a common premise to assume that the standard operations from relational algebra such as *selection, union, intersection* and *difference are also suitably applicable* relationship evaluation between any set of spatial object.

SPATIAL INDEXING AND INFORMATION RETRIEVAL

According to Güting (1994), a spatial database is any database that is able to provide at least a spatial indexing method and a spatial join operation. With this, the system would be able to retrieve from a large collection of objects in some space in a particular area without scanning the whole set. Indexing spatial data according to Lungu and Velicanu, (2009) is a method of decreasing the number of searches, this mechanism helps to locate objects in the same area of data (window query) or from different locations. The main goal of indexing is to optimize the speed of database query (Ajit and Deepak, 2011) Given a user query say for example "What is the cheapest, and fastest path from location Q to P?" the spatial database could be indexed (sorted - implicitly) so that even if p is changed to another location say Z within that same geometric region, there would not be any need to resort the data in other to answer the query efficiently. This facilitates the information retrieval process and could also improve database integrity and general performance. Since generally there is no ordering that exists in dimensions greater than 1 without transforming of the data to one dimension according to Cazals (2013), then indexing could be used as a way of finding a better sort procedure on the database in other to accelerate search query performance. Generally speaking, in a database management system, every record can be conceptualized as a point in a multidimensional space to Güting (1994). Unfortunately, this comparison is not always appropriate for spatial data because the dimensionality of the representative point may be too high and that poses a problem when considering spatial data (although we may decide to reduce the dimensionality of the representing point in other to approximate the spatial object). But then, using this form of transformation (such as merely mapping spatial data into points in another space) proximity would not be preserved. Such transformation as mentioned above would be fine for storage purposes and for queries that only involve the points that embrace the line segments (including their end points). For example, finding all the line segments that intersect a given point or set of points or a given line segment. However (Samet, 1995), the method is not good for queries that involve points or sets of points that are not part of the line segments as they are not transformed to the higher dimensional space by the mapping). If we have to use a representative point to represent a line object, each line segment can then be represented by its end points. As such the line segments are represented by a tuple of four items (i.e., a pair of x coordinate values and a pair of y coordinate values). Therefore, we have constructed a mapping from a two-dimensional space (i.e., the space from which the lines are drawn) to a four-dimensional space (i.e., the space containing the representative point corresponding to the line). Thus the present challenge of data analyst would be to find techniques suitable to overcome the problems of inappropriate mapping of spatial objects to point data. These techniques possibly will be the use of data structures that are based on sorting the spatial objects by spatial occupancy (Samet, 2009). Spatial occupancy methods decompose the space from which the data is drawn (e.g., the two dimensional space containing the lines as described above) into regions called buckets. Spatial indexing methods preserve order in other words, objects in close proximity should be placed in the same bucket or at least in buckets that are close to each other in the sense of the order in which they would be accessed (i.e., retrieved from secondary storage in case of a false hit, etc.). In large databases especially spatial – temporal ones, the efficiency of searching is dependent on the extent to which the underlying data is sorted (Samet 2009). The sorting is encapsulated by the data structure known as an *index* that is used to represent the spatial data thereby making it more accessible. According to Cazals (2013), in order to store objects in these databases, it is common to map every object to a feature vector in a (possibly high-dimensional) vector space. The feature vector then serves as the representation of the object. The traditional role of the indexes is to sort the data, which means that they order the data. However, since generally no ordering exists in dimensions greater than 1 without a transformation of the data to one dimension, the role of the sort process is one of differentiating between the data and what is usually done is to sort the spatial objects with respect to the space that they occupy. The resulting ordering should be implicit rather than explicit so that the data need not be resorted (i.e., the index need not be rebuilt) when the queries change. The indexes are said to order the space and the characteristics of such indexes are explored further (Samet 2009). In Park et al (2013) spatial indexing techniques are one of the most effective optimization methods to improve the quality of large dynamic databases, this is achieved by applying ordering tools (e.g. Z-order curve, Hilbert curve) which linearizes multidimensional data. A key property of these ordering functions is that it can map multidimensional data to one dimension while preserving the locality of the data points. Once the data is sorted according to these ordering then a spatial data structure is then built on top of it and query results are refined, if necessary, using information from the original feature vectors. Any n-dimensional data structure can be used for indexing the data, such as binary search trees and B-trees, R-trees X-trees e.t.c. Cazal et al., (2013). According to Güting (1994) rectangles are more difficult to model than points because they do not fall into a single cell of a bucket partition.

Indexing Points and Rectangular Objects

Because of the non - linearity that exists among large spatial data set, an effective data structure which has the ability to tackle the branched structures that exists among a given spatial data is required. This complex spatial dataset trait according to Candan and Sapino, (2010) are better represented using graphs and trees because the larger datasets are always made up of other minor events or objects which are always difficult to be ordered to form of sequences. Spatial objects can be indexed in the form of point or region (rectangles), this can be achieved using a point access method (PAM) or a spatial access method (SAM).

Point Access Methods

Representing multidimensional point data is a central issue in a spatial database design according to Samet (2006), this means that there is one dimension specified for each attribute or key. In a multi-dimensional data space, shared data such as documents, music files, and images, are frequently specified as points based on expressed features, as such requires a systems to provide an efficient multi-dimensional query processing (Jagadish et al. 2006; Samet, 2006). Point access method works by defining space decomposition of disjoint points, as such in most tree indexing structures for point data, it is expected that the leaf nodes will not overlap (Leutenegger et al, 1997). Figure 17 illustrates some well-known point access methods as Mamoulis (2012) has identified. Point access methods can simply be seen as a data structures and algorithms that primarily search for points that are defined in multidimensional space examples including *EXCELL, Grid file, hB-tree, Twin grid file, Two-level grid file, K-d tree, BSP-tree, Quad-tree, UB-tree, Buddy tree, Locality-sensitive hashing (LSH)*...(Paul, 2008).

In Figure 18, two different methods were presented for indexing the same point dataset: (i) the R-tree and the (ii) Quad-tree. The presentation shows a set of points P = {A, B...}. Point C, D, E are close to each other in space so we have clustered them in the same leave node (that is the minimum bounding rectangle labelled Z1 outlined in red). The next upper level is the MBRs Z1, Z2 and Z3 (which encloses

Figure 17. Efficient point access methods (Mamoulis, 2012)

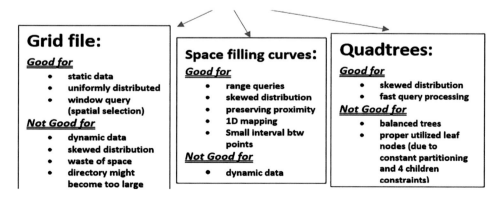

Figure 18. Comparison between different tree structures to represent the same point location dataset: (a) and (b) R-tree (c) and (d) Quad-tree

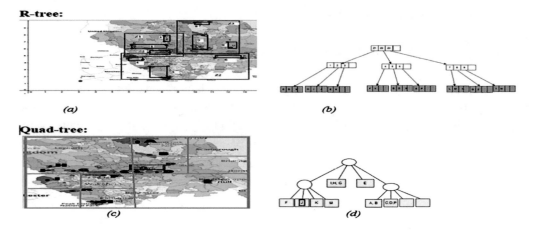

leave nodes 1….9) these two non-leave nodes are yet grouped into the next higher level which in this case is the root. We have assumed the capacity of a node to be four (4) entries for the r-tree and four for the Quad-tree (following the normal conventional Quad-tree partitioning).

Task 1

Points A through M (in Figure 8) shows point locations (modelling them as points means we have considered them as locations on the map that do not have extents but have a spatial reference in the 2D plane) of towns around the Yorkshire and the Humber County where the percentage of women in professional occupation are 26 and above, examples of point query using point data:

1.   Find the distance between town A and town C.
2.   Which of the locations is closest to the centre of the county (point P).
3.   Find all town that are < 50 miles from P.

Note that the extent of each point locations will not alter the outcome of the query result.

Region Access Methods

For range queries, a data structure that can search for lines, polygons, etc would be required. Point access methods have been known not to fully support region, overlap, enclosure, etc., so methods like *cell tree*, *extended k-d tree*, *GBD-tree*, *multilayer grid file*, *D-tree*, *P-tree*, *R-file*, *R⁺-tree*, *R*-tree*, *R-tree*, *Skd-tree* according to Paul (2008) have been proposed to manage these sort of data. Most spatial objects are better stored as rectangles. Storing spatial objects as rectangles is an important task of spatial database as this provides a basic approximation of the actual geometry of the object. Spatial approximation according to Mamoulis (2012) helps to reduce the computational complexity associated with actual geometries of the spatial objects. The usefulness of storing regions as rectangles cannot be overemphasized for instance when handling a range query, we consider all the rectangles that intersects the region of the query. Many objects in 2-dimensional spaces represents objects using their MBRs by so doing, the MBRs identify the region of the larger data space that each object represents and then an Intersection tests is performed to determine which objects intersect with the spatial query using an *R-tree o*rganizes all the spatial objects by pruning the search space Jagadish et al. (2006). According to Güting (1994) The use of bounding boxes, demands that most spatial data structures be designed to store either a set of points (for point values) or a set of rectangles (for line or region values). Güting (1994) added that rectangles are more difficult to model than points because they do not fall into a single cell of a bucket partition, therefore three strategies have been developed to be able to handle rectangle data partitioning, these include: (a) Transformation approach, (b) overlapping bucket regions, (c) clipping. Figure 19 presents an R-tree for indexing region data. In this case a set of rectangles {A, B… L}. Rectangles A, B are close to each other in space so we have clustered them in the same leave node (that is the minimum bounding rectangle labelled 8).We have assumed the capacity of a node to be four entries (M) for the r-tree. The MBRs in green are the leaf nodes and they contain the index record (*b, obj_pointer*). *b* is the number of the page of the smallest MBR that contains the spatial object which is referenced by *obj_pointer*. The rectangles in blue (containing M child nodes), are the non-leaf nodes with entries (*b, child_pointer*) where *b* in this case is the number of the page of the smallest MBR that contains the MBRs in the child node that is being referred to by *child_pointer*. Finally, these entry nodes are grouped into the root (labelled 1). Note that the rectangles marked blue in the actual tree are the rectangles that have some kind of spatial relationship with the query window *P* as such that determines the rectangles that are involved in the query operation.

Tree Indexing Data Structures a Brief Comparison

One would have noticed the ubiquitous nature of the R-tree indexing structure, this is attributed to the fact that the R-tree and its variant have proven very useful in management of multidimensional database and handles both points and spatial data efficiently. R–tree according to Mamoulis 2012 is known as the most dominant spatial access method (SAM). The main idea behind the data structure according to Guttman (1984) is to group nearby objects by representing them using their minimum bounding rectangle (the "R" in R-tree) in the next higher level of the tree. In Samet (1995), it is established that the R-tree and its variant performs remarkably well when applied to indexing arbitrary spatial objects especially

Figure 19. R-tree for representing the regions

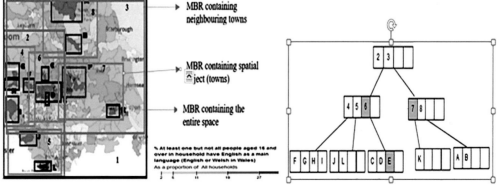

rectangles (in two (2) or d-dimension). The most important argument in Samet (1995) is that the smallest rectangles that represents the object under consideration must be axis-aligned (see Baum and Hanebeck (2010) for more on axis aligned rectangle). The main reason the R-tree index structure has been widely accepted and used according to Berchtold et al. (2001) is because the index structure supports both points data as well as data with extent whereas most of the other structures like the kdB-trees, grid files etc. do not support both types of data concurrently, also the R-tree index structure proves efficient for spatial clustering (which is a vital issue in the performance of tree based indexing structures) since it doesn't require point transformation in other to store spatial data. Guttman (1984) describes the functionalities of the R-tree and most importantly identified the basic strategy for building an efficient R-tree structure with respect to its clustering technique and partitioning strategy. Nevertheless, despite its popularity and efficiency, basic limitations of this tree-based index structure (which majorly has to do with increase in overlap of the MBRs of directory nodes when dimension increases) has rendered it incompetent to some limit and has warranted research into new methods for enhancing its performance by refining the way the tree is built. Among the many specialized indexes proposed to offer better performance than the R–tree for high-dimensional data include: the X–tree, the VA–file, TV-tree, SR-tree, the pyramid-technique, A-tree, X+-tree, PL-tree, the hybrid-tree etc. overall, indexing structures for multidimensional spatial databases according to Mamoulis (2012) can only perform optimally if they provide an efficient underlying paradigm for similarity and nearest neighbour (NN) search in high-dimensional space. In Figure 20, the authors have listed some of the basic definition encountered in indexing a spatial database using a tree data structure.

ISSUES ON SPATIAL DATABASE

Dimensionality

In some application domain, the underlying data (spatial or not) are made up of sets of objects and storing these objects in a database usually involve mapping every object to a feature vector in a (possibly high-dimensional) vector space the objects are described using a collection of features which forms the feature vector and this serves as the representation of the object in the database (Cazals et al., 2013).

Figure 20. Basic terms and terminologies used in constructing a tree structure for spatial indexing

- Entry: Entries represent a single piece of data in the tree. It represents a point paired with non-geographic data (an ID, an object, etc.).
- Point: A point on the map, defined as a pair of coordinates (x, y).
- Box: A rectangle, defined by its lower-left point (x, y) and its upper-right point (x2, y2).
- Node: Nodes make up the tree, and are defined by a bounding box, and a list of children. There are two kinds of nodes: branches and leaves.
- Branch: A node whose children are also nodes.
- Leaf: A node whose children are entries

High dimensionality that is, the measurement of the degree or size of the feature space according to Katayama and Satoh (2002); Samet (2006), is one of the properties of feature spaces and in most cases queries always relate to similarity retrieval from such a feature space of vectors, which in multidimensional informational systems boils down to nearest neighbour search in the space, therefore the challenge that faces such a data mining task is management of the dimensionality of the space. Furthermore according to Böhm et al. (2001), in multidimensional spatial database management systems (SDBMs), high dimensionality is characterized by the presence of excess attribute exceeding the total of at least 15. Some examples of application areas where the data is of considerably higher dimensionality (though they may not be spatial) include, pattern recognition and image databases where the data is made up of other set of objects, and the high dimensionality comes as a result of result of trying to describe the objects via a collection of features (also known as a feature vector) examples colour, moments, textures, shape descriptions, and so on (Samet, 2006). High-dimensional means a situation where the number of the unknown parameters which are to be estimated is one or several orders of magnitude larger than the number of samples in the data (Bickel et al., 2001). In large spatial databases, *High-dimensional data* can be seen as data that is described by a large number of attributes, where this is the case then as the dimensionality increases there is always an impending notion that the complexity of computational process would also increase thereby leading to the ineffectiveness of various existing spatial data mining algorithm (Assent, 2012). In Bouveyron et al. (2007), it is stated that many scientific domains consider measured observations as high-dimensional and in such high dimensional (feature) space clustering always proofs to be difficult due to the fact that the high-dimensional data are always embedded in different low-dimensional subspaces which are hidden in the original space. It is worthy to note that in similarity search operation, computing the Euclidean distance between two points in a high-dimensional space for instance d, involves d multiplication operations and $d-1$ addition operations, and most importantly, the computation requires the definition of what it means for two objects to be similar which according to Samet (2006) is not always so obvious. Also Keim et at (2008) ascertained that feature-based approach has several advantages compared to other approaches for implementing similarity search, the extraction of features from the source data is usually fast and easily parametrizable, and metric functions for feature vectors, as the Minkowski distances, can also be efficiently computed. Novel approaches for computing feature vectors from a wide variety of unstructured data are proposed regularly. As in many practical applications the dimensionality of the obtained feature vectors is high. The X-tree spatial index data structure is a valuable tool to perform efficient similarity queries in spatial databases. Some examples of High dimensional variables as identified by Mosley (2010) include: (mostly variables with many units or levels) like ZIP code, Vehicle classification, etc. The author also identified the complications associated with these types of high dimensional variable which include: Credibility at individual levels and Determining proper groupings

1. Credibility at individual levels examples:
   a. Convergence errors (from models).
   b. Results that do not make sense.
2. Determining proper groupings example:
   a. Thousands of ZIP codes.

Handling High Dimensional Data

Though searches through an indexed space usually involve relatively simple comparison tests, searching in high-dimensional spaces is generally time-consuming according to Samet (2006), but performing point and range queries are considerably easier (from the standpoint of computational complexity) than performing similarity queries because point and range queries do not involve the computation of distance. Suggestions have been made regarding the best possible ways to handle the problems of high dimension in large databases. Cazals et al. (2013) has suggested several methods for handling high dimensional datasets including: i) Dimension reduction ii) Embedding methods, iii) Clustering, and iv) Nearest neighbour methods

Dimension Reduction (DR)

Dimension reduction has been seen as one major way of tackling the problem of high-dimension in largely correlated spatial data. Cazal et al. (2013) describes Dimension reduction as a processes of computing a mapping function f from the high-dimensional feature space R^m to a lower-dimensional space R^k (upon which a spatial data structure is built) with the goal of preserving the properties of the feature vectors that are relevant for the application at hand. According to Parsons et al., (2004), dimension reduction has to do with two main specific kind of task;

1. **Feature Selection:** This technique selects only the most significant of the dimensions from a dataset that shows a group of objects that are similar on only a subset of their attributes. Though this method of dimension reduction have difficulty when clusters are found in different subspaces, they are quite successful on many datasets.
2. **Feature Transformation:** This techniques tries to summarize a dataset using fewer dimensions by creating combinations of the original attributes. The techniques is very successful in uncovering hidden structure in a large datasets. Nevertheless, they preserve the relative distances between objects, thereby making them less effective when there are large numbers of irrelevant attributes that hide the genuine clusters in deep noise.

Other dimension reduction techniques according to (Kushilevitz et al., 2000), is the principal component analysis (PCA) which is a statistical technique that uses a kind of transformation to convert a set of observations of probably correlated variables into a set of values of linearly uncorrelated variables called principal components.

Embedding Methods

These methods for handling high dimensionality deals with Data embedding i.e., they embed the objects into a vector space within which a distance metric approximating the original one can be used (Samet, 2006). This method also tends to ease the calculation of (costly) distances between spatial objects Cazals et al., (2013). In Weinberger and Saul (2006), discovering clever representations (which are used to simplify problems in some application areas using symbolic input) automatically, from large amounts of unlabelled data, remains a fundamental challenge as such, an algorithm that will faithfully learn low dimensional representation of high dimensional data was examined and proposed. The algorithm relies on modern tools in convex optimization which is obtainable in non-linear embedding method. According to Cazal et al., (2013). Non-linear embedding methods of handling high dimensionality leads to easy to implement polynomial-time algorithms and they prove more efficient with larger data sets than the ones usually involved in iterative or greedy methods (like e.g. the ones involving EM or EM-like algorithms). A majority of data embedding methods are isometric. In other words, they take a metric space (inter-point distances) as input and try to embed the data to a low dimensional Euclidean space such that the inter-point distances are preserved as much as possible (Yang 2006). Semi Definite Embedding (SDE) also known as the maximum variance unfolding – MVU is a kind of embedding method (Non-linear dimensionality reduction technique) that attempt to map high-dimensional data onto a low-dimensional Euclidean vector space using semidefinite embedding. The main intuition behind the maximum variance unfolding – MVU (Weinberger and Saul, 2004; 2006) is to exploit the local linearity of manifolds and create a mapping that preserves local neighbourhoods at every point of the underlying manifold. The method can be used to analyse high-dimensional data that lies on or near a low dimensional manifold as can be seen in the Semi-definite embedding (SDE).

Clustering Methods

Improvements to the traditional clustering algorithms solves the various problems such as curse of dimensionality and sparsity of data for multiple attributes (Paithankar and Tidke, 2015). Clustering methods are used according to Steinbach et al., (2004) to partition a large dataset similar functionality into groups as a means of data compression. The process of finding clusters reveals meaningful homogenous groups of objects embedded in subspaces of high dimensional data and also helps to extract the relevant information from such high dimensional dataset (Paithankar and Tidke, 2015). The essence of this task is to achieve scalability, proper understanding of data mining results, and insensitivity to the order of input records in a database management system (Agrawal et al., 1998). According to the definition in Berchtold et al (1997), an object or a data record typically has dozens of attributes and the domain for each attribute can be large. It is therefore not meaningful to look for clusters in such a high dimensional space as the average density of points anywhere in the data space is likely to be quite low. Thus according to IBM (1996), such problem of high dimensionality is often attempted by requiring the user to specify the subspace (a subset of the dimensions) for a given cluster analysis, (i.e. bearing in mind that user identification of subspaces is quite prone to error). In a high dimensional dataset (having millions of data points that exist in many thousands of dimensions-i.e. having many attributes- representing many thousands of clusters), dimensionality can be handled by performing a two way clustering (ensemble method) by first dividing the data into a group of overlapping subsets (using one distance metrics) and then using a different distance measurements to estimate accurate clusters (McCallum et al., 2000). One other way of handling high dimensionality using a clustering algorithm according to (Paithankar and Tidke, 2015) is by combining the two basic methods suggested in this section (subspace clustering and ensemble clustering).

It is worthy to note the difference between the two classes of datasets that one can encounter within a spatial database

1. Low dimensional dataset:
   a. Limited number of clusters.
   b. Low feature dimensionality (few attributes for each object).

c.   Small number of data points.
2.   High dimensional dataset:
a.   Large number of data points.
b.   Many thousands of dimensions-i.e. having many attributes.
c.   Many thousands of clusters.

Generally, in high dimensional spaces, the data are inherently sparse and the distance between each pair of points is almost the same for a wide variety of data distributions and distance functions (Muller et al., 2009).

Nearest Neighbour Methods

Hinneburg et al. (2015) argued that there can be several reasons for the meaninglessness of nearest neighbour search in high dimensional space especially in a case of sparsity of data objects in space which is unavoidable. Moreover Beyer et al. (1999) also supported the premise by claiming that in high dimensional space, all pairs of points are almost equidistant from one another for a wide range of data distributions and distance functions, thereby giving rise to the problem of instability. However it is also important to know that Searching for a nearest neighbour among a specified database of points is a fundamental computational task that arises in a variety of application areas (including information retrieval, data mining, pattern recognition, machine learning, computer vision, data compression, and statistical data analysis) where the database points are represented as vectors in some high dimensional space (Kushilevitz et al., 2000). High-dimensional nearest neighbour problems arise naturally when complex objects are represented by vectors of d numeric features (Arya et al., 1994). Therefore one solution of the problem of high dimensionality using nearest neighbour search techniques applies an approximation of the nearest neighbour query as a method for high dimensional filtering where queries are compared against their most relevant candidates. The seemingly difficulty of obtaining algorithms that are efficient in the worst case with respect to both space and query time for dimensions higher than 2, according to (Arya et al., 1994, Cazal et al., 2013) suggests that the alternative approach of finding approximate nearest neighbours (which do not require heavy resource and is a less demanding computational task) is worth considering. Description of the approximate nearest neighbour object search is given below in Figure 21:

Curse of Dimensionality: What Is It?

The curse of dimensionality - as explained by Bellman (1957) who defined the term originally - is a term used to express the fact that the number of samples needed to estimate an arbitrary function with a given level of accuracy grows exponentially with the number of variables (dimensions) that it comprises.

Figure 21. Approximated nearest neighbour model

Given a parameter $k > 1$, a *k-approximate* nearest neighbour *(k-NN)* to a query q is a point p in P with $d(q, p) \leq k * d(q, p')$ where p' is a *NN to q*. Hence, under approximation, the answer can be any point whose distance from q is at most times larger than the distance between q and its *NN*.

This means that the number of objects (points) in the dataset that needs to be examined in deriving the estimates in a similarity search (i.e., finding nearest neighbours), grows exponentially with the underlying dimension and thereby giving rise to the question "is nearest neighbour search meaningful in such a domain?" Curse of dimensionality simply described as a situation whereby an extra dimension is added to an already existing Euclidean space. Curse of dimensionality is also defined by Kouiroukidis and Evangelidis (2011), as a phenomenon which states that in high dimensional spaces distances between nearest and farthest points from query points become almost equal as such, nearest neighbour calculations cannot discriminate candidate points. Though the above elucidation is faced by many database systems, suggestions has been put forward towards fighting the curse of dimensionality. Ding (2007), suggested Feature selection using SVM-RFE (Support Vector Machine-Recursive Feature Elimination) as a solution to the problem. Generally according to Verleysen and François (2005), the curse of dimensionality is the expression of all phenomena that appear with high-dimensional data, and that have most often unfortunate consequences on the behaviour and performances of learning algorithms.

Optimizing Spatial Databases

Optimizing spatial databases is one of the most important aspects of working with large volumes of data. Basically, some of the issues to consider in trying to optimise a large spatial database include: reducing the access rate and times to external memory, reading and writing in multiples of pages and reducing number of disk accesses. In Figure 22 an illustration is shown on different ways of possibly optimizing spatial database as suggested by Samet (2010), some of the ways of improving the behaviour of search in a large spatial database includes:

Goal 1: Minimizing the number of children of a node that must be visited by search operations (i.e. minimize the area common to children (overlap).

Goal 2: Reducing the likelihood of each node (say q) being visited by the search (i.e. minimize the total area spanned by the bounding box of q (coverage).

In addition to the methods mentioned above, Katayama and Satoh (2002), has suggested another better way to optimise spatial databases by considering reducing the amount of disk page accesses because reading and writing to external storage in disk- based data structures is much slower than doing same

Figure 22. Different way of optimizing a spatial database

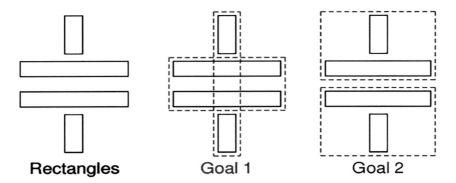

141

with the main memory. Bulk loading disk-based data structures is another way of optimizing spatial database, this is because external storage are organised in fixed data blocks of typically 4 to 16kb. A good bulk loading method according to (Mamoulis, 2012; 2011) would build fast for static objects and will ensure a lesser amount of wasted empty spaces on the tree pages. Giao and Anh (2015) identified the advantages of the bulk loading a tree structure as the follows: 1. Faster loading of the tree with all spatial objects at once 2. Reducing empty spaces in the nodes of the tree and 3. Better splitting of spatial objects into nodes of the tree. Belciu and Olaru (2011) has also added that the best way to improve the optimization of spatial databases is through spatial indexes. Using spatial indexes such as Grid index, Z-order, Quadtree, Octree, UB-tree, R-tree, kd-tree, M-tree etc. improves the performance and integrity of spatial databases in terms of storage and time costs. According to Lungu and Velicanu (2009) indexing spatial data is a way to decrease the number of searches, and a spatial index (considered logic) is used to locate objects in the same area of data (window query) or from different locations. Using approximations, spatial indexing methods organize space and the objects in it in such a way that only parts of the space and a subset of the objects need to be considered to answer such a query Güting (1994).

Autocorrelation

Autocorrelation is basically seen as a measure of the similarity or interdependence of an object in space with surrounding objects. According to Samson et al., (2014), the presence of spatial auto-correlation and the fact that continuous data types are always present in spatial data makes it important to create methods, tools and algorithms to mine spatial patterns in a complex spatial data set. In Jerrett et al (2003) Failure to control for autocorrelation can lead to false positive significance tests and may indicate bias resulting from a missing variable or group of variables. Spatial autocorrelation is an optimal method for systematically ascertaining spatial patterns. According to Legendre and Fortin (1989) Spatial autocorrelation frequently occurs in ecological data, and many ecological theories and models implicitly adopt an underlying spatial pattern in the distributions of organisms and their environment. Autocorrelation arises from the fact that elements of a given population or community (or even the geographic/social environment as a whole) that are close to one another in space or time are more likely to be influenced by the same generating process. According to Chen et al. (2011) spatial autocorrelation shows correlation of a variable with itself through space. In their own view, Rossi and Queneherve, (1998); Legendre, (1993) acknowledged that spatial autocorrelation measures the similarity between samples for a given variable as a function of spatial distance. Spatial autocorrelation as seen by Dale and Fortin (2009) simply portrays self-dependence of spatial data (meaning that the individual observations made from the chosen samples include information present in other observations, so that the effective sample size, say n, is less than the number of observations, m); this dependence according to them poses a great problem that affects the significance rates of statistical test when it is positive and as such must be corrected in other to produce a better measurement of goodness-of-fit.

DISCUSSION

The most basic spatial query types are spatial selection, nearest neighbour search, and spatial joins. Extending a DBMS to support spatial data requires changes at all layers: data modelling, query languages, storage and indexing, query evaluation and optimization, transaction management, etc. Nowadays more users are interested in retrieving information related to the locations and geometric properties of spatial objects. Users of mobile devices may want to find the nearest hotel to their location, Astrologers may want to study the spatial relationships among objects of the universe, Army commanders may want to schedule the movements of their troops according to the geography of the field, Scientists may want to study the effects of object positions and relationships in a 2D/3D space to some scientific or social fact (e.g., spatial analysis of protein structures, relationship between the residence of subjects and their psychic behaviour and so on (Mamoulis 2012). The efficiency of searching is dependent on the extent to which the underlying data is sorted in other words an appropriate index structure is required to be put in place in other to achieve an optimal database efficiency (Samet (2009). In the search and retrieval process of a spatial database for handling data query according to Mamoulis (2012), two major problem are most likely

- First, the geometry of the objects could be too complex; therefore, testing a query predicate against each object in a database would result in a high computational cost.
- Secondly, exhaustively testing all objects of the relation against a spatial query predicate requires a significant amount of I/O operations, for large databases

SOLUTIONS

1.   The first problem is mainly handled by storing the spatial objects together with their exact geometry using an appropriate *spatial approximation example minimum bounding rectangle (MBR), the minimum bounding rectangle* encloses the convex hull covering the geometry of the spatial object; the MBR of an object is the minimum rectangle which *encloses* the geometric extent of the object. Thus in other to overcome the first problem mentioned above,

    a.   First, the query predicate is tested against the MBR of the objects, if the MBR passes the *filter step then the refinement operation set is applied*. Filtering allows us selects the objects whose *minimum bounding box* satisfies the spatial predicate - Intersection, adjacency, containment, etc.- which are examples of spatial predicates a pair of objects to be joined must satisfy. The filtering step consists of traversing the index, and applying the spatial test on the *MBRs*. An *mbr* might satisfy a query predicate, whereas the exact geometry may not. (In other words, filtering is a way of being able to allocate a spatial object's natural geometry to a minimum bounding box and then extracting the bounding boxes that for instance intersects with a given query window).

    b.   Then the exact geometry of the object is tested against the query predicate. The refinement stage searches each stored MBR of the spatial objects (extracted by filtering) and then test the specific geometry of the object against the query predicate. The final spatial test is done on the actual geometries of objects whose *mbr* satisfies the filter step.

For many spatial databases, many indexing methods that try to cope with the dimensionality curse in high dimensional spaces have been proposed, but, usually these methods end up behaving like the sequential scan over the database in terms of accessed pages when queries like k-Nearest Neighbours are examined. Kouiroukidis and Evangelidis (2011), examined a multi-attribute indexing methods and try to investigate when these methods reach their limits, namely, at what dimensionality a kNN query requires visiting all the data pages.

CONCLUSION

More users these days are interested in retrieving information related to the locations and geometric properties of spatial objects. Unlike the classical relational database management system which store data as numbers, alphabets, alphanumeric or even symbols, spatial databases store abstract data types (ADTs) such as points, lines, polygons, coordinates, topology or other data types that can be mapped. Traditional database systems have great difficulties to cope with these kinds of data, because they have been customised to fixed-length data of very simple internal structure. It is quite tedious to build a spatial database directly using a classical database model, therefore the traditional system needs to be extended and equipped to manage and support spatial data types (or data models), spatial functions, and spatial indexes. The essential features of spatial databases that distinguishes them from alphanumeric data includes a complex internal structure, arbitrary finite representation of shapes. Thus, domain-specific knowledge is necessary for traditional/classical databases to be able to support non-standard database applications. In this chapter (for the sake of efficient information retrieval) we have examined spatial data bases, its architecture, optimization technique, methods of improving their internal and optimal storage capacity. Because of the non - linearity that exists among large spatial data set, an effective data structure which has the ability to tackle the branched structures that exists among a given spatial data is required. These complex spatial dataset behaviors are better represented using graphs and trees due to the larger datasets that are always made up of other minor events or objects and are always difficult to be ordered to form of sequences. The main goal of indexing is to optimize the speed of database query in other to facilitates information retrieval process and also improve database integrity and general performance. Developing a spatial database normally starts with developing a data model (which relates to the conceptual, logical and physical data modelling), that describes the contents of the database and their relationship. Therefore to achieve this, data analyst constantly seek an appropriate data structure that efficiently stores the objects data in the database and allows for a better and efficient database management.

REFERENCES

Agrawal, R., Gehrke, J., Gunopulos, D., & Raghavan, P. (1998). Automatic subspace clustering of high dimensional data for data mining applications. ACM.

Ajit, S., & Deepak, G. (2011). Implementation and Performance Analysis of Exponential Tree Sorting. International Journal of Computer Applications, 24(3), 34-38.

Akinyemi, F. A. (2010). Conceptual Poverty Mapping Data Model. *Transactions in GIS, 14,* 85–100. doi:10.1111/j.1467-9671.2010.01207.x

Arya, S., Mount, D. M., Netanyahu, N., Silverman, R., & Wu, A. Y. (1994, January). An optimal algorithm for approximate nearest neighbor searching in fixed dimensions. In *Proc. 5th ACM-SIAM Sympos. Discrete Algorithms* (pp. 573-582).

Asaeedi, S., Didehvar, F., & Mohades, A. (2013). *Alpha-Concave Hull, a Generalization of Convex Hull.* arXiv preprint arXiv:1309.7829

Baum, M., & Hanebeck, U. D. (2010, September). Tracking a minimum bounding rectangle based on extreme value theory. In *Multisensor Fusion and Integration for Intelligent Systems (MFI), 2010 IEEE Conference on* (pp. 56-61). IEEE. doi:10.1109/MFI.2010.5604456

Belciu, A. V., & Olaru, S. (2011). *Optimizing spatial databases.* Available at SSRN 1800758

Bellman, R. E. (1957). *Dynamic programming.* Princeton, NJ: Princeton University Press.

Berchtold, S., & Keim, D. A. (1996). The X-tree: An Index Structure for High-Dimensional Data. *Proceedings of the 22nd VLDB Conference.*

Berchtold, S., Keim, D. A., & Kriegel, H. P. (2001). An index structure for high-dimensional data. Readings in multimedia computing and networking.

Berchtold, S., Bohm, C., Keim, D., & Kriegel H.-P. (1997). A cost model for nearest neighbor search in high-dimensional data space. In *Proceedings of the 16th Symposium on Principles of Database Systems* (PODS).

Beyer, K., Goldstein, J., Ramakrishnan, R., & Shaft, U. (1999). When is Nearest Neighbors Meaningful? *Proc. of the Int. Conf. Database Theorie*, (pp. 217-235).

Böhm, C., Berchtold, S., & Keim, D. A. (2001). Searching in high-dimensional spaces: Index structures for improving the performance of multimedia databases. *ACM Computing Surveys*, *33*(3), 322–373. doi:10.1145/502807.502809

Bolstad, P. (2002). GIS Fundamentals: A First Text on GIS. Eider Press.

Bourne, M. (2015). *Applications of integration.* Retrieved from http://www.intmath.com/applications-integration/5-centroid-area.php

Candan, K. S., & Sapino, M. L. (2010). *Data management for multimedia retrieval.* Cambridge University Press. doi:10.1017/CBO9780511781636

Cazals, F., Emiris, I. Z., Chazal, F., Gärtner, B., Lammersen, C., Giesen, J., & Rote, G. (2013). *D2. 1: Handling High-Dimensional Data.* Computational Geometric Learning (CGL) Technical Report No.: CGL-TR-01.

Census. (2011). *Wards in Yorkshire and the Humber.* Available at http://ukdataexplorer.com/census/yorkshireandthehumber/#KS206EW0007

Chen, L., & Brown, S. D. (2014). Use of a tree-structured hierarchical model for estimation of location and uncertainty in multivariate spatial data. *Journal of Chemometrics*, *28*(6), 523–538. doi:10.1002/cem.2611

Ding, Y. (2007). *Handling complex, high dimensional data for classification and clustering.* University of Mississippi.

Dröge, G. & Schek. (1993). Query-Adaptive Data Space Partitioning Using Variable-Size Storage Clusters. *Proc. 3rd Intl. Symposium on Large Spatial Databases.*

Eberly, D. (2015). *Minimum-Area Rectangle Containing a Set of Points*. Geometric Tools, LLC. Retrieved from http://www.geometrictools.com/

Efunda. (2016). *Solids: Centre of Mass*. Available at http://www.efunda.com/math/solids/CenterOfMass.cfm

Ernest, R., & Djaoen, S. (2015). *Introduction to SQL Server Spatial Data*. Retrieved from https://www.simple-talk.com/sql/t-sql-programming/introduction-to-sql-server-spatial-data

Ester, M., Kriegel, H. P., & Sander, J. (1997). Spatial data mining: A database approach. In *Advances in spatial databases* (pp. 47–66). Springer Berlin Heidelberg. doi:10.1007/3-540-63238-7_24

Ester, M., Kriegel, H. P., & Sander, J. (1999). *Knowledge discovery in spatial databases*. Springer Berlin Heidelberg.

Fortin, M. J., & Dale, M. R. (2009). Spatial autocorrelation in ecological studies: A legacy of solutions and myths. *Geographical Analysis*, *41*(4), 392–397. doi:10.1111/j.1538-4632.2009.00766.x

Freeman, H., & Shapira, R. (1975). Determining the minimum-area encasing rectangle for an arbitrary closed curve. *Communications of the ACM*, *18*(7), 409–413. doi:10.1145/360881.360919

GADM. (2009). *Global Administrative Areas: Boundaries without limit*. Available at http://www.gadm.org/download

Ganguly, A. R., & Steinhaeuser, K. (2008). Data mining for climate change and impacts. In ICDM Workshops. doi:10.1109/ICDMW.2008.30

Giao, B. C., & Anh, D. T. (2015). Improving Sort-Tile-Recusive algorithm for R-tree packing in indexing time series. In *Computing & Communication Technologies-Research, Innovation, and Vision for the Future (RIVF), 2015 IEEE RIVF International Conference on* (pp. 117-122). IEEE.

Güting, R. H. (1994). An introduction to spatial database systems. *The VLDB Journal—The International Journal on Very Large Data Bases, 3*(4), 357-399.

Güting, R. H., & Schneider, M. (1993). Realms: A foundation for spatial data types in database systems. In Advances in Spatial Databases (pp. 14-35). Springer Berlin Heidelberg. doi:10.1007/3-540-56869-7_2

Hinneburg, A., Aggarwal, C. C., & Keim, D. A. (2000). What is the nearest neighbor in high dimensional spaces? In *26th Internat. Conference on Very Large Databases* (pp. 506-515).

International Business Machines. (1996). IBM Intelligent Miner User's Guide, Version 1 Release 1, SH12-6213-00 edition. Author.

Jagadish, H. V., Ooi, B. C., Vu, Q. H., Zhang, R., & Zhou, A. (2006). Vbi-tree: A peer-to-peer framework for supporting multi-dimensional indexing schemes. In *Data Engineering, 2006. ICDE'06. Proceedings of the 22nd International Conference on* (pp. 34-34). IEEE. doi:10.1109/ICDE.2006.169

Jain, A. K., Murty, M. N., & Flynn, P. J. (1999). Data clustering: A review. *ACM Computing Surveys*, *31*(3), 264–323. doi:10.1145/331499.331504

Jerrett, M., Burnett, R., Willis, A., Krewski, D., Goldberg, M., DeLuca, P., & Finkelstein, N. (2003). Spatial Analysis of the Air Pollution Mortality Relationship in the Context of Ecologic Confounders. *Journal of Toxicology and Environmental Health. Part A.*, *66*(16-19), 1735–1778. doi:10.1080/15287390306438 PMID:12959842

Jiawei-Han, M. K. (2001). *Data Mining: Concepts and Techniques*. Morgan Kaufmann Publishers.

Katayama, N., & Satoh, S. (2002). Experimental evaluation of disk based data structures for nearest neighbour searching. *AMS DIMACS Series, 59*, 87.

Kouiroukidis, N., & Evangelidis, G. (2011). The effects of dimensionality curse in high dimensional knn search. In *Informatics (PCI), 2011 15th Panhellenic Conference on* (pp. 41-45). IEEE. doi:10.1109/PCI.2011.45

Kushilevitz, E., Ostrovsky, R., & Rabani, Y. (2000). Efficient search for approximate nearest neighbor in high dimensional spaces. *SIAM Journal on Computing*, *30*(2), 457–474. doi:10.1137/S0097539798347177

Legendre, P. (1993). Spatial autocorrelation: Trouble or new paradigm? *Ecology*, *74*(6), 1659–1673. doi:10.2307/1939924

Legendre, P., & Fortin, M. J. (1989). Spatial pattern and ecological analysis. *Vegetatio*, *80*(2), 107–138. doi:10.1007/BF00048036

Lifshits, Y., & Zhang, S. (2009). Combinatorial algorithms for nearest neighbors, near-duplicates and small-world design. In *Proc. SODA*. doi:10.1137/1.9781611973068.36

Lungu, I., & Velicanu, A. (2009). Spatial Database Technology Used In Developing Geographic Information Systems. *The 9th International Conference on Informatics in Economy – Education, Research & Business Technologies*. Academy of Economic Studies, Bucharest.

Mamoulis, N. (2012). *Spatial data management* (1st ed.). Morgan & Claypool Publishers.

McCallum, A., Nigam, K., & Ungar, L. H. (2000, August). Efficient clustering of high-dimensional data sets with application to reference matching. In *Proceedings of the sixth ACM SIGKDD international conference on Knowledge discovery and data mining* (pp. 169-178). ACM. doi:10.1145/347090.347123

Mosley, R. C. (2010). *Handling High Dimensional Variables*. Pinnacle Actuarial Resources, Inc.

Muller, E., Gunnemann, S., Assent, & Seidl, T. (2009). Evaluating Clustering in Subspace Projections of High Dimensional Data. *VLDB '09*. Lyon, France: VLDB Endowment.

Paithankar, R., & Tidke, B. (2015). *A H-K Clustering Algorithm for High Dimensional Data Using Ensemble Learning*. arXiv preprint arXiv:1501.02431

Papadias, D., Zhang, J., Mamoulis, N., & Tao, Y. (2003). Query processing in spatial network databases. In *Proceedings of the 29th international conference on Very large data bases* (vol. 29, pp. 802-813). VLDB Endowment.

Parsons, L., Haque, E., & Liu, H. (2004). Subspace clustering for high dimensional data: A review. *ACM SIGKDD Explorations Newsletter*, *6*(1), 90–105. doi:10.1145/1007730.1007731

Patel, P., & Garg, D. (2012). *Comparison of Advance Tree Data Structures*. arXiv preprint arXiv:1209.6495.

Paul, E. B. (2008). Point access method. In *Dictionary of Algorithms and Data Structures*. Available from: http://www.nist.gov/dads/HTML/pointAccessMethod.html

Ramakrishnan, R., & Gehrke, J. (2003). *Database management systems* (3rd ed.). New York: McGraw-Hill.

Rigaux, P., Scholl, M., & Voisard, A. (2003). Spatial Databases with Application to GIS. *SIGMOD Record, 32*(4), 111.

Rossi, J. P., & Quénéhervé, P. (1998). Relating species density to environmental variables in presence of spatial autocorrelation: A study case on soil nematodes distribution. *Ecography, 21*(2), 117–123. doi:10.1111/j.1600-0587.1998.tb00665.x

Samet, H. (1995). *Spatial data structures, Modern database systems: the object model, interoperability, and beyond*. New York, NY: ACM Press/Addison-Wesley Publishing Co.

Samet, H. (2006). *Foundations of Multidimensional and Metric Data Structures*. Morgan Kaufmann.

Samet, H. (2009). Sorting spatial data by spatial occupancy. In *GeoSpatial Visual Analytics* (pp. 31–43). Springer Netherlands.

Samet, H. (2010, December). Sorting in space: multidimensional, spatial, and metric data structures for computer graphics applications. In ACM SIGGRAPH ASIA 2010 Courses (p. 3). ACM. doi:10.1145/1900520.1900523

Samson, G. L., Lu, J., & Showole, A. A. (2014). Mining Complex Spatial Patterns: Issues and Techniques. *Journal of Information & Knowledge Management, 13*(02), 1450019. doi:10.1142/S0219649214500191

Samson, G. L., Lu, J., Wang, L., & Wilson, D. (2013). An approach for mining complex spatial dataset. *Proceeding of Int'l Conference on Information and Knowledge Engineering*. Retrieved from http://worldcompproceedings.com/proc/proc2013/ike/IKE_Papers.pdf

Schneider, M. (1997). Spatial Data Types for Database Systems - Finite Resolution Geometry for Geographic information systems. *LNCS, 1288*.

Schneider, M. (1999). Spatial Data Types: Conceptual Foundation for the Design and Implementation of Spatial Database Systems and GIS. In *Proceedings of 6th International Symposium on Spatial Databases*.

Shekhar, S., & Chawla, S. (2003). Spatial databases: A tour. Upper Saddle River, NJ: Prentice Hall.

Shekhar, S., Chawla, S., Ravada, S., Fetterer, A., Liu, X., & Lu, C. (1999). Spatial Databases - Accomplishments and Research Needs. *IEEE Transactions on Knowledge and Data Engineering, 11*(1), 45–55. doi:10.1109/69.755614

Shekhar, S., Evans, M. R., Kang, J. M., & Mohan, P. (2011). Identifying patterns in spatial information: A survey of methods. *Wiley Interdisciplinary Reviews: Data Mining and Knowledge Discovery, 1*(3), 193–214.

Singh, S. P., & Singh, P. (2014). Modelling a Geo-Spatial Database for Managing Travelers 'demand. *International Journal of Database Management Systems, 6*(2), 3–47. doi:10.5121/ijdms.2014.6203

Steinbach, M., Ertöz, L., & Kumar, V. (2004). The challenges of clustering high dimensional data. In *New directions in statistical physics* (pp. 273–309). Springer Berlin Heidelberg. doi:10.1007/978-3-662-08968-2_16

Stonebraker, M., Rowe, L. A., Lindsay, B. G., Gray, J., Carey, M. J., Brodie, M. L., & Beech, D. et al. (1990). Third-generation database system manifesto. *SIGMOD Record, 19*(3), 31–44. doi:10.1145/101077.390001

Velicanu, A., & Olaru, S. (2010). Optimizing Spatial Databases. *Informatica Economica, 14*(2), 61–71.

Verleysen, M., & François, D. (2005, June). The curse of dimensionality in data mining and time series prediction. In *International Work-Conference on Artificial Neural Networks* (pp. 758–770). Springer Berlin Heidelberg. doi:10.1007/11494669_93

Weinberger, K. Q., & Saul, L. K. (2004). Unsupervised learning of image manifolds by semidefinite programming. In *Proceedings of the IEEE Conference on Computer Vision and Pattern Recognition (CVPR-04)*.

Chapter 4
The Impact of the Mode of Data Representation for the Result Quality of the Detection and Filtering of Spam

Reda Mohamed Hamou
University of Saïda, Algeria

Abdelmalek Amine
University of Saïda, Algeria

Moulay Tahar
University of Saïda, Algeria

ABSTRACT

Spam is now of phenomenal proportions since it represents a high percentage of total emails exchanged on the Internet. In the fight against spam, we are using this article to develop a hybrid algorithm based primarily on the probabilistic model in this case, Naïve Bayes, for weighting the terms of the matrix term -category and second place used an algorithm of unsupervised learning (K-means) to filter two classes, namely spam and ham (legitimate email). To determine the sensitive parameters that make up the classifications we are interested in studying the content of the messages by using a representation of messages using the n-gram words and characters independent of languages (because a message may be received in any language) to later decide what representation to use to get a good classification. We have chosen several metrics as evaluation to validate our results.

INTRODUCTION TO THE PROBLEM

Unsolicited email, or spam, is a type of electronic communication that currently represents up to 95% of email processed on some servers. This is an ethical and economic issue that effectively fight against this scourge. The decision to classify an email as spam or not spam is most effectively done by a hu-

DOI: 10.4018/978-1-5225-2058-0.ch004

man. A message in circulation prevents the address from manually sorting the acceptable email from spam. Spam is a massive, global phenomenon. According to the CNIL (The Commission Nationale de L'Informatique and Freedoms), spam is defined as follows: "The" spamming "or" spam "is to send massive and sometimes repeated, unsolicited emails, to individuals with whom the sender has never had contact, he has captured the email address erratically." It was not until the late 90s that the problem of detection and spam filtering by content, drew attention to three areas of research that were not directly affected by email: the Retrieval (IR), the Data Mining (DM) and Machine Learning (ML).

Detection and spam filtering are a binary classification problem in which the email is classified as either ham or spam. This area has experienced a wide range of methods for the classification among its techniques; the use of Bayes' theorem is the most famous. Bayesian filters work by establishing a correlation between the presence of certain elements (usually words) in a message and the fact that they usually appear in messages (spam) or in legitimate email (ham) to calculate the probability that the message is spam. Bayesian filtering spam is a powerful technique for the treatment of unwanted email. It adapts to the habits of the user and produces a false positive rate low enough to be acceptable.

This problem leads us to do a study as to the representation of data (message corpus) to try to identify sensitive parameters that can improve the results of classification and categorization around detections and spam filtering. We know very well that supervised learning techniques yield the best results. For this reason that we have tried to inject a clustering algorithm (k-means) to try to minimize the intervention of expert.

STATE OF THE ART

Among the anti-spam techniques that exist in the literature include are those based on machine learning and those not based on machine learning.

The Techniques Not Based on Machine Learning

Heuristics, or rules-based, this analysis uses regular expression rules to detect phrases or characteristics that are common in spam, and the amount and severity of identified features will propose the appropriate classification of the message. The history and the popularity of this technology has largely been driven by its simplicity, speed and accuracy. In addition, it is better than many advanced technologies of filtering and detection in the sense that it does not require a learning period. Techniques based on signatures generate a unique hash value (signature) for each message recognized spam. Filters signature compare the hash value of all incoming mail against those stored (the hash values previously identified to classify spam e-mail). This kind of technology makes it statistically unlikely that a legitimate email will have the same hash of a spam message. This allows filter signatures to achieve a very low level of false positives. The blacklist is a technique that is simple common among almost all filtration products. Also known as block lists, blacklists filter e-mails from a specific sender. White lists, or lists of authorization, perform the opposite function, to correctly classify an email automatically from a specific sender. Currently, there is a spam filtering technology based on traffic analysis that provides a characterization of spam traffic patterns where a number of attributes per email are able to identify the characteristics that separate spam traffic from non-spam traffic.

The Techniques Based on Machine Learning

Filtering techniques based on machine learning can be further categorized into, comprehensive solutions and complementary solutions. Complementary solutions are designed to work as part of a larger filtering system, providing support to the primary filter (whether or not based on a machine learning approach). The solutions aim to build a comprehensive knowledge base that classifies independently all incoming messages.

Bayesian filtering spam (of the mathematician Thomas Bayes) is a system based on a large amount of spam and legitimate e-mails to determine whether an email is legitimate or not (Sahami,1998). To function properly, the corpus of spam and ham (legitimate email) should ideally contain several thousand "specimens." The support vector machine (SVM) is generated by the mapping of the data forming a non-linear characteristic of a space of higher dimension, where a hyperplane is formed that maximizes the margin between the sets. The hyperplane is then used as a nonlinear decision boundary when exposed to real data. Drucker (1999) applied this technique to spam filtering, testing it against the other three classification algorithms text: Ripper, Rocchio and building decision trees. Both trees stimulating and SVM provided a performance "acceptable." Neural networks are generally optimized by methods of learning probabilistic, in particular Bayesian. They are placed one hand in the family of statistical applications, that they enrich with one set of paradigms allowing to create fast classifications (Kohonen networks in particular), and on the other the family of artificial intelligence methods that they provide a perceptual mechanism independent of designer's own ideas and providing input information to formal logical reasoning.

Chhabra (2004). present a classifier based anti-spam on a Markov random field (MRF) model. This approach allows the spam classifier to consider the importance of the neighborhood relationship between words in an email message. Dependency between the words of natural language can be incorporated into the classification process, which is generally ignored by Bayesian classifiers (Chhabra, 2004). Characteristics of incoming e-mails are decomposed into feature vectors and are weighted super-increasing.

There are other anti-spam methods such as envelope filtering, filtering content, filtering by keywords or addresses, regular expression filtering, virus scanning and attachments, filtering server sender's Realtime Black hole List (RBL), SPF (Sender Policy Framework), integrity SMTP priority MX records, the gray list, and heuristic filtering or RPD Recurrent Pattern Detection.

Figure 1 shows the classification of different approaches to spam filtering.

Figure 1. Classification of different approaches to spam filtering

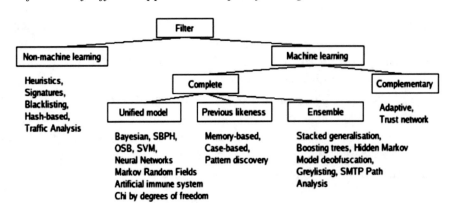

REPRESENTATION OF DATA

The natural language text cannot be directly interpreted by a classifier or by classification algorithms from which the need for a mathematical representation of the text in such a way that it can perform analytical processing thereon, retaining maximum semantics. The mathematical representation generally used is the use of a vector space representation as a target. The main feature of the vector representation is that each language is associated with a specific dimension in the vector space. Two texts using the same textual segments are therefore projected onto identical vectors.

Several approaches for the representation of texts exist in the literature, among which are the representation of sentences bag of words which constitutes the simplest and most used; representation bag phrases, lexical roots and of course the n-grams representation which is independent representation of natural language (Shannon, 1948).

In general, the n-gram character is defined as a sequence of n consecutive characters and n-gram word as a sequence of n words. The principle of the n-gram character for a string of k characters surrounded by white, we generate (k +1) n-grams. An example of cutting the word "porte" in 2-gram is the following: "_porte_" _p, po, or, rt, te e_.

Once we extract all n-grams of a document we define the list of n-grams sorted in descending order of their frequency of occurrence. These methods are independent of language and neither the segmentation into linguistic units or pretreatments are needed. After the step of representing the n-grams, indexing documents are required. Once the components of the vectors chosen to represent a text, we must decide how to encode each coordinate of the vector. Given the occurrence of a term t_k in document d_j, each component of a vector is coded f (t_k d_j) where the function f must be determined.

A very simple function is the Boolean function defined by:

$$F = \begin{cases} 1 \text{ if the term } t_k \text{ appear in document } d_i \\ 0 \text{ if not} \end{cases}$$

This function is rarely used in statistical methods because this coding removes information that can be useful: the appearance of the same word several times in a text can be an important decision. The most used function is the coding tf.idf.

This encoding uses a function of occurrence multiplied by a function which involves the inverse of the number of different documents in which a term appears. Function TFIDF [Salton & Buckley, 88)], defined as follows (Dziczkowski, 2008):

$$tfidf(t_k, d_j) = \#(t_k, d_j) . \log \frac{|T_r|}{\# T_r(t_k)}$$

where #(t_k, d_j) denotes the number of times tk occurs in dj, and # (t_k) denotes the frequency of term t_k in document corpus - ie the number of documents in which tk occurs, $|$ Tr $|$ number of documents in the corpus. This function shows that the more often a term appears in a document, it is more representative, more the number of documents containing a term are important, this term is less discriminatory.

TF×IDF coding does not fix the length of texts, to this end, the coding TFC is similar to TF×IDF, but it sets the length of texts by cosine normalization, not to encourage longer.

$$TFC(t_k, d) = \frac{TF.IDF(t_k, d)}{\sqrt{\sum^{r} (TF.IDF(t_k, d))^2}}$$

At the end of this phase we obtain our document vector where each component indicates the weight of the term tk in the document.

We experienced in our study 2,3,4 and 5 grams characters, and 1 gram words.

In all areas of computing in which you want to automatically analyze a set of data, it is necessary to have an operator that can accurately assess the similarities or dissimilarities that exist within the data. On this basis, it becomes possible to order the elements of the set, prioritize or to extract invariants.

To describe this operator in our area which is supervised and unsupervised classification of text document we use the term "similarity". This similarity is expressed by several types of vector distances.

THE PROPOSED APPROACH

In our experiments we used a corpus of data already categorized that we will detail in the next section, where we will speak of the learning base. The Bayesian network that we construct will allow us to calculate the probability of a new message being spam.

After representation of textual documents corpus of spam, by various techniques of n-grams that are character n-grams and word n-grams, we construct the matrix term document for each type of representation, which represent the presence or absence of the document in terms coded as 1 and 0 respectively. We can find terms that appear in both spam and ham and it is for this reason that we use the naive Bayes probabilistic model to calculate the new weighting of terms in the document-term matrix that we call the matrix category term. By the same model we do categorization (supervised learning) constructing the matrix document category using similarity distances. The points obtained are represented in a two-dimensional landmark (2D) which are displayed in Figures 2 and 3. Subsequently, we perform a clustering algorithm (k-means) (Figures. 4 and 5) to obtain two new classes that we evaluate by measures based on recall and precision in this case the entropy and F-measure to know the percentage of documents correctly classified and unclassified ones. For each technical representation of texts, we note the best results for classification that at the end we can make a decision on what type of representation chosen for the detection and spam filtering. Before analyzing the results, we explain the methodology treatments (Hamou, 2010, 2012, 2013).

The Detection and Bayesian Filtering of Spam

Bayesian filtering spam (of mathematician Thomas Bayes) is a system based on a large amount of spam and legitimate e-mails to determine whether an email is legitimate or not.

Some words have probabilities of appear in spam and legitimate mail. For example, most people frequently will encounter the word "Viagra" in their spam, but they rarely will encounter it in their legitimate emails. The filter does not know in advance the probabilities, which is why it takes a long time learning to evaluate them.

Learning is the responsibility of the user, who must manually indicate whether a message is spam or not. For every word of every message "learned", the filter adjusts the probabilities of encountering this word in spam or legitimate mail and stores them in its database. For example, Bayesian filters are likely to have a high probability of spam for the word "Viagra", but a very low probability for words encountered in legitimate emails, such as names of friends and relatives of the user. After learning, the probabilities of words (also called likelihood functions) are used to calculate the probability that a message (all these words) is spam. Each word of the message, or at least every word "interesting" message contributes to the likelihood that the message is spam. This contribution is calculated using Bayes' theorem. Once the calculation for the entire message is finished, we compare its probability of being spam to an arbitrary value (eg 95%) to mark or unmark a message as spam.

Mathematical Foundations

The Bayesian spam filters based on Bayes' theorem. Bayes' theorem is used repeatedly in the context of spam:

- A first time to calculate the probability that the message is spam, since a given word appears in this message;
- A second time, to calculate the probability that the message is spam, considering all his words, or a significant subset of the words.
- Sometimes, to treat rare words.

Calculate the probability that a message containing a given word is a spam:

Suppose the suspicious message contains the word "Word". In 2009 most of the people accustomed to receive e-mail know that it is likely that the message is spam. The spam detection software ignores these facts; however, all he can do is calculating probabilities.

The formula for determining this probability is derived from Bayes' theorem, it is, in its most general form, to:

$$P(S \setminus M) = \frac{P(S \setminus M).P(S)}{P(M \setminus S).P(S) + P(M \setminus H).P(H)}$$

where,

- P (S / M) is the probability that the message M is spam, knowing that the word "Word" is included.
- P (S) is the absolute probability that any message is spam.
- P (M / S) is the probability that the "Word" appears in spam messages.
- P (H) is the absolute probability that any message is not spam (ie, the "ham").
- P (M / H) is the probability that the "Word" appears in messages ham.

The Spamicity

Recent statistics show that the current probability that any message being spam is at least 80%: ie: P (S) = 0.8 and P (H) = 0.2.

Most software Bayesian spam detection believe that there is no a priori reason that a received message is spam instead of ham, and consider the two cases as having equal probabilities of 50%, ie: P (S) = P (H) = 0.5.

Filters that make this assumption are called "non-biased", which means they do not have prejudices about incoming mail. This assumption simplifies the general formula:

$$P(S \setminus M) = \frac{P(M \setminus S)}{P(M \setminus S) + P(M \setminus H)}$$

This quantity is called spamicity the word "Word" and can be calculated. The number P (M\S) that appears in this formula is approximated by the frequency of messages containing "Word" among the messages identified as spam during the learning phase. Similarly, P (M\H) is approximated by the frequency of messages containing "Word" among the messages identified as the ham during the learning phase.

Of course, determine whether a message is spam or not relying solely on the presence of the word "Word" can lead to error, which is why the anti-spam software tries to consider several words and combine spamicités for determine the probability of assembly to be spam.

Figure 2. Graphical representation of data by 1-gram word after weighting of Naïve Bayes

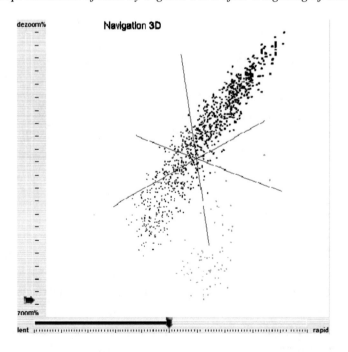

Figure 3. Graphical representation of data by the 4-gram characters after weighting Naïve Bayes

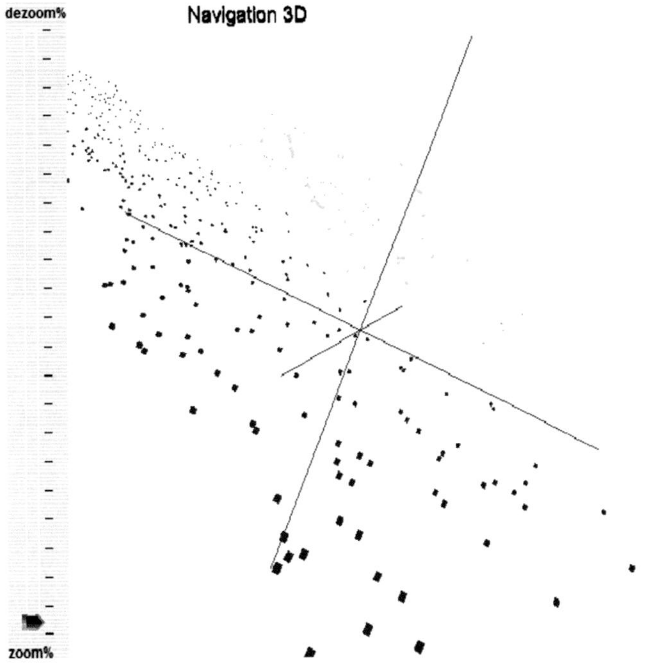

The Clustering by k-Means

Clustering by K-means (MacQueen, 1967) is a commonly used technique to automatically partition a data set into k groups. It does this by selecting k initial cluster centers, and then iteratively refines them as follows:

Initialize centers $\mu_1, \cdots \mu_K$

- Repeat.
- Assigning each point to its nearest cluster.

$$Cl \leftarrow x_i such.as.l = \arg\min d(x_i, \mu_k)$$

- Recalculate the center μ_k of each cluster.

$$\mu_k = \frac{1}{N_k} \sum_{i \in C_k} x_i$$

- Where N_k is the number of data in the cluster C_k.
- While $\|\Delta\mu\| > \varepsilon$.

Complexity: $O(K_{nI})$ for I: iterations

A visual result after clustering by k-means is illustrated in Figures 4 and 5.

It should be noted that 3D navigation software has been designed to represent the data and the different classifications performed in our study. The points in red represent ham and green points represent the spam.

RESULTS AND EXPERIMENTS

The Data Used

The SMS Spam Corpus v.0.1 (hereafter the corpus) is a set of SMS tagged messages that have been collected for SMS Spam research. It contains two collections of SMS messages in English of 1084 and 1319 messages, tagged according being legitimate (ham) or spam.

This corpus has been collected from free or free for research sources at the Web:

- A list of 202 legitimate messages, probably collected by Jon Stevenson, according to the HTML code of the Webpage. Only the text of the messages is available. We will call this corpus the Jon Stevenson Corpus (JSC). It is available at: http://www.demo.inty.net/Units/SMS/corpus.htm
- A subset of the NUS SMS Corpus (NSC), which is a corpus of about 10,000 legitimate messages collected for research at the Department of Computer Science at the National University of Singapore. The messages largely originate from Singaporeans and mostly from students attending the University. These messages were collected from volunteers who were made aware that their

Figure 4. Graphical representation of data by 1-gram word after clustering by k-means

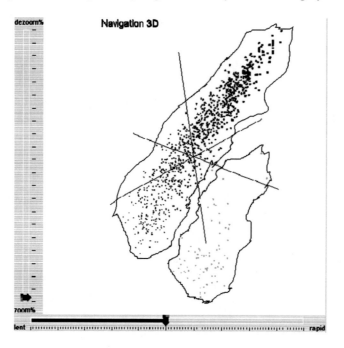

Figure 5. Graphical representation of data by the 4-gram characters after clustering by k-means

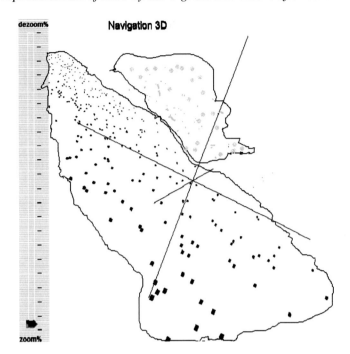

contributions were going to be made publicly available. The NUS SMS Corpus is avalaible at: http://www.comp.nus.edu.sg/~rpnlpir/downloads/corpora/smsCorpus/

- A collection of between 82 and 322 SMS spam messages extracted manually from the Grumbletext Web site. This is a UK forum in which cell phone users make public claims about SMS spam messages, most of them without reporting the very spam message received. The identification of the text of spam messages in the claims is a very hard and time-consuming task, and it involved carefully scanning hundreds of web pages. The Grumbletext Web site is: http://www.grumbletext. co.uk/

RESULTS AND DISCUSSIONS

To carry out our experiments, we opted by the following methodology:

1. Representation of documents in the corpus by:
   a. The 1-gram words.
   b. The 1-gram characters.
   c. The 2-gram characters.
   d. The 3-gram characters.
   e. The 4-gram characters.
   f. The 5-gram characters.
2. For each representation defined above, we performed experiments with and without cleaning the documents in the corpus.

3.   Calculate the matrix document-term.
4.   Compute the matrix-term category. by probabilistic weightings.
5.   Make a categorization (supervised learning) by the model-Naïve Bayes.
6.   Data Visualization in a 3D coordinate system.
7.   From the data thus found, we run a clustering algorithm (unsupervised learning) based on k-means to identify two classes of documents in this case the new ham and spam and therefore determine the confusion matrix or more precisely contingency table.
8.   Evaluation of results measures based on recall and precision (F-measure and Entropy).

The corpus used contains 1084 documents divided into 82 spams and 1002 ham.

Referring to Tables 1 and 2, we will explain the results based on the contingency tables of the best results of the model in this case the 4-gram representations characters and 1-gram words with cleaning data, and 3-gram representation characters without data cleansing.

Contingency table (or table of co-occurrence) is a tool often used when it is desired to study the relationship between two variables that take discrete values (or categories). In our case, the variables are in the columns, actual (also known as "Gold Standard") and in the lines, the result of the filter. The sum of each column gives the actual number of elements in each class and of each line gives the number of elements seen by the classifier in each class. Table 3 shows the form of the contingency table.

Tables 4, 5 and 6 show the contingency matrix representations that have given the best results with the evaluation criteria which we outline below.

We present some evaluation metrics that we used in our experiments to validate our results.

Table 1. Results of learning naïve bayes with data cleaning

Representation	# Term	# Spam	# Ham	Learning Time (s)	F_measure	entropy	Confusion matrix	
							Spam	Ham
1-Gram Char	27	253	831	5	0, 8284	0,1522	72	181
							10	821
2-Grams Char	555	131	953	11	0,9433	0.0554	76	55
							6	947
3-Grams Char	3907	82	1000	17	0.9888	0.0111	77	7
							5	995
4-Grams Char	12074	74	1010	62	0.9929	0.0067	74	0
							8	1002
5-Grams Char	23516	56	1028	89	0.9798	0.0163	56	0
							26	1002
1-Gram Word	2270	71	1013	16	0.9905	0.0088	71	0
							11	1002

Table 2. Results of learning naïve bayes without data cleaning

Representation	# Term	# Spam	# Ham	Learning Time (s)	F_measure	entropy	Confusion matrix	
							Spam	Ham
1-Gram Char	98	94	990	7	0.9851	0,0148	80	14
							2	988
2-Grams Char	2005	86	998	13	0.9944	0.0056	81	5
							1	997
3-Grams Char	**9175**	**79**	**1005**	**53**	**0.9972**	**0.0028**	**79**	**0**
							3	**1002**
4-Grams Char	20951	68	1016	83	0.9881	0.0107	68	0
							14	1002
5-Grams Char	33233	51	1033	96	0.9767	0.0176	51	0
							31	1002
1-Gram Word	4224	62	1022	34	0.9837	0.0139	62	0
							20	1002

Table 3. Form of the contingency table

	True Spam	True Ham
Ranking Spam	VP	FP
Ranking Ham	FN	VN

Where

VN: True negatives: Hams seen by the filter as hams or hams correctly classified.

FN: False negative: Spam seen as hams or spams not correctly classified.

VP: True positives: Spam seen as spam or spam correctly classified.

FP: False positive: Hams seen as spams or hams not correctly classified.

Table 4. Contingency table for 4-grams Characters with cleaning

	True Spam	True Ham
Ranking Spam	74	0
Ranking Ham	8	1002

Table 5. Contingency table for 1-gram Word with cleaning

	True Spam	True Ham
Ranking Spam	71	0
Ranking Ham	11	1002

Table 6. Contingency table for 3-grams Characters without cleaning

	True Spam	True Ham
Ranking Spam	79	0
Ranking Ham	3	1002

Error Rate by Class

(False positives and false negatives): it is the fraction of the number of objects in a category erroneously classified in another class.

$$FPR = \frac{FP}{VN + FP}$$

$$FNR = \frac{FN}{VP + FN}$$

Based on Tables 4 and 5, which relate the results by doing the cleaning data before doing learning, and the above formulas, we calculate the error rate per class (spam and ham).

1. 4-grams Characters with cleaning: FPR = 0; FNR = 8/82 = 0.0975.
2. 1-gram words with cleaning: FPR = 0; FNR = 11/82 = 0.134.
3. 3-gram characters without cleaning: FPR = 0; FNR = 3/82 = 0.0365.

Based on these evaluation results and the error rate for each class, we note that 3-grams Characters have the better performance than other types of representations and data cleansing reduces the performance of results.

Rate of Good Ranking

(True positives and true negatives or sensitivity and specificity)

$$VPR = \frac{VP}{VP + FN} = 1 - FNR$$
$$VNR = \frac{VN}{VN + FP} = 1 - FPR$$

1. 4-grams Characters with cleaning: VPR = 74/82 = 0.9025; VNR = 1002/1002 = 1.
2. 1-gram words with cleaning: VPR = 71/82 = 0.865; VNR = 1002/1002 = 1.
3. 3-gram characters without cleaning: VPR = 79/82 = 0.963; VNR = 1002/1002 = 1.

We see that the representation of data by 3-gram characters without data cleansing gives very good results given the very high sensitivity (VPR= 0.963) and a specificity equal to 1 (VNR).

Precision and Recall

The precision indicates the proportion of spam messages among detected as spam, while the recall is the ratio between the number of detected spam rightly and the total number of spams.

$$Pr\,ecision = \frac{VP}{VP + FP}$$
$$Re\,call = \frac{VP}{VP + FN}$$

1. 4-grams Characters with cleaning: Precision = 1; Recall = 74/82 = 0.9025.
2. 1-gram words with cleaning: Precision = 1; Recall = 71/82 = 0.865.
3. 3-gram characters without cleaning: Precision = 1; Recall = 79/82 = 0.963.

Both criteria have their origin in retrieval applications and are sometimes found in the assessment results spam filters.

It should be noted that the f-measure and entropy are defined as follows:

$$F - measure = 2x\,\frac{Pr\,ecision.\,Re\,call}{Pr\,ecision + Re\,call}$$
$$Entropy = -Pr\,ecision.Ln(Pr\,ecision)$$

Hence,

1. 4-grams Characters with cleaning: f-measure = 0.9929; Entropy ≈ 0.
2. 1-gram words with cleaning: f-measure = 0.9905; Entropy ≈ 0.
3. 3-gram characters without cleaning: f-measure = 0.9972; Entropy ≈ 0.

As regards the assessment by the F-measure and the entropy, we note very good results with almost zero entropy (close to zero) and F-measure close to 1.

Accuracy

This is the total error rate, the two classes combined.

$$Accuracy = \frac{VP + VN}{VP + FN + VN + FP}$$

a. 4-gram characters with cleaning:: Accuracy = 1076/1084 = 0.993.
b. 1-gram words with cleaning:: Accuracy = 1073/1084 = 0.990.
c. 3-gram characters without cleaning: Accuracy = 1081/1084 = 0.997.

All evaluation results are summarized in Tables 7 and 8 as follows:

The following graphs provide an illustration on the sensitivity of the mode of representation on the quality of the result of our classifier.

Figure 6 shows that the 3-gram character provides better results (For the corpus used) compared to other forms of data representation since all documents ham were correctly classified because the clas-

Table 7. Evaluation results for different modes of representation without data cleaning

	Rate of rank well		Precision	Recall	Accuracy
	Spam	**Ham**			
1-Grams Char	97.56%	98.60%	85.11%	97.56%	98.52%
2-Grams Char	98.78%	99.50%	94.19%	98.78%	99.45%
3-Grams Char	96.34%	**100.00%**	**100.00%**	96.34%	**99.72%**
4-Grams Char	82.93%	100.00%	100.00%	82.93%	98.71%
5-Grams Char	62.20%	100.00%	100.00%	62.20%	97.14%
1-Gram Word	75.61%	100.00%	100.00%	75.61%	98.15%

Table 8. Evaluation results for different modes of representation with data cleaning

	Rate of rank well		Precision	Recall	Accuracy
	Spam	**Ham**			
1-Grams Char	87.80%	81.94%	28.46%	87.80%	82.38%
2-Grams Char	92.68%	94.51%	58.02%	92.68%	94.37%
3-Grams Char	93.90%	99.30%	91.67%	93.90%	98.89%
4-Grams Char	90.24%	**100.00%**	100.00%	90.24%	**99.26%**
5-Grams Char	68.29%	100.00%	100.00%	68.29%	97.60%
1-Gram Word	86.59%	100.00%	100.00%	86.59%	98.99%

sification error rate of ham is zero and is the case as for 4 and 5 grams characters, and 1 gram words, but the difference is that one of the modes of representation mentioned, ie the 3-gram characters, have the lowest rate of spam classification (3.66%).

We can clearly see for Figures 8 and 9 show that the best results are achieved for 3-gram characters, and especially without data cleaning because they have a high f-measure and low entropy.

COMPARATIVE STUDY

We experienced a metaheuristic for the detection and spam filtering in this case the social bees (ABC algorithm) for the same corpus and we found the following results in Table 9.

Based on some evaluation criteria, we present the following table for comparison between the two algorithms studied.

CONCLUSION AND PERSPECTIVES

In this paper, we were interested in modes of representation of textual data in this case, the n-gram characters and words because it's modes, which operate independently of languages, and lexical roots

Figure 6. Error rate per class for representation without cleaning

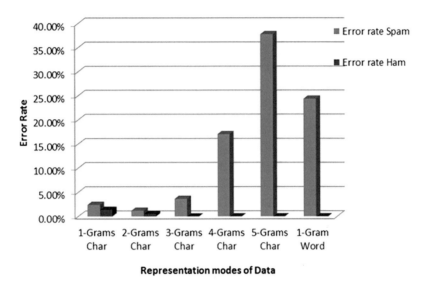

Figure 7. Rate of rank well for representation without cleaning

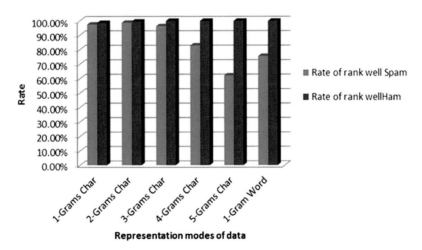

are automatically captured and are tolerant to the misspellings. The advantages of n-grams have led us to use them because spam is text document written in any language and can contain text full of mistakes, written by anyone.

The results obtained have proven that the 3-gram characters are most likely to be used for these kinds of problems, detection and spam filtering without the cleaning step is to remove data terms (words tools) and 4-gram characters were the best with the data cleaning step.

Another index that emerged as significant is the use of data cleaning because the best results were obtained without data cleansing, this is interpreted by the fact that the elimination of terms in this stage could harm the quality of classification because a term may have eliminated its importance to the calculation of the probability that the document is or is not spam.

Figure 8. Results of learning by hybrid algorithme (F-measure)

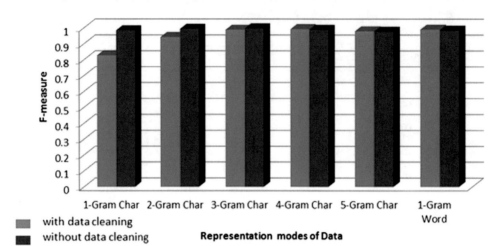

Figure 9. Results of learning by hybrid algorithme (Entropy)

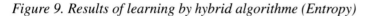
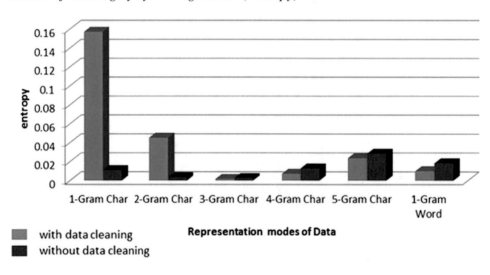

Table 9. The artificial bee colony algorithm (ABC)

	Jaccard		Cosinus		Euclidian		Manhattan		Minkovsky		Manahalobis	
Learning Time	6695		16397		64270		59572		74399		5225	
Recall	0.4362		0.4937		0.5325		0.5330		0.5157		0.5309	
Precision	0.4821		0.4982		0.5091		0.5092		0.5044		0.5086	
Entropy	0.165		0.196		0.216		0.216		0.207		0.215	
F-Measure	0.4580		0.4960		0.5205		0.5209		0.5100		0.5195	
accuracy	0.4649		0.5092		0.4981		0.4990		0.4981		0.5055	
confusion Matrice	471	531	513	489	493	509	494	508	496	506	502	500
	49	33	43	39	35	47	35	47	38	44	36	46

Table 10. Result of evaluation of the two approaches studied

	Our Algorithm	ABC Algorithm
F-measure	98.13%	52.09%
Accuracy	99.72%	50.92%
Entropy	0%	16.5%

In the future, we plan to experimenting unsupervised learning techniques because supervised learning techniques are very expensive.

REFERENCES

Chhabra, S., Siefkes, C., Assis, F., & Yerazunis, W. S. (2004, September). Combining winnow and orthogonal sparse bigrams for incremental spam filtering. In *European Conference on Principles of Data Mining and Knowledge Discovery* (pp. 410-421). Springer Berlin Heidelberg.

Drucker, H., Wu, D., & Vapnik, V. N. (1999). Support vector machines for spam categorization. *IEEE Transactions on Neural Networks*, *10*(5), 1048–1054. doi:10.1109/72.788645 PMID:18252607

Dziczkowski, G., & Wegrzyn-Wolska, K. (2008, December). An autonomous system designed for automatic detection and rating of film reviews. In *Proceedings of the 2008 IEEE/WIC/ACM International Conference on Web Intelligence and Intelligent Agent Technology* (pp. 847-850). IEEE Computer Society. doi:10.1109/WIIAT.2008.262

Hamou, R. M., Amine, A., & Lokbani, A. C. (2013a). Study of Sensitive Parameters of PSO Application to Clustering of Texts. *International Journal of Applied Evolutionary Computation*, *4*(2), 41–55. doi:10.4018/jaec.2013040104

Hamou, R. M., Amine, A., Lokbani, A. C., & Simonet, M. (2012). *Visualization and clustering by 3D cellular automata: Application to unstructured data.* arXiv preprint arXiv:1211.5766.

Hamou, R. M., Amine, A., Rahmouni, A., Lokbani, A. C., & Simonet, M. (2013b). Modeling of Inclusion by Genetic Algorithms: Application to the Beta-Cyclodextrin and Triphenylphosphine. *International Journal of Chemoinformatics and Chemical Engineering*, *3*(1), 19–36. doi:10.4018/ijcce.2013010103

Hamou, R. M., Lehireche, A., Lokbani, A. C., & Rahmani, M. (2010a). Representation of textual documents by the approach wordnet and n-grams for the unsupervised classification (clustering) with 2D cellular automata: A comparative study. *Computer and Information Science*, *3*(3), 240–255.

Hamou, R. M., Lehireche, A., Lokbani, A. C., & Rahmani, M. (2010b, October). Text clustering by 2D cellular automata based on the N-grams. In *Cryptography and Network Security, Data Mining and Knowledge Discovery, E-Commerce & Its Applications and Embedded Systems (CDEE), 2010 First ACIS International Symposium on* (pp. 271-277). IEEE.

MacQueen, J. (1967, June). Some methods for classification and analysis of multivariate observations. In *Proceedings of the fifth Berkeley symposium on mathematical statistics and probability* (*Vol. 1*, No. 14, pp. 281-297). Academic Press.

Sahami, M., Dumais, S., Heckerman, D., & Horvitz, E. (1998, July). A Bayesian approach to filtering junk e-mail. In *Learning for Text Categorization:Papers from the 1998 workshop* (*Vol. 62*, pp. 98-105). Academic Press.

Salton, G., & Buckley, C. (1988). Term-weighting approaches in automatic text retrieval. *Information Processing & Management*, *24*(5), 513–523. doi:10.1016/0306-4573(88)90021-0

Shannon, C. E. (1948). A note on the concept of entropy. *The Bell System Technical Journal*, *27*, 379–423. doi:10.1002/j.1538-7305.1948.tb01338.x

Chapter 5

Debunking Intermediary Censorship Framework in Social Media via a Content Retrieval and Classification Software

Baramee Navanopparatskul
Chulalongkorn University, Thailand

Sukree Sinthupinyo
Chulalongkorn University, Thailand

Pirongrong Ramasoota
Chulalongkorn University, Thailand

ABSTRACT

Following the enactment of computer crime law in Thailand, online service providers are compelled to control illegal content including content that is deemed harmful or problematic. This situation leads to self-censorship of intermediaries, often resulting in overblocking to avoid violating the law. Such filtering flaw both infringes users' freedom of expression and impedes the business of OSPs in Thailand. The Innovative Retrieval System (IRS) is thus developed to investigate intermediary censorship in online discussion forum, Pantip.com, as a case study of social media. The result shows that there is no consistency of censorship pattern on the website at all. The censorship criteria depend on type of content in each forum. Overblocking is also high, over 70% of removed content, due to intimidation of governmental agencies, lawsuits from business organizations, and fear of intermediary liability. Website administrator admitted that he would cut off some users to avoid business troubles.

INTRODUCTION

Intermediary censorship has emerged as a contentious issue in the scholarly area of Internet filtering in recent years. In the context of Web 2.0, online service providers (OSPs) or social media like online discussion forums, social networking services and blogging services have become important public sphere whereby users are provided with space to generate their own content. This should, in any general

DOI: 10.4018/978-1-5225-2058-0.ch005

context, promote freedom of expression of Net users. However, many regimes around the world have not been accommodating for this novel opportunity as they have made OSPs new choking points for Internet control by transferring to them the liability related to content published online, which Zuckerman (2009) refers to as "intermediary censorship". In fact, cyber crime laws in some countries have made intermediary liability a major regulatory component. Such is the case with Thailand's relatively new, yet highly controversial, Computer-Related Offence Act B.E. 2550 (2007) which requires online intermediaries to remove potentially infringing content, particularly those that may fall under lèse majesté – damaging or defaming the king and royal family – a historically serious crime in Thailand (Bangkok Post, 2009).

According to a local research on control and censorship of online media through the use of laws and the imposition of Thai state policies (iLaw, 2010), censorship and lawsuits have dramatically increased particularly under charges of defamation and lèse majesté as shown in Figure 1 and Figure 2. Also, according to the study on the impact of defamation law on freedom of expression in Thailand by ARTICLE 19 (2009), the Ministry of Information and Communications Technology (MICT) has shut down more than 2,000 websites alleged to have contained lèse majesté material. Based on reviews of related research and unobtrusive observation, however, the emerging filtering scheme at the intermediary level has led to a subjective censorship practice of sort (MacKinnon, 2009).

Online social media such as discussion forums, social networking, blogging and video sharing sites are among the most popular technologies emerging in the Web 2.0 age. Such applications enable ordinary users to post their own content, share information, and connect with large audiences. They have changed how people communicate and connect to each other. Not only have they enabled users to present themselves more easily and freely than before, but they also played a vital role in political and social activism. In Egypt, Tunisia, Iran, and Thailand, for example, democracy advocates have relied heavily on Facebook and Twitter to mobilize supporters and organize mass rallies.

Figure 1. Number of cases under Computer Crime Act in 2007 - 2010 (iLaw, 2010)

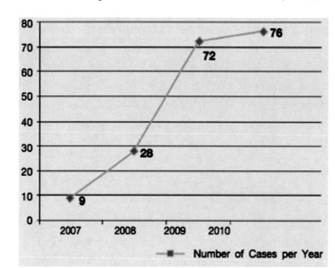

Figure 2. Numbers of cases segregated by content (iLaw, 2010)

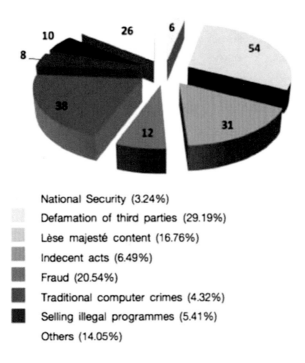

National Security (3.24%)
Defamation of third parties (29.19%)
Lèse majesté content (16.76%)
Indecent acts (6.49%)
Fraud (20.54%)
Traditional computer crimes (4.32%)
Selling illegal programmes (5.41%)
Others (14.05%)

RESEARCH QUESTIONS

Most social media services utilize both manual and auto filtering method to cope with a broad range of content on the website. However, some intermediaries have resorted to excessive removal of content or overblocking to avoid violating the law. Inevitably, Internet users' freedom of expression has been violated as well. Overblocking not only threatens free expression and Internet companies, but also innovation and economic growth. This situation of Internet control in Thailand and filtering flaw in social media has led to an important line of inquiry about censorship in online intermediaries, which has been formulated into the following questions:

1. What are the criteria of censorship in online social media in Thailand?
2. What types of content are filtered by intermediaries in Thailand?
3. Does overblocking happen in online social media in Thailand?

To answer those questions, a framework of Innovative Retrieval System (IRS) is introduced to investigate the intermediary censorship scheme by exploring and retrieving the content filtered by OSPs. The classification of filtered content will be identified to show what content is blocked and what influence has induced the censorship.

APPROACHES AND CONTEXT OF INTERNET FILTERING

There are four principal mechanisms that are at play in Internet regulation – law, technology or architecture, markets and social norms (Lessig, 1999), while OpenNet Initiative (ONI) has concluded that one of the most common and effective approaches of Internet censorship and content restrictions normally used today is induced self-censorship. It would induce through the threat of legal action, the promotion of social norms, or informal intimidation.

Deibert (2009) has documented the blocked content in his research, which mainly includes pornography and other culturally sensitive material. However, in some countries including Thailand, content beyond pornography, for instance political, social, conflict-related, and security content, is targeted for filtering as well. Similarly, Weckert (2000) stated that three areas of content on the Internet subject to regulation are pornography, hate language, and potentially harmful information. He indicated that there are moral justifications for regulation of the media and they should be applied to the Internet as well.

According to Faris and Villeneuve (2008), there are basically three main contexts for filtering Internet content, which are politics, social norms and morals, and security issues. Subjects, including Internet tools i.e. social networking services, blogging services, and other Web-based applications, are subject to filtering (see Table 1). Filtering political dissent is also a common form of censorship founded in many countries including Thailand. Pornographic and gambling-related content are basic examples of what is filtered for social and cultural reasons. Hate speech and political satire are also the target of Internet filtering in some countries. Infringing content, including those that may fall under lèse majesté – damaging or defaming the king and royal family – has been widely blocked in Thailand.

However, the regulation or restriction comes with a negative side effect, so called chilling effect. It is a situation where speech is suppressed by fear of penalization at the interests of an individual or group. It may prompt self-censorship and therefore hamper free speech. Klang (2006) stated that many different bodies of legislative rules might cause chilling effect or affect the way in which communication occurs. Those that are most common are privacy, defamation, copyrights and trademarks. Then the

Table 1. Categories subject to Internet Filtering

Free expression and media freedom	Sex education and family planning
Political transformation and opposition parties	Public health
Political reform, legal reform, and governance	Gay/lesbian content
Militants, extremists, and separatists	Pornography
Human rights	Provocative attire
Foreign relations and military	Dating
Minority rights and ethnic content	Gambling
Women's rights	Gaming
Environmental issues	Alcohol and drugs
Economic development	Minority faiths
Religious conversion, commentary, and criticism	Hate speech
Sensitive or controversial history, arts, and literature	

Source: Faris and Villeneuve (2008)

content involving these issues tend to be censored as well. CDT (2012) also indicated that chilling effect could happen in the level of intermediary due to fear of potential liability. Intermediary liability not only threatens Internet companies, but also innovation, free expression, and economic growth.

CONTROVERSY OF INTERNET CENSORSHIP

Censorship has long been a contentious issue especially when it comes to new types of media content like that on the Internet content. It is not necessarily a debate between conservatives and liberals as has been the case with media censorship in the past but also posits new angles like the necessity and justification of the censorship across international jurisdictions and cultures.

The primary concern of censorship lies in possible violation of rights to free expression. People have rights, in a free society, to decide for themselves and not be told how to think and what to access. In the contest of Web 2.0, where users are allowed to generate their own content into the public sphere, there should be even more democracy and freedom of expression in the media landscape. But Internet censorship would undermine those advantages of Web 2.0 and would involve massive intrusions on privacy (Weckert, 2000).

As mentioned earlier, Weckert (2000) agreed that Internet should be regulated to some extent and offensive materials must be justified that they would not harm or infringe on rights of others. It would not be easy to show that people have rights to express themselves through pornography, hate speech and the potentially harmful information. Therefore, the Internet could be reasonably and justifiably regulated. However, Akdeniz (2004) stated that harmful content should be regulated differently from illegal content because the former is not criminalized by national laws even though it is deemed objectionable, offensive, or harmful. Akdeniz (2004) concluded that Internet content considered harmful includes sexually explicit material, political opinions, religious beliefs, views on racial issues, and sexuality. Particularly, pornography is not always considered illegal, even though is often problematic, depending upon its nature and the laws of a specific State as mentioned by Akdeniz (2004) that there is no international attempt to regulate sexually explicit content.

The problem is Internet filtering schemes are usually generated through a combination of manual and automatic search for targeted content. The error, thus, could happen from both human error and technological limit. Filtering software is not foolproof. For instance, forbidden Webpages could easily be given new name and offensive users could register in different account. More effective technology for certain Internet content filtering will be possibly developed, but it is not yet available today (Weckert, 2000). According to CDT (2012), there is no sophisticated technology or enough resources, human and financial, for Internet companies to prevent all illegal content posted on their services. However, this technological problem is not an excuse not to regulate the Internet content. Even though the amounts of harmful content are reduced to some extent, perhaps not significantly, there are still benefits to children and the society in reducing such offensive materials. This is enough in itself to justify regulation.

What follows from this argument relates to what extent of content the regulations should apply. In many cases the censorship applies beyond pornography, hate speech, and potentially harmful information. Political dissent, political satire, terrorism and lèse majesté are examples of sensitive issues that tend to be filtered in some countries even though it is internationally accepted that freedom of expression should apply to political issues as indicated by UN Human Rights Committee (1996):

The free communication of information and ideas about public and political issues between citizens, candidates and elected representatives is essential. This implies a free press and other media able to comment on public issues without censorship or restraint and to inform public opinion.

Many opponents of the Internet censorship claim that political content and related issues should not be blocked based on freedom of expression, and that the profusion of Internet censorship often incorrectly block content that are not subject to be blocked, in other words, overblocking. Also, OSPs are intermediaries made liable under computer crime law, which are often not subject to the standards of review common in government mandates. The danger happens when the OSPs work alongside undemocratic regimes in order to set up nationwide content filtering schemes or reveal sensitive information about users. For instance, Yahoo!'s Hong Kong office complied with Chinese government requests for the identity of a user who forwarded a memo documenting government pressure on Chinese journalists to an overseas website. With information from Yahoo!, Chinese authorities arrested journalist Shi Tao and eventually sentenced him to ten years on charges of leaking state secrets (Reporters Without Borders, 2005). Zuckerman (2009) also claimed that OSPs might trade off their business risk and reward with free speech and human rights.

Moreover, Klang (2006) concluded that the threat of privatized censorship of service providers should not be underestimated. Once the opposing view or information is censored, what remains online is a form of consensus. This makes it even more difficult for anyone with an opposing view to speak out. This problem normally occurs in some countries such as China, South Korea, Thailand and Vietnam, where sensitive issues are abundant and significant amount of censorship has been performed according to Faris and Villeneuve (2008). However, in the case of Thailand, over the past two years online censorship has increased in both scale and scope due to political turmoil in 2009 and 2010 affecting tens of thousands of websites by the end of 2010, which turns out to be "Not Free" in the 2011 Internet freedom status of the country and selective political censorship has become substantial (Freedom House, 2011).

INTERNET CENSORSHIP IN THAILAND

The Ministry of Information and Communications Technology (MICT) is the main state agency with the authority to regulate the Internet in Thailand. MICT has used some of the approaches as outlined by ONI researchers to filter Internet content. As shown in Figure 3, the suppression on the dissemination of computer data by Court orders has dramatically increased from 2007 to 2010 according to a local research on control and censorship of online media through the use of laws and the imposition of Thai state policies (iLaw, 2010).

It is obvious that online censorship has steadily been on the rise after the Computer Related Offence Act B.E. 2550 (2007) was enacted in 2007. Particularly, social media services have become prime targets for the censorship due to the open nature and high participation of users who wish to mobilize political action or just share similar ideologies (Bunyavejchewin, 2010). In addition, filtering or censorship is inconsistent, with different Internet service providers (ISPs) blocking different information due to different interpretations of the provisions of the computer crime law in 2007, which are generally vague (ARTICLE 19, 2011). For example, the provisions in Article 14 and 15 of Computer-Related Offence Act B.E. 2550 (2007) allow the prosecution of any service provider who intentionally support or consent to the dissemination of computer data that cause damage or harmful to national security, third party or

Figure 3. Content suppression by Court orders in Thailand (2007 – 2010) (iLaw,2010)

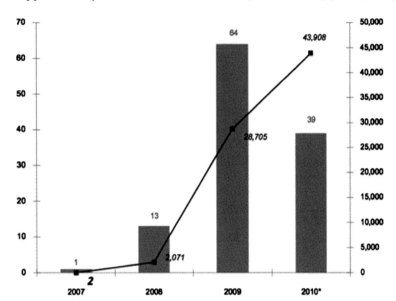

the public. The question is: what type of content is deemed harmful? Akdeniz (2004) stated that the regulation or governance of harmful content might differ from country to country. The criterion on harm depends upon cultural differences.

Sometimes Webmasters or administrators have failed to control the problematic content, considered harmful by the government, and have been charged under Article 15 for content posted by other users on websites or discussion board they hosted. In Thailand, Webmaster or moderators can be sentenced to a maximum of five years imprisonment or a THB 100,000 fine or both according to the provision in Article 15 of Computer-Related Offence Act B.E. 2550 (2007) for intermediary liability.

In March 2009, for instance, Thai police arrested Chiranuch Premchaiporn, the director and moderator of the political news site www.prachatai.com, under Section 15 of the Computer Crimes Act for allegedly allowing a comment defaming the royal family to remain on the site for 20 days (Macan-Markar, 2009; Head, 2009). Observers and critics have noted that lèse majesté is frequently used as a 'political tool to discredit opponents' (ARTICLE 19, 2005). Noticeable consequences are online service providers or OSPs are inevitably induced to control such harmful or potentially problematic content as political dissent, political satire, and sensitive issues including content that are deemed lèse majesté (defaming the royal family). Especially, intermediaries hosted with critical views about the monarchy or politically dissenting viewpoints have resorted to self-censorship to avoid prosecution, resulting in overblocking. Such filtering flaw both infringes users' freedom of expression and impedes the business of OSPs in Thailand. In accordance with the study by Freedom House (2011), Thailand is at particular risk of suffering setbacks related to Internet freedom in 2011 and 2012.

INFLUENCES TO INTERMEDIARY CENSORSHIP

Influence from Governmental Sector

According to Freedom House (2009), censorship could take place through technical filtering, formal or informal government intimidation, requests from private sectors, and judicial decisions. Many regimes around the world have not been accommodating for this novel opportunity as they have made OSPs new choking points for Internet control by transferring to them the liability related to content published online, which Zuckerman (2009) refers to as "intermediary censorship". Sniderman (2011) stated that France's government banned the use of the words "Twitter" and "Facebook" on broadcast news saying that it constituted unsolicited advertising, while U.Kn also end up in enemy hands.

Influence from Private Sector

Censorship has been outsourced to private companies such as Internet Service Providers (ISPs), Online Service Providers (O. government has warned British soldiers about how they use social media lest that informatio SPs), cyber-cafes, and mobile phone operators, to censor and monitor information and communication technologies (ICTs) (Freedom House, 2009). Zuckerman (2009) stated that if the costs exceed the profit margins, which actually are quite tight in a highly competitive market, OSPs are likely to sacrifice a handful of customers in exchange for avoiding legal review.

Influence from Civil Society

Weckert (2000) stated that there are moral justifications for regulation of the media and they should be applied to the Internet as well. In the past, civil society or representatives of non-governmental organizations (NGOs) was not involved in the traditional media. However, in new media era, civil society organizations were increasingly voicing their concerns about many issues to regulate the content on the Internet (Kleinsteuber, 2004). According to Haraszti (2008), business and labor, religious and minority organizations, traditional and newly established interest groups, and individual members of the public could be main providers of complaints or criticism of the media. This complaint mechanism would induce media to preserve editorial freedom on what to report and what opinions to express.

Influence from User

The involvement of governments, industries, users and citizen action groups is crucial for successful regulation (Kleinsteuber, 2004). Kleinsteuber (2004) also stated that users who wanted to utilize the Internet in a civilized way could induce self-regulation or self-censorship of the Internet by using informal code of conduct, so called Netiquette. An example of influence from users to intermediary censorship is family-based filtering, which parents control the Internet content for their children. Akdeniz (2004) indicated that Internet users or parents play an important role to report illegal and harmful content like child pornography to protect children and vulnerable people.

IMPACT OF INTERMEDIARY CENSORSHIP

The impact of intermediary censorship might be more far-reaching than it appears. There are a number of impacts that could be summarized in three main areas as follows:

Impact on Usability and Online Business

When users feel lack of free speech online or cannot speak out in a certain social media service, they would move to another easily and that would diminish the business of the deserted OSP. But if an OSP develops a reputation for aggressively defending user rights particularly right to free expression, it is likely to attract more users who generate infringement claims (Zuckerman, 2009). However, architecture and engineering effort have to be added up with some expense to defend user rights and avoid violating the law in the same time. If the costs exceed profit margins, which actually are quite tight in a highly competitive market, OSPs are likely to sacrifice a handful of customers in exchange for avoiding legal review (Zuckerman, 2009). Therefore, an approach to investigate the over-blocking in intermediaries would be useful to affirm the justification of censorship, which would lead to transparency of filtering scheme of OSPs. This transparency advantage would attract more users and reduce the costs of defending filtering infrastructure required.

Impact on Freedom of Expression

When intermediaries are liable for the content created others, they will strive to reduce their liability risk (Center for Democracy & Technology, 2010). Consequently, they are likely to overcompensate, blocking even lawful content. Freedom of expression is thus restricted by the chilling effect of intermediaries. So when users feel lack of free speech online or cannot speak out in social media, they would move to another easily and that would diminish the business of the OSP itself. But if an OSP develops a reputation for aggressively defending user rights, it is likely to attract more users who generate infringement claims (Zuckerman, 2009). However, infrastructures and engineering effort have to be added up with some expense to defend user rights and avoid violating the law in the same time. Intermediary providers are spared the heavy costs linked to supervision and filtering – technically difficult to implement, of dubious effectiveness and involving significant cost (Council of Europe, 2008; Angelopoulos, 2009). If the costs exceed profit margins, which actually are quite tight in a highly competitive market, OSPs are likely to sacrifice a handful of customers in exchange for avoiding legal review (Zuckerman, 2009).

Impact on Innovation

Center for Democracy & Technology (2010) stated that intermediary liability could create disincentives for innovation in information and communications technologies. Companies could less likely to develop new ICT products and services. It also tends to close the market to start-ups, which are often unable to afford expensive compliance staffs. Many businesses may choose to move to operate in countries where intermediaries are granted broad liability protections, resulting in less foreign direct investment in those countries that do not grant such protections. In addition, Von Hippel (1988) indicated that the emergence of technologies that facilitate information sharing and collaboration could induce user-centered innovation. Since the Internet has increased the amount of creative information available to individuals and businesses with low cost of accessing such information, intermediary censorship in social media could create barriers to information exchange and inhibit potential innovation in several markets.

Montero and Van Enis (2011) conclude that despite a precise and effective technology to filter the content at present, it appears that implementation of a filtering measure difficult to reconcile with the right to freedom of expression. They raise the question: how does the filtering measure work without infringing freedom of expression. An approach is to investigate the over-blocking in intermediaries to affirm the criteria in censorship, which would reflect the transparency of filtering scheme of OSPs. This transparency advantage would shield the intermediary providers from liability actions and reduce cost to undertake supervision and other infrastructure of filtering systems. Consequently, it would thus promote freedom of expression, attract more users and encourage the boom in information society services.

HOW TO COPE WITH PROBLEMATIC AND ILLEGAL CONTENT ON THE INTERNET

Akdeniz (2004) indicated that the approaches to cope with problematic or harmful content are to encourage self-regulatory, content-monitoring schemes, development of rating and filtering schemes, and increase awareness of users. He also suggested that there should be a partnership or co-operation between government and industry including individual Internet users to involve in Internet governance, in other words, co-regulation. The balance of such partnership is vital to both protect Internet users from harmful and illegal content, and respect the rights to freedom of expression of individual Internet users.

According to Kleinsteuber (2004) who authors 'The Internet between regulation and governance', he called co-regulation as regulated self-regulation, where the government does not involve. He suggested that regulated self-regulation is the best way for Internet governance, while conventional law or regulation should be limited as much as possible. This way all relevant stakeholders including representatives of governments, industry, users and citizen action groups can be involved. Without this joint involvement, regulation of Internet will never be successful. Similarly, Marsden (2004) stated that filtering tools to limit access to harmful and illegal content have had only limit success. What is more effective and flexible than censorship by government regulation is co-regulation, which involves multiple stakeholders and balances between government regulation and pure self-regulation. It is vital to keep balance between each actor's participation to achieve intended regulatory objectives of Internet governance.

RESEARCH FRAMEWORK

From the literature review, the research framework is developed as shown in Figure 4. The intermediary censorship in Thailand is influenced by several factors, mainly governmental sector, private or business sector, civil society and user. The content that is to be censored comprises both illegal and problematic content, which is the focus of this research study. It is postulated that the impact of excessive censorship by intermediaries, based on harm issue, would lead to inconvenience and inefficient of Internet use, lack of diversity of opinions, violation of citizen's rights in public sphere and inhibition of innovation.

Illegal and problematic content could be categorized into three groups of context: political, social, and security. Illegal content is basically removed under the computer crime law, while content that tends to be problematic is removed under the judgment of OSPs. Table 2 shows the categories of content subject

Figure 4. Research framework of Intermediary censorship in Thailand

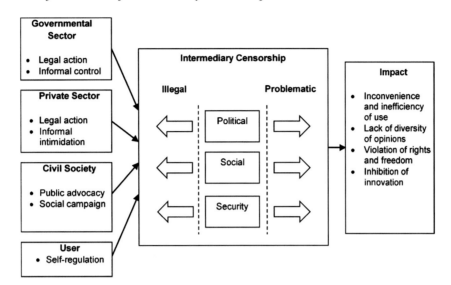

to intermediary censorship based on review of related research and the Computer-Related Offence Act B.E. 2550 (2007). It might be noticed that lèse majesté content is classified under national security group. This is because lèse majesté is classified under 'Offences Relating to the Security of the Kingdom' in Thailand's Section 112 of the Penal Code. Also, Section 8 of the 2007 Constitution indicates as:

The King shall be enthroned in a position of revered worship and shall not be violated. No person shall expose the King to any sort of accusation or action.

This implies that any person commit an offence to the King would commit an offence to the national security as well.

Hate speech is another issue that is unclear and problematic. Oftentimes, it gets mixed up with cyberbullying, of which the meaning is quite similar. However, based on the Additional Protocol to the Convention on Cybercrime (2003), hate speech is defined as 'any written material, any image or any other representation of ideas or theories, which advocates, promotes or incites hatred, discrimination or violence, against any individual or group of individuals, based on race, color, descent or national or ethnic origin, as well as religion if used as a pretext for any of these factors'. On the other hand, cyberbullying is more about harm and harassment in general issues on the Internet. It is a global concerned issue for parents, whose kids spend a lot of their time online these days. In the United States, cyberbullying gets attention from U.S. Federal Legislative Responses as the Megan Meier Cyberbullying Prevention Act (2009) stating that 'Youth who create Internet content and use social networking sites are more likely to be targets of cyberbullying'. This is why cyberbullying is classified only in social category, while hate speech is addressed in all categories.

Table 2. Content subject to intermediary censorship

Content	Illegal	Problematic
Political	-	• Hate speech • Political dissent and satire
Social	• Alcohol and drugs • Defamation • False or forged computer data • Gambling • Piracy • Pornography • Privacy • Prostitution	• Absurdity or nonsensical issue • Commercial use • Conflict • Cyberbullying • Dating • Free expression and media freedom • Hate speech • Human rights • Minority faiths, rights and ethnic • Misuse • Public and health issues • Sensitive or controversial history • Sex education and family planning • Sex orientation / Gender Identity

Security	• National security
	  o Lèse majesté
	  o Religious commentary and criticism
	• Terrorism and separatism
		• Foreign relations and military
		• Hate speech
		• Militants and extremists

Source: Based on review of related research and the Computer-Related Offence Act B.E. 2550 (2007)

MODEL OF INNOVATIVE RETRIEVAL SYSTEM (IRS)

As shown in Figure 4, self-censorship of intermediary in Thailand has not been studied in term of filtering scheme, impact of the business and users, and pattern of censorship in social media. We cannot monitor the self-censorship without a special tool that can monitor missing threads or comments all the time. Therefore, an Innovative Retrieval System (IRS) model is introduced to investigate this study gap expected to promote users' freedom of expression and transparency in social media and to assist the censorship practices of OSPs by exposing the overblocking and criteria used in content censorship. The model of IRS is shown in Figure 5.

There are three modules in the IRS.

Gathering Module

A web crawler or a spider periodically collects data from target websites every five minutes and store the retrieved content in content database. The gathering process can be automated or designated as frequently as possible.

Analyzing Module

The collected data from content database is transferred to the time frame analyzer. In the time frame analyzer, the content is compared to the content collected previously to identify the missing data using standard shortest edit distance method. In this study, the missing content is assumed to be removed by censorship policy of the website owner so it is retrieved and classified by human based on context of

Figure 5. Framework of Innovative Retrieval System (IRS)

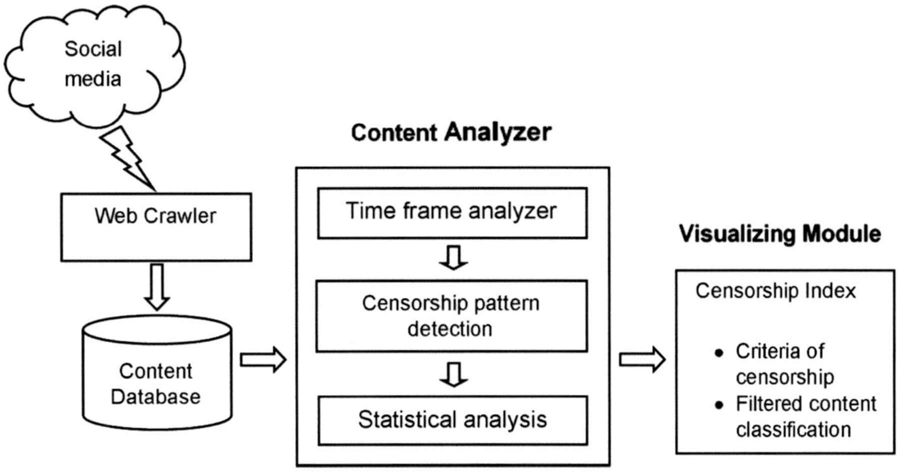

censorship i.e. political, social, or national security. It is also compared against computer law to detect the overblocking. All data are thus analyzed further on statistics of censorship and content filtering pattern that appear in a certain social media.

Visualizing Module

Finally the analyzed data will be reported as 'intermediary censorship index' in the visualizing module. The result includes criteria of censorship, filtered content classification and overblocking. The censorship criteria of social media are also determined to reveal the influences of censorship such as politics, society, and chilling effect.

A CASE STUDY OF PANTIP.COM

Pantip.com is an online social media as it is a public space for any user to share information and content. Despite serving as a form of entertainment space, Pantip.com has also played a vital role in political and social activism due to its popularity, which had attained a traffic rank of 9th in Thailand (Alexa, 2011), and was one of the first websites established in Thailand when the Internet was being introduced in the country in the 1990s. Due to diversity of forums and dynamic participation from users, Pantip.com has faced many issues of illegal content on the website. It has then resorted several tools to limit the adverse effect from illegal content posted by users. One of the most well known filtering schemes is the "one ID one account" policy, which is the process requiring 13-digit national ID number or passport ID number for subscription. Users have to comply with the policy and try not to break the rules of the forum; otherwise they would be banned and could not re-subscribe again. Demographics of users, traffic, policy and current issues of Pantip.com can be summarized as follows:

1. Total number of users is more than 600,000 unique IPs per day.
2. Most registered users are aged between 25-34 years old. Next groups are 35-44, 65+, 45-54, 55-64 and 18-24 years old respectively.
3. There are more female users than male users in the website.
4. The majority of users holds a higher degree than bachelor's degree.
5. Users access the website from their home rather than work and school.

Pantip.com has several features and its subsidiaries e.g. Tech-Exchange, PantipMarket, Chat, Pantown and BlogGang. But the most popular feature of the site is PantipCafe, which consists of 25 separate discussion forums dedicated to particular topic as shown in Table 3.

Table 3. Discussion forums in PantipCafe

Discussion Forum	Description
Siam Square	Teenager
Chalermthai	Entertainment
Chalermkrung	Music and art
Jathujak	Pet, gardening, hobby
Gonkrua	Food and drink
Chaikha	Property, furniture and electrical appliance
Rachada	Car
Maboonkrong	Communication
Supachalasai	Sport
BluePlanet	Travel
Klong	Photography and camera
Suanlumpini	Health
Ruammit	All topics
Toh Krueng Pang	Fashion and cosmetic
Chanruen	Family
Klaiban	Foreign issue
Hongsamut	Book and literature
Sassana	Religion
Whakor	Science and technology
Silom	Business and management
Sinthorn	Finance and investment
Ratchadamnoen	Politics
Sala Prachakom	Social, economic and law issue
Rai Sungkat	Not subject to any tables
Toh Khao	News and current issues

METHOD

A multi-step, multi-method design was used to investigate the removed content on Pantip.com and to analyze types or context, frequency, and influence of censorship. Table 4 summarizes the basic research procedure, along with the methods and research questions associated with each step in the study.

A semi-structured, in-depth interview was conducted with Wanchat Padungrat – managing director – in July 20, 2011 and Worapoj Hirunpraditkul – Webmaster in August 30, 2012. In order to best achieve the aim of answering the research questions relating to intermediary censorship, it was important to use the research framework described above as a guide to data collection. Thus, interview questions were broadly related to the framework. Questions were open-ended giving interviewee the opportunity to develop his answers and to provide narratives as broad as he deemed appropriate.

IRS was used to collect content removed from forums in PantipCafe, which is the most popular feature in Pantip.com. The collection time frame was four days from May 25-28, 2012. Frequency of data collection was every five minutes. Targets of data collection were sampled from four discussion forums in PantipCafe: Chalermthai, Ratchadamnoen, Siamsquare and Toh Khao. These forums were randomly selected. Chalermthai contains entertainment content. Ratchadamnoen contains political content. Siamsquare contains teenager content. Toh Khao contains news or current issues content.

FINDINGS AND ANALYSIS

Step 1: The in-depth interview questions were conducted regarding to the research framework. The data collected were then analyzed descriptively as follows.

Influence from Governmental Sector

In the recent political crisis, Pantip.com has received a few notifications from the ministry of information and communication technology (MICT) and ad-hoc security body like the Center for Resolution in Emergency Situation (CRES) to remove 'problematic' content in the forum. Wanchat admitted that the websites has to comply with the requests regardless of the legal and moral justifications.

There are two times that we received a call from the authorities to take some action on the PantipCafe. The first time was from the MICT and the second was from the military junta.

Table 4. A multi-step, multi-method process to investigate censorship in Pantip.com

Step	Research Questions	Methods
1	What are the criteria of censorship in online social media?	In-depth interview
2	What types of content are filtered by intermediaries?	IRS and Content analysis
	Does overblocking happen in online social media in Thailand?	

Even we have a strict rule about political expression, there will still be a lot of satire, especially in Ratchadamnoen forum. However, we won't censor as long as it is not obviously an infringing content except lèse majesté that we would not let it go.

Influence from Private or Business Sector

Wanchat stated that most of the notifications, follows with legal actions, were not originated from governmental sector, but rather from private sector. And some are not reasonable.

Most of notices are from businesses rather the government. We would consider whether the notices are reasonable. If not, we would keep the content and that could probably cause the lawsuit. We got many lawsuits in a year, mostly about defamation case.

Worapoj also stated that since Pantip.com contains a large amount of commercial content, which oftentimes include infringement or defamation issue, the content would then be deleted immediately to prevent offense under computer law. Worapoj indicated that although defamation issue is not directly addressed in the Computer-Related Offence Act B.E. 2550 (2007) but it could be claimed under Section 326 in the Criminal Code, which states that any person commit an offence in a manner that is likely to impair the third party's reputation or cause that third party to be isolated, disgusted or embarrassed, shall be subject to imprisonment for not longer than one year or a fine of not more than 20,000 baht, or both. This, according to Worapoj, would lead to chilling effect of intermediary like Pantip.com, follows with overblocking in the website even if the take-down notifications were not reasonable.

Influence from Civil Society

Not only does Pantip.com comply with the law, the website also bases its content filtering criteria on issues which are public concern as advocated by civic society particularly children protection groups and other underlying moral standards.

Gambling-related content and other moral concerns are not founded in Pantip.com since we have made clear our policy and have strong filtering schemes against those kind of content. However, commercial use still exists. We usually found that some users post content for their own benefit. Most of them are marketing officer or business owner.

Worapoj indicated that users and civic group should become more involved in regulating the forum to inhibit cyberbullying and other immoral issues. Direct influence or intervention from civil society in Pantip.com is actually hardly found but instead social sanction from user is prevalent.

Influence from User

Pantip.com has built self-regulation scheme in the forum using flagging system. Users can flag the problematic or illegal content to notify the moderator. If the flagging takes place more than three times, the flagged content will be removed. Not only illegal content e.g. pornography or gambling is prohibited, but also absurd or nonsensical content is considered problematic, which tends to be removed from the website.

This is because the great expectation of Pantip.com is to create culture of knowledge and credibility in the website, as Worapoj mentioned. On the other hand, users can notify the good content or comment, same as "like" in Facebook, so the content owner would get self-esteem and award from the websites.

We are usually notified by users who have learnt what is illegal and not acceptable in community. There is social norm in PantipCafe that is strong enough to regulate users' practices and we believe it is a good sign for what is called self-regulation.

Wanchat and Worapoj believe that self-regulation is the way to balance filtering scheme and user's freedom of expression. However, there must be monitoring system by moderator as well. So co-regulation of the website by OSP is the best choice to achieve the Internet governance.

Usually we give users freedom to express their political view. However, in some situation we considered it would cause chaos or heavy conflict in the forum when the debate was too intense or related to security concerns. So, we censored or even shut down some forums, if necessary. We believe in freedom of expression but there should be a limit. I would call regulation rather than filtering. There were many cases that we had to sacrifice some users to keep order of the community and keep our business going.

Step 2: IRS was used to collect the content removed from four forums in PantipCafe. After four days of data collection, it is found that removed content in the four discussion forums comprises both comments and threads as shown in Table 5. Each thread and comment is then coded to classify types of content subject to intermediary censorship as shown in Table 2.

At this point, it is obvious that the trend of censorship in Pantip.com is to remove threads rather than comments. Ratchdamnoen is the only forum that the comments were removed rather than threads. Then all threads and comments were classified by human using method of coding, which is based on context of censorship in review of related research and the Computer-Related Offence Act B.E. 2550 (2007). The results of coded data are shown in Figure 6 - 9.

According to Figure 6, the first fifth highest removed or censored content in Chalermthai forum was conflict, misuse, defamation, absurdity, and miscellaneous content. Chalermthai forum is provided for exchanging the opinions about entertainment in all media. Most opinions usually came from fans of performing artists, television programs, radio programs, or cinemas, which differ in accordance with individual tastes. Consequently, opposing opinions would likely end with debate and conflict, and of-tentimes involve alluding each other. Thus conflict and defamation content were largely removed from

Table 5. Removed content in PantipCafe

Forum	Threads	Comments
Chalermthai	31	9
Ratchadamnoen	18	31
Siamsquare	28	13
Toh Khao	24	10

Figure 6. Removed content in Chalermthai forum

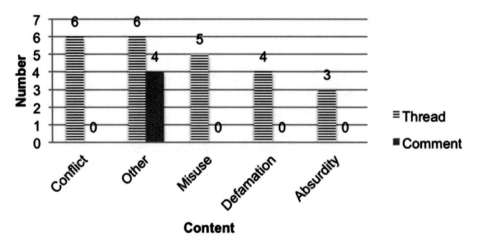

Figure 7. Removed content in Ratchadamnoen forum

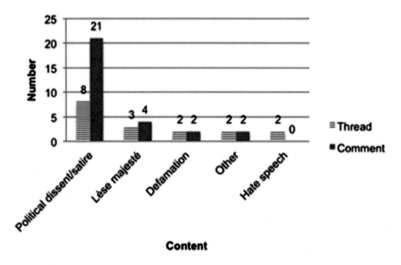

Figure 8. Removed content in Siamsquare forum

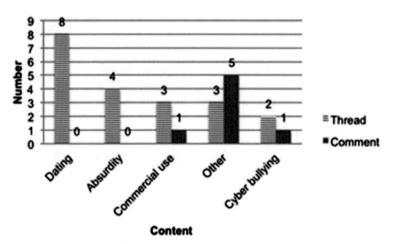

Figure 9. Removed content in Toh Khao forum

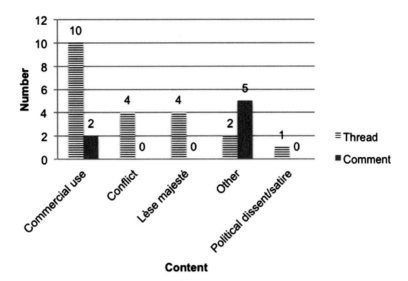

Chalermthai forum. Whereas the advertising and commercial content were also greatly removed as they were considered content misuse, which is prohibited in certain forums in PantipCafe including Chalermthai. In some cases, advertising content concerning artists or TV programs led to conflict of their fans as well. Moreover, it is noticeable that the removed content was mostly threads (blue bar), which implies that problematic or illegal comments were so abundant and interconnected. Thus it is obvious that the pattern of censorship in Chalermthai forum focuses on the conflict of fans.

Ratchadamnoen forum is a space basically provided for political content. This forum oftentimes has debate and conflict among users with different political view. It was occasionally shut down or changed to 'only thread without comment' system depending on the political contest in which Thailand is. Particularly, after military coup in 2006 lèse majesté content in several websites had been suppressed by MICT (Figure 3). Pantip.com had consequently proceeded more rigorous policy on such content resulted in a dramatic drop in the posting of the defamation and lèse majesté content in Ratchadamnoen forum. According to Figure 7, only a few threads and comments about defamation and lèse majesté were removed from the forum, which indicated that there were not many of these sorts of content floating around in the forum. On the other hand, political dissent and satire content were removed significantly showing that these types of content still prevalently remain in the forum. It is noticeable that although political dissent and satire are not illegal but website administrator still did not allow this sort of content to be disseminated in the forum. This apparently shows that Pantip.com has been affected from the chilling effect under the influence of the governmental sector. Furthermore, the removed content was mostly comments instead of threads, which implied that only some comments, not the whole threads, tended to provoke the debate or conflict in the forum. They were more like cyberbullying camouflaged as political opinion. Thus the website administrator tried to keep the conversation in the threads and chose to remove only such problematic comments. Obviously, the pattern of censorship in Ratchadamnoen forum is under chilling effect, focusing on political dissent, satire and cyberbullying.

Siamsquare forum (Figure 8) is basically for adolescent content but it appears that the removed content was mainly about dating and flirting. The researcher thus conducted another in-depth interview with Worapoj to gain additional information about this issue. Worapoj claimed that there were some users in this forum who caused disturbance to other users by continuously changing their login name and posting the same pattern of content of dating and flirting. He stated that the reason of doing that was not found and considered absurdity. Thus the website administrator had kept an eye on these users by monitoring their IP address and would immediately remove their content even it was not illegal. Obviously, the pattern of censorship in Siamsquare forum is targeted censorship focusing on individual users.

Toh Khao forum (Figure 9) is fundamentally provided as an alternative news channel for users who wants to seek additional point of view rather than conventional media channel. However, the content in this forum mostly contained the commercial content such as announcement, advertisement, and public relation. Therefore, this sort of content was removed significantly in the forum due to violation of the policy of the website. In addition, the second-ranking removed content was conflict and lèse majesté content similar to those removed in Ratchadamnoen forum. This might imply that some users avoided posting in Ratchadamnoen forum, which is monitored stringently, and chose to post in Toh Khao forum, which contains several sorts of news-related issues, instead. Thus the pattern of censorship in Toh Khao forum mainly focuses on commercial and illegal content, which was moved from other forums to avoid censorship.

According to categories of content subject to censorship in Table 3, the removed threads and comments in each forum can be categorized into three groups of content: political, social, and national security as shown in Figure 10.

Figure 10 shows that removed content in all forums was social-related issue, excluding Ratchadamnoen forum that mainly removed political content. The result is in accordance with the basic characteristics of each forum as Chalermthai, Siamsquare, and Toh Khao forum are provided for social issue e.g. adolescence, entertainment, and news while Ratchadamnoen forum is provided for political issue. Moreover, it is obvious that threads in social forums like Chalermthai, Siamsquare, and Toh Khao were more removed than comments whereas comments in Ratchadamneon forum were more removed than threads. These findings may be analyzed as follows:

1. Users tended to avoid stringent policy in Ratchadamneon forum and moved to post problematic or illegal threads in other forums instead. Thus the number of removed threads in this forum was low comparing with those in other forums.

Figure 10. Censorship in Chalermthai, Ratchadamnoen, Siamsquare, and Toh Khao

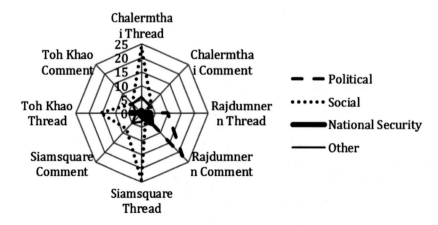

2. As described earlier, some users in Ratchadamneon forum are cyberbullies and tried to provoke the debate and conflict in camouflaged as political opinion. They avoided being censored by posting comments rather than threads because comments are usually hidden in different page view from threads. These problematic comments are also commonly posted in a popular thread, as they are hard to be found especially in the webpage structure of Pantip.com where new comment will be posted at the bottom of the page, not the top. It thus turned out that the illegal content or conflict often happened at the very bottom of the page in a thread. The more comments a thread had, the possibility of the conflict happened. Therefore, as shown in Figure 11, there are a large number of comments in Ratchadamnoen forum considered problematic under judgment of website administrator, which tended to remove such comments solely, not the whole thread.

3. Chalermthai, Siamsquare, and Toh Khao forum were monitored in less stringent manner than Ratchadamneon forum. Illegal or problematic content thus tended to be posted in both threads and comments. Most threads, therefore, were removed as website administrator who chose to end the illegal or problematic content at the beginning without opportunities for users to share any conversation in comments at all.

The situation of thread removal also represents the infringement of freedom of expression since those removed thread usually contains not illegal comments, which were impacted from censorship inevitably. Some removed threads contained more than 40 comments with only few illegal or problematic comments.

Lastly, according to research framework in Figure 4, all removed content can be classified into two groups under determinant of removal: illegal and problematic content as shown in Figures 11-15.

It is obvious that the majority of removed content in all four forums was problematic content, which was not illegal but potentially harmful under the judgment of website administrator. The remainder was illegal content, which was only a quarter or less from overall removed content. For instance, 73% of problematic content was removed under judgment of website administrator whereas 27% of illegal content was removed in Chalermthai forum. Similarly, 78% and 79% of problematic content was re-

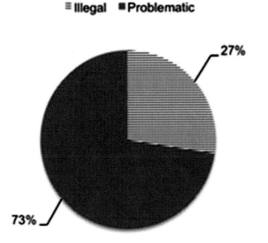

Figure 11. Determinant of removal in Chalermthai

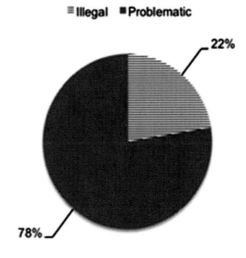

Figure 12. Determinant of removal in Ratchad-amnoen

Figure 13. Determinant of removal in Siamsquare   *Figure 14. Determinant of removal in Toh Khao*

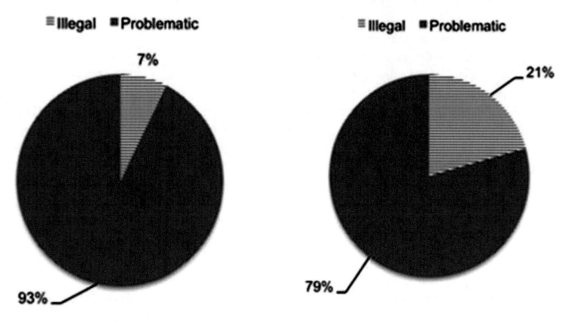

Figure 15. Determinant of removal in all four forums

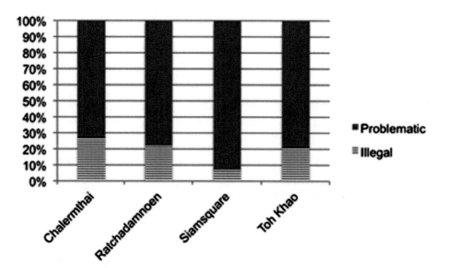

moved respectively under judgment of website administrator whereas 22% and 21% of illegal content was removed in Ratchadamneon and Toh Khao forum respectively. Particularly in Siamsquare forum, the problematic content was removed up to 93% while the illegal content was removed only 7%.

It is the problematic content that indicates the overblocking or excessive removal of content in a website. In the case of Pantip.com, removal of problematic content in each forum could indicate the overblocking level as overblocking score. The higher the overblocking score is, the more problematic the judgment of website administrator is. Thus overblocking score of four forums would be summarized in Table 6.

Table 6. Overblocking score of four forums in Pantip.com

Forum	Illegal content removal (%)	Overblocking score (%)
Chalermthai	27	73
Ratchadamneon	22	78
Siamsquare	7	93
Toh Khao	21	79

It appeared that Chalermthai forum had the lowest overblocking score (73) indicating that censorship practice in this forum was the best among other four forums. Whereas Siamsquare forum had the highest overblocking score (93) indicating that censorship practice in this forum was the worst among other four forums.

DISCUSSION

As mentioned earlier, Internet filtering schemes are usually generated through a combination of manual and automatic search for targeted content. The error, thus, could happen from both human error and technological limit. In the same way, this research has shown the error of filtering scheme in Pantip.com with the high level of overblocking. As designed to collect output data on the webpage, IRS gathers only what is removed by the secondary manual filtration, not the primary automatic filtration in back office of the website. The secondary manual filtration is proceeded under the judgment of website administrator, which is basically subjective and potentially inaccurate according to Weckert (2000) and CDT (2012) stating that nowadays there is no effective technology or enough resources, both human and financial, to provide a certain Internet content filtering.

High level of overblocking in Pantip.com also implies that OSP tried to protect its interests rather than users' interests, which is similar to the statement of Wanchat and Worapoj indicating that it is acceptable to sacrifice some users to protect the social order in the website and to keep the business run. Similarly, Zuckerman (2009) stated that OSPs might cut off some users to avoid legal review and avoid adding up some expense in filtration if it affects to the profit margins of the business. In addition, Pantip.com has tried to build self-regulation scheme and involved multiple stakeholders in order to create co-regulation according to Akdeniz (2004), Kleinsteuber (2004), and Marsden (2004) stating that co-regulation with all relevant stakeholders, for instance governmental sector, private or business sector, civil society, and users, is more effective and flexible than censorship by conventional law or government regulation. However, the level of overblocking of Pantip.com is still high. This might be because of what is called chilling effect as mentioned earlier, which attributes to three main factors as follow:

1. Chilling effect from government interference. According to Kleinsteuber (2004), co-regulation is the best way for Internet governance where the government is not involved. In case of Pantip.com, Wanchat and Worapoj accepted that there were intimidations from the governmental sector and the military junta (during the coup period in 2006).

2. Chilling effect from threats of lawsuits. Wanchat stated that Pantip.com has received several notices or lawsuits concerning the problematic content. He accepted that it is necessary to remove such problematic content if the litigation expenses exceed the legal budget of the website.

3. Chilling effect from intermediary liability provision in computer crime law. The provisions in Article 14 and 15 of Computer-Related Offence Act B.E. 2550 (2007) allow the prosecution of any service provider who intentionally support or consent to the dissemination of computer data that cause damage or harmful to national security, third party or the public. It is not clear what type of content is deemed harmful as ARTICLE 19 (2011) indicating that filtering or censorship is inconsistent due to different interpretations of the provisions of the computer crime law, which are generally vague. Also, OSP like Pantip.com is suppressed by fear of heavy penalty (imprisonment for not more than five years or a fine of not more than one hundred thousand baht or both under the provision in Article 15 for intermediary liability) as CDT (2012) also indicated that chilling effect could happen in the level of intermediary due to fear of potential liability.

CONCLUSION

This research shows that overblocking is still prevalent in Pantip.com even though co-regulation is administered. It is because of chilling effect attributing to several influences intervening censorship practices of the website. However, external influences are not only the problems in intermediary censorship, it is also the criteria of censorship that could not be overlooked. With different judgment of website administrator, the criteria of censorship would be inconsistent. In case of Pantip.com, it is apparently found that pattern of censorship is quite different in each forum depending on several factors e.g. types of content and users characteristics. Even in the same website, the criteria of censorship are dissimilar in each forum. Consequently, users cannot acknowledge whether their content disseminating to the public will be censored or not or under which criteria.

Therefore, the IRS aims to identify pattern of censorship and to increase accountability and transparency of OSPs to users, which would likely contribute to not only users' informed judgment in use selection of social media websites but also to users' freedom of expression. However, government interference and intermediary liability provision in computer crime law causing the chilling effect to OSPs are likely to be main obstacles threatening not only ingenious communication of the public, but also Internet business, innovation, and economic growth. The investment and growth in the Internet industry in Thailand would be deterred as long as these obstacles remain.

LIMITATION

This research has three main limitations.

1. Limitation on IRS investigation. The IRS is an application collecting removed content on the webpages to study online censorship. Such removed content including illegal and problematic content will be categorized for analysis on over-blocking of the websites. However, there still be some illegal content that is not removed from the websites, which is called underblocking. This

underblocking rate will be another indicator showing how websites manage the content among the provision of the computer crime law.

2.   Limitation on the social media platform. The IRS is not a universal compatible platform. Since each social media on the Internet has been built in different architecture and platform, IRS has to be tailor-made for every website. This first version of IRS is designed only for Pantip.com.

3.   Limitation on the scope of the study. As mention earlier, government interference and intermediary liability provision in computer crime law causing chilling effect to OSPs are likely to be main obstacles for communication of the public. This study only indicates the problem but does not go through the solution.

RECOMMENDATIONS

1.   This study only focuses on censorship in social media. Thus over-blocking has been researched for constructing censorship index, showing how websites manage the content. However, underblocking should be studied to fulfill the other side of censorship because the website that does not block at all, absolute freedom, is not good as well. The future study should focus on illegal and problematic content that is not blocked in social media.

2.   Since each social media has different platform, for instance web board and social networking, technology on IRS architecture could be further researched for universal compatibility with every website.

3.   The research has found the causes and problems of censorship but has not go through the solution due to the limitation on scope of study. The future study should focus on how intermediary liability provision in computer crime law could be amended to protect OSPs from chilling effect. Also, prevention of government interference should be studied to find a solution for Internet business in Thailand.

REFERENCES

Additional Protocol to the Convention on Cybercrime. (2003). *Concerning the criminalisation of acts of a racist and xenophobic nature committed through computer systems.* Council of Europe. Retrieved July 19, 2013, from http://conventions.coe.int/Treaty/en/ Treaties/Word/189.doc

Akdeniz, Y. (2004). Who watches the Watchmen? The role of filtering software in Internet content regulation. In C. Moller & A. Amouroux (Eds.), *The Media Freedom Internet Cookbook* (pp. 101–121). Vienna: Academic Press.

Alexa. (2011). Top sites in Thailand. *Alexa.* Retrieved July 21, 2013, from http://www.alexa.com/top-sites/countries/

Article 19. (2005). Freedom of expression and the media in Thailand. *Article 19.* Retrieved July 22, 2013, from http://www.article19.org/data/files/pdfs/publications/thailand-baseline-study.pdf

Article 19. (2009). Impact of defamation law on freedom of expression in Thailand. *Article 19.* Retrieved July 24, 2013, from http://www.article19.org/data/files/pdfs/analysis/thailand-impact-of-defamation-law-on-freedom-of-expression.pdf

Article 19. (2011). Article 19's Submission to the UN Universal Periodic Review: Kingdom of Thailand. *Article 19.* Retrieved June 29, 2013, from http://www.refworld.org/docid/4d8073465b9.html

Bangkok Post. (2009, January 6). Web censoring needs a debate. *Bangkok Post.* Retrieved June 23, 2013, from http://www.bangkokpost.com/opinion/opinion/9202/

Bunyavejchewin, P. (2010). Internet politics: Internet as a political tool in Thailand. *Canadian Social Science, 6*(3), 67–72.

CDT. (2012). *Shielding the messengers: CDT travels to Thailand to argue against intermediary liability.* Center for Democracy & Technology (CDT). Retrieved July 19, 2013, from https://www.cdt.org/blogs/kevin-bankston/0504shielding-messengers-cdt-travels-thailand-argue- against-intermediary-liabil

Deibert, R. J. (2009). The geopolitics of Internet control: Censorship, sovereignty, and cyberspace. In A. Cbadwick & P. N. Howard (Eds.), *The Routledge Handbook of Internet Politics* (pp. 323–336). New York: Routledge.

Faris, R., & Villeneuve, N. (2008). Measuring global Internet filtering. In R. J. Deibert, J. G. Palfrey, R. Rohozinski, & J. Zittrain (Eds.), *Access Denied: The Practice and Policy of Global Internet Filtering* (pp. 5–27). Cambridge, MA: MIT Press.

Freedom House. (2009). Freedom on the Net: A global assessment of Internet and digital media. *Freedom House.* Retrieved June 30,2013, from http://www.freedomhouse.org/uploads/specialreports/NetFreedom2009/FreedomOnTheNet_FullReport.pdf

Head, J. (2009, March 6). Police arrest Thai website editor. *BBC News.* Retrieved June 21,2013, from http://news.bbc.co.uk/mobile/i/bbc_news/asia_pacific/792/79281/story7928159.shtml

iLaw. (2010). Situational report on control and censorship of online media, through the use of laws and the imposition of Thai state policies. *iLaw.* Retrieved June 27,2013, from http://www.scribd.com/doc/44962197/Situational-Report-on-Control-and-Censorship-of-Online-Media-through-the-Use-of-Laws-and-the-Imposition-of-Thai-State-Polocies

Klang, M. (2006). Social informatics: An information soceity for all? IFIP International Federation for Information Processing, 223, 185-194.

Kleinsteuber, H. J. (2004). The Internet between regulation and governance. In C. Moller & A. Amouroux (Eds.), *The Media Freedom Internet Cookbook* (pp. 61–75). Vienna: Academic Press.

Lessig, L. (1999). *Codes and other laws of cyberspace.* New York: Perseus Book.

Macan-Markar, M. (2009, March 8). Media-Thailand: Police target websites unflattering to royalty. *IPS.* Retrieved July 1,2013, from http://www.ipsnews.net/news.asp?idnews=46023

MacKinnon, R. (2009). Chinas censorship 2.0: How companies censor bloggers. *First Monday, 14*(2), 2089. doi:10.5210/fm.v14i2.2378

Marsden, C. (2004). Co- and self-regulation in European media and Internet sectors: The results of Oxford university's study. In C. Moller & A. Amouroux (Eds.), The Media Freedom Internet Cookbook (pp. 76–100). Vienna: Academic Press. Retrieved from www.selfregulation.info

Megan Meier Cyberbullying Prevention Act (2009). H.R. 1966, 111th Congress.

OpenNet Initiative. (n.d.). *About filtering*. Retrieved June 15, 2013, from http://opennet.net/about-filtering

Reporters Without Borders. (2005, September 6). Information supplied by Yahoo! Helped journalist Shi Tao get 10 years in prison. *Reporter Without Borders*. Retrieved June 17, 2013, from http://www.rsf.org/article.php3?id_article=14884

Weckert, J. (2000). What is so bad about Internet content regulation? *Ethics and Information Technology, 2*(2), 105–111. doi:10.1023/A:1010077520614

Zuckerman, E. (2009). Intermediary censorship. In R. J. Deibert, J. G. Palfrey, R. Rohozinski, & J. Zittrain (Eds.), *Access Controlled: The Shaping of Power, Rights, and Rule in Cyberspace* (pp. 71–85). Cambridge, MA: MIT Press.

Chapter 6
Semantic Approach to Web-Based Discovery of Unknowns to Enhance Intelligence Gathering

Natalia Danilova
City University London, UK

David Stupples
City University London, UK

ABSTRACT

A semantic Web-based search method is introduced that automates the correlation of topic-related content for discovery of hitherto unknown intelligence from disparate and widely diverse Web-sources. This method is in contrast to traditional search methods that are constrained to specific or narrowly defined topics. The method is based on algorithms from Natural Language Processing combined with techniques adapted from grounded theory and Dempster-Shafer theory to significantly enhance the discovery of related Web-sourced intelligence. This paper describes the development of the method by showing the integration of the mathematical models used. Real-world worked examples demonstrate the effectiveness of the method with supporting performance analysis, showing that the quality of the extracted content is significantly enhanced comparing to the traditional Web-search approaches.

INTRODUCTION

The quality of decisions made in business and government correlates directly to the quality of the information used to support these decisions. Most of the information used for intelligence analysis may, in the future, be harvested from the Web as this is fast becoming the richest source. An organisation's Intranet knowledge base can be efficiently searched using enterprise search systems based upon either semantics such as ontologies, or meaning-based computing. These technologies require comprehensive (and often automatic) clustering, indexing and tagging of the Intranet knowledge base information. The

DOI: 10.4018/978-1-5225-2058-0.ch006

existing Web, as originally envisaged by Berners-Lee (2001), was expected to form into a Semantic Web, that encourages simply the inclusion of semantic content in Web-pages, making it both human readable and machine readable. However, most of the current Web remains poorly semantically tagged, making it impossible to apply enterprise search methods for Web-based information extraction.

Traditional information retrieval often violates one of the fundamental laws associated with handling complexity. One of them is the "Law of Requisite Variety" (Ashby, 1956), which states that only variety can master variety, reducing disturbances and promoting harmonious order. When applied to the task of Web-based discovery of unknowns, if the retrieval algorithm does not involve enough variety to deal with the scope and complexity of the Web, its results appear to be attenuated, thus losing information in the process. In effect, we need to identify a search solution for the Web that can handle the vast variety and quantity of information involved and then to filter relevant Web-pages of high quality and discarding information that is either too topically remote or irrelevant information noise.

The main contribution of this paper is that it addresses this variety search issue and presents a novel semantic approach method to Web-based discovery of previously unknown intelligence. It provides a comprehensive theoretical background to the proposed solution together with as demonstration of the effectiveness of the method from results of the experiments, showing how the quality of collected information can be significantly enhanced.

The rest of the paper contains research background on Web-based search of unknowns, detailed discussion on the semantic approach, results of real-world experiments, and post-analysis and conclusions.

BACKGROUND ON WEB-BASED SEARCH OF UNKNOWNS

If the Web is to be used for improving decision-making, then a more effective search method is needed to collect and correlate the best information.

Government and business decisions are made with varying degrees of certainty. Donald Rumsfeld (2002) stated: "There are 'known knowns' – that is things we know we know; there are 'known unknowns' – that is some things we know we do not know; but there are also 'unknown unknowns' – that is things we don't know we don't know." Effective decision-making requires trusted, focused and relevant information. We should be comfortable with both 'known knowns' (KKs) and 'known unknowns' (KUs), as these are straightforward to find. The problem being that much of the rich information required for good decisions may be in the category of 'unknown unknowns' (UUs). So an important question to ask is how can we find the relevant UUs to enrich the knowledge on the topic, reduce the associated uncertainty and improve decision-making (Figure 1)?

Recent research projects aimed at discovery of UUs focus primarily on ontology-based knowledge acquisition techniques. Lehmann et al. (2007) presented a new user interface 'DBpedia' to explore a large ontology-based data set by finding connections between different objects, thus, discovering UUs. The core of DBpedia is in the form of an ontology that represents background knowledge comprising structured information extracted from Wikipedia. However, this solution is limited to searches within the DBpedia data set only.

Further work in the discovery of UUs was undertaken by the TORISHIKI-KAI project (Torisawa et al., 2010) which displays all relevant keywords extracted from a large Web-archive as having a particular semantic relationship to the search topic. Even though TORISHIKI-KAI summarises a large volume

Figure 1. Discovery of unknowns reduces uncertainty and enhances decision quality

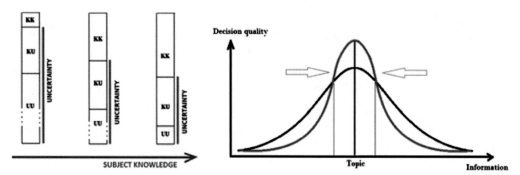

of Web documents, the search system is designed to suggest relevant UUs under just three semantic categories: troubles, methods and tools.

Another noteworthy method is the 'Pattern-based Understanding and Learning System' (PULS) which is designed to extract news information from several domains (Huutunen et al, 2012). Its Web-crawler finds relevant articles using a keyword-based Web-search. The rule-based information extraction module analyses the plain text from the news feed and transforms this text into database records. Its declassifier determines the relevance of the selected events to a particular use.

In contrast to the above identified research, which tends to focus on specifically selected topics, the solution presented in this paper has no limitations for Web-sources and is open to perform search and analysis through any Web-page available to the search engine. This new search method may be used to harvest Web-wide data in accordance with controlled parameters and subsequently transfer this data to a knowledge base where enterprise search technologies may be applied in the traditional way.

DETAILED DISCUSSION ON THE SEMANTIC APPROACH

The proposed method comprises three integrated processes that operate iteratively (see Figure 2). First, the application of Natural Language Processing (NLP) methods enables the filtering of Web-search results to form a set of relevant information, thus overcoming the traditional search engine keyword and ranking mechanisms that limit the search scope as a result of using meaning-based parameters. Thus, the captured sets of KKs, KUs and UUs are semantically related and, therefore, relevant to the search topic being considered. The resulting set of pages is subjected to an application of grounded theory

Figure 2. General level process flow diagram

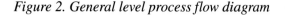

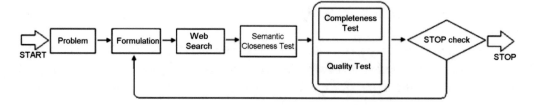

where UUs are specifically identified and used to test the completeness of evidence. The last process sees the application of the Dempster-Shafer theory which tests the quality of gathered information and subsequently sets a quality figure for the efficacy of the eventual decision. The three processes together are applied iteratively to the Web with an expanding query base using converted UUs to identify the best information for inclusion in the final information set. The algorithm can be seen as divided into two parts – preparation and main.

Collecting the Data and its Preparation for Analysis

The preparation involves the definition of the intelligence requirement. Initial target knowledge and search objectives are identified manually by analysts and recorded in text format. This text comprises the KKs and KUs in preparation for the initial search. An initial set of queries is formulated and a traditional search engine is used to create a list of Web-search results. Three steps are involved: formulation, Web-search, and search results pre-processing.

Step 1 (Formulation)

Information search, regardless of the environment, can be seen as following a sequence of actions. On any topic the information source content is compared against the explicit and tacit knowledge of the searching analyst. Regardless of the source, the information discovery process is always accompanied by conversion of UUs into KUs and KKs. At this stage it is important to identify all available explicit knowledge on the search topic in order to understand the information need. This is related to semantic closeness or the level of confidence assigned to a given document and may allow calculating its quality value. Hence, all the knowledge available on the search topic is collected, written in natural language and recorded in a single text file. The list of associated queries for the search topic is held separately. Each query is used with a Web-search engine. The above procedure is undertaken in a traditional manner with each query associated with a single iteration of the search and analysis process. Thus, the set of KKs forms the initial knowledge base and the queries contain KUs and reflect the information need as part of the uncertainty of the search topic. The rest of the uncertainty is formed by UUs and remains unidentified as shown in Figure 1.

Step 2 (Web-Search)

Google is used for this research as it has a substantial Web-based index. Our task was to build not only accurate, but also complete evidence, and we take advantage of Google's keyword search algorithm that ignores content duplication resulting in up to 1000 unique Web-pages in the search results list. Any of the search results that are irrelevant to the search topic expressed in the knowledge base will be removed later. Each query corresponds to a single iteration. The resulting list of Web-pages found by Google in response to the query then progresses for pre-processing. The extraction of the final list of links from a Google search results is a semi-automated process and involves analysis of source pages. Link extraction is a universal way of scraping Google search results that can be adapted to the frequent changes in Google system. The list of links to Web-pages is recorded in a separate text file. The links follow the same order as they appear in the search engine results.

Step 3 (Search Results Pre-Processing)

Starting from the beginning of the link list, each Web-page is opened. The Web contains a significant volume of valuable information. However, in practice, due to the complicated and flexible layout, the main content of a Web-page is accompanied by noisy information (such as advertisement, decoration, navigation bar/list, etc.). We are interested in the main content only. Our filtering method employs AlchemyAPI software (http://www.alchemyapi.com/) for the extraction of the main content. Once the content is extracted, it is parsed for stop-words to eliminate frequently used words, thus, leaving only those that form up the meaning. Out of several stop-word extraction techniques available in NLP applications (Van Rijsbergen 1979; Luhn 1958; Fox 1990), we have selected a classic list of 250 stop-words proposed by van Rijsbergen (1979) to create an approach that is applicable to any subject domain. After the stop-words are removed from the text, the content is passed to the "main part" of analysis and processing.

Applying the Main Processing to the Collected Data

The main part comprises a combination of three integrated processes. First, the application of NLP methods enables the filtering of Web-search results to form a set of KKs, KUs and UUs that are semantically close to the meaning of the search topic. This part of the method combines statistical and semantic approaches to analyse texts for semantic relatedness. In addition, the collected evidence is assessed for completeness and quality.

Step 4 (Natural Language Processing)

The NLP element calculates the semantic distance between the initial knowledge base and each of the Web-search results. The issue associated with information retrieval lies in the diversity of the language different people use to describe same subject. Hitherto, there have been a number of knowledge-based measures to estimate semantic distance between words or concepts. These measures can be classified as (1) lexical – measures that rely on the structure of a knowledge source; and (2) distributional – measures that rely on the distributional hypothesis, which states that two words are semantically close if they tend to occur in similar contexts (Firth, 1957). For this research, we have chosen a hybrid approach proposed by Mohammad and Hirst (2006) and Mohammad (2008) that combines the co-occurrence statistics of a distributional measure with the information in a lexical resource. The concept distance is calculated as the distance between the Distributional Profiles (DPs) of concepts – vectors that represent strength of association (SOA) values between words and concept for a given text. The closer the distributional profiles of two concepts, the smaller is their semantic distance. For the lexical source we use Roget's Thesaurus (www.roget.org) that, in contrast to traditionally used WordNet (Fellbaum, 1998), classifies all English words into 1044 categories.

Each single Web-page's text from the list of search results is further analysed and compared against the initial knowledge base text. The algorithm starts with creating SOA matrices for the both texts. The SOA matrix of the initial knowledge base remains the same throughout the whole iteration. The words within the text are associated with corresponding concepts in Roget's Thesaurus. A Text-Concept Matrix (TCM) is built. The columns represent 1044 concepts from the Thesaurus and the rows represent the n_u unique words within the text. Thus, the TCM matrix has dimensions $[n_u \times 1044]$. Each cell contains either a "1" indicating that the word is associated with the Thesaurus concept or "0" otherwise. Using the TCM, a Word-Concept Co-occurrence Matrix (WCCM) is created by placing word types "*w*" as one dimension and Thesaurus categories "*c*" as the other. The resulting matrix is of the size [*N* x 1044], where *N* is the number of all words in the texts excluding stop-words. The WCCM is of the type:

	c_1	c_2	...	c_j	...
w_1	m_{11}	m_{12}	...	m_{1j}	...
w_2	m_{21}	m_{22}	...	m_{2j}	...
...	...	...	...	...	...
w_i	m_{i1}	m_{i2}	...	m_{ij}	...
...	...	...	...	...	...

To build the WCCM, the text is parsed for the words that are positioned within a text window of ±5 words of the target word. The values for these neighbour 10 words are then found in the TCM and the rows summed. Thus, each value C_{ij} corresponds to a number of times a word w_i co-occurred with any word listed under the category c_j within the text window of ±5 words. A contingency table is generated for every word and Thesaurus category – the cells for all other words and categories are joined into one and their frequencies summed. The contingence table is of the type:

	c	$\neg c$
w	n_{wc}	$n_{\neg w}$
$\neg w$	$n_{\neg c}$	$n_{\neg \neg}$

The contingency table calculates the conditional probabilities $P(w|c)$ that a word w co-occurs with a concept c within the text window. The conditional probability values form the SOA matrix as part of calculating of DPs of concepts. The augmented list of unique words in both texts is created to ensure the DP vectors for both texts are of the same dimension. The list is sorted in alphabetical order, and for each vector its elements (SOA values) follow the order of the corresponding words in the augmented list of unique words.

Before calculating the semantic closeness between the two texts, we calculate the similarity between each of the concepts in the two texts. Based on a detailed survey of semantic distance measures (Mohammad & Hirst, 2006), we have chosen the adapted Cosine method to estimate distributional distance between two concepts to accommodate the highest level of correlation with human rated word pairs of automatic rankings (Rubenstein & Goodenough, 1965). The Cosine similarity is an accepted measure of similarity between two vectors that measures the Cosine of the angle between them. Given two vectors of attributes, *A* and *B*, the Cosine similarity $Cos(\theta)$ is calculated using a dot product and magnitude:

$$Cos(\theta) = \frac{A \cdot B}{\|A\|\|B\|} = \frac{\sum_{i=1}^{n} A_i \times B_i}{\sqrt{\sum_{i=1}^{n}(A_i)^2} \times \sqrt{\sum_{i=1}^{n}(B_i)^2}} \ . \tag{1}$$

In essence, vectors A and B are DPs of two concepts. The attributes of each of the vector are SOA values as per the DP. Out of n unique words in the list some words belong to both texts, but have the corresponding SOA values. As per (Mohammad and Hirst, 2006) the Cosine distributional distance measure for two concepts c_1 and c_2 is denoted by:

$$Cos(c_1, c_2) = \frac{\sum_{w \in C(c_1) \cup C(c_2)} (P(w \mid c_1) \times P(w \mid c_2))}{\sqrt{\sum_{w \in C(c_1)} (P(w \mid c_1))^2} \times \sqrt{\sum_{w \in C(c_2)} (P(w \mid c_2))^2}}, \tag{2}$$

where $w \in C(c)$ is the set of words that co-occur with concepts and within a text window of ± 5 words in both texts. Thus, (2) measures the semantic distance between each concept from each text, and treats the distributional profiles of concepts as vectors of the size equal to the number of all unique words in both texts. Conditional probabilities $P(w|c)$ are used as SOA between each word and each concept in both texts, and are taken from the DPs of concepts. The value for Cosine measure lies between 0 and 1, indicating semantic remoteness of two concepts when the value approaches 0 (orthogonal vectors) and semantic closeness when the value is close to 1.

The use of Thesaurus categories as concepts allows pre-computing of all concept distance values required in a form of concept-concept distance matrix of a size much smaller than word-word distance matrix. The results are recorded in a form of a matrix with dimension [1044 x 1044].

Having obtained the semantic distances between each of the concepts in each of the texts, it is possible to define the semantic closeness between the initial knowledge base and the Web-page text. We have adapted the formula for measuring similarity between texts, proposed by Corley et al. (2006). Their original method measures the semantic similarity between two texts by exploiting the information that can be drawn from the similarity of the component words. This research specifically adapts their method by involving concept-to-concept distance instead of word-to-word distance (Danilova & Stupples, 2012). The similarity between the two texts T_1 and T_2 is determined using the following function:

$$sim(T_1, T_2) = \frac{1}{2} \left(\frac{\sum_{c \in \{T_1\}} (\max Sim(c, T_2) * idf(c))}{\sum_{c \in \{T_1\}} idf(c)} + \frac{\sum_{c \in \{T_2\}} (\max Sim(c, T_1) * idf(c))}{\sum_{c \in \{T_2\}} idf(c)} \right). \tag{3}$$

First, for each concept c in the initial knowledge base text T_1 we identify the concept in the candidate text T_2 that has the highest semantic similarity $\max Sim(c, T_2)$, according to Cosine measure results $Cos(c_1, c_2)$ as per (2). Next, the same process is applied to determine the most semantically close concepts in T_2 compared to the concepts in T_1 $\max Sim(c, T_1)$. The concept similarities are then weighted with the corresponding concept idf. Finally, concept similarities are summed up, and the resulting scores are combined using an average. The semantic closeness has value between 0 and 1; the closer the value is to 1, the closer the texts are in their meaning. If the Web-page text is semantically close to the initial knowledge base text by at least 85% threshold, then the Web-page text is passed on to the second stage of the framework algorithm – the grounded theory analysis.

Step 5 (Grounded Theory Analysis)

The volume of information that would be considered enough to build the evidence leading to sensible decision making is unknown. However, we assume that the topic is exhausted if no new information can be added, or if new information does not significantly enhance the knowledge known on the topic. Grounded theory (Martin & Turner, 1986), (Corbin & Strauss, 2008) has been successfully used for building a hypothesis (theory) using interviews. Grounded theory is a systematic methodology from the social sciences involving the generation of intelligence evidence from data. An important characteristic of grounded theory is that it does not use any prior information, and that it builds theory only based on information that is obtained throughout the research, making it suitable in the context of evidence building with very limited prior information. We apply grounded theory to analyse the amount of new information coming from the Web-pages and to test the completeness of gathered information. Only the information from the initial knowledge base is classified as known. Every Web-page that is considered relevant at the previous stage of the algorithm is compared to the knowledge base and analysed for the amount of new concepts within the text of this Web-page. Grounded theory is an integral part in our approach to identify the set of UUs in newly gathered information through comparison of the conversion rate of KUs and UUs (new concepts) into KKs (evidence). Total knowledge on a topic K_{total} is the collection of all three sets. It is the sum of initial knowledge base concepts KK_0, initial search objective concepts KU_0, while 'unknown unknowns' UU_0 are undefined:

$$K_{total}\left(0\right) = KK_0 + KU_0 + UU_0. \tag{4}$$

After each iteration, newly identified concepts are added to the initial knowledge base, thus expanding the evidence:

$$K_{total}\left(i\right) = K_{total}\left(i-1\right) + KU_i, \tag{5}$$

where "KUs" represent new concepts on each iteration, and $KU(i-1) \neq KU(i)$. A change in KU represents the conversion rate $\delta(KU)$ of new concepts in evidence and is defined as:

$$\delta(KU) = KU_i - KU_{(i-1)}. \tag{6}$$

If $\delta(KU) > 0$, then there are still possible concepts that can be identified for evidence expansion. If $\delta(KU) < 0$, then we are not identifying new information and can assume that the topic is tending to exhaustion. Conversion rate (6) is used to analyse the change in new concepts after each iteration. The comparison is done for the cumulative amount of new concepts calculated for previously checked Web-pages' content added to the initial knowledge base. In conjunction with quality test (Step 6), conversion rate provides a basis for the decision of acceptance of the Web-page content. When $\mid \delta(KU) \mid \approx 0$ and the conversion function converges to a number, we can consider that the search topic is exhausted. Having identified the effect of the information from the Web-page on the completeness of the initial knowledge base, quality of the Web-page is then tested.

Step 6 (Evidence Quality Test)

Evidential analysis is fundamental to the practice of intelligence analysis and requires the ability to represent, store, and manipulate evidence. We apply evidential analysis to estimate the quality of collected information, hence, setting a quality parameter for the efficacy of the eventual decision-making. There are a variety of formal theories we could have used for this purpose. We have chosen Dempster-Shafer theory of evidence (Dempster, 1968), (Shafer, 1976) as it is a well-understood, formal framework for judging the evidence under uncertainty. The mathematical connection between information retrieval and Dempster-Shafer theory was suggested by Van Rijsbergen (1992). Dempster-Shafer theory (DS) is utilised for measurement of the quality level associated with gathered information. The quality is measured considering semantic closeness values only. However, there is an option to expand the scope of the quality metric and broaden its parameters by including some Web-site statistics, as proposed in (Danilova & Stupples, 2012). The total quality score for each Web-page is calculated as a Belief function; the higher the value of Belief for a Web-page, the higher its quality value and the higher the Web-page will be ranked in the final list of results. Next, we describe the main concepts of DS theory as presented by Shafer (1976) and relate them with the context of Web-based discovery of unknowns.

Frame of discernment. In the DS theory propositions are represented as subsets of a given set. The hypotheses (in context – texts as combination of concepts) represent all the possible states of the system considered. It is required that all hypotheses are elements (singletons) of the frame of discernment, which is given by the finite universal set U. The set of all subsets of U is its power set 2^U. A subset of those 2^U sets may consist of a single hypothesis or a conjunction of hypotheses. Moreover, it is required that all hypotheses are unique, not over-lapping and mutually exclusive.

If the value of some quantity is u, and the set of its possible values is U, then the set U is called a frame of discernment. "The value of u is in A" is a proposition for some $A \subseteq U$. The proposition $A = \{a\}$ for $a \in U$ constitutes a basic proposition "the value of u is a". Thus, each text can be represented as a set of Thesaurus categories, where each element is a Boolean value corresponding to whether the text includes any words from the category. Hence, the set of 1044 Thesaurus categories and all their possible combinations is a universal set $\underline{U} = \{c1, ..., c1044\}$. Each Web-page text as a combination of Thesaurus categories is a member of the power set $2^U = \{\varnothing, \{text\_1\}, \{text\_2\}, \{text\_3\}, ..., U\}$.

Basic probability assignment. In order to express the uncertainty of propositions, Beliefs can be assigned to them. The Beliefs are usually computed using a basic probability assignment (*bpa*) or mass function m: $2^U \rightarrow [0,1]$. It has two properties: the mass of the empty set is zero, and the masses of the remaining members of the power set add up to a total of 1:

$$m(\varnothing) = 0 \text{ and } \sum_{A \subseteq U} m(A) = 1. \tag{7}$$

Mass function $m(A)$ expresses the proportion of all relevant and available evidence that supports the claim that the actual state belongs to A but to no particular subset of A. The value of $m(A)$ pertains only to the set A and makes no additional claims about any subsets of A, each of which have, by definition, their own mass. If there is positive evidence for the value of u being in A then $m(A) > 0$, and A is called a focal element. No Belief can ever be assigned to a false proposition. The focal elements and the associated *bpa* define a body of evidence. The mass function for a text, as a proportion of all evidence that supports the text, is a normalised value of the NLP analysis result according to (3). The calculated semantic distance has a value between 0 and 1, and the total evidence is scaled to fall between 0 and 1 in order to satisfy the definition of *bpa*.

Belief function. Given a body of evidence with *m*, we can compute the total Belief provided by that body of evidence for a proposition. This is done with a Belief function *Bel: $2^U \to$* [0, 1] defined upon *m*. Probability values are assigned to sets of possibilities and Belief in a hypothesis is constituted by the sum of the masses of all sets enclosed by it.:

$$Bel(A) = \sum_{B \subseteq A} m(B).$$

(8)

Bel(A) is the total Belief committed to *A*, i.e. the *m(A)* itself plus the mass attached to all subsets of *A*. *Bel(A)* is then the total positive effect the body of evidence has on the value of *u* being in *A*. The quality of information in each text is associated with the value of the Belief function for corresponding texts and reflects the amount of evidence supporting each text directly. Each text can be seen as a combination of Thesaurus concepts. For example, the Belief in the text_1 as a set of concepts {c1 U c2} is the sum of its own basic assignment with those of all of its subsets. Thus, if text_1 = {c1, c2}, text_2 = {c1} and text_3 = {c2}, the Belief function of the text_1 is:

$$Bel(text\_1) = m(text\_3) + m(text\_2) + m(text\_1).$$

(9)

Step 7 (Decision on the Next Iteration)

The Web-pages with the highest quality from semantic view point are placed at the top of the list. The Web-pages with a quality value of 10% and higher that have passed through the grounded theory test will be suggested for transferring to the organisation's knowledge base. And those Web-pages with quality value over 85% will be considered as "high quality" information. At this stage, the list of Web-pages suggested by the search engine is significantly reduced. It contains only Web-pages that have passed all three main filtering stages of the algorithm. The pages are highly relevant to the subject of the initial knowledge base. They contain new information that will expand the knowledge on the search topic, and will be ordered based on the quality of collected evidence rather than popularity. The decision on whether to iterate or stop is based on evidence tests for completeness and quality. Table 1 shows all possible combinations of results from the grounded theory test and the evidence quality test.

To summarise, the decision on the next iteration depends on the amount of the discovered and converted UUs coming into the knowledge base as well as the change in quality of knowledge base, if new information is to be added. The overall process is iterative and applied to the Web. The discovered

Table 1. Choice of next step

Conversion rate, $\delta(KU)$	Quality	Action
Positive	Positive	Continue (expand query)
Positive	Negative	Stop searching
Negative	Positive	Continue (expand query)
Negative	Negative	Stop (change formulation)

unknowns are used as a basis for new query expansion in order to identify the best information for the target decision process.

RESULTS OF REAL-WORLD EXPERIMENTS

The main objective of the experiments is to evaluate whether the suggested method significantly improves the process of decision making by extracting only relevant high quality information from the Web. The evaluation experiments cover a set of chosen test topics with corresponding lists of queries. A working prototype is implemented using Python. The experimental element of this research is semi-automated – the initial knowledge base and the corresponding list of queries for a search engine are manually defined, together with the search engine lists of results. Two experiments have been chosen for the illustration purposes of this paper. The first experiment had an objective of assessing how well the system can find topic-related quality information from the Web when the topic is well understood and well defined. The second experiment was aimed at assessing the ability of the system to identify relevant information of high quality assuming that the topic understanding is incomplete and the chosen queries were only slightly relevant to the search topic.

Experiment 1: Cocaine Smuggling

To assess the system's ability to find and filter the Web-pages given a well defined initial knowledge base and relevant queries, the topic of the initial knowledge base was "cocaine smuggling" and the chosen queries were Q1 "cocaine production and distribution", Q2 "cocaine trafficking UK", Q3 "cocaine smuggling UK", Q4 "cocaine cartels", Q5 "Mexican drug cartels". The chosen queries are semantically focused around the search topic. This experiment was aimed to test the performance of the system when each new Web-page content is compared against the same knowledge base initiated at the beginning. The experiment resulted in the significant reduction of information provided by Google search across all five queries (Figure 3a, Figure 3b).

Thus, out of 2903 Web-pages suggested by Google across all five queries, 82% were recognised as relevant, 8% were identified to contain quality information with approximately 1% as "high-quality" Web-pages. The high proportion of relevant pages is a result of close semantic distance between the search topic and the chosen queries. Grounded theory analysis explores how well the information from the extracted Web-pages expands the search topic.

Analysing the KU conversion rate throughout the five iterations the cumulative KU function (Figure 4a) becomes close to convergence after about ¾ of the processed Web-pages. This can indicate that the information obtained with the chosen queries spans the search topic well and new Web-pages will not add a significant amount of new information. The quality of the top rated pages after the five iterations has improved compared to the Google PageRank order results (Figure 4b).

The average quality at the top of the list increased from 4% to 28%, with the average quality of highest positioned Web-pages of 77%. Noteworthy, the resulting list of Web-pages did not follow the order of Google PageRank and had Web-pages from the middle and end of Google list closer to the top of the reordered list of results. This indicates no correlation exists between the Web-page quality and the depth of the search results list.

Figure 3a. Distribution of semantic closeness values across five queries

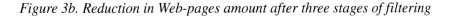

Figure 3b. Reduction in Web-pages amount after three stages of filtering

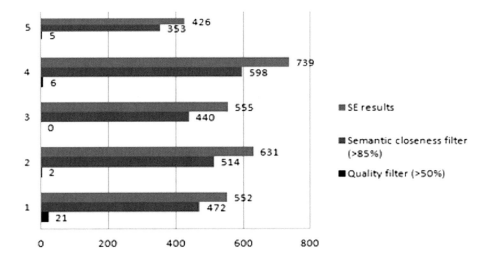

Experiment 2: Coffee Production

This experiment was aimed at assessing how well the system filters relevant Web-pages assuming the level of uncertainty on the subject is high, thus, the chosen queries are semantically remote from the search topic. The second set of experiments was carried out with regard to the search topic "coffee production". The corresponding queries were chosen to be semantically remote from the meaning of the initial knowledge base. The list of queries consists of Q1 "tobacco industry competition", Q2 "tobacco criminal", Q3 "tobacco financial market", Q4 "tobacco smoking statistics", Q5 "tobacco investment opportunities". The distribution of semantic closeness results across five queries is shown in Figure 5a. The reduction in the amount of pages is shown in Figure 5b.

Figure 4a. Cumulative KU conversion rate across five queries

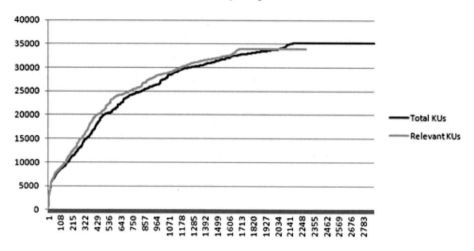

Figure 4b. Quality change for top search results

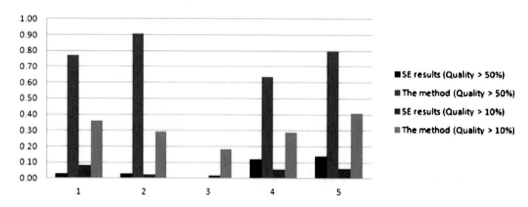

Figure 5a. Distribution of semantic closeness values across five queries

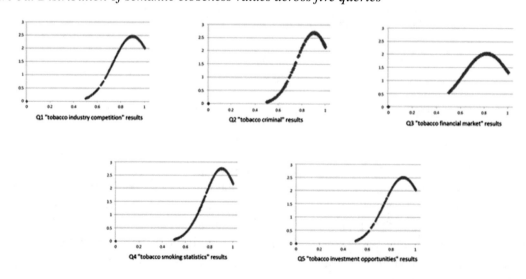

Figure 5b. Reduction in Web-pages amount after three stages of filtering

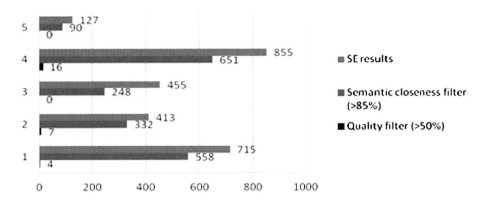

Thus, the total number of Web-pages suggested by Google across five queries was 2565, 73% were identified as relevant information and 6% as quality information. Approximately 0.5% of all results were rated as "high-quality" information sources.

Grounded theory analysis for the five iterations shows that the cumulative KU function continuously grows throughout the whole search procedure (Figure 6a). This indicates that the chosen queries do not cover the search topic well enough and iterating further is suggested. After the list of Web-pages had been reordered, there was a significant quality improvement in the top of the list (Figure 6b). The average quality of top-rated pages from the initial search engine results list was 3.5% and increased to 29% with the average quality of the highest rated Web-pages of 75%.

The relatively high proportion of the relevant pages can be explained as a small level of semantic remoteness between the topics, i.e. "coffee" and "tobacco" have a lot in common, but have different meanings. Similarly to the previous experiment, the reordered search results list did not follow the PageRank order. For each experiment the conversion rate of KUs was taken as a parameter for identifying

Figure 6a. Cumulative KU conversion rate across five queries

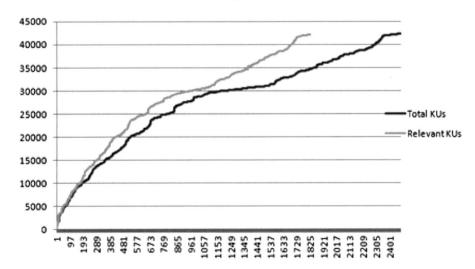

Figure 6b. Quality change for top search results

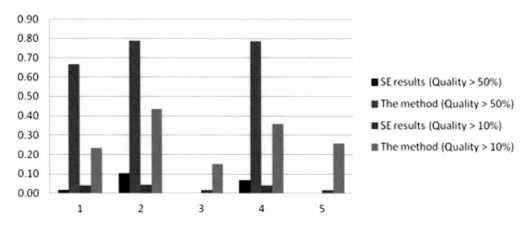

when the iterating should stop. The cumulative sum of discovered unknowns was analysed and, if the next iteration has a little conversion rate, it is assumed that the topic is close to be exhausted and new iteration on the same topic will not significantly enhance the knowledge base.

POST ANALYSIS

Part of this research has investigated the ability of a traditional search engine to find relevant information based on the keywords match technique. Clearly, the better knowledge the analyst has on the search topic, the greater chance there is that the selected keywords formulate the query that will more accurately describe the topic. Moreover, one may apply "advanced search" option and use Boolean operators to improve search results. For the purpose of this research the "advanced search" option was not used. Nevertheless, the major part of the search results (approximately 70%) was still considered relevant to the search topic with relatively high semantic closeness value of 0.85-1.0. The experiments revealed that approximately 30% of the Web-pages in the results list have little or no relevance to the search topic, meaning that these Web-pages may contain the words from the query but discuss a completely different subject. Thus, up to almost one third of the search results may turn out to be irrelevant to the search topic and the experiments have shown that some of these irrelevant Web-pages are placed at the top of the results list. When analysing the 'search engine' results and deciding which Web-pages are relevant, only a rare user goes beyond the first 100 snippets presented by the search engine. This means that the relevant high quality Web-pages placed towards the end of the long search results list are likely to remain ignored.

Even if the analyst views all snippets in the search results list before choosing which Web-pages to open and further explore, the experiments have shown that it should take approximately 5 minutes to view one results page of 50 snippets. Thus, for average 2500 results across 5 queries it would take the user approximately 250 minutes or 4 hours and 10 minutes just to look through the snippets without opening the Web-pages. As for the content on each of the Web-pages, a number of studies have been conducted that explore reading habits of Web users when scanning the Web content (Chaparro et al., 2004), (Nielsen Norman Group, 2006), (Nielsen Norman Group, 2008). These eye-tracking studies revealed that when skimming a Web-page most users tend to concentrate on the content which is placed towards to the left as well as content that fits an F-shaped pattern, such as headings followed by paragraphs.

Studies on reading behaviours of people reveal that only 28% of the text is read on a Web-page and this figure decreased the more text there is on a page, meaning that if an important piece of information is placed towards the bottom of a long document, there is a high chance that this information will not be noticed by the user. Moreover, the studies show that users will read about 20% of the text on the average page with 593 words. According to (Chaparro et al., 2004), if the average reading speed is 200 words per minute, it would take 36 seconds for the user to read 120 words or to skim 2 average Web-pages in one minute.

In contrast, we demonstrate the solution that overcomes the human factor and analyses the full amount of textual content despite its length, layout or reading age. Taking our example of 2500 Web-pages it would require 1250 minutes or almost 21 hours to skim 20% of the total content. Considering the unlikely scenario when the user looks through the 100% of the textual content, it would take 6250 minutes or 104 hours to look through all the Web-pages for our 5 queries. While the proposed solution is able to process the same amount of information in approximately 5 hours, which is 20 times faster comparing to the human processing, if the system's code gets optimised, the processing time can be significantly reduced.

The analysis of values of the probability density function (Figures 3a and 5a) in the relevance test results may help to understand how good the corresponding query reflects the search topic well in the eyes of the SE. A narrower bell curve indicates that the chosen query accurately matches the search topic and results in more relevant pages after the Web-search. A wider bell curve indicates that the chosen query brings back a broader spectrum of information and expands the search topic. Hence, it is possible to adjust the scope or direction of the Web-search. Precise queries that are themselves highly semantically close to the search topic will fill up the gaps in the knowledge on the subject without expanding it. On the contrast, queries that go beyond the meaning of the search topic will unveil possible directions of the topic expansion. This is the case where the initial knowledge on the topic is limited and, as a result, the queries formed on that limited information can be very remote semantically from the initial search topic.

When the traditional search engine presents its search results, they are ordered in accordance with some Web-page quality criteria. In our example, Google uses PageRank algorithm for ordering search results based on the Web-page popularity metric. This research refutes the idea that the more popular a Web-page is the more relevant content it contains. The proposed quality measurement based on the Dempster-Shafer theory employs semantic closeness parameter to estimate the quality of Web-pages for a particular query based on their meaning rather than popularity. This technique allows rearranging the search results list and moving the relevant Web-pages of higher quality to the top of the results list. Hence, the search list becomes not only reduced in its size after the irrelevant Web-pages are excluded, but also has high-quality pages at the top of the list.

CONCLUSION

In this paper we have presented the detail for a new method for Web-based discovery of unknown unknowns for intelligence gathering. This method relies on the combination of NLP techniques with grounded theory and the Dempster-Shafer theory in order to facilitate discovery of previously unknown useful Web-sourced intelligence. The results of the experiments outlined in this paper show that the quality of collected information is significantly enhanced with the use of the proposed method. A set of experiments carried out with different queries has proven that within the list of search engine results there is a large portion of Web-pages containing high-quality previously unknown information which would have not been identified using traditional methods.

REFERENCES

Ashby, W. R. (1956). *An Introduction to Cybernetics.* Chapman and Hall.

Berners-Lee, T., Hendler, J., & Lassila, O. (2001, May). The Semantic Web. *Scientific American, 284*(5), 34–43. doi:10.1038/scientificamerican0501-34 PMID:11323639

Chaparro, B., Baker, J. R., Shaikh, A. D., Hull, S., & Brady, L. (2004, July). *Reading Online Text: A Comparison of Four White Space Layouts. Usability News, 6*(2). Retrieved from The Psychology Department of Wichita State University: http://psychology.wichita.edu/surl/usabilitynews/62/whitespace.htm

Corbin, J., & Strauss, A. (2008). *Basics of qualitative research: techniques and procedures for developing grounded theory* (3rd ed.). London: Sage Publications. doi:10.4135/9781452230153

Corley, C., Mihalcea, R., & Strapparava, C. (2006). Corpus-based and Knowledge based Measures of Text similarity.*AAAI'06: Proceedings of the 21st national conference on Artificial intelligence.* AAAI Press.

Danilova, N., & Stupples, D. (2012). Application of Natural Language Processing to Web-based Intelligence Information Acquisition. *EISIC2012 Proceedings.* Odense, Denmark: IEEE Computer Society.

Dempster, A. P. (1968). A generalization of the Bayesian inference. *Journal of the Royal Statistical Society. Series A (General), 30*, 205–447.

Fellbaum, C. (1998). *WordNet: An Electronic Lexical Database.* Cambridge, MA: The MIT Press.

Firth, J. (1957). A Synopsis of Linguistic Theory, 1930-55. *Studies in Linguistic Analysis, 1952*(59), 168-205.

Fox, C. J. (1990). A Stop List for General Text. *ACM Special Interest Group on Information Retrieval Forum, 24*, 19-35.

Huutunen, S., Vihavainen, A., Du, M., & Yangarber, R. (2012). *Predicting Relevance of Event Extraction for the End User. In Multi-source, Multilingual Information Extraction and Summarization* (pp. 163–176). Berlin, Germany: Springer.

Lehmann, J., Schüppel, J., & Auer, S. (2007). Discovering Unknown Connections - the DBpedia Relationship Finder. CSSWeb'07 Proceedings.

Luhn, H. (1958). The Automatic Creation of Literature Abstracts. *IBM Journal*, 159-165.

Martin, P., & Turner, B. (1986). Grounded Theory and Organizational Research. *The Journal of Applied Behavioral Science, 22*(2), 141–157. doi:10.1177/002188638602200207

Mohammad, S. (2008). *Measuring Semantic Distance Using Distributional Profiles of Concepts.* Toronto, Canada: University of Toronto.

Mohammad, S., & Hirst, G. (2006). *Measuring semantic distance, using distributional profiles of concepts.* New York: Association for Computational Linguistics.

Nielsen Norman Group. (2006, April 17). *F-Shaped Pattern For Reading Web Content.* Retrieved from Nielsen Norman Group: http://www.nngroup.com/articles/f-shaped-pattern-reading-Web-content/

Nielsen Norman Group. (2008, May 6). *How Little Do Users Read?* Retrieved from Nielsen Norman Group: http://www.nngroup.com/articles/how-little-do-users-read/

Rubenstein, H., & Goodenough, J. (1965, October). Contextual Correlates of Synonymy. *Communications of the ACM, 8*(10), 627–633. doi:10.1145/365628.365657

Rumsfeld, D. (2002). *News Transcript: DoD News Briefing.* Washington, DC: U.S. Department of Defence.

Shafer, G. (1976). *A Mathematical Theory of Evidence.* Princeton, NJ: Princeton University Press.

Torisawa, K., De Saeger, S., Kazama, J., Sumida, A., Noguchi, D., Kakizawa, Y., & Yamada, I. et al. (2010). Organizing the Webs Information Explosion to Discover Unknown Unknowns. *New Generation Computing, 28*(3), 217–236. doi:10.1007/s00354-009-0087-7

Van Rijsbergen, C. J. (1979). *Information Retrieval.* London: Butterworths.

Van Rijsbergen, C. J. (1992). Probabilistic retrieval revisited. *The Computer Journal, 35*(3), 291–298. doi:10.1093/comjnl/35.3.291

Chapter 7

Securing Financial XML Transactions Using Intelligent Fuzzy Classification Techniques:
A Smart Fuzzy–Based Model for Financial XML Transactions Security Using XML Encryption

Faisal Tawfiq Ammari
University of Huddersfield, UK

Joan Lu
University of Huddersfield, UK

ABSTRACT

The eXtensible Markup Language (XML) has been widely adopted in many financial institutions in their daily transactions. This adoption was due to the flexible nature of XML providing a common syntax for systems messaging in general and in financial messaging in specific. Excessive use of XML in financial transactions messaging created an aligned interest in security protocols integrated into XML solutions in order to protect exchanged XML messages in an efficient yet powerful mechanism. However, financial institutions (i.e. banks) perform large volume of transactions on daily basis which require securing XML messages on large scale. Securing large volume of messages will result performance and resource issues. Therefore, an approach is needed to secure specified portions of an XML document, syntax and processing rules for representing secured parts. In this research we have developed a smart approach for securing financial XML transactions using effective and intelligent fuzzy classification techniques. Our approach defines the process of classifying XML content using a set of fuzzy variables. Upon fuzzy classification phase, a unique value is assigned to a defined attribute named "Importance Level". Assigned value indicates the data sensitivity for each XML tag. The research also defines the process of securing classified financial XML message content by performing element-wise XML encryption on selected parts

DOI: 10.4018/978-1-5225-2058-0.ch007

defined in fuzzy classification phase. Element-wise encryption is performed using symmetric encryption using AES algorithm with different key sizes. Key size of 128-bit is being used on tags classified with "Medium" importance level; a key size of 256-bit is being used on tags classified with "High" importance level. An implementation has been performed on a real-life environment using online banking system in Jordan Ahli Bank one of the leading banks in Jordan to demonstrate its flexibility, feasibility, and efficiency. Our experimental results of the system verified tangible enhancements in encryption efficiency, processing-time reduction, and resulting XML message sizes. Finally, our proposed system was designed, developed, and evaluated using a live data extracted from an internet banking service in one of the leading banks in Jordan. The results obtained from our experiments are promising, showing that our model can provide an effective yet resilient support for financial systems to secure exchanged financial XML messages.

INTRODUCTION

eXtensible Markup Language (XML) (Bray, Paoli, Sperberg-McQueen, Maler, & Yergeau, 2008) has been widely adopted in many financial institutions in their daily transactions; this adoption has been due to the flexible nature of XML in providing a common syntax for systems messaging in general and for financial messaging in particular. Excessive use of XML in financial transactions messaging has created an aligned interest in security protocols integrated into XML solutions in order to protect exchanged XML messages by using an efficient yet powerful mechanism. There have been several approaches proposed by researchers to secure XML messages and there is a comprehensive collection of related works.

XML is designed based on text format and has a tree structure. It is natural that data integrity, data authentication, information confidentiality, and other security benefits should be applied to entire XML data or portions of XML data. XML security solutions should provide a high level of security to ensure the confidentiality of information represented using the XML format. XML security must be integrated with XML data features and characteristics to keep the flexible nature of XML while integrating essential security technologies.

Due to the sensitive nature of financial transactions that use XML as their main messaging protocol, a security requirement should be fulfilled to protect exchanged XML messages by using a dynamic and efficient mechanism. The security mechanism should encrypt portions of XML data rather than whole messages, e.g. element-wise encryption should be used to protect sensitive parts within the XML message.

The specifications related to XML security published by W3C define the basic framework and rules that can be utilized across applications. The basic idea for XML security is to perform data encryption on XML messages whereby XML data confidentiality is achieved to ensure that the XML data structure, data content, and other sensitive information in XML data may only be accessed by legitimate parties. Confidentiality is generally associated with encryption mechanisms or access control technologies. XML key management (Hallam-Baker & Mysore, 2005) provides the basic key requirements for XML data confidentiality.

However, on a daily basis, financial institutions (i.e. banks) perform large volumes of transactions that require XML encryption on a large scale. Encrypting large volumes of messages in full will result in performance and resource issues. Therefore, an approach is needed to encrypt defined parts within the XML document, to identify syntax for representing encrypted portions, and to identify the processing rules for decrypting those portions. W3C XML encryption has a feature called element-wise encryption, which is the process of encrypting parts of an XML document. The encryption process can be applied to more than one element in a given XML document; each is contained in another element. The element might enclose sub-elements, attributes, texts, or a mix of all mentioned items. The remaining parts of the document should remain intact as plaintext.

To avoid any performance or resource issues, a mechanism should be considered to choose which parts of the XML document should be encrypted on the fly, whereby the parts are selected based on smart criteria for detecting sensitive information within an XML document.

The fuzzy logic (FL) (L.A. Zadeh, 1965) approach can be used to distinguish sensitive parts within each XML document. FL provides an easy way to reach to a definite conclusion based upon noisy, vague, imprecise, ambiguous, or missing information. FL's approach for controlling problems imitates how a person would make a quick decision. FL includes a rule-based 'IF X AND Y, THEN Z' approach for solving a control problem, rather than attempting to design a system in mathematical way. The FL model is relying on an operator's experience rather than their technical understanding of the system.

The FL approach is quantified based on a combination of historical data and expert input. FL has been used in many fields especially in computer information systems, and computer science to combine expert input with computer models for a large scale of applications. The main advantage of the fuzzy approach is that it can process imprecisely defined variables and variables which mathematical relationships cannot define their corresponding relationships. FL has the ability to integrate expert human knowledge and judgment to define the variables and corresponding relationships. By integrating expert human judgment the more realistic models are available (Mahant, 2004)

Research Motivation

Many businesses and financial institutions use XML in their basic transaction messaging, due to its flexible nature and structure. A solid security approach is required to ensure safe and trustworthy transactions either within the same institution or between different institutions (business to business). XML security specifications published by W3C have addressed XML encryption (Imamura, Dillaway, & Simon, 2002). XML encryption is mainly used to ensure XML data confidentiality and authenticity. However, institutions that deal with large volumes of transactions on a daily basis require a flexible and solid mechanism to process XML messages that performs element-wise encryption in a timely and efficient manner.

Encrypting sensitive information only within the XML document is a complicated issue to analyse; it needs to take into consideration the process of encrypting different portions within the XML document every time the message is transmitted. This is complex to analyse because the classification requires set of factors to consider.

Despite there are handful of applications available to secure XML messages, there are no known solutions that utilize fuzzy classification techniques in detecting sensitive information within each XML document.

The motivation behind our research is to create an effective, powerful, and intelligent model to classify XML messages by detecting sensitive information within XML documents, in order to perform element-wise encryption on selected parts.

We have conducted a quantitative methodology in our research, and it explores fuzzy XML classification systems. The technique uses FL to process XML data features and patterns, for extracting the message's fuzzy classification rules into the data miner, and then for applying element-wise encryption algorithms on selected portions extracted from XML data features and patterns. The proposed XML security model combines fuzzy techniques for the purpose of automating the fuzzy rules. The automation process is completed by extracting the set of fuzzy rules that are going to be deployed inside the fuzzy inference engine. Therefore, a set of IF-THEN rules are constructed using these fuzzy rules. The IF-THEN rules reflect the relations between different transaction characteristics and patterns and their associations with one another. These rules can then be used for the final stage, which uses element-wise encryption with different key sizes based on the importance levels assigned.

Our previous expertise in the banking and financial sector in Jordan shed the light on the importance of securing business and financial transactions based on XML. Many researches and case studies have been reviewed and evaluated in order to find a robust and flexible solution that can be used with ease and efficiency.

Aims and Objectives

Our prime aim is to build a system that secure financial XML messages that uses FL to classify XML content to perform XML encryption, in order to provide necessary data confidentiality for classified portions within an XML document. This mechanism enhances the performance of encrypting XML documents on high-volume transactions. In order to reach this aim, there are several objectives:

Our objectives can be summarized with the following points:

1. Conduct a literature review to illustrate the current and existing approaches concerning XML security, fuzzy XML models, and XML data confidentiality.
2. Build a resilient, intelligent, dynamic, and secure XML messaging system that uses artificial intelligence and FL to fetch and classify sensitive information within XML documents. The outcome system has to be adaptive, flexible, and efficient.
3. Illustrate feasibility and adaptability after analysing a large number of actual transaction datasets fetched over period of time reflecting internet banking transactions, phone banking transactions, and mobile banking transactions.
4. Present the applicability of applying an FL expert system in order to classify and find out importance levels within XML documents. Fuzzy rules are being used for and driven by human expert knowledge on creating flexible and secure XML messaging systems.
5. Provide a solution that improves existing XML encryption approaches and illustrates a performance improvement over well-known XML encryption models, like W3C XML Encryption Recommendations. We illustrate the enhancements and processing improvements by securing only the necessary parts with high importance levels within XML documents.

We have implemented a quantitative research methodology to enable us achieving all above objectives, taking into consideration experimental studies, case analysis, data collection, testing, evaluation, and comparing final results.

Contributions

This research will contribute to the fields of XML security, fuzzy XML in general, XML encryption, and fuzzification, specifically in the following areas:

1. A robust XML security model has been introduced performing element-wise encryption to encrypt critical and sensitive parts within XML documents that are used in business and financial institutions. This technique encrypts XML documents efficiently by encrypting only the sensitive parts within each XML document by using a set of fuzzy variables. Significant processing time improvements have been recorded against a well-known approach (W3C XML Encryption Recommendations).

2. An efficient and secure XML model has been created to reduce encrypted XML file sizes, due to the fact that only essential parts within each XML document are encrypted, leaving other nodes intact without encryption. Reduce file sizes will reduced bandwidth used on large scale.

3. A fuzzy classification engine has been created to determine which parts within each XML document require encryption. The fuzzification engine works by assigning an importance level to each tag within the XML document. The importance level value is set by the engine for later encryption processing; the importance level is assigned using one of three values (high, medium, or low). The fuzzification process itself is based on fuzzy logic, which uses a combination of human expert knowledge and a set of IF-THEN operators.

4. A resilient XML encryption system has been created whereby future enhancements can be achieved without the need to redesign the whole system. The encryption standards and algorithms used within the system are flexible and can be changed when needed; different encryption algorithms can be used to replace existing algorithms either to improve performance or to add more security.

5. A set of XML fuzzy classification characteristics has been created that were fetched from actual financial XML transactions. There are ten main characteristics that were created by using a hybrid of personal expertise, onsite financial analysts, a set of questionnaires, and a set of surveys. These ten characteristics define the classification criteria we will use in our fuzzy classification stage.

A desktop application has been designed and developed to test and validate our proposed model. Application developed based on reliability, feasibility, and extraction process of the mechanism. The application was programmed using the Java programming language.

BACKGROUND

This section introduces the XML model with all its detailed components. Cryptographic algorithms and types are presented. The XML security model is presented as well. Specifically, we present XML digital signatures, XML Encryption, XML key management, SAML, and XACML security models. We then present the information retrieval mechanism in general and XML fuzzy classification specifically. Finally, we introduce the fuzzy logic model in details.

XML Model

EXtensible Markup Language (XML) was first announced in 1998 (W3C, 1998). This proposed markup language became the standard for data exchange and representation among many online and offline applications, providing the flexibility of exchanging different digital content among applications. An XML document is formed in a hierarchical structure with the ability to define its element contents, define tags, create nested document structures, and build document types by specifying a set of regular expression patterns (XML Schema or Document Type Definitions (DTD)). An XML document incorporates structure and data in one entity. Therefore, XML data is semi-structured data (S. Abiteboul, 1996).

The solid set of XML characteristics created an interest in building effective solutions to support the following advantages:

- **Extensibility:** New fields and tags can be created when they are needed. There are no fixed set of fields.
- **Self-Description:** This feature allows any XML field to process an unlimited number of attributes.
- **Readability:** XML is easy for humans or machines to read and understand. This feature facilitates the usage of XML by different applications and users.
- **Simplicity:** XML code is easy to understand; also, it can be easily processed and deployed in different practices. Updating the existing XML Schema is an easy and straightforward operation.
- **Supports Multilingual Documents and Unicode:** This is important for the internationalization of applications.
- **Interoperability:** There is the ability to use XML documents in any industry without the need to make changes to the data itself. XML is treated as an independent unit from both the machine and software levels.
- **Portability:** An XML document has the ability to represent different data types, such as ordinary text and binary files (images, videos, and sounds).

However, there are some drawbacks in XML, which include:

- **Syntax Redundancy:** This can affect human readability and system efficiency, and this can result in higher storage requirements and resource usage. Bandwidth limitations can prevent XML being deployed in certain applications.
- **A Number of Vague, Unneeded Features within XML:** Efforts were made to create "Minimal XML", which led to the discovery that there was no consensus on which features were in fact obscure or unnecessary.
- **A Wide Range of Data Types are Not Supported in the Basic Parsing Requirements:** Some additional work might be required to process the desired data in the XML document.
- **A Significant Overhead for Various Uses of XML:** This mainly applies where resources may be limited. This might happen because of the parser's limitations in recusing arbitrarily nested data structures or the missing feature of performing additional checking and validation for improperly formatted syntax or data.
- **Security Concerns:** These may arise when XML input is fed from unknown or untrusted sources
- **Difficulty in Modeling Overlapping Data Structures:** This requires extra effort.

Well-Formed XML

A well-formed XML document is one which corresponds to the XML 1.0 (Bray, Paoli, Sperberg-McQueen, Maler, & Yergeau, 2007) grammar specified by W3C. It has just one root element, which is known as the document element. Each starting element tag must have a corresponding closing tag. Each element ought to be nested within one another. Nesting rules with defined labels enable information to be represented by XML hierarchically. Figure 1 illustrates a sample of a well-formed XML message.

Figure 1. Sample of a well-formed XML message

```
<?xml version = "1.0" encoding="UTF-8" standalone="yes"?>
<document>
  <employee>
    <name>
      <lastname>Faisal</lastname>
      <firstname>Ammari</firstname>
    </name>
    <hiredate>January 2, 2000</hiredate>
      <project>
        <product>Laptop</product>
        <id>002</id>
        <price>JD500.125</price>
      </project>
    </projects>
  </employee>
</document>
```

XML Components

An XML document consists of elements that represent a piece of information. More specific information can be found in nested elements, such as character data, attributes, and entity references. These elements are marked up by the tags in a specific document. Between the start tag and end tag of an element there is the element content, presented as text content.

1. **Elements:** Elements start with an opening tag (<t>) and end with an ending tag (</t>). Everything between the starting and ending tags is called the element content. Each element has an element name (e), which should follow the following rules:
   a. The element name should not start with "XML" or "xml".
   b. The element name is case sensitive.
   c. The element name starts with a character or an underscore.
   d. The element name consists of characters, numerals, underscores, and tabs.
2. **Attributes:** Attributes are information that can provide more information about the element and often define an instance of an element. Attributes have a name defined. For example, <book name="Learn C++ in 24 days"> is a book element with an attribute name that has the value "Learn C++ in 24 days".
3. **Comments:** Comments can be placed anywhere inside the XML document for further explanation or description. Comments are not part of the main document and can be used by using the start tag (<!—) and the end tag (-->).
4. **XML Declaration:** An XML declaration supplies the XML processor with information such as encoding, version, and any other information related to the document. A declaration can be defined with a start tag (<?xml) and an end tag (?>).
5. **Processing Instructions (PIs):** PIs may occur anywhere in the XML document. Their main purpose is to carry specific instructions to the application. A PI is represented within the document in the form of: <?Target instructions for command?>.
6. **CDATA Sections:** Using CDATA will tell the XML parser that there is no markup in the characters during the time of processing. Sections can be defined by using: <! [CDATA]!>.

Figure 2. A DTD Example

```
<!DOCTYPE family [
    <!ELEMENT title (#PCDATA)>
    <!ELEMENT parent (#PCDATA)>
    <!ATTLIST parent role (mother | father) #required>
    <!ELEMENT child (#PCDATA)>
    <!ATTLIST child role (daughter | son) #required>
    <!NOTATION gif system "image/gif">
    <!ENTITY JENN system
    "http://images.about.com/sites/guidepics/html.gif"
    NDATA gif>
    <!ELEMENT image empty>
    <!ATTLIST image source entity #required>
    <!ENTITY footer "Brought to you by Jennifer Kyrnin">
]>
```

XML Schema Languages

XML schema languages, like XML Schema (D. C. Fallside & Walmsley, 2004), DTDs, DSDs (M\oller, 2005), Schematron (Jelliffe, 2006), and RELAX NG (Makoto, Walsh, & McRae, 2001), are used to certify XML documents. The reason for certifying/validating a document is to verify whether the XML document conforms to a set of structural and content rules expressed in one of many schema languages. The validation procedure happens on at least four primary levels (Ray, 2003):

1. **Structure:** Relates to the placement and use of markup elements and attributes.
2. **Data Typing:** Relates to the set of numbers, dates, and texts (patterns of character data).
3. **Integrity:** Relates to the linkage between resources and corresponding nodes.
4. **Business Rules:** Relates to collections of tests such as spelling checks, checksum results, etc.

Document Type Definition (DTD)

The Document Type Definition (DTD) (Hunter, Cagle, Dix, & Cable, 2001) is a set of rules that define the hierarchical structure of any XML document. The XML parser utilizes these rules to determine whether the XML document is valid or not. The DTD consists of four basic parts: elements, attributes, tags, and entities. A declared element specifies the name of the element and the valid content. Tags are used to indicate elements. Attributes are used to provide additional details about an element and can be used to describe element properties as well. Entities are the variables that can be reused within the document. Figure 2 illustrates a sample DTD example.

XML Schema

XML Schema (Hunter et al., 2001) is a DTD alternative that is based on XML. Users can exploit XML Schema to represent an XML document structure. An XML Schema Definition (XSD) is regarded as XML Schema language.

Figure 3. A RELAX NG Schema example

```
<?xml version="1.0" encoding="UTF-8"?>
<element name="books"
xmlns="http://relaxng.org/ns/structure/1.0">
  <element name="book"
  <attribute name="price"/>
  <attribute name="id"/>
  <element name="name"><text/></element>
  <element name="authors"
    <element name="author"><text/>
    <attribute name="id"/>
    <optional>
      <attribute name="address"/>
    </optional>
    </element>
  </element>
  <element name="ISBN"><text/></element>
  </element>
</element>
```

XML Schemas can take the place of DTDs in most web applications. XML Schemas are written in XML and are present in well-formed XML documents. XML Schemas support data types such as string, date and time, and integers. XML Schemas can be used to construct complex data types as well.

RELAX NG

RELAX NG is a schema language for XML developed by ISO/IEC JTC1/SC34/WG1 (Makoto et al., 2001). RELAX NG is based on two languages. The first language is the Tree Regular Expressions for XML (TREX) designed by James Clark (Clark, 2001); the second language is the Regular Language description for XML (RELAX) designed by Murata Makoto (Makoto, 2002). The primary idea of RELAX NG consists of patterns that are formed to widen the range of the idea of the content model. In RELAX NG, a pattern is an expression of elements, text nodes, and attributes. The definitions of data types may be utilized for constraining the sets of values of text nodes and attributes. Figure 3 demonstrates an example of a RELAX NG Schema.

Document Structure Description (DSD)

A Document Structure Description is a schema language developed by combined efforts from BRICS and AT&T Labs (Klarlund, Møller, & Schwartzbach, 2000; M\oller, 2005). Constraints form the basic concept of a DSD. A restraint is used to define the content of an element, corresponding attributes, and its particular context. A pair consisting of an element name and a restraint forms the definition of an element. Element content is constrained by means of a content expression, which is a regular expression over element definitions. To force constraints on the context of an element, context patterns are used.

Schematron

Schematron is schema language based on rules developed by Rick Jelliffe at the Academia Sinica Computing Centre (ASCC) (Jelliffe, 2006). The main functionality of Schematron is to perform co-constraints checking in XML instance documents. A sequence of rules is defined by a Schematron document, which is grouped in a logical way in pattern elements. A context attribute is included within each rule and used by an XPath pattern to determine the elements to which the rule applies. Within each rule, a sequence of reports and elements are specified with a testing attribute, which considered an XPath expression. This expression is evaluated to a value of Boolean type for each node within the context.

XML API

Application Program Interfaces (APIs) are used by many programming languages to access XML document information without the need to create and write a parser in the specific used language.

DOM Parser

The DOM (Document Object Model) parser is utilized as a hierarchical object model to get XML document information (Hégaret, Whitmer, & Wood, 2005). The whole XML document's information is being read by DOM parser, and establishes the corresponding DOM object tree of nodes. The construction is being performed in main memory. This XML parser is appropriate for small to medium XML documents that may fit in memory. DOM can be utilized in document-centric document whereby the sequence of elements within the document is essential. The sequence of elements is preserved due to direct read from the document. It has multiple functions for traversing XML trees and other relevant functions like (insert, delete, and access nodes).

SAX Parser

The Simple Application Interface for XML (SAX) parser provides accessibility to XML information as a series of events. For every open tag, closing tag, and every #PCDATA and CDATA section, SAX activates an event. These events along with the corresponding sequences need to be interpreted by the document handler. SAX is suitable for medium to large XML documents; this is because there is no need to parse XML documents in main memory first. SAX is suitable for structured XML documents as well, as the sequence for elements not essential.

Java API for XML

The Java programming language (and some other languages) provides different types of XML Application Programming Interfaces (APIs), such as SAX, DOM, and XSLT (Mclaughlin & Edelson, 2006; Violleau, 2001; Williams, 2009), in order to process XML documents by means of writing a computer program using several programming languages. SAX (Simple API for XML) scans the XML document sequentially and throws up events that the programmer can handle. These events are thrown up by the parser when it detects the start document and end document tags, as well as the start element tag, including a list of all its attributes, end elements, and characters. The programmer should write suitable code

Figure 4. A generic encryption system

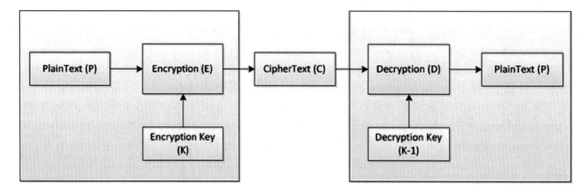

for each event to process an entire XML document. Since each event occurs only once for each element, all the required work needed to process the document should be done in one cycle.

CRYPTOGRAPHIC ALGORITHMS FOR CONFIDENTIALITY

Encryption Mechanism

The encryption mechanism is the process of transforming plaintext into ciphertext and vice versa. Plaintext is readable content that needs rendering to be unreadable. Ciphertext is encrypted plaintext in which no semantic content is available. An encryption mechanism transforms plaintext into ciphertext. A decryption mechanism transforms ciphertext back into plaintext. In order to be able to re-use a particular algorithm in many systems, the algorithm is parameterized by a key. Figure 4 illustrates encryption mechanisms.

Key: "A sequence of symbols that controls the operations of encryption and decryption."

As illustrated in Figure 4, to encrypt plaintext (P), the encryption algorithm (E) is parameterized with a confidentiality encryption key (K). Ciphertext (C) is decrypted using the confidentiality decryption key (K^{-1}).

Encrypting plaintext (P) under the key (K) produces ciphertext (C) and is denoted as $C = E_K\left(P\right)$. The decryption of C under the key K^{-1} reproduces the plaintext P and is denoted as $P = E_{K^{-1}}\left(C\right)$.

Cryptography uses two different types of encryption systems: symmetric encryption systems and asymmetric encryption systems.

Symmetric Cryptography

- **Symmetric Encryption System:** This type of encryption system is based on symmetric cryptographic techniques that use one secret key for both the encryption and decryption algorithms.
- **Symmetric Cryptographic Technique:** This cryptographic technique uses a shared secret key. Symmetric encryption systems have the property that both the encryption key and the decryption key have the same value.

Figure 5. Symmetric cryptographic cycle

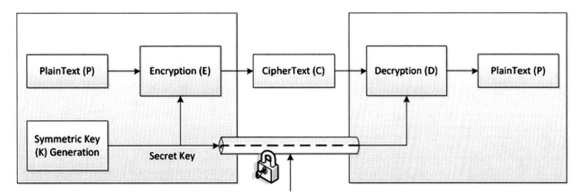

Secret Key: "A key that is used with a symmetric cryptographic algorithm. Possession of a secret key is restricted (usually to two entities)" (ISO10181-1). The secret key can be generated in various ways:

- By the encrypting entity (encryptor) illustrated in Figure 5;
- By the decryptor;
- By a trusted third party (TTP), like a key distribution centre (KDC); or
- It can be derived from parameters in a key agreement protocol that is performed by both the encryptor and the decryptor.

If the key is not computed using a key agreement protocol, the key must be transported through a secure channel that is protected in terms of confidentiality and integrity. Additionally, the recipient(s) of the secret key must know the source of the key, i.e. data origin authentication for the transported key is necessary.

The ciphertext itself can be transported through an unprotected channel.

- **Symmetric Cryptographic Algorithm:** "An algorithm for performing encryption or the corresponding algorithm for performing decryption in which the same key is required for both encryption and decryption" (ISO10181-1).

Algorithms that perform symmetric encryption are grouped into two classes:

1. Block ciphers
2. Stream ciphers

A block cipher processes blocks of plaintext to create blocks of ciphertext. A block is a string of n bits; such a block cipher is called an n-bit block cipher. Typical algorithms that are used in today's systems include:

- AES (Advanced Encryption Standard).

Figure 6. Asymmetric cryptographic cycle

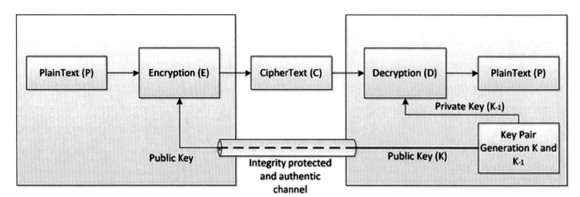

- 3DES (Triple DES (Data Encryption Standard), also known as TDEA: Triple Data Encryption Algorithm).
- IDEA (International Data Encryption Algorithm).
- Various other block ciphers, like the other AES candidates (e.g. Blowfish or RC6).

The plaintext bit sequence is segmented into n-bit blocks, as the block cipher needs n bit as its input. To allow cases where the input length is not a multiple of n bit, a padding mechanism is usually used with a block cipher. The padding algorithm defines an unambiguous way in which each plaintext is extended to a length of a multiple of n bit. This is done even if the length of the plaintext is already a multiple of n bit. So, if a padding mechanism is used, the length of the ciphertext is larger than the length of the plaintext. After decrypting with the block cipher, the padded bits are removed from the decrypted data.

The mechanisms closely related to block ciphers are modes of operation. Modes define how the inputs and outputs of consecutive block cipher operations are combined. This is done to ensure that the same plaintext block results in different ciphertext blocks throughout the ciphertext stream and to chain the blocks together to prevent substitution attacks.

A stream cipher combines a sequence of plaintext symbols with a sequence of keystream symbols, one symbol at a time, using an invertible function (for single bits as a symbol, the function is usually an exclusive bit or a between-keystream bit and a plaintext bit). Typical stream cipher algorithms include RC4 and A5, which are n-bit block ciphers that operate in a specific mode to create a key symbol stream.

Asymmetric Cryptography

- **Asymmetric Encryption System:** "Encryption system based on asymmetric cryptographic techniques whose public transformation is used for encipherment and whose private transformation is used for decipherment" (ISO/IEC9798-1, 1997).
- **Asymmetric Cryptographic Technique:** "Cryptographic technique that uses two related transformations, a public transformation (defined by the public key) and a private transformation (defined by the private key). The two transformations have the property that, given the public transformation, it is computationally infeasible to derive the private transformation" (ISO/IEC11770).

In an asymmetric encryption system, the encryption key K (also called the public key) and the decryption key K^(-1) (also called the private key) have distinct values, but these values have a mathematical relationship that is defined by the underlying cryptographic algorithm, as illustrated in Figure 6.

- **Private Key:** "A key that is used with an asymmetric cryptographic algorithm and whose possession is restricted (usually to only one entity)" (I.-T. X. I. 10181-1, 1996).
- **Public Key:** "A key that is used with an asymmetric cryptographic algorithm and that can be made publicly available" (I.-T. R. X. I. I. 10181-1, 1996).

A key pair consists of a public and the corresponding private key. The generation of a key pair can be performed by different parties:

- The key pair can be generated by the decryptor. In this case, the decryptor can publish the public key in a directory service or directly send the public key to the encryptor. This case is shown in Figure 6. Note that the channel for transporting the public key does not have to be protected in terms of confidentiality.
- The key pair can be generated by a trusted third party. In this case, the private key must be transmitted to the decryptor via a channel that is protected in terms of confidentiality.

The private key must be protected by the decryptor. Regardless of which entity undertakes the key pair generation, the public key must be made available to the encryptor. The encryptor must be confident that the public key belongs to the decryptor. This can be achieved using digital certificates (if a trusted third party is available) or by transport through integrity-protected channels with data origin authentication enabled.

- **Asymmetric Cryptographic Algorithm:** The most commonly used asymmetric encryption algorithm is the RSA algorithm, named after its inventors (Rivest, Shamir, & Adleman, 1978). The RSA algorithm is based on the difficulty of factoring large integers.

XML Security Models

XML security standards present the major processing rules for the fulfilment of security requirements. Basically, XML security standards use traditional cryptographic protocols and security standards, all combined with XML technologies. The XML security standards include XML Encryption (Imamura et al., 2002) to provide confidentiality, XML digital signatures (Bartel, Boyer, Fox, LaMacchia, & Simon, 2002) to cover integrity, XML key management (XKMS) (Hallam-Baker & Mysore, 2005) to provide public key registration and validation, XML Access Control Mark-up Language (XACML) (GODIK & MOSES, 2002) for stating authorization rules, and security assertion markup language -SAML (OASIS, 2002) to cover authentication and attribute assertions.

An XML security model needs to support the following:

1. A robust authorization mechanism whereby it can control accessibility to content and structure.
2. Ability to reuse existing security and cryptographic technologies when needed.

Figure 7. XML Signature structure

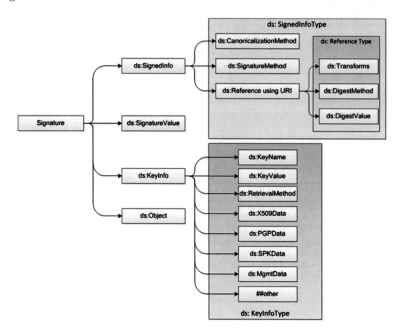

3. The ability to enforce security policies efficiently without the need to look up the underlying document.
4. Schema information, characterizing exactly those elements accessible to each type of user.

XML Signature

XML Signature was first introduced by (Bartel et al., 2002), XML Signature defines a standard format to represent digital signatures in XML, it provides a method for efficiently employing digital signatures to XML resources. However, XML Signature may also be utilized to sign binary resources like videos, images, and sound files. Several resources within XML can be covered by one signature, whether it is a whole document, part of a document, or a binary document.

W3C has established related specifications that are required when the actual XML Signature is deployed. These specifications are:

1. Exclusive XML Canonicalization Version 1.0, published by W3C (JOHN BOYER, EASTLAKE, & REAGLE, 2002).
2. Canonical XML Version 1.0, published by W3C Recommendation (J. Boyer, 2001).
3. XML Signature XPath Filter 2.0, published by W3C Recommendations (J. Boyer, Hughes, & Reagle, 2003).

The above specifications led W3C to publish a second edition (Bartel, Boyer, Fox, LaMacchia, & Simon, 2008). Figure 7 represents the XML Signature element's basic structure.

As illustrated in Figure 7, the structure of XML Signature starts from the *<ds:Signature>* element at the top of the document. The root element *<ds:Signature>* contains four main sub-elements,

Figure 8. Enveloped, detached, and enveloping signatures

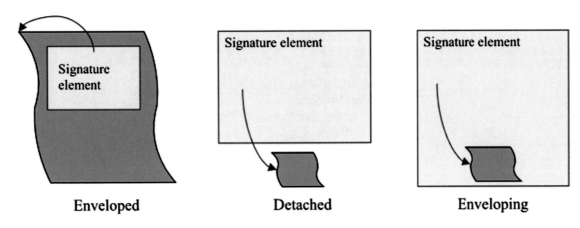

which are: *<ds:SignedInfo>*, *<ds:SignatureValue>*, *<ds:KeyInfo>*, and *<ds:Object>*. The element *<ds:SignedInfo>* includes references to the applied algorithms used in XML Signature generation, the hash value, and the target in the XML data (Weerasinghe, Elmufti, Rajarajan, & Rakocevic, 2006). Signature results are stored in the element *<ds:SignatureValue>*; element *<ds:KeyInfo>* contains the public key information that is used when the XML Signature is verified. The element *<ds:Reference>* within the element *<ds:SignedInfo>* is connected with each resource; A Uniform Resource Identifier (URI) identifies all resources. A digest of the referenced resource is included in the *<ds:Reference>* element. The *<ds:SignedInfo>* element can contain multiple *<ds:Reference>* elements. The element *<ds:SignedInfo>* contains references to the resources being signed. Therefore, an XML signature might be enveloping, enveloped, or detached taking into consideration each referenced resource. Figure 8 illustrates enveloped, detached, and enveloping signatures.

If the Signature element is within the referenced XML resource, then we call this signature an enveloped signature. If the signature references a resource that is separate from the Signature element, then we call this signature a detached signature. Finally if the signature references a resource that is contained within the Signature element, then we call this signature an enveloping signature. When the signature is enveloping, an instance of the object element is used to contain the resource.

As the Signature element of an enveloped signature is actually located within the XML document being signed, an enveloped signature transform is defined. This transform removes the entire Signature element from the digest calculation, so that the Signature element is not included in the digest of the XML resource being signed. Otherwise it would not be possible to calculate the correct digest, considering that the resource (from which the digest is to be calculated) would be subject to change when adding the digest to the Signature element. XML Encryption also uses *<ds:KeyInfo>* element, this element is defined by XML Signature. The *<ds:KeyInfo>* element is extended by XML Encryption with an *<EncryptedKey>* element, which might support the transport for a symmetric/secret key. The <KeyInfo> element is used by the XML Key Management Specification as well.

Figure 9. XML Encryption structure

```
<EncryptedData Id? Type? Encoding?>
  <EncryptionMethod/>
  <ds:KeyInfo>
    <EncryptedKey/>
    <AgreementMethod/>
    <ds:KeyName/>
    <ds:RetrievalMethod/>
  </ds:KeyInfo>
  <CipherData>
    <CipherValue/>
    <CipherReference URI/>
  </CipherData>
  <EncryptionProperties/>
</EncryptedData>
```

XML Encryption

XML Encryption was first released by W3C as a proposed recommendation (Eastlake & Reagle, 2002; Imamura et al., 2002), providing encryption for different sizes of units. The units may be a whole XML document, an element within a document, XML element content, or an attribute.

XML Encryption is an encryption technology that is optimized for XML data. A format is provided for using the XML processing rules in encryption and decryption processes. XML Encryption can be performed partially, which encrypts selected tags within the XML document, or multiple times, which enables the data to be encrypted multiple times. XML can be used to facilitate resolving XML data eavesdropping.

Generally, an XML element containing encrypted XML information can act as a container for the encrypted data, keys, or both. XML Encryption is able to encrypt the whole XML document and is also capable of encrypting parts of the XML document (Geuer-Pollmann, 2002). The inclusion of encrypted content can be as a reference via the transform machine or can be included in the container. Key management is offered by XML Encryption to facilitate the symmetric wrapping of the private keys being used, private key transportation, and key agreements using a Diffie-Hellman key (Diffie & Hellman, 1976) exchange. By using the XML Encryption standard, we gain a number of benefits, including:

- An XML element can act as a container for encrypted data, as a container for encrypted key material, or as a container for both. However, in order to act like a container, the XML element should contain XML Encryption information.
- User data can be encrypted by using XML Encryption, like:
  ◦ Full XML documents (Geuer-Pollmann, 2002).
  ◦ Single elements inside an XML document.
  ◦ The content of an element inside an XML document.
  ◦ Arbitrary binary content outside of an XML document.
- The ability to allow direct inclusion of the encrypted content in the container.
- The ability to de-reference the encrypted content via the URI / transforms mechanism.

Figure 10. <EncryptedData> element and components

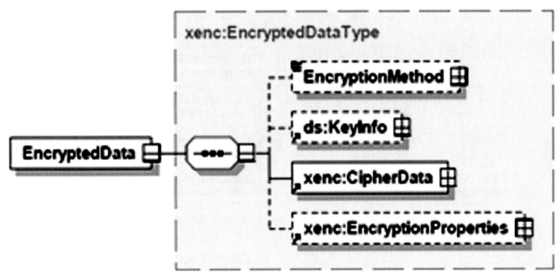

- XML Encryption offers key management facilities for:
  - The symmetric wrapping of secret keys.
  - Key transport of secret keys.
  - Key agreement using a Diffie-Hellman key.

Figure 9 illustrates the structure of XML Encryption provided by W3C. Data objects are encapsulated within a defined encryption element called *<EncryptedData>*. This element contains essential sub-elements that describe how the data is encrypted; the first sub-element is *<EncryptionMethod>*, which determines which encryption algorithm is used within the XML message. The second sub-element is *<EncryptedKey>*, which is used to transport encryption keys between the sender and receiver; it can also be used individually in a separate XML message. *<KeyInfo>* is the third sub-element and is used to specify the associated keying material. Another major element is *<CipherData>*, a mandatory element that provides the encrypted data. It must contain the encrypted octet sequence of the base64 encoded text of the *<CipherValue>* element. Another way is by providing a reference to an external location that contains an encrypted octet sequence location via another element called *<CipherReference>*. Figure 10 and Figure 11 represent both the *<EncryptedData>* element and the *<EncryptedKey>* element with all their sub-elements.

The W3C XML Encryption Recommendation allows two different granularity levels: encryption of full sub-trees whereby a single element and all its descendants are encrypted, and encryption of sequences of sub-trees whereby a sub-tree can be a single node or a mixed sequence (comments, elements, text, and processing instructions).

- Drawing A in Figure 12 presents the encryption of a sub-tree rooted by the element 'X'. The element and all its descendants are encrypted into a single <EncryptedData> element.
- Drawing B in Figure 12 presents the encryption of the content of element 'X'. All children of the element and their respective descendants are encrypted into a single <EncryptedData> element.

Figure 11. <EncryptedKey> element and components

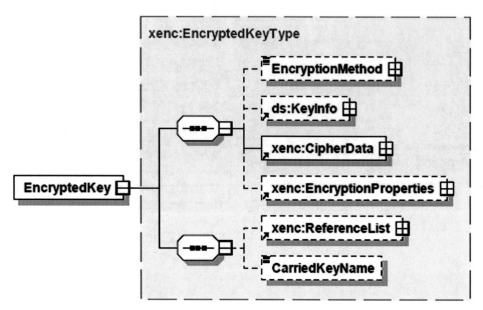

Figure 12. W3C Encryption possibilities (modes)

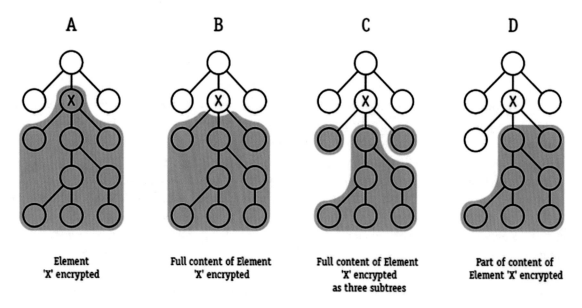

- Drawing C in Figure 12 presents sub-tree encryption applied three times to each child of element 'X'. Each sub-tree rooted by a child node of element 'X' is encrypted into a separate <EncryptedData> element.
- Drawing D in Figure 12 presents a way to use content encryption: two subsequent sub-trees are grouped together and are encrypted together.

Figure 13. Encrypting the encrypted content for multiple recipients (super-encryption)

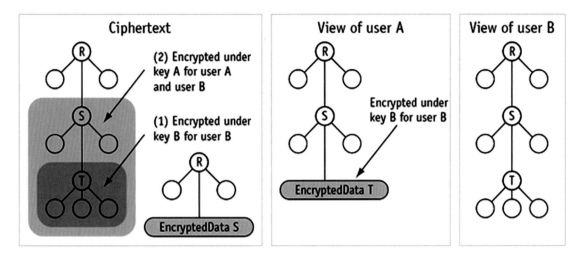

The decryption in drawings A and C leads to single elements. The octets resulting after the decryption in drawings B and D are not directly parse-able but must be wrapped in a start tag / end tag combination.

Encryption for Multiple Recipients

1. **Encrypting the Same Content:** There are different ways to encrypt any resource intended for multiple recipients. The basic case is where all recipients have the privilege to see the same portion of the document, which means the content is encrypted only once, whereas the content encryption key is encrypted multiple times (once for each recipient). The document should include a single <EncryptedData> element for the encrypted content and an <EncryptedKey> element for each recipient, which includes the content encryption key encrypted under the recipient's key.
2. **Super Encryption:** When recipients are allowed to see different portions of a document, then there is a way to encrypt content for multiple recipients. Figure 13 illustrates the process of encrypting encrypted content multiple times.

The process of encrypting parts of an XML tree leads to the substitution of the existing plaintext structure with the appropriate XML Encryption element *<EncryptedData>*. Super-encryption applies when the *<EncryptedData>* element or its ancestors are encrypted.

As illustrated in Figure 13, the element 'T' sub-tree is encrypted under a key B for a recipient B. After the first step, the element 'S' sub-tree is encrypted under key A for both recipients A and B. Keys A and B are processed by recipient B. Key A is processed only by recipient A. After the two encryption steps, the main document contains the 'R' element and two unencrypted notes along with the *<EncryptedData>* element, which has the encrypted element 'S' and its descendants. Both recipients A and B can decrypt the outer *<EncryptedData>* element because they have key A. The decrypted element 'S' contains the inner *<EncryptedData>* element.

The inner *<EncryptedData>* element can only by decrypted by recipient B because recipient B is the only one who possesses key B. There is a part in the document where recipient A is aware that he

Figure 14. Sample XML financial message

```
<?xml version="1.0"?>
<Transfers>
  - <Transaction xmlns="http://example.org/paymentv2" ImportanceLevel="001">
        <TransactionAmount>250</TransactionAmount>
        <From_Account>3214569987456321457</From_Account>
        <Transaction_Currency Code="USD">001</Transaction_Currency>
        <Account_Type Code="001">Personal</Account_Type>
        <Payee_Name>Faisal Ammari</Payee_Name>
        <Branch_Code>Amman</Branch_Code>
    </Transaction>
</Transfers>
```

is not able to decrypt it. Recipient A can make an estimation of how large the plaintext (undecrypted) portion is. This estimation is based on the number of octets of the undecryptable ciphertext. Recipient B has both content decryption keys A and B and performs the decryption in two stages: decrypting the *<EncryptedData>* element containing 'T' is performed after decrypting the *<EncryptedData>* element that contains the 'S' plaintext.

After performing the decryption process, the document is decrypted in full and is available to recipient B. Recipient B acknowledges that super-encryption of the innermost *<EncryptedData>* is done in order to prevent other users accessing the inner information

Serialization of XML for XML Encryption

Usually, symmetric encryption algorithms such as DES and AES are used for encrypting large amounts of data. Symmetric encryption algorithms transform a plaintext octet string into a ciphertext octet string and vice versa. Due to the tree-structured nature of XML, it must be converted into an octet string prior the encryption process, and then converted back from an octet string into a tree-based structure after the decryption process.

In order to encrypt portions of a given XML document, the application selects balanced portions of XML and serializes them into a UTF-8 encoded octet sequence.

Namespace nodes and associated attributes in the XML namespace need to be taken care of: moving encrypted data into a different context can lead to inconsistent results after the decryption process. Such issues happen if the decrypted plaintext uses namespace prefixes without defining them.

Example of XML Encryption

Figure 14 illustrates a sample XML message fetched from a real production environment. Considering the plaintext shown in Figure 14, this represents a financial transaction containing public information about the transaction (payee name and branch code) and sensitive information (payee account).

Parts of the XML message shown in Figure 14 will be encrypted. Figure 15 illustrates the sample XML message after deploying XML encryption on the selected tag <From_Account>, which denotes the full account number of the payee.

Figure 15. Sample XML financial message after partial W3C encryption

```
<?xml version="1.0"?>
- <Transfers>
    - <Transaction xmlns="http://example.org/paymentv2">
          <TransactionAmount>250</TransactionAmount>
        - <EncryptedData xmlns="http://www.w3.org/2001/04/xmlenc#" Type=
          "http://www.w3.org/2001/04/xmlenc#Element">
          - <CipherData>
                  <CipherValue>Vtbfzl75UFx3pKYBWzJGzrpZy1XzM2zxuz2DJbMl5
                  weHXGTUH </CipherValue>
            </CipherData>
          </EncryptedData>
          <Transaction_Currency Code="USD">001</Transaction_Currency>
          <Account_Type Code="001">Personal</Account_Type>
          <Payee_Name>Faisal Ammari</Payee_Name>
          <Branch_Code>Amman</Branch_Code>
    </Transaction>
</Transfers>
```

The *<Transaction>* element was substituted by an *<EncryptedData>* element of type element. The *<EncryptedData>* element contains the *<CipherData>* element, which uses a *<CipherValue>* element to save the encrypted *<Transaction>* element and all its descendants.

Example Implementations of XML Encryption

One of the most well-known implementations of XML encryption is XEnc (Imamura et al., 2002). XEnc is a stream-based prototype implementation that uses the Xerces Native Interface (XNI) of Xerces2. The implementation using XNI API achieves a reduction in processing time of 0.27%–26% for XML documents encryption that have sizes larger than 2KB and 34-88% reduction in decryption of XML documents of any size. Despite the reduced processing time, the issue has been raised as to whether XNI SAX API capable of parsing decrypted data efficiently.

XEnc uses DOM in many if not most of the implmentations, rather than using SAX API. preferring DOM than SAX as DOM because that DOM has the ability to parse decrypted data in an efficient way. However, Implementing DOM cost more time and space compared to SAX API due to XML document being parsed in memory.

Issues Regarding Attribute Values

XEnc uses element-wise encryption as a security mechanism, which secures both elements and content. Despite the flexible nature of XEnc. However, it is impossible to handle attribute encryption due to the XML Encryption Syntax and Processing rules. There are two solutions proposed by Simon (Ed, 2000), who first uncovered this issue. It is assumed that the alt attribute of the video element in Figure 16 will be encrypted.

Figure 16. The alt attributes (to be encrypted) of a video element

```
<video alt="C++ tutorial in 10 days" src="tutorial1.mpeg"/>
```

Figure 17. Output of encrypting the alt attribute of the video element

```
<video src="tutorial1.mpeg" enc:EncryptedDataManifest="./EncryptedDataManifest"
xmlns:enc="http://www.w3.org/xml/encryption/...">
    <EncryptedDataManifest xmlns="http://www.w3.org/xml/encryption/...">
    <EncryptedData Type="video/mpeg Name="tutorial1.mpeg">
        <CipherText URI="secret.enc"/>
    </EncryptedData>
    <EncryptedData Type="AttributeValue" Name="alt">
        <CipherText>AbCd...WxYz</CipherText>
    </EncryptedData>
    </EncryptedDataManifest>
</video>
```

The first solution was proposed to replace the targeted attribute that needs encryption with the *<EncryptedDataManifest>* attribute and adding other encryption details within the element. The output of this solution is illustrated in Figure 17.

The second solution was proposed to transform the attribute into elements by using XSLT to be used for encryption. However, this proposed solution is inefficient because the decrypted needs to be transformed back into attributes. Transformation is needed to validate the document against its XML Schema (if there is one).

XML Key Management

XKMS stands for XML Key Management Specification. XKMS Version 1.0 was first submitted to the W3C in 2001 (Phillip M & Ford, 2001). XKMS Version 2.0 was proposed and published in 2005 by Hallam-Baker (Hallam-Baker & Mysore, 2005). The main objective of XKMS is to provide a way to implement a Public Key Infrastructure (PKI) in web services and applications (King, 2003). XKMS has been developed to facilitate PKI handling, providing a simplified interface through which the application can pass. XKMS simplifies PKI handling by moving the complexity of dealing with the PKI from the application to the XKMS service itself. The application is thus protected from primary complexities (O'Neill, 2003).

In both cases, X-KRSS provides mechanisms for authenticating clients. X-KISS defines two main services: locate service and validate service. <KeyInfo> element provides the data format that is needed for communicating key information; this element is defined by XML Encryption. Thus, it will facilitate the utilization of XKMS together with XML Encryption and XML Signature.

XKMS consist of two parts. The first part is called X-KRSS, which stands for XML Key Registration Service Specification. The second part is called X-KISS, which stands for XML Key Information Service Specification. X-KRSS defines the services for the processes of registering, revoking, recovering, and reissuing keys. The client or provided service can perform the process of new public keys registration. If the client generates the key pair, then the client is required to provide or present the authenticity of

Figure 18. Obtaining a validated public key by sender B for sender A

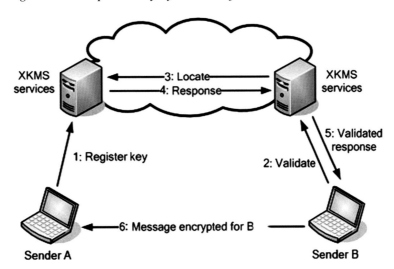

their owning the private key to be able to register for public key. Regardless of whether the client or the provided service generates the key pair, KRSS provides mechanisms to authenticate clients. There are two services defined by X-KISS: locate service and validate service. The locate service allows a client to fetch information about a public key or it allow a client to fetch a public key. The validate service allows a client to fetch information about a public key or it allow a client to fetch a public key but it confirms that the information returned matches specific validation rules. The <KeyInfo> element defined by XML Encryption is used to provide the data format that is used to communicate key information.

Figure 18 illustrates how XKMS operates in steps. In Figure 18, sender B target is to submit the encrypted document to sender A using the public key in possession. Though, sender B does not have sender A's public key. Although sender A has the public key registered using XKMS service, within the sender A's domain there is no trust relationship established between sender B and the XKMS service. This can be resolved by sender B contacting the validate service within sender B's domain, requesting a public key for sender A to be used in the encryption process. This request might be forwarded by the validate service to the locate service within sender A's domain. Validate service will validate the response within its own domain; validation process is performed before the sender B has the response returned.

Security Assertion Markup Language (SAML)

SAML stands for Security Assertion Markup Language (Cantor, Kemp, Philpott, & Maler, 2005). SAML defines the representation of security assertions within XML documents. An assertion process is a set of pre-defined statements, created by an assertion authority, which a relying party may trust. Figure 19 represents the assertion process, whereby the required assertion is identified by the issuer element. There are three statement types defined by SAML: authorization, authentication, and attribute statements. The same abstract type derives the three statement types, from which any additional statement types may be derived as well. Any number of statements can be included in a SAML assertion. In cases where the assertion has all three assertion types, it is necessary to indicate the subject type to which assertion type can be applied, in order to utilize the subject element. Subjects' confirmation methods can be specified

Figure 19. SAML assertion elements

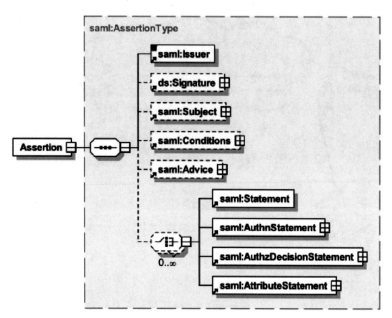

by the subject element. Such methods can be used to ensure that the message origin is exactly from the subject identified in the assertion. There are many methods for subject confirmation (Hughes et al., 2005). Usually, the message is signed by the subject and by using a private key associated with the assertion. Signing the message can be performed by other applications' specific procedures.

XML Extensible Access Control Markup Language (XACML)

XACML stands for Extensible Access Control Markup Language and is an open standard XML-based language designed to explain the security policies and access privileges to data and information for digital rights management (DRM), web services, and enterprise security applications. XACML was first introduced by OASIS (Organization for the Advancement of Structured Information Standards) in 2003 (Godik & Moses, 2003). The main objective of XACML is to set a basic standard for access control through XML language.

XACML can work in conjunction with SAML, whereby a rule engine with policies expressed in XACML can compare such information with established criteria to ascertain user rights.

Figure 20 illustrates the basic components of XACML. As seen in Figure 20, the policy enforcement point and the policy decision point can be shared with SAML.

An access request arrives for authorization at the Policy Enforcement Point (PEP). An XACML request is created by the PEP and submitted to the Policy Decision Point (PDP), which then evaluates all incoming requests and sends it back with responses (either accepted or denied).

A decision is made by the PDP after evaluating the relevant policies and the rules within them. Not all policies are evaluated; only relevant policies are picked up for the evaluation process, which depends on the policy target.

Figure 20. XACML components

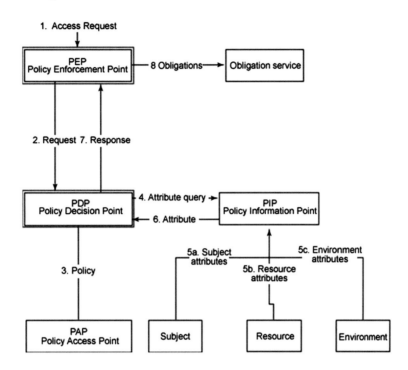

The Policy Access Point (PAP) is used by the PDP to fetch all policies, write policies and policy sets, and to ensure the policies are available to the PDP. In order to retrieve the attribute values associated with the subject, resources, or the environment, the PDP may invoke the Policy Information Point (PIP). The PEP fulfills the needed requirements once the authorization decision arrived at by the PDP either permits or denies access.

Text Categorization

Text categorization is the process of assigning text documents to a predefined set of categories/classes. There are two main phases involved in the categorization process: the training phase and the fuzzification phase. In the training phase, sets of documents belonging to each category are used to create representations of the categories. The classification phase compares the representations resulting from the training phase with a new document in order to assign a new document to one or more category. Many algorithms that can be used to perform the process of text categorization, including k-nearest neighbour classification (kNN) (Guo, Wang, Bell, Bi, & Greer, 2006), support vector machines (SVMs) (Brank, Grobelnik, Milic-Frayling, & Mladenic, 2003), neural networks (Ng, Goh, & Low, 1997), linear least squares fit mapping (LLSF) (Yang & Chute, 1993), the vector space method (Gauch, Madrid, Induri, Ravindran, & Chadlavada, 2004), and naïve Bayes classification (NB) (McCallum & Nigam, 1998). (Yang & Liu, 1999) conducted a performance comparison of all these classification systems and found that SVMs and kNN significantly outperform all other classifiers.

Figure 21. Characteristic function of a crisp set

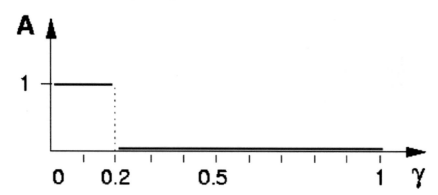

Fuzzy Logic Model

Fuzzy logic (FL) was first introduced by (L.A. Zadeh, 1965). Fuzzy logic is based on multi-value logic, which allows intermediate values to be defined between conventional evaluations in the form of Yes/No, True/False, etc. Different concepts like "very short" or "rather slow" can be formulated in mathematical notations and processed by computers, in order to apply a more human-like way of thinking (L. A. Zadeh, 1984).

FL provides a powerful method to reach a certain conclusion that is based on vague, uncertain, or noisy information. In order to make faster decisions, FL provides a mechanism to control problems. FL provides the ability to integrate rule-based approach (consist of IF X and Y THEN Z rules) to solving control problems.

The FL approach provides essential information to assist financial decision makers in effectively measuring and identifying sensitive information, essential parts and important figures within financial transactions, more so than the existing qualitative approaches. This is because, using FL, the degree of importance within each financial transaction is quantified based on a combination of financial historical data and input by experts.

Over the years, FL has been used to integrate expert input into computer models for a large scope of applications in different categories. The main advantage of the fuzzy methodology is that it enables the processing of ambiguously defined variables and variables whose relationships cannot be defined by any mathematical relationships. In order to define those variables along their relationships, fuzzy logic can incorporate expert human judgment for that purpose.

Fuzzy Sets and Crisp Sets

The fuzzy subset is the basic concept of fuzzy systems. In mathematics, we call it a crisp set. Figure 21 illustrates the characteristic function of a crisp set.

In Figure 21, the elements that have been assigned the number 1 can be interpreted as the elements that are in set A, whereas the elements that have been assigned the number 0 are the elements that are not in set A. This concept lacks flexibility for some applications. The upper range is difficult to define. So, the upper range is set to 0.2. Thus, we get B as a crisp interval defined as following: (B= [0, 0, 2]). However, this means that a value of 0.21 is not considered low while a value of 0.20 is considered low.

Figure 22. Characteristic function of a fuzzy set

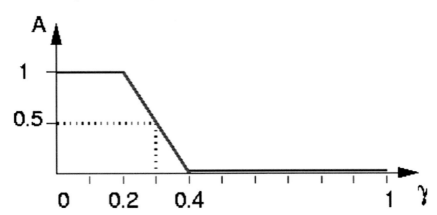

To construct the set B in a more natural way is by relaxing the strict separation between low and not low. This can be achieved by allowing more flexible rules like "fairly low" rather than allowing only the crisp decisions. A fuzzy set will enable us to define such a notion.

The intention is to utilize fuzzy sets to be able to make computers more 'intelligent'. And so, the idea above needs to be coded more formally. A straight method to generalize this concept would be to enable more values between 0 and 1. Actually, infinitely many choices could be permitted between the bounds 1 and 0, specifically the unit interval $I = [0, 1]$. A gradual membership is reflected by all other values to establish B. This really is proven in Figure 22. The membership function is a graphical representation of the magnitude of contribution of every input signal. It associates a weighting with all of the inputs which are processed, identifies functional overlap between inputs, and ultimately determines an output result. The rules utilize the input membership values as weighting factors to ascertain their influence in the fuzzy output sets of the final output conclusion.

The membership function, functioning in this instance in the fuzzy set of interferometric coherence g, returns a value between 0.0 and 1.0. It's significant to indicate the distinction between probability and fuzzy logic. Both operate over exactly the same numeric range and have similar values: 0.0 represents non-membership (or False) and 1.0 represents full membership (or True). However, there's a distinction to be made between the two statements. The probabilistic approach yields the natural language statement, "There is a 50% likelihood that g is low", as the fuzzy language corresponds to "g's degree of membership within the set of low interferometric coherence is 0.50." The semantic difference is critical: the first view supposes that g is or isn't low; the chance to know which set it is in is only 50%. Fuzzy terminology assumes that g is "more or less" low or, corresponds to the value of 0.50.

Fuzzy Inference Process

FL can allow the use of degrees of truth in order to calculate results. FL techniques allow one to represent concepts that could be considered to be in more than one category. which means the representation of overlapping and partial membership in sets or categories is allowed (Bridges & Vaughn, 2001). There are four main steps involved in the FL inference process (Cox, 2001b), which are:

Figure 23. Fuzzy inference process

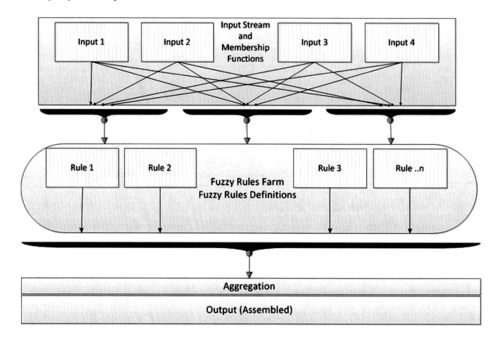

Step 1 (Fuzzification): Taking the crisp input X and input Y, the process determines the degree to which these inputs belong to and where they fit in the fuzzy set.

Step 2 (Rule Evaluation): Taking the fuzzy inputs, the qualified fuzzy rules are applied. Fuzzy operators (AND / OR) are used in case of any uncertainty to get a single value. The outcome value is called a "Truth Value", which will be applied to the membership function for rule evaluation.

Step 3 (Aggregation of the Rule Outputs): The outputs of all the rules are unified. Scaled rules are combined into a single fuzzy set for each variable.

Step 4 (Transforming the Fuzzy Output into a Crisp Output): The output should have a clear, crisp value and it will be assigned to each tag classified.

Figure 23 illustrates the FL inference process, showing the four major steps required to perform the FL inference lifecycle.

Fuzzy logic is needed because of the ability that FL has to accept vaguely defined data. It has the ability to model non-linear functions of arbitrary complexity and can build on the experience of experts.

Summary

This section introduces the XML model and its basic components and the schema languages involved. This section also introduces the main XML security techniques that are utilized in XML security specifications. The XML security specifications published by W3C and OASIS are the core of XML security technology, such as XML Encryption. XML Encryption makes XML data confidential and it ensures this using XML Encryption technology.

Text categorization has been discussed as well to describe the classification methods for the text documents and their associated algorithms to categorize data into relevant categories properly.

Finally, fuzzy logic has been introduced to explain the methodology we are using in this research to identify how we will classify XML content and find the importance level for each tag included within the XML document.

THE STATE OF THE ART TECHNOLOGY

Models are the key factor inspiring and supporting this research. Classifying XML messages using fuzzy logic (FL) is the other key part of this research and is also discussed and analyzed in this section.

XML Encryption Models

Companies and financial institutions adopted XML as a standard in their data communication and exchanges among different platforms due to its independency, flexibility, and ability to enable custom structures and creations. XML documents are exchanged via variant communication mediums, which in some cases have weak security measurements; they may use unsecured channels or may even be hacked by an unknown party. XML documents are well known to be verbose, which make them readable by machines and humans as well. Any plaintext editor should be enough to read, modify, or change the contents to cause real damage.

Therefore, some XML encryption models have been proposed and published to ensure the confidentiality of transferred XML messages and to make sure they reach their destinations without any issues.

(W3C, 2001) first published the XML Encryption Standard (XEnc) by describing the syntax needed to represent encrypted XML data and the process of encrypting and decrypting XML data. Data confidentiality is achieved by the XML encryption by hiding sensitive information so that it can only be understood by targeted recipients. The XEnc structure syntax is defined by using XML Schema.

Element-wise encryption is the security provided by XEnc, where elements and content are integrated with each other. Due to the flexible and extensible nature, the XEnc standard can be used and processed by XML tools. However, it is impossible to expand their capability handling attribute encryption due to the current XML Encryption Syntax and Processing rules.

(Maruyama & Imamura, 2000), (E & B, 2000), and (Takeshi & Hiroshi, 2000) have worked on XML element-wise encryption, which supports W3C in delivering a candidate specification for XML encryption (Imamura et al., 2002). The candidate specification specifies a process for encrypting data and representing the result of the encryption process in XML. Data might be in different format, for example it could be arbitrary data, XML elements, or XML element content.

The encrypted data element is called *<EncryptedData>*. This element identifies the format of the encrypted data; the identification does not include user's ability to identify how the XML document is encrypted. It is impossible to handle attribute encryption due to the *<EncryptedData>* element's syntax.

(Ed, 2001) explained the attribute encryption as following: Elements and attributes are identified by XML for information structuring and applications that uses attributes in a frequent basis. Author urged the support of attributes encryption unless it is impossible to support.

(Steve, 2001) explained the difficulty of redesigning a legacy application and XML vocabularies in cases of existing attributes containing data. Such redesigning can be onerous when there are pre-existing XML data and applications. The main goal is to find a simple yet effective way of handling the encryption of attribute data.

(D. Fallside, 2001) presented some negative sides of attribute encryption that might trigger issues. The first possible issue is that the encrypted XML document cannot be validated against the original XML schema. This will result amending the original schema so that it can identify particular encrypted elements. Briefly, assuming an XML document (X) with its schema (S) defining both structure of the document and content. Next, the encrypted document (Xs) will not follow (S), because it is impossible to present XML encryption without schema changes during the encryption process, as described in (Blair, 2001) and (Ed, 2001).

Without attribute encryption in XML, sensitive data cannot be stored securely in the attributes of XML documents. Also, we have to tell the users to redesign their legacy XML documents if they wish to apply XML encryption to them. We consider that the only acceptable reason for not including attribute encryption in XML is if it is impractical or impossible to do so. After much discussion about the requirements, complexities, and alternatives of attribute encryption, the working group decided to proceed under the requirement of element encryption while remaining open to further comment, experimentation, and specification of attribute-encryption proposals or alternatives that satisfy the requirement to encrypt sensitive attribute values (Joseph, 2001). (Ed, 2001) also mentioned the possibility of leaving out attribute encryption until version 2.0 of XML encryption.

(Geuer-Pollmann, 2002) proposed an encryption approach called pool encryption: the approach has the ability to remove sensitive information from the resulting file. Each XML document is parsed into a DOM tree for encryption purposes. DOM tree nodes are labelled, the corresponding node has the position information attached to it. Each node is individually encrypted whereby it has an encryption key specified for each node. These nodes are removed later from their unique position located in the source document and placed into a pool of encrypted notes.

The pool of nodes can be stored either in different documents or in the source document; the choice will depend on the pre-defined security requirements. A unique node key is assigned to each node. The node keys are grouped into a pool of node keys to ease nodes management. The sender identifies the decryption competences of the different users by assuring that the recipient has the pool of node keys. The more keys the pool receives, the more nodes it can decrypt. The recipient will only be able to view parts within encrypted document taking into consideration the corresponding pool of node keys. This is because the pool is encrypted with the recipient's key before it is submitted to the recipient. Any node that does not match keys will be hidden and the recipient will not be able to view it. The individual nodes which have the bundled original position information uses this information during decryption process in order to restore any specific node back to its original position within the XML document. The pool encryption method is able to remove confidential information from the document; this method is also able to hide both the size and the existence of encrypted content. By performing this method, it prevents information leakage to unauthorized users to access the document. However, there are number of disadvantages related to this method due to the change in the size of the encrypted document to prevent any traffic analysis attack. Disadvantages defined as following:

- The encrypted document size is changed due to the pool of node keys.
- Increase in encrypted document size due to added position information.
- For each node, the encryption process and decryption process are executed separately.
- Each node has to have a unique node key generated.
- The original position information has to be attached to particular individual nodes.

- At the contrary of the ordinary encryption/decryption processes, the process of reassembling and flattening nodes requires intensive resource usage.

The above disadvantages cause high memory usage, large storage requirements, high bandwidth consumption, and high processor power consumption.

(Rosario, 2001) introduced the concept of XML access control (XAC), which is a server-side access control whereby a trusted access control processor allows security policies and procedures to be established based on policies. XAC presents a way to control the access of users to specific portions of a full XML document that is stored on a server.

XAC encrypts an XML element with the ability to exclude its descendants. This specific feature of XAC gives an advantage over XEnc because XEnc requires the encryption of a full sub-tree.

XAC pruning process refers to the authorization of a user and in the next step it removes elements labelled with "deny (-)" from the tree.

Thus, it declines the requesting user from reading sensitive information and also it prevents the user from gaining information about any existing sensitive content. In brief, only elements with "permit (+)" labels remains in the resulting file. The pruning process is executed online at the same time the client issues a query (similar to SQL query). It is similar to XEnc but without encryption after pruning process. However, a form of additional security is needed (like SSL) to transmit the document in a secure mode to users.

However, XAC restricts the user's access to a document. Some of the techniques used: mandatory access control, rule-based access control, access control list, discretionary access control, role-based access control, and lattice-based access control.

Table 1 illustrates the three main XML encryption approaches with their advantages and disadvantages.

Fuzzy XML Modelling

Over the years, fuzzy systems have been used successfully in many fields to handle the imprecise and uncertain information that is commonly found in real-world applications, such as business and financial systems, data mining, and decision-making systems.

(L.A. Zadeh, 1965) addressed the representation of fuzzy information with fuzzy set theory. Fuzzy set theory has been successfully identified as a working technique to model imprecise and uncertain data and it has been introduced into many application areas, such as business intelligence (Petrovic, Roy, & Petrovic, 1999; R. R. Yager, 2000; Ronald R. Yager & Pasi, 2001) and database, semantic web, and information systems (Galindo, 2008; Klir & Yuan, 1995; Lukasiewicz & Straccia, 2008; Ortega, 2008; Smets, 1996).

XML is not able to represent and process vague and unclear data. Currently, less research has been done on modelling and querying imperfect XML data. XML documents with incomplete information have been researched by (Serge Abiteboul, Segoufin, & Vianu, 2006) and probabilistic data has been researched by (Nierman & Jagadish, 2002). (Lee & Fanjiang, 2003) developed a fuzzy-object-oriented modelling technique based on the XML language to model requirement specifications and incorporated the notion of stereotypes to facilitate the modelling of imprecise requirements.

(Gaurav & Alhajj, 2006) presented an approach to integrate fuzziness with XML. They base their approach on identifying possible entities in XML that might have fuzzy values. Their approach based on analysing XML document structure to identify which parts within the document that can be handled using

Table 1. XML encryption approaches

Approach	Advantages	Disadvantages
W3C XML Encryption Standard (2001)	• Only users that know the key can decrypt and read the message. Each recipient can only decrypt the parts of a message that are intended for them; they are unable to decrypt the rest. • *EncryptedData* is an XML element that replaces the data to be encrypted. The *EncryptedData* and the *EncryptedKey* are composed of other sub-elements, such as the encryption method, key information, and cipher value. • The entire XML message or only some parts can be encrypted. • If both the sender and the receiver have not exchanged the keys previously, the key can be sent in the message encrypted using a public key system.	• Unable to handle attribute encryption. • Leaves descendants visible. • Needs style sheets. • New recipients cannot be added without re-encrypting the content. • Neither of DTD nor schema definition is encrypted, both are exposed to "plaintext attack". Therefore, there is a risk of information leakage.
XML Pool Encryption (Christian Geuer-Pollmann – 2002)	• Uses a secure, complete sub-tree. • Has the ability to secure attribute values. • A new recipient can be added without re-encrypting the content.	• The original position information has to be attached to particular individual nodes. • The encrypted document size is changed due to the pool of node keys. • For each node, the encryption process and decryption process are executed separately. • Each node has to have a unique node key generated. • Increase in encrypted document size due to added position information. • At the contrary of the ordinary encryption/decryption processes, the process of reassembling and flattening nodes requires intensive resource usage.
XML Access Control (XAC) (Ricardo Rosario – 2001)	• Involves the automation of encryption/access decisions. • Attribute encryption is possible.	• Needs additional transport security. • Needs trustworthy servers.

fuzziness. They then specified the appropriate mechanism to integrate fuzziness. Their approach focused on XML being a structured (logical and physical) and well-formed language. They were interested in the logical structure as a key issue, defining the content (data) of an XML document. Then, they identified different parts of an element that can have fuzzy data. there are five items that might have fuzzy data: 1) simple elements "text only"; 2) complex or empty elements - the attribute value "val"; 3) complex element -only the element "val" and occurrence of <subElmt> within <elmt>; 4) complex or text only elements - attribute value "val" & "text"; 5) complex and mixed elements - attribute value "val", element content "text", and the occurrence of <subElmt> within <elmt>. This means that the elements content "text", the attribute value "val", and the <subElmt> of an <elmt> might be fuzzy entities within an XML document. this is declared from their evaluation of including the attribute "val", fuzzy data, and element content "text" as they are similar in nature and are all equivalent, as opposed to the <subElmt> of an <elmt>. Therefore, there are two main categories of entities in an XML document that might be fuzzy: the first category is when having an element content "text", or the attribute value "val", and the sub-element <subElmt> of an element <elmt>.

However, their approach does not tackle the production of nested, fuzzy XML schema or the provision of techniques to make vague queries on a vague XML document.

(Ma & Yan, 2007) introduced a fuzzy XML data model to manage fuzzy data in XML, based on possibility distribution theory, by first identifying the multiple granularity of data fuzziness in UML and XML. A fuzzy UML data model and a fuzzy XML data model that address all types of fuzziness were developed. Further, the author developed the formal conversions from the fuzzy UML model to the fuzzy XML model, as well as the formal mapping from the fuzzy XML model to fuzzy relational databases. It is noted that the fuzzy extension of XML in the author's model only focuses on XML DTD, because it has traditionally been the most common method for describing the structure of XML instance documents. However, XML DTD lacks enough expressive power to describe highly structured data properly, and XML Schema provides a much richer set of structures, types, and constraints for describing data.

(Tseng, Khamisy, & Vu, 2005) presented an XML methodology to represent fuzzy systems for facilitating collaborations in fuzzy applications and design. DTD and XML Schema are proposed to define fuzzy systems in general. One fuzzy system can be represented in different formats understood by different applications using the concept of XSLT style sheets. As an example, they represent a given fuzzy system in XML and transform it into comprehensible formats for Matlab and FuzzyJess applications.

(Tseng et al., 2005) methodological components consist of: a) an input base that consists of a collection of inputs (linguistic variables) containing terms and membership functions; b) a membership function repository that contains all the membership functions used to describe the fuzzy system; c) an inference engine that defines all operators used to perform inferencing; d) an operator repository that contains all the operators ("And", "Or", "Aggregations") used to describe the fuzzy system; e) a rule base that is a collection of fuzzy IF-THEN rules; f) defuzzification, which translates fuzzy set output values into crisp values; and g) an output base that consists of a collection of outputs (each being a linguistic variable data type).

On the lower side of their methodology, (Tseng et al., 2005) proposed fuzzy system data types that consist of: linguistic variables, linguistic terms, membership functions, operators, and rules. They then proposed a DTD as a kind of schema to describe fuzzy systems in XML; one DTD is defined per component and main data type. Fuzzy system schema can also be used to define fuzzy systems in XML; they define an individual XSD for each major component.

However, Tseng did not pay much attention to the design of reverse style sheets to transform fuzzy system descriptions in given software into an XML document that is compliant with their proposed XML schema.

(Turowski & Weng, 2002) introduced a formal syntax for the important fuzzy data types that are used to store fuzzy information. They defined appropriate DTDs as they show how fuzzy information, whose description is based on these DTDs, can be exchanged between application systems by using XML. As a result, they introduced a better approach for business applications integration using fuzzy approaches to business application systems. This allows better collaboration with application systems and development tools that use fuzzy approaches. Their approach focuses on encapsulating fuzzy information, and any related fuzzy data that describes fuzzy information in XML tags is named according to a standardized term set. By performing encapsulation, the messages that contain fuzzy information from other application systems get a meaning and can subsequently be processed. They defined a DTD as defining constraints on the logical structures of XML documents.

(Zhang, Ma, & Yan, 2013) proposed an approach along with an automated tool called FXML2FOnto for constructing fuzzy ontologies from fuzzy XML models. They also investigated how constructive fuzzy ontologies may be useful for improving some fuzzy XML applications (i.e. reasoning in fuzzy XML models). They first proposed a definition of fuzzy XML models that includes the XML document structure's fuzzy DTDs and the XML document content's fuzzy XML documents. Based on this definition, they proposed an approach to constructing fuzzy OWL DL ontologies from fuzzy XML models.

They used two key steps to construct the fuzzy OWL DL: first, transforming the fuzzy DTD into a fuzzy ontology at the structure level; second, transforming the fuzzy XML document into a fuzzy ontology at the instance level. They gave proof of the correctness of the transformation by providing a detailed construction example. Following the proposed approach, they implemented a prototype tool called FXML2FOnto, which automatically constructs fuzzy OWL DL ontologies from fuzzy XML models.

In the final stage of their approach, they reduced reasoning in fuzzy XML models to reasoning in fuzzy OWL DL ontologies, so that by using existing fuzzy ontologies' reasoning, the reasoning of fuzzy XML models can be automatically checked. The reasoning results may provide several simple optimization steps in answering queries over a fuzzy XML document base. By using this approach, it is possible to improve some fuzzy XML business and financial applications.

(Herrera-Viedma, Peis, Morales-del-Castillo, Alonso, & Anaya, 2007) proposed an evaluation model for websites that are based on XML documents that are user centred and based on a fuzzy linguistic approach. The evaluation model consists of two components: an evaluation scheme that contains the evaluation criteria to be considered in the website quality evaluation; and a computing method of linguistic quality ratings. In the evaluation scheme phase, they analysed the information quality of websites from the information user's perspective, considering the following: a) different quality approaches to information quality; b) generating quality ratings on websites provided by evaluators; c) not including an excessive number of quality dimensions to avoid conflicting users; and d) analysing websites that store information in multiple types of documents structured in XML format (i.e. scientific articles). Based on these considerations, they defined a user-centric evaluation scheme of websites that anticipates four quality categories with the following evaluation dimensions: 1) intrinsic quality of websites; 2) contextual quality of websites; 3) representational quality of websites; and 4) accessibility quality of websites. The second component in their model is a computing method of linguistic quality rating that is used to evaluate the information quality of websites that are based on XML documents. Linguistic ratings are obtained from the linguistic evaluation judgements provided by a non-determined number of web visitors. After a visitor has used an XML document stored in a website, they are invited to complete a quality evaluation questionnaire as per the quality dimensions created in the evaluation scheme.

Ratings of the linguistic quality are obtained by performing an aggregation function of the linguistic evaluation judgements by means of the LWA and LOWA operators, which are a linguistic family of OWA operators (R. R. Yager, 1988). These operators are used to allow inclusion of the concept of a "fuzzy majority" (Herrera, Herrera-Viedma, & Verdegay, 1996) in the computation of the rankings. The "fuzzy majority" is represented by the linguistic quantifier that is used to compute the weighting vector of the OWA operator.

However, their model has the following limitations. First, it uses little information about web users; the model is designed to compute quality ratings only. Therefore, the performance could be improved if user profiles are used in the computation process of quality ratings. Second, it is a user-dependent model, so the quality of the websites can be evaluated only if users' perceptions can be gathered.

Summary

In this section, we have presented various approaches to XML encryption standards. It discussed the capabilities, functions, and mainly primary criteria of the XML Encryption Standard.

During the study of existing approaches, various issues have been addressed, such as super encryption, attribute value encryption, and other security issues. XML encryption models have been compared with one another. Implementations are considered as well for a few of the models.

W3C may have to reconsider attribute value encryption, because it's not supported by the present XML Encryption Standard. If not, confidential information should be stored inside an element, consequently deprecating the use of attributes.

We have evaluated the W3C XML Encryption Syntax and Processing rules. The security offered by XEnc is element-wise encryption, content and comprising elements. It may be utilized together with XML Signature. Its flexibility and extensibility enables XEnc to be processed and used by XML family tools. However, it is impossible to extend the capability of the current XML Encryption Syntax and Processing rules to handle attribute encryption. We have also discussed XML access control (XAC) and made a comparison with XEnc: attribute encryption is possible in XAC. As its descendants can be excluded by the encryption of an element, XAC has greater flexibility over XEnc. This isn't permitted in XEnc as it requires the encryption of a complete sub-tree. However, XAC restricts the user's access to a document using several techniques, such as: discretionary access control, mandatory access control, role-based access control, rule-based access control, and lattice-based access control.

Pool encryption has also been reviewed as one of the encryption models that are used to encrypt XML documents. XML pool encryption has the capacity of removing sensitive content from the encrypted XML document. However, this model introduces a number of disadvantages, like the increase in the size of the encrypted document due to added position information. Such disadvantages lead to high storage, high bandwidth and memory requirements, and high processor power consumption.

Additionally, we have reviewed a number of fuzzy XML models and studies. Some of the studies tried to encapsulate fuzzy system descriptions in common elements that can be used to represent any fuzzy system. Some models proposed a DTD/XML schema to describe fuzzy systems in XML. Also, we have introduced studies presenting fuzzy XML data models that can be used to manage fuzzy data in XML, based on possibility distribution theory. Some models presented an approach to incorporating fuzziness in XML by identifying the possible entities in XML that might have fuzzy values. Potential entities that can handle fuzziness are identified by analyzing the XML document structure to incorporate fuzziness.

INTELLIGENT FUZZY-BASED FINANCIAL XML SECURITY MODEL

This section proposes a secure XML management model named SXMS. The model consists of two major parts. Each part has a discrete scope acting as an independent unit and forming an essential part of the whole system. Content is classified using a set of fuzzy classification techniques and encrypted using an element-wise encryption on selected parts within each XML message. This section also describes the combination of the model with XML message requirements and specifications.

The proposed model has been designed based on two major phases, each with a discrete scope acting as an independent unit and forming an essential part of the whole system. Phase one of the proposed models involves performing a set of fuzzy classification techniques on the targeted XML messages. The fuzzy classification process is designed mainly to decide the similarity between the different standards within the same message. Basically the main target is to classify XML content to find out which parts are essential to have a specific security standards deployed. Upon fuzzy classification, a new value is generated and assigned to an existing XML tag. The XML tag named "Importance Level" will be used as an identifier for the next phase. The "Importance Level" tag presents a value which is used to identify the sensitivity level for the carrying tag and corresponding nodes. Phase two involves applying element-wise encryption to different parts within each XML message. Encryption could be for the whole message or elements of an XML message. The "Importance Level" value assigned in phase one is also used to decide which type of encryption and key size is to be deployed. Element-wise encryption is based on W3C's recommendation (Maruyama & Imamura, 2000).

Proposed Model for Securing XML Financial Documents

This work presents a novel approach to securing XML financial messages by using a combination of fuzzy classification techniques and element-wise encryption. Main reason behind choosing FL technology for our classification stages is the ability of FL system to combine human expertise into computer-assisted decision making, facilitating more human-like decisions. FL is used in our proposed model to characterize XML message content sensitivity factors as fuzzy variables within each XML message, which determines the sensitivity level within the XML message to perform security measures on selected parts. The importance level rate for pre-selected nodes is a key factor to determine which encryption algorithm and keys are to be deployed. The importance level values are interpreted as "High", "Medium" or "Low".

During the fuzzification phase, element-wise encryption is performed on selected parts defined in the previous phase. Encryption type and key size is selected based on the "Importance Level" value. AES symmetric encryption with a 256-bit key size is deployed on tags with an "Importance Level" classified with a "High" value, and AES symmetric encryption with a 128-bit key size is deployed on tags with an "Importance Level" classified with a "Medium" value. Tags with a "Low" value are forwarded to the message assembler without performing any kind of encryption.

Model Requirements

The system is designed to achieve a set of goals ensuring secure and efficient exchange of XML banking messages. The following requirements are needed to form the system core:

1. **Messaging Interface:** Defines the syntax and semantics for the outgoing financial XML messages and ensures that our model understands them fully.
2. **XML Parser:** Deciphers incoming XML messages to ensure they are fully understood prior to further processing.
3. **Valid XML Message:** Submitted messages should be valid in terms of message structure whereby it represents the schema defined in the originating channel.
4. **Stamped XML Message:** The first security layer which identifies that the incoming XML message is valid and from a trusted source. The stamp is added in the message header ensuring the originating channel, date of transmission, and service ID are all presented in a pre-defined sequence.
5. **Communication Port:** A dedicated communication port needs to be used in our XML submission, which is different from the one used in service messaging.

Figure 24. Main system components

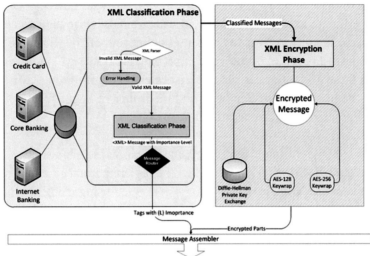

6. **XML Fuzzy Classification Characteristics:** The 10 characteristics that define each transaction, each item should be available in the XML message; this will allow our system to build the classification criteria using our fuzzy classification phase.

7. **Encryption Algorithm:** An encryption algorithm is needed to perform element-wise encryption. The AES encryption standard is being used in our model; we have chosen AES encryption over other algorithms for the following reasons:

    a.   Fast deployment for encryption/decryption processes in both software and hardware.

    b.   AES uses three key sizes: 128, 192, and 256 bits.

    c.   Advanced Encryption Standard not only assures security but also improves the performance in a variety of settings such as smartcards, and hardware implementations.

    d.   Currently there is no known non-brute-force direct attack against AES.

    e.   However, this can be replaced with other symmetric encryption standards.

8. **Encryption Key Management:** The encryption keys that are going to be used in our encryption phase must be managed.

9. **D-H Key Exchange:** The "public-key" or "asymmetric" cryptographic keys must be utilized.

10. **Message Assembler:** To assemble different XML parts coming from different stages, encrypted or forwarded parts should be received and combined in one final message.

System Architecture and Design

Based on system requirements, the system architecture is illustrated in Figure 24. Major system components are described in details in Figure 24. System modules act as independent units whereby each unit can act as separate system; modules are combined to form SXMS.

As illustrated in Figure 24, the system architecture core is built based on two main modules forming the system core:

1. **Fuzzy Classification Module:** In our fuzzy classification module, we categorized 10 transaction characteristics into three different layers according to their type. The characteristics were chosen after exploring different experts' opinions and backgrounds, reviewing financial analysis tools, reviewing technical reports, researching different online and offline financial systems conducted within the financial institution, and performing a set of internal surveys among banking group heads. We categorized these 10 transaction characteristics extracted from the XML message into three layers (Account Segment, Details Segment, and Environment Segment). Grouping will facilitate and simplify the process of fuzzy classification.

This phase performed a set of intelligent fuzzy classification techniques to assign a new value to an existing tag within each XML message. We called the tag "Importance Level", and the main idea is distinguish which parts of the XML message is to be encrypted using element-wise AES asymmetric encryption, and which parts are to be forwarded directly to the message assembler without further processing. The key size for AES encryption is dependent on the "Importance Level" value assigned in this stage. The 10 characters are defined as follows:

2. **Transaction Amount:** Financial institutions set pre-defined transaction limits. The limits allow users to perform transactions with specified limits on a daily basis. The range of transaction limits is defined based on the local policy within each institution. Banks normally treat the transaction amount as an alert to any critical transaction; the amount is used in most banks to measure the weight of the total transaction performed. Source, destination, and amount all combine to act as an alert which is already pre-defined based on the bank's policy. Large transaction amounts will affect the importance of the transaction itself, which can be used in our model as a measurement item in our importance-level evaluation.

3. **Transaction Currency:** There is a well-defined list of allowed currencies that can be used online or offline. Each currency has its own set of risk variables depending on usage and importance. Foreign currency uses exchange rates, operational interference, and market value for the transaction the moment occurred. Banks treat each FX transaction with high importance, because it involves buying and selling with bank's rate. We have used this factor in our importance evaluation.

4. **Account Type:** Accounts are segmented within each institution. Segmentation is performed to enable application of a set of internal rules on selected segments. Each segment has its own value and weight, for example corporate account segments are listed with high importance and priority because most of the transactions involve large volumes which can benefit the bank for each transaction. We used this factor due to its role in deciding the importance level for the whole transaction.

5. **Transaction Notes:** Exceptions are placed upon unusual activity on a specific account, and such exceptions will raise a flag in any transaction being processed to handle the exception before the process is completed. Having a flagged transaction will raise the importance level and trigger an alert to monitor that specific transaction due to its importance; we have used this factor to measure the importance level in terms of a transaction's critical weight.

6. **Profile ID:** A unique identifier for the destination account owner, the value is set during the system integration and profile creation process. Companies or individuals with custom profile IDs have a high potential to be monitored for transactions, and monitoring is based on the transaction amount after classifying each profile ID whereby a range of IDs are listed in the high importance zone, all after deploying a bank's methods and procedures.

7. **Account Tries:** How many times the account is used in the system; more usage means more trust whereby the history of the account is known and trusted. A historical log is kept and evaluated on a regular basis to confirm trusted accounts and suspicious ones. The evaluation will result in a set of important ranges of trusted accounts to be used in the transaction evaluation and setting the importance level.

8. **Incorrect Password Tries:** The number of times users try to enter the password incorrectly to complete the financial transaction. This factor adds a slight level of importance to each transaction, with a high rate of incorrect tries giving an indication of high importance.

9. **Time Spent on the Service:** The time spent navigating the service before performing the transaction. The time range is set based on the bank's policy, taking into consideration peak hours. This factor considers technical factors to measure the importance level of the transaction which is based on non-financial elements.

10. **Daily Transactions:** How many transactions are performed before the financial transaction is carried out. The number of daily transactions puts a weight on the overall importance level for the transaction itself, whereby the number of transactions to be performed is set based on the bank's policy within the allowed ranges.

11. **Transaction Time:** The financial day is categorized in three periods: peak period, normal hours, and dead zone. Periods are defined separately by the financial institution based on local policy and the historical transactions range. Each period has its own value which adds a level of importance and how the occurrence of any transaction is affected by the time of occurrence. Ranges are set to weigh an importance level when the transaction is performed.

12. **Encryption Module:** This module operates by performing an element-wise encryption using the AES encryption algorithm. Element-wise encryption is performed on selected portions of an XML document and their corresponding nodes defined previously in the fuzzy classification module. The encryption process can be applied to any number of elements whereby it is encoded using base64. Two key sizes are being used in this module, a 256-bit key and a 128-bit key, and usage depends on the "Importance Level" tag value classified earlier. Attributes with a value of "High" are encrypted using a 256-bit key size, attributes with a value of "Medium" are encrypted using a 128-bit key size, and finally the attributes with a value of "Low" are forwarded directly to the message composition stage without performing any kind of encryption.

13. **Message Assembly Module:** This module is responsible for gathering all pieces together, all in sequence of arrival. Encrypted and non-encrypted parts are being assembled for final submission to the message destination channel.

In section 5 we will test and evaluate above components. While we design the system, we took in consideration the following points:

- Ability to test against main requirements, each requirement should be tested with ease.
- System should be structured and well-defined. System code should be readable and easy to understand.
- Ability to reuse components, system design should be reusable.

Figure 25. Fuzzy Inference System

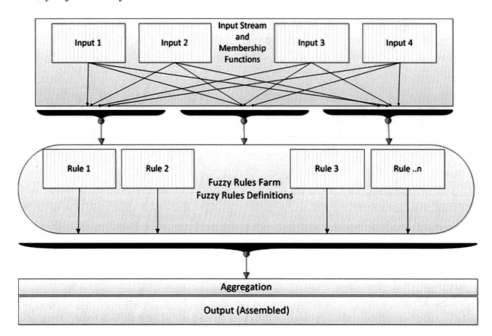

Fuzzy Classification Methodology

Methodology main technique involves the fuzzification of input variables based on 10 characteristics extracted from the XML message, Figure 25 illustrates the whole fuzzy classification process and internal stages, rule evaluation, aggregation of the rule outputs, and defuzzification phases are displayed.

The fuzzy inference system involves four phases. A comprehensive description for each phase will be explained in order to understand main functionality behind each phase. Connection between each phase is described as well.

Fuzzily Input Stage

The first step is to take the inputs extracted from the 10 characteristics within each XML message and determine the degree to which they belong to each of the appropriate fuzzy sets via membership functions. The input is always a crisp numerical value limited to the universe of discourse of the input variable (in our case it is an interval between 0 and 10) and the output is a fuzzy degree of membership in the qualifying linguistic set (interval between 0 and 1). Fuzzification of the input amounts to a function evaluation. A decision mechanism for identifying importance-level values within each XML message will be provided.

We built this stage on three rules, and each of the rules depends on resolving the inputs into a number of different fuzzy linguistic sets: the factor is non-sensitive, the factor is normal, and the factor is sensitive. Before the rules can be evaluated, the inputs must be fuzzified according to each of these linguistic sets. For example, the transaction amount can range from "Non-sensitive" to "Sensitive" with other values being taken into account. The degree of membership decides the degree of belongingness of the values of variables to any class. We have designed a membership function for each transaction's characteristic

Figure 26. Input variable for transaction amount factor

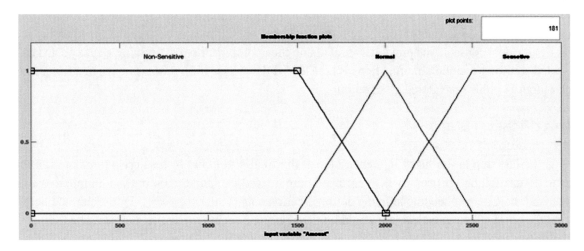

indicator, which clearly defines how each input is mapped to a membership value between [0, 1]. Linguistic values are assigned to each transaction factor as non-sensitive, normal, and sensitive and for the final layer rate as High, Medium, and Low. Figure 26 represents an example of the linguistic descriptors used to illustrate one of the key transaction characteristics, transaction amount, with a plot of the fuzzy membership functions. The range of possible values for the corresponding key importance characteristic (Non-Sensitive, Normal, and Sensitive) is represented in x-axis. The linguistic descriptor represents the degree to which a value for the importance level characteristic and it is represented in y-axis.

Transaction Amount: (Non-Sensitive, Normal, Sensitive).
Linguistic Variable: Transaction Amount value.
Linguistic Value: Range (in Numbers).
Sensitive: [2000, 2500, 3000, 3000].
Normal: [1500, 2000, 2500].
Non-Sensitive: [0, 0, 1500, 2000].

Rule Evaluation Stage

The second step is to take the fuzzified inputs and apply them to the antecedents of the fuzzy rules. If a given fuzzy rule has multiple antecedents, the fuzzy operator (AND or OR) is used to obtain a single number that represents the result of the antecedent evaluation. This number (truth value) is applied to the consequence membership function. Then we specify how the importance level probability is different as a function of the main importance level characteristic factors. A set of fuzzy rules are represented in form of (IF-THEN) statements and provided by experts; these statements connect to the importance level probability of different levels of importance characteristic factors based on previous experience.

Aggregation of the Rule Output Stage

This is the process of unification of the outputs of all the rules. It means we take the membership functions of all rules' consequents previously scaled and then combine them in one single fuzzy set. The list of scaled resulting membership functions is considered the aggregation process input, one fuzzy set for each output variable considered as an output.

Defuzzification Stage

This is the last step in the fuzzy inference model; the final output has to be a crisp number. The input for the defuzzification process is the aggregate output fuzzy set and the output is a number. We have conducted the Centroid technique in the defuzzification stage (Sugeno, 1985). This technique helps us to find the point where a vertical line would hit the aggregate set into two equal masses. The final output is the importance level rate which is defined in fuzzy sets ("High", "Medium", and "Low"). Figure 27 illustrates the final output ranges.

Linguistic Variable: Importance Level.
Linguistic Value: Range (In Numbers).
High: [6, 8, 10, 10].
Medium: [3, 5, 7].
Low: [0, 0, 2, 4].

High: If the importance level of the tag is considered "High", this will impact upon the overall transaction within the XML message.

Medium: This might affect the overall transaction rate in some way; the content could be important for further attention.

Low: With a low importance level, no impact is to be considered in the XML transaction.

Fuzzy Classification Model

In our fuzzy classification model, we categorize the 10 transaction field characteristics into three different layers (Transaction Layer, Details Layer, and Environment Layer) based on their nature among overall transaction type whereby each element within the layer has its own importance measures. To improve the final importance level rate (fuzzy output), we have conducted a layering process for these features. Table 2 illustrates the grouping mechanism and layering details based on XML message content.

Figure 28 illustrates architecture design of the fuzzy inference classification model. As seen in the figure, each layer has an output which indicated that the tag rate that depends on the evaluation (fuzzy outputs) of the layer components.

Our fuzzy classification model is performed based on three layers: Transaction Layer, Details Layer, and Environment Layer. Each layer has a set of components that are distributed based on the component nature and usage; the total number of components is 10 and they are distributed among the three layers as follows: transaction amount, transaction currency, and account type are fitted in layer 1 (account segment layer); account tries, transaction notes, profile ID, and incorrect password tries are fitted in layer

Figure 27. Output variable and ranges

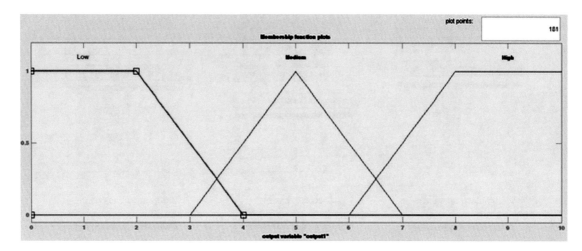

2 (details segment layer); and finally, the daily transactions, transaction time, and time spent on site are fitted in layer 3 (environment segment layer).

Fuzzy Rule Base and Layers Categorization

Rule Base for Layer 1

The rule base for layer 1 has three inputs and one output. The rule has all the "IF-THEN" conditions of the system. For each entry of the rule base, each component is assumed to be one of the three values and each criterion has three components. This means that rule base 1 contains 27 entries (3^3). The output of rule base 1 is one of the importance level fuzzy sets (High, Medium, or Low) representing the account

Table 2. XML message content components and layers

Components	Sequence	Layer Name	Layer
Transaction Amount	1	**Account Segment**	Layer 1
Transaction Currency	2		
Account Type	3		
Components	**Sequence**	**Layer Name**	**Layer**
Account Tries	4	**Details Segment**	Layer 2
Transaction Notes	5		
Profile ID	6		
Incorrect Password Tries	7		
Components	**Sequence**	**Layer Name**	**Layer**
Daily Transactions	8	**Environment Segment**	Layer 3
Transaction Time	9		
Time Spent on Service	10		

Figure 28. Classification Architecture of the importance level fuzzy mode (TAG Classification)

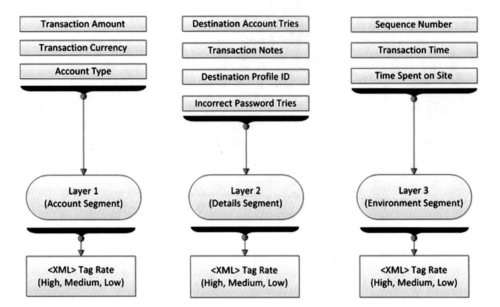

segment layer importance level. Table 3 illustrates a sample structure along with sample entries of rule base 1 for layer 1.

The system structure for the account segment layer is the result of joining the three basic components (transaction amount, transaction currency, and account type), which generates the layer importance level. Figure 29 and Figure 30 illustrate the structure of the system and the three-dimensional surface structure, respectively. MATLAB R2010R has been used in the process.

Table 3. Rule base 1 for the account segment layer – layer 1

Transaction Amount	Transaction Currency	Account Type	Account Layer Importance Level Rate
Non-Sensitive	Non-Sensitive	Non-Sensitive	**Low**
Non-Sensitive	Non-Sensitive	Normal	**Low**
Non-Sensitive	Sensitive	Non-Sensitive	**Low**
Normal	Normal	Normal	**Medium**
Normal	Non-Sensitive	Sensitive	**Medium**
Normal	Sensitive	Normal	**Medium**
Sensitive	Non-Sensitive	Sensitive	**High**
Sensitive	Non-Sensitive	Non-Sensitive	**Low**
Sensitive	Sensitive	Non-Sensitive	**High**

Figure 29. Layer 1 system structure (inputs and outputs)

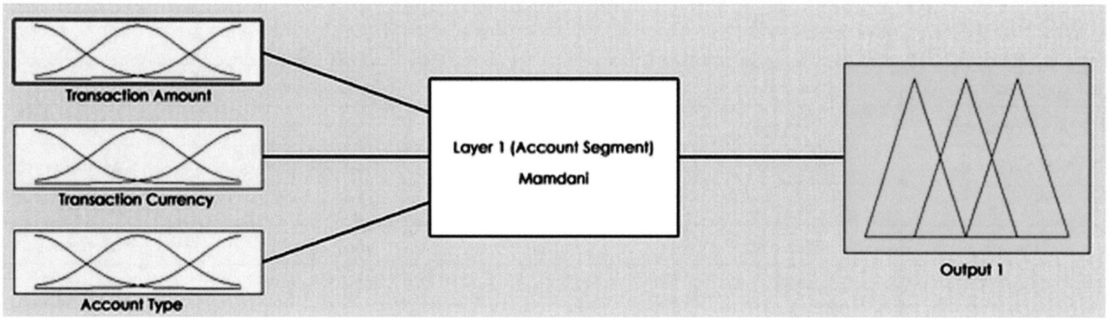

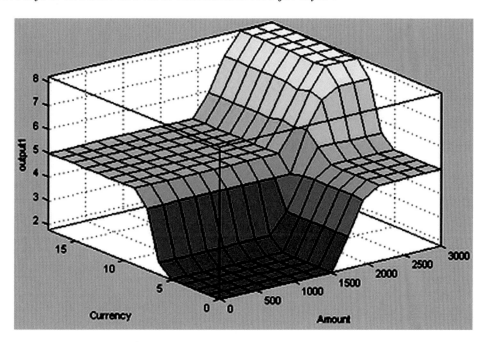

Rule Base for Layer 2

The rule base for layer 2 has four inputs and one output. The rule has all the "IF-THEN" conditions of the system. For each entry of the rule base, each component is assumed to be one of the three values and each criterion has four components. This means the rule base for layer 2 contains 81 entries (34).

The output of rule base is one of the importance level fuzzy sets (High, Medium, or Low) representing the details segment layer importance level. Table 4 illustrates a sample structure along with sample entries of rule base for layer 2.

The details segment layer system structure is the result of joining the four basic components (transaction notes, profile ID, account tries, and incorrect password tries), which generates the layer importance

Figure 30. Surface structure in a three-dimensional view for layer 1

Table 4. Rule base 1 for the details segment layer – layer 2

Transaction Notes	Profile ID	Account Tries	Incorrect Password Tries	Details Layer Importance Level Rate
Non-Sensitive	Sensitive	Sensitive	Sensitive	**High**
Non-Sensitive	Normal	Sensitive	Sensitive	**High**
Non-Sensitive	Sensitive	Non-Sensitive	Non-Sensitive	**Medium**
Normal	Sensitive	Non-Sensitive	Normal	**Medium**
Normal	Sensitive	Normal	Non-Sensitive	**Medium**
Normal	Non-Sensitive	Normal	Non-Sensitive	**Low**
Sensitive	Sensitive	Non-Sensitive	Non-Sensitive	**Medium**
Sensitive	Non-Sensitive	Non-Sensitive	Non-Sensitive	**Medium**
Sensitive	Non-Sensitive	Non-Sensitive	Sensitive	**High**

level. Figure 31 and Figure 32 illustrate the structure of the system and three-dimensional surface structure, respectively. MATLAB R2010R has been used in the process.

Rule Base for Layer 3

The rule base for layer 3 has three inputs and one output. All of the "IF-THEN" conditions of the system reside within the rule. Each component of each entry of the rule base is assumed to have one of the three values. This means the rule base has 27 entries (3^3). The rule base output is one of the importance level fuzzy sets (High, Medium, or Low) representing the environment segment layer importance level. Table 5 illustrates a sample structure and sample entries of the rule base for layer 3.

The system structure for the environment segment layer is the result of joining the three basic components (Time on Service, Daily Transactions, and Transaction Time), which generates the layer importance level. Figure 33 and Figure 34 illustrate the structure of the system and the three-dimensional surface structure. MATLAB R2010R has been used in the process.

Figure 31. Layer 2 system structure (inputs and output)

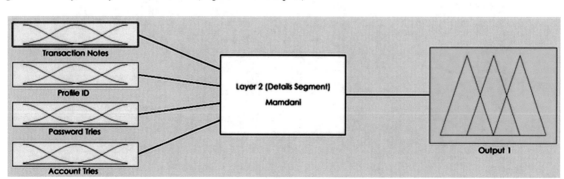

Figure 32. Surface structure in a three-dimensional view for layer 2

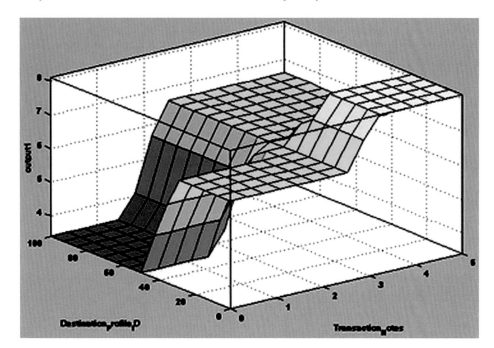

Encryption Model

Element-Wise Encryption

In the previous step, we conducted fuzzy classification techniques on the XML messages in order to classify the included tags. The main idea of the process is to distinguish between the sensitive parts that require the deployment of security measures and the other parts that need no processing. Therefore the second phase in our model is to apply element-wise encryption on the classified parts within each XML

Table 5. Rule base 1 for the environment segment layer – layer 3

Time on Site	Daily Transactions	Transaction Time	Environment Layer Importance Level Rate
Non-Sensitive	Normal	Sensitive	**High**
Non-Sensitive	Sensitive	Sensitive	**High**
Non-Sensitive	Sensitive	Normal	**Medium**
Normal	Non-Sensitive	Normal	**Medium**
Normal	Sensitive	Non-Sensitive	**Medium**
Normal	Non-Sensitive	Non-Sensitive	**Low**
Sensitive	Normal	Sensitive	**High**
Sensitive	Sensitive	Sensitive	**High**
Sensitive	Non-Sensitive	Sensitive	**High**

Figure 33. Layer 3 system structure (inputs and output)

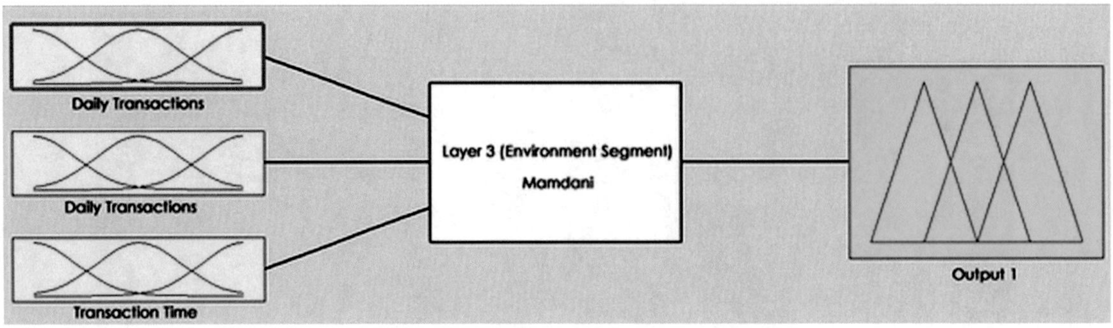

message. Element-wise encryption was first introduced by (Maruyama & Imamura, 2000). Figure 35 illustrates the system structure when deploying element-wise encryption on selected parts.

As displayed in Figure 35, the tags with an importance level of "High" or "Medium" are being encrypted using different keys depending on the importance level value, and tags with an importance level of "Low" are being forwarded without any need of encryption.

Element-Wise Encryption Standard

In order to deploy element-wise encryption on selected parts within XML message, the following list of requirements need to be fulfilled first:

Figure 34. Surface structure in a three-dimensional view for layer 3

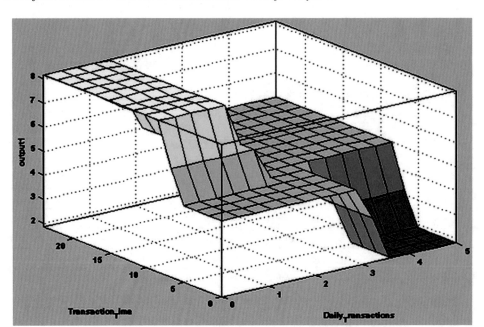

Figure 35. Encryption module architecture and design

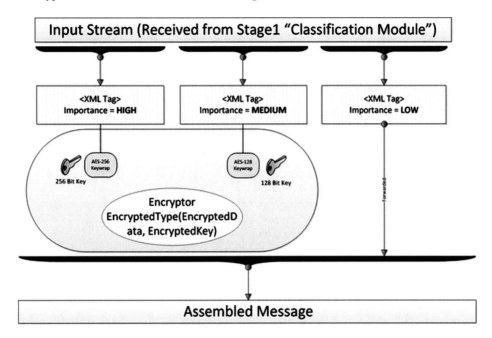

1. **Element-Wise Confidentiality:** Elements within the XML document should be able to be encrypted. Elements might enclose different types; the remaining parts of the XML document should remain in plaintext.
2. **The Encrypted Document Should Be Well-Formed:** The resulting document (after encryption has been deployed on the selected parts) has to be a well-formed XML document. Encryption can be nested within the document.
3. The same set of basic information items must be exactly provided as the original document (when decrypting an encrypted document). Comments can be ignored. CDATA and entity references sections are not preserved.
4. **Independence From Encryption Algorithm:** Symmetric and asymmetric encryption must be supported, whereby the encrypted elements syntax should be isolated from the encryption algorithm used.
5. **Flexible key Delivery Mechanism:** Two main key exchanges should be supported, the first is the certificate-based key exchange (encryption key is embedded in the syntax) and the second is the out-of-band key exchange (no key elements are embedded in the syntax).
6. **Content Independency:** The outer text should not play a role in decrypting the encrypted parts. For instance, the character encoding for the outer context might be changed without affecting the encrypted document content.
7. **Verification and Validation by Receiver:** The incoming decrypted XML document should be validated by the receiver.
8. **Intermediary Validation:** This refers to the ability of an intermediary to validate the encrypted document without the decryption keys and without the need to decrypt the element. No need to validate the included content models, but the validation of any outer text.

Figure 36. Classified XML message to be encrypted using element-wise encryption

```
<?xml version="1.0"?>
- <Transfers>
    - <Transaction ImportanceLevel="Low" xmlns="http://paymentv2">
          <Transaction_Notes>002</Transaction_Notes>
          <Profile_ID>92</Profile_ID>
          <AccountTries>02</AccountTries>
          <PasswordTries>01</PasswordTries>
      </Transaction>
    - <Transaction ImportanceLevel="Low" xmlns="http://paymentv2">
          <Posting_Date>2011/01/07</Posting_Date>
          <Service_ID>WWW60</Service_ID>
          <Customer_Language>E</Customer_Language>
      </Transaction>
    - <Transaction ImportanceLevel="Medium" xmlns="http://paymentv2">
          <TransactionAmount>755</TransactionAmount>
          <Transaction_Currency Code="JOD">001</Transaction_Currency>
          <Account_Type Code="001">Indivisual</Account_Type>
      </Transaction>
    - <Transaction ImportanceLevel="High" xmlns="http://paymentv2">
          <IPAddress>128.200.3.212</IPAddress>
          <From_Account>390230101401043000</From_Account>
          <To_Account>120130101155414000</To_Account>
      </Transaction>
</Transfers>
```

9. **Content Model Confidentiality:** It should be feasible to maintain the content model of the encrypted data confidential. By knowing the content model of the element, there is a good chance to have an idea of which element to attack (if the XML document has multiple encrypted elements).

Figure 36 illustrates a sample XML message after the fuzzy classification phase is performed, showing the "Importance Level" attribute values.

Figure 37 illustrates the same XML message after element-wise encryption is deployed. The tag attribute marked with a "Low" importance level will have no encryption deployed, while the tags with an "Importance Level" value of "High" or "Medium" will be encrypted using the AES encryption algorithm.

Design Consideration

All of the fuzzy rules employed in our fuzzy classification model were obtained based on our banking and financial expertise, combined with financial experts knowledge and supported by a set of experimental stages empowered by real life examples. Next we will show all fuzzy rules for all XML content characteristics.

1. **Element Serialization:** XML documents (with sub-elements) need to be converted into a byte sequence before encryption because the AES encryption algorithm (which is used in our model to encrypt the selected tags) treats the inputs as a byte sequence. Our conversion tries to minimize the loss of any non-essential information during the encryption process, like DOCTYPE declaration, use of namespace prefixes, and character encoding of the document. In our encryption phase we preserve the XML information set during the serialization operation by using canonical XML (W3C, BOYER, EASTLAKE, & REAGLE, 2002). We use C14N because of the implementation language independency. Encryption and decryption processes can be achieved in normal ways once the element is converted into byte array.

Figure 37. XML message after deploying element-wise encryption on selected parts

```
<?xml version="1.0"?>
- <Transfers>
    - <Transaction ImportanceLevel="Low" xmlns="http://example.org/paymentv2">
        <Transaction_Notes>002</Transaction_Notes>
        <Profile_ID>92</Profile_ID>
        <AccountTries>02</AccountTries>
        <PasswordTries>01</PasswordTries>
      </Transaction>
    - <Transaction ImportanceLevel="Low" xmlns="http://example.org/paymentv2">
        <Posting_Date>2011/01/07</Posting_Date>
        <Service_ID>WWW60</Service_ID>
        <Customer_Language>E</Customer_Language>
      </Transaction>
    - <Transaction ImportanceLevel="Medium" xmlns="http://example.org/paymentv2">
        - <EncryptedData xmlns="http://www.w3.org/2001/04/xmlenc#" Type="http://
            - <CipherData>
                <CipherValue>i66xTe5hmF/siLFCXDPXTucE9wJZFd pbSV3yYwN7pBZKIC
                    0KoZS9B1gKOalZUjE8Sp8AI8qKgrxbfx3CR7fIdEKPdO47t6hrswwL7l
                    uXp268jX5dL0dlUDOEqdtgfPUXxROUetbLP1AmtO8riJWVh/Qyd3pvV
              </CipherData>
          </EncryptedData>
      </Transaction>
    - <Transaction ImportanceLevel="High" xmlns="http://example.org/paymentv2">
        - <EncryptedData xmlns="http://www.w3.org/2001/04/xmlenc#" Type="http://
            - <CipherData>
                <CipherValue>6N28UemsjUz4vegVtDE1wNNgNkvTvC6Pxi9k2vcHcGIhSe
                    DWGvHlebDHA7DgNjmm+D37lU1DuzsB094b8cUPZH9gCjX0VDRntfL
                    pxnBFo35XheoJQFcLv21Kxz7Tzffh9ZCaqYU8HBE</CipherValue>
              </CipherData>
          </EncryptedData>
      </Transaction>
  </Transfers>
```

2. **Packaging Encrypted Elements in XML:** When inserting the encrypted elements (binary data) into an XML document, Base64 is used as a text encoding method. Additionally, it is necessary to attach additional information for the decryption process like initialization vector, encryption algorithm, and keys. Usage of an existing cryptographic message would alleviate the burden of having security flaws.

The cryptographic message format that is used in S/MIME (PKCS7/CMS) considered one of the most popular formats. In S/MIME, the encrypted process is performed by packing the cipher text alongside related information in a single MIME entity (media type should be application/pkcs7-mime). It can be included in an XML document in one of the standard ways to embed MIME objects.

Child nodes related to the parent tag are also encrypted using the same level of encryption. Child tags' behaviour is taken from the parent "Importance Level" value. In Figure 37, tags (Transaction Amount, Currency, and Account Type) are encrypted using AES encryption with a 128-bit key size as per their parent "Account" layer. Basically we inherit the encryption behaviour from parent to child as per our categorization process.

XML Message Schemas

Syntax: Schema for XML core encryption, Figures 38, 39, 40, 41, 42, and 43 illustrate XML schema for core encryption and other sub elements.

Figure 38. XML Schema for core encryption
Syntax: Schema for XML core encryption

```
<?xml version="1.0"?>
<schema targetNamespace="http://www.w3.org/xmlenc">
        xmlns="http://www.w3.org/1999/XMLSchema"
        xmlns:xenc="http://www.w3.org/xmlenc">

<simpleType name="base64-encoded-binary" base="binary">
  <encoding value="base64"/>
</simpleType>
```

Figure 39. XML schema for EncryptionInfos element
Syntax: Schema for the EncryptionInfos Element

```
<element name="EncryptionInfos">
  <complexType>
    <choice minOccurs="1" maxOccurs="unbounded">
      <element ref="xenc:EnvelopeInfo" />
      <element ref="xenc:EncryptionInfo" />
    </choice>
  </complexType>
</element>
```

Figure 40. XML schema for KeyValue element
Syntax: Schema for the KeyValue Element

```
<element name="KeyValue">
  <complexType>
    <choice>
      <any minOccurs="1" maxOccurs="unbounded" />
      <element ref="xenc:AESKeyValue" />
    </choice>
  </complexType>
</element>
```

Figure 41. XML schema for the ContentEncryptionMethod element
Syntax: Schema for the ContentEncryptionMethod Element

```
<element name="ContentEncryptionMethod">
  <complexType>
    <any minOccurs="0" maxOccurs="unbounded" />
    <attribute name="Algorithm" type="uriReference"
use="required" />
  </complexType>
</element>
```

Figure 42. XML schema for the Reference element
Syntax: Schema for the Reference Element

```
<element name="Reference">
  <complexType>
    <element ref="xenc:CanonicalizationMethod" minOccurs="0"
maxOccurs="1" />
      <attribute name="URI" type="uriReference" use="optional" />
      <attribute name="Id" type="ID" use="optional" />
      <attribute name="MimeType" type="string" use="optional" />
  </complexType>
</element>
```

Figure 43. XML schema for the EncryptedContent element
Syntax: Schema for the EncryptedContent Element

```
<element name="EncryptedContent">
<complexType base="xenc: base64-encoded-binary"
derivedBy="extension">
<attribute name="Id" type="ID" use="optional" />
<attribute name="URI" type="uriReference" use="optional" />
</complexType>
</element>
```

Diffie–Hellman Key Exchange

The DH Algorithm, first introduced by (Diffie & Hellman, 1976), was the first system to utilize "Public-key" cryptographic keys. We used the DH system because of its ability to manage public keys easily. As we use symmetric encryption "AES" with different key sizes, both sides of the communication must have identical keys. Securing the submitted keys has been an issue, so we use our model (symmetric-based encryption system) to encrypt the XML documents and DH system (asymmetric-based system) to encrypt the symmetric keys for distribution. In brief, we use the DH algorithm for public key exchange.

D-H Process

Use Diffie-Hellman to secure exchanged keys, not the actual content which is already encrypted using our element-wise encryption module. To achieve the efficient exchange, we create a shared secret key, which we call "Key Encryption Key - KEK", between the two entities (the sending channel and the receiving channel). Later the shared secret key encrypts the symmetric key for secure submission. The resulting symmetric key is called the traffic encryption key (TEK) for the data encryption key (DEK). This means KEK secures the delivery of TEK, while TEK provides the secure delivery of the XML document itself.

The process starts just after the generation of private keys by each side (sending and receiving channels). Each side then generates a public key, which is derived from the private key because both keys are mathematically linked. Then the two entities (sender channel and receiver channel) exchange their public keys. Each side now has its own private key and the other entity public key.

Figure 44. Key exchange using the DH method

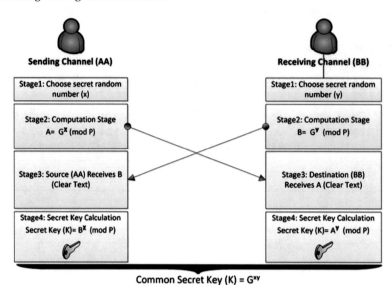

During the key exchange process, the DH protocol generates "shared secret" keys that are identical and shared by both entities. A set of mathematical operations are performed against the sender's private key and the receiver's public key which generate a value. The reverse process (performing mathematical operations against the sender's public key and the receiver's private key) is performed to generate another value. The two values should be identical. The combination of the two values is called the "Shared Secret" which encrypts the information between the two entities. In our model, the shared secret of the Diffie-Hellman protocol encrypts a symmetric key for our AES encryption algorithm, transmits it securely, and the distant end decrypts it with the shared secret. Figure 44 shows how the DH process operates. The sender is the one who actually generates and transmits the symmetric key in most cases. However, it can be handled by both sender and receiver.

As seen in Figure 45, we require two large numbers, one prime (P), and (G), which is a primitive root of (P). P should be at least 512 bits. In stage 2 we compute public values for both sender and receiver (A, B) using:

$$A = G^X \left(mod\, p \right)$$

where X is the generated number by sender in stage 1

$$B = G^Y \left(mod\, p \right)$$

where Y is the generated number by receiver in stage 1

Now we compute the shared and secret keys by applying:

$K_a = B^x \, (mod\, p)$ Where K_a is the secret key for sender.

Figure 45. Represents the DH key agreement schema

```
<element name="DHKeyValue" type="xenc:DHKeyValueType"/>
<complexType name="DHKeyValueType">
    <sequence>
        <sequence minOccurs="0">
            <element name="P" type="ds:CryptoBinary"/>
            <element name="Q" type="ds:CryptoBinary"/>
            <element name="Generator"type="ds:CryptoBinary"/>
        </sequence>
        <element name="Public" type="ds:CryptoBinary"/>
        <sequence minOccurs="0">
            <element name="seed" type="ds:CryptoBinary"/>
            <element name="pgenCounter" type="ds:CryptoBinary"/>
        </sequence&gy;
    </sequence>
</complexType>
```

$K_b = A^y \ (mod \ p)$ Where K_b is the secret key for receiver.

Message Utilization

Message security is the main concern to be handled in our model. However, deploying our framework will enable us to utilize outgoing messages and save resources by reducing outgoing messages. Figure 46 illustrates how the outgoing messages are utilized whereby only essential parts are being secured; other parts are just forwarded to the message assembler without the need for any type of processing.

Once the utilization process is completed, messages are ready for final submission to the selected destination.

Summary

A novel approach for securing financial XML messages using intelligent mining fuzzy classification techniques has been proposed. This approach will secure financial XML messages using element-wise XML encryption, fuzzy classification techniques that allow us to classify XML messages on the fly without the need to define a set of rules prior to the process.

Mining fuzzy classification techniques have been used to evaluate and measure the data sensitivity level within each XML message to find a degree of sensitivity for each tag in the XML message. The mining fuzzy classification process allowed us to assign a value to a new attribute added to the parent XML nodes. A value is determined by applying a set of fuzzy classification processes based on Mamdani inference (Mamdani & Assilian, 1975). A new value has been used to determine which type of encryption algorithm is being performed on selected tags, allowing us to secure only the needed parts within each message rather than encrypting the whole message. XML encryption is based on W3C XML recom-

Figure 46. Message utilization

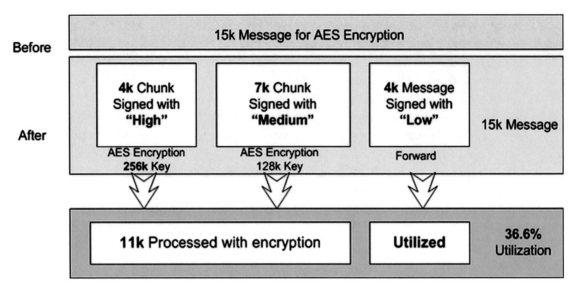

mendations. Nodes that are assigned an importance level value of "High" will be encrypted using the AES encryption algorithm with a 256-bit key size to ensure maximum security. Nodes that are assigned an importance level value of "Medium" will be encrypted using the AES encryption algorithm with a 128-bit key size. An implementation was performed on a real-life environment using online banking systems to demonstrate its flexibility, feasibility, and functionality. There are many possible directions for future work which will be discussed in next section.

SXMS MODEL IMPLEMENTATION AND TESTING

This section presents the main system components, system functionalities, and implementation tools that have been used to evaluate our secure XML management model. The detailed testing of SXMS model is presented in general and the testing of the main parts of the SXMS model in specific. The testing strategy will involve testing each stage on its own. Additionally, we present the XML sample set extracted from our collected financial messages which have been used in our testing and evaluation stages. Finally, we summarize and conclude the section.

Development Architecture and Used Tools

Used Tools

System designed to achieve set of goals ensuring secure and efficient exchange of XML financial messages among different systems. Following measures are key factors in system design:

1. **Technical Computing (MATLAB R2010a):** Since we are performing fuzzy classification, we require a high-performance language for technical computing. It has the capability to integrate

computation, visualization, and plotting of functions and data. Also it allows interfacing with other applications written in other programming languages such as Java, C, and C++. In our case we require the integration with our Java application that is used to encrypt classified documents. Solutions are presented in an easy to understand and familiar mathematical notation.

2. **Stylus Studio 2011 XML Enterprise Suite:** Dealing with XML documents is the core of our model, since the files are in XML format we require an easy way to edit and manipulate XML files, XML schemas, and DTD codes. This tool allows us to check the validity of XML files, XML well-formedness checking, and parsing as well. Also we require the ability to edit XML schemas, DTD with inline capability.

3. **Netbeans IDE 7.0:** Our fuzzy classification module is built using Java J2EE, Netbeans Integrated development environment (IDE) is a platform framework for Java applications. The NetBeans Platform is a reusable framework for simplifying the development of Java Swing desktop applications. The NetBeans IDE bundle for Java SE contains what is needed to start developing NetBeans plugins and NetBeans Platform based applications.

4. **Microsoft Office Excel:** Used as a graphical and chart presentation, as we will compare models and present results in graphical presentation. Excel allows us to have a clear and easy to understand presentation with measures presented on the graph.

Development Architecture

Our proposed secure XML management system has the ability to extract all of the 10 transaction characteristics and patterns for each XML transaction. Our fuzzy classification module main functionality is to classify XML messages based on these characteristics and by deploying Mamdani fuzzy system. Once classified, the fuzzy classification module will assign a value to the "Importance Level" tag within the messages. Classified messages are being processed by our encryption module to perform element-wise encryption on selected classified parts.

System design includes three primary parts all of which signifies a crucial element of the requirements need. Those parts are:

- **Parsing Incoming XML Messages:** To check for validity and well-formedness by using XML Sax parser. In case of any issues, messages should be handled by error handler component for either return an error code or halt the operation.

- **Classifying Valid XML Messages:** Fuzzy classification is done by using the fuzzification of input variables that is based on 10 characteristics extracted from the XML message.

- **Routing Messages:** Messages are being routed either to final message assembler or to the XML encryption phase.

- **Encrypting Incoming Messages Where "Importance Level" Tag is Labelled with "High" or "Medium":** Tags with "Importance Level" set to "High" are being encrypted using 256-bit key, tags with "Importance Level" set to "Medium" are being encrypted using 128-bit key.

- **Private Key Exchange:** Using Diffie-Hellman private key exchange to exchange keys between sender and receiver.

In this section, a set of testing and evaluation for the above listed components will be performed. During our design and development we took the following measures into consideration:

Figure 47. Model development architecture

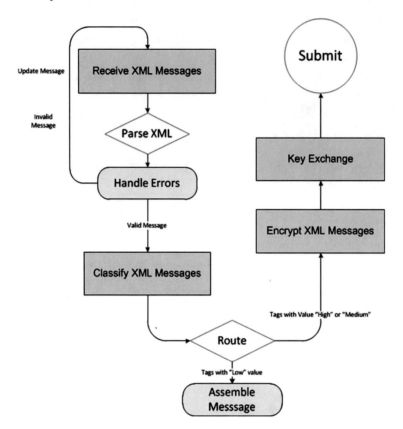

- **Reusability:** Ability to reuse included components or the system in complete.
- **Testability:** Ability to test the system against requirements.
- **Structured:** Ability to read code and structure easily.

Figure 47 presents the development architecture and design.

System Implementation

SXMS Implementation Requirements

Table 6 represents the minimum software and hardware requirements needed for NetBeans IDE 7.0 and Stylus Studio 2011 XML Enterprise Suite to perform system testing and implementation.

SXMS Implementation Process

Based on approaches in section 4, SXMS fuzzy classification module generates on-the-fly fuzzy classification value; this value is assigned to the Importance Level attribute in each XML message. The major steps for the fuzzy classification module are shown in Figure 48.

Table 6. Minimum hardware requirements to run main tools

Operating System	Microsoft Windows 7 – Ultimate edition, 64-bit / SP1
Environment	Java Development Kit JDK v7.0
Processor	PC / Intel based technology 2.0 MHz or faster processors
Memory	512 MB of RAM
Disk Space	750 MB of free disk space
Display	1280x 768 px
Drive	DVD Drive

Figure 48. Process for XML data fuzzy classification

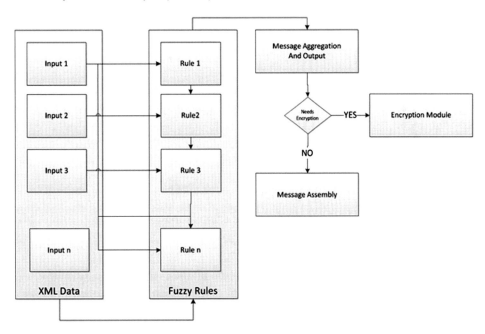

Step 1: This is the process of generating membership values for a fuzzy variable using membership functions. The first step is to take the crisp inputs from the 10 characteristics which stamp the importance level and determine the degree to which these inputs belong to each appropriate fuzzy set.

Step 2: The fuzzified inputs are applied to the antecedents of the fuzzy rules. Since the fuzzy rule has multiple antecedents, the fuzzy operator (AND or OR) is used to obtain a single number that represents the result of the antecedent evaluation.

Step 3: This is the process of unification of the outputs of all the rules. In other words, we are combining the membership functions of all the rules' consequents previously scaled into single fuzzy sets (output). Thus, input of the aggregation process is the list of scaled consequent membership functions, and the output is one fuzzy set for each output variable.

Step 4: This is the last step in the fuzzy inference process, where a fuzzy output of a fuzzy inference system is transformed into a crisp output. The input for the defuzzification process is the aggregate

Figure 49. Process for XML data encryption

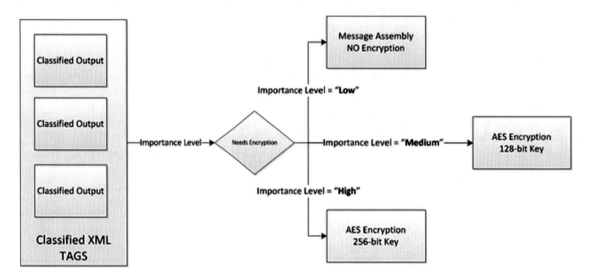

output fuzzy set where the output is a number. Centroid technique (Cox, 2001a) has been used to complete this step.

The encryption process starts just after the fuzzy classification phase, Figure 49 illustrate the encryption process deployment which consists of three steps.

Step 1: This is the process of reading the value of the crisp output. Crisp output is the XML tag named "Importance Level" classified in the previous fuzzy classification process; output has one of the values (Low, Medium, and High).

Step 2: This process involves performing AES encryption on the coming XML Tags has an "Importance Level" value of "Medium" or "High". Values set to "Medium" will be encrypted using AES-128 bit key, values set to "High" will be encrypted with 256-bit key.

Step 3: This process involves redirecting message content that need no further processing into message aggregator for final message assembly.

Testing Strategy

For the purposes of testing SXMS complete model, the testing strategies are to be identified first. The next sections describe the performance testing strategy used and then the functional testing strategies.

Testing SXMS Behaviour

First we defined the state diagram in order to describe the behavioural activities of SXMS. State Figure 50 illustrates the behaviour state.

Phase-A: This phase is the GUI of the designed model. It represents the starting phase in order to deal with all the other phases. This phase has two outputs:

Figure 50. Model behaviour states

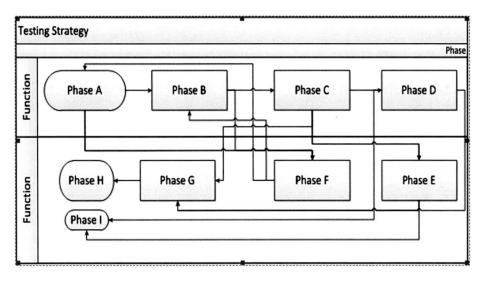

Out-1: To form an XML document, go to phase-B.

Out-2: To handle invalid XML document, go to phase-F.

***Phase-B*:** This phase represents the process of parsing incoming XML documents. It has two outputs:

Out-4: To classify valid XML message, go to phase-C.

Out-5: To re-construct invalid XML message, go to phase-F.

***Phase-C*:** This phase represents the process of classifying incoming XML messages using Mamdani fuzzy inference system and it has three outputs:

Out-6: Classified tags whereby Importance Level assigned value set to "High", go to phase-D.

Out-7: Classified tags whereby Importance Level assigned value set to "Medium", go to phase-E.

Out-8: Classified tags whereby Importance Level assigned value set to "Low", go to phase-G.

***Phase-D*:** This phase represents the process of encrypting XML tags marked with "High" importance level using 256-bit AES encryption and it has two outputs:

Out-9: Encrypted tags using 256-bit key, go to phase-G.

Out-10: Generated private key, go to phase-I.

***Phase-E*:** This phase represents the process of encrypting XML tags marked with "High" importance level using 128-bit AES encryption and it has two outputs:

Out-11: Encrypted tags using 128-bit key, go to phase-G.

Out-12: Generated private key, go to phase-I.

***Phase-F*:** This phase represents the process of handling incoming error cases from different phases and it has two outputs:

Out-13: Rejected XML message, go to phase-A.

Out-14: Message to be modified or re-phrased, go to phase-B.

***Phase-G*:** This phase represents the process of aggregate and assembles incoming XML tags from different phases for final composition and it has one output:

Out-15: Successfully assembled message, go to phase-H.

***Phase-H*:** This phase represents the process of message submission to final and it has one output:

Out-16: Message for final submission, submitted successfully.

Phase-I: This phase represents the process of exchanging private keys between sender and receiver and it has one output:

Out-17: Private keys for receiver.

Testing SXMS's Functionality

White-box and Black-box testing (IEEE, 1990) have been conducted to test the functionality of SXMS. The following describes both white-box and black-box testing steps:

White-Box Testing

For our white-box testing strategy, all subroutines in our system were tested carefully by checking every statement written. Therefore, different types of XML documents were tested to guarantee all decisions, loops, nested loops, paths, and data structure have been tested. To facilitate the testing for better tracking our testing strategy, we have divided SXMS into two main sub-systems: XML Classifier, and XML Encryptor. Later we have divided each sub-system into smaller units to follow the unit testing. We have used white-box testing for the following types:

1. **Unit Testing (IEEE, 1990):** In this testing we performed white-box testing on each unit and associated sub-units. Test cases have been written to make sure the coding is deployed correctly for further integration. We have performed this testing in an accurate way as we eliminated more than 60% of system bugs during this testing.
2. **Integration Testing:** In this testing we tested and evaluated the interaction between units and sub-units, interfaces between the different units are examined carefully based on test cases created earlier, some of the test cases can be used as black-box test cases as well.
3. **Regression Testing:** We have performed a selective retesting of a set of components, sub-components, or the whole system. testing have been deployed to make sure that modifications have not caused a major effects on system behaviour, also to make sure that the system still complies with the requirements we defined (IEEE, 1990).

Black-Box Testing

Although black-box testing is performed when the system is intended to be published or distributed, we performed the black-box testing to determine whether or not the system does what it supposed to do based on the functional requirements we defined. In our test we attempts to find errors and issues in external behaviour in the following categories (Pressman, 2009): (1) incorrect or missing functionality; (2) interface errors; (3) errors in data structures used by interfaces; (4)behaviour or performance errors; and (5) initialization and termination errors.

In our black-box testing a different specialist performed the testing knowing main functionality of system but without knowing all details. The following types are the black-box testing strategy types we adopted:

- **Integration Testing:** Same as white-box integration testing but without knowing internal procedures and lifecycle. Testers performed their testing based on system functionality following provided work flow. Verification has been made that different units work together without issues and they are integrated into a larger code base.
- **Functional and System Testing:** We examined the high-level designs. Our functional testing involved ensuring that the functionality specified in the requirement specification works as it meant to be. System testing involves measuring the system in many different environments to ensure the program works in typical financial environments with different types of operating systems.
- **Acceptance Testing:** Testing was made based on end-user expectations of the functionality. Such testing is performed to decide whether or not the system satisfies the acceptance criteria. Test cases were pre-specified and given to the testing team.

Testing Validation

In this research, we have assembled a testing framework whereby it can evaluate the encryption part of our model against the well-known W3C Encryption standard (W3C, 2001). To evaluate the effectiveness of our fuzzy XML encryption model, we have used this framework as measuring tool. We have selected data set from one of the electronic channels, which is the internet banking service in Jordan Ahli Bank (one of the leading banks in Jordan). The main goal of our testing against W3C Encryption standard is to prove the effectiveness of using SXMS model as a secure XML management tool for financial messages. Table 7 illustrates the factors we use in our testing and evaluation.

Testing Environment

All experiment tests are performed on a PC (Intel core i5) 2.3 GHz CPU, 6.00 GB RAM, running Windows 7 Ultimate 64-bit operating system. NetBeans IDE 7.0 is used to implement SXMS model, and Stylus Studio 2011 XML Enterprise Suite is used as an XML editor and validator.

Testing Data Preparation

We have used two sets of data in our implementation and testing: A sample of 1,000 financial XML messages and a sample of 1,500 financial XML messages representing an internet banking service, messages extracted from Jordan Ahli Bank (JAB, 2013), one of the leading banks in Jordan. Sample has been taken for a period of seven months extracted randomly; we choose Jordan Ahli Bank as a source of our sample since the information is accessible due to our working nature within the bank and concerned departments. The extracted sample contain massive amount of historical transactions reflecting our need to test the model. Sample has the transaction amount recorded, transaction time, logged IP address, account tries, and other details used to build our fuzzy classification layers.

The collected dataset of 2,500 XML messages presenting the periods: three months (starting January 2010 until March 2010) for the first sample, and four months (April 2010 until August 2010) for the second sample of data. Both samples covered the 10 fuzzy classification characteristics we defined in our model. We have collected our samples on CD's in XML format; we arranged the documents and renamed each file to reflect the sample name and date of the transactions.

Table 7. Testing Factors

Module	Testing Factors
SXMS – Fuzzy Classification Model	• Efficiency classifying XML messaging • Functionality test
SXMS – XML Encryption	• Improve encryption processing time • File size reduction for encrypted files

Figure 51. Sample data captured from the first set

TO_ACCOUNT_NO	TO_Account Currency	Transaction Amount	Transaction Currency	Posting_Date	Time_On_Site	Transaction_Time	Commission	Subscription_Number	Destination ProfileID	Destination Account T.
	Account Layer_Calc	Account Layer	Account Layer		Environment	Environment			Details Layer	Details Layer
120130101155414000	01	122.22	17	2011/03/20	2:36	7:03:00	000	999999	22	3
120130106451259000	01	100	16	11/21/2010	1:26	0:34:55	000	999999	92	3
390130106155820000	01	210	01	11/21/2010	23:46	12:54:50	000	999999	71	1
120130101100553000	01	104	02	11/21/2010	21:31	10:34:35	000	999999	68	2
120130106455673000	01	300	17	11/21/2010	11:17	10:25:12	000	999999	17	2
230230101434067000	02	800	17	11/21/2010	19:53	14:59:20	000	999999	17	2
420130106457750000	01	50	02	11/21/2010	10:04	1:49:58	000	999999	94	2
540130101478629000	01	7550	03	11/21/2010	1:24	2:56:40	000	999999	73	2
120130103100539000	01	100	01	11/21/2010	5:59	22:29:53	000	999999	32	2
420130101420248000	01	1.725	02	11/21/2010	6:13	20:02:37	000	999999	100	2
340130101415880000	01	80	16	11/23/2010	23:02	22:46:20	000	999999	15	2
250130101438706000	01	303	06	11/23/2010	9:06	21:38:38	000	999999	96	2
120230101155532000	02	1455	12	11/23/2010	16:34	4:56:40	000	999999	61	2
120130103103035000	01	30	03	11/23/2010	21:42	23:00:45	000	999999	3	2
620130101429139000	01	20000	13	11/23/2010	17:43	0:28:31	000	999999	106	2
120130106455800000	01	250	06	11/23/2010	16:05	6:28:40	000	999999	102	2
390130103103755000	01	100	16	11/23/2010	17:08	13:56:44	000	999999	49	2
580130101135295000	01	245	16	11/23/2010	8:41	13:44:14	000	999999	53	2
390130103103759000	01	100	09	11/23/2010	23:59	20:06:27	000	999999	0	2

Figure 52. Sample data captured from the second set

Channel_ID	Service_ID	Daily_Transactivity	Transaction ID	Customer_Lang	Num_Of_Accounts	Account_Sign_Flag	Account_Currency	Account_Balance	Account_Type	FROM_ACCOUNT_NO	Transaction_Notes Code	TO_ACCOUNT_NO
		Environment					Account Layer_Calc		Account Layer		Details Layer	
WWW	60	01	123456	E	01	D	17	1500	001	390230101401043000	00	120130101155414000
WWW	60	01	61520	E	01	C	16	-779.736	001	120130101451259000	00	120130106451259000
WWW	60	02	61653	E	01	C	01	-16815.021	001	390130101155820000	03	390130106155820000
WWW	60	01	62559	E	01	C	02	-10518.11	001	120130101100553000	02	120130101100553000
WWW	60	02	62612	E	01	c	17	-365.44	001	120130101455673000	02	120130106455673000
WWW	60	01	62706	E	01	C	17	-24.27	001	30130101434067600	00	230230101434067000
WWW	60	02	62782	E	01	C	02	-10518.11	001	520130101457750000	02	420130106457750000
WWW	60	01	62937	E	01	C	03	-365.44	001	560130101478629000	00	540130101478629000
WWW	60	02	47307	E	01	C	01	-24.27	001	390130106100539000	00	120130103100539000
WWW	60	03	63873	E	01	C	02	-11840.74	001	420130101420248000	00	420130101420248000
WWW	60	02	72931	E	01	D	16	59298.873	003	340130106415880000	00	340130101415880000
WWW	60	01	73210	E	01	D	06	0	001	250130106438706000	00	250130101438706000
WWW	60	01	73355	E	01	D	12	0	001	120130101155532000	02	120230101155532000
WWW	60	01	73891	E	01	C	03	-11840.74	001	120130101103035000	04	120130103103035000
WWW	60	01	73925	E	01	D	13	0	001	180130101429139000	00	620130101429139000
WWW	60	01	74112	E	01	D	06	0	001	120130106455800000	02	120130106455800000
WWW	60	02	74820	E	01	C	16	-96813.765	001	390130101103755000	00	390130103103755000
WWW	60	03	75153	E	01	C	16	-94882.42	001	580130103135295000	00	580130101135295000
WWW	60	04	75812	E	01	D	09	0	001	390130101103759000	00	390130103103759000

As seen in Figure 51, and Figure 52, the two sample sets contain large amount of data extracted from the transaction files and arranged in two separate files. Each file has number of columns presenting the raw value that is captured during the transaction. However, we only used the 10 characteristics defined earlier to be used in our fuzzy classification stage.

Fuzzy Classification and Encryption Testing

Testing Fuzzy Classification

There are two implementations of the fuzzy classification model developed. The first implementation is using the first set of XML transactions presenting the internet banking service. We have selected internet banking service because it uses XML as the main messaging for data exchange between back-end host and the front-end. System has been deployed as a middleware connected to the application backend. Few customizations have been placed to match XML message structure; mapping took place as well for final message fuzzy classification.

Phase 1: First implementation conducted using a sample of 1,000 records; Records have been selected randomly presenting various transaction types like money transfers, fund transfer, and wire transfer for a period of seven months. System classified sample messages into three layers depending on 10 characteristics described in section 4. A sample of the structure and the records of the rule base for layer 1 are shown in Table 8. System main structure for layer 1 is the combination of Transaction Amount,

Table 8. Sample of data classified for Layer 1

Transaction Amount	Transaction Currency	Account Type	Account Layer Importance Level Rate
Non-Sensitive	Non-Sensitive	Non-Sensitive	**Low**
Non-Sensitive	Non-Sensitive	Normal	**Low**
Non-Sensitive	Sensitive	Non-Sensitive	**Low**
Normal	Normal	Sensitive	**Medium**
Normal	Normal	Normal	**Medium**
Sensitive	Non-Sensitive	Sensitive	**High**
Sensitive	Non-Sensitive	Non-Sensitive	**Low**
Sensitive	Sensitive	Non-Sensitive	**High**

Table 9. Sample of data classified for Layer 2

Transaction Notes	Profile ID	Account Tries	Incorrect Password Tries	Details Layer Importance Level
Non-Sensitive	Normal	Non-Sensitive	Normal	**Low**
Non-Sensitive	Normal	Sensitive	Sensitive	**High**
Non-Sensitive	Sensitive	Sensitive	Sensitive	**High**
Normal	Sensitive	Normal	Sensitive	**High**
Normal	Sensitive	Non-Sensitive	Sensitive	**Medium**
Normal	Sensitive	Non-Sensitive	Non-Sensitive	**Medium**
Sensitive	Non-Sensitive	Normal	Non-Sensitive	**Low**
Sensitive	Sensitive	Sensitive	Non-Sensitive	**Medium**
Sensitive	Non-Sensitive	Non-Sensitive	Non-Sensitive	**Medium**

Table 10. Sample of data classified for Layer 3

Time on Service	Daily Transactions	Transaction Time	Environment Layer Importance Level Rate
Non-Sensitive	Normal	Sensitive	High
Non-Sensitive	Non-Sensitive	Sensitive	Medium
Normal	Non-Sensitive	Normal	Medium
Normal	Sensitive	Non-Sensitive	Medium
Sensitive	Normal	Sensitive	High
Sensitive	Sensitive	Sensitive	High
Sensitive	Non-Sensitive	Sensitive	High

Transaction Currency, and account type. The rule base contains (3^3) which are 27 entries and the output of this rule base is one of the Importance Level attribute fuzzy sets (High, Medium, Low) for layer 1.

Same implementation sample has been conducted, a sample of the structure and the records of the rule base for layer 2 are shown in Table 9. System main structure for layer 2 is the combination of Transaction Notes, Profile ID, Account Tries, and Incorrect Password Tries. The rule base contains (3^4) which are 81 entries and the output of this rule base is one of the Importance Level attribute fuzzy sets (High, Medium, Low) for layer 2.

Same implementation sample has been conducted, a sample of the structure and the records of the rule base for layer 3 are shown in Table 10. System main structure for layer 3 is the combination of Time on Service, Daily Transactions, and Transaction Time. The rule base contains (3^3) which are 27 entries and the output of this rule base is one of the Importance Level attribute fuzzy sets (High, Medium, Low) for layer 3.

The aggregated surface of the rule evaluation is defuzzified using the Mamdani method to find the Centre of Gravity (COG). Centroid defuzzification technique shown in Equation (1) can be expressed as:

$$COG = \frac{\int \mu_i\left(x\right) x\ dx}{\int \mu_i\left(x\right) dx} \tag{1}$$

$\mu i(x)$: Aggregated membership function.
x: Output variable.

Figure 53 illustrate the set of fuzzy rules extracted from layer 1 using MATLAB R2010a, rules are based on a set of IF-THEN statements describing the effect of each factor in layer 1 on overall layer importance level. Figure 54 shows the surface view for layer 1 as well.

After deploying the fuzzy classification methodology on the three layers using MATLAB R2010a, we then have a list of classified tags with an importance level attribute defined and assigned.

The fuzzy classification phase successfully processed the selected sample of 1,000 messages, The account segment layer recorded 267 out of the 1,000 sample with a "High" importance level representing

Figure 53. Set of fuzzy rules for layer 1

1. If (Amount is Non-Sensitive) and (Currency is Non-Sensitive) and (Account_Type is Non-Sensitive) then (output1 is Low) (0.4)
2. If (Amount is Non-Sensitive) and (Currency is Non-Sensitive) and (Account_Type is Normal) then (output1 is Low) (0.4)
3. If (Amount is Non-Sensitive) and (Currency is Non-Sensitive) and (Account_Type is Sensetive) then (output1 is Medium) (0.4)
4. If (Amount is Non-Sensitive) and (Currency is Normal) and (Account_Type is Non-Sensitive) then (output1 is Low) (0.4)
5. If (Amount is Non-Sensitive) and (Currency is Normal) and (Account_Type is Normal) then (output1 is Medium) (0.4)
6. If (Amount is Non-Sensitive) and (Currency is Normal) and (Account_Type is Sensetive) then (output1 is Medium) (0.4)
7. If (Amount is Non-Sensitive) and (Currency is Sensetive) and (Account_Type is Non-Sensitive) then (output1 is Low) (0.4)
8. If (Amount is Non-Sensitive) and (Currency is Sensetive) and (Account_Type is Normal) then (output1 is Medium) (0.4)
9. If (Amount is Non-Sensitive) and (Currency is Sensetive) and (Account_Type is Sensetive) then (output1 is Medium) (0.4)
10. If (Amount is Normal) and (Currency is Non-Sensitive) and (Account_Type is Non-Sensitive) then (output1 is Medium) (0.4)
11. If (Amount is Normal) and (Currency is Non-Sensitive) and (Account_Type is Normal) then (output1 is Medium) (0.4)
12. If (Amount is Normal) and (Currency is Non-Sensitive) and (Account_Type is Sensetive) then (output1 is High) (0.4)
13. If (Amount is Normal) and (Currency is Normal) and (Account_Type is Non-Sensitive) then (output1 is Medium) (0.4)
14. If (Amount is Normal) and (Currency is Normal) and (Account_Type is Normal) then (output1 is Medium) (0.4)
15. If (Amount is Normal) and (Currency is Normal) and (Account_Type is Sensetive) then (output1 is High) (0.4)
16. If (Amount is Normal) and (Currency is Sensetive) and (Account_Type is Non-Sensitive) then (output1 is Medium) (0.4)
17. If (Amount is Normal) and (Currency is Sensetive) and (Account_Type is Normal) then (output1 is Medium) (0.4)

Figure 54. Surface view for layer 1

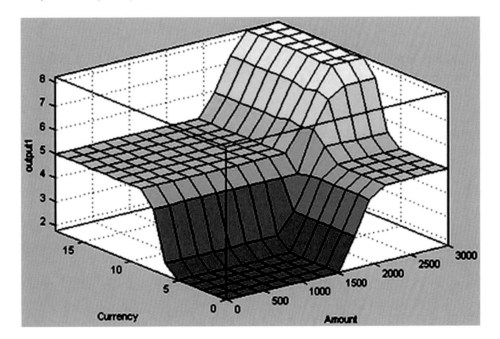

26.7% positively qualified for high level of encryption of key size of 256k. 62 out of 1,000 messages classified with a "Medium" importance level, representing 6.2% qualified for an encryption of 128k key size.

Finally 671 out of 1,000 classified with a "Low" importance level representing 67.1% of the total skipping the encryption process to be forwarded directly to message assembler.

Details segment layer achieved 401 occurrences out of the same 1,000 sample messages with a "High" importance level, representing 40.1% of the total positively qualified for high level encryption of key size of 256k. 410 out of 1,000 messages have been classified with a "Medium" importance level, representing

Figure 55. Fuzzy classification chart for sample implementation

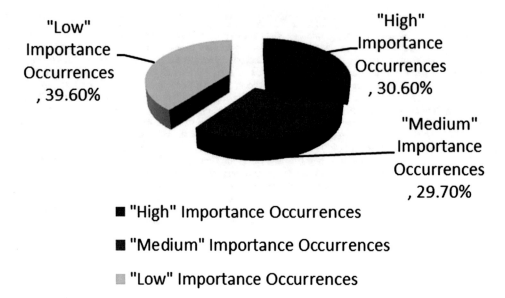

41% qualified for an encryption of size 128k key. The remaining 189 out of the 1,000 sample marked with "Low" importance level, representing 18.9% which require no encryption processing.

Environment segment layer recorded 250 occurrences out of the same 1,000 sample messages with a "High" importance level, representing 25% of the total positively qualified for high level encryption of key size 256k. 421 occurrences recorded with a "Medium" importance level to be encrypted with a 128k key size. The final 329 occurrences marked with a "Low" importance level to be forwarded without any further processing. 30.6% of the occurrences average across the three layers achieved "High" importance level, 29.7% achieved "Medium" importance level, and 39.6% of the total marked "Low" importance level across the three layers.

The results clearly indicate as shown in Table 11 and Figure 55 that 26.8% of the sample 1,000 messages have a fuzzy classification level of "high" which require high encryption mechanism to secure the sensitive parts. 67% of the sample messages have been marked as "low" which have been forwarded directly without performing any encryption mechanism. The remaining 6.2% will adopt a high level of encryption but with lower key size.

As seen in Table 11, the highest occurrences for "High" and "Medium" importance level combined is 32.9% in layer 1, which means only 32.9% of the 1,000 records sample data require an encryption processing either using 128bit key or 256bit key, leaving a 67.1% of the sample data to be forwarded

Table 11. Fuzzy Classification table for first sample implementation

Fuzzy Classification Layer	"High" Appearances	"Medium" Appearances	Percentage (High + Medium)
Layer1 (Account)	267	62	32.9%
Layer 2 (Details)	401	410	81.1%
Layer 3 (Environment)	250	421	67.1%

Figure 56. Sample XML message after fuzzy classification phase

```xml
<?xml version="1.0"?>
<Transfers>
  - <Transaction ImportanceLevel="High" xmlns="http://example.org/paymentv2" Segment="Account">
        <TransactionAmount>2500</TransactionAmount>
        <Transaction_Currency Code="USD">001</Transaction_Currency>
        <Account_Type Code="001">Corporate</Account_Type>
    </Transaction>
  - <Transaction ImportanceLevel="Medium" xmlns="http://example.org/paymentv2" Segment="Details">
        <Transaction_Notes>154</Transaction_Notes>
        <Profile_ID>44</Profile_ID>
        <AccountTries>01</AccountTries>
        <PasswordTries>02</PasswordTries>
    </Transaction>
  - <Transaction ImportanceLevel="Medium" xmlns="http://example.org/paymentv2" Segment="Environment">
        <Posting_Date>2011/01/08</Posting_Date>
        <Transaction_Time>14:22:12</Transaction_Time>
        <Time_On_Service>00:25:13</Time_On_Service>
        <Daily_Transactions>2</Daily_Transactions>
        <Customer_Language>A</Customer_Language>
    </Transaction>
  - <Transaction xmlns="http://example.org/paymentv2" Segment="Additional">
        <IPAddress>128.2000.3.10</IPAddress>
        <From_Account>321456987456321457</From_Account>
        <To_Account>96325874193214587</To_Account>
    </Transaction>
</Transfers>
```

Figure 57. Sample XML message after encryption phase

```xml
<?xml version="1.0"?>
<Transfers>
  - <Transaction ImportanceLevel="High" xmlns="http://example.org/paymentv2" Segment="Account">
    - <EncryptedData xmlns="http://www.w3.org/2001/04/xmlenc#" Type="http://www.w3.org/2001/04/xmlenc#Element">
        - <CipherData>
            <CipherValue>/a91RXq4nGfSa6vCArk/zhzPoFWQK8UkqkC8TrdDhIlrYYUQ5nNIIWNAeGU0Jy0fMFdNt7VvjDQt
            nqgF1diLYLosR3hkGvqbfcbxh17JPbbpDp71hcCXhYvjwQ9uWZ5H/goFwkl/2U48GDHKHLx5MClg
            DeYrpGYIXBrWgiBE0/6fUBu6aGYrmOGsAsUH6pDpe785DHn3fSwbw1WG3ngBJQ==</CipherValue>
          </CipherData>
      </EncryptedData>
    </Transaction>
  - <Transaction ImportanceLevel="Medium" xmlns="http://example.org/paymentv2" Segment="Details">
    - <EncryptedData xmlns="http://www.w3.org/2001/04/xmlenc#" Type="http://www.w3.org/2001/04/xmlenc#Element">
        - <CipherData>
            <CipherValue>2Z8omknbXS8w2Nd2ji4uV1bf++nQTZtWcIV770zTshgbh7/dVc54Pze88VTbry06WIZZBHBj9UU+
            xXzoMCSZkH58y16MW4JD4r6U7Cbty6xPot5QDh4hgAXlOKyYp2LneTOTT2JVEpZ4mKFPL95gDx4h +vvalHBd9m98DOE4sKU=</CipherValue>
          </CipherData>
      </EncryptedData>
    </Transaction>
  - <Transaction ImportanceLevel="Low" xmlns="http://example.org/paymentv2" Segment="Environment">
        <Posting_Date>2011/01/08</Posting_Date>
        <Transaction_Time>14:22:12</Transaction_Time>
        <Time_On_Service>00:25:13</Time_On_Service>
        <Daily_Transactions>2</Daily_Transactions>
        <Customer_Language>A</Customer_Language>
    </Transaction>
  - <Transaction xmlns="http://example.org/paymentv2" Segment="Additional">
        <IPAddress>128.2000.3.10</IPAddress>
        <From_Account>321456987456321457</From_Account>
        <To_Account>96325874193214587</To_Account>
    </Transaction>
</Transfers>
```

directly to message assembler without the need of the encryption process. In brief, instead of performing full encryption for the whole XML message or even performing partial encryption on pre-selected parts, we were able to produce secured, optimized, and utilized messages, performing encryption only on needed parts selected using our fuzzy classification techniques based on the Mamdani method.

Testing XML Encryption

Assigned importance level is used as an indicator for which type of encryption is needed on corresponding node. Figure 56 illustrates a real XML message after fuzzy classification phase.

As seen in the figure, the classified XML message has the "Importance Level" attribute with value depending on the fuzzy classification phase, "Importance Level" attributes with a "Medium" value is entitled to have an AES Encryption using 128-bit key, "Importance Level" attributes with a "High" value is entitled to have an AES Encryption using 256-bit key, Tags with no "Importance Level" assigned will be forwarded to message assembler without performing any type of encryption. Figure 57 presents the XML message after deploying AES encryption on selected parts.

As seen in Figure 57 only selected parts that are classified earlier are being encrypted whereby two different keys are deployed, first is AES 128-bit key on tags marked with "Medium" "Importance Level", second is AES 256-bit key on tags marked with "High" "Importance Level". Tags marked with "Low" or not marked with any value will be forwarded to message assembler without performing any type of encryption.

Summary

In this section, extensive tests were carried out to check the performance of our model. The model was tested against W3C XML Encryption standard. Testing took place taking into consideration element-wise encryption and full encryption. Element-wise encryption was performed and evaluated based on two cases, the first by encrypting a pre-defined list of tags within each XML message and measuring the results against our model which uses element-wise encryption on a classified list of tags, tags were selected based on a previous step which classify the XML messages deploying fuzzy classification techniques. The second case is by encrypting the whole messages and comparing the results against our element-wise based encryption model. Results showed a significant improvement in both cases presenting the superiority of our basic concept which uses on-the-fly fuzzy classification mechanism for the final goal which is encrypting necessary parts.

PERFORMANCE EVALUATION: IMPLEMENTATION TO SECURE FINANCIAL XML MESSAGES USING INTELLIGENT FUZZY-BASED TECHNIQUES

This section presents the performance evaluation, evaluation methods, and actual testing that have been performed on real data sets to properly evaluate our secure XML management model. We also present the main application classes that have been used to classify outgoing XML documents, encrypt classified XML documents, and forwarders that used to aggregate message parts. Main application code which was built using Java J2EE also presented, describes module functionality and interface. XML sample set extracted from our collected financial messages which have been used in our testing and evaluation stages. Finally, we summarize and conclude the section.

SXMS Performance Evaluation

For our implementation of the secure XML management system and for performance measurement, we have developed our own desktop application built based on Java technology. Our application is used to perform both fuzzy classification and encryption of XML messages. We used Java programming language (J2SE1.6) to build the main application and user interface. Application is independent and can be used on different operating systems.

Evaluation Method

Two parameters have been taken into account in the evaluation process: the processing time that is used to encrypt the classified messages and the size of each message after encryption process. The results are compared against the W3C Encryption standard.

- **Processing Time:** Measure the time needed to fetch essential parts within each XML message and then encrypt needed tags using different key sizes, the measurement is based on the time needed from the starting point which is start of the XML message until the closing tag. Encryption process is performed on the whole message, selected tags, or no tags. All depending on the fuzzification stage prior to message encryption phase.
- **Processing File Size:** Measure the file size for each XML message, size is calculated after the encryption process take place. Resulting file size from our model will be compared against the file size from the W3C Encryption standard.

Evaluation Preparations

Prior to the encryption phase which will be comparing SXMS model with W3C XML Encryption recommendation, we deployed the fuzzification stage whereby we classified XML message sets that are going to be used in the evaluation stages. Fuzzification process took place to assign an importance level value to the 10 characteristics extracted from the financial XML messages. Fuzzification stage performed by deploying set of "IF-THEN" conditions, these conditions reflect the relations between the different financial features and characteristics, and also it reflects the association with each other. Relation and association with each other are used for the final importance level value. Figure 58 shows

Figure 58. Fuzzification stage (IF-THEN operators)

```
46. If (Transaction_Notes is Normal) and (Destination_Profile_ID is Non-Sensitive) and (Password_Tries is Non-Sensitive) and (Destination_Account_Tries is Sensetive) then (output1 is Medium) (0.3)
47. If (Transaction_Notes is Normal) and (Destination_Profile_ID is Non-Sensitive) and (Password_Tries is Non-Sensitive) and (Destination_Account_Tries is Normal) then (output1 is Low) (0.3)
48. If (Transaction_Notes is Normal) and (Destination_Profile_ID is Non-Sensitive) and (Password_Tries is Non-Sensitive) and (Destination_Account_Tries is Non-Sensitive) then (output1 is Low) (0.3)
49. If (Transaction_Notes is Normal) and (Destination_Profile_ID is Non-Sensitive) and (Password_Tries is Normal) and (Destination_Account_Tries is Sensetive) then (output1 is Medium) (0.3)
50. If (Transaction_Notes is Normal) and (Destination_Profile_ID is Non-Sensitive) and (Password_Tries is Normal) and (Destination_Account_Tries is Normal) then (output1 is Medium) (0.3)
51. If (Transaction_Notes is Normal) and (Destination_Profile_ID is Non-Sensitive) and (Password_Tries is Normal) and (Destination_Account_Tries is Non-Sensitive) then (output1 is Medium) (0.3)
52. If (Transaction_Notes is Normal) and (Destination_Profile_ID is Non-Sensitive) and (Password_Tries is Sensetive) and (Destination_Account_Tries is Sensetive) then (output1 is Medium) (0.3)
53. If (Transaction_Notes is Normal) and (Destination_Profile_ID is Non-Sensitive) and (Password_Tries is Sensetive) and (Destination_Account_Tries is Normal) then (output1 is Medium) (0.3)
54. If (Transaction_Notes is Normal) and (Destination_Profile_ID is Non-Sensitive) and (Password_Tries is Sensetive) and (Destination_Account_Tries is Non-Sensitive) then (output1 is Medium) (0.3)
55. If (Transaction_Notes is Sensetive) and (Destination_Profile_ID is Sensetive) and (Password_Tries is Non-Sensitive) and (Destination_Account_Tries is Sensetive) then (output1 is High) (0.3)
56. If (Transaction_Notes is Sensetive) and (Destination_Profile_ID is Sensetive) and (Password_Tries is Non-Sensitive) and (Destination_Account_Tries is Normal) then (output1 is High) (0.3)
57. If (Transaction_Notes is Sensetive) and (Destination_Profile_ID is Sensetive) and (Password_Tries is Non-Sensitive) and (Destination_Account_Tries is Non-Sensitive) then (output1 is Medium) (0.3)
58. If (Transaction_Notes is Sensetive) and (Destination_Profile_ID is Sensetive) and (Password_Tries is Normal) and (Destination_Account_Tries is Sensetive) then (output1 is High) (0.3)
59. If (Transaction_Notes is Sensetive) and (Destination_Profile_ID is Sensetive) and (Password_Tries is Normal) and (Destination_Account_Tries is Normal) then (output1 is High) (0.3)
60. If (Transaction_Notes is Sensetive) and (Destination_Profile_ID is Sensetive) and (Password_Tries is Normal) and (Destination_Account_Tries is Non-Sensitive) then (output1 is High) (0.3)
61. If (Transaction_Notes is Sensetive) and (Destination_Profile_ID is Sensetive) and (Password_Tries is Sensetive) and (Destination_Account_Tries is Sensetive) then (output1 is High) (0.3)
62. If (Transaction_Notes is Sensetive) and (Destination_Profile_ID is Sensetive) and (Password_Tries is Sensetive) and (Destination_Account_Tries is Normal) then (output1 is High) (0.3)
```

a sample group of IF-THEN rules used in fuzzification process that is used to assign an importance level attribute a value between (High, Medium, and Low).

Evaluation Stages

Using two sets of XML messages; each set represent a period in which the messages were extracted. Each set has number of XML messages to test. Collected XML messages present online banking service transactions fetched from Jordan Ahli Bank, one of the leading banks in Jordan.

We have selected to deploy full and partial encryption on selected sets of XML messages, whereby we will deploy full encryption on first set of XML messages, and partial encryption on the second set of XML message. The two sets have been selected randomly taken for a period of seven months (between January 2012 until August 2012) representing financial transactions in specific. In the first set we collected 1,000 random XML messages presenting a period of three months taken between January 2012 and March 2012. In the second set we used 1,500 XML messages presenting a period of four months taken between April 2012 and August 2012. Sample sets have been collected after taking necessary approvals and authorizations from the bank's concerned departments. Table 12 illustrates the two sets of XML messages in details.

As seen in Table 12, the first set has 1,000 XML messages with 4,000 root nodes and total size of 947KB. The second set has 1,500 XML messages with 6,000 root nodes and total size of 1380KB.

To ensure we are evaluating our model in a fair and comprehensive manner, we divided our evaluation into two stages. Evaluation stages are compared against W3C XML Encryption Recommendations. In each stage there are two experiments performed, each experiment presents an encryption using different key sizes. In first stage we have deployed full message encryption using W3C encryption standard with different key sizes. In the second stage we have deployed partial encryption using W3C encryption standard with different key sizes. Results from both stages are compared against our model which uses element-wise encryption and mixture of key sizes. Table 13 illustrates stage 1 evaluation details.

Stage 1: Evaluation for this stage has been conducted by performing two experiments; first experiment deployed performing full encryption using W3C XML encryption standard with a 128-bit key size deployed on the first set of 1,000 sample XML messages. SXMS uses the same sample of XML messages to deploy element-wise encryption. SXMS model uses symmetric AES encryption with mixed key values (128-bit, 256-bit), Key size used in the encryption process depends on the importance level attribute value assigned by the fuzzification stage for selected set of tags within each XML message. Second experiment has been conducted performing full encryption using W3C XML encryption standard with a 256-bit key deployed on the same 1,000 sample XML messages. SXMS uses the same sample of XML messages to deploy element-wise encryption. Later we compared results for both experiments against results from our model.

Table 12. Stage 1 Sets detail

Set	Number of XML messages	Total Root Nodes	Total Messages Size	Period	Encryption Performed
1	1,000 messages	4,000 node	**947 KB**	3 Months Jan 12-Mar12	Full Encryption
2	1,500 messages	6,000 node	**1380 KB**	4 Months Apr12-Aug12	Partial Encryption

Table 13. Performance evaluation for stage 1

Stage	Number of XML Messages	Model	Experiment 1 Used Key Size	Experiment 2 Used Key Size
1	1,000 Messages (4,000 Nodes)	W3C (Full Encryption)	128 bit	256 bit
		SXMS (Element-Wise)	(128 bit or 256 bit or NO Encryption)	(128 bit or 256 bit or NO Encryption)

Table 14. Processing time and resulting file sizes using SXMS and W3C-128

Stage 1 – Experiment 1 (Full Encryption)	Processing Time		File Size	
XML Message Set	SXMS Model	W3C 128 bit	SXMS Model	W3C 128 bit
1 XML File	0.0018 ms	0.0023 ms	1.14 KB	1.87 KB
300 XML Chunk	0.562 ms	0.702 ms	167.9 KB	263 KB
600 XML Chunk	0.873 ms	1.264 sec	342.6 KB	541.9 KB
900 XML Chunk	1.271 sec	1.825 sec	501.9 KB	799.7 KB
1,000 XML (Set 1)	**1.625** sec	**2.456** sec	**652.4 KB**	**988 KB**

Table 14 illustrates time needed and resulting file size to encrypt the XML message set using our model compared against W3C XML encryption model using a key size of 128 bit encrypting each message in full.

The XML messages are encrypted in chunks of 1, 300, 600, 900, and 1,000 messages. The SXMS model processed the XML chunks with a significant improvement in processing time compared to W3C XML encryption model which uses a 128-bit key size to encrypt the whole XML message.

SXMS uses a 128-bit key in the cases where the importance level attribute value equals to "Medium" and 256-bit key used when the importance level attribute value equals to "High". As seen in table 14, the encryption process for the whole XML 1,000 messages using W3C Encryption standard with a 128-bit key size took 2.456 seconds to complete, compared to 1.625 seconds using SXMS model. The result reflects a 33.8% improvement in processing time for the 1,000 messages. Figure 6.2 illustrates the comparison between the two models and performance improvement using SXMS. Table 14 also illustrates files size reduction encrypting XML messages using SXMS model, table shows a significant reduction in file size, whereby the total size of the encrypted 1,000 XML messages was 988 KB using W3C model with a key size of 128-bit encrypting each XML message in full. SXMS achieved smaller sizes for the same set of 1,000 encrypted XML messages which is 652.4 KB showing a size reduction of 34% from the encrypted file size using W3C model. Such improvement can save a significant amount of space and bandwidth on large scale. Figure 59 illustrates the processing time needed to encrypt the sample messages in the first experiment compared to our model.

As seen in Figure 59, the x-axis present the number of XML messages being processed, while y-axis present the processing time encrypting XML messages in seconds.

Figure 60 presents file size comparison for the encrypted XML messages using SXMS and W3C XML Encryption syntax and processing model using a key size of 128-bit performing full message encryption.

Figure 59. Comparison chart between SXMS and W3C model using 128-bit key

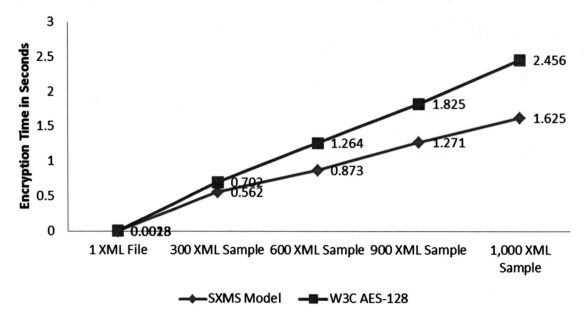

In the second experiment of stage 1, we deployed W3C Encryption standard to fully encrypt the same sample of 1,000 XML messages but this time using 256-bit key size. SXMS uses the same sample of XML messages to deploy element-wise encryption. SXMS model uses symmetric AES encryption with mixed key values (128-bit, 256-bit), Key size used in the encryption process depends on the importance level attribute value assigned by the fuzzification stage for selected set of tags within each XML message.

Figure 60. File size comparison between SXMS and W3C model using 128-bit

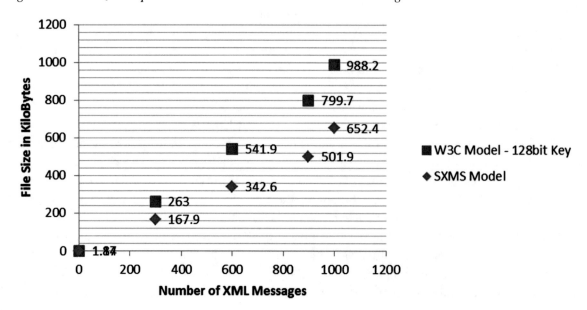

Table 15. Processing time table using SXMS and W3C-256 Model (Full Encryption)

Stage 1 – Experiment 2 (Full Encryption)	Processing Time		File Size	
XML Message Set	SXMS Model	W3C 256 bit	SXMS Model	W3C 256 bit
1 XML File	0.0018 ms	0.0027 ms	1.14 KB	1.98 KB
300 XML Chunk	0.562 ms	0.811 ms	167.9 KB	283.4 KB
600 XML Chunk	0.873 ms	1.591 sec	342.6 KB	601 KB
900 XML Chunk	1.271 sec	2.137 sec	501.9 KB	864.8 KB
1,000 XML (Set 1)	**1.625** sec	**2.8** sec	**652.4 KB**	**1112 KB**

Table 15 represents the time needed for each model performing the encryption process on selected sample of messages.

As seen in Table 15, the encryption process for the whole message using the W3C Encryption standard with a 256-bit key size took 2.8 seconds to complete, compared to 1.625 seconds using SXMS model. The result reflects a 41.9% improvement in processing time for the 1,000 messages.

Table 15 also illustrates files size reduction encrypting XML messages using SXMS model, table shows a significant reduction in file size, whereby the total size of the encrypted 1,000 XML messages was 1112 KB using W3C model with a key size of 256-bit encrypting each XML message in full. SXMS achieved smaller sizes for the same set of 1,000 encrypted XML messages which is 652.4 KB showing a size reduction of 41.3% from the encrypted file size using W3C model. Such improvement can save a significant amount of space and bandwidth on large scale. Figure 61 illustrates the performance comparison between SXMS model and W3C encryption standard using key size of 256-bit. Figure 62 presents file size comparison for the encrypted XML messages using SXMS and W3C XML Encryption syntax and processing model using a key size of 256-bit performing full message encryption.

Finally, Figures 63, 64 illustrates the final performance and file size reduction comparison between SXMS and W3C model for both experiments which uses 128-bit key and 256-bit key performing full encrypting for each XML message in the first message set. Figure presents a significant amount of performance improvement using SXMS model.

Stage 2: Evaluation for this stage has been conducted by performing two experiments; first experiment deployed performing partial encryption on a pre-defined list of tags using W3C XML encryption standard with a 128-bit key size deployed on the second set of 1,500 sample XML messages (Table 16). SXMS uses the same sample of XML messages to deploy element-wise encryption. SXMS model uses symmetric AES encryption with mixed key values (128-bit, 256-bit), Key size used in the encryption process depends on the importance level attribute value assigned by the fuzzification stage for selected set of tags within each XML message. Second experiment has been conducted performing partial encryption on a pre-defined list of tags using W3C XML encryption standard with a 256-bit key deployed on the same 1,500 sample XML messages. SXMS uses the same sample of XML messages to deploy element-wise encryption. Later we compared results for both experiments against results from our model.

Figure 61. Performance comparison between SXMS and XML using 256-bit

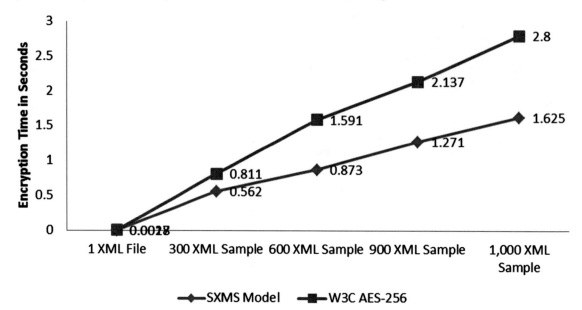

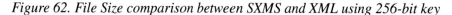

Figure 62. File Size comparison between SXMS and XML using 256-bit key

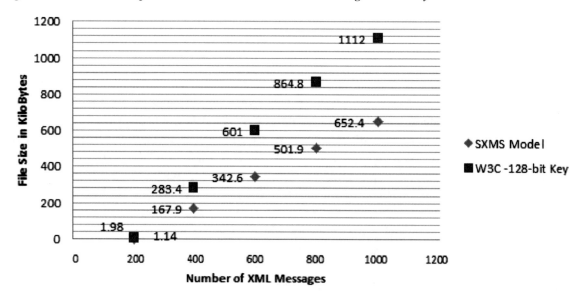

Table 17 presents time needed to encrypt the sample messages using our model compared against W3C XML encryption model using a key size of 128 bit to encrypt part of the message for the whole set.

As seen in Table 17, the encryption process for part of the message using the W3C Encryption standard with a 128-bit key size took 2.218 seconds to complete, compared to 1.963 seconds using SXMS model. The result reflects an 11.4% improvement in processing time for the 1,500 messages.

Table 17 also illustrates files size reduction encrypting XML messages using SXMS model, table shows a significant reduction in file size, whereby the total size of the encrypted 1,500 XML messages

Figure 63. Final performance comparison between SXMS and W3C models

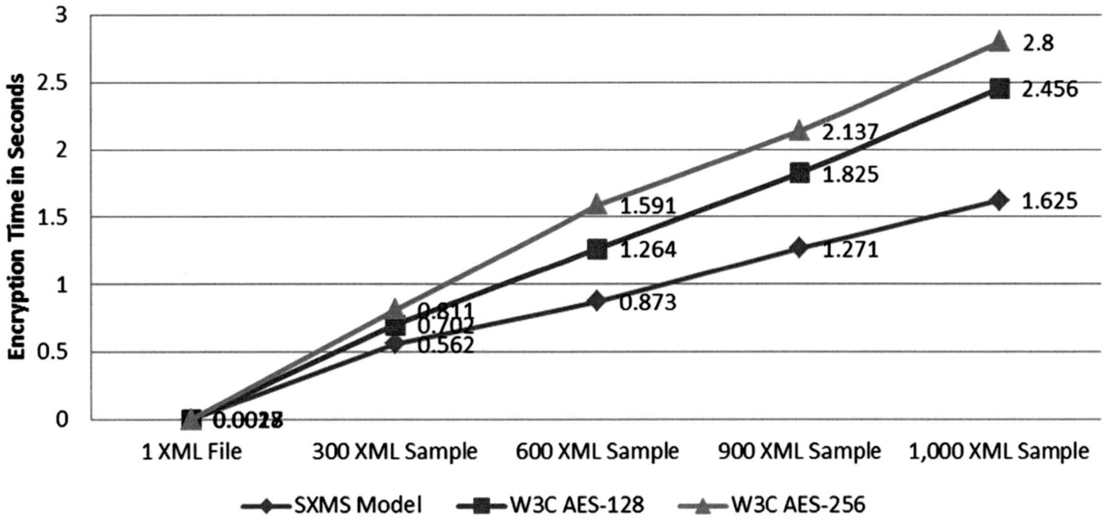

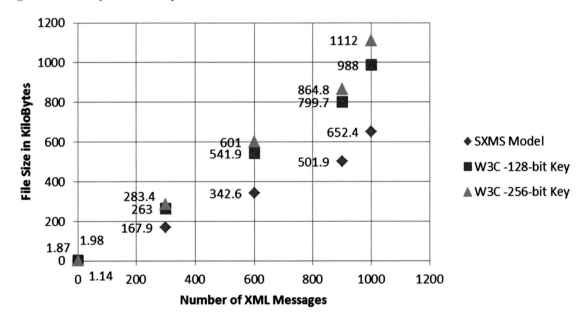

Figure 64. Final file size comparison between SXMS and W3C models

Table 16. Performance evaluation for stage 2

Stage	Number of XML Messages	Model	Experiment 1 Used Key Size	Experiment 2 Used Key Size
2	1,500 Messages (6,000 Nodes)	W3C (Partial Encryption)	128 bit	256 bit
		SXMS (Element-Wise)	(128 bit or 256 bit or NO Encryption)	(128 bit or 256 bit or NO Encryption)

Table 17. Processing time table using SXMS and W3C-128 Model (Partial Encryption)

Stage 2 – Experiment 1 (Partial Encryption)	Processing Time		File Size	
XML Message Set	SXMS Model	W3C 128 bit	SXMS Model	W3C 128 bit
1 XML File	0.0018 ms	0.0019 ms	1.14 KB	1.61 KB
300 XML Chunk	0.562 ms	0.578 ms	167.9 KB	244 KB
600 XML Chunk	0.873 ms	0.984 sec	342.6 KB	510.2 KB
900 XML Chunk	1.271 sec	1.422 sec	501.9 KB	740.7 KB
1,500 XML (Set 2)	**1.963** sec	**2.218** sec	**810.1 KB**	**1203.6 KB**

Figure 65. Performance comparison between SXMS and W3C Standard using AES-128 Key

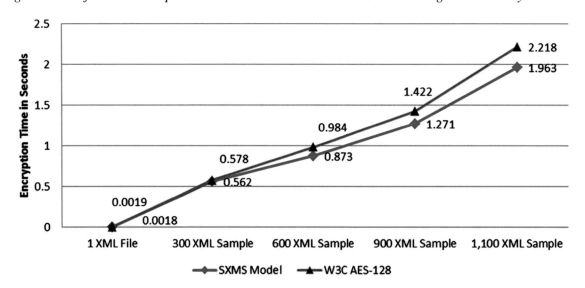

was 1203.6 KB using W3C model with a key size of 128-bit encrypting each XML message partially. SXMS achieved smaller sizes for the same set of 1,500 encrypted XML messages which is 810.1 KB showing a size reduction of 32.6% from the encrypted file size using W3C model. Such improvement can save a significant amount of space and bandwidth on large scale. Figure 65 illustrates the comparison between SXMS model and W3C encryption standard using key size of 128-bit.

Figure 66 presents file size comparison for the encrypted XML messages using SXMS and W3C XML Encryption syntax and processing model using a key size of 128-bit performing partial message encryption.

In the second experiment of stage 2, we deployed W3C Encryption standard to partially encrypt the XML messages to same sample of 1,500 XML messages but this time using 256-bit key size. SXMS uses the same sample of XML messages to deploy element-wise encryption. SXMS model uses symmetric AES encryption with mixed key values (128-bit, 256-bit), Key size used in the encryption process depends on the importance level attribute value assigned by the fuzzification stage for selected set of

Figure 66. File size comparison between SXMS and W3C Standard using AES-128 Key

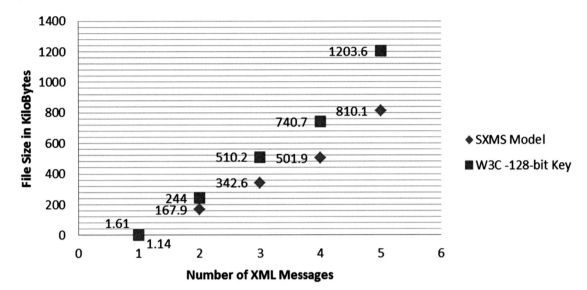

Table 18. Processing time table using SXMS and W3C-256 Model (Partial)

Stage 2 – Experiment 2 (Partial Encryption)	Processing Time		File Size	
XML Message Set	SXMS Model	W3C 256 bit	SXMS Model	W3C 256 bit
1 XML File	0.0018 ms	0.0021 ms	1.14 KB	1.72 KB
300 XML Chunk	0.562 ms	0.687 ms	167.9 KB	269 KB
600 XML Chunk	0.873 sec	1.42 sec	342.6 KB	588.4 KB
900 XML Chunk	1.271 sec	2.026 sec	501.9 KB	813.9 KB
1,500 XML (Set 2)	**1.963** sec	**2.899** sec	**810.1 KB**	**1399.6 KB**

tags within each XML message. Table 15 represents the time needed for each model performing the encryption process on selected sample of messages.

As seen in Table 18, the encryption process for part of the message using the W3C Encryption standard with a 256-bit key size took 2.899 seconds to complete, compared to 1.963 seconds using SXMS model. The result reflects a 32.2% improvement in processing time for the 1,500 messages. Table 18 also illustrates files size reduction encrypting XML messages using SXMS model, table shows a significant reduction in file size, whereby the total size of the encrypted 1,500 XML messages was 1399.6 KB using W3C model with a key size of 256-bit encrypting parts of the XML message. SXMS achieved smaller sizes for the same set of 1,500 encrypted XML messages which is 810.1 KB showing a size reduction of 42.1% from the encrypted file size using W3C model. Such improvement can save a significant amount of space and bandwidth on large scale. Figure 67 illustrates the comparison between SXMS model and W3C encryption standard using key size of 256-bit encrypting parts of the XML message for the second sample set.

Figure 67. Comparison between SXMS and W3C Standard using AES-256 Key

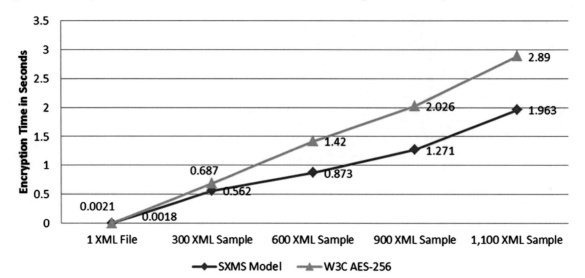

Figure 68. File size comparison between SXMS and W3C model using 256-bit key

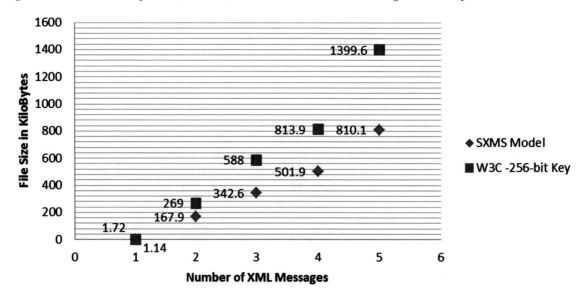

Figure 68 presents file size comparison for the encrypted XML messages using SXMS and W3C XML Encryption syntax and processing model using a key size of 256-bit performing partial message encryption.

Finally, Figures 69, 70 illustrate performance improvements and file size reduction comparison between SXMS model and W3C model for both experiments in stage 2 showing a significant amount of performance improvement and size reduction on a large scale using SXMS model.

We have presented evidence that implementing element-wise encryption based on the fuzzy classification techniques to encrypt only necessary parts within XML messages can improve performance of the encryption process, and can reduce encrypted file sizes which eventually will save space and bandwidth on a large scale.

Figure 69. Comparison between SXMS and W3C Standard using different keys

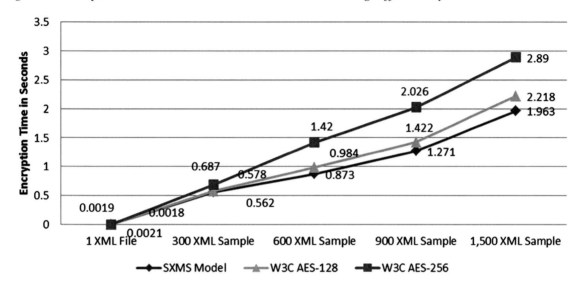

Figure 70. File size comparison between SXMS and W3C Standard using different keys

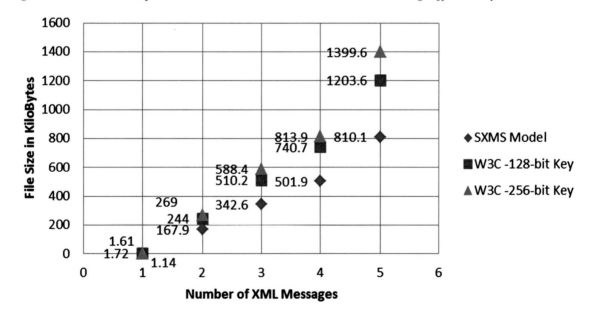

Screenshots, Source Codes, and Pseudo Code Examples

Screenshot Examples

Figure 71 and Figure 72 demonstrates screenshots of our application that is used in our testing and evaluation. Our intelligent model checked all extracted 10 characteristics within each XML message. Then using the fuzzification approach adopted by our main application, for the final importance level assigned

Figure 71. SXMS Main application interface

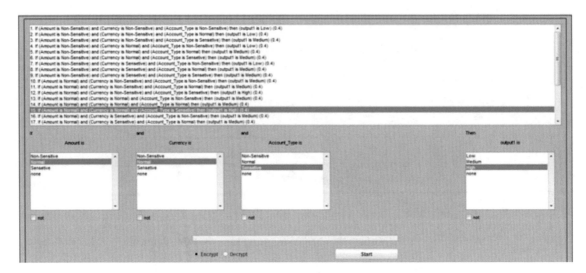

Figure 72. Main application result files after encryption process

for each tag, we have associated and classified all patterns with each other. Then we used our element-wise encryption embedded within the application to perform encryption using mixed keys depending on importance level value assigned by the fuzzification stage. The usage of AES encryption with a specific key value depends on the importance level assigned. Whereby, tags assigned the value "High" will be encrypted and their descendants using AES encryption with a key value of 256-bit, tags assigned with "Medium" will be encrypted using a key value of 128-bit. Finally tags with "Low" importance level will be forwarded to message assembly without any encryption performed.

Source Codes Examples

In this section we represent some source code examples used in our application.

- **Main Application Source Code (Java):**

```
new Thread(new Runnable(){
    public void run(){
        File dir = new File(settings.srcDir);
        File[] xmls = dir.listFiles();
        progress.setMaximum(xmls.length);
        progress.setValue(0);
        ArrayList<Object[]> times = new ArrayList<Object[]>();
    //It will store xml name and time take for encryption or decryption.
        for(File xmlName: xmls){
            Date timeStampStart = new Date();
                            //Starting time of encryption/decryption.

            progress.setValue(progress.getValue()+1);
            String fileName = xmlName.getPath();
            String xml = "";
            try {
                xml = getXmlString(new File(fileName));
                            //Getting xml string from a xml file.
            } catch (Exception ex) {
                javax.swing.JOptionPane.showMessageDialog(null,"Error
while opening input xml file!!");
                return;
            }
            String tagName = settings.tagName;
            String attName = settings.priorityAttribute;

            ArrayList<Data> datas = Data.parseXml(xml, tagName, attName);
            //Getting list of data which need to be encrytped or decrypted.
            for(Data data: datas){
                                        //Checking for key code.
                int keycode = 128;
                if(data.priority.equals(settings.aes256)) keycode = 256;
                else if(data.priority.equals(settings.aes128))keycode = 128;
                else {
                    //If key code does not match it will simply ignore it.
    //javax.swing.JOptionPane.showMessageDialog(this, "Key code does not match.
                    Skipping "+data.startIndex+" To "+data.endIndex);
                    data.data2=data.data;
                    continue;
```

```
                }

                if(radioEncrypt.isSelected()){
                    byte[] cipherBytes=null;
                    try {
                        cipherBytes = AES.encrypt(data.data, settings.
password, keycode);
                                            //Getting Encrypted data.
                    } catch (Exception ex) {
                        javax.swing.JOptionPane.
showMessageDialog(null,"Error at the time of encryption"+ex.toString());
                        continue;
                    }
                    data.data2= "\r\n<EncryptedData
Type='http://www.w3.org/2001/04/xmlenc#Element'
xmlns='http://www.w3.org/2001/04/xmlenc#'> \r\n" +
                        "<CipherData>\r\n<CipherValue>" + new sun.misc.
BASE64Encoder().encode(cipherBytes) +
                        "</CipherValue>\r\n</CipherData>\r\n</
EncryptedData>\r\n";
                }else{
                    try {
                                            //Getting decrypted data.
                        byte[] decoded =AES.decrypt(new sun.misc.BASE64De-
coder().decodeBuffer(data.getCipherData()), settings.password, keycode);
                        data.data2 = new String(decoded);
                    } catch (Exception ex) {
                        javax.swing.JOptionPane.
showMessageDialog(null,"Error at the time of decryption"+ex.toString());
                        return;
                    }
                }
            }

            int startIndex = 0;
            String newXml = "";
                    //Recreating the xml after encryption or decryption.
            for(Data data: datas){
                newXml += xml.substring(startIndex, data.startIndex);
                newXml += data.data2;
                startIndex=data.endIndex;
            }
            newXml += xml.substring(startIndex);
                        //Saving the new file to the destination folder.
            try {
                String dstFile = settings.dstDir+"\\"+xmlName.getName();
```

```
                    PrintWriter pw = new PrintWriter(dstFile);
                    pw.print(newXml);
                    pw.flush();
                    pw.close();
              } catch (FileNotFoundException ex) {
                    javax.swing.JOptionPane.showMessageDialog(null,"Error when
writing final xml!!\n"+ex.toString());
                    }

                              //Storing the orginal file into archive folder.
              String archName = settings.arcDir+"\\"+ xmlName.getName();
              while(!xmlName.renameTo(new File(archName))){
                  archName=archName.substring(0, archName.length()-4)+"_"+".xml";
              }
                                             //Processing ending time.
              Date timeStampEnd = new Date();
              long timeTook = timeStampEnd.getTime()-timeStampStart.get-
Time();
                                 //Calculating time took for the process.
              times.add(new Object[]{xmlName.getName(),timeTook});

          }
          javax.swing.JOptionPane.showMessageDialog(null,"Done");

                          //Showing time took for each file and total time.
          if(times.size()>0){
              int n = JOptionPane.showConfirmDialog(null, "Do you like to
save time stat?","AESEncrypt",JOptionPane.YES_NO_OPTION);
                  if(n==JOptionPane.YES_OPTION){
                      final JFileChooser fc = new JFileChooser();
                      int returnVal = fc.showSaveDialog(null);
                      if (returnVal == JFileChooser.APPROVE_OPTION) {
                          File file = fc.getSelectedFile();
                          try {
                              PrintWriter pw = new PrintWriter(file.getPath());
                              pw.println("FILE NAME\t\t\t\tTIME TOOK\r\n--------
-\t\t\t\t---------\r\n");
                              long total=0;
                              for(Object[] obj: times){
                                  String fileName = (String)obj[0];
                                  long time = (Long)obj[1];
                                  total += time;
                                  pw.println(fileName+"\t\t\t\t"+time);
                              }
                              pw.println("---------\t\t\t\t---------\r\nTotal
Time\t\t\t\t"+total+" or "+(total/1000)+"."+(total%1000)+" Sec");
                              pw.flush();
                              pw.close();
```

```
                    javax.swing.JOptionPane.showMessageDialog(null,"Done");
                } catch (FileNotFoundException ex) {}
            }
        }
    }

    btnContinue.setEnabled(true);
    radioEncrypt.setEnabled(true);
    radioDecrypt.setEnabled(true);
    }
}).start();
}
```

In the above code, we started by initializing the components that will be used in our process, at first we initialize the counter to check-up the processing speed needed for the whole process. Then reading XML files form incoming XML documents by getXMLString() function. Then we execute the parsing step to know which parts to be encrypted by calling Data.parseXml() function, later we define which key value to be used upon reading key string value. After deploying the encryption process for selected parts, we read the encrypted values by executing AES.encrypt(data.data, settings.password, keycode); function. Final stage is by assembling the message (with encrypted parts and forwarded parts) which requires file re-creation. Encryption time is calculated by initiating the variable *timeStampStart* of Date() type and running cross the application to start the counter, later another variable initiated at end of the encryption process called *timeStampEnd* which reads the time at the finishing stage.

- **Parse XML Code:**

```
public String getXmlString(File xml) throws Exception{
        String fileContent = "";
        try {
            BufferedReader reader = new java.io.BufferedReader(new java.
io.FileReader(xml.getPath()));
            String row = reader.readLine();
            while(row!=null){
                fileContent+=row+"\r\n";
                row = reader.readLine();
            }
            reader.close();
        } catch (IOException ex) {
            throw ex;
        }
        return fileContent;
    }
```

In the above class, we parse XML messages by using XPath function. getXMLString() is used to read the file by getting full file path and then read it line by line. Function returns file content to be used later in the encryption process.

- **Read Encrypted XML Data:**

```
public String getCipherData(){
        String retVal="";
        Pattern p = Pattern.compile("<([\\s]*)CipherValue([^>]*)>([\\w\\
W]*?)<([\\s]*)/([\\s]*)CipherValue([\\s]*)>");
        Matcher m = p.matcher(data);
        while(m.find()){
            retVal = m.group();
            int s = retVal.indexOf(">")+1;
            int e = retVal.lastIndexOf("<");
            retVal=retVal.substring(s, e).trim();
        }
        return retVal;
    }
}
```

In the above class, we read encrypted data by using GetCipherData() function which gets the base64-encoded data representing the encrypted form of the plaintext data.

- **AES Encryption Class (Encryption):**

```
public class AES {
    /**
     * Encrypt a string using AES Encryption.
     *
     * @param  data  String data to be encrypted.
     * @param  pass  Password for symmetric encryption.
     * @param  encryptSize  128 or 256 .
     */
    public static byte[] encrypt(String data, String pass, int encryptSize)
throws Exception{
        try{
                byte[] keyBytes = getPassBytes(pass, encryptSize);
                byte[] input = data.getBytes();
                SecretKeySpec key = new SecretKeySpec(keyBytes, "AES");
                Cipher cipher = Cipher.getInstance("AES");
                cipher.init(Cipher.ENCRYPT_MODE, key);
                byte[] cipherText = cipher.doFinal(input);
                return cipherText;
            }catch (Exception ex) {
                throw ex;
            }
    }
```

In the AES encryption class, the cipher object is initialized. The initialization is done in cipher.init (Cipher.ENCRYPT_MODE, key); method. The first parameter determines the operation mode of the cipher. As we want to encrypt a file, we use the ENCRYPT_MODE. The second parameter is the secret key which should be used for encryption.

- **AES Decryption Class:**

```
public static byte[] decrypt(byte[] data, String pass, int encryptSize) throws
Exception{
        try{
                byte[] keyBytes = getPassBytes(pass, encryptSize);
                byte[] input = data;//data.getBytes();
                SecretKeySpec key = new SecretKeySpec(keyBytes, "AES");
                Cipher cipher = Cipher.getInstance("AES");
                cipher.init(Cipher.DECRYPT_MODE, key);
                byte[] cipherText = cipher.doFinal(input);
                return cipherText;
        }catch (Exception ex) {
                throw ex;
        }
    }
```

In the AES decryption class, we start the decryption process based on the incoming message. Function calls the data string, encryption size and assign read ciphered data to a variable. Then we use the same cipher as for encryption, but we initialize it for decryption with the previously generated secret key.

Pseudo Codes Examples

Below are some important pseudo examples for extracting importance level value for the fuzzy classification phase in our system implementation.

- **Read XML Tag "Importance Level":**

```
Value XML_Tag_Value = "Importance Level"
Number_Of_Tags;
Get Parsed_XML_Message;
Get XML_Tag_Value;
While count <= Number_Of_Tags
Check XML_Tag_Value
        If XML_Tag_Value = "High"
          Encryption_Algorithm = "AES"
                Encryption_Key = "256"
Do_Encryption_Function1 for the XML Tag: XML_Tag_Value AND Childs
        If XML_Tag_Value = "Medium"
          Encryption_Algorithm = "AES"
                Encryption_Key = "128"
Do_Encryption_Function2 for the XML Tag: XML_Tag_Value AND Childs
        If XML_Tag_Value = "Low" OR XML_Tag_Value = ""
          Encryption_Algorithm = ""
                Encryption_Key = ""
Do_Message_Forward_Function for the XML Tag: XML_Tag_Value AND Childs
```

Summary

In this section, extensive tests were carried out to check the performance of SXMS model and file size reduction. The basic idea of testing is to measure the encryption processing time and resulting file sizes. SXMS model was tested against W3C XML Encryption standard. Testing took place taking into consideration element-wise encryption and full encryption. Element-wise encryption was performed and evaluated based on two cases, the first by encrypting a pre-defined list of tags within each XML message and measuring the results against SXMS model which uses element-wise encryption on a fuzzified list of tags, tags were selected based on a previous step which classify XML messages deploying fuzzification techniques. The second case performed by encrypting the whole messages and comparing the results against our element-wise based encryption model. Results showed a significant improvement in both cases presenting the superiority of our basic concept which uses on-the-fly fuzzy classification mechanism encrypting only critical information within XML messages.

The other achievement is the encrypted file size reduction, whereby deploying SXMS produced smaller file sizes post the encryption process which saves both time and bandwidth on a large scale.

CONCLUSION AND FUTURE DIRECTIONS

Conclusion

This research has characterized an intelligent and secure XML management system has been proposed for securing financial XML messages. System has been designed to secure the essential parts within the financial XML messages. Fuzzy logic has been used to provide an efficient technique for creating an intelligent model to fetch the important parts within each XML message, which involves selecting the important parts and assigning them an attribute value called the importance level. An element-wise encryption model is used to encrypt selected parts from the fuzzy classification phase; encryption uses different key sizes during the encryption process depending on the importance level value. Set of experiments have been deployed to analyse different transaction features and patterns, with all corresponding relations. Experiments result presented the need for deploying a secure yet efficient system to handle exchanged messages in business applications in general and in financial applications in particular. The importance is not only in securing the transactions but in securing them in an efficient and robust way. The SXMS model covered the concept of providing an efficient yet robust security mechanism for exchanging XML messages.

Phase one of SXMS uses a fuzzy-logic-based model to detect the important parts within XML messages. The fuzzy logic model we have proposed consisted of the main four stages (fuzzification stage, rule evaluation stage, aggregation stage, and finally defuzzification stage). Financial XML message features are characterized as fuzzy variables with specific fuzzy sets. For the purpose of final calculation of the XML importance level attribute value, the fuzzy rules are processed by the operations performed by fuzzy set into the inference engine.

The experiments are securing only the needed parts within each XML message that is an effective mechanism to use on a large scale. In our results, we were able to achieve a significant improvement in encryption processing speed. In our first experiment, we achieved a 33.8% improvement in processing time for our sample messages. Using same sample messages, we were able to reduce file sizes for encrypted XML messages. A significant size reduction of 34% achieved using our model compared to encrypted XML messages using W3C Encryption.

In our second experiment on the same data sample, we were able to achieve improvement in encryption processing time whereby we reached 41.9% improvement using different key size. File size reduction is achieved as well hitting 41.3% improvement in our second experiment using same data sample.

Additional two experiments are conducted using a different data sample consist of 1,500 messages. Using the same key size our model achieved 11.4% improvement in processing time and 32.6% in file size reduction.

Using same sample set of data but with different key size, we were able to achieve another improvement in encryption processing time marking 32.2% faster to encrypt the same sample and a 42.1% file size reduction for resulted encrypted files.

A desktop application has been developed and implemented. This application has extracted all the XML message features. Verification of the extracted features has been plugged into the model to identify importance level values effectively. An element-wise encryption module has been integrated into the solution to perform element-wise encryption effectively on the selected parts. The importance level attributes within each XML message that have values of "High" or "Medium" are then processed. Different key sizes are used depending on the importance level value.

The results from our evaluation stages and testing stages illustrated that our proposed solution outperformed the existing XML security solutions. Our solution outperformed these existing models in terms of efficiency, accuracy, and the speed of importance level detection, using fuzzy classification techniques.

We have presented a comparative performance of proposed system in order to illustrate the capabilities through testing stages.

Potential contributions can be deduced from our research that could enhance overall model deployment in different niches and fields. The following are the main contributions and achievements described in detail:

1. Significant improvement in processing time performing either element-wise encryption or full encryption, an average improvement in encryption processing time of 22.6% achieved compared to W3C Encryption model using the same key size. An average 34.5% improvement also achieved using different key size.
2. Significant file size reduction achieved, an average file deduction of 33.3% achieved compared to W3C Encryption model using the same key size, and a 41.2% size reduction achieved using different key size.
3. The ten features and patterns that characterize financial XML messages were extracted in a successful way and distributed in three main layers, depending on the transaction attribute nature.
4. A resilient, secure, and intelligent XML model has been proposed. The mechanism uses fuzzy logic to process the features of XML messages. The model performs element-wise encryption on selected parts with attribute values set to "High" or "Medium".
5. A desktop application has been designed and developed to test and validate our proposed model. The testing was done to prove the reliability, feasibility, and extraction process of the mechanism. The application has been developed using Java programming language; our application successfully extracted the critical and important parts within two chunks of sample messages. The two samples reflected 1,000 and 1,500 XML messages.
6. The SXMS model was built with flexibility taken into consideration. The system was designed to handle future enhancements and modifications, so researchers would be able to make core changes either at the fuzzy classification stage or at the encryption stage. Such core changes could include changing the fuzzy classification technique and how it is used; this could be used in conjunction with data mining and classification techniques, or could even be completely replaced with well-known classifiers like decision trees (Quinlan, 1979, 1986, 1998) or Classification based on association

(CBA) (Liu, Hsu, & Ma, 1998). Core changes could also include changing the encryption algorithm and used keys: the AES encryption could be replaced with DES or triple DES encryption, if the researchers could prove this change's feasibility. The flexibility of our model leaves a wide range of space for enhancements and new contributions.

Future Directions

A secure XML management system has been introduced for handling the exchanging of XML messages in a secure and efficient way. Our proposed solution is based on two main phases: the first phase involves fetching the important parts within XML messages by implementing a fuzzy based classification technique. This technique uses an intelligent fuzzy methodology based on a layered structure to collect and analyses all of the XML message features and patterns. The second phase involves adopting an element-wise encryption mechanism that uses different key sizes to encrypt the parts selected in the previous stage. The level of encryption used on the selected parts depends on the attribute values assigned in the fuzzy classification stage: if the attribute value for an importance level tag is set to "High", AES encryption with a key value of 256 bits is used. A key value of 128 bits is used in the case of a "Medium" attribute value. Finally, tags with no attribute values assigned or those set to "Low" are forwarded without deploying any type of encryption.

This kind of intelligent and supervised machine learning technique provides a large amount of room and potential for future improvements and enhancements.

Each unit in our SXMS model acts independently as a separate system. This flexible nature allows and motivates future work and enhancements. Despite the significant improvement on the processing time and file size reduction, the proposed system has some limitations in term of automating the whole process, especially rule evaluation stage whereby we need to inject the expert knowledge manually during fuzzification stage. The following points describe the future work that could be achieved to improve system functionality and automation of certain areas:

Fuzzy classification phase: We can employ supervised machine learning for fuzzy rule generation process automation. By performing this automation we can reduce the human expert involvement with high potential to increase fuzzy classification phase performance. This could be achieved by generating classification rules using well-known classifiers. For example, we could use PRISM (Cendrowska, 1987), C4.5 Decision Tree (Quinlan, 1996), Ripper (Cohen, 1995), Classification based on association (CBA) (Liu et al., 1998), k-nearest neighbour classification (kNN) (Guo et al., 2006), support vector machines (SVM) (Brank et al., 2003), naïve bayes classification (McCallum & Nigam, 1998), neural networks (NN) (Ng et al., 1997), linear least squares fit mapping (Yang & Chute, 1993), or the vector space method (Gauch et al., 2004). These association classification rules could be shared with a fuzzy logic inference engine to provide importance level extraction in an efficient way.

Encryption phase: We could utilize a different encryption scheme; asymmetric algorithms could be deployed. We have deployed symmetric encryption due to its efficiency and processing time; it outperforms asymmetric encryption algorithms. However, we could change the symmetric encryption algorithm to something different like DES, triple DES, or blowfish encryption. Researchers will be able to test and measure the performance for any replaced encryption algorithm. Also, usage of the encryption keys could be change to reflect different key sizes for each importance level assigned. For example, we could assign an encryption key size of 192 bits instead of 256 bits for the importance level "High" value.

There is also the ability to add the concept of XML classification instead of fuzzy classification or associative classification. XML classification focuses on structure similarity rather than content. We could use the classification technique using hierarchical taxonomies proposed by (Fuhr & Weikum, 2002), or we could use the well-known classifier called XRules proposed by (Zaki & Aggarwal, 2003), which focuses on the structural classification of XML documents. We also might consider a hybrid combination of content and structural classification as proposed by (Denoyer & Gallinari, 2004), which is based on a generative Bayesian classifier.

Finally, regarding the ability to generalize the Fuzzy-based Model for Financial XML Transactions Security adoption, we can expand our work in fuzzy classification phase to enable XML message parsing without the need to create a pre-defined structure. By performing this kind of improvement, we will be able to adopt the model with ease and without the need to create a pre-defined structure for message extraction. Successful adoption of this generalization enables commercial packaging for broader use in commercial and financial areas.

REFERENCES

10181-1, I.-T. R. X. I. I. (1996). *Information technology — Security Frameworks in Open Systems: Overview*. Author.

10181-1, I.-T. X. I. (1996). *Information technology — Security Frameworks in Open Systems: Overview*. Author.

W3C. (1998). *Extensible Markup Language*. Retrieved October 2009, from http://www.w3.org/TR/1998/REC-xml-19980210

W3C. (2001). *XML Encryption Syntax and Processing*. W3C.

W3C, Boyer, J., Eastlake, D. E., & Reagle, J. (2002). *Exclusive XML Canonicalization, Version 1.0*. Retrieved April 2011, from http://www.w3.org/TR/2002/REC-xml-exc-c14n-20020718/

Abiteboul, S. (1996). *Querying Semi-Structured Data*. Stanford InfoLab.

Abiteboul, S., Segoufin, L., & Vianu, V. (2006). Representing and querying XML with incomplete information. *ACM Transactions on Database Systems, 31*(1), 208–254. doi:10.1145/1132863.1132869

Bartel, M., Boyer, J., Fox, B., LaMacchia, B., & Simon, E. (2002). *XML-Signature Syntax and Processing*. W3C Recommendation.

Bartel, M., Boyer, J., Fox, B., LaMacchia, B., & Simon, E. (2008). XML signature syntax and processing (2nd ed.). Academic Press.

Blair, D. (2001). *Re: attribute encryption (from XML encryption mailing list)*. Academic Press.

Boyer, J., Eastlake, D. E., & Reagle, J. (2002). *Exclusive XML Canonicalization, Version 1.0*. Retrieved from http://www.w3.org/TR/2002/REC-xml-exc-c14n-20020718/

Boyer, J. (2001). *Canonical XML Version 1.0*. RFC Editor.

Boyer, J., Hughes, M., & Reagle, J. (2003). *XML-Signature XPath Filter 2.0*. RFC Editor.

Brank, J., Grobelnik, M., Milic-Frayling, N., & Mladenic, D. (2003). *Training text classifiers with SVM on very few positive examples*. Academic Press.

Bray, T., Paoli, J., Sperberg-McQueen, C. M., Maler, E., & Yergeau, F. (2007). *Extensible Markup Language (XML) 1.0* (4th ed.). Academic Press.

Bray, T., Paoli, J., Sperberg-McQueen, C. M., Maler, E., & Yergeau, F. (2008). *Extensible Markup Language (XML) 1.0* (5th ed.). Retrieved from http://www.w3.org/TR/REC-xml/

Bridges, S. M., & Vaughn, R. B. (2001). *Fuzzy Data Mining And Genetic Algorithms Applied To Intrusion Detection*. Paper presented at the 23rd National Information Systems Security Conference.

Cantor, S., Kemp, J., Philpott, R., & Maler, E. (2005). *Assertions and Protocols for the OASIS Security Assertion Markup Language (SAML) v2.0*. Academic Press.

Cendrowska, J. (1987). PRISM: An algorithm for inducing modular rules. *International Journal of Man-Machine Studies*, *27*(4), 349–370. doi:10.1016/S0020-7373(87)80003-2

Clark, J. (2001). *TREX - Tree Regular Expressions for XML*. Academic Press.

Cohen, W. W. (1995). Fast Effective Rule Induction In *Proceedings of the Twelfth International Conference on Machine Learning* (pp. 115-123): Morgan Kaufmann.

Cox, E. (2001a). Fuzzy logic and the measures of certainty in eCommerce expert systems. *PC AI*, *15*(3), 16–22.

Cox, E. (2001b). *Fuzzy Logic and the Measures of Certainty in eCommerce Expert Systems*. Scianta Intelligence.

Denoyer, L., & Gallinari, P. (2004). Bayesian network model for semi-structured document classification. *Information Processing & Management*, *40*(5), 807–827. doi:10.1016/j.ipm.2004.04.009

Diffie, W., & Hellman, M. E. (1976). New directions in cryptography. *Information Theory. IEEE Transactions on*, *22*(6), 644–654. doi:10.1109/tit.1976.1055638

E, S., & B, L. (2000). *XML encryption strawman proposal*. Retrieved from http://lists.w3.org/Archives/Public/xml-encryption/2000Aug/0001.html

Eastlake, D., & Reagle, J. (2002). *XML Encryption Syntax and Processing*. Academic Press.

Ed, S. (2000). *XML Encryption: Issues Regarding Attribute Values and Referenced*. Retrieved from http://www.w3.org/Encryption/2001/Minutes/0103-Boston/simon-attribute-encryption.html

Ed, S. (2001). *Re: attribute encryption, schema validation, role of XSLT, scope of XML encryption document (from XML encryption mailing list)*. Academic Press.

Fallside, D. (2001). *XML schema part 0: primer*. W3C Recommendation.

Fallside, D. C., & Walmsley, P. (2004). XML Schema Part 0: Primer Second Edition. W3C Recommendation.

Fuhr, N., & Weikum, G. (2002). Classification and Intelligent Search on Information in XML. *Bulletin of the IEEE Technical Committee on Data Engineering, 25,* 51–58.

Galindo, J. (2008). *Handbook of Research on Fuzzy Information Processing in Databases.* IGI Global. doi:10.4018/978-1-59904-853-6

Gauch, S., Madrid, J. M., Induri, S., Ravindran, D., & Chadlavada, S. (2004). *KeyConcept: A Conceptual Search Engine.* University of Kansas.

Gaurav, A., & Alhajj, R. (2006). *Incorporating fuzziness in XML and mapping fuzzy relational data into fuzzy XML.* Paper presented at the 2006 ACM symposium on Applied computing, Dijon, France. doi:10.1145/1141277.1141386

Geuer-Pollmann, C. (2002). *XML pool encryption.* Paper presented at the 2002 ACM workshop on XML security, Fairfax, VA. doi:10.1145/764792.764794

Godik, S., & Moses, T. (2002). *XACML 1.0 - The OASIS extensible Access Control Markup Language (XACML).* Retrieved from http://www.oasis-open.org/committees/xacml/

Godik, S., & Moses, T. (2003). *eXtensible Access Control Markup Language (XACML) Version 1.0.* Retrieved from http://www.oasis-open.org/committees/xacml/repository/

Guo, G., Wang, H., Bell, D., Bi, Y., & Greer, K. (2006). Using kNN model for automatic text categorization. *Soft Computing, 10*(5), 423–430. doi:10.1007/s00500-005-0503-y

Hallam-Baker, P., & Mysore, S. H. (2005). *XML Key Management Specification (XKMS 2.0).* Retrieved June, 2010, from http://www.w3.org/TR/xkms2/

Hégaret, P. L., Whitmer, R., & Wood, L. (2005). *Document Object Model (DOM).* Retrieved from http://www.w3.org/DOM/

Herrera, F., Herrera-Viedma, E., & Verdegay, J. L. (1996). Direct approach processes in group decision making using linguistic OWA operators. *Fuzzy Sets and Systems, 79*(2), 175–190. doi:10.1016/0165-0114(95)00162-X

Herrera-Viedma, E., Peis, E., Morales-del-Castillo, J. M., Alonso, S., & Anaya, K. (2007). A fuzzy linguistic model to evaluate the quality of Web sites that store XML documents. *International Journal of Approximate Reasoning, 46*(1), 226–253. doi:10.1016/j.ijar.2006.12.010

Hughes, J., Cantor, S., Hodges, J., Hirsch, F., Mishra, P., Philpott, R., & Maler, E. (2005). *Profiles for the OASIS Security Assertion Markup Language (SAML) V2.0.* Academic Press.

Hunter, D., Cagle, K., Dix, C., & Cable, D. (2001). *Beginning XML* (2nd ed.). Wrox Press.

IEEE. (1990). IEEE Standard Glossary of Software Engineering Terminology. *IEEE Std 610.12-1990,* 1-84. doi: 10.1109/ieeestd.1990.101064

Imamura, T., Dillaway, B., & Simon, E. (2002). *XML Encryption Syntax and Processing.* Academic Press.

ISO10181-1, I.-T. X. (n.d.). *Information technology — Security Frameworks in Open Systems: Overview.* ISO.

ISO/IEC11770. (n.d.). *Information technology — Security techniques — Key management*. ISO.

ISO/IEC9798-1. (1997). *Information technology — Security techniques — Entity authentication — Part 1: General*. ISO.

JAB. (2013). *Jordan Ahli Bank*. Retrieved from http://www.ahli.com/

Jelliffe, R. (2006). *Resource Directory (RDDL) for Schematron 1.5*. Retrieved June 2010, from http://xml.ascc.net/schematron/

Joseph, R. (2001). *XML Encryption Requirements*. Retrieved November, 2011, from http://www.w3.org/TR/xml-encryption-req

King, S. (2003). Threats and Solutions to Web Services Security. *Network Security, 2003*(9), 8–11. doi:10.1016/S1353-4858(03)00907-3

Klarlund, N., Møller, A., & Schwartzbach, M. I. (2000). *DSD: A Schema Language for XML*. Paper presented at the Workshop on Formal Methods in Software Practice, Portland, OR. Retrieved from http://www.brics.dk/DSD/dsd.html

Klir, G. J., & Yuan, B. (1995). *Fuzzy sets and fuzzy logic: theory and applications*. Prentice-Hall, Inc.

Lee, J., & Fanjiang, Y.-y. (2003). Modeling imprecise requirements with XML. *Information and Software Technology, 45*(7), 445–460. doi:10.1016/S0950-5849(03)00015-6

Liu, B., Hsu, W., & Ma, Y. (1998). Integrating Classification and Association Rule Mining. Academic Press.

Lukasiewicz, T., & Straccia, U. (2008). Managing uncertainty and vagueness in description logics for the Semantic Web. *Web Semantics: Science, Services, and Agents on the World Wide Web, 6*(4), 291–308. doi:10.1016/j.websem.2008.04.001

Ma, Z. M., & Yan, L. (2007). Fuzzy XML data modeling with the UML and relational data models. *Data & Knowledge Engineering, 63*(3), 972–996. doi:10.1016/j.datak.2007.06.003

Mahant, N. (2004). Risk Assessment is Fuzzy Business—Fuzzy Logic Provides the Way to Assess Off-site Risk from Industrial Installations. Bechtel, Australia. *Risk (Concord, NH)*.

Makoto, M. (2002). *RELAX (Regular Language description for XML)*. Retrieved June 2010, from http://www.xml.gr.jp/relax/

Makoto, M., Walsh, N., & McRae, M. (2001). *TREX and RELAX Unified as RELAX NG, a Lightweight XML Language Validation Specification*. Academic Press.

Mamdani, E. H., & Assilian, S. (1975). An experiment in linguistic synthesis with a fuzzy logic controller. *International Journal of Man-Machine Studies, 7*(1), 1–13. doi:10.1016/S0020-7373(75)80002-2

Maruyama, H., & Imamura, T. (2000). *Element-Wise XML Encryption*. Retrieved February 2008, from http://lists.w3.org/Archives/Public/xml-encryption/2000Apr/att-0005/01-xmlenc

McCallum, A., & Nigam, K. (1998). *A comparison of event models for Naive Bayes text classification*. Academic Press.

Mclaughlin, B., & Edelson, J. (2006). *Java and XML* (3rd ed.). O'Reilly.

Moller, A. (2005, December). *Document Structure Description 2.0.* Academic Press.

Ng, H. T., Goh, W. B., & Low, K. L. (1997). Feature selection, perceptron learning, and a usability case study for text categorization. *SIGIR Forum, 31*(SI), 67-73. doi:10.1145/278459.258537

Nierman, A., & Jagadish, H. V. (2002). ProTDB: Probabilistic data in XML. In *Proceedings of the 28th VLDB Conference* (pp. 646-657). Springer.

O'Neill, M. (2003). Web Services Security. McGraw-Hill Osborne Media.

OASIS. S. S. T. C. o. (2002). *Oasis security services (saml).* Retrieved October 2010, from http://www.oasis-open.org/committees/security/

Ortega, F. B. (2008). *Managing Vagueness in Ontologies* (PhD Dissertation). University of Granada, Spain.

Petrovic, D., Roy, R., & Petrovic, R. (1999). Supply chain modelling using fuzzy sets. *International Journal of Production Economics, 59*(1–3), 443–453. doi:10.1016/S0925-5273(98)00109-1

Phillip, M. H.-B., & Ford, W. (2001). *XML Key Management Specification (XKMS).* Retrieved from http://www10.org/cdrom/posters/1129.pdf

Pressman, R. (2009). Software Engineering: A Practitioner's Approach (7th ed.). McGraw-Hill.

Quinlan, J. R. (1979). *Discovering rules from large collections of examples: a case study.* Academic Press.

Quinlan, J. R. (1986). Induction of Decision Trees. *Machine Learning, 1*(1), 81–106. doi:10.1007/BF00116251

Quinlan, J. R. (1996). Improved Use of Continuous Attributes in C4.5. *Journal of Artificial Intelligence Research, 4*, 77–90.

Quinlan, J. R. (1998). *Data Mining Tools see5 and c5.* Academic Press.

Ray, E. T. (2003). *Learning XML - creating self-describing data: cover schemas* (2nd ed.). O'Reilly.

Rivest, R. L., Shamir, A., & Adleman, L. (1978). A method for obtaining digital signatures and public-key cryptosystems. *Communications of the ACM, 21*(2), 120–126. doi:10.1145/359340.359342

Rosario, R. (2001). *Secure XML An Overview of XML Encryption.* Academic Press.

Smets, P. (1996). *Imperfect Information: Imprecision and Uncertainty.* Uncertainty Management in Information Systems.

Steve, W. (2001). *Re: attribute encryption (from XML encryption mailing list).* Academic Press.

Sugeno, M. (1985). An introductory survey of fuzzy control. *Information Sciences, 36*(1-2), 59–83. doi:10.1016/0020-0255(85)90026-X

Takeshi, I., & Hiroshi, M. (2000). *Specification of element-wise XML encryption.* Retrieved from http://lists.w3.org/Archives/Public/xml-encryption/2000Aug/att-0005/01-xmlenc-spec.html

Tseng, C., Khamisy, W., & Vu, T. (2005). Universal fuzzy system representation with XML. *Computer Standards & Interfaces, 28*(2), 218–230. doi:10.1016/j.csi.2004.11.005

Turowski, K., & Weng, U. (2002). Representing and processing fuzzy information — an XML-based approach. *Knowledge-Based Systems, 15*(1–2), 67–75. doi:10.1016/S0950-7051(01)00122-8

Violleau, T. (2001). *Java Technology and XML.* Academic Press.

Weerasinghe, D., Elmufti, K., Rajarajan, M., & Rakocevic, V. (2006). *XML Security based Access Control for Healthcare Information in Mobile Environment.* Paper presented at the Pervasive Health Conference and Workshops.

Williams, I. (2009). *Beginning XSLT and XPath: Transforming XML Documents and Data.* Wrox Press.

Yager, R. R. (1988). On ordered weighted averaging aggregation operators in multicriteria decision-making. *Systems, Man and Cybernetics. IEEE Transactions on, 18*(1), 183–190. doi:10.1109/21.87068

Yager, R. R. (2000). Targeted e-commerce marketing using fuzzy intelligent agents. *Intelligent Systems and their Applications, IEEE, 15*(6), 42-45. doi: 10.1109/5254.895859

Yager, R. R., & Pasi, G. (2001). Product category description for web-shopping in e-commerce. *International Journal of Intelligent Systems, 16*(8), 1009–1021. doi:10.1002/int.1046

Yang, Y., & Chute, C. G. (1993). *An application of least squares fit mapping to text information retrieval.* Paper presented at the 16th annual international ACM SIGIR conference on Research and development in information retrieval, Pittsburgh, PA. doi:10.1145/160688.160738

Yang, Y., & Liu, X. (1999). *A re-examination of text categorization methods.* Paper presented at the 22nd annual international ACM SIGIR conference on Research and development in information retrieval, Berkeley, CA.

Zadeh, L. A. (1965). Fuzzy Sets. *Information and Control, 8*(3), 338–353. doi:10.1016/S0019-9958(65)90241-X

Zadeh, L. A. (1984). Making computers think like people: The term `fuzzy thinkingÂ¿ is pejorative when applied to humans, but fuzzy logic is an asset to machines in applications from expert systems to process control. *Spectrum, IEEE, 21*(8), 26-32. doi: 10.1109/mspec.1984.6370431

Zaki, M. J., & Aggarwal, C. C. (2003). *XRules: an effective structural classifier for XML data.* Paper presented at the ninth ACM SIGKDD international conference on Knowledge discovery and data mining, Washington, DC. doi:10.1145/956750.956787

Zhang, F., Ma, Z. M., & Yan, L. (2013). Construction of fuzzy ontologies from fuzzy XML models. *Knowledge-Based Systems, 42*(0), 20–39. doi:10.1016/j.knosys.2012.12.015

APPENDIX A: RULES FOR LAYER 1, LAYER 2, AND LAYER 3

The complete list of rules extracted from MATLAB is listed in Appendix A. rules represent the three layers, layer 1 which is the account segment, layer 2 which is the details segment, and layer 3 which is environment segment. There are 135 rule defined in this list.

Rules for Layer 1 (Account Segment)

There are 27 rules extracted from MATLAB fuzzy set, layer 1 represent account segment.

Fuzzy Rules

Rule 1: If (Amount is Non-Sensitive) and (Currency is Non-Sensitive) and (Account_Type is Non-Sensitive) then (output1 is Low) (0.4)

Rule 2: If (Amount is Non-Sensitive) and (Currency is Non-Sensitive) and (Account_Type is Normal) then (output1 is Low) (0.4)

Rule 3: If (Amount is Non-Sensitive) and (Currency is Non-Sensitive) and (Account_Type is Sensitive) then (output1 is Medium) (0.4)

Rule 4: If (Amount is Non-Sensitive) and (Currency is Normal) and (Account_Type is Non-Sensitive) then (output1 is Low) (0.4)

Rule 5: If (Amount is Non-Sensitive) and (Currency is Normal) and (Account_Type is Normal) then (output1 is Medium) (0.4)

Rule 6: If (Amount is Non-Sensitive) and (Currency is Normal) and (Account_Type is Sensitive) then (output1 is Medium) (0.4)

Rule 7: If (Amount is Non-Sensitive) and (Currency is Sensitive) and (Account_Type is Non-Sensitive) then (output1 is Low) (0.4)

Rule 8: If (Amount is Non-Sensitive) and (Currency is Sensitive) and (Account_Type is Normal) then (output1 is Medium) (0.4)

Rule 9: If (Amount is Non-Sensitive) and (Currency is Sensitive) and (Account_Type is Sensitive) then (output1 is Medium) (0.4)

Rule 10: If (Amount is Normal) and (Currency is Non-Sensitive) and (Account_Type is Non-Sensitive) then (output1 is Medium) (0.4)

Rule 11: If (Amount is Normal) and (Currency is Non-Sensitive) and (Account_Type is Normal) then (output1 is Medium) (0.4)

Rule 12: If (Amount is Normal) and (Currency is Non-Sensitive) and (Account_Type is Sensitive) then (output1 is High) (0.4)

Rule 13: If (Amount is Normal) and (Currency is Normal) and (Account_Type is Non-Sensitive) then (output1 is Medium) (0.4)

Rule 14: If (Amount is Normal) and (Currency is Normal) and (Account_Type is Normal) then (output1 is Medium) (0.4)

Rule 15: If (Amount is Normal) and (Currency is Normal) and (Account_Type is Sensitive) then (output1 is High) (0.4)

Rule 16: If (Amount is Normal) and (Currency is Sensitive) and (Account_Type is Non-Sensitive) then (output1 is Medium) (0.4)

Rule 17: If (Amount is Normal) and (Currency is Sensitive) and (Account_Type is Normal) then (output1 is Medium) (0.4)

Rule 18: If (Amount is Normal) and (Currency is Sensitive) and (Account_Type is Sensitive) then (output1 is Medium) (0.4)

Rule 19: If (Amount is Sensitive) and (Currency is Non-Sensitive) and (Account_Type is Non-Sensitive) then (output1 is Medium) (0.4)

Rule 20: If (Amount is Sensitive) and (Currency is Non-Sensitive) and (Account_Type is Normal) then (output1 is Medium) (0.4)

Rule 21: If (Amount is Sensitive) and (Currency is Non-Sensitive) and (Account_Type is Sensitive) then (output1 is High) (0.4)

Rule 22: If (Amount is Sensitive) and (Currency is Normal) and (Account_Type is Non-Sensitive) then (output1 is Medium) (0.4)

Rule 23: If (Amount is Sensitive) and (Currency is Normal) and (Account_Type is Normal) then (output1 is High) (0.4)

Rule 24: If (Amount is Sensitive) and (Currency is Normal) and (Account_Type is Sensitive) then (output1 is High) (0.4)

Rule 25: If (Amount is Sensitive) and (Currency is Sensitive) and (Account_Type is Non-Sensitive) then (output1 is Medium) (0.4)

Rule 26: If (Amount is Sensitive) and (Currency is Sensitive) and (Account_Type is Normal) then (output1 is High) (0.4)

Rule 27: If (Amount is Sensitive) and (Currency is Sensitive) and (Account_Type is Sensitive) then (output1 is High) (0.4)

Number of Rules: 27

Rules for Layer 2 (Details Segment)

There are 81 rules extracted from MATLAB fuzzy set, layer 2 represent details segment.

Fuzzy Rules

Rule 1: If (Transaction_Notes is Non-Sensitive) and (Destination_Profile_ID is Sensitive) and (Password_Tries is Non-Sensitive) and (Destination_Account_Tries is Sensitive) then (output1 is Medium) (0.3)

Rule 2: If (Transaction_Notes is Non-Sensitive) and (Destination_Profile_ID is Sensitive) and (Password_Tries is Non-Sensitive) and (Destination_Account_Tries is Normal) then (output1 is Low) (0.3)

Rule 3: If (Transaction_Notes is Non-Sensitive) and (Destination_Profile_ID is Sensitive) and (Password_Tries is Non-Sensitive) and (Destination_Account_Tries is Non-Sensitive) then (output1 is Low) (0.3)

Rule 4: If (Transaction_Notes is Non-Sensitive) and (Destination_Profile_ID is Sensitive) and (Password_Tries is Normal) and (Destination_Account_Tries is Sensitive) then (output1 is Medium) (0.3)

Rule 5: If (Transaction_Notes is Non-Sensitive) and (Destination_Profile_ID is Sensitive) and (Password_Tries is Normal) and (Destination_Account_Tries is Normal) then (output1 is Medium) (0.3)

Rule 6: If (Transaction_Notes is Non-Sensitive) and (Destination_Profile_ID is Sensitive) and (Password_Tries is Normal) and (Destination_Account_Tries is Non-Sensitive) then (output1 is Medium) (0.3)

Rule 7: If (Transaction_Notes is Non-Sensitive) and (Destination_Profile_ID is Sensitive) and (Password_Tries is Sensitive) and (Destination_Account_Tries is Sensitive) then (output1 is High) (0.3)

Rule 8: If (Transaction_Notes is Non-Sensitive) and (Destination_Profile_ID is Sensitive) and (Password_Tries is Sensitive) and (Destination_Account_Tries is Normal) then (output1 is High) (0.3)

Rule 9: If (Transaction_Notes is Non-Sensitive) and (Destination_Profile_ID is Sensitive) and (Password_Tries is Sensitive) and (Destination_Account_Tries is Non-Sensitive) then (output1 is Medium) (0.3)

Rule 10: If (Transaction_Notes is Non-Sensitive) and (Destination_Profile_ID is Normal) and (Password_Tries is Non-Sensitive) and (Destination_Account_Tries is Sensitive) then (output1 is Low) (0.3)

Rule 11: If (Transaction_Notes is Non-Sensitive) and (Destination_Profile_ID is Normal) and (Password_Tries is Non-Sensitive) and (Destination_Account_Tries is Normal) then (output1 is Medium) (0.3)

Rule 12: If (Transaction_Notes is Non-Sensitive) and (Destination_Profile_ID is Normal) and (Password_Tries is Non-Sensitive) and (Destination_Account_Tries is Non-Sensitive) then (output1 is Low) (0.3)

Rule 13: If (Transaction_Notes is Non-Sensitive) and (Destination_Profile_ID is Normal) and (Password_Tries is Normal) and (Destination_Account_Tries is Sensitive) then (output1 is Medium) (0.3)

Rule 14: If (Transaction_Notes is Non-Sensitive) and (Destination_Profile_ID is Normal) and (Password_Tries is Normal) and (Destination_Account_Tries is Normal) then (output1 is Medium) (0.3)

Rule 15: If (Transaction_Notes is Non-Sensitive) and (Destination_Profile_ID is Normal) and (Password_Tries is Normal) and (Destination_Account_Tries is Non-Sensitive) then (output1 is Low) (0.3)

Rule 16: If (Transaction_Notes is Non-Sensitive) and (Destination_Profile_ID is Normal) and (Password_Tries is Sensitive) and (Destination_Account_Tries is Sensitive) then (output1 is Medium) (0.3)

Rule 17: If (Transaction_Notes is Non-Sensitive) and (Destination_Profile_ID is Normal) and (Password_Tries is Sensitive) and (Destination_Account_Tries is Normal) then (output1 is Medium) (0.3)

Rule 18: If (Transaction_Notes is Non-Sensitive) and (Destination_Profile_ID is Normal) and (Password_Tries is Sensitive) and (Destination_Account_Tries is Non-Sensitive) then (output1 is Medium) (0.3)

Rule 19: If (Transaction_Notes is Non-Sensitive) and (Destination_Profile_ID is Non-Sensitive) and (Password_Tries is Non-Sensitive) and (Destination_Account_Tries is Sensitive) then (output1 is Low) (0.3)

Rule 20: If (Transaction_Notes is Non-Sensitive) and (Destination_Profile_ID is Non-Sensitive) and (Password_Tries is Non-Sensitive) and (Destination_Account_Tries is Normal) then (output1 is Low) (0.3)

Rule 21: If (Transaction_Notes is Non-Sensitive) and (Destination_Profile_ID is Non-Sensitive) and (Password_Tries is Non-Sensitive) and (Destination_Account_Tries is Non-Sensitive) then (output1 is Low) (0.3)

Rule 22: If (Transaction_Notes is Non-Sensitive) and (Destination_Profile_ID is Non-Sensitive) and (Password_Tries is Normal) and (Destination_Account_Tries is Sensitive) then (output1 is Medium) (0.3)

Rule 23: If (Transaction_Notes is Non-Sensitive) and (Destination_Profile_ID is Non-Sensitive) and (Password_Tries is Normal) and (Destination_Account_Tries is Normal) then (output1 is Medium) (0.3)

Rule 24: If (Transaction_Notes is Non-Sensitive) and (Destination_Profile_ID is Non-Sensitive) and (Password_Tries is Normal) and (Destination_Account_Tries is Non-Sensitive) then (output1 is Low) (0.3)

Rule 25: If (Transaction_Notes is Non-Sensitive) and (Destination_Profile_ID is Non-Sensitive) and (Password_Tries is Sensitive) and (Destination_Account_Tries is Sensitive) then (output1 is Medium) (0.3)

Rule 26: If (Transaction_Notes is Non-Sensitive) and (Destination_Profile_ID is Non-Sensitive) and (Password_Tries is Sensitive) and (Destination_Account_Tries is Normal) then (output1 is Medium) (0.3)

Rule 27: If (Transaction_Notes is Non-Sensitive) and (Destination_Profile_ID is Non-Sensitive) and (Password_Tries is Sensitive) and (Destination_Account_Tries is Non-Sensitive) then (output1 is Low) (0.3)

Rule 28: If (Transaction_Notes is Normal) and (Destination_Profile_ID is Sensitive) and (Password_Tries is Non-Sensitive) and (Destination_Account_Tries is Sensitive) then (output1 is High) (0.3)

Rule 29: If (Transaction_Notes is Normal) and (Destination_Profile_ID is Sensitive) and (Password_Tries is Non-Sensitive) and (Destination_Account_Tries is Normal) then (output1 is High) (0.3)

Rule 30: If (Transaction_Notes is Normal) and (Destination_Profile_ID is Sensitive) and (Password_Tries is Non-Sensitive) and (Destination_Account_Tries is Non-Sensitive) then (output1 is Medium) (0.3)

Rule 31: If (Transaction_Notes is Normal) and (Destination_Profile_ID is Sensitive) and (Password_Tries is Normal) and (Destination_Account_Tries is Sensitive) then (output1 is High) (0.3)

Rule 32: If (Transaction_Notes is Normal) and (Destination_Profile_ID is Sensitive) and (Password_Tries is Normal) and (Destination_Account_Tries is Normal) then (output1 is Medium) (0.3)

Rule 33: If (Transaction_Notes is Normal) and (Destination_Profile_ID is Sensitive) and (Password_Tries is Normal) and (Destination_Account_Tries is Non-Sensitive) then (output1 is Medium) (0.3)

Rule 34: If (Transaction_Notes is Normal) and (Destination_Profile_ID is Sensitive) and (Password_Tries is Sensitive) and (Destination_Account_Tries is Sensitive) then (output1 is High) (0.3)

Rule 35: If (Transaction_Notes is Normal) and (Destination_Profile_ID is Sensitive) and (Password_Tries is Sensitive) and (Destination_Account_Tries is Normal) then (output1 is High) (0.3)

Rule 36: If (Transaction_Notes is Normal) and (Destination_Profile_ID is Sensitive) and (Password_Tries is Sensitive) and (Destination_Account_Tries is Non-Sensitive) then (output1 is High) (0.3)

Rule 37: If (Transaction_Notes is Normal) and (Destination_Profile_ID is Normal) and (Password_Tries is Non-Sensitive) and (Destination_Account_Tries is Sensitive) then (output1 is Medium) (0.3)

Rule 38: If (Transaction_Notes is Normal) and (Destination_Profile_ID is Normal) and (Password_Tries is Non-Sensitive) and (Destination_Account_Tries is Normal) then (output1 is Medium) (0.3)

Rule 39: If (Transaction_Notes is Normal) and (Destination_Profile_ID is Normal) and (Password_Tries is Non-Sensitive) and (Destination_Account_Tries is Non-Sensitive) then (output1 is Medium) (0.3)

Rule 40: If (Transaction_Notes is Normal) and (Destination_Profile_ID is Normal) and (Password_Tries is Normal) and (Destination_Account_Tries is Sensitive) then (output1 is Medium) (0.3)

Rule 41: If (Transaction_Notes is Normal) and (Destination_Profile_ID is Normal) and (Password_Tries is Normal) and (Destination_Account_Tries is Normal) then (output1 is Medium) (0.3)

Rule 42: If (Transaction_Notes is Normal) and (Destination_Profile_ID is Normal) and (Password_Tries is Normal) and (Destination_Account_Tries is Non-Sensitive) then (output1 is Medium) (0.3)

Rule 43: If (Transaction_Notes is Normal) and (Destination_Profile_ID is Normal) and (Password_Tries is Sensitive) and (Destination_Account_Tries is Sensitive) then (output1 is High) (0.3)

Rule 44: If (Transaction_Notes is Normal) and (Destination_Profile_ID is Normal) and (Password_Tries is Sensitive) and (Destination_Account_Tries is Normal) then (output1 is Medium) (0.3)

Rule 45: If (Transaction_Notes is Normal) and (Destination_Profile_ID is Normal) and (Password_Tries is Sensitive) and (Destination_Account_Tries is Non-Sensitive) then (output1 is Medium) (0.3)

Rule 46: If (Transaction_Notes is Normal) and (Destination_Profile_ID is Non-Sensitive) and (Password_Tries is Non-Sensitive) and (Destination_Account_Tries is Sensitive) then (output1 is Medium) (0.3)

Rule 47: If (Transaction_Notes is Normal) and (Destination_Profile_ID is Non-Sensitive) and (Password_Tries is Non-Sensitive) and (Destination_Account_Tries is Normal) then (output1 is Low) (0.3)

Rule 48: If (Transaction_Notes is Normal) and (Destination_Profile_ID is Non-Sensitive) and (Password_Tries is Non-Sensitive) and (Destination_Account_Tries is Non-Sensitive) then (output1 is Low) (0.3)

Rule 49: If (Transaction_Notes is Normal) and (Destination_Profile_ID is Non-Sensitive) and (Password_Tries is Normal) and (Destination_Account_Tries is Sensitive) then (output1 is Medium) (0.3)

Rule 50: If (Transaction_Notes is Normal) and (Destination_Profile_ID is Non-Sensitive) and (Password_Tries is Normal) and (Destination_Account_Tries is Normal) then (output1 is Medium) (0.3)

Rule 51: If (Transaction_Notes is Normal) and (Destination_Profile_ID is Non-Sensitive) and (Password_Tries is Normal) and (Destination_Account_Tries is Non-Sensitive) then (output1 is Medium) (0.3)

Rule 52: If (Transaction_Notes is Normal) and (Destination_Profile_ID is Non-Sensitive) and (Password_Tries is Sensitive) and (Destination_Account_Tries is Sensitive) then (output1 is Medium) (0.3)

Rule 53: If (Transaction_Notes is Normal) and (Destination_Profile_ID is Non-Sensitive) and (Password_Tries is Sensitive) and (Destination_Account_Tries is Normal) then (output1 is Medium) (0.3)

Rule 54: If (Transaction_Notes is Normal) and (Destination_Profile_ID is Non-Sensitive) and (Password_Tries is Sensitive) and (Destination_Account_Tries is Non-Sensitive) then (output1 is Medium) (0.3)

Rule 55: If (Transaction_Notes is Sensitive) and (Destination_Profile_ID is Sensitive) and (Password_Tries is Non-Sensitive) and (Destination_Account_Tries is Sensitive) then (output1 is High) (0.3)

Rule 56: If (Transaction_Notes is Sensitive) and (Destination_Profile_ID is Sensitive) and (Password_Tries is Non-Sensitive) and (Destination_Account_Tries is Normal) then (output1 is High) (0.3)

Rule 57: If (Transaction_Notes is Sensitive) and (Destination_Profile_ID is Sensitive) and (Password_Tries is Non-Sensitive) and (Destination_Account_Tries is Non-Sensitive) then (output1 is Medium) (0.3)

Rule 58: If (Transaction_Notes is Sensitive) and (Destination_Profile_ID is Sensitive) and (Password_Tries is Normal) and (Destination_Account_Tries is Sensitive) then (output1 is High) (0.3)

Rule 59: If (Transaction_Notes is Sensitive) and (Destination_Profile_ID is Sensitive) and (Password_Tries is Normal) and (Destination_Account_Tries is Normal) then (output1 is High) (0.3)

Rule 60: If (Transaction_Notes is Sensitive) and (Destination_Profile_ID is Sensitive) and (Password_Tries is Normal) and (Destination_Account_Tries is Non-Sensitive) then (output1 is High) (0.3)

Rule 61: If (Transaction_Notes is Sensitive) and (Destination_Profile_ID is Sensitive) and (Password_Tries is Sensitive) and (Destination_Account_Tries is Sensitive) then (output1 is High) (0.3)

Rule 62: If (Transaction_Notes is Sensitive) and (Destination_Profile_ID is Sensitive) and (Password_Tries is Sensitive) and (Destination_Account_Tries is Normal) then (output1 is High) (0.3)

Rule 63: If (Transaction_Notes is Sensitive) and (Destination_Profile_ID is Sensitive) and (Password_Tries is Sensitive) and (Destination_Account_Tries is Non-Sensitive) then (output1 is High) (0.3)

Rule 64: If (Transaction_Notes is Sensitive) and (Destination_Profile_ID is Normal) and (Password_Tries is Non-Sensitive) and (Destination_Account_Tries is Sensitive) then (output1 is Medium) (0.3)

Rule 65: If (Transaction_Notes is Sensitive) and (Destination_Profile_ID is Normal) and (Password_Tries is Non-Sensitive) and (Destination_Account_Tries is Normal) then (output1 is Medium) (0.3)

Rule 66: If (Transaction_Notes is Sensitive) and (Destination_Profile_ID is Normal) and (Password_Tries is Non-Sensitive) and (Destination_Account_Tries is Non-Sensitive) then (output1 is Medium) (0.3)

Rule 67: If (Transaction_Notes is Sensitive) and (Destination_Profile_ID is Normal) and (Password_Tries is Normal) and (Destination_Account_Tries is Sensitive) then (output1 is High) (0.3)

Rule 68: If (Transaction_Notes is Sensitive) and (Destination_Profile_ID is Normal) and (Password_Tries is Normal) and (Destination_Account_Tries is Normal) then (output1 is Medium) (0.3)

Rule 69: If (Transaction_Notes is Sensitive) and (Destination_Profile_ID is Normal) and (Password_Tries is Normal) and (Destination_Account_Tries is Non-Sensitive) then (output1 is Medium) (0.3)

Rule 70: If (Transaction_Notes is Sensitive) and (Destination_Profile_ID is Normal) and (Password_Tries is Sensitive) and (Destination_Account_Tries is Sensitive) then (output1 is High) (0.3)

Rule 71: If (Transaction_Notes is Sensitive) and (Destination_Profile_ID is Normal) and (Password_Tries is Sensitive) and (Destination_Account_Tries is Normal) then (output1 is High) (0.3)

Rule 72: If (Transaction_Notes is Sensitive) and (Destination_Profile_ID is Normal) and (Password_Tries is Sensitive) and (Destination_Account_Tries is Non-Sensitive) then (output1 is High) (0.3)

Rule 73: If (Transaction_Notes is Sensitive) and (Destination_Profile_ID is Non-Sensitive) and (Password_Tries is Non-Sensitive) and (Destination_Account_Tries is Sensitive) then (output1 is Medium) (0.3)

Rule 74: If (Transaction_Notes is Sensitive) and (Destination_Profile_ID is Non-Sensitive) and (Password_Tries is Non-Sensitive) and (Destination_Account_Tries is Normal) then (output1 is Medium) (0.3)

Rule 75: If (Transaction_Notes is Sensitive) and (Destination_Profile_ID is Non-Sensitive) and (Password_Tries is Non-Sensitive) and (Destination_Account_Tries is Non-Sensitive) then (output1 is Low) (0.3)

Rule 76: If (Transaction_Notes is Sensitive) and (Destination_Profile_ID is Non-Sensitive) and (Password_Tries is Normal) and (Destination_Account_Tries is Sensitive) then (output1 is Medium) (0.3)

Rule 77: If (Transaction_Notes is Sensitive) and (Destination_Profile_ID is Non-Sensitive) and (Password_Tries is Normal) and (Destination_Account_Tries is Normal) then (output1 is Medium) (0.3)

Rule 78: If (Transaction_Notes is Sensitive) and (Destination_Profile_ID is Non-Sensitive) and (Password_Tries is Normal) and (Destination_Account_Tries is Non-Sensitive) then (output1 is Medium) (0.3)

Rule 79: If (Transaction_Notes is Sensitive) and (Destination_Profile_ID is Non-Sensitive) and (Password_Tries is Sensitive) and (Destination_Account_Tries is Sensitive) then (output1 is High) (0.3)

Rule 80: If (Transaction_Notes is Sensitive) and (Destination_Profile_ID is Non-Sensitive) and (Password_Tries is Sensitive) and (Destination_Account_Tries is Normal) then (output1 is Medium) (0.3)

Rule 81: If (Transaction_Notes is Sensitive) and (Destination_Profile_ID is Non-Sensitive) and (Password_Tries is Sensitive) and (Destination_Account_Tries is Non-Sensitive) then (output1 is High) (0.3)

Number of Rules: 81

Rules for Layer 3 (Environment Segment)

Fuzzy Rules

Rule 1: If (Daily_Transactions is Sensitive) and (Transaction_Time is Non-Sensitive) and (Time_On_Site is Sensitive) then (output1 is Medium) (0.3)

Rule 2: If (Daily_Transactions is Sensitive) and (Transaction_Time is Non-Sensitive) and (Time_On_Site is Normal) then (output1 is Medium) (0.3)

Rule 3: If (Daily_Transactions is Sensitive) and (Transaction_Time is Non-Sensitive) and (Time_On_Site is Non-Sensitive) then (output1 is Medium) (0.3)

Rule 4: If (Daily_Transactions is Sensitive) and (Transaction_Time is Normal) and (Time_On_Site is Sensitive) then (output1 is Medium) (0.3)

Rule 5: If (Daily_Transactions is Sensitive) and (Transaction_Time is Normal) and (Time_On_Site is Normal) then (output1 is High) (0.3)

Rule 6: If (Daily_Transactions is Sensitive) and (Transaction_Time is Normal) and (Time_On_Site is Non-Sensitive) then (output1 is High) (0.3)

Rule 7: If (Daily_Transactions is Sensitive) and (Transaction_Time is Sensitive) and (Time_On_Site is Sensitive) then (output1 is High) (0.3)

Rule 8: If (Daily_Transactions is Sensitive) and (Transaction_Time is Sensitive) and (Time_On_Site is Normal) then (output1 is High) (0.3)

Rule 9: If (Daily_Transactions is Sensitive) and (Transaction_Time is Sensitive) and (Time_On_Site is Non-Sensitive) then (output1 is High) (0.3)

Rule 10: If (Daily_Transactions is Normal) and (Transaction_Time is Non-Sensitive) and (Time_On_Site is Sensitive) then (output1 is Low) (0.3)

Rule 11: If (Daily_Transactions is Normal) and (Transaction_Time is Non-Sensitive) and (Time_On_Site is Normal) then (output1 is Medium) (0.3)

Rule 12: If (Daily_Transactions is Normal) and (Transaction_Time is Non-Sensitive) and (Time_On_Site is Non-Sensitive) then (output1 is Medium) (0.3)

Rule 13: If (Daily_Transactions is Normal) and (Transaction_Time is Normal) and (Time_On_Site is Sensitive) then (output1 is Low) (0.3)

Rule 14: If (Daily_Transactions is Normal) and (Transaction_Time is Normal) and (Time_On_Site is Normal) then (output1 is Medium) (0.3)

Rule 15: If (Daily_Transactions is Normal) and (Transaction_Time is Normal) and (Time_On_Site is Non-Sensitive) then (output1 is High) (0.3)

Rule 16: If (Daily_Transactions is Normal) and (Transaction_Time is Sensitive) and (Time_On_Site is Sensitive) then (output1 is Medium) (0.3)

Rule 17: If (Daily_Transactions is Normal) and (Transaction_Time is Sensitive) and (Time_On_Site is Normal) then (output1 is Medium) (0.3)

Rule 18: If (Daily_Transactions is Normal) and (Transaction_Time is Sensitive) and (Time_On_Site is Non-Sensitive) then (output1 is High) (0.3)

Rule 19: If (Daily_Transactions is Non-Sensitive) and (Transaction_Time is Non-Sensitive) and (Time_On_Site is Sensitive) then (output1 is Low) (0.3)

Rule 20: If (Daily_Transactions is Non-Sensitive) and (Transaction_Time is Non-Sensitive) and (Time_On_Site is Normal) then (output1 is Low) (0.3)

Rule 21: If (Daily_Transactions is Non-Sensitive) and (Transaction_Time is Non-Sensitive) and (Time_On_Site is Non-Sensitive) then (output1 is Medium) (0.3)

Rule 22: If (Daily_Transactions is Non-Sensitive) and (Transaction_Time is Normal) and (Time_On_Site is Sensitive) then (output1 is Low) (0.3)

Rule 23: If (Daily_Transactions is Non-Sensitive) and (Transaction_Time is Normal) and (Time_On_Site is Normal) then (output1 is Medium) (0.3)

Rule 24: If (Daily_Transactions is Non-Sensitive) and (Transaction_Time is Normal) and (Time_On_Site is Non-Sensitive) then (output1 is Medium) (0.3)

Rule 25: If (Daily_Transactions is Non-Sensitive) and (Transaction_Time is Sensitive) and (Time_On_Site is Sensitive) then (output1 is Medium) (0.3)

Rule 26: If (Daily_Transactions is Non-Sensitive) and (Transaction_Time is Sensitive) and (Time_On_Site is Normal) then (output1 is Medium) (0.3)

Rule 27: If (Daily_Transactions is Non-Sensitive) and (Transaction_Time is Sensitive) and (Time_On_Site is Non-Sensitive) then (output1 is High) (0.3)

Number of Rules: 27

APPENDIX B: SAMPLE EXTRACTED DATA USED IN EXPERIMENTS

Sample of data used in our real evaluation experiments. Data is extracted from the internet banking system used in Jordan Ahli Bank. Data reflects a specific period of time.

- Sample extracted data for Layer 1 (before and after mapping) (Table 19 and Table 20).

Table 19. Extracted data to be processed for layer 1 (before mapping)

Account_Currency	TO_Account_Currency	Transaction ID	Transaction_Amount	Transaction_Currency	Same/To Same Curr
02	01	123456	122.22	USD	No
01	01	61520	100	JOD	Yes
01	01	61653	210	JOD	Yes
01	01	62559	104	JOD	Yes
01	01	62612	300	JOD	Yes
01	02	62706	800	JOD	No

continued on following page

Table 19. Continued

Account_Currency	TO_Account_ Currency	Transaction ID	Transaction_ Amount	Transaction_ Currency	Same/To Same Curr
01	01	62782	50	JOD	Yes
01	01	62937	7550	JOD	Yes
01	01	47307	100	JOD	Yes
01	01	63873	1.725	JOD	Yes
01	01	72931	80	JOD	Yes
01	01	73210	303	JOD	Yes
01	02	73355	1455	JOD	No
01	01	73891	30	JOD	Yes
01	01	73925	20000	JOD	Yes
01	01	74112	250	JOD	Yes
01	01	74820	100	JOD	Yes
01	01	75153	245	JOD	Yes
03	01	75812	100	EUR	No
01	01	75973	125	JOD	Yes
01	01	76096	1000	JOD	Yes
01	01	76175	60	JOD	Yes
01	02	76286	500	JOD	No
01	02	76296	450	JOD	No
01	01	76350	10000	JOD	Yes
01	01	77327	110	JOD	Yes

Table 20. Extracted data for layer 1 (after mapping)

Transaction Amount	Transaction Currency	Account Type	Account Layer Importance Level Rate
Non-Sensitive	Non-Sensitive	Non-Sensitive	Low
Non-Sensitive	Non-Sensitive	Normal	Low
Normal	Normal	Sensitive	Medium
Normal	Normal	Normal	Medium
Sensitive	Non-Sensitive	Sensitive	High
Normal	Non-Sensitive	Sensitive	Medium
Sensitive	Non-Sensitive	Non-Sensitive	Low
Non-Sensitive	Sensitive	Non-Sensitive	Low
Non-Sensitive	Normal	Normal	Low
Non-Sensitive	Sensitive	Non-Sensitive	Low
Sensitive	Sensitive	Non-Sensitive	High
Normal	Sensitive	Normal	Medium

continued on following page

Table 20. Continued

Transaction Amount	Transaction Currency	Account Type	Account Layer Importance Level Rate
Non-Sensitive	Sensitive	Normal	**Low**
Non-Sensitive	Normal	Non-Sensitive	**Low**
Non-Sensitive	Non-Sensitive	Sensitive	**Low**
Non-Sensitive	Non-Sensitive	Non-Sensitive	**Low**
Non-Sensitive	Normal	Sensitive	**Low**
Normal	Sensitive	Non-Sensitive	**Low**
Non-Sensitive	Non-Sensitive	Non-Sensitive	**Low**
Sensitive	Non-Sensitive	Non-Sensitive	**Low**
Sensitive	Sensitive	Non-Sensitive	**High**
Normal	Non-Sensitive	Sensitive	**Low**
Sensitive	Sensitive	Normal	**High**
Sensitive	Non-Sensitive	Normal	**Low**
Sensitive	Non-Sensitive	Non-Sensitive	**Low**
Normal	Non-Sensitive	Non-Sensitive	**Low**
Sensitive	Sensitive	Non-Sensitive	**High**
Non-Sensitive	Non-Sensitive	Non-Sensitive	**Low**
Non-Sensitive	Non-Sensitive	Normal	**Low**
Sensitive	Sensitive	Normal	**High**
Normal	Sensitive	Non-Sensitive	**Low**
Non-Sensitive	Non-Sensitive	Normal	**Low**
Non-Sensitive	Normal	Sensitive	**Low**
Non-Sensitive	Normal	Non-Sensitive	**Low**
Sensitive	Sensitive	Non-Sensitive	**High**
Sensitive	Normal	Normal	**Medium**

- Sample extracted data for Layer 2 (before and after mapping) (Table 21 and Table 22).

Table 21. Extracted data for layer 2 (before mapping)

Transaction ID	Account_Type	Transaction_ CODE	Destination_ ProfileID	Destination_ Account_Tries	Incorrect_ Password_Tries
123456	002	00	962002	3	0
61520	001	00	962001	3	0
61653	002	00	962002	1	0
62559	001	00	962001	2	1
62612	001	00	962001	2	1
62706	001	00	962001	2	1

continued on following page

Table 21. Continued

Transaction ID	Account_Type	Transaction_ CODE	Destination_ ProfileID	Destination_ Account_Tries	Incorrect_ Password_Tries
62782	001	00	962001	2	1
62937	002	00	962002	2	0
47307	001	00	962001	2	0
63873	001	00	962001	2	0
72931	003	02	962001	2	0
73210	001	00	962001	2	0
73355	001	00	962001	2	0
73891	001	00	962001	2	0
73925	001	00	962001	2	0
74112	001	00	962001	2	0
74820	001	00	962001	2	0
75153	001	00	962001	2	0
75812	001	00	962001	2	0
75973	001	00	962001	2	0
76096	001	00	962001	2	0
76175	001	00	962001	1	0
76286	002	00	962002	1	0
76296	002	00	962002	1	0
76350	001	00	962001	1	0
77327	001	00	962001	3	0

Table 22. Extracted data for layer 2 (after mapping)

Transaction Notes	Profile ID	Account Tries	Incorrect Password Tries	Details Layer Importance Level Rate
Normal	Sensitive	Non-Sensitive	Non-Sensitive	**Medium**
Sensitive	Non-Sensitive	Non-Sensitive	Non-Sensitive	**Medium**
Non-Sensitive	Normal	Non-Sensitive	Normal	**Low**
Non-Sensitive	Normal	Sensitive	Sensitive	**High**
Non-Sensitive	Sensitive	Sensitive	Sensitive	**High**
Normal	Sensitive	Non-Sensitive	Non-Sensitive	**Medium**
Normal	Non-Sensitive	Normal	Non-Sensitive	**Low**
Normal	Non-Sensitive	Normal	Non-Sensitive	**Low**
Normal	Sensitive	Non-Sensitive	Non-Sensitive	**Medium**
Normal	Non-Sensitive	Non-Sensitive	Non-Sensitive	**Low**
Non-Sensitive	Normal	Sensitive	Sensitive	**High**
Non-Sensitive	Sensitive	Non-Sensitive	Non-Sensitive	**Medium**

continued on following page

Table 22. Continued

Transaction Notes	Profile ID	Account Tries	Incorrect Password Tries	Details Layer Importance Level Rate
Sensitive	Non-Sensitive	Sensitive	Sensitive	**High**
Normal	Sensitive	Non-Sensitive	Non-Sensitive	**Medium**
Sensitive	Normal	Sensitive	Normal	**High**
Non-Sensitive	Normal	Sensitive	Sensitive	**High**
Non-Sensitive	Normal	Sensitive	Non-Sensitive	**Medium**
Non-Sensitive	Non-Sensitive	Sensitive	Normal	**Medium**
Sensitive	Non-Sensitive	Sensitive	Sensitive	**High**
Non-Sensitive	Normal	Sensitive	Sensitive	**High**
Sensitive	Normal	Sensitive	Normal	**High**
Sensitive	Normal	Sensitive	Sensitive	**High**
Non-Sensitive	Normal	Sensitive	Non-Sensitive	**Medium**
Sensitive	Normal	Sensitive	Sensitive	**High**
Normal	Non-Sensitive	Normal	Sensitive	**Medium**
Non-Sensitive	Non-Sensitive	Sensitive	Normal	**Medium**
Normal	Non-Sensitive	Normal	Sensitive	**Medium**
Non-Sensitive	Normal	Normal	Sensitive	**Medium**
Sensitive	Sensitive	Non-Sensitive	Sensitive	**High**
Non-Sensitive	Normal	Sensitive	Non-Sensitive	**Medium**
Normal	Non-Sensitive	Normal	Non-Sensitive	**Low**
Non-Sensitive	Normal	Sensitive	Sensitive	**High**
Normal	Sensitive	Non-Sensitive	Non-Sensitive	**Medium**
Sensitive	Sensitive	Normal	Normal	**High**
Non-Sensitive	Normal	Sensitive	Sensitive	**High**
Non-Sensitive	Normal	Sensitive	Sensitive	**High**

Table 23. Extracted data for layer 3 (before mapping)

Transaction ID	Sequence_NO	Posting_Time	Logged_IP
123456	01	7:07:50	128.100.22.121
61520	01	8:46:37	77.241.64.34
61653	01	9:54:20	77.245.0.12
62559	01	9:57:21	79.134.128.64
62612	01	10:05:44	79.173.192.11
62706	01	10:11:11	80.64.208.112
62782	01	10:24:06	80.90.160.93.1
62937	01	10:33:02	80.249.208.108.6
47307	01	11:47:16	81.28.112.124.1

continued on following page

Table 23. Continued

Transaction ID	Sequence_NO	Posting_Time	Logged_IP
63873	01	7:58:08	82.212.64.139.6
72931	01	9:00:46	84.18.32.155.1
73210	01	9:15:45	84.18.64.170.6
73355	01	10:07:49	86.108.0.186.1
73891	01	10:09:59	91.186.224.201.6
73925	01	10:32:11	92.62.112.217.1
74112	01	12:14:24	92.241.32.232.6
74820	01	1:05:35	94.142.32.248.1
75153	01	2:46:01	94.249.0.263.6
75812	01	3:25:49	95.140.160.75
75973	01	3:40:17	95.141.208.43
76096	01	3:54:27	95.172.192.32
76175	01	4:11:19	188.123.128.112
76286	01	4:12:27	188.123.160.90.5
76296	01	4:18:45	188.244.96.100.5
76350	01	12:19:27	188.247.64.110.5
77327	01	7:25:19	193.188.64.120.5

Table 24. Extracted data for layer 3 (after mapping)

Time on Service	Daily Transactions	Transaction Time	Environment Layer Importance Level Rate
Sensitive	Normal	Sensitive	High
Non-Sensitive	Normal	Sensitive	High
Non-Sensitive	Sensitive	Sensitive	High
Normal	Non-Sensitive	Normal	Medium
Sensitive	Non-Sensitive	Sensitive	High
Non-Sensitive	Normal	Sensitive	High
Non-Sensitive	Sensitive	Sensitive	Medium
Normal	Sensitive	Non-Sensitive	Medium
Sensitive	Non-Sensitive	Sensitive	High
Normal	Non-Sensitive	Normal	Low
Non-Sensitive	Non-Sensitive	Sensitive	Medium
Normal	Sensitive	Non-Sensitive	Medium
Normal	Non-Sensitive	Normal	High
Non-Sensitive	Non-Sensitive	Sensitive	Medium
Sensitive	Non-Sensitive	Non-Sensitive	Medium
Sensitive	Normal	Normal	Medium

continued on following page

Table 24. Continued

Time on Service	Daily Transactions	Transaction Time	Environment Layer Importance Level Rate
Normal	Non-Sensitive	Normal	**Medium**
Non-Sensitive	Normal	Sensitive	**High**
Sensitive	Normal	Sensitive	**High**
Sensitive	Normal	Sensitive	**High**
Non-Sensitive	Sensitive	Sensitive	**High**
Non-Sensitive	Sensitive	Sensitive	**Medium**
Non-Sensitive	Sensitive	Sensitive	**High**
Sensitive	Non-Sensitive	Non-Sensitive	**Medium**
Non-Sensitive	Normal	Non-Sensitive	**Low**
Non-Sensitive	Normal	Sensitive	**Medium**
Non-Sensitive	Non-Sensitive	Sensitive	**Low**
Non-Sensitive	Normal	Sensitive	**High**
Sensitive	Normal	Sensitive	**High**
Normal	Non-Sensitive	Non-Sensitive	**Low**
Non-Sensitive	Non-Sensitive	Sensitive	**Medium**
Non-Sensitive	Sensitive	Non-Sensitive	**Low**
Normal	Non-Sensitive	Normal	**Medium**

APPENDIX C: SAMPLE XML MESSAGES AND SAMPLE DTDS

Sample Source XML Messages

```xml
<?xml version='1.0'?>
<Transfers>
<Transaction xmlns='http://example.org/paymentv2' ImportanceLevel="000">
        <Transaction_Notes>002</Transaction_Notes>
        <Profile_ID>92</Profile_ID>
        <AccountTries>02</AccountTries>
        <PasswordTries>01</PasswordTries>
</Transaction>
<Transaction xmlns='http://example.org/paymentv2' ImportanceLevel="000">
        <Posting_Date>2011/01/07</Posting_Date>
        <Service_ID>WWW60</Service_ID>
        <Customer_Language>E</Customer_Language>
</Transaction>
<Transaction xmlns='http://example.org/paymentv2' ImportanceLevel="002">
        <TransactionAmount>755</TransactionAmount>
        <Transaction_Currency Code='JOD'>001</Transaction_Currency>
        <Account_Type Code='001'>Individual</Account_Type>
</Transaction>
```

```
<Transaction xmlns='http://example.org/paymentv2' ImportanceLevel="001">
        <IPAddress>128.200.3.212</IPAddress>
        <From_Account>390230101401043000</From_Account>
        <To_Account>120130101155414000</To_Account>
</Transaction>
</Transfers>
```

Sample Encrypted XML Messages

```
<?xml version='1.0'?>
<Transfers>
<Transaction xmlns='http://example.org/paymentv2' ImportanceLevel="Low">
        <Transaction_Notes>002</Transaction_Notes>
        <Profile_ID>92</Profile_ID>
        <AccountTries>02</AccountTries>
        <PasswordTries>01</PasswordTries>
</Transaction>
<Transaction xmlns='http://example.org/paymentv2' ImportanceLevel="Low">
        <Posting_Date>2011/01/07</Posting_Date>
        <Service_ID>WWW60</Service_ID>
        <Customer_Language>E</Customer_Language>
</Transaction>
<Transaction xmlns='http://example.org/paymentv2' ImportanceLevel="Medium">
        <EncryptedData Type='http://www.w3.org/2001/04/xmlenc#Element'
         xmlns='http://www.w3.org/2001/04/xmlenc#'>
                <CipherData>
                        <CipherValue>i66xTe5hmF/siLFCXDPXTucE9wJZFd
                        pbSV3yYwN7pBZKIOTdRdD6LtOgunRVgjxKirSWpLx0yZ3l
                        0KoZS9B1gKOalZUjE8Sp8Al8qKgrxbfx3CR7fIdEKPdO47t6hrsw-
wL7lewxZnrJo5Whd2kw/XRUb
                        uXp268jX5dL0dlUDOEqdtgfPUXxROUetbLP1AmtO8riJWVh/Qyd-
3pvVZtNOn9mo0CbclDn0UsntXHFEfst8=
                        </CipherValue>
                </CipherData>
</EncryptedData>
</Transaction>
<Transaction xmlns='http://example.org/paymentv2' ImportanceLevel="High">
<EncryptedData Type='http://www.w3.org/2001/04/xmlenc#Element' xmlns='http://
www.w3.org/2001/04/xmlenc#'>
        <CipherData>
                <CipherValue>6N28UemsjUz4vegVtDE1wNNgNkvTvC6Pxi9k2vcHcGIhSeH+k
UIdd2IWvb/62gepoBCDhFGI+XQ9
                DWGvHlebDHA7DgNjmm+D37lU1DuzsB094b8cUPZH9gCjX0VDRntfDTFyeiUtLU
KIdH1vUi/m+ok/
                pxnBFo35XheoJQFcLv21Kxz7Tzffh9ZCaqYU8HBE
                </CipherValue>
        </CipherData>
</EncryptedData>
</Transaction>
</Transfers>
```

Chapter 8
Building a Secured XML Real–Time Interactive Data Exchange Architecture

Yousef E. Rabadi
University of Huddersfield, UK

Joan Lu
University of Huddersfield, UK

ABSTRACT

TCP and UDP communication protocols are the most widely used transport methods for carrying out XML data messages between different services. XML data security is always a big concern especially when using internet cloud. Common XML encryption techniques encrypt part of private sections of the XML file as an entire block of text and apply these techniques directly on them. Man-in-the-Middle and Cryptanalysts can generate statistical information, tap, sniff, hack, inject and abuse XML data messages. The purpose of this study is to introduce architecture of new approach of exchanging XML data files between different Services in order to minimize the risk of any alteration, data loss, data abuse, data misuse of XML critical business data information during transmission; by implementing a vertical partitioning on XML files. Another aim is to create a virtual environment within internet cloud prior to data transmission in order to utilise the communication method and rise up the transmission performance along with resources utilisation and spreads the partitioned XML file (shredded) through several paths within multi agents that form a multipath virtual network. Virtualisation in cloud network infrastructure to take advantage of its scalability, operational efficiency, and control of data flow are considered in this architecture. A customized UDP Protocol in addition to a pack of modules in RIDX adds a reliable (Lossless) and Multicast data transmission to all nodes in a virtual cloud network. A comparative study has been made to measure the performance of the Real-time Interactive Data Exchange system (RIDX) using RIDX UDP protocol against standard TCP protocol. Starting from 4 nodes up to 10 nodes in the domain, the results showed an enhanced performance using RIDX architecture over the standard TCP protocol.

DOI: 10.4018/978-1-5225-2058-0.ch008

INTRODUCTION

From the industrial age the world has become more in need to connect businesses together and globally migrate to an informational age, and exchanging information has increasingly become a part of its requirements. However, technology is used not only by ethical users but unfortunately by unethical users too; they grab any opportunity to manipulate or spy on the data during transmission for their immoral purposes. The need to set up an interoperable framework for exchanging data between different domains plays an important and essential role in doing business. As XML increasingly becomes a standard format for transmitting data on networks between different businesses, the need for finding secured and efficient techniques of transmitting XML data files is an essential matter. Real-time interactive data exchange system (RIDX) aims to place a multi-layer of defence of exchanging XML data information electronically between businesses, organisations, and other groups using Internet cloud network as a platform. The RIDX goal in this study is to build a clear infrastructure required for managing XML data real-time interactive exchange, taking into consideration the enormous security threats that face XML data files during transmission. The proposed system adapts as part of its transport protocol by using a multicast data distribution mechanism in order to reduce network resources, minimise the hindrance and expenditure. Thus far, there has been little stimulus to utilise multicast data distribution, because it lacks a protection mechanism for the data being delivered.

Although there has been significant progress in presenting secured multicast data distribution different drawbacks, threats and attacks can be addressed during the traditional transmission process:

- Communication channels that are not secured will jeopardise data integrity, from modification, data misuse, and data abuse. A man-in-the-hub can tap the stream of data including encryption keys, sensitive data etc.
- Operating system security breaks including memory observation; invaders can forecast sensitive secrets concealed inside memory.
- To prevent a service from providing its ordinary functions that may result to a noncontemporary information, this denial of service (DoS) can cost the organisation a large amount of service time and money.
- When transmitting data across a shared network, some tools can be used to sniff network packets in order to reveal sensitive information especially if no data encryption measurements have been taken.
- When encryption methods are applied on sections of XML file assumable confidential parts, cryptanalysts can generate statistical information and extract some useful data that can be used unlawfully, and if the encryption is applied on XML as one block of data, efficiency problems might occur.
- Validating messages transmitted from the originator is always a concern. Therefore an authentication process as a security measurement has to be established.
- Failing to preserve data integrity from any alteration, maliciously or accidentally, is a challenge during data transmission.
- Failing to guarantee that the data transferred can stay confidential and convey assurances that the data is not revealed by any unauthorised parties.

CONTRIBUTION AND IMPORTANCE OF THIS STUDY

A significant contribution of this study is to create a virtual multi agent decentralised domain network using Internet cloud. A group of nodes communicate and establish a ground for various communication protocols and interoperable XML data exchange among them. Process and embedded security measurement stages such as automation, authentication, encryption and tunnelling protocols are used to ensure communication security and service availability and to sustain service on demand prior to XML data transmission in order to conduct a secured XML data exchange between domain members, businesses and organisations. The aim is to build embedded multi-level security prevention and defence mechanism in order to transmit XML data files in a secured manner coupled with reliability, quality of communication, independence, scalability, and flexibility.

Another contribution for this system architecture is to implement multicast reliable communication to deliver XML data files in multi-concurrent connections to achieve the best transmission efficiency during multi-concurrent transmissions, which will widen the simultaneous number of connections to serve data transmissions and enhance transmission performance in terms of speed, message rate and throughput. Using a multicast reliable communication technique can take advantage of the availability of RIDX instances which reside as decentralised multiagents in the Internet cloud; this will allow the sender to elect the most efficient nodes including the utilised communication paths and routers that will carry out messages to different destinations.

A constructive contribution to this approach is by fragmenting vertically an XML data file into customised smaller chunks, to form a meaningless set of characters in each chunk in order to hide the structure of the XML file, and to conceal sensitive information that the XML file might contain. Furthermore, apply encryption techniques on each chunk to add another layer of security on each partition, and then send the fragmented/shredded chunks of each piece into different paths through RIDX virtual multi agents' domain network which reside on Internet cloud, until all parts (chunks or messages) reach the final destination from all around network multi agents (domain nodes) and merge back into its original file structure through a set of modules. This method will utilise the network resources for better performance by avoiding a network bottleneck problem, and in addition, it will minimise the risk of tapping messages and analysing data messages, furthermore, distributing the load and breaking down the risk among its multi agents that form the domain group.

Research Motivation

XML has come into view as the de facto preferable structure for saving and interchanging data through the Internet. While data is exchanged over the Web, security matters become progressively more essential. Such issues extend from one level to another: data security level to network security stage up to high level access controls; the author's focus is on how to create an environment which employs precautionary security steps in order to secure XML data transmission in the Internet cloud.

Developing a system that enhances both XML security and communication efficiency within Internet cloud architecture is a challenge. In cloud computing, different networks and various computers' software interact with each other, there are always security measurements that need to be considered and network efficiency needs to be enhanced.

By taking different threats into consideration when building a system, there is a belief that this new approach contains a mechanism that is apposite to achieve the security requirements for various threats; a minimum requirement is at hand such as authentication, integration and confidentiality.

Adding multi-level stages of defence is the key to this project:

Level 1: Create a multiagent virtual network domain group within Internet cloud and establish connectivity between all nodes in the domain prior to any data transmission, while enforcing methods of communication by ensuring authenticity, encryption and transmission efficiency using reliable multicast techniques.

Level 2: Vertical data shredding of the XML file to create a data set of characters into data chunks to hide XML data structure and sensitive information to be ready for transmission and spread across the virtual domain multiagent network until they reach the ultimate destination side.

Level 3: Adding another security layer by applying tunnelling and virtual private network techniques between domain members and initiating tunnelling techniques within the automation process of establishing secured connectivity.

Level 4: An embedded and automated process flow and employing a communication set of rules such as node authentication and public/private key encryption, in addition to accessing the system by understandable API routines to govern the processes from initiation stage until the process termination without any human interference, and relatively lowering the complexity of establishing a combination of security measurements and lowering the operational cost.

Research Hypothesis

This thesis scrutinises various XML security threats, especially during XML transmission. Being able to preserve security throughout XML transmission along with a high transmission performance are crucial elements of any XML transmission and XML security techniques.

Following on from the arguments developed in the previous section, the research hypothesis is:

1. Creating a virtual domain network in an Internet cloud prior to data transmission can increase system availability and enforce process automation.
2. Customising and adding functionality on standard UDP can enhance data transmission efficiency and utilise resources over standard TCP protocol.
3. A multipath multicast connectivity transmission can present better transmission performance in terms of speed, message rate and throughput rather than point-to-point connectivity transmission.
4. Applying embedded security measurements such as authentication, encryption, XML data vertical partitioning and tunnelling in a virtual network domain between members will enhance security against threats.

Below, a real-time interactive XML data exchange system is presented and evaluated to assess its features and the performance improvements, taking into consideration the enhancement of the automation of the security methods that has been used.

BACKGROUND

One of the protocols and services that have been used to transmit XML data format is SOAP (Simple Object Access Protocol). Evaluation studies of SOAP XML transmission protocol have been made, specifically of the SOAP and XML performance, with several of them concluding that the performance of SOAP and XML acquire a considerable price when compared to binary transmission protocols.

An evaluation experiment was conducted about SOAP implementation latency performance, comparing CORBA/IIOP and Java RMI protocols. As a conclusion, SOAP is much slower; therefore, SOAP XML messages are not appropriate for transmitting bulk data. Another comparison has been made while SOAP did fare poorly when compared to both binary CDR and the established industry protocol FIX.

Another implementation of exchanging messages is the FIX protocol, which stands for "Financial Information eXchange". This protocol was developed to form a standardisation protocol for exchanging transactions electronically for trading securities in a real-time manner within and between stock markets, and also formed as standard protocol between brokerage houses or investors with stock markets. FIX messages consist of tag-value pairs separated by a special delimiter character (SOH, which is ASCII value 0x01), messages in FIX protocol hold different types of values, such as integer, floating point values and strings. It is a fast and reliable protocol that guarantees data delivery, but this approach does not comply with XML structure, and FIX protocol is purely for financial trades, stock markets and securities trades, and the purpose of it is not transmitting XML data files between different types of businesses.

Another implementation which is derived from FIX protocol, is FpML and FIXML protocols, which is also used for pure financial interchange trading systems, and does not solve the XML data file transmission between different applications or different types of businesses, furthermore, it depends on a predefined DTD structure of a message including tags and values, which means it is not designed for transmitting XML data files as an independent middleware interchange between other types of businesses.

Another approach is REST (representational state transfer), which is a Web service depend on method of Request-Respond over HTTP protocol (methods such as PUT, GET, POST etc) that transfers data in a form of XML document. Therefore, a limitation of over 4 KB of data makes GET versus POST impossible, and also impossible to encode such data of URI, which gives an error "HTTP Code 414 - Request-URI too long".

CLOUD COMPUTING

Businesses have turned out to rely on the Internet for their advertising, supply chain, and sales. E-commerce has gone through a wonderful expansion in the last period. Associations are searching for novel ways to purchase the Internet for business growth. Web services are a rising technique in the Information Systems field. Information Management is also an ever-increasing endeavour for several associations. The requirement for detail is enhancing as they build up all the way through the detail age. Presently, several associations have static information architecture. They appraise the biggest requirement for information that the association possibly needs, add a security feature, and then buy and expand an information infrastructure focused on that evaluation (Wilkinson, 2005). A review of the utilisation and architecture is carried out, and the benefits and drawbacks of procedure are surveyed. Various products are discussed as well.

Areas and Functions in Cloud Computing

Cloud computing can offer a variety of functions, from applications to data storage. IBM refers to cloud computing as "a term used to describe both a platform and a type of application". Weinberg (2009) claims that cloud computing "is less a new technology than it is a way of using technology to achieve economies of scale and offer self-service resources that are available on demand". The use of cloud computing to handle overflow requests is sometimes referred to as 'cloud bursting'. This technology enables an organisation to handle and control infrastructure and applications while leveraging the cloud to expand and contract dynamically. Cloud bursting investigates two issues that many organisations entertain:

An organisation periodically needs the additional capacity but return on investment for this capacity is long because of the sporadic use of the additional capacity.

Companies are hesitant to move their entire infrastructure to a cloud due to security and reliability concerns.

InfoWorld provides seven areas where cloud computing can provide an impact:

1. **Software as Service (Saas):** Provides a single tool through a web browser. The consumer doesn't demand straight servers, licences or investment.
2. **Utility Computing:** Presents virtual servers and storage on demand that an organisation can access and use.
3. **Web Services in the Cloud:** Instead of delivering full applications, this service allows users to access APIs for added services.
4. **Platform as a Service:** This offers an environment to develop as a service. This technology can be used to develop customised applications that dash on provider's server.
5. **Managed Service Provider (MSP):** This is a service provided application that actually resides in the vendor's cloud. Examples are anti-virus and anti-spam applications.
6. **Service Commerce Platforms:** This type provides a service hub in order for the user to interact with. It is a mixture of SaaS and MSP. It can be thought of as an automated service bureau (Amer-Yahia, 2002).
7. **Internet Integration:** This service is in its infant stages. This will provide the ability to provide integrated solutions to its customers. The concept is that giant clouds could be melded together.

Cloud computing was anticipated to be one of the main Information Systems styles in 2009. Weinberg defines cloud computing among his Nine Hot Technologies for 2009 (2008). He describes three levels of clouds. The first level is infrastructure in the cloud. The customer is aware and informed about their infrastructure and they make selections about the type of infrastructure desired. The customer only pays for the resources used and can scale up or down as needed. The next level or layer is the web development platform. Google's App Engine $_{for}$ example allows web developers to develop and upload web-based code and rely on Google's infrastructure to install the application and allocate computer resources. The third level is running application enterprises in the cloud. A cloud vendor can take over an organisation's enterprise and manage the availability and performance of the enterprise. E-mail may be the most likely and common enterprise to be managed by cloud computing. To get an insight into the features of cloud computing it is useful to investigate products that have emerged. Amazon, Google, and IBM all offer cloud computing services. Microsoft is beginning to roll out its own cloud computing endeavour (Wilkinson, 2005).

Amazon's Role in Cloud Computing

Amazon Web Services (AWS) emerged from the challenges and experiences that amazon.com has grown through. Amazon features two levels of cloud computing:

- **Raw Computing Resources:** Offers traditional resources such as processors, memory, file systems, and messaging. Amazon supplies and manages the resources and charges on a peruse basis.
- **Ready-To-Go Appliances:** Build applications or services on top of raw computing resources. Amazon has partners who generally provide the ready-to-go appliance. The partners charge a surcharge on top of Amazon's charge for the service. In this case, Amazon is purely an enabler; it depends on yourself or the partners to create the applications. Some vendor solutions manage the AWS resources directly.

Amazon's AWS consists of five services:

1. **Elastic Compute Cloud (EC2):** This product offers virtual equipment containing raw resources: storage, memory and processors. All of the virtual machines are based on Linux. Amazons with its various applications that work in cloud can allocate and deal with locating the virtual machines. EC2's virtual machines range from 32 bit to 64 bit, complete with associated memory and storage. EC2 is currently in beta stage and does not offer any service level agreements (SLA). For security, a virtual machine can have a firewall attached and forms a security group. Also, a security group features protection to and from IP ports, IP protocol, or group. The Amazon Web Services site lists the following functionality:
   a. Produce an Amazon machine image (AMI) comprising libraries, applications, and data and connected configuration settings. Or use pre-configured, template pictures to get up and working instantly.
   b. Upload the AMI into Amazon S3. Amazon EC2 presents applications that keep securing the AMI simple. Amazon S3 presents a secure, fast and reliable repository to keep images.
   c. Apply Amazon EC2 web service to arrange network and security access.
   d. Select which instance styles and working system you wish, and then begin, terminate, and observe different examples of your AMI as required, applying the Web service APIs or the range of management tools presented.
   e. Decide whether you wish to perform in multiple areas, apply static IP endpoints, or connect constant block storage to your examples.
   f. Pay only for the resources that are used, like data transfer or instance-hours.
2. **Simple Storage Service (S3):** This is a simple, direct, large storage service. A customer obtains buckets and places data objects into the buckets. A security profile controls access for the bucket. There are several options or added features available. Third-party vendors offer an application that offers a file system view of the buckets you have purchased. URLs for direct access to a bucket are also available. Specific functionality includes:
   a. Read, write and remove aims comprising from 1 byte to 5 gigabytes of data each. The number of aims that can be secured is unrestricted.
   b. Every aim is secured in a bucket and retrieved through an exclusive, developer-planned key.
   c. A bucket can be situated in America or the UK. All aims within the bucket will be kept in the location of the bucket, but the aims can be contacted from anywhere.

Table 1. Interface correlation methods

	Rest	Query	SOAP
EC2	--	X	X
S3	X	--	X
SQS	X	X	X
Simple DB	--	X	X

d. Authentication systems are presented to assure that information is secured from unofficial contact. Aims can be prepared publicly or privately, and privileges can be given to particular consumers.

e. Implements standards-based REST and SOAP conditions prepared to perform with any toolkit of Internet-development.

f. Made to be flexible so that functional layers or protocol can simply be added. Protocol of default download is HTTP. A Bit Torrent protocol line is presented to lower costs for high scale distribution.

g. Consistency backed with the Amazon S3 Service Level Agreement.

3. **Simple Queue Service (SQS):** Provides a message queue. This service provides message storage and provides guaranteed message delivery. SQS is highly reliable and can store messages for later delivery if desired. It interconnects with all of the other AWS services.

4. **Simple DB:** Provides a rudimentary query language interface for textual data. It is currently in a limited beta stage. Up to 256 attributes can be associated with your data and basic Boolean operations are used for queries (Muehlen, Nickerson and Swenson, 2005).

5. **Cloud Front:** Delivers access to Amazon's worldwide distributed configuration of servers. Cloud Front integrates with S3, supplies high transfer rates and low latency. S3 contains the original data and relocates it to the necessary edge server. The price for this service varies with use (Abiteboul, 2001).

For access and activation, one must obtain an account. The account is accessed by use of an access key or security certificate. There are three interfaces that your applications can interact with:

- **Rest**: Assembles an HTTP request message containing data wrapped within a request main body.
- **Query:** Relies on HTTP but utilises basic browsers using names and parameters.
- **SOAP:** Uses XML documents described in a WSDL.

The AWS applications correlate to the interface methods as described in Table 1.

There are also two other types of interfaces available that are useful to the user: the AWS toolkit and third party vendor products. Persistence when using AWS revolves around S3. When one sets up an account they have the ability to create up to ten persistent storage buckets, with each being unique. The storage buckets can be associated with a URL if desired. A third party vendor can be used to view the storage as if it were a file system and also will provide the ability to back up your storage directly into the cloud (Muehlen, Nickerson and Swenson, 2005).

Google's Role in Cloud Computing

The Google Application Engine (GAE) relies on computing capabilities as for AWS it is more focused on computing resources. The GAE features application resources featuring an agile computer language (Python) and will shortly include the Java programming language. The application engine allows a customer to perform web applications utilising the GAE infrastructure (Wilkinson, 2005). The application promises that it is easy to use, easy to maintain, and scalable. GAE offers e-mail and collaboration applications, including video streaming. The applications can be tailored to the needs of the individual or corporation.

When using GAE applications files can be shared or tightly controlled. They can be accessed by a URL if desired. Documents and presentations can be imported and exported into the service as needed, providing flexibility for the customer (Abiteboul, 1997). In its messaging service, Google promises a cost benefit (the degree according to size) and the following services:

- E-mail accounts with 25 GB per user and search tools.
- Instant messaging, voice and video chat.
- Group calendars.
- Mobile access.
- Spam and virus filtering.
- Web-based collaboration applications.

With its collaboration applications, Google claims the following features:

- **Essential Collaboration Applications:** It offers a website, document and video applications.
- **Continuous Innovation:** Google claims to be continuously upgrading the site to provide up-to the-minute technology. It recently expanded its programming applications to include Java.
- **Smoother Information Sharing:** The application site will enhance current productivity suites, can be stored on the site or copied externally, and provides myriad coverage of file extensions and compatibilities.
- **Worker Mobility:** The data can be accessed anywhere, from any computer.
- **Information Access Control:** Information can be declared as public for open file sharing or private when stringent security measures are needed.
- **Enterprise Class Service:** Google Apps offers phone support and a 99% uptime Service Level Agreement.
- **Secure Infrastructure:** Google Apps claims security advantages for several reasons. First, its use eliminates the need for file copying to external devices (a huge source of external virus and worms) and attachments since files can be directly accessed. Also, Google Apps has a dedicated security team and has installed perimeter defences (firewalls and intrusion detection). In addition Google is built from the ground up with security as a priority (Whitemore, 2009). An application goes through routine security reviews from Google as it is being developed. Finally, Google fractures its data across many servers and is non comprehensible to humans. Data is replicated in multiple data centres for redundancy for backup assurance. Finally, Google builds with only necessary software components, and homogeneous server architecture ensures rapid and clear updates.

IBM's Role in Cloud Computing

IBM has also entered the cloud computing forum, but in a different capacity to Google or Amazon. They offer to set up cloud computing organisations, by providing infrastructure, hardware and software, and information management to a potential cloud vendor. They can also provide APIs for potential third party vendors.

IBM claims two major areas of cloud computing: cloud infrastructure and cloud services. These consist of four major features:

- Dynamic Infrastructure. IBM offers technology to build an infrastructure that is agile, quick and flexible. This allows an organisation to meet the demands of modern day business.
- Service Management. Software that provides management services built around visibility (to see the inner workings of business), control (to manage business), and automation (to optimise business).
- Information on Demand presents an important vision for unlocking the business worth of knowledge for aggressive benefit through allowing corporations to make and influence confirmed data to maximise performance of business.
- Service Oriented architecture is a business-centric IT system that encourages incorporating your business as connected, repeatable, business services or tasks.

Microsoft's Role in Cloud Computing

Microsoft has entered the cloud computing fray by offering Windows Azure. They are venturing into the Web services environment offering known development platforms in an Internet-based environment. Windows Azure offers a development platform and applications for customer use.

The developer features eliminate the need for up-front purchase of software. They offer development in the Visual Studio and .NET platforms. Currently programming can be done in languages supported by .NET, and Azure plans to add more languages. Azure provides an on demand compute and storage environment that is automated and configured for dynamic scaling to match the needs of the customer with a pay-as-you-go option provided.

Microsoft also provides applications that are ready for use by its customers. These include database and storage applications. They also offer an application and service that allows collaboration.

It would be beneficial to discuss the implementation of a cloud computing architecture. At the physical bottom layer the hardware is virtualised to present a flexible and agile platform that can present maximum implementation of resources. The next two layers represent the key to cloud computing infrastructure: management and virtual environment. These two layers ensure that the data centre is effectively managed and that its resources are properly configured and allocated (Whitemore, 2009).

Disadvantages of Cloud Computing

There are some risks with cloud computing and there are several controversies surrounding its use. Ashford cautions that cloud computing does not work in every context (2008). He stresses that many legal complications could arise with the use of cloud computing, especially in a highly regulated medium such as financial services. The Data Protection Act requires businesses to control how personal data is used and stored but this can be difficult when cloud computing is employed. Businesses must only select cloud computing services that allow them to avoid risk entirely or manage it at a reasonable level.

Another issue surrounding cloud computing is that it is still a new technology and is still an immature process. Most companies that are offering cloud computing services are offering short term gain but have no plan for long term sustainability. Companies can save as much as 40% on customer relationship models by employing cloud computing but these services generally do not include aids to improve processes over time (Grötschel, Alevras and Wessäly, 1998). Being able to deploy an enterprise level application quickly at a low cost does not always mean success.

Cloud computing is especially attractive during economic hardship. Low costs, fast deployment, and the lack of maintenance concerns are a strong pull for many companies. Some estimates claim that up to 60% of businesses intend to employ some sort of cloud computing. These factors may pull many companies who are not a good fit for this service into employing it by the promise of short term business savings without realising its long term implications. A full study on the short and long term benefits of cloud computing needs to be conducted to see if it is useful for an organisation, keeping in mind that there are also legal implications (Grötschel, Alevras and Wessäly, 1998).

Cloud computing has many benefits, it comes at a price. The following lists five concerns with cloud computing:

1. Security. One of the advantages of cloud computing is that a client company does not have to worry about maintenance of the systems in the cloud. At the same time, security of the data falls to the provider of the cloud services. Data privacy, therefore, is out of the client company's control. They cannot directly guarantee the security of these systems. For some companies that demand a high level of security, even though a cloud provider may promise a high quality, secure service, the risk from the use of cloud computing is too great to utilise this service (Ioannidis, Keromytis and Smith, 2000).

2. Reliability. Reliability is a worry faced by cloud computing customers. Organisations not only require dependable applications, but also services as well. E-mail and messaging have to be delivered on a consistent basis. As an example, in the summer of 2008 Google's e-mail and Apps services were out of commission, and on July 20, Amazon S3 was out of service for eight hours (Bushell-Embling, 2010).

3. Privacy. Privacy is a main concern in all aspects of information technology, and it is no different in cloud computing. The major issue is that the customer does not manage their data. Another concern is that the cloud computing company itself may outsource part of its storage capacity so that the customer does not even know who is managing the data (Curbera and Duftler et al, 2002).

4. The Cost of Failure. If a failure occurs in a cloud, either through system breakdown or security breach, all of the data and services maintained in the cloud will be at risk. As more organisations join a cloud the cost of failure increases dramatically. If a large super cloud is created, it is possible that a catastrophic failure could cause devastating losses. It could be damaging enough to put a cloud service out of business.

5. Cost Versus Risk. Although the possibility of financial loss is mentioned above, many organisations are joining cloud services because they promise short term gains, or the costs outweigh the risks (Bushell-Embling, 2010). Many of the cloud companies are still new and the technology is in its infant stages so reliability will be an issue for some time, until the technology matures. An organisation needs to ensure that the savings gained by a cloud computing service will overcome the risks associated with using it.

Advantages and Benefits of Cloud Computing

There are a myriad of advantages to using cloud computing. With cloud computing, an organisation or individual can take advantage of a potentially endless array of processors, storage and bandwidth, and also a vast array of software and application services. The concept behind cloud computing is pay-as-you go: an organisation only pays for the utilities that they use. This is a big advantage for an organisation that needs flexibility in certain aspects of their information systems. One example is an organisation that has a peak demand for data storage, perhaps a spike in storage needs for a few months for every year. This organisation can purchase the extra storage needed for its peak period through a cloud, or it can purchase all of its storage through the same organisation and allow their data storage to dynamically expand and contract as needed, paying only for what is used.

Elasticity is a main selling point of cloud computing. It can expand and contract to add or drop resources as needed, purchase resources it does not have (from a vendor) and allocate resources to assure efficient storage. It allows scalability up or down without a huge cost increase. Another major attraction is the ability to have direct connections to software and applications. The cloud can hold more than your software. It can host its own databases and software as well as third party vendors' products as well. The direct connection provides high performance and avoids latency issues that can plague a distributed Web service (Comer, 2006).

Study notes benefits for both individuals and businesses. Personal benefits to using cloud computing include:

- **Ease of Use:** 51% of personnel who use cloud computing note that ease and convenience are the major reason for their choice. Cloud computing eliminates the need for setup, anti-virus checks, etc.
- **Accessibility:** Cloud computing allows software developers the ability to design applications without the concern for hardware constraints. Any computer may be used as long as it is connected to the Internet.
- **Information Sharing:** Files can be created, uploaded and shared by end users. Data files can be spread widely across the Internet and can be easily accessed. Cloud computing is more reliable and faster than information sharing through e-mail. Collaboration allows consistency across a large number of users, a change by one user is instantly available to all other users of the file.
- **Low Risk of Losing Data:** Total systems failures of home computers happen frequently; at a much higher rate than a large corporation. The major reason for this is the organisations have a more robust virus and attack system, and have in place a hardware and software management system that is managed by professionals.

Businesses have the following benefits when utilising cloud computing:

- **Fast Start Up of Companies and Projects:** Organisations that run a multitude of businesses can reap large benefits by using cloud computing. Most SaaS in the clouds are designed to enlarge capabilities or capacity instantly, with no increase in infrastructure, or purchasing any new licensing for software or even the need for any training of new personnel (Rabhi and Benatallah, 2002). Organisations can expand and grow without the burden of taking on new worries; new projects can be opened efficiently. This will increase profitability of many companies, and ensure professional support from new technologies they are trying to utilise.

- **Comparatively Small Cost:** Servers, software, hardware, licensing, and training can amount to a high cost. For small to mid-sized organisations this cost can be excessive. Cloud computing organisations allow a customer to rent vast resources at a comparatively low cost with a vast array of plans and options to choose from.

- **Flexibility:** In the current paradigm, an organisation must develop its own network and data management system. The process of development is lengthy, generally features cost overruns and schedule delays. If outsourcing is used, the process is controlled by an outsider and the organisation is dependent on their end product. Contracts for vendors must be written, and management must still track the progress of the project. With cloud computing the process becomes much easier and quicker. An organisation can switch applications and user software, buy or delete resources, and use new technologies without a long time lag needed in the development process. A variety of applications and software are instantly available on the Web (Dan, 2011).

- **Maintainability:** Computer systems maintenance is expensive and cumbersome. Organisations allocate a significant budget (sometimes in the hundreds of thousands to million dollars) for information system maintenance. A significant cost saving can be incurred if the organisation utilises a cloud computing system. Responsibilities of upgrades and replacing faulty hardware, etc. fall to the cloud provider instead of the organisation (Rabhi and Benatallah, 2002).

- **Safety:** Protecting sensitive information becomes more difficult and complex every day. Many organisations do not have the resources to build the security measures needed to ensure information privacy and data integrity. Some organisations may not be aware of the urgency of the need for information security. Cloud computing organisations can provide many of these services (Rabhi and Benatallah, 2002).

Summary of Cloud Computing

Cloud computing is one of the hot topics in information systems today. One survey of 1,300 software buyers disclosed that 11% planned on deploying cloud computing. Another survey of business technology professionals disclosed that 38% of their organisations are already using cloud computing or are seriously considering it. It is apparent that cloud computing is becoming more than a fantasy story; it is a reality and is rising as a viable force in the Information Systems profession. One Information Technology writer estimates that cloud computing grew in excess of 20% in 2009 (Dan, 2011).

Many advantages and disadvantages in the deployment of cloud computing have been discussed. It is clear that cloud computing can be a great benefit to many organisations, but it is also evident that the organisation must have a need and a long term plan for its use. Deployment of these solutions must be made after careful consideration of the impact that this service can have on the organisation, both positive and negative.

Currie (2011) contends that as organisations move to the cloud their solutions will become more complicated in some respects and less complicated in others. Information systems will become more complicated in that technology is likely to be spread out or distributed across many vendors. Managing and controlling security will become a challenging operation for these organisations. Project management of all these solutions can be an equal challenge. The less complicated features for these organisations are that the working and functional mechanisms of hardware and software are moved off campus. These functions will not have to be managed.

The key to the successful use of cloud computing is planning. When using cloud architecture, assume things will fail. Design and deploy features from the cloud assuming failure will occur. Assume and plan for hardware failure. Four strategies can help plan for difficulty:

1. Plan for consistent back-up and restore.
2. Put up a procedure that will resume when rebooting.
3. Permit the condition of the system to re-sync the messages from queues.
4. Maintain preoptimised and preconfigured data images to sustain the reboot and re-launch.

Cloud computing appears to be a permanent fixture in the Information Systems world. It can provide cost savings, flexibility, and provide applications and data storage services to organisations that could not afford or manage them. It can be a wonderful and versatile tool if it is used and deployed properly. But, it comes with a risk, and with any associated business risks, mitigations and proper risk management must be employed if the deployment is to be successful.

XML SECURITY THREATS

Security is a critical issue (arguably the most critical one) for Web applications. Not surprisingly, there is a lot of activity around XML, Web services and security. The W3C promotes standardisation efforts for security, e.g. for XML encryption, XML signature or cryptographic keys. The security assertion mark up language is an XML-based framework promoted by the Oasis consortium for exchanging security information. The next example illustrates how basic security features may be supported in SAML. Suppose for instance that an SAML peer, Joe, wants to send a message to an SAML peer, Linda, with a portion of the message encrypted. In SAML, the portion of the message to be encrypted is a sub-tree rooted at some particular node, say n. To encrypt it, Joe has to remove the children sub-trees of n, say t1 to tm, and to replace them with their encrypted value.

In an SAML setting, encrypted XML data will be represented using the standard XML encryption with the following syntax:

```
<Encrypted Data Id? Type? Mime Type? Encoding?> <Encryption Method/>? <ds: Key
Info> <Encrypted Key>?
<Agreement Method>?
<ds: Key Name>?
<ds: Retrieval Method>?
<ds:*>?
</ds: Key Info>? <Cipher Data>
<Cipher Value>?
<Cipher Reference URI?>?
</Cipher Data>
<Encryption Properties>?
</Encrypted Data>
```

SAML rely on a public key encryption scheme. Each participant has a unique public/private key pair denoted PUK/PRK. As usual, the private key is private, while the public one is made accessible to the world, through the following service:

```
Public Key@ peer () -> string
```

A similar Private Key@ peer () service exists, that can only be invoked by the peer itself. It is assumable that each peer has the following generic services, which respectively perform encryption and decryption.

A main goal is to show how SAML provides a uniform framework for addressing standard query processing issues as well as issues such as security for data management, that are typically considered separately. The author believes that, in a Web context where various functionalities may be supported by different peers, it is important to provide an abstract model for distributed data management that captures these various viewpoints in a unique framework. Such a uniform model allows addressing issues such as data exchange protocol verification in a rigorous manner.

A Complete Framework

A whole threat-protection framework requires covering three key operations: prevention, protection and screening.

Prevention

A prevention framework should make sure that during the period of messages transmission to prevent through blocking possible message-level feats similar to the placing of attacks into the message. Message contracting, succession amounts, and the utilisation of PKI (public key infrastructure) among clients and services assists make sure to content and offers particular security next to man-in-the-middle and rematch assaults.

Protection

Software or infrastructure should be capable to defend it and downstream methods next to approaches that are planned to deliver it terminal. Long-familiar Web space assaults for example DDoS, payload poisoning, and exterior commands are as great a menace in XML and Web services usage. A well-designed treating architecture mixed with important safeguards may assist defends next to approaches.

Screening

Message-level testing must cover every traditional firewall and operates also as permission to the supervisor to permit or deny particular actions or messages. These operations comprise inclusive schema sustention, integrity enforcement, decryption/encryption; message capacity questions, biometric authentication, and some other permit or refuse criteria. The capability to assign or unload particular payload dispensation to some other best-in-class methods - for example a virus scan locomotive - permits safety controllers to tailor the assessment of the screening as needed.

DISCUSSION OF GENERIC COMPRESSION TECHNIQUES

XML is recognised mainly as a helpful and significant technique that was issued as an outcome of the huge reputation of the World Wide Web and HTML. Because of the

effortlessness of its principle ideas and fundamental premises, XML has been utilised in figuring out several troubles, for example offering neutral information among wholly varied architectures, linking over the space among software systems with negligible attempt and putting in large amounts of semi-structured information. Nevertheless, this self-describing factor offers an enormous suppleness except conversely; it also brings in the important factor of verboseness of XML documents which have outcomes in vast sizes of documents. As XML practice is growing, the enormous demand for competent XML compaction equipments have been subsisted. There are various research attempts to improve compression techniques. The utilisation of compaction equipments have several benefits, for example: diminishing the connection bandwidth needed to exchange data, diluting the storage capacity needed to minimise the storage and memory for query to process XML documents (Ho, Vincent and Cheng, 2009).

XML is a text agency for tree prearranged information. Therefore, an above board proportional access for compacting XML documents is to utilisation of the conventional all-purpose text solidity tools. Several algorithms were developed so far to expeditiously squeeze text information. The mainly famous also competent examples are: PPM, gzip, and bzip2 compactions. The gzip compaction is focused on the lossless DEFLATE information density algorithm that utilises the mixture of the LZ77 algorithm and Huffman coding. LZ77 algorithm gets compaction through swapping parts of the information with mentions to corresponding information that has previously moved during each decoder and encoder. Huffman coding employs an important technique for selecting the delegacy for every sign where the mainly ordinary qualities employ smaller strings of bits which are employed for fewer ordinary signs. bzip2 compaction utilises the Burrows-Wheeler transmute for changing often chronic character series into equal letters draw, and after that attempts a move-to-front transmute, lastly doing the Huffman coding. Adaptive statistical information firmness method (PPM) focused on framework of the context modelling along with anticipation. It employs a set of statistical modelling methods, which may be deemed blending jointly various contexts in fixed-order to forecast next character in the input string. Forecast possibilities in every context in the model are computed as of occurrence calculates that are efficient adaptively. Even though PPM is merely effective of the compactions obtainable, thus far, it is as well computationally the mainly high operational priced.

XML NON-QUERIABLE COMPACTIONS

Suciu and Liefke (2000) demonstrated the initial execution of an XML witting compaction. XMill has brought in few novel plans for XML witting firmness which are pursued through various XML compactions. The important and most significant plan emphasised, is by dividing the XML structure as of information and the division of the information assesses into containers that are homogenously focused on the associative paths of these containers in a form of tree according to their information kinds. The XMill method does the compaction for XML files individually, one for the structure and one for the data values. XML tags and the features are put in the structure section and encoded in a dictionary-based style previous to allowing it to a back-end general text compaction method. XMill allots every separate part and assigns an integer code, this name/code provides the key within the attribute and element name

Figure 1. XMILL compaction (Suciu and Liefke, 2000)

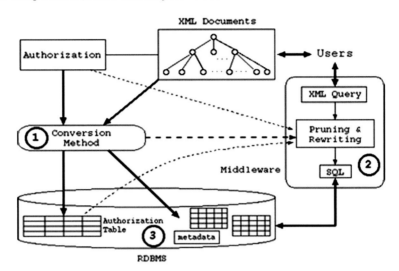

dictionaries. In the information section, information assesses are sorted into semantically and homogenous associated containers in accordance to the path type and information.

Then every container is packed in individually employing specified compaction, which is suitable to the information kind of the container and the grouping procedure provides the restriction of the repetitions and thus raises the degree of compaction. The newest versions of the XMill spring dispersion, the compacted format of the intermediary binaries, may use one of three compaction methods (gzip, PPM, bzip2), which is a substitute of the back-end general intention compactions. Swacha and Skibinski have used the Word Replacing Transmute compaction that attempts a similar plan to XMill. It employs a dictionary-based solidity method (XWRT) (Swacha and Skibinski, 2007). The plan of the XWRT method is to return commonly happening words with orientations into a dictionary that is sustained through a preliminary go through by above the information. Encoded outcomes presented by XWRT of the pre-working action to three substitutes common reason compaction schemes: PPM, gzip and LZMA. Figure 1 illustrates the process using XMill compression methods.

Weimin Li (2003) has illustrated the operation of some other XML compaction that attempts the same plan of XMill with a trivial alteration. For example with XComp, the XML file is analysed initially, the constituents are re-arranged and sent on to the density engine. The analysed stage detail is utilised to limit containers' size in the memory. XComp exacted the effectiveness of the usage of the memory, which may be enhanced through attempting a storage window when setting a value.

XML AND ENCRYPTION

The World Wide Web Consortium (W3C) proposed several techniques to encrypt XML data, especially techniques that encrypt parts of XML files; their methods are flexible, thus even when encrypting parts of the document, but still preserving the structure of the XML file, therefore, this file can be encrypted many times from different parties also on various sections. In Ho Lam and James' point of view (2009), these approaches have some drawbacks, because W3C concentrated on the flexibility side of the method but not the efficiency of queries or the level of security, therefore, it does not gratify the needs of several applications where information safety and query effectiveness is imperative.

In Figure 2, the example covers XML fragment, the plain text segment as of '<Credit Card Id>' to '</Credit Card Id>' to be encrypted and restored by the encrypted information node. But this encrypted data is yet processed as a complete text block, at the same time interior structure is dismissed. A problem may occur where the redundancy inserted through the format of the XML document may be browbeaten to assault the encryption. For example, the encrypted section constantly terminates with the tag '</Credit Card Id>', and this may employ and be vulnerable to the cryptanalysis techniques. Another concern may be noticed especially when the secret section is returned through its representing blocks of encrypted data, the circumstances surrounding it possibly will be oppressed through the antagonist. For example, it may be noticed that the Credit Card ID for the encrypted block returns to John Rabadi. In addition, the facts that John Rabadi has some sensitive data (in our example the credit card ID) as displayed in the information file. Another case may be noticed that when numbers of purchased items are encrypted jointly, cryptanalysts could discover number of items by estimating the length of the encrypted text block, therefore, they can generate statistical studies about it. In addition to these safety drawbacks, using this technique of encrypting data will create efficiency drawbacks. For example, the XPath query: //Payment Info [//Issuer = "Bank of Scotland"]/Name

Along with details of Payment Info, just detail regarding issuers is important to retrieve this question. Although the data that has been encrypted forms a whole block, it is not possible to extract the issuer information alone without bringing the whole block or maybe several blocks together. Accordingly, a prominent total of needless decryption is executed, which will eventually reduce speed query and exhaust the bandwidth.

Figure 2. XML file before and after encryption

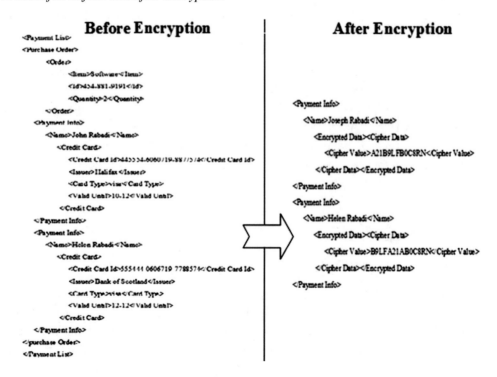

By considering both the effectiveness and the drawbacks, Ng and Yang (2006) proposed a new XML encryption technique (XQEnc); they focused on the expansions of XML repositories, which is the compaction using vectorization and skeleton methods. They demonstrate the results of their method with other existing techniques; XQEnc showed an efficient ability in processing in the query retrieval and XQEnc method attempts to combine the security enhancement and query efficiency along with flexibility.

The foremost idea of XQEnc is to make XML data outsourcing secure. Safe XML outsourcing information makes it doable to save XML data in undependable servers and save XML information in a secured manner, moreover, reallocating the workload of querying the XML data on the server side as feasibly as it can, at the same time, making sure that the data is not exposed to the server outsourcing providers. The argument to outsource the server storage from a business standpoint is to take advantage of the service providers to manage the data in terms of back-ups, restores, archiving, managing the data efficiently etc, while the organisation can focus on the core of their business.

SKELETON AND VECTORIZATION XML COMPACTION

In the XQEnc technique, the two Skeleton and Vectorization methods have been used; the latter take a broad view of 'Vertical Partitioning' technique, where the purpose is to optimise the query performance, especially in a relational database (Yang et al, 2006). An uttermost shape of vertical partition is to save every column separately in relational tables. So the main purpose of vectorization is to divide the XML document into vector paths. The outcome of this division is a series of information assesses happening beneath every path and posturing the similar path labelling.

Skeleton Compaction

Some other significant technology named 'skeleton compaction' was initially suggested for sustaining query working of compacted XML data. The purpose of this is to discard the severance included in the tree that has been formed for the XML file, through partaking an ordinary sub-tree and swapping consecutive and matching sub-trees (branches) with one branch and a diversity annotation. In the XML example above (Figure 2), it is noticed that the two (<Payment Info>) stubs after running skeleton and encryption methods are packed into one branch and one diversity notation. The results showed that the pressed XML skeleton is small and sufficient to fit substantially in the memory.

Vectorization

Vectorization is the technique of dividing the XML file into two divisions, one represents the structure of XML, and the other division is the data information values. It divides them into containers that are homogenously focused on the associative paths of these containers in a form of tree according to their information kinds. XML tags and the features are put in the structure section and encoded in a dictionary-based style, then the compression techniques allot every separate part and assign and integer code. This name/code provides the key within the attribute and element name dictionaries. In the information section, information assesses are sorted into semantically and homogenously associated containers in accordance with the path type and information.

SECURING XML OUTSOURCE DATA

Lately, the main concern of outsourcing and securing sensitive data has strained substantial consideration. In the outsourcing concept, customers rent a data storage server from services providers to store their data in, but as organisations hold sensitive information about their clients, they need to secure their data when outsourcing it with a service provider, therefore, even when querying obtaining certain information from the server, there should be a way to secure the data within the server and to secure the requested data, also to keep the efficiency of the query high, therefore, the data should be stored in an encrypted form. In the meantime the server requires few details regarding the information (for instance the utilisation of 'cryptoindex') so as to process questions. The outcome of an inquiry is typically an encrypted superset of the real outcome and is moved to the clients. The aim is to move query treating as far as possible to the server slope whereas sustaining information safety throughout information transfer and working.

A simplified architecture of information outsourcing method is an overview of the information outsourcing method as follows: a query from a user interpreted by the translator and dividing the query into two subordinate-queries. The first part of the query goes over the encrypted information, which is implemented at the server part through the assistance of a cryptograph index. The second part of the query filters the inquiry in the client part, the outcomes from the first part come up to the client and then chooses the actual answer. In order to do filtration, the data must first decrypt knowing that the outcomes from the server are in a form such as tuples. Various propositions suggested a way of forming the cryptography index; the purpose is to give helpful information to the server to progress the inquiries. The main suggestion is to initially divide name spaces into displaced containers, and then save the container IDs in a server repository.

While the query is processed, assessments are made to the inquiries and are interpreted into their representations of the ID of the container. This technique exposes the container IDs from the actual saved information, and then the server retrieves a super set of the original outcomes. An extra effective method utilising the order conserves algorithm that ensures no detail outflow along with the optimal communication traffic. Most similar methods used to retrieve XML data have the retrieval methods only in the relational structure, and so far are not appropriate in XML structure (Yang et al 2006). Consequently basically replacing values through cryptographic indexes possibly exposes the detailed structure to the service provider or the host. In their campaigning instance, keeping sensitive information such as bank details or credit card information along with only assesses encrypted reveals the interior structure of the credit card chunk.

Overview of XML Query Encryption

The traditional methods used to encrypt XML files (such as DES) encrypt the file as an entire piece, but these methods have some drawbacks. Therefore, the vital idea in the transmutation is how to create encoded values based on the actual file. The fundamental plan of XQEnc is to initially calculate the compacted skeleton and the consequent vector that represent the data set, in addition to encrypting both units individually. While implementing XQEnc, the latter takes on the advance of using skeleton compaction plus vectorization to create the structural index tree (SIT). SIT assists in discarding the redundant and the replica formation in an XML file. In effect, prominent sections of the formation of several XML files are surplus and may be terminated (Atay, 2007).

By executing these methods, it avoids a complete decryption by grouping the information into several small blocks (chunks). Then utilising the algorithm for encrypting the data (similar to triple DES algorithm) for encrypting every part that is obstructed in XQEnc. Afterward, the inscribed obstructs are joined to create the encoded values for the original file. To process queries in XQEnc, it needs initially to decrypt the related encrypted obstruct in order to reply back to the query.

Overview of XQEnc

As an XML file has an assorted nature, in several issues only sections of the original XML file require encryption, and these sensitive data sections possibly dispel over and are done without or with obvious patterns. A non-proportional way is to employ the techniques defined in the former part on every sensitive section of the file individually, that fulfil the W3C standards.

Nonetheless, there are various downsides along with processing this approach (Miklau, 2006). For instance, if they utilise the XQEnc method on the payment info sections (see Figure 2), the two obstructs detail individually, and substitute them with their equivalent encoded text, the ensuing XML file is similar to the transformed file, excluding that the encoded text assesses are created by utilising XQEnc. Then the safety related issues remain that the content may still be victimised to assault the encrypted data and deduce analytical detail. Furthermore, the sensitive sections have precisely the same interior formation and the similar compacted skeletons are carried out several times. For now, the information vectors for a single sensitive section are frequently not big enough to occupy an information block, which badly affects storage use and inquiry effectiveness. Instead of encrypting every sensitive section separately, XQEnc places them jointly and creates only one part of encoded data, introduced as the very last position of the root tree. Utilising their campaigning instance, XQEnc creates the outcome as demonstrated in the following transmuted document:

```
<Payment Info List>
<Payment Info>
<Name>John Rabadi<Name/>
</Payment Info>
<Payment Info>
<Name>Helen Rabadi<Name/>
</Payment Info>
<Encrypted Information><Cipher Information>
<Cipher Value>E7FDA243B745CC586</Cipher Value>
</Cipher Information></Encrypted Information>
</Payment Info List>
```

As a result of the process, it derives two components for the encoded text: the compacted skeleton of the file (F), and the sensitive information shredded in vectors, the two components are encoded. Maintaining the compacted skeleton file (F) makes sure that there is no structural loss. The compacted skeleton file is generally not large, with a comparison between the original and the compacted one, is less than 1 MB for a file that extends several megabytes, or even a lesser amount of 1% of the total file size (Jianyong and Cunying, 2011). Therefore, the required memory is generally available in most devices nowadays, especially the tremendous enhancement of RAM size. Moreover, the option is still available by keeping just the 'partial' compacted skeleton that is applicable to the sensitive information. By doing so it will even create a slighter encoded value, but definitely the expenditure of processing the query is higher.

The sensitive data are kept in the shredded vectors along with their file position and the encoded value. Then to reply when XPath query is received, initially the compacted skeleton of the file is decrypted (Jianyong and Cunying, 2011). The XQEnc method is fired to process the decrypted data from the previous step and treats both the values and the tags as two separate entity resources. Any non-sensitive values needed by the processor are retrieved directly from file. XQEnc shreds the file into chunks, and encodes each chunk separately. The smallest unit that is retrieved by the method is the chunk (Block). In their execution the non-encoded sections are initially analysed throughout the pre-processing stage, and evaluation of a non-encoded node may be simply fetched. If any details included in the encoded text node are required, the process of retrieving the encrypted chunks within the vector in accordance with the position of the text inside the file, when requesting a data from the file to retrieve the names of the purchasers, the data has been retrieved directly from file as text, because it is not part of the encrypted data block. On the other hand, when requested to retrieve data about the name of the issuer, the data was recalled and retrieved from the vector block.

Summary

XQEnc utilised both skeleton compression techniques along with vectorization method to encrypt XML data. The method is functional to assist XML query processing data in an environment of outsourcing. Furthermore, it offers enhanced safety as well as efficiency of data query processing (Buneman, 2007). After applying XQEnc, the resulting document obeys with the standard of W3C encryption, which permits diverse treatments and handlings to be utilised on various sections of the XML file. The methods can be employed among the conventional compaction methods to minimise the exchange of data overhead in the communication (Arnold, 2010).

Skeleton and vectorization showed how to protect the XML information while outsourcing can be accomplished employing XQEnc; this included the data relational technique for storing and retrieving from outsourced services. The given method ensures vigorous security for both textual and structural information.

Message learnt and some concerns:

- There is more than one step for processing the query results, and interpreting it on both the server side and the client side. On the other hand, saving structures and other data in the client metadata makes this client site the only node that can access the outsourced server.
- On the server side, when observing the query requests and the results, it can be derived from the data structure of the XML file, and then derives useful statistical data.
- The fact that the client performs multi steps for processing the query, means that the overhead on the connection becomes higher if the retrieved data is big, and this leads to a communication efficiency drawback.
- When requesting specific information from the server, the retrieved chunk or block of data may contain unnecessary information; this will put unnecessary overheads on the network, especially if there are a large number of requests happening on the outsourced server simultaneously.
- Memory usage of the server is not monitored by this method, therefore, if the number of requests is high and the queries retrieve a large amount of data, this might overflow the memory allocations.

- Converting the original XML file into a three step transformation will add a security level by concealing sensitive data and hiding the original XML data structure; on the other hand, it might slow down the processing time, both in bidirectional ways.
- The method proposed is built on top of HTTP protocol, XPath and other query processing techniques, which are also built on top of TCP/IP protocol. This technique works only in a case of outsourcing XML database storage in a third party service. On the other hand, the concept of vectorization can be expanded to be applied on the transport layer level.

SOAP

OAP permits both COM and objects in Java objects to communicate to one another in a decentralised Web-based and distributed environment (Dan, 2011). Furthermore, it permits any type of objects, in any language and on any podium, to communicate with each other. Currently, it has been applied in more than around 20 platforms and over 60 different languages. Unexpectedly objects all over the place, small and large, local and far-flung are competent to interoperate. Two so dissimilar types of object are ultimately capable to talk. In this section about the technology, it demonstrates SOAP at first in the wider Web-based services perspective, in universal description, discovery and integration (UDDI) as a protocol to facilitate messaging services as well as registry amongst different businesses. This review is to discourse the Web based foundation of the rising model of 'publish-find-bind', along with the delivery and transport techniques in the SOAP system.

Network Tiers

In the development of Web-based services, three network tiers are obvious: TCP/IP, HTTP/HTML and XML. Such networks lay successively on top of one another as well as remaining compatible now (Bryant, Atallah and Stytz, 2004).

First, TCP/IP protocol is the bottom network tier, which is concerned mainly with transferring information in packets through the wire. TCP/IP is considered as a reliable protocol to transmit data across various networks (private and public), and it also stresses dependability about the physical connectivity as well as data transport. Currently, still TCP/IP considers being the key the web mostly used protocol as a transport layer and relies on it a standard to high-level protocols such as HTTP protocol (Dan, 2011).

The next network tier is HTTP protocol, which comes on top of the HTML protocol. HTML is a tier for presentation and refers to it as browser-based, sharing as well as retrieval of data. This presentation layer is stressed as GUI-based direction-finding and the handling of the layouts. In several behaviours, HTML protocol is more a demonstration than go, and needs both extensile and accurate encoding control. However, the concept of hypertext documents can be shared in an environment of browser based changed radically the method human's converse textbased data to each other. The environments of 'networked desktop', loaded with possessory of operating systems and software to rely on platforms, are gradually but definitely providing the mode in the Internet to adapt the open systems computation.

XML's Role in Web Services

The best solution/method to make all this feasible is the PC-to-PC communication, a region wherein XML stands out. To describe the syntax of data, XML excels is definition driven

(by the employ of schemas and DTDs) and permits programmatically the data to be controlled. It indicates that all the presumed works can be taken beyond the communication of business to business. Settlements of tags can be agreed upon, the description of interfaces can be done and standardisation can be worked out. The components of Web services are recyclable to be utilised XML standard, extensile frame of communication to be provided to C2C type of business (Buneman, 2000).

Interfaces provided by Web services facilitate the transfer of data components' data on top of HTTP along with its business logic. Web browsers can access a large quantity of information that sits under the scripts of the service provider server and in their depositaries. Web services guarantee to revive business published information, and also lay inactive in several scheme spheres (Dan, 2011).

The contributing role of XML is very important to integrate Web-tenant information into the applications of the organisation to be able to systematise the components and reform the business logic collectively. Particular services and tasks in business (comprising business and workflow logic, transaction logic, component sequencing logic, etc) can be closed in the documents of XML and integrated into business atmospheres. It permits organisations to control current resources and works and reveal the data as Web services, providing business transactions and interaction between Web services (Chamberlin, 2000).

Due to the XML being totally text-based as well as readable for humans, it is perfect as a structure of transport between Web services in a loosely coupled manner. The outcome would be: computerised business transactions enhance output, decrease costs and enhance the entire service. Standardisation makes computerised transactions of business promising, resulting in more productivity (Gregorio, 2009).

XML standard is the base of XML-RPC, and the latter was driven to produce a higher technology which is SOAP, in other logic, indications of rising standards known as electronic business XML or eb-XML.

CORBA's Contribution in Web Services

BEA, Sun and IBM collaborate with the very firms they fight with. The protocols of 'standardised network transport', platform-independent languages of programming such as XML, Java or industry-specific accents, and the server with open component-based computer structural design all participate in this non-propriety free-for-all. Web services current guarantees of application regarding the broader inter-operability appear as the eventual 'glue' to develop such new technologies that are interrelated, except seamlessly, leastwise without the overload that came with past technologies such as RMI and CORBA (Dan, 2011).

On the other hand, CORBA was introduced as a second approach in Web services. But, whereas it was a binary IIOP-based communications and object-oriented structure, loaded with stubs and ORB vendor-specific, Web services are frivolous, piloted in XML, based on HTTP, and totally language/platform neutral.

Service Providers and Web Services

Web services framework comprises of a publish-find-bind sequence, whereas the service providers develop services or data accessible to "requesters are registered service" who utilise reliable resources by binding and situating to desired services. Web services description language (WSDL), employed for requesting applications themselves, which facilitates little altitude procedural data regarding the desired service, granted the applications to access the schematic information of XML for data programming, making sure the exact works are raised over the correct protocols (Thornycroft, 2010).

The mechanisms of 'Publish, bind and find' have their particular foil in 3 different concepts except to some extent the same protocols that constitute the network in the stack of Web services: UDDI, WSDL and SOAP.

Going deep on the CORBA correlation, IIOP was contributed by SOAP. It is the mechanism of binding between discoursing endpoints. Conversely, WSDL contributes a part of 'interface definition language' (IDL). Herein capabilities, Web services within WSDL were described as the ports' operations and collection. A WSDL port is similar to an interface; WSDL operations are analogous to a technique and the port introduces the interfaces to parties involved in the process of communication transversely to various platforms.

However, WSDL goes further than only being an interface, meaning language which allows you to interpret the information and the address of protocol for the desired Web services for you to distribute (Govindaraju and Bramley, 2000). Regarding WSDL, the attractive aspect is that it explains a theoretical interface for Web services whereas at the same time permitting the user, in agonising aspect to connect a Web service to a precise mechanism of transfer, such as HTTP. While the interface is considered, functions of the WSDL are a recyclable technology of Web services. By connecting to a particular mechanism of transport, WSDL develops the abstract solid. The mechanism of transport might be altered, but the payload perseveres.

Lastly, registering into UDDI is like positioning and publishing Web services. Then the service provider reveals information for connecting to the interfaces in the registry of Webbased, giving a shared index for users as well as businesses to find each other's Web services.

SOAP Clients and Servers

SOAP requester is actually computer software that develops a XML file comprising the data required to invoke remote methods in a distributed system. This program need not be traditional. Additionally a SOAP client could be a server application on the Web or computer desktop software (Balmin, 2005).

From SOAP clients, requests and messages are usually delivered over the HTTP protocol. Consequently, the SOAP documents are capable of traversing any firewall, allowing the data exchange across different types of servers. A SOAP service is merely a unique service that accepts requests from SOAP clients and performs as an interpreter and distributor of SOAP data. Other Web services externally may interrelate with application servers using J2EE, which processes the requests of SOAP by a range of different users.

SOAP services make sure that the data obtained using HTTP protocol is transformed to objects that the requester can interpret. Due to the complete process of communications being developed in terms of XML, Java language objects may interact through SOAP services with some other languages such as (C++/C#). It is the SOAP server's job to ensure the end points understand the SOAP they are being served.

Java Technology and SOAP

In accordance with SOAP version 1.1 descriptions, SOAP is "a lightweight protocol for exchanging data in a decentralised and distributed atmosphere".

SOAP obviously is not specified for a single programming model, nor specifies the connection methods for a particular programming language. For example, in Java, it is up to the Java developers to describe the binding of a particular language. Also Java uses JAX-RPC for interconnection technique as one of the language methods.

Having comprehensively organised the stage for SOAP and defined it's very important contributing part in the Web as a service it is necessary to have a close look at the functionality of SOAP. It is totally a text-based and extensible framework for allowing the interconnection between various entities, generally, objects in different platforms can interact between each other without having the knowledge of each other. Furthermore, a loosely-coupled concept environment has made it possible to interact between different applications and to locate and connect energetically to services devoid of any pre-agreed method of interaction between them.

SOAP enforces a text-based framework, therefore it is extensible, due to the SOAP clients, protocol and the servers it can develop devoid of breaking the existing applications. Moreover, SOAP is flexible in forms of assisting mediators and architecture of multi-layered structure. It indicates the nodes of processing can stay on the passageway a call acquires between the server and client. Such mediates nodes interpret the messages' elements specified by SOAP by the headers and these headers permit clients to address which of the nodes operates on what component of the message. This mediate header working is carried out through some agreement between the user software and the mediate processing node. It facilitates the features that must be understood for headers that permit the user to identify whether the process is compulsory or elective. For example, if the header sets to a value = 1, then the server has either to execute the mediate interpretation identified in the header or return an error.

Moreover, SOAP describes the rules of encoding data, known as 'Section 5 encodings' or 'base level encodings', a part of SOAP specification that defines it. Then it is noticeable that the encoding section in SOAP version 1.1 occupies a big part in the 40-page specification. Devoid of getting swamped intensely in the data of XML specifications, inundate continues being debilitated through professionals at the group of XML Schema, encoding as in SOAP is an accumulation of both plain and complex values.

Simple and plain values can be very simple types, such as strings, floats, or integers, or integrals as described in XML Schema description Part 2. They also comprise arrays of enumerations as well as bytes (Gont, 2008).

Complex values comprise arrays, structures and compound types as described, again, through the group of XML Schema. Finally, rules of serialisation the objects in SOAP that is identified by data encodings; it is the mechanism for marshalling and unmarshaling the stream of data on the net. It is also very significant to observe that such 'Section 5 encodings' are not compulsory at all, thus both the servers and clients are able to employ dissimilar standards for data encoding as far as the format is agreed on.

Lastly, SOAP develops the rules that allow both the servers and clients to perform distant process invocation employing the framework of communications. On the other hand, an oriented protocol such as SOAP-RPC operates very well using a base message of SOAP, and this is possible because of the object serialisation.

SOAP-RPC

SOAP-RPC is basically 'in single direction' message transmission from a transmitter to a recipient; however the SOAP message is frequently blended to execute the mechanisms of request/response (Wilkinson, 2005). To do RPC employing SOAP, some conventions must be pursued. Firstly, the messages of response and request must be programmed as encoded as structures. There must be an element for every input parameter of a process (structure should contain the input as part of it) and the parameter also has an identical name. In the same sense, each element must have an identical parameter for the output. To demonstrate the response and request messages, the following example demonstrates our example above:

The Request Message side:

```
< SOAP-ENV: Body >
< m: Get Last Trade Buy Price xmlns: m = "some - URI" >
< Trade Symbol > MSFT < /Trade Symbol >
< /m: Get Last Trade Buy Price >
< /SOAP - ENV: Body >
The Response Message side:
< SOAP-ENV: Body >
< m: Get Last Trade Buy Price Response xmlns: m = "some - URI" >
< Buy Price > 23.35 < /Buy price >
< /m: Get Last Trade Buy Price Response >
< /SOAP - ENV: Body >
```

The request calls for the method of 'Get Last Trade Price'. Notice that the response describes an operation of 'Get Last Trade Price Response' (Wilkinson, 2005). A standard normal to SOAP invokes adding Response to the Request operation's end to develop a 'Response structure'. This structure of output comprises an element known as price, which comes back to the outcomes of the method invocation, most probably like a float.

It is also very significant that the SOAP envelope contains data types that are clearly defined, thus we still cannot recognise the type of data by looking to it. 'Data types' are defined by the 'Client applications' either generally by the 'Section 5 encodings', or agreed through concurred-upon agreement with service providers. In either situation, such classifications are not clearly comprised in the SOAP envelope.

Lastly, in order to apply RPC, HTTP protocol at the lower-level is required and deploying the latter as a transport protocol, the newer versions of SOAP (containing both attachments along with message) allow the employ of other transport protocols such as SMTP, FTP etc.

A SOAP Use Case

By observing the SOAP envelope thoroughly, it helps to stand back a little and analyse the process of the round trip that happens in the environment of web distribution (Wilkinson, 2005) for a wide review scheme that creates the abstract stamina for SOAP and its services.

- A user software someplace on the Web uses the services.
- Services using SOAP reveal the objects and its methods.
- Remote methods of objects can retrieve data from any place in the Internet.

Figure 3. SOAP use case

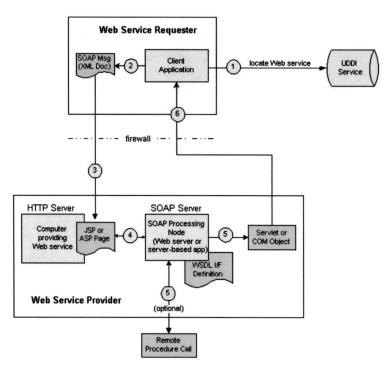

Implementing the transitive sense to such propositions, we can realise the entire aim of SOAP and similar services: users someplace use data anyplace on the Internet.

As a thorough description for use case (Figure 3), the figure contains process numbers which are described in the process sequence as follows:

1. Services (in our case SOAP) registered in UDDI can be located and found by users. Instead of using WSDL straight away, SOAP services will mainly be installed to employ a specific type of port as well as binding style, and it will energetically arrange the service address to be requested to be equivalent to the ones exposed by the UDDI.
2. A SOAP message developed by the client application, which is a document of XML and able to execute the coveted operation of request/response.
3. Users send their message requests to SOAP via ASP or JSP or any other language to the server who is listening to these message requests.
4. SOAP service analyses the message, passes the parameters that are contained in the message and requests the suitable object's method in its area. As mentioned above, the headers' values are set to optionally process unique works before receiving the rest of the message.
5. The requested object carries out the pointed work and brings back the data or information to the SOAP service, then the latter wraps the data outcomes and forms it as a SOAP envelope. After that, the envelope is enclosed in an object of Servlet or COM or any other object form to be sent back to the original requester.
6. The requester (user) shreds the SOAP envelope object and dissolves the desired data back to the user software; in this way, finalizing the request and response sequence.

SOAP ADVANTAGES AND DISADVANTAGES

SOAP is a layer of communication for message interaction protocol; it uses HTTP protocol as a transport layer. Also it can be applied in amalgamation with different bottom layer protocols such as JMS, SMTP, and FTP etc. Even though the broadest protocol that SOAP uses as a transport layer is HTTP, vendors start to use other transport layers such as SMTP. In general cases, messages in SOAP can pass through various transport layers before it reaches the final target.

SOAP Advantages

- Platform, language and vendor independent.
- Decoupling the runtime from the communications and the encoding environment. Platforms have no relation with the service or in the structure of the message or payload from a remote service.
- Programming language independence gave the capability to various developers (C++, Perl, J2EE etc) to contribute in a SOAP exchange, with a comparatively small barrier to development.
- Message structure uses XML to receive and send data.
- Uses an easy technique to get remote components or objects. Because it uses an XML structure, understanding the structure of SOAP is relatively swift.
- Standard HTTP used as a transport protocol layer.
- Because of using HTTP, this removes firewall complications.
- Easy to understand and deploy in comparison with DCOM, CORBA, and RMI. Since it does not transact with particular additional but essential features of remote object systems.
- Used for interchanging as protocol the knowledge in a distributed and decentralised structure.
- It can utilise different transport protocols for exchanging messages.

SOAP Disadvantages

- No protection or security mechanism mentioned in SOAP specifications.
- Message body in version 1.1 specification does not define a default encoding. An encoding is defined to be compliant in a way that any custom encoding is defined in the attribute of the encoding style or of entity aspects within the message. Therefore, in comparison with CORBA, SOAP deals with plain text to serialise the objects and not with "stringified remote object references (interoperable object references, IORs, as described in CORBA), therefore, distributed garbage collection has no meaning".
- Remote objects do not keep condition indications at the user side (client).

Summary

XML is the foundation structure of SOAP for delivering different messages and creating RPCs in an environment of distributed. Text data in SOAP can be serialised regardless of a particular bottom layer transport protocol, even though the HTTP protocol is in general the choice protocol. SOAP is excellent for developing the language-neutral systems and platform that interoperate. In general, Web services and SOAP comprise the whole thing required to construct a decentralised distributed structure of application. It reduces the trouble of different platforms used inconsistencies in retrieving information through settling the dispute between object models (either Java or COM elements) or any other object modelling.

As a conclusion, SOAP is considered to be ideal as middleware between object elements of different kinds, to employ as a medium for communications.

XML KEY MANAGEMENT SPECIFICATION

Encryption as well as the signature of XML as specifications offers the mechanisms to encrypt and sign the documents of XML in the critical scenario of electronic-services and they engage the employ of crypto-keys. The necessity to incorporate digital certificates and PKIs with applications that use XML structure grows. W3C in particular is formulating an unwrapped description called 'XML key management specification' denoted by XKMS. It describes a mechanism to register as well as distributing the public keys, employed among XML encryption and XML signature (Carlos, Miguel and Jaime, 2006). The major task of it is to permit the progress of the trusted services, which an XML-based structure is running on the keys of PKIbased cryptograph. XKMS is intended to minimise the difficulty of PKI mechanism by involving a trusted third party to rely on when interacting with various applications that adopt XML as an interchanging medium file type for every action associated with the tasks of PKI.

XKMS defines the techniques for distributing (register and process) the public keys which are completely integrated with XML encryption and signature (Nicholas and David, 2006). At an elevated degree, the protocol describes the services of predefined, communication protocols connections, a set of message formats, error models, rules for processing, and responsibilities. It is made of two main components that are explained below.

XML Key Information Service Specification

Key information service specification is denoted as XKISS and specifies a protocol that controls the public key information facilitating with two major services as 'locates and validates', employed to process as well as validate the public keys, in that order. Specifically, it also offers assistance to process 'ds': Key Info entity employed by XML encryption and signature. Depending on this service, applications are obviously not engaged in every action involving a communication with the infrastructure of public key, which could need some knowhow regarding particular standards like 'Simple PKI', 'X.509', etc. X-KISS also permits the description of the data which provides to the authenticator ideas to employ the public key (FIXML, 2010). It is also described as a service that contains three layers; in layer-0 'ds': Key Info is processed by applications; in layer-1 'ds': Key Info is deputed to a service; in layer-2 'ds': Key Info is deputed to a service that offers further details on the data described in the 'ds': Key Info entity.

XML Key Registration Service Specification

This is denoted as XKRSS which acknowledges the PKI registration and is also in charge for the whole management of the key lifecycle. Particularly, it assists the next four major functions engaged in the process and offered through the registration process. The procedure of registration permits all the entities to register a specific key (in our case Public), attaching required data to it. Creating PUK might be carried out by the registration server as well as by a client. The service of registration may need the user to give more information to validate the request, and also checks if the user has already created the Pair-key (Private & Public) himself. The registration process obliges the user to facilitate an evidence of ownership of the matching key (Private part) (Nicholas and David, 2006). The operation of revocation permits all the entities to cancel a formerly issued key registration. The operation of recovery permits all the entities to retrieve the PK correlated with a registered PUK. Knowing that in this process may take time, along with process of Registration Service frequently to execute XML Security and invalidate the process after a request of recovering. The regeneration process permits a formerly registered pair of keys to be reproduced. The process of registration requires certifying the legality of every request of its integrity as well as legitimacy, and also requires handling verification of holding of PUKs (Yu and Liu, 2006). For that reason, the service of registration sets a policy of authentication defining a mechanism of authentication that develops offline a covert with the user.

XML-BASED ACCESS CONTROL LANGUAGE

In the initial stage, XACL were functioned to secure the resources that were themselves XML files. New suggestions however employ the XML to specify languages for showing the requirements of protection or security for any type of resources or data. The two pertinent to

Web Service Policy (WS-Policy) and the XACLs are the extensile approach mark-up language (XACML), whereas WS-Policy offers the syntax to express the policy of Web services. XMLbased access control mark-up language (XACML) is the effect of an OASIS organisation; they suggested a language based on XML to demonstrate and exchange and set a policy for access control mechanisms. XACML is intended to state a policy set of authorisation structured in XML alongside objects that can themselves be addressed in XML. Whereas the Web security policy and XACML split a few general features, XACML has the benefit of relishing a fundamental model of policy as a foundation, resulting in a fresh and univocal language's meaning. In the rest of the section, we describe the major characteristics of WS-Policy and XACML (Nicholas and David, 2006).

Access Control Mark-up Language

The main tasks provided by access control mark-up language (XACML) can be summarised below:

- **Mixture of Policy:** It facilitates a way for aggregating ruling separately defined. Various elements can then specify these rulings on the similar resource. If a request is received to access the resource, the methods have to consider the mixture of various policies combined.
- **Aggregating Algorithms:** Given that it assists the specification of policies separately defined, there is a requirement for a technique for integrating these different rules when their assessment is conflicting. It also assists the various aggregating algorithms, all of them representing an approach of combining manifold verdicts into a solitary resolution.
- **Attribute-Based:** Limitations or boundaries. It also assists the specification of rules reliant on attributes or properties connected with resources and subjects except the identities. It also permits the classification of strong ruling relied on common properties connected with themes such as addresses and names.

Setting Rules and Policies

The representations of the format used in XACML consented to control the security access by setting rules and policies as well as its function. This stage of modelling is necessary to ensure an apparent and univocal language, or else it will be subject to various assessments and interpretations. The primary goal on setting the structure of this language is to come up with clear rules, policies and set policies. Policies in XACML have, as a core element, either Policy Set or Policy. 'Policy Set' is an accumulation of Policies or Policy Set entities. Also it contains a target, an optional set of obligations, a set of rules, and a mixture of ruling algorithms. As for the target, it essentially includes a basic set of situations, actions, resources or the subject that should be met for a strategy that is relevant to a provided petition. In cases where every situation of a Target has been met, then the related Policy (or set of Policies) attempts to the petition (AlWasil, 2006).

The set of elements of a rule forms an object, a condition and effect. This object (target) identifies a list of actions, themes and resources, in order for this list of elements to be applied to (Nicholas and David, 2006). The consequence of the rule may be 'allow' or 'reject'. In the theme element, which can be denoted also as condition, the representation of it is a form of Boolean expression, which by its function can treat pertinence of the policy (Biddle, Peinado and Willman, 2008). Keep in mind that the object element is not an obligatory one; policies with no specified object or a target will affect every probable request. A compulsion rule will be executed in concurrence with the implementation of an approval selection. For example, a compulsion may affirm that every approach to mechanical information must be registered. Keep in mind that just strategy that is assessed and responded of allowing or refusal may return compulsory action. This derives that the rule state is Not Applicable then the compulsion element is not relevant. The last assessment value, called the approval assessment, appended to the context of XACML information via PDP is the output or the rule as described through the mixture of the algorithm (Nicholas and David, 2006). XACML describes various mixture algorithms.

A significant option of XACML is rules that focus on the description of characteristics representing particular attributes of an action, theme, atmosphere or sources. For example, a mechanic at a factory possibly has the capability to be an investigator, an expert in a few fields, or several further job roles (Rizzolo and Mendelzon, 2001). In accordance to these assigns, the mechanic may be capable of executing various functions inside the factory. These components employ the Attribute Value element to describe the requested outcome of a special assign. On the other hand, the Attribute Selector element may be employed to identify where to put back a specific attribute. Notice that every attribute-designator and Attribute Selector elements may get back more than one value. For this cause, XACML offers an assign kind named bag, an ungraded compilation that may include repeat values for a special attribute (Rittinghouse, 2009).

Request and Response

Request and Response is defined as a common structure within XACML. When submitting a request by evaluation point, the interpreter interprets the request and transforms the request into a canonical structure; the transformed request will be directed to the decision point module for assessment. In its structure, it contains the three elements (action, subject and resource) and a non-compulsory element (environment). Each message contains only a single set of attributes for each element. There possibly several collections of subject assigns which is named through a class URI. A resulting component includes one or more outcomes representing an assessment. Every outcome includes three components (obligations, status and decision). The latter component identifies the status of permission returned (that is, allow, refuse, undefined, not applicable), as for the status component, if any error is returned during the assessment step, and the last component (obligations) must be filled by the evaluation point module (Rittinghouse, 2009).

OVERVIEW OF RIDX ARCHITECTURE

Internet cloud communication is admittance over an unrestricted access available to the public. A secured and reliable communication environment is a big challenge for almost all businesses operating under Internet cloud. Nevertheless, Internet cloud provides a cost-effective platform for different businesses, services and type of communication to choose.

A Real-Time Interactive Data Exchange system (RIDX) virtually provides an environment to carry out secured communication between different services for transferring XML data. In chapter 2, the author has discussed several areas of cloud computing including types of services which operate under Internet cloud. Some services work as SaaS (Software as a Service) or as an integrated cloud solution etc. RIDX can simply be a combination of Software as a service and integrated cloud solution that work as a middleware for distributing XML files between different nodes, services or any domain group members.

The main functionality that can describe the RIDX system is as follows:

- RIDX is a software system that contains a pack of modules written in Java and run in any Java Virtual Machine environment. It can be run on various different platforms and operating systems that support Java virtual machine. Also it is considered as lightweight software that can reach between 15 to 20 KLOC depending on the number of modules used in the pack of modules.
- Modules in RIDX that form the system have a flexible configuration and scalability that can be set by XML configuration file which contains the definition of pack of modules used, the order of them, and the parameters needed for each module as initial setup values. These values can be customised and vary depending on the desired setup, for example, the encryption key size can be set to 256 bit key or 512 bit key, or maybe the Ping module has a periodic packet check which is set to every two seconds or every five seconds, or a parameter to set the XML shredding message size to 1K or 5K etc. On the other hand, the order of modules can be flexible depending on the functional priority needed in the system, or flexibility to add a new module to solve a specific case requirement.
- RIDX can be installed on a node or group of nodes spread across the Internet cloud WAN and LAN that will form a domain, each node has the ability to initialise, join and leave the domain group at any time, furthermore, it can establish a secured communication and exchange data among each other. A virtual environment can be set up ahead prior to any data interchange; this gives RIDX the option to establish a multipath secured communication ground for any XML data transmission between domain members and group of nodes. RIDX architecture can be used to be a bottom most transport layer for most common used protocols, such as HTTP, or can be used for Web services such as SOAP etc.

- A failure detection mechanism that detects any unreachable members and eliminates them from the domain, also joining or leaving the domain is automatically detected; it notifies all other members in the domain.
- A shredder/assembly module which contains an algorithm to vertically shred and fragment XML files to a desired message size. Each output part resulting from the vertical partitioning process of the XML file can be formed in separate chunks, each chunk contains a group of unrelated characters that hold no useful meaning in case sniffed by an intruder of neither readable nor understandable data. This method can add another level of security in case a man-in-the-middle is trying to tap messages. The assembler module algorithm is the reverse process of shredder, the assembler rejoins the separate chunks (messages) at the receiver side into its original XML file state.
- Authentication and encryption modules are used in RIDX architecture. Authentication is used to authenticate any domain joiner and the encryption module is used to encrypt all messages between domain members.
- A reliable transmission between all members with a guaranteed message delivery and no data loss during transmission, means that the receiver will receive all messages with zero tolerance of message loss on the contrary of standard UDP. In addition, using RIDX UDP transport protocol is a multicast data transfer method, which means that every node can simultaneously send messages to multi nodes and receive from multi nodes, meanwhile, it can route messages simultaneously to other nodes.
- A module is used to tunnel and create a virtual private network between different domain members and add an additional level of security to protect data during transmission.

RIDX is an instance that resides on a node or a host at Internet cloud, WAN or LAN. It is possible to run more than one instance on the same host, each instance can be part of a domain group, this domain group usually has a mutual agreement between members (Grötschel, Alevras and Wessäly, 1998). Domains can be identified by giving a name to the PIPELINE; a pipeline is created by a process which is initiated by a domain creator (first member of this domain), by default; the domain creator will act as domain coordinator, if the domain coordinator leaves the domain, the second oldest domain member will be elected to be a coordinator, and so on. In order to join a domain, members can connect to a domain by creating a process with the same domain name. The handler between domain members is the pipeline; this means that all domain members that hold the same pipeline name can send and receive messages among each other. A domain member can be a part of different domain groups at the same time.

Pipelines are the handler between domain members, applications and pack of modules, therefore applications can connect to a pipeline to send XML data files, then the pipeline passes the data to the pack of modules to be processed until RIDX UDP transport protocol puts the processed data on to the network.

In reverse order, when the destination receives the data, the RIDX UDP transport protocol listens to incoming data via the network and passes it to the pack of modules to be processed back into the original state, and then the data are pushed to the receiver pipeline. The pipeline queues the data until the application guzzles all the data.

Whenever there is a connection request by the application to use a pipeline, the pipeline starts the pack of modules to be ready for use, and the modules will be stopped when the application disconnects from the pipeline.

The directional order of the pack of modules is defined in an XML file; this file contains the parameter list for each module, and the order of them.

RIDX and Virtualization of Cloud Computing

A key element in RIDX architecture of using cloud computing is virtualization. Virtualization is "the abstraction of logical resources away from their underlying physical resources in order to improve agility and flexibility, reduce costs and thus enhance business value" (Antonopoulos and Gillam, 2010). Computing environments that are virtualized can be adapted to the required use. It can be expanded, contracted, moved, and created dynamically as required by the particular application (Wilkinson, 2005). Virtualization is a perfect fit for a cloud computing environment, as the resources need to be fluid, agile, and responsive and adaptive to the frequently changing needs of a customer. When virtualization is used, and one portion of the system is underused, it can be allocated to another operation. This improves flexibility and efficiency of architecture (Ioannidis, Keromytis and Smith, 2000).

Virtualization comes in many different forms and its precise implementation and definition can vary from user to user (or vendor to vendor). RIDX virtualization is generally considered to map a single sender into multi-connection paths or to several path alternatives into a single receiver. Virtualization in RIDX is not restricted to a centralised point of connection; it is a decentralised communication into multi-agent networking.

A virtualized network environment can allow an outside node (a customer or a service) to join and behave as if they are part of the domain group, unacquainted that they may be sharing it.

The systems are kept separate from one another. Virtualization constitutes a complete layer of a cloud computing architecture.

Administration and management of a virtualised system is a complex chore if manually processed and is paramount to the success of the system. IBM stress that automation is the key to managing a virtual environment. Automation simplifies management of the hardware layer that make available the needed resources. The two most recurrent tasks performed in a cloud computing data-centre are on boarding and off boarding of applications (dynamic provisioning). On boarding is the installing of RIDX and configuring it and additional modules added to the pack of modules in order to be prepared obtainable to perform helpful work. Off boarding presents to the stages important to recoup automatically to obtain different aims. When performed manually, these tasks can be time-consuming. Automation makes these tasks efficient.

Another key area that is automated is reservation and scheduling of resources (Ioannidis, Keromytis and Smith, 2000).

Along with automation, a self-service API access is a vital part of the management architecture. This handles requests and automates management. It allows customer/service to access through a Web service or through direct API listeners to request a service. Monitoring is an essential part of the system management architecture as it collects real-time and historic data and measures performance. Capacity planning is an important element that needs to be managed. This becomes complex in a virtualized environment, because it is less predictable in terms of size of domain members, and the size of XML data files usage than a static environment.

Topology

The Real-Time Interactive Data Exchange (RIDX) system resides on a host within the domain area (group of nodes that share same domain/interest) in the Internet cloud (Ho, Vincent and Cheng, 2009). Each RIDX system contains modules, processes and listeners, some responsible for keeping track of domain

Figure 4. RIDX instances distributed in the cloud, domain interest is 'Financial Sector'

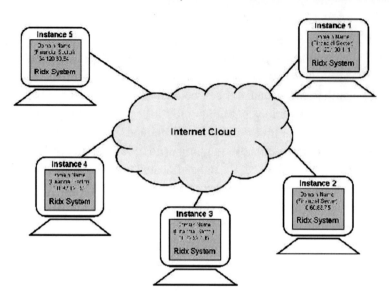

members, some for delivering and receiving messages, others for routing messages and for shredding/joining messages etc.

Architecture

RIDX architecture is divided into three major parts:

1. Pack of modules containing classes to process XML data which includes data encryption, XML vertical partitioning, data assembling, message sequencer, data flow control and group of modules that administer domain states and membership control.
2. Transport protocol which consists of three layers, the bottom most layer is tunnelling; on top of it a router module, and then the higher transport protocol layer is RIDX UDP protocol.
3. The interface (API) which provides the accessibility to different types of applications to enable users to access RIDX pack of modules in order to facilitate the pack of modules to interact and work as a middleware software for exchanging XML data between different parties.

Figure 5 shows the hierarchical layers in the RIDX system, for example, Instance (1) shows that the highest layer is the application layer; applications can be any software application that uses an XML file structure to interact with other applications. The application layer can also be any Web service on the Internet, such as SOAP, CORBA or various application servers etc. These applications can integrate and communicate with RIDX through RIDX APIs. The next sections explain about different layers as follows:

Figure 5. Instance structure and different modules which are used to facilitate major functionality

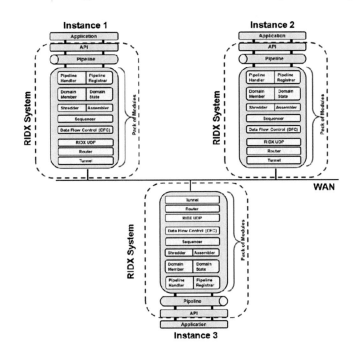

THE CONCEPTUAL MODEL DESIGN AND COMPONENTS

A pack of modules facilitates the functionality of the system; the Application Programming Interface (API) is the interface between the RIDX system and the application software layer accessing it to allow using various services and resources, along with different modules and protocols. Each XML file sent by the application/user through a pipeline/API will be processed by the hierarchical layered modules until it reaches the lowest layer (UDP or tunnelling layer). Messages received by transport layer during transmission session will process and hand over each message to the next upper layer through the pack of modules up until it reaches back to the application layer. System parameters, configuration setup and initial values are saved in XML file structure; the values that are kept in this file can drive the system to perform the desired outcomes from the system, for example, the message size can be controlled by setting (Partition Size) the variable to a desired shredding size, or the number of credits in the Data Flow Control module can be set to a certain number in order to control the data flow etc.

The following modules describe the components from top layer to bottom used by the system as in Figure 5; the transport layer, which consists of three modules (RIDX UDP, Router, Tunnel), will be discussed in chapter 4:

Listeners/Interfaces (APIs)

- **Message Handler:** Whenever this listener receives a message, a push style event handler notifies the receiving of the message, number of methods is invoked to determine the state of the message in order to be processed. When a message is received, the method receive() will be called. Both getState() and setState() methods are used to get hold of domain member's state. In addition, when a message is received, a byte buffer is allocated for this message, and then appends this buffer into its queue, this queue is dedicated for input messages (received messages), and another queue is dedicated for output messages (sent messages). Append process eventually is a copy of the first initialised byte buffer, this copy is done in sequence to un-serialise the message in the copied buffer at the input queue instead. Ultimately this is prepared in order to free the message handler thread to receive new messages. This is due to the time needed to finish the serialisation/unserialisation process, but doing so gives the ability to continuously pass the un-serialised messages to the modules above to be processed.

- **Domain Members:** Each domain member has a list of active members that is joining the domain, whenever a new member asks to join or leave the domain; a snapshot is taken of the list and distributes it after registering the new status to all domain members. The domain coordinator is in charge of accepting/leaving and announcing the new snapshot. When suspecting one of the domain members of crashing without announcing leaving the domain group by disconnecting from the Pipeline, the suspect() call-back is raised. The viewAccepted () method will notify the requester and all the other members in the group that a new domain member has joined the domain and been accepted. At the same time, it will notify domain members that the domain member has left (disconnected) from the domain group. In case of two or more requests received from different new requesters to join the domain, the block() method is invoked in order to block all the request messages until the current request is determined and finalises the status of the new requester and synchronises the status with all domain members.
- **Pipeline Registrar:** In order to send and receive messages, the user needs to register in a pipeline, the pipeline name identifies the domain and the coordinator holds the state of the pipeline whether it is active, inactive or closed. To register in Pipeline, a method Pipeline.setPipelineListener () is used for implementing a class PipelineListener () in order to obtain the state of the pipeline and any other information to declare the pipeline state. A call-back will be raised whenever a pipeline is opened, disconnected or closed.
- **Pipeline Handler:** The pipeline handler passes all XML files from the application to the pack of modules or from the pack of modules to the application.

Pipeline

Pipeline is similar to a socket; a new joiner must create a pipeline and join a domain in order to send and receive messages, a process will handle creating a pipeline. Connecting to a pipeline will give a name of the domain that would like to join. Whenever a pipeline is active and in a connected state, it is always allied with a particular domain. A pack of modules look out so that pipelines that are holding the same domain name can find each other. A finder module is loaded when a pack of modules are loaded, the main job of it is to search and find an active member on the net, it triggers a message with the help of Ping module to locate any member on the LAN. If there is any positive response from a member during the Finder process, the member will respond to the request by sending back the status of it along with the coordinator IP/Port address. The Finder module will extract the coordinator address and pass it to the AML module for further communication to join the domain.

A pipeline has three main states (Not Connected, Connected, and Closed), sending and receiving messages is only compelling when the state of the pipeline is connected, Figure 6 shows the states and the process of changing the state.

Figure 6. Different states of the pipeline and the process of changing between them

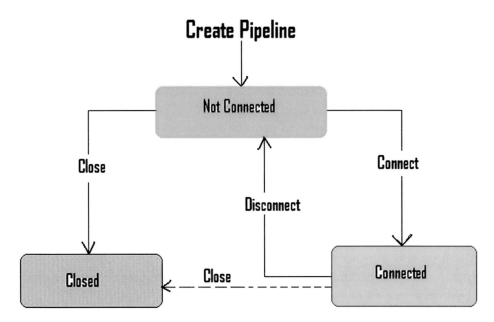

Whenever a successful connection has been made, the system will prepare the pack of modules for this connection to be ready; an XML file grasps the configuration parameters including the desired list of modules needed for the system along with the parameter list for each module.

Shredder and Assembler

The shredder and assembler modules are one of the defence mechanisms of this architecture. The first purpose of these modules is to break down the XML file into several chunks (small pieces) by applying a vertical partitioning, adding an identifier to each chunk, then attaching this identifier to a message along with the data; the ID can be added separately either by adding a header to the message or embedding it in the message body. At the final destination (Receiver), all messages are re-assembled again.

The size of the chunk is predetermined in the configuration file; this decision depends on what level of partition size needs to be applied. For example if a high level of security is required depending on the sensitivity of the data, a smaller size of each chunk is imposed.

Although fragmentation is part of a standard TCP protocol by its nature, it has several concerns:

- The performance and inefficiency can be affected negatively when reassembling fragmented data.
- The performance and high cost of retransmitting can be affected when number of lost fragments is high.
- In a standard UDP case, the performance can be affected when using more resources because of unfortunate choice of datagram size, this happens because of lack of guessing the Maximum Transmission Unit (MTU) size. MTU size varies depending on the hardware, router and operating system that have been used given that when UDP sends a message, it does not expect any feedback from the receiver, and therefore, the fragmentation is controlled by the operating system and not UDP protocol itself.

The Shredder algorithm reads the XML file and splits it into several 1K size chunks as a default system parameter partition size. The 1K chunk size is preferred to be used to keep the whole message that might include additional headers under the standard MTU size (1.5K), by doing this, the fragmentation of messages larger than the MTU size can be avoided and this eliminates any possible retransmission cost and enhances transmission performance (see chapter 5). Eventually, the number of partitions depends on the whole XML file size. The process starts from top down vertically to form an array that might be similar to a set of byte arrays of character type. A dataset of $X = \{X0, X1, X2...Xn\}$ where X represents XML file and X0... Xn represents numbers of partitions generated from partitioning File X. In Figure 7, which illustrates an XML file shredded into 15 chunks, an ID is assigned for each partition in order to preserve the order of messages at the receiver side.

At the receiver side, the assembler reconstructs the file by verifying and reassembling chunks according to message sequences. The message sequence is unique in conjunction with Sender ID (obtained from Active Member List), and a process ID which is unique generated by shredder layer and assigned to a specific XML file, and a partition ID which is unique per partition sequence number within this specific XML file process. Any additional information that needs to be included can be attached to the message header. As shown in performance results in chapter 5, the best results are obtained when keeping the chunk/partition size 1K or under per message size.

Figure 7. XML shredded file example

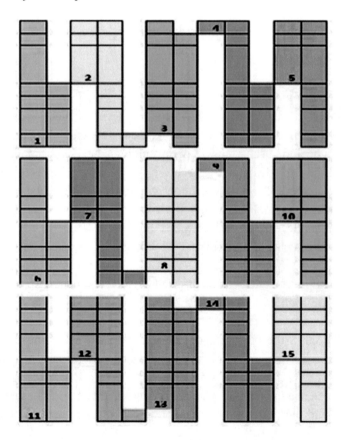

Sequencer

In this module, a reliable and vigorous mechanism is applied. Among them included the use of sequence number to ensure the orders when receiving the packets, also to detect the duplicate RIDX UDP segments, as well as employing the checksum technique to detect errors, and enforcing acknowledgments and timers for leaks and delays.

When the connection is established, initially the sender and the receiver exchange and swap sequence numbers between them, this identifies and counts the data segment in the byte stream which has been received through the application layer. A pair of numbers is always formed as part of the packet, one for sequence and one for the acknowledgement. At the sender side, the sequence number reflects the sequence of the data being sent, as for the acknowledgement number reflecting the receiver's sequence number. To sustain reliable communication, a recipient replies back the location of the segments received representing a part of the continuous stream of bytes.

One of the keys to preserve the forcefulness and security of RIDX communication is the choice of initial sequence number (Initial Sequence Number - ISN). The sender computes the 16bit checksum by counting the summation of the data and header ones' complement values, and appends this number in the transmission segment. The receiver recalculates the checksum of the header and data, and simply calculates the summation of the 1s complement with the checksum included; the outcome must be zero. Therefore, it is presumed that the segment has arrived intact and without errors, and needs to mention that checksum in RIDX UDP protocol including the destination and source addresses. This gives protection adjacent to misdirected packages for errors in addresses.

The acknowledgments (ACKs or Acknowledgments) of data between the sender and the receiver can benefit from it; the sender in particular can understand network conditions between them. When a timer is employed during the transmission, both the sender and the receiver can adjust the performance of the data flow. To accomplish high performance and circumvent any congestion in the network in RIDX, there are some techniques used by RIDX UDP protocol for controlling the flow of data (the sender sends as fast as the receiver can receive). A dedicated module for controlling data flow is produced and discussed in the next section, and there is a sequence number generated by each side, thus helping to establish that connections cannot be falsified (spoofing).

When a sender starts transmitting messages, the first message is given an initial sequence number, the receiver tags this message as a starting sequence number and creates a negative acknowledge window. On the sender side, a specific timeout is set to monitor messages which is delivered to the receiver. If the receiver did not acknowledge receiving all messages, the sender resends messages that have not been acknowledged, a specific timeout is set in case during transmission the sender has crashed or lost connection and eventually stops an endless retransmission process. The same case is monitored in the receiver side; when the sender requests retransmission of non-received messages, a timeout is set to control endless retransmission requests and considers whether the sender is crashed or lost connection, therefore the file transmission is considered as failed.

Data Flow Control

Data Flow Control is responsible for controlling the speed of transmitting when the receiver is slower than the sender. When messages overflow the receiver, it starts to drop any new messages, and this will cause the sender to retransmit the dropped messages, leading to a higher cost and lower performance.

There are several techniques to control data flow used by standard TCP protocol such as stop-and-wait, sliding window etc. None of these techniques can be deployed in RIDX communication structure because these techniques assume a Unicast oneto-one connection and will not work within Multicast RIDX architecture. Therefore another approach has to be implemented; this approach should cope with the characteristics of the connection topology (1-N, N-1), where one sender sends messages simultaneously to number of RIDX routers (N), then number of RIDX routers (N) routes back the messages to one receiver. The receiver receives number of N messages simultaneously; the sender processes a group of N messages until the whole XML file is transferred.

Consequently, this process can cause an overflow state on the receiver side over time. A simple technique is implemented in RIDX to overcome this problem by using a data flow control (DFC) module. For instance, one of the techniques used is 'Bank Account', which controls the

transmitter to send information within the receiver's buffer and flow control algorithms, such as the algorithm for congestion avoidance, the slow start (Slow-start), the fast retransmit and the fast recovery (Fast Recovery).

This module is similar to an acclaim bank account transaction; each member holds a number of credits parameter, this parameter is defined in the configuration file (see Figure 8) and the account credit number can be preconfigured to meet certain conditions. When a sender initiates the process and starts sending messages to a receiver, it initiates the maximum number of credits defined in the system specifically for that receiver. In each new process of transmission, the credit number is initiated again along with it. When the sender starts sending messages, the sender decrements from a maximum bank account value by 1, if the account value is decreased below 0, the sender stops sending messages. On the receiver side, whenever a receiver receives a message, it reimburses the sender bank account value by 1. Therefore, the sender keeps sending messages as long as the credit number is greater than 0. Messages in the receiver side will be processed and queued in the pipeline until all messages are received and reconstructed back to their original XML file structure.

Identifier

Each domain member has to be identified, when using UDP transport layer, the IP Address is the unique identifier for each node plus the port number (Socket Number) on which the message handler will be receiving messages. If it is desired to run more than one RIDX instance on the same node, then all instances have the same identifier (IP Address) except for the port number. Therefore port numbers differentiate between multiple instances on the same node.

In order to determine if the IP address (Identifier) is a multicast IP address, RIDX must have solid implementation methods to sort and compare the addresses and to allow all probable types of addresses (e.g. ATM etc), RIDX UDP protocol generates the actual implementations of addresses and the interface should not be implemented directly to preserve the unique identity of RIDX node.

Active Member List

When Domain Coordinator (First Member) initiates a Pipeline, an Active Member List is created, this list will be identified by an ID, and it contains all the existing active domain members. Whenever a new joiner to the domain is registered into a pipeline, the domain coordinator will release a new AML (Active Member List), then the coordinator will distribute this list to all domain members. The list identifier

(ID) identifies the version of this list and sequences any new ID whenever a new list has issued. In the same sense, whenever a domain member leaves the domain, either by disconnecting or leaving or even by crashing, the coordinator will issue a new AML and all domain members will be notified of the new AML sequence along with the new Active Member List.

The Active Member List contains current and active members which forms the domain; active member means that the member is reachable with a positive response when firing a Ping message and the member has RIDX modules including the initialisation of RIDX Pipeline along with all modules needed to communicate with other members. The active list has two main columns, one column contains the IP/Port address for each active member, the second column contains the current coordinator for each member, so each row contains a pair of one of the domain members and its coordinator.

Maintaining the AML is very important because the list is the main and primary reference to maintain the communication modules used by RIDX, for example, RIDX Router totally depends on AML to control routing messages between the sender and the receiver. The Authentication, Encryption and Tunnelling modules depend on this list always being maintained and periodically checked for continuous updates. The coordinator plays a major role in governing this process and maintaining it periodically.

MODULES AND GENERAL WORK OF RIDX

Initiation of Process

- **Initiating a Pipeline:** Initiating a pipeline can be done in two ways, one by creating it directly using a constructor (e.g. new Pipeline()) which is an instance of a sub-class of (Pipeline), the other way is to create a Pipeline Factory upon request. The following is by using the first method to create a Pipeline: Public Dpipeline (String props) throws PipelineException{ }.

The configuration parameters for this method are read from an XML file which contains all the parameters needed to configure the pipeline. If the pipeline was not created, an exception will be thrown, a wrong or missing parameter is mostly the possible reason that causes an exception. The RIDX UDP XML configuration file looks as follows (Figure 8).

Every element in the configuration file delineates one of the modules in the pack. For example, in Figure 8, a parameter is set to identify the node by assigning IP address and port number in 'Multicast' address and port parameters. The receiving and sending buffers are set to a size in bytes. Two main thread pools are set which include maximum and minimum number of threads per pool, and the policies related to it. The main thread pool is for handling RIDX data messages, the Auxiliary pool handles messages which are marked as Aux messages, for example, the Ping heartbeat message is marked as an Aux message, therefore, it will be processed in the Auxiliary pool threads. This method is very helpful for processing RIDX data messages quickly and separately from utility messages, because data messages do not need to wait until utility messages are processed especially if it is from the same sender. Ping, Failure Detection, Active List, Authentication and Synchronise encryption keys are considered as part of utility messages, therefore it will be processed separately by Aux Pool. Failure detection and Ping parameters are set to timeout in micro seconds to determine when nodes in group are continuously available or crashed. The last two parameters in Figure 8 are set to initialise the data flow control maximum credits and the shredding size of each message when processing the shredding module on XML

Figure 8. RIDX system configuration file

```
<config>
    <RIDX_UDP
    mcast_addr="${ridx.udp.mcast_addr:182.0.0.10}"
    mcast_port="${ridx.udp.mcast_port:45588}"
    mcast_recv_buf_size="25000000"
    mcast_send_buf_size="640000"
    loopback="false"
    discard_incompatible_packets="true"
    max_bundle_size="64000"
    max_bundle_timeout="30"
    use_incoming_packet_handler="true"
    ip_ttl="${ridx.udp.ip_ttl:2}"
    enable_diagnostics="true"
    use_concurrent_stack="true"
    thread_pool.enabled="true"
    thread_pool.min_threads="2"
    thread_pool.max_threads="8"
    thread_pool.keep_alive_time="5000"
    thread_pool.queue_enabled="true"
    thread_pool.queue_max_size="1000"
    Aux_thread_pool.enabled="true"
    Aux_thread_pool.min_threads="1"
    Aux_thread_pool.max_threads="8"
    Aux_thread_pool.keep_alive_time="5000"
    Aux_thread_pool.queue_enabled="false"
    Aux_thread_pool.queue_max_size="100"
    Aux_thread_pool.rejection_policy="Run"/>
    <PING timeout="2000" num_initial_members="3"/>
    <FD timeout="10000" max_tries="5"/>
    <VERIFY_SUSPECT timeout="1500"  />
    <pbcast.acknak retransmission="true"
    exponential_backoff="150"
    retransmit_timeout="50,300,600,1200"
    discard_delivered_msgs="true"/>
    <pbcast.router stability_delay="1000"
      desired_avg_router="50000"
     max_bytes="1000000"/>
    <AML_SYNC avg_send_interval="60000"   />
    <pbcast.AML print_local_addr="true" join_timeout="3000"
    view_bundling="true"/>
    <DFC max_credits="500000" min_threshold="0.20"/>
    <Shred shred_size="60000"  />
</config>
```

files. The XML configuration file is used to preserve the independency and scalability, each module is implemented by a separate Java Class; also each element can represent a layer in RIDX.

- **Pipeline Naming:** When a pipeline is created, a Universally Unique Identifier (UUID) is assigned to this pipeline, instead of using the pipeline address; we can set a more useful logical name for this pipeline. For example, the UUID creates an identifier such as: '29f96f2d0a77-9a0e-9581-7804-ae25e7c3', instead, we can set a more meaningful name that might illustrate the function of the pipeline, for example: 'No1-domain-accounting', this name is more understandable than the UUID. To set the logical name, a method is invoked to do so. The pipeline will hold the logical name until the pipeline is destroyed. Setting the logical name happens before connecting to a pipeline.
- **Connecting to Pipeline:** To join as a member to a domain, it needs to specify the name of the domain: Connect (String DomainName) throws PipelineClosed. A domain in RIDX is the group of members connecting to the same Pipeline name. When a user or client invokes this method, it checks the state of the domain if it already subsists. If it exists, it will check the state of the domain whether the domain is in close state or open (see Figure 6). If the domain name does not exist, then it will create a new domain name and the client will act as a coordinator for this domain member, therefore, the coordinator will be responsible for governing the initiated new group and controls the new members' joining process.

- **Retrieving Name and Address:** Generating an address generally happens in the lower bottom layer (RIDX UDP) module. If the state of the pipeline is closed or disconnected, we cannot retrieve the address, otherwise we use this method to retrieve the local address and the name of the domain.

- **Sending Multicast Message:** Sending a message in multicast mode needs to specify the source and destination addresses (Sender & Receiver Addresses) and also needs to serialise objects, then build a message according to the selected parts of the XML document that has been shredded from the shredder/assembler module. Then it sends the message; exceptions occur if the pipeline is disconnected or closed.

- **Message Receiver:** Pipeline can accept registration by message receiver, as a replacement for pulling out a message from the pipeline; this will save one thread to serve this issue, as a result, queuing messages is not the pipeline responsibility to maintain it, because it can get large if the receiver thread cannot process the data message swift enough. To register a Receiver Interface in a pipeline, all the call-backs will be invoked in case of AML changes or receiving messages.

The pipeline can hold different types of messages, one for XML data message, one for updating the Active Member List, and one for exchanging the State Transfer of any RIDX node.

- **Disconnect from Pipeline:** The following method is used to disconnect from the pipeline: public void disconnect(); when invoking this method, it will inform the coordinator by sending a disconnect message, this will remove the user (pipeline address for this user) from the domain members. The coordinator will issue a new member list and distribute it to all domain members. The pipeline will be in a disconnect state after a successful disconnect, this can be reconnected if the user requested it to do so.

- **Close a Pipeline:** Closing a pipeline means that all the resources for the RIDX modules will be released and destroyed; no more possible operations can be made if the state turns to close. The Java Runtime system will free all the resources and invoke a Garbage Collection process.

When requesting to transfer XML data initiated by the user at the data application layer, the system will initiate the first step by creating a pipeline process; this pipeline process is the handler between the user application layer and RIDX system. A set of properties belonging to the pipeline process is created at the time of initiation and then registering to a domain by specifying the name of this domain, e.g. Domain name ('ABC'), every member in the domain ABC will see each other. A request from the new joiner to get AML (Active Member List) from the coordinator, the coordinator accepts the new member and provides the new AML to all domain members.

The XML file sent by the user will be shredded into several chunks; the size of each piece is specified according to the parameter set in the RIDX XML configuration file. Each piece is encrypted and encapsulated in the RIDX message structure, each RIDX message contains all the information needed to be transferred until it reaches the final destination. The system will choose a different path for each chunk according to the Active Members List and transmit simultaneously in a UDP multicast reliable transmission. The next graph represents a sample of transmitting a XML file after shredding it and sending each partition into different paths from sender to receiver through virtual RIDX domain group, several modules will be invoked before the transmission operation starts, for example, the module Shredder/Assembler vertically partitions an XML file into chunks and prepares them into a table in the buffer

Figure 9. RIDX Internet cloud domain members: domain name 'ABC'

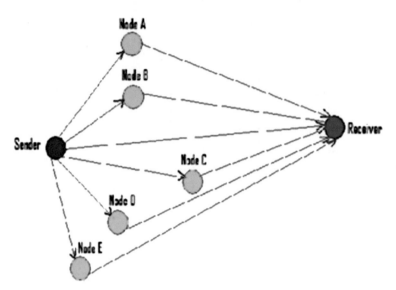

ready to be sent, then the table is handed to the next layer which is the Sequencer to sequence each chunk for maintaining the ordering and acknowledging messages by the receiver. The Sequencer holds the prepared sequenced chunks into a table in the buffer to be handled by the transport protocol to form all messages that will send all messages in a reliable multicast transmission.

At the final destination (Receiver), all messages are sequenced; therefore messages will be reordered, decrypted and joined/merged together until the XML file is constructed again into its original state. In case of any packet loss, the receiver requests the sender to re-transmit the lost messages. As in Figure 9, Nodes (A, B, C, D, E) work as routers to route all messages to the final destination.

Data Encryption in RIDX

The main methods used to encrypt messages are Asymmetric or Symmetric encryption methods. The two methods vary from each other in the usage of the encryption key. For example in symmetric encryption, the same key is used for both decryption and encryption of the data, whereas in the encryption using asymmetric algorithm, the keys are in pairs but are not equal, one key is applied for encryption and another key for decryption. Symmetric encryption is considered faster and easier than asymmetric encryption. The security strength of the encrypted data is related to the length of the key. Asymmetric encryption has one private key that is recognised just to a specific user who is using it to encrypt information; this private key should not be distributed and shared with any other users, and one public key that is known between different users (Matuszek, 1999).

Secret and private keys are very similar and are often used interchangeably. The difference is that secret keys are used for both encryption and decryption, while a private key is part of the public/private key system and is used only for decryption (Cryptography, 2005). In both cases, the key may be known only to a single person or a limited group of people in order to keep the key secure.

In RIDX, communication between domain members can be encrypted, this can be done in two scenarios, one is to assign the encryption process to the coordinator, or it can be preconfigured within the RIDX configuration setup files. The following will illustrate the two scenarios provided:

Scenario 1: (Asymmetric RSA)

The coordinator plays a primary role in controlling the process of distributing and synchronising encryption keys between all domain members. This mode depends on using customised encryption key size and configurable algorithms, and the key size according to the encryption methods used, for example, a 512 bytes as a default key size in case of Asymmetric encryption algorithm used, and a 128 bytes size for symmetric algorithms. When the Asymmetric algorithm has been chosen to be used in RIDX, then the configuration parameter needs to be set to a default key size (512 bytes), whenever a new domain member requests to join the domain, the coordinator will issue a new Active Member List (AML). The joiner requests a private key after sending its own public key to the coordinator, the coordinator generates a new private key and encrypts it with the public key which was sent by the requester (new joiner) and then sends it back to the joiner. The new member decrypts the key and extracts the private key to be installed and used for further data and communication encryption. Whenever there is a new AML issue, this process is repeatedly triggered again. During this process, if any messages have currently been sent, it will be queued in the outgoing and incoming queues until the coordinator regenerates the new key and synchronises the public/private keys with the new joiner and all other domain members.

Scenario 2: (Symmetric Triple DES)

Java (Sun – Oracle) provides a library for cryptographic support through JDK standard.

They provide two options for applying cryptographic methods using a key store file basis, one is abbreviated as 'JKS' (Java Key Store), and the other comes as an extension and it is abbreviated as 'JCEKS', (Java Cryptography Extension Key Store) as part of Java Cryptography Extension library 'JCE'. JCEKS uses Triple DES (Digital Encryption Standard) encryption which is considered as "stronger protection for stored private keys than JKS" (Java SunPKCS11, 2001). RIDX can be set up to use triple DES algorithm with the implementation of password protection based encryption (MD5) algorithm.

Using these methods in RIDX is considered much simpler to implement than the Asymmetric technique because it eliminates the complexity and the overheads of exchanging the encryption keys between domain members, therefore, it is faster in processing time. The key store file contains the secret key, which is generated by API key tool method provided within the Java JDK. This file must be synchronised with all domain members and all members must have the same file. This encryption technique can be used in any part of RIDX modules, and can encrypt any event of type MESSAGE without the need of a coordinator.

In the two scenarios, both parts of RIDX message (Data & Headers) can be encrypted, the encryption key version and the encryption identifier and all the information needed by the receiver can be attached to the message as a header.

Authentication in RIDX

The purpose of Authentication mechanism in RIDX is to authenticate any request of joining the domain and reject any attempt of un-authorised joining requests. This module is processed before the Active Member module (AML), whenever a joining request is received. The Authentication module initiates the authentication process, if the answer back from this module returns 'Allow' as a result, then it will pass the request to the AML module for further processing. Otherwise the authentication module will result in a reject state and discard this request and send back the security exception error along with the type of error.

The authentication process has some differences in the techniques used as in the certificate authorities approach. For example, the Public-Key Infrastructure (PKI) is a method of verifying users on a network, while a digital certificate is a reference from a neutral company that confirms the identity of an Internet site. Certificate Authority (CA) for instance (VeriSign) provides digital certificates, as for the registration authorities (RA) which operate to recognise the user and be a reference to it, and use a directory that holds the certificate and can revoke a company's digital status. The PKI technology is at the core of the digital certificates used in almost all transactions on the Internet. The PKI uses a cryptographic key pair, one of which is public and one which is private, to authenticate the owner of the certificate (Stanton, 2005).

The authentication mechanism used in RIDX is a software security token, which is simply a text encrypted string which is considered as a key for accessing the system. This key is a way to prove that the user is the one it is claiming to be. Tokens in Java are used as part of the utility library under the name 'Auth Token'. The Authentication Token utility is an abstract class used to generate and validate authentication tokens, and also using Java tokens is considered as a single step for the user to sign into the authentication system. An external file contains the authentication string token (credentials), this file has a limited access and can be accessed only by a certain RIDX process initiated by authentication class, and this process can extract the credentials from the file. The authentication token file is protected and distributed within RIDX configuration files.

Security threats can always be a concern when trying to establish a secured communication; therefore one single authentication file and unencrypted token string can always be a concern, especially when the hacker can sniff or spoof the message or have unauthorised access to the authentication token file. Hence another process is added to increase the level of security to the authentication process of member joining request. Encryption methods can be used to encrypt the token string while sending it for verification along with the certificate implementation. This identity certificate combines and binds the identity of a member along with the public key to form a digital signature. For example, certificates contain the domain member information which forms the identity of it along with the encryption/decryption public key. The next algorithm illustrates the authentication process using digital certificates and authentication tokens:

- A new member wants to join the domain by sending a joining request message to the coordinator along with its digital certificate.
- The domain coordinator checks the chain of the certificate and verifies if it is a valid certificate and decides if the member is trusted to continue with the joining request or not. If the certificate verification results return a negative state (Not Verified), then the coordinator responds back to the requester with a negative response with an exception error and no further action taken.
- If the coordinator verifies the certificate, then it will send an authentication request to the new joiner, which also contains the coordinator's certificate to be verified by the new domain joiner,

the message encapsulates the private key that will be used by the new joiner to encrypt all the next messages. The new joiner decrypts the message using the public key and verifies the certificate and extracts the private key.

- The new joiner responds to the coordinator and sends the authentication token, and encrypts the message using the private key which was sent by the coordinator.
- The coordinator verifies the authentication token string, if it is successfully authenticated or not, and then the coordinator passes the request to the Active Member List module to process the joining request.
- The AML module prepares a new list of all members including the new joiner; the list contains two columns paired with the coordinator's IP/Port address and all other member IP/Port addresses. The AML distributes the new public key encryption and synchronises the public key between all domain members including the new member.

The authentication process including the Public/Private encryption has five to six steps to authenticate, but it is acceptable, first because it preserves a higher security control and second this process does not happen very often, and triggers only when a new member wants to join the domain, and third, whenever a member joins or leaves the domain, RIDX ensures to issue new encryption keys to all members, in this case the new joiner cannot decrypt old messages and the member that has left the domain also cannot decrypt any current messages.

RIDX Transport Layer

The RIDX Transport Layer resides on the bottom of the RIDX pack modules (see Figure 5). It is responsible for sending and receiving data through LAN and WAN networks. This layer consists of three main modules and a set of supporting modules to implement and support the fully functional transport layer. The main modules are consequently ordered from bottom to top as Tunnelling, Router and RIDX UDP. The tunnelling module level is the bottom-most level; it encapsulates all messages coming from upper modules by multiplexing/de-multiplexing when sending data from one end to another. More discussion is made about Tunnelling, Routing and RIDX UDP in this chapter along with the supporting modules and their functionality.

In chapter 2, the author has discussed some Internet cloud services (SOAP, CORBA etc) and Access Security Modules (XACML etc), they all use the XML file structure as the intermediate, and they adopt XML as a communication file structure between these systems and services, also some of these systems and services work on top of TCP/IP Protocol or Standard UDP protocol directly or indirectly. For example in case of SOAP services, SOAP uses HTTP protocol as a communication method, whereas the latter uses TCP/IP protocol as a bottom-most transport layer for communication. In some other systems such as multimedia streaming services use standard UDP protocol as the bottom-most transport layer for its communication. One of the techniques used in Media Resource Control Protocol implemented a different method by using Real-Time Transport protocol (RTP). RTP protocol is considered as a sub-protocol of UDP (Internet Engineering Task Force (IETF) RFC 3550, 2003), there are two concerns of using this protocol first as it "can tolerate packet losses" and second, RTP protocol is formed within the structure of standard UDP protocol, this made RTP protocol inherit the characteristics of UDP protocol.

The motivation behind RIDX is to create a virtual network structure throughout Internet cloud as a platform, without the need to invest in several technologies in order to secure the communication within this virtual network, no additional hardware for creating VPN connection, and no third party solutions to automate the authentication process, or encryption or even depend on hardware routers to route messages. The ultimate goal is to establish a secured environment for data exchange, especially XML data files. In addition, to combine features from well known and widely spread protocols such as TCP and UDP into a system that can guarantee data delivery in a multicasting ability, along with an enhanced performance in terms of transmission speed, throughput, data security, and utilisation of the resources available. Section 4.1 gives an overview of the main characteristics for TCP and UDP protocols and how RIDX benefit from its features.

TCP AND UDP PROTOCOLS OVERVIEW

TCP and UDP protocols occupy the major share of Internet, LAN and WAN networks, and are used as a transport layer for most implementations. Between TCP and UDP, RIDX comes as a common ground that combines characteristics from both protocols; combining the reliability of TCP connectivity with a high transfer speed of UDP, RIDX was built to benefit from TCP and UDP and to perform the best out of them. The next sections contain an overview of TCP and UDP protocols, and a description of RIDX UDP. Some major differences are discussed between standard TCP and standard UDP, and then discuss the enhancements that have been made to construct and implement RIDX UDP.

Standard TCP

TCP is a highly developed and complex protocol. Nevertheless, although major improvements have been proposed and implemented over a period of time TCP has retained the most fundamental operations unchanged from the specification published in 1981 (RFC 793). The document 'Host Requirements for Internet Hosts' referenced at RFC-1122, specifies the amount of requirements for an implementation of the TCP-protocol. The 'TCP Congestion Control' in RFC-2581 is considered as the most significant document relating to TCP recently. It describes new techniques to pass up excessive congestion. Another document, written in 2001 (RFC-3168), described a new approach, which is 'Explicit Congestion Notification' (ECN), a form of mechanism to avoid congestion of signalling. In the early stages of the Internet, TCP occupied 95% of the total packets circulating on the Internet. Among the most familiar implementations that adopted TCP protocol were: e-mail family (POP3, SMTP and IMAP), Internet (HTTP and HTTPS), and other utilities such as Telnet and FTP. Its large extension has been tested for the original developers of its creation were outstanding.

Most recently, a new technique for controlling congestion was introduced and denoted as FAST-TCP which stands for 'Fast Active queue management Scalable Transmission Control Protocol' by developers from the California Institute of Technology. It detects congestion from delays in the queues experienced by packets to be sent to their destination. There is still an open debate on whether this is an appropriate symptom control congestion.

Operation Details

TCP connections are composed of three steps: establishing a connection, transferring the data and lastly ending the connection. To connect using the procedure called negotiation in three steps (3-way handshake); disconnection used a four-step negotiation (4-way handshake). When establishing the connection, initialising some values of the parameters is done in order to guarantee the delivery of the data is in order and to guarantee the healthiness of the communication.

Establishment of Bargaining

When a sender tries to send data to a receiver, usually the receiver opens a socket on a particular TCP port, and this port listens for any data being sent by the sender. This is called a 'passive open', plus the connection determines the server side. The connection on the client side performs an 'active open' port by sending a primary SYN packet to the receiver side (client) as part of the negotiation in three steps. The server side checks whether the port is open, i.e. if there is a process listening on that port. Should it not be, send to the client a response packet with the RST bit set, which means the rejection of the connection attempt? If we do open the port, the receiver side (server) would reply to the legitimate SYN request with a SYN/ACK. Lastly, the sender side (client) should reply with an ACK to the receiver (server), thus carrying out the negotiations in three steps (SYN, SYN/ACK and ACK) and establishing the connection step.

Sliding Window and Window Size

The acknowledgments (ACKs or Acknowledgments) of data between the sender and the receiver can benefit from it; the sender especially can understand network conditions between them. When a timer is employed during the transmission, both the sender and the receiver can adjust the performance of the data flow. To accomplish high performance and circumvent any congestion in the network in TCP, there are some techniques used by TCP protocol for controlling the flow of data (the sender sends as fast as the receiver can receive). For instance, one of the commonly used techniques is 'Sliding Window', which controls the transmitter to send information within the receiver's buffer and flow control algorithms, such as the algorithm for congestion avoidance (congestion avoidance), the slow start (Slow-Start), the fast retransmit, the fast recovery (Fast Recovery), and others.

The data bytes received is the window size that can be crammed into the receive buffer for the connection. The issuer may send a certain amount of data but you must wait for a nod of the window size update from the receiver.

An example would be: a receiver starts with a window size of x bytes received and then your window size is x - y and the transmitter can only send packets with a maximum size of data (x - y) bytes. The following packages received will reduce the size of the receive window. This situation will remain until the receiving application collects data from the receive buffer. For efficiency in networks of high bandwidth, you should use a larger window size.

End Connection

The completion phase of the connection uses a negotiation in four steps (four-way handshake), ending the connection from each side independently. When one of the two sides wants to end his side of the connection, it sends a FIN request message and the other party nods with an acknowledgement. Consequently, a classic off requires a pair of FIN and Acknowledgement packets from both sides.

Figure 10. Trading in three steps or three-way handshake

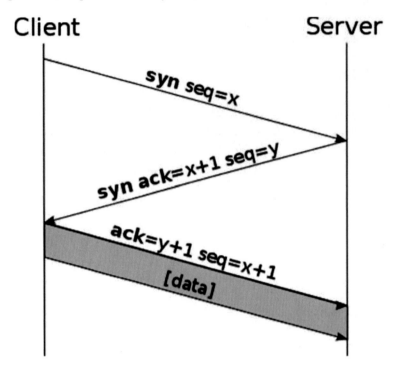

If one ended the connection but not the other, then the connection status is 'Half Open'. The side that has ended the connection cannot send more data but the other can still.

UDP Protocol

User Datagram Protocol is a transport level for exchanging datagrams. It allows sending datagrams through the network without having previously established a connection, since the same datagram includes enough addressing information in its header. Nor does it confirm or flow control, so that packages can anticipate each other, and it is not known if he has arrived correctly, and no delivery confirmation or receipt. Its primary use is for protocols such as DHCP, BOOTP, DNS and other protocols that exchange packets, or are not profitable with respect to the information provided, as well as streaming audio and video in real time, where broadcasts are not possible because of the strict delay requirements you have in these cases.

Description

The family of Internet protocols, UDP, presents a simple edge between the application and network layer. UDP does not provide any guarantee to deliver messages, and the source does not retain the states of the UDP messages that are sent to the network. It does the checksum on the data (payload) and the header. Any guarantees for transmission of the data should be done in a higher level.

Headers contain four fields from which two are optional. The 16-bit fields present the ports of the source and destination which identifies the origin and reception operation. Because UDP message is pertaining to state the message at the destination side, therefore the source may not know or ask for replies, and the source port can optionally be used, or else it should be reset to (0) The destination port field is mandatory and contains the destinations' port number. The data and the header length are calculated and set into the Length field, the 8-bytes length of the header in addition to the maximum 65,527-bytes length of data forms the maximum length number can be put in the length field, assuming that the data field contains no data, therefore the minimum length is 8-bytes. The 16-bit checksum field comprises the header data and a header with source and destination IP, protocol, the datagram length, and 0's to complete a multiple of 16, but not the data. According to IPv4, checksum field is optional, if not used it needs to be set to zeros, but as in the specification of IPv6 it does not.

The UDP protocol is used, for example, when you need to transmit voice or video and it is most important to speed to ensure that absolutely all the bytes arrive.

RIDX UDP PROTOCOL

RIDX UDP protocol is part of the transport layer for RIDX system. Transport layer consists of three main modules: RIDX UDP, ROUTER and TUNNEL respectively (see Figure 5). The following sections describe the main characteristics of each module with its functionality and major security threats to be considered especially on the OSI level. The common parts of this transport layer that are shared with other conventional protocols is the standardisation of port numbers and data transfer concept. The following points describe further:

Port Numbers

Port numbers are used to distinguish between different applications used by the sender and the receiver. Both sides of the connected parties have linked to an unsigned 16-bit number (a possibility of 65,536 different port numbers) assigned by application on both the sender and the receiver. It is calculated by the total range of 2 to the power 16, and covers 65,536 numbers, from 0 to 65,535. The port classification defines three classes: Registered, Dynamic (private) and Well-Known. The latter ports are assigned by the 'Internet Assigned Numbers Authority' (IANA), ranging from 0-1023; these ports are commonly used by the operating system.

Applications that use these ports are implemented as servers and are listening for connections. For instance: HTTP uses port number 80, SSH, FTP, Telnet, and SMTP uses consecutive port numbers 22, 21, 23 and 25. Users can connect to these ports on a temporary basis. The Registered port class represent services that are listed by a third party (registered port range:1024 to 49,151). Dynamic ports/private class is to be used by user and application customisation. Dynamic-private ports have no meaning outside the RIDX UDP connection in which they were used (dynamic range of ports/private: 49,152 to 65,535). Rules for port numbers are implied on the transport protocols (TCP, UDP and RIDX UDP).

Data Transfer

Data stream through Transport layer to be sent to the network. The Shredder/Assembler module in RIDX divides and partitions the XML file vertically into a byte stream returned from the application into segments (chunks) of appropriate size and add headers. Then, RIDX UDP hands over the resulting segment to the IP layer, where through the network, it arrives at the RIDX UDP layer of the destination entity. Sequencer in RIDX assigns sequence numbers in order to check that no segment is missing, which is also used to ensure that the packets have reached the target entity in the correct order. Assent RIDX returns a byte that has been received correctly, a timer on the origin of the consignment entity states timeout status if the packet did not acknowledge that it received within a reasonable time, therefore, the probable missing packet will then be retransmitted. The Assembler module checks that no damage happened to the data packet during shipment, and it is calculated by the issuer in every packet before being sent, and checked by the receiver.

RIDX Message Structure

The main components comprised in RIDX message are the body which is compulsory and an optional header. The body is always aimed for the last message's recipient, whereas the interpretation of the message is processed according to header entry. Binary or other types of data can be attached to the message body.

Message header considers an orthogonal relation with the main or primary content of the message, therefore, it is a useful feature to be offered for the user, and it is so helpful in accumulating the data to the message that does not affect the message body's interpretation.

For instance, headers perhaps employed to give digital signatures for an appeal comprised in the message's body. Therefore for example, an authorisation or authentication service can use headers for this purpose, and strip out the data to authenticate the digital signature. And when the authentication is confirmed, the remaining part of the message will pass to the higher pack of modules and process the whole body message. A very close observation of the message will assist in making the function clear as well as positioning the header as well as the elements of the body.

The RIDX message structure is similar to IPv6 packet; XML data is shredded into smaller chunks, encrypted and encapsulated into RIDX message (Data Field), then the message can be sent to other domain members (Grötschel, Alevras and Wessäly, 1998). The message structure is shown in Figure 11.

The RIDX message contains:

- **Message Headers:** Different methods can be used to operate headers, for example, one method is responsible to attach/add headers to a message, another method is to detach/delete, and so on. Headers are attached whenever data should not be put in the Data Field. Headers indicate that both communicated RIDX nodes formerly concurred leading that the semantic who rule the interpretation of the header entity, with the intention that the service understands precisely what to perform with the elements' value. When the service obtaining the respond does not interpret the meanings of the header value, then the message will refuse the entire request and return an error. Therefore, this error response has to be as an element of the respond message body and forms a unique component, and should be defined as part of the response mechanism answering back the client if any message interpretation error happens. In addition to describing the interpretation of nodes as mentioned above, a RIDX message may in an optional manner comprise the header entries specifying nodes which execute the processing of authorisation, business logic processing, encryption, persistence of state, etc. Headers assist to develop RIDX as a modular, extensible model of packaging, taking into account that the body element of RIDX message and the header entity is processed independently.

Figure 11. RIDX UDP message structure used in transport protocol layer

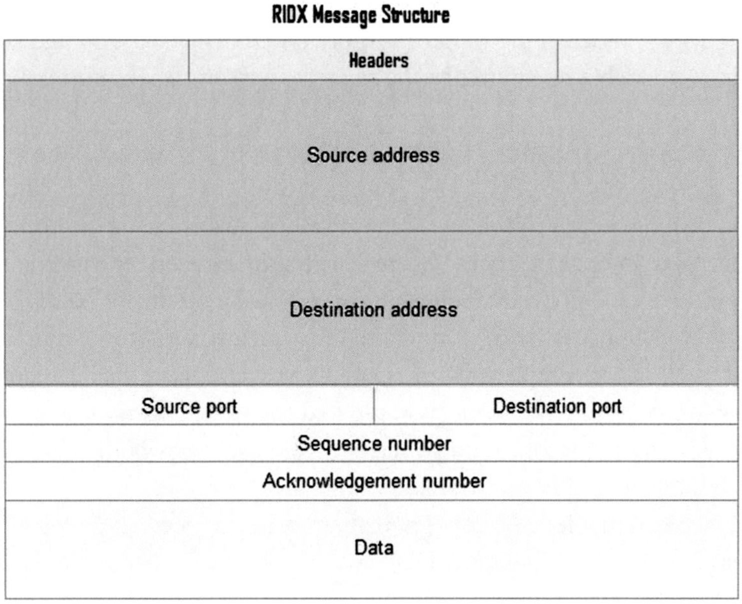

RIDX Message Structure

| Headers |
| Source address |
| Destination address |
| Source port / Destination port |
| Sequence number |
| Acknowledgement number |
| Data |

- **Source/Destination Address:** Usually the RIDX UDP transport protocol will fill the source address (Sender) automatically, but in some cases, the source wants the message responses to be delivered to a different address or other domain member.
- **Data Field:** It is the desired data to be transferred between domain members. RIDX message body comprises a payload devoid of not evident for hackers to realise and understand. Therefore RIDX is not only a cryptic model of packaging, but also a modular packaging model. In the body, sniffers see the message as a combination of character set entity that has no meaningful sequence assuming that there is no encryption applied yet, this is due to the vertical fragmentation of the original XML file by the Shredder module; then it is up to the service and its configuration to interpret the meaning of the message and perform the correct response. Pack of modules effectively offers a clear form for handling the payloads in a meaningful and significant way. Here, the word 'meaningful' means the domain member requests to initiate procedures in order to invoke the pack of modules desired to interpret the payload of the message.
- **Source/Destination Ports:** The port number (Socket Number) that will differentiate between RIDX instances; the socket number will also work as Pipeline identifier.
- **Sequence Number:** The sequencer module will generate sequence numbers to the shredded/fragmented data (chunks) from the original XML file. This sequence number will preserve the data ordering when merged in the destination side. And the destination node will rearrange messages, as well as identifying each segment of the data (Peterson and Davie, 2000).
- **Acknowledgement Number:** RIDX is a Multicast reliable delivery, therefore message acknowledgement is to guarantee delivery of all messages, in case of lost packets/messages, and the source will retransmit the lost packets.

Protocols Comparison Chart

Differences and similarities between the three transport protocols TCP, UDP and RIDX UDP can be summarised in Table 2; this table recapitulates the main features for each protocol and the differences between them.

The RIDX UDP transport layer employs IP Multicast with added features to become a Multicast Reliable Transport Protocol transmission functionality. In addition it is a reliable transmission by adopting a ACK-NACK (Acknowledgment & Negative Acknowledgment) message control mechanism, which provides as an option a 'first in first out' (FIFO) technique for guaranteed message delivery transmission. The summary in Table 3 concluded the differences between protocols and shows differences in terms of reliability. In Unicast and Multicast transmissions, the row header represents both unreliable and reliable model, and the column header represents the Unicast and Multicast transmission. Therefore, items in each cell in the table meet both the delivery mode and the transmission mode criteria together, for example, TCP protocol lie under Reliable and Unicast, which satisfies both characteristics, and RIDX UDP satisfies both Reliable and Multicast transmissions.

In order to define what Reliable Delivery Transmission is, we need to understand what unreliable delivery is; for example in Table 3, standard UDP is categorised as unreliable delivery transmission, because of the following two main reasons:

- Messages can be dropped during transmission because the size of the message is too big, and no fragmentation mechanism is invoked to control message size, or the buffer at the receiver has reached an overflow state, then the receiver starts dropping messages. Or the switch buffer (NIC/IP network buffer) can also reach an overflow state and start dropping messages.
- No guarantees at the receiver side to receive messages in sequence, because UDP sends messages without acknowledgement mechanism, which means that if any message is dropped during transmission, the receiver will not request any dropped messages from the sender to be resent. Furthermore, the sender does not know the state of the message whether received or not.

RIDX ROUTER

In RIDX domain, a group of RIDX instances that share the same domain name will form a domain group. RIDX conducts and maintains the communication between its members. The connectivity between domain members is governed by the domain coordinator through a periodic and continuous check up on the connection between all members. On the other hand, each RIDX instance checks and maintains the connectivity between other instances using a PINGER module; the latter is similar in functionality to the Ping utility used in TCP protocol. The coordinator and all other members schedule timed intervals to issue Ping packets in order to check if the connection is 'Alive'. In case of a crashed member or any lost connection to a node, the coordinator announces to all active members that a certain node has crashed, and drops the node from the active list, then distributes the list again to all members.

The Active Member List is a crucial element to be used by the RIDX router, it is considered as a routing table to the routing module. Routing in RIDX is considered to be a single delivery to a specific node and a Unicast forwarding message to the target machine or instance, and resides between the sender and the receiver, plus the routing node performs as an intermediate member for forwarding messages

Table 2. Protocols comparison chart

	TCP	UDP	RIDX UPD
Packet Ordering:	Orders of the data packets rearrange as specified.	No orders of the data packets. To preserve ordering, techniques should be added in a higher layer.	A sequencer module added to sequence the packets and manage the ordering
Error Checking:	Error checking is available	No option for error checking	Checking errors on a higher level
Headers:	Header is 20 bytes size	Header is 8 bytes size.	More headers can be added, the size of 8 bytes
Weight:	Sockets need 3 packets to set up the connection, afterwards data can be sent. Also responsible for congestions and reliability control.	Lightweight protocol, no tracking connections	Lightweight protocol, no need to track connections because connection is already established
Data Stream:	Interpret the data as a byte stream, bounded in a segment data size	Data Stream has no boundaries while packets has, data integrity checked only on arrival, packets are sent individually	Data Stream has no boundaries while packets has, data integrity checked only on arrival, packets are sent individually
Transmission speed:	Slower than UDP and RIDX UDP because of errorchecking, 3 way handshaking…etc	Faster than TCP because there is no error-checking for packets	Result showed that it is faster than TCP protocol
Reliability of	An absolute guarantee for	No guarantee at all for the	A feature was added (Ack-
	TCP	**UDP**	**RIDX UPD**
data:	the data to reach destination	data to reach destination	Nack) & sequencer to guarantee delivery and order
Operational:	3 way handshaking or 4 way handshaking to establish a connection	No need to establish a connection	Connection already established in step ahead by Pipeline registration
Reliability of connection:	Reliable on Two way Connection	Reliable on one way Connection	Reliable on Multi Way Connection
Flow Control:	Contains Flow Control technique	No option for data flow control	A Data Flow Control (DFC) module was added

from the sender to the ultimate destination. RIDX routing module is designed to route messages only for a one level depth or distance, and the router can only route a message to the final destination and not to another RIDX router. For example, if a domain contains four domain members (A, B, C and D), and member A wants to send a message to D, the possibility in our case here has three possibilities to send from A to D, one by sending messages directly from A to D, or sending from A through B to D, or sending from A through C to D. Node B cannot route the message to C through D.

Table 3. Summary of protocols differences

	Unreliable Delivery	Reliable Delivery
Unicast Transmission	U D P	T C P
Multicast Transmission	IP Multi-cast	RIDX UDP

Standard UDP and RIDX UDP share the same characteristics in terms of operational transmission; both protocols do not have a dialogue for implicit handshaking model as in the case of TCP protocol, RIDX rather uses customised modules at the application level. This technique can save the operational processing time at the communication level and avoid the overhead of requiring special paths or prior communication setup to transmit data. Therefore, setting up the communication ground between all RIDX domain members prior to transmission time can save communication processing time, improve the transmission speed and as a result improve the overall performance of data interchange. Section 4.1.2 showed that UDP protocol is considered as a non-reliable protocol which means no guarantees to deliver data and no consideration of data integrity or message ordering. The RIDX system has well thought-out these shortcomings by adding modules to support the transport layer and modules that the transport layer is set on top of, such as routing and tunnelling modules (see Figure 5).

The RIDX Router module is a simple yet effective technique to forward messages. It simply reads and interprets a stateless nature of RIDX UDP message by reading the Source/Port and Destination/Port addresses together with the headers of the message (see Figure 11). If the destination address does not match the routers' address, then the router looks up into the active

member list to match the address with one of the addresses within its list, and if it exists, it directly forward the message to its destination. If the address does not exist then it will check the headers for a specific code parameter or any attached instructions. In certain cases some instructions or parameters can be attached to the message in order to pass these instructions to other members. For example, when one of the members resides behind a firewall and the group members need to maintain communication with the hidden member through a dedicated router; this case is discussed more in section 4.5 when applying the tunnelling technique.

OSI AND SECURITY THREATS

The OSI model contains different layers, and each one has its own security risks, which developers are working on overcoming. The physical layer is a layer that must be approached from a physical point of view, because access to this layer is most likely to come from outside the device level. The threats to the physical layer include people taking the equipment itself, packet sniffing, tapping, electric failure or disaster damage.

These threats can be combated by using identifying badges, locks and surveillance equipment to reduce the exposure of outsiders to the equipment as well as sniffer equipment to identify leaks on the cabling. To protect against disasters, electromagnetic shielding and distributed data backups may be used along with backup power supply.

Establishing the identity by knowing the MAC address occurs on the data link layer; at this layer, spoofing this address can occur at the upper layer. Additionally, faults when introduced can cause loops with spanning tree protocols. There is vulnerability at this layer with the use of virtual LANs, where the interconnection of LANs and wireless LANs with VLAN policies can be used to perform VLAN hopping, creating data pathways to bypass firewalls and subnet addressing.

These threats can be mitigated by separating the sensitive areas from the rest of the physical network and by using security at other layers to establish security for VLANs. Wireless networks must be secured and unauthorised wireless access points should be detected and removed as soon as they are discovered.

VPNs also provide a level of security at this layer by allowing encrypted data transfer. Network Intrusion Detection (NID) systems can be implemented here to watch the data and look for suspicious packets.

At a third layer, security controls are a challenge for both Internet and routing protocols. Security threats can be used such as route and address spoofing, using a machine's own address to send out malicious packets that appear to be from within the network. Firewalls that can be configured at the edge of a network to closely examine packets coming in from outside a network will reduce the chances of these kinds of attacks. Routing controls and filters should be used alongside ARP monitoring software. IPSec will also prevent insertion at the transport layer of any packets.

Error checking occurs at the transport layer and uses UDP or TCP protocols to route packets around the network and ensure successful delivery of data. When the transport layer receives packets, which are not well defined, some protocols have difficulty handling those packets. This is the layer where Denial of Service (DOS) and DDOS attacks occur (Stanton, 2005).

The solution to problems at this layer is the use of firewalls with stateful packet inspection and dynamic NAT (Arizona Enterprise Architecture, 2005). Some controls used to filter unwanted packets to prevent the DOS attacks; these controls can use software or hardware devices such as firewalls to do so (Arizona Enterprise Architecture, 2005). Part of the security from this layer involves the methods used in the session layer to implement encryption and prevent man in the middle attacks; SSL and SSH also come into play here.

The session layer begins, manages and ends dialogues between devices or applications (Song, 2004). At this layer, application program interfaces (APIs) such as NetBIOS and remote procedure calls (RPCs) allow communication among the upper layer applications. It is also at this layer that problems with authentication and session identification can occur, as can brute force attacks and information leakage. It is feasible to encrypt passwords alongside SSL, SSH or transport layer security (TLS), with wireless TLS when required, to provide greater security.

Expirations and timeouts can also improve security at the session layer (Mazurczyk and Szczypiorski, 2009).

The presentation layer handles the compression, encryption and standardisation of the data for the application layer to the session layer to remove differences in the format of data. Unicode vulnerabilities can allow users access to the root directory when it is kept in the same place as the files for the Internet. Buffer overflows are also an issue in the presentation layer, when temporary storage areas are flooded with more information than the interface can handle. The vulnerabilities of input weaknesses can be limited by careful coding and testing interfaces before implementation (Stanton, 2005).

The application layer is perhaps the most difficult to keep secure because of the wide variety of applications in use. Back doors, security flaws, which are inherent or written unintentionally into the application code, and new threats that were not apparent when the application was written, are all factors at this layer. Trojans, viruses, worms, spyware attacks and password issues all come into play at the application layer. The use of strong passwords and enforcement of password policies can reduce issues with access, and application firewalls can reduce the misuse of applications. Digital certificates using PKI and encryption can also assist in network security. Additionally, anti-virus software and anti-malware programs can keep machines free of Trojans, adware and spyware (Mazurczyk and Szczypiorski, 2009). SQL injections, cross-site scripting and parameter tampering are three very common application layer attacks which require a new way of approaching security. In some cases, there is a need for testing of the application before it is put into production, but in other cases, companies are justified in bringing in outside companies to test for weaknesses in the network's application layer (Stanton, 2005).

In building any network, there are many things to be aware of that can create vulnerabilities in the system, but with research and persistence, a network administrator can plan for most instances of failure and keep the majority of the network and its data safe. Backups of data and a good knowledge of the physical and virtual layout of the network are imperative for keeping most of the network assets from becoming vulnerable to attack from inside the company or outside (Fielding, 2007).

Tunnelling

Firewalls stop any attempt to contact an internal method from outside the corporation through the Internet on other open ports (Stanton, 2005). Firewalls will moreover evade users of internal networks from communicating with particular Internet sites which could be offensive or risky (Shay, 2004). The firewall performs at the OSI model's layers three and four through looking packets for particular kinds of headers. So, firewalls vary from file safety as anyone inside the corporation can supposedly contact files behind the firewall, whereas security of files presents internal safety against staff of a corporation (Chaudhury, 2005).

One of the obstacles that can face RIDX is conducting proper communication when an RIDX instance resides behind a firewall. Due to a great risk in using public Internet communication, organisations use a firewall to protect the organisation against attacks, and impose access control. For that reason, firewalls mostly prevent the connection from outside to inside, but allow some inside applications to connect to outside services and machines.

Tunnelling is a protocol that encapsulates other protocols, and provides a mechanism to allow RIDX to operate through firewall systems and security gateways (Figure 12).

The question we need to ask is: "Is it feasible to implement VPN tunnelling between all RIDX instances using external or third party hardware and software?" In order to answer this question, we need to look at different aspects when applying it.

First, implementing tunnelling can be expensive mostly due to the need for different technologies involved, such as hardware, software and security network specialists to implement and maintain it (Leonov, 2004).

Second, when hosting RIDX instances internally in the intranet organisation, tunnelling is not applied, and still the transferred data can be exposed by man-in-the-hub.

Third, when using embedded tunnelling mechanism within RIDX modules, performance is a considerable factor that needs to be investigated. Therefore, an experiment has been made to measure the throughput before and after a VPN tunnelling on different data frame sizes. More details about the experiment test results are discussed in chapter 5.

Considering the communication structure of RIDX, which depends on IP networking (multi-casting), RIDX has followed the recommendation stated by the Internet Engineering Task Force organisation (IETF) standards by using Layer-2 Tunnel Protocol (L2TP) over IP networking. The second available option for tunnelling is widely used especially in a Windows environment such as point-to-point tunnelling technique (PPTP), but the latter does not comply with IETF standards, and the encryption method which is used for this tunnelling type is not considered strong enough compared with Internet Protocol Security (IPSec) encryption method used with L2TP (Wanger et al, 2006). One of the two main schemes in IPSec is encapsulating the message using ESP, which stands for 'Encapsulating Security Payload'. Most implementations of IPSec use ESP as a base module, as it is considered to be more secure than the other IPSec scheme pointed as Authentication Header (Arturo Perez et al, 2006). Therefore, RIDX

Figure 12. Creating a tunnel between a node behind the firewall

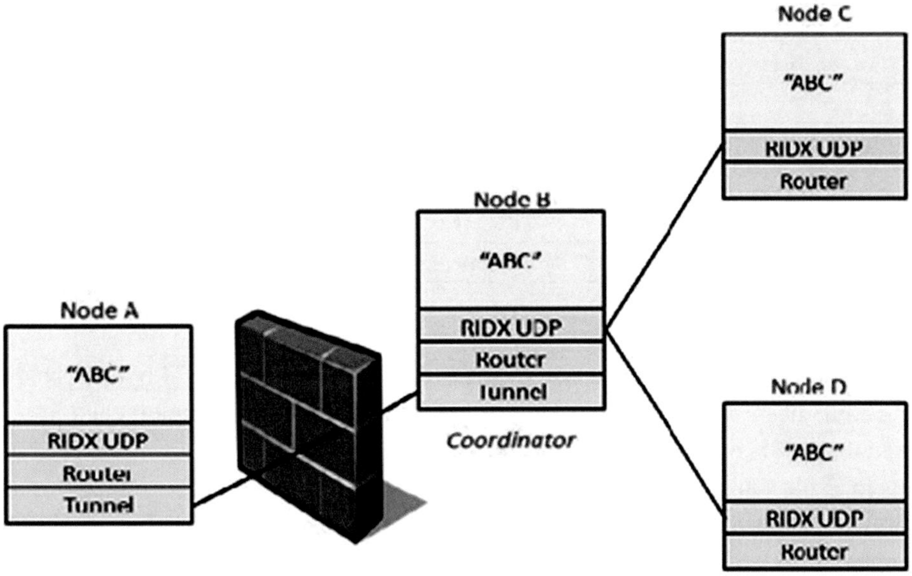

has adopted the L2TP/IPSec/ESP methods for tunnelling through firewalls and Internet cloud. A test has been made to measure the performance of tunnelling the connection over Layer-2 Tunnelling Protocol using IPSec/ESP scheme, and the results are as shown in chapter 5.

EXPERIMENTAL RESULTS AND CASE STUDIES

Ridx Tunnelling Performance Test

In a previous section, Tunnelling was presented as part of RIDX modules and a technique to create a secured connectivity between RIDX domain members as well as how it can be applied in different situations. For example one case is to penetrate the firewall, or in some cases, through an un-trusted Internet cloud, or maybe across shared infrastructure network connectivity. The purpose of tunnelling is to create secured layer between two RIDX systems or multi tunnelling connection between domain group members. A test is made to measure two things:

1. The throughput before and after tunnelling in Megabit per second for different frame sizes.
2. The Latency before and after tunnelling in microsecond for different frame sizes.

The test is conducted on SUN 3 GHz with 4GB RAM on 2.6.9-14 RedHat Enterprise Linux 4 / 64 bit system that the kernel natively include and support the IPSec, and the tunnelling passes through a CISCO switch which is 1GBps along with Gigabit Ethernets installed on RIDX nodes, a SUN JVM 1.6.0_3 is installed on Two nodes which contain RIDX system. The tunnelling connection was established between two nodes, and all messages were sent in a unidirectional way (only one way) from node A to node B,

Table 4. Throughput Data of VPN (Before and after)

Frame Size	Throughput BEFORE Tunnelling	Throughput AFTER Tunnelling
64-bytes	34.4 Mbps	7.1 Mbps
128 bytes	68.7 Mbps	12.3 Mbps
256 bytes	137.3 Mbps	19.2 Mbps
512 bytes	**210.4 Mbps**	**26.8 Mbps**
1024 bytes	190.5 Mbps	33.5 Mbps

and different frame sizes used, the frame sizes varied from 64 bytes up to 1024 bytes. Table 4 shows the experimental results of measuring the throughput before and after tunnelling on each frame size used. Traffic generated at 100% of the line rate of (1000 Mbps).

The results in Table 4 and Figure 13 showed that there is a significant effect on the throughput when using tunnelling techniques over IP networking, The effect of tunnelling varied in relation to the frame size, for example, on 64 bytes frame size, the throughput has dropped down by 79% approximately, and on 1024 bytes frame size, the throughput has dropped down by around 82%. The significant effect was noticed on the 512 bytes frame size which dropped down the throughput by 87% and the second highest throughput drop down is on 256 bytes frame size.

The delay of delivering the packets from node A to node B is measured before and after tunnelling, the tunnelling test is applied under the same setup conducted above, time is measured in microseconds for 1 packet traffic per second. Different frame sizes are used and varied from 64 bytes up to 1450 bytes. Table 5 shows the result of this test.

The results showed that there is a noticeable effect on the packet delay time when conducting the tunnelling techniques, the delay time fluctuates depending on the frame size used, for example a significant jump in delay time by almost 3 times before and after tunnelling, was noticed when using 1024 bytes frame size and above.

As a result of this experiment, using tunnelling technique between all RIDX nodes needs a significant amount of overhead processing, although the results showed that there is considerable latency when using tunnelling techniques, consequently, choosing tunnelling in certain situations is acceptable where RIDX resides behind a firewall and has limited access in and outside the RIDX cloud. A module TUNNEL is responsible for this process. In all cases, there must be at least two ports open through firewall inside-out to be able to connect and conduct the tunnelling.

As in Figure 12, the initial process of conducting a secured tunnel starts from (Node A) which is assumed to be behind the firewall by requesting to join a domain from the coordinator, the coordinator accepts the new joiner, Node A establishes the secured connection after the coordinator accepts it, then (Node B) the coordinator announces that (Node A) is only accessible by (Node B). Eventually, if any RIDX node in the cloud other than Node B tries to ping (using the Pinger Module) Node A, it will return a negative response and will fail, therefore Node B will act as a router for all messages to/from Node A.

Nevertheless, tunnelling technique in RIDX has several downsides. First, using Node B as a dedicated router might exhaust and consume the resources from Node B. second, It isn't always possible to control firewalls owned by a third party to setup and enable the desired ports needed to establish the tunnelling.

Figure 13. Tunnelling Throughput Before and after

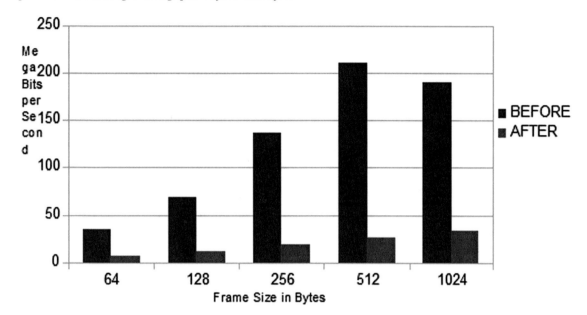

RIDX Performance Test Parameters

A test is conducted on SUN 3 GHz with 4GB RAM on 2.6.9-14 RedHat Enterprise Linux 4 / 64 bit system, a CISCO switch of 1GBps, SUN JVM 1.6.0_3. Each node (box) contains RIDX system, it sends number of M messages to all cloud nodes; receiver can be a sender at the same time, the timer starts when first message is received, again the timer will stop when last message is received, number (M) and size (S) of messages is known to all RIDX nodes. The computation of message rate in each RIDX with its throughput is calculated by multiplying {number of senders N} times {number of messages M}. A configuration file contains same parameters for all RIDX nodes:

- N = 4 then 6 then 8, senders are same receivers, that means N equals to number of RIDX nodes also
- M = 1,000,000

Table 5. Before and after VPN one-way tunneling

Frame Size	Delay BEFORE VPN tunnel (µs)	Delay AFTER VPN tunnel (µs)
64 bytes	165 µs	315 µs
128 bytes	169 µs	334 µs
256 bytes	171 µs	374 µs
512 bytes	196 µs	445 µs
1024 bytes	228 µs	612 µs
1450 bytes	**260 µs**	**736 µs**

Figure 14. Delay before and after tunnelling

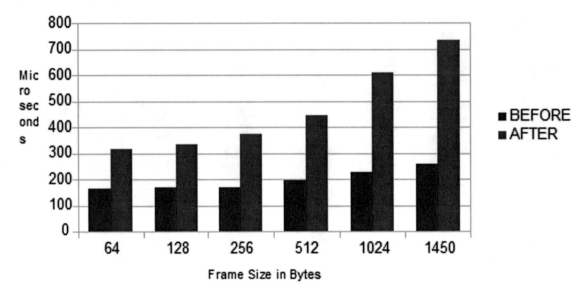

- S = 1 then 2.5 then 5 KB the size of each message

Experimental Results

The computation of message rate = (M * N) / T, where T is the total time of receiving all messages. Therefore, X & Y axis represents (S) and (Rate & throughput) simultaneously. For example: a collection of data results when the test is done, we need to calculate the average rate of number of messages received per second, this can be done by summing up the data collected and divide it by (N), then we calculate the throughput by multiplying the (S * average message rate) (FIX Protocol Ltd, 2009).

When compared standard TCP against RIDX UDP, a TCP & UDP variance between four to ten nodes, we notice that the TCP begins at 49 MB per Second until it drops down to 34 MB per second, on the other hand, RIDX UDP begins at 56 MB per Second until it drops down to 51

MB per second, this shows that a significant better performance accomplished by RIDX UDP. But we also notice that when S = 2.5k, UDP drops down from 94 to 65 MB per second, and the same for larger message size; this is due to Maximum Transmission Unit system OS kernel parameter limitation to size of 1500, so whenever message size gets large and exceeds the Maximum Transmission Unit size, then the UDP packet split into more IP packets,, reasoning more delays to following packets, this problem we do not find it in TCP protocol because it creates IP packets which is always under than Maximum Transmission Unit size, and Shredder/Joiner modules is responsible of keeping the MTU size controlled by RIDX.

Case Study 1: Four Domain Members

This test is conducted on 4 RIDX domain members, Node A, B, C and D. Each node is capable of sending, receiving and routing messages at the same time; therefore, each node will send 4000000 messages and will receive 4000000 messages in total. For example, Node A will send 1000000 messages to node

B; in this case node C and D will act as routers. And then node A will send 1000000 messages to node C; in this case node B and D will act as routers, and so on. While node A sends messages, Node B is also sending 1000000 messages to node A and in this case node C and D acts as routers, in the same sense, node D sends 1000000 messages to node C while node A and B will act as routers, and so on. The last considered case is when node A for example sends 1000000 messages to itself (node A to node A), in this situation the nodes B, C and D will act as routers. The loopback is not used in any test, and the sender must use other nodes to route back the messages to and from the sender.

The test was conducted on three different message sizes. The first message size is 1K, which is less than the MTU size, as mentioned in the previous section, the 1K size in this test is chosen to eliminate the possibility of fragmenting any messages which is over the MTU size (1.5K). Then the 2.5K and 5K message sizes were chosen to test the effect of the message fragmentation done by the operating system on the performance of the RIDX system, also to measure the effect of the use of the node resources (such as CPU time, Memory...etc).

The following next two graphs illustrate the test results, one for measuring the message rate which shows the number of sending messages per second per message size, and one for measuring the throughput rate which represents the capability of transmitting Megabits per second per message size. The results below show a comparison between RIDX UDP and standard TCP under the same configuration environment setup (Figure 15).

Figure 15 shows a comparison of the message rates between RIDX UDP and TCP for various message sizes. A significant improvement is noticed when using RIDX UDP over TCP.

For example, on 1K message size, RIDX sent about 56 thousand message per second, whereas TCP sent about 49 thousand message per second. On 2.5K message size, RIDX sent about 37 thousand message per second compared to 31 thousand message per second sent by TCP, The last comparison based on 5K message size again showed better rating for the RIDX UDP over TCP with 21 & 17 thousand messages per second consequently.

Figure 16 shows a comparison of the message throughput between RIDX UDP and TCP for various message sizes. A significant improvement is noticeable using RIDX UDP over TCP on all message sizes. The throughput for example on 5K message size in TCP has achieved around 89MB/Sec while RIDX UDP has exceeded 107MB/Sec. On 2.5 message size, TCP has achieved around 79MB/Sec while RIDX has achieved around 94MB/Sec. And on 1K message size, TCP reached to 49MB/Sec while RIDX reached to around 56MB/Sec.

Case Study 2: Six Domain Members

The test parameters and the setup environment is the same setup explained in section 5.2, and these settings were used in all case studies that measure the message rate and the throughput. Figures 17 and 18 shows the comparison results between RIDX UDP and TCP, it shows the comparison of message rate and the throughput comparison respectively, In this case study, 6 members have formed the domain and established a connectivity between each other. Every domain member holds a list of other domain members in a form of paired field list which contains the coordinator IP address and the IP addresses/Port Numbers for all members. Each member will send 1000000 messages to every member in the domain; therefore, each member will send 6000000 messages and receive 6000000 messages in total including the loopback messages, as explained in the case study 1, the loopback here means that the node will send messages to itself through the domain members and not using the internal loopback.

Figure 15. Message Rate for 4 Members

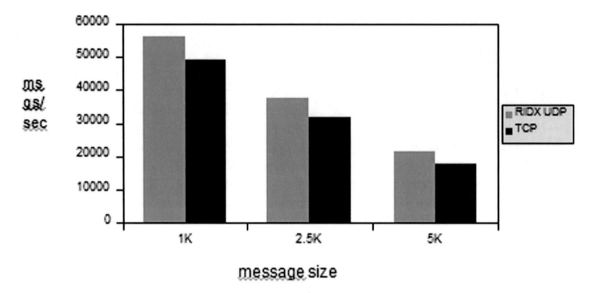

Figure 17 shows a significant improvement using RIDX UDP over TCP on a 1K message size, RIDX has sent about 52 thousand message per second, whereas TCP sent about 44 thousand message per second. On the other hand, the 2.5K and 5K message sizes has ranged nearly closed to each other when comparing the message rate between RIDX and TCP.

In Figure 18, the results show that there is a significant improvement using RIDX UDP over TCP on both 1K and 5K message sizes. But the throughput on 2.5K message size on both RIDX and TCP has achieved almost the same rate which varied between 76 and 77 MB/Sec.

Figure 16. Throughput for 4 Members

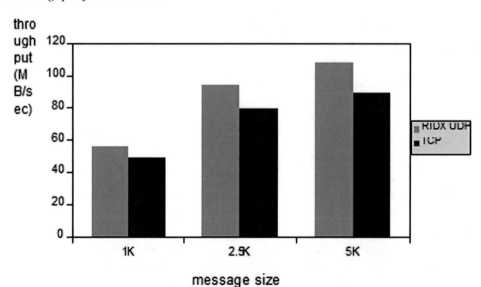

Figure 17. Message Rate for 6 Members

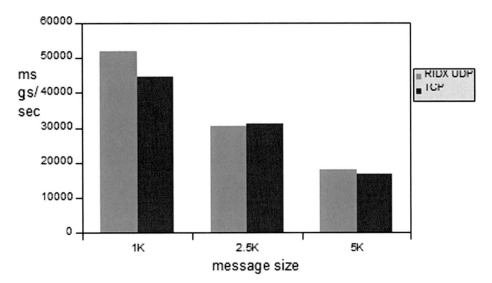

Case Study 3: Eight Domain Members

In this case study, the same test parameters have been used as in the previous case study, but adding another two members to the domain to become a total of 8 members in the same domain, and to study the effect of number of the domain members on message rate and the throughput. Every member will send, receive and route simultaneously 1000000 messages to/from each domain member, the total messages would be 8000000 per node. Using the multicasting techniques via multi threading pool of IP multicast, this gave the ability to send messages from one member simultaneously to all other members, and receive messages from all members at the same instance, and also routes all the messages that are not targeted the node.

Figure 19 shows the message rate comparison test results between RIDX and TCP on different message sizes.

The results showed in Figure 19 that there is a significant improvement using RIDX UDP over TCP on a 1K message size, RIDX was capable of sending around 50 thousand messages per second, whereas TCP sent around 42 thousand messages per second. While the 2.5K and 5K message sizes has achieved almost the same message rate.

In Figure 20, the results showed that there is also a significant improvement on throughput using RIDX UDP over TCP on 1K message size. The 2.5K and 5K message sizes both achieved almost the same throughput rate with a slight improvement on 5K message size to RIDX UDP (86MB/Sec to RIDX against 84MB/Sec to TCP).

Case Study 4: Ten Domain Members

This last case study has used 10 domain members and joined in a single domain. The configuration setup and the environment parameters were preserved for consistency purposes and used the same setup as in the previous case studies. The connection between all members was established and by default,

Figure 18. Throughput for 6 Members

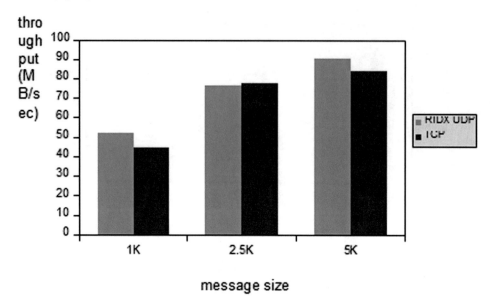

the coordinator governs this process. As in previous case studies, each node is going to send 1000000 messages for each domain member including itself, therefore each member will send in total 10,000,000 messages and receive the same. At any instance, each node can send, receive and route messages to/ from all members at the same time.

Figures 21 and 22 shows the results for message rate and throughput of this test.

Figure 21 shows a significant improvement using RIDX UDP over TCP on a 1K message size, RIDX has sent about 51 thousand message per second, whereas TCP sent about 34 thousand message per

Figure 19. Message Rate for 8 Members

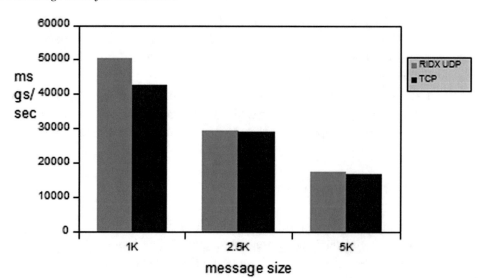

Figure 20. Throughput for 8 Members

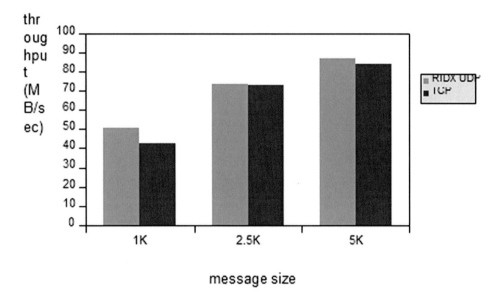

second. On the other hand, the 2.5K and 5K message sizes has ranged nearly closed to each other when comparing the message rate between RIDX and TCP.

In Figure 22, the results show that there is a significant improvement using RIDX UDP over TCP, RIDX throughput has achieved around 51MB/Sec whereas TCP throughput has achieved around 34MB/Sec. But the throughput on 2.5K and 5K message sizes on both RIDX and TCP has achieved almost the same rate which varied between 65 and 81 MB/Sec.

Test Results Discussion

Many factors could affect the results when conducting the experiments, some of these factors have a direct effect, and other factors have an indirect effect. In this section, the author wanted to shed light on some of these factors, and also study the consequence of the experiment test on the resources used during these tests, such as CPU time, Memory usage...etc. In section 5.2, the configuration parameters were set to be as a fixed setup for experimental tests for all the case studies conducted. The purpose of setting up the same configuration parameters and the same environment setup is to study the effect of the results when expanding the domain by adding members to the domain in terms of message rate, throughput, memory usage and CPU processing time, and to pinpoint the important parameters that might have an influence of the results. By identifying these parameters, it can be adjusted to enhance the performance and achieve better results.

A Comparison between the Case Studies Results

Figure 23 compares RIDX against TCP on message rates between the 4 case studies (5.3.1 to 5.3.4) above, and groups them according to number of domain members and the size of the message. Each bar represents the number of messages sent per second per domain member. The X axis represents the

Figure 21. Message Rate for 10 Members

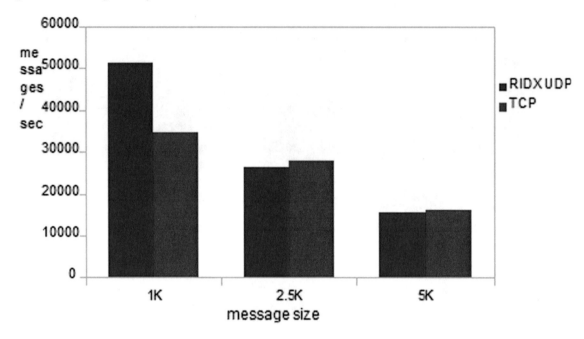

number of domain group (between 4 to 10 members per domain), and the Y axis represents the number of messages scaled in 10000 messages.

Figure 22. Throughput for 10 Members

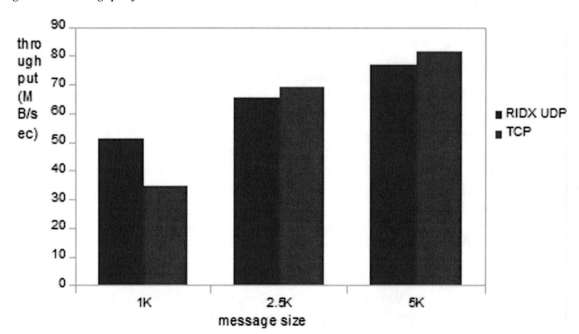

Figure 23. Message Rate Scalability

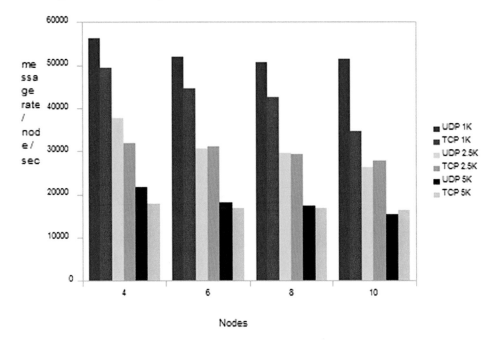

Figure 24 compares RIDX against TCP on message throughput between the 4 case studies (5.3.1 to 5.3.4) above, and groups them according to number of domain members and the size of the message. Each bar represents the Megabits sent per second per domain member. The X axis represents the number of domain group (between 4 to 10 members per domain), and the Y axis represents the throughput in Megabits per second scaled in 20MB/sec.

The comparison graphs in Figures 23 and 24 showed that there was a slight affect in both the message rate and the throughput to the number of members per domain, it can be noticed that this digression happens when the number of domain members increase. The cause of this affect might have a couple of reasons that influenced the results. First, as mentioned earlier, in all case studies, the test setup and the environment parameters has set to the same setting regardless the number of members involved, therefore Data Flow Control (DFC) might affect the message rate and the throughput because number of credits in this module was set statically in a fixed number and was not set according to number of nodes, and when setting the number of credit parameter less than the required, it will slow down the data flow between domain members, this parameter can have a direct effect on both the message rate and the throughput. Second, the network switch might have reached to an overwhelmed state and starts to drop packets which lead to retransmitting the dropped packets again and this process might delay the delivery especially in a reliable packet transmission as in RIDX case.

RIDX Processing Time and Memory Usage

During the experimental tests, a log files were set to collect all the data results from the experimental outputs, the log file includes number of messages sent, the system time in Micro seconds, number of messages sent per second, the throughput per second, the free and total memory in kilobytes. The purpose

Figure 24. Throughput Scalability

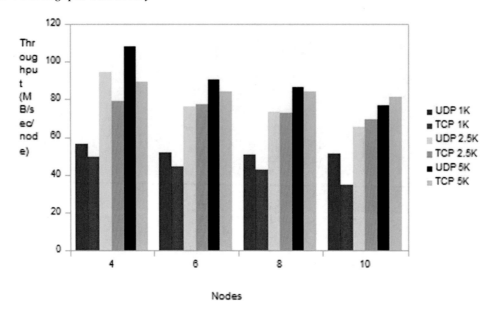

of this data log file is to calculate the average usage of the memory and the average CPU time needed to finish the transmission task to all the messages. A sample test result for both RIDX UPD as in table 7and Standard TCP as in Table 8 for a message size 1K and number of messages (1000000) will be sent by each member simultaneously in a 4 domain members, the throughput is calculated for each member, and the average throughput for all members. The parameters for this test along with the log file interval are shown in Table 6.

The test results for the configured parameters as shown in Table 7.

The output results represented in table 7 shows that the average free memory during the transmission period is about 284 Megabyte, and the total memory reserved by RIDX for the full operation is about 403 Megabyte. The actual usage of the total memory averaged to 119 Megabytes. The total physical memory is 4Gegabytes of RAM thus the percentage of the actual memory used is about 3%, and the percentage of the actual memory used from the reserved memory for this operation is about 30%. These percentages are well acceptable to complete a successful full transmission.

Table 7 represents the log data file for only one RIDX domain member, the other three domain members was setup to log the data in a similar way, and each domain member holds its own log file which contains the same parameters. To consolidate the four domain members' data log, the summary of the four log files are discussed as follows:

- An IP address and a port number was set to identify each domain member, the summation of number of messages received and the time needed to receive all the messages, also the percentage of the loss rate, and the message rate along with the throughput. The summation results per node as the following:

    182.100.3.15:46280:

    Number of messages expected =4000000, Number of messages received=4000000 (loss rate=0.0%), received=4GB, time=71054ms, Messages/Sec=56295.21, throughput=56.3MB

Table 6. The configuration parameters to setup and run the RIDX performance test program

Log Interval	100000 Bytes
Message Size	1000 Bytes
Number of Senders	4 Senders
Number of Messages	1000000 Messages
Number of Members	4 Members

    182.100.0.15:52377:

    Number of messages expected=4000000, Number of messages received=4000000 (loss rate=0.0%),
        received=4GB, time=71094ms, Messages/Sec=56263.54, throughput=56.26MB

    182.100.2.15:47440:

    Number of messages expected=4000000, Number of messages received=4000000 (loss rate=0.0%),
        received=4GB, time=71083ms, Messages/Sec=56272.25, throughput=56.27MB

    182.100.1.15:50924:

    Number of messages expected=4000000, Number of messages received=4000000 (loss rate=0.0%),
        received=4GB, time=71094ms, Messages/Sec=56263.54, throughput=56.26MB

- The consolidated data combined from all log files were averaged on both the message rate and the throughput, the results calculated as: (56273.63 Messages/Sec) averaged over all receivers and the throughput is (56.27MB/sec)

- It is noticeable from the results that the loss rate is Zero percent, this means that there was no packets lost during the transmission, and the message transmission using RIDX UDP is a reliable and guaranteed to deliver all the messages, and retransmit any undelivered message.

TCP Processing Time and Memory Usage

The case study conducted in section 5.3.1 was done for both RIDX UDP and standard TCP. The data test results using TCP protocol was collected in data log files, the log file parameters includes number of messages sent, the system time in Micro seconds, number of messages sent per second, the throughput per second, the free and total memory in kilobytes.

Table 8 represents the data test results for a message size 1K and the number of messages (1000000) will be sent by each member simultaneously in a 4 domain members, the throughput is calculated for each member and the average throughput for all members. The TCP transport protocol data log results is shown in Table 8.

The output results represented in Table 8 shows that the average free memory during the transmission period is about 280 Megabyte, and the total memory reserved by RIDX for the full operation is about 402 Megabyte. The actual usage of the total memory averaged approximately 122 Megabytes. The total physical memory is 4Gegabytes of RAM thus the percentage of the actual memory used is about 3%, and the percentage of the actual memory used from the reserved memory for this operation is approximately 31%.

Every domain member was set to log the data individually, and each domain member contains the same log file parameters. The consolidation of the data for the four domain members was summed up as the following:

Table 7. RIDX UDP Test Results

#msgs	SysTime in (ms)	Msgs/Sec	Throughput/Sec [KB]	Free Mem [KB]	TotalMem [KB]
100000	1218786077887	11061.95	11061946.90	330166.07	397869.06
200000	1218786080227	17574.69	17574692.44	347983.49	397869.06
300000	1218786081788	23182.13	23182134.30	399585.12	415629.31
400000	1218786083351	27578.60	27578599.01	250748.66	415367.17
500000	1218786084925	31098.40	31098395.32	281613.07	414973.95
600000	1218786086425	34133.58	34133576.06	288874.70	413663.23
700000	1218786087955	36633.87	36633870.63	384390.09	413728.77
800000	1218786089524	38690.33	38690332.25	245139.47	413859.84
900000	1218786091048	40538.71	40538714.47	339123.56	413794.30
1000000	1218786092598	42103.49	42103490.38	205260.48	413859.84
1100000	1218786094073	43605.80	43605803.54	293514.23	414056.45
1200000	1218786095620	44821.28	44821275.17	387482.82	414253.06
1300000	1218786097080	46045.41	46045407.86	255355.52	414711.81
1400000	1218786098653	46970.41	46970408.64	338720.49	414973.95
1500000	1218786100188	47860.63	47860629.85	183764.79	414842.88
1600000	1218786101681	48729.98	48729975.03	268914.70	415105.02
1700000	1218786103218	49460.30	49460300.84	361359.14	415170.56
1800000	1218786104773	50102.99	50102989.48	223336.59	415694.85
1900000	1218786106270	50770.92	50770916.28	311141.94	415301.63
2000000	1218786107789	51358.43	51358430.49	397084.15	415825.92
2100000	1218786109328	51876.19	51876188.83	286094.67	415694.85
2200000	1218786110869	52353.53	52353529.10	292625.78	414580.74
2300000	1218786112464	52731.73	52731733.04	321395.52	413138.94
2400000	1218786113971	53186.77	53186774.22	348513.61	412483.58
2500000	1218786115437	53659.58	53659583.60	186308.17	412745.73
2600000	1218786117008	53985.59	53985590.00	259691.78	413204.48
2700000	1218786118533	54341.26	54341263.13	309087.55	413597.70
2800000	1218786120079	54653.34	54653341.66	372126.06	413859.84
2900000	1218786121611	54961.72	54961716.32	234858.52	413728.77
3000000	1218786123146	55249.64	55249636.27	311938.29	413401.09
3100000	1218786124614	55588.43	55588430.43	182914.83	413663.23
3200000	1218786126124	55868.85	55868847.88	224531.46	413990.91
3300000	1218786127717	56055.72	56055715.98	272061.95	414253.06
3400000	1218786129437	56114.87	56114870.44	343830.19	414515.20
3500000	1218786131170	56159.04	56159042.41	387312.80	414777.34
3600000	1218786133000	56115.85	56115848.05	223535.50	414646.27
3700000	1218786134732	56158.46	56158457.92	250990.13	414711.81
3800000	1218786136411	56242.97	56242969.63	268208.58	415105.02
3900000	1218786138132	56289.24	56289240.10	281911.22	414580.74
4000000	1218786139941	56263.54	56263538.41	192717.91	415301.63

- Using TCP protocol, a combination of IP address and a port number identifies each domain member, considered that the system is installed on separate units. A common port number opened and known to all domain members to establish the connection. The connection initiated based on a 3 way handshaking technique and terminates when all the message transmission is accomplished. The summation is calculated to include number of messages received and the time needed to receive all the messages, also the percentage of the loss rate, and the message rate along with the throughput. The summation results per node as the following:

  182.100.3.15:7700:

  Number of messages expected =4000000, Number of messages received=4000000 (loss rate=0.0%), received=4GB, time= 81073ms, Messages/Sec= 49338.25, throughput=49.34MB

  182.100.0.15:7700:

  Number of messages expected=4000000, Number of messages received=4000000 (loss rate=0.0%), received=4GB, time= 81072ms, Messages/Sec= 49338.86, throughput=49.34MB

  182.100.2.15:7700:

  Number of messages expected=4000000, Number of messages received=4000000 (loss rate=0.0%), received=4GB, time=81044ms, Messages/Sec=49355.91, throughput=49.63MB

  182.100.1.15:7700:

  Number of messages expected=4000000, Number of messages received=4000000 (loss rate=0.0%), received=4GB, time=81037ms, Messages/Sec=49360.17, throughput=49.36MB

- The averaged data for message rate and the throughput summed as: (49348.30) Messages/Sec averaged over all receivers and the throughput is (49.35MB/sec)

- In standard TCP transmission protocol the delivery of packets is a Unicast (point-to-point) reliable delivery, therefore It shows in the results that the loss rate is also (0.0) percent.

- When comparing CPU time and memory usage in RIDX and TCP, RIDX has a slight improvement over TCP in terms of utilizing the memory usage and the CPU time needed to accomplish the transmission.

SUMMARY OF PERFORMANCE TEST RETULTS

In the performance test results, the throughput and the message rate is trivially demeaned when we increase the number of members in the domain. But it is noticeable from all case studies that in most cases RIDX has achieved better message rate and better throughput, especially on a 1K message size, the improvement on 1K message size has a significant advancement regardless the number of domain members, furthermore, the utilization of memory and CPU processing time using 1K message size (less than MTU size) has also a significant improvement. On the other hand, when using 2.5K and 5K message sizes, the results showed that RIDX has achieved a slight improvement over TCP, and in other cases, the results averaged nearly to each other, the probable cause is that the Data Flow Control has not many credits to maintain a continuous data flow without any delays or the network switch begins dropping data packets. The current DFC module does not have a dynamic setting for the bank credit to adjust the pre-setting credit numbers according to number of domain members. The throughput and the message rate for all messages can be collectively averaged over the whole domain, and then it can be scaled the rate up almost around 100%, that means we can distribute 5,000,000 messages of 1K in a domain with 10 members, and the throughput can reach over 800MB/Sec.

Table 8. Standard TCP Test Results

#msgs	SysTime in (ms)	Msgs/Sec	Throughput/Sec [KB]	Free Mem [KB]	TotalMem [KB]
100000	1218786691748	9545.63	9545628.1	218965.75	397869.06
200000	1218786693883	15859.17	15859170.57	369874.02	397869.06
300000	1218786695716	20769.87	20769869.84	237457.40	414973.95
400000	1218786697553	24568.52	24568515.45	311860.92	412352.51
500000	1218786699419	27552.76	27552763.54	354295.24	412745.73
600000	1218786701239	30049.58	30049581.81	193283.33	412745.73
700000	1218786703028	32175.03	32175032.18	208764.91	413007.87
800000	1218786704857	33919.86	33919864.32	276655.47	413007.87
900000	1218786706574	35570.31	35570310.65	232425.24	413007.87
1000000	1218786708346	36935.81	36935805.57	184918.25	413401.09
1100000	1218786710139	38105.80	38105795.55	221633.88	413138.94
1200000	1218786711948	39118.53	39118529.14	243869.42	413466.62
1300000	1218786713725	40057.93	40057929.93	271953.07	413794.30
1400000	1218786715496	40906.97	40906965.87	379450.01	413794.30
1500000	1218786717245	41697.94	41697940.12	252284.27	413204.48
1600000	1218786719041	42362.78	42362784.29	335518.22	412483.58
1700000	1218786720851	42952.07	42952070.54	188578.70	411303.94
1800000	1218786722625	43527.68	43527676.35	265635.89	410845.18
1900000	1218786724433	44021.22	44021222.86	334603.47	410386.43
2000000	1218786726248	44468.16	44468160.80	383264.92	411041.79
2100000	1218786727969	44970.77	44970769.00	362625.70	404881.41
2200000	1218786729743	45387.96	45387963.94	184358.97	411041.79
2300000	1218786731499	45792.10	45792103.85	300320.62	411041.79
2400000	1218786733276	46150.30	46150296.13	324522.50	411041.79
2500000	1218786735067	46472.72	46472720.51	267699.86	409468.93
2600000	1218786736819	46807.21	46807208.31	281638.55	410845.18
2700000	1218786738633	47070.31	47070309.10	307599.27	411369.47
2800000	1218786740446	47318.08	47318078.89	330946.09	411762.69
2900000	1218786742221	47580.76	47580764.25	345182.05	412155.90
3000000	1218786743966	47851.47	47851469.04	368708.06	412680.19
3100000	1218786745748	48079.91	48079905.70	379184.38	413138.94
3200000	1218786747528	48297.51	48297512.68	244953.00	411697.15
3300000	1218786749272	48529.41	48529411.76	286501.25	412024.83
3400000	1218786751003	48758.80	48758801.68	199740.78	412614.66
3500000	1218786752774	48949.68	48949679.73	332359.59	412680.19
3600000	1218786754851	48927.00	48927003.63	247119.20	412614.66
3700000	1218786756644	49089.85	49089847.69	380152.54	412942.34
3800000	1218786758533	49183.93	49183934.97	298092.46	413663.23
3900000	1218786760390	49293.46	49293460.40	215528.99	413466.62
4000000	1218786762344	49338.86	49338859.29	351471.90	413925.38

Another factor that can positively affect the performance of RIDX is the size of the Maximum Transmission Unit (MTU), in all previous results, the MTU size was set to its default size (1500 Bytes). A preliminary test results showed even better performance when setting the MTU to 9000 bytes (Jumbo Frames). Using the same hardware environment setup as shown in case studies, but setting the MTU to a Jumbo Frame size (9000 bytes), the results showed that the achievement in a domain of 4 members and each member sends 5,000,000 message of a 1K size has jumped from 56MB/Sec to 137MB/Sec. On a 2.5K message size, the throughput jumped from 94MB/Sec to 149MB/sec. On a 5K message size, the throughput has raised to 155MB/Sec.

A Comparison Case Study

Eric Gamess and Rina Suros (2008) have made a performance test and measure the throughput for both IPv4 and IPv6, and made a comparison of the throughput between the two TCP versions. They tested a point-to-point connection between TCP/IP and UDP transport protocols for transferring the data. In addition, they did a test comparison using different platforms (e.g. Windows XP 2, Solaris 10 and Debian 3.1). They did the same performance test to measure the throughput between IPv4 and IPv6 UDP protocol on the same environment. The MTU has a length of 1500 bytes, and the RAM has 2GB with a dual core AMD CPU (2GHz). They calculated the maximum (theoretical) throughput as shown in Figure 25 for a pointto-point connection:

The data payload in both IPv4 & IPv6 varies between 1 byte to 5K (5000 bytes), and as noticed in the graph above, the lower curve is for the IPv6 TCP version, this made the superior upper one (IPv4) due to the size of the IP message header, for IPv6 is 40 bytes as for the IPv4 is only 20 bytes, and effected the theoretical throughput of about 5% difference.

The actual test results to measure the throughput has been made on different platforms (Windows, Solaris and Debian) against the Maximum theoretical throughput, the next graph represents the throughput for IPv4 TCP between different platforms (operating systems):

In their findings, they estimated the difference in the performance between IPv4 and IPv6 is about 5%. As noticed from the outputs, there is an amount of variation between different platforms. In Figure 26 showed that the performance for example Windows platform achieved better performance in certain message sizes, but in other cases Debian platform gave better performance than others. Therefore, the performance between the three platforms under the same environment test varied depending on message size, for that reason, when comparing these findings for these different platforms used, we need to calculate the average throughput value on each message size in different platforms, and then compare the mean values with the RIDX UDP throughput. It needs to be mentioned here some facts for better understanding of the comparison:

1. The four RIDX domain members model is chosen for comparison because it represents the simplest module to be compared with against point-to-point communication module.
2. The four RIDX domain members model contains the main factors to complete the benchmark of RIDX architecture, and the ideal model to represent a multi path virtual domain network that contains a sender, a receiver and two routers, and has an acceptable performance outcome in terms of throughput and message rate.
3. This case study uses a point to point transmission, which are one source and one destination only.

Figure 25. Max Theoretical Throughput (Eric Gamess and Rina Suros 2008)

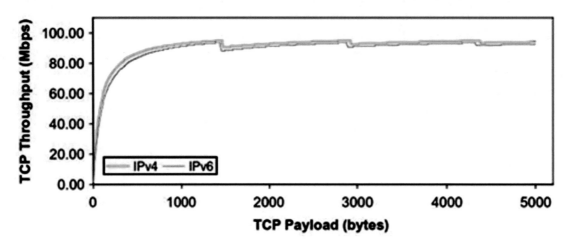

4.   A Unicast UDP transport protocol measurement from this case study is included in this comparison; therefore, this can be another performance indicator between Unicast UDP transmission method against Multicast RIDX UDP transmission method.

From the comparison table results in Table 9 and the Bar graph Figure 27 RIDX has a significant better performance than the standard TCP transport protocol, at the same time, preserving the security measurements that RIDX architecture is enforcing. As a result, we can conclude that reliable multicast transmission showed better performance than a single point to point transmission.

Figure 26. IPv4 Comparison Throughput (Eric Gamess and Rina Suros 2008)

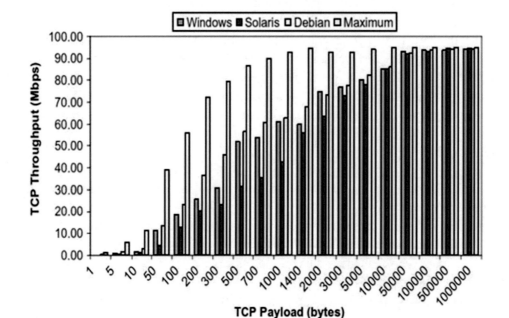

Table 9. Comparison throughput results

	1K	**2.5K**	**5K**
RIDX UDP	56.27	94.24	107.92
TCP Ipv4	52.01	80.21	85.33
TCP Ipv6	51.2	78.76	82.44
UDP Ipv4	52.87	82.43	86.53
UDP Ipv6	52.12	80.33	85.04

CONCLUSION AND RECOMMENDATIONS

Conclusion

Security data threats are always subject under improvement & development. Securing XML file during transmission is one of the challenges system developers can face, protecting XML data from any threats, attacks and exposure during transmission is an essential subject to be thoroughly studied. Different techniques are applied to protect XML data, but this study proposed architecture of how to build an embedded multilevel line of defence for securing XML data during transmission between different organizations, businesses and services. The experimental test is made to measure the performance, considering preserving the security methods and techniques that was implemented in this approach. The experimental results showed that RIDX UDP transport protocol has better performance than a standard TCP transport protocol. As a result, protecting the data and maintaining the transmission performance coupled with a reliable delivery is an achievement to this research.

As a summary, achievements summed up as follows:

- Multi agent domain members spread across the internet cloud WAN and LAN, with ability to form a secured virtual domain network that can initialises, joins, leaves the domain in an automated process flow.
- An automated authentication process during member joining stage, and automated Public/Private encryption key mechanism for all messages during transmission between domain members
- Automatic detection for all nodes that joins, leaves, and crashes, then notifies all domain members and update the Active Member List for the use of routing and other services.
- Vertical XML file shredding into several chunks, each chunk contains a combination of unrelated set of characters to hide XML file structure and conceal confidential information.
- Use RIDX UDP transport protocol to transmit XML data in a reliable and multicast transmission as a bottom-most transfer protocol in order to enhance transmission efficiency in terms of message rate, throughput, and memory/CPU usage.
- Routing capabilities to route messages between multi agent domain group members
- An automated Tunnelling technique process between members to add another security layer to the communication pipelines.

Figure 27. A comparison throughput between RIDX and other case studies

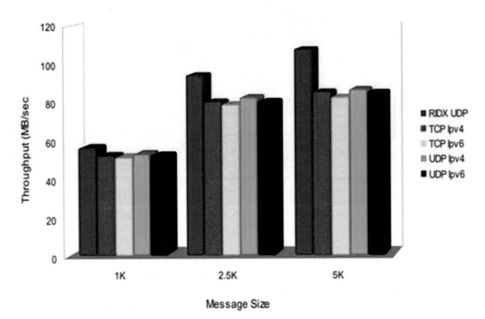

The conclusion summary is that when creating a virtual multi agent domain group network using RIDX UDP protocol prior to data transmission improve the communication efficiency and enhances the transmission by achieving higher message rate and throughput.

Furthermore, embedding and automating security measurements in RIDX such as Authentication, Partitioning, Encryption and Tunnelling has lowered the operational running cost, lowered the complexity of achieving the security layers, and utilized the resources usage.

Adding to this lightweight infrastructure to satisfy high security measurements and simultaneously provide a global framework for interoperability by an efficient bottom-most transport layer for data exchange in an unsecured environment.

RECOMMENDATIONS FOR FUTURE DIRECTIONS

RIDX is a middleware for transmitting XML data files that uses the internet cloud as a platform. Many factors can affect this approach due to wide variances that can exist in the internet cloud, such as using different hardware, different operating systems, different routing techniques and different security measures. Some improvements can be considered to this approach to expand the capabilities of the system, the following is the summary of these concerns and future work:

- A comparative study and a thorough testing of data vulnerability for the embedded security methods used in RIDX and the formal security methods
- Test, Analyse and study the communication efficiency for message rate and throughput when scaling up the number of domain members over 50 or 100 groups members together in one single domain group.

- Studying and Analysing in depth the effect of various security attacks on RIDX system before and during data transmission.
- When registering to a domain, all members in the domain works as a group, regardless the geographical locations, a case my arose when the ISP (Internet Service Providers) or any middle routing hardware might fail or crashes, which results to separating the domain members into more than one group, which will lead to electing domain coordinator for each separated group, therefore, a mechanism should be applied to re-join and merge back all groups into one domain group whenever the routing connection has been restored.
- Due to the factor of using different hardware and routing techniques, packet speed varies depending on the route the message has taken, creating a slow delivery for some packets to the final destination. Therefore, a module can solve this existing downside by calculating network fastest and least cost path between all RIDX members. A list of members with best routing performance options can be distributed to be used as preferred routing list members.
- Tunnelling experiments showed a significant overhead processing in both throughput and the packet delays. A study could be made to compare the throughput and the latency between the software tunnelling implementation and the hardware implementation, or use different types of transport protocols and compare the throughput and the latency before and after tunnelling.
- Study the effect of compression techniques on the system performance in terms of message rate and throughput and the usage of the resources.
- Study the network efficiency when using RIDX as middleware for Wireless and mobile implementations
- Enhancement can be made to the Data Flow Control module by adapting a dynamic credit bank technique, instead of pre-configuring number of credits; the new enhancement could be done by calculating the free memory allocations and packet loss rate dynamically.

REFERENCES

Abiteboul, S. (1993). Querying and updating the file. In *Proceedings of 19th International Conference on Very Large Databases*.

Abiteboul, S. (1997). Queries and Computation on the Web.*International Conference on Database Theory ICDT*. doi:10.1007/3-540-62222-5_50

Abiteboul, S. (1997). Querying Semi Structured Data. In *Proceedings of International Conference on Database Theory ICDT*. doi:10.1007/3-540-62222-5_33

Abiteboul, S. (1997). The Lorel Query Language for Semistrucutred data. *International Journal on Digital Libraries*, *1*(1), 68–88.

Abiteboul, S. (1999). Data on the Web: From Relations to Semi structured Data and XML. Morgan Kaufmann.

Abiteboul, S. (2001). Semistructured Data: from Practice to Theory. In *Proceedings of the 16th Annual IEEE Symposium on Logic in Computer Science LICS*. IEEE Computer Society. doi:10.1109/LICS.2001.932513

Adeel, M., & Iqbal, A. (2004). TCP Congestion Window Optimization for CDMA2000 Packet Data Networks. *International Conference on Information Technology (ITNG'07)*. doi:10.1109/ITNG.2007.190

Al-Wasil, F. (2006). Query Translation for Distributed Heterogeneous Structured and Semi structured Databases.*British National Conference on Databases BNCOD*. doi:10.1007/11788911_6

Al-Wasil, F. (2006a). Establishing an XML metadata knowledge base to assist integration of structured and semi-structured databases. In *Proceedings of the 17th Australasian Database Conference*.

Amer-Yahia, S. (2002). A Mapping Schema and Interface for XML Stores. In *Proceedings of the 4th international Workshop on Web information and Data Management WIDM*. doi:10.1145/584931.584937

Ardagna, C., Damiani E., Vimercati, S., & Samarati, P. (2007). *Security, Privacy, and Trust in Modern Data Management Data-Centric Systems and Applications.* DOI: 10.1007/978-3-540-69861-6_6

Arnab, A., & Hutchion, A. (2005). *Requirement analysis of enterprise DRM systems.* Academic Press.

Arnold, J. (2010). *Why businesses need to think differently about cloud communications.* Academic Press.

Atay, M. (2004). Mapping XML data to relational data: A DOM-based approach. In *8th IASTED International Conference on Internet and Multimedia Systems and Applications*.

Atay, M., Chebotko, A., Liu, D., Lu, S., & Fotouhi, F. (2007). Efficient schema based XML-to-Relational data mapping. *Information Systems*, *32*(3), 458–476. doi:10.1016/j.is.2005.12.008

Balmin, A., & Papakonstantinou, Y. (2005). Storing and Querying XML data using demoralized relational databases. *The VLDB Journal*, *14*(1), 30–49. doi:10.1007/s00778-003-0113-1

Barbosa, D. (2001). ToX: The Toronto XML Engine. In *Proceedings of the Workshop on Information Integration on the Web*.

Barre, P., Paasch, C., & Bonaventure, O. (2011). *MultiPath TCP: From Theory to Practice.* IFIP Networking.

Barre, R., Greenhalgh, P., & Handley, W. (2011). Improving datacenter performance and robustness with multipath TCP. *Proceedings of the ACM SIGCOMM 2011 Conference*.

Biddle, P., England, P., Peinado, M., & Willman, B. (n.d.). *The darknet and the future of content distribution*. Retrieved from http://msl1.mit.edu/ESD10/docs/darknet5.pdf

Birman, K., Hillman, R., & Pleisch, S. (2005). Building network-centri military applications over service oriented architecture. *SPIE Defence and Security Symposium*, Orlando, FL.

Blahut, R. (2004). *Algebraic Codes for Data Transmission.* Cambridge University Press.

Bryant, D., Atallah, J., & Stytz, R. (2004). A survey of Anti-Tamper technologies CrossTalk. *The Journal of Defense Software Engineering*, *17*(11), 12–16. Retrieved from http://www.arxan.com/ATknowledge-Portal/pdfs/Crosstalk-Article-A-Surve-ofAntiTamper-Technologies.pdf

Buneman, P. (1996). A query language and optimization techniques for unstructured data. In *Proceedings of ACMSIGMOD International Conference on Management of Data*. doi:10.1145/233269.233368

Buneman, P. (1997). Adding Structure to unstructured data. In *Proceeding of the international conference on Database Theory* (pp. 336–350). Springer Verlag.

Buneman, P., Choi, B., Fan, W., Mann, R., & Hutchison, R. (2005). Vectorizing and Querying Large XML Repositories. Academic Press.

Buneman, P., Fernandez, M., & Suciu, D. (2000). UnQL: A query language and algebra for semi structured data based on structural recursion. *The VLDB Journal, 9*(1), 76. doi:10.1007/s007780050084

Bushell-Embling, D. (2010). Malaysia's pricey leased lines. *Telecom Asia, 21.*

Bustamante, F., Eisenhauer, G., Schwan, K., & Widener, P. (2000). Efficient wire formats for high performance computing. In *Proceedings of the ACM/IEEE 2000 Conference on Supercomputing*. doi:10.1109/SC.2000.10046

Cattell, R. (2000). *The Object Data Standard ODMG 3.0*. Morgan Kaufmann.

Chamberlin, D. (2000). *An XML Query Language for Heterogeneous Data Sources*. International Workshop on the Web and Databases (WebDB'2000), Dallas, TX.

Chaudhuri, S., Chen, Z., Shim, K., & Wu, Y. (2005). Storing XML (with XSD) in SQL Databases: Interplay of Logical and Physical Designs. *IEEE Transactions on Knowledge and Data Engineering, 17*(12), 1595–1609. doi:10.1109/TKDE.2005.204

Chawathe, S. (1994). The TSIMMIS Project: "Integration of Heterogeneous Information Sources". In *Proceedings of 10th Meeting of the Information Processing Society Conference.*

Chen, J., Hu, C., & Ji, Z. (2011). Self-Tuning Random Early Detection Algorithm to Improve Performance of Network Transmission. *Educational Researcher, 39*(7), 515 – 524.

Christophides, V. (1994). From structured documents to novel query facilities. *SIGMOD Record, 23*(2), 313 – 324.

Davis, D., & Parashar, M. (2002). Latency performance of SOAP implementations. In *Proceedings of the 2nd IEEE/ACM International Symposium on Cluster Computing and the Grid*. doi:10.1109/CCGRID.2002.1017169

Deering, S., & Hinden, R. (1998). *Internet Protocol, Version 6 (IPv6) Specification, Internet Engineering Task Force*. RFC 2460.

Douglas, C. (1995). Internetworking with TCP/IP, Volume 1: Principles, Protocols, and Architecture. Prentice Hall.

Douglas, C. (2006). *Internetworking with TCP/IP: Principles, Protocols, and Architecture (5th Ed.)*. Prentice Hall.

Duftler, C., Khalaf, M., Nagy, R., Mukhi, W., & Weerawarana, S. (2002). Unraveling the web services web: An introduction to SOAP, WSDL, UDDI. *IEEE Internet Computing, 6*(2), 86–93. doi:10.1109/4236.991449

Emina, S., Liu, R., & Spasojevic, P. (2004). *Hybrid ARQ with Random Transmission Assignments*. Retrieved from http://ect.bell-labs.com/who/emina/papers/hatc.pdf

Fan, W., Chan, C., & Garofalakis, M. (2004). Secure XML querying with security views. In *Proceedings of the 2004 ACM SIGMOD international conference on Management of data*. doi:10.1145/1007568.1007634

Felten, W., & Halderman, A. (2006). *digital rights management, spyware, and security*. Los Alamitos, CA: IEEE Comput.Soc.

Fernando, G. (2009). On the implementation of TCP urgent data. *73rd IETF meeting Gregorio J. URI Templates*. Retrieved from http://bitworking.org/projects/ URI-Templates/

Fielding, R. (2007). A little REST and Relaxation. *The International Conference on Java Technology (JAZOON07)*, Zurich, Switzerland

FIX Protocol Ltd. (n.d.). *FIXML: A markup language for the FIX application message layer. Version 4.4*. Retrieved from http://www.fixprotocol.org/specifications/fix4.4fixml

FIX Protocol Ltd. (n.d.). *The Financial Information Exchange Protocol (FIX), version 5.0*. Retrieved from http://www.fixprotocol.org/specifications/FIX.5.0SP2

FIXML. (n.d.). *FpML Overview of the schema FIXML 4.4*. Retrieved from http://www.fixprotocol.org/specifications/fix4.4fixml

Gamess, E., & Suro, R. (2011). An upper bound model for TCP and UDP throughput in IPv4 and IPv6. *Internet Technology and Applications (iTAP),2011 International Conference*.

Harms, J., & Holte, R. (2005). Impact of Lossy Links on Performance of Multihop WirelessNetworks. In *Proceedings of the 14th International Conference on Computer Communications and Networks* (pp. 303 - 308). Retrieved from http://www.gont.com.ar/talks/hacklu2009/fgont-hacklu2009-tcp-security.pdf

Ioannidis, S., Keromytis, D., Bellovin, M., & Smith, M. (2000). Implementing a Distributed Firewall. In *Proceedings of Computer and Communications Security* (pp. 190–199). CCS.

Jacobi, J. (2011). Optimize Your Router for VoIP and Video Streams. *PC World, 29*(3).

Kenneth, P., Chen, B., Hopkinson, K., Thomas, R., Thorp, J., Renesse, R., & Vogels, W. (2005). Overcoming Communications Challenges in Software for Monitoring and Controlling Power Systems. *International Conference on Data Engineering*. ICDE.

Kent, C., & Mogul, J. (1995). Fragmentation Considered Harmful. *ACM SIGCOMM Computer Communication Review, 25*.

Kim, S. (2002). A Data Model and Algebra for Document-Centric XML Document. *Information Networking, Wireless Communications Technologies and Network Applications,International Conference*. doi:10.1007/3-540-45801-8_67

Kohloff, C., & Steele, R. (2003). *Evaluating SOAP for High Performance Business Applications: Real-Time Trading Systems*. Retrieved from http://www2003.org/cdrom/papers/alternate/P872/p872\kohl

Kudrass, T. (2002). Management of XML Documents in Object- Relational Databases. In. Lecture Notes in Computer Science: Vol. 2490. *EDBT2002 workshops* (pp. 210–227). Springer-Verlag. doi:10.1007/3-540-36128-6_12

Kurose, F., & Ross, W. (2010). *Computer Networking: A Top-Down Approach* (5th ed.). Boston, MA: Pearson Education.

Lau, H., Ng, W., Yang, Y., & Cheng, J. (2006). An efficient Approach to Support Querying Secure Outsourced XML Information. In *Proceedings of the 18th international conference on Advanced Information Systems Engineering*. Springer-Verlag.

Leonov, A., & Khusnutdinov, R. R. (2004). Construction of an Optimal Relational Schema for Storing XML Documents in an RDBMS without Using DTD/XML Schema. *Programming and Computer Software, 30*(6), 323–336. doi:10.1023/B:PACS.0000049510.04348.ee

Martin, G., Dimitris, A., & Roland, W. (1998). Cost-efficient network synthesis from leased lines. *Annals of Operations Research, 76*, 1-20.

Mazurczyk, W., & Szczypiorski, K. (2009). *Cryptography and Security*. Retrieved from http://arxiv.org/abs/1006.0495

McHugh, J., & Widom, J. (1999). Query Optimization for XML. In *Proceedings 25th International Conference on Very Large Databases*. Morgan Kaufmann.

Miklau, G. (2006). *The XML data repository*. Retrieved from http://www.cs.washington.edu/research/xmldatasets/

Möller, B., & Löf, S. (2009). *A Management Overview of the HLA Evolved Web Service API*. Retrieved from http://www.pitch.se/images/06f-siw-024.pdf

Murphy, D., & Heffernan, D. (2003). *Assembly Automation*. Academic Press.

Novak, L., & Zamulin, A. (2005). Algebraic Semantics of XML Schema. *LNCS, 3631*, 209–222.

Olovsson, T., & John, W. (2008). Detection of malicious traffic on back-bone links via packet header analysis. *Campus-Wide Information Systems, 25*(5), 342 – 358.

Pautasso, C., Zimmermann, O., & Leymann, F. (2008). RESTful Web Services vs. Big Web Services: Making the Right Architectural Decision. *17th International World Wide Web Conference,* Beijing, China. doi:10.1145/1367497.1367606

Perez, A., Zarate, V., Montes, A., & Garcia, C. (2006). Quality of Service Analysis of IPSec VPNs for Voice and Video Traffic. *Telecommunications, 2006. AICT-ICIW '06.International Conference on Internet and Web Applications and Services/Advanced International Conference.* doi:10.1109/AICT-ICIW.2006.157

Peterson, L., & Davie, B. (2000). Computer Networks: A Systems Approach. Morgan Kaufmann.

Popoviciu, C., Levy-Abegnoli, E., & Grossetete, P. (2006). *Deploying IPv6 networks* (1st ed.). Cisco Press.

Rabhi, F., & Benatallah, B. (2002). An integrated service architecture for managing capital market systems. *IEEE Network*, *16*(1), 15–19. doi:10.1109/65.980540

RFC 2460. (1998). *Internet Protocol, Version 6 (IPv6) Specification*. Author.

Rittinghouse, J., & Ransome, J. (2009). *Cloud Computing: Implementation, Management, and Security*. doi:10.1201/9781439806814

Rizzolo, F., & Mendelzon, A. (2001). *Indexing XML Data with ToXin*. WebDB.

Robie, J. (1998). *XML Query Language (XQL) online*. Available from http://www.w3.org/TandS/QL/QL98/pp/xql.html

Rosasco, N., & Larochelle, D. (2003). *How and Why More Secure Technologies Succeed in Legacy Markets: Lessons from the Success of SSH*. Dept. of Computer Science, Univ. of Virginia. Retrieved from http://www.cs.virginia.edu/~drl7x/sshVsTelnetWeb3.pdf

Schaffer, D. (2011). Network security in the Automation world. *InTech*, *58*(2).

Serrão, C., Dias, M., & Delgado, J. (2006). *Bringing DRM Interoperability to Digital Content Rendering Applications*. DOI: 10.1007/1-4020-5261-8_50

Shiau, W., Li, Y., Chao, H., & Hsu, P. (2006). Evaluating IPv6 on a large-scale network. *Computer Communications*, *29*(16), 3113–21.

Staken, K. (2001). *Introduction to Native XML Database*. Available from: http://www.xml.com/lpt/a/2001/10/31/nativexmldb.html

Stanton, R. (2005). Securing VPNs: comparing SSL and IPsec. *Computer Fraud & Security*, (9), 17-19.

Thornycroft, P. (2010). *Moving communications into the cloud*. Retrieved from http://agentsandbrokers.phoneplusmag.com/articles/moving-communications-into-thecloud.html

Weinberg, J. (2010). *2G Applications, An emerging media channel in developing nations*. Retrieved from http://nydigitallab.ogilvy.com/2010/05/19/2g-applications-an-emerging-media-channelin-developing-nations/

Whitemore, J. (2009). *Unified communications for the enterprise: hosted VoIP or cloud communications*. Retrieved from http://www.westipc.com/blog/2009/06/04/hosted-voip-or-cloud-communications/

Wilkinson, P. (2005). Construction Collaboration Technologies: The Extranet Evolution. Academic Press.

Yu, J., & Liu, C. (2006). Performance Analysis of Mobile VPN Architecture. *4th Annual Conference on Telecommunications, and Information Technology*, Las Vegas

Zuleita, H., Lau, V., & Cheng, R. (2009). Cross-Layer Design of FDD-OFDM Systems based on ACK/NAK Feedbacks. *Information Theory. IEEE Transactions on*, *55*(10), 4568–4584.

Zur-Muehlen, M., Nickerson, J., & Swenson, K. (2005). Developing Web Services Choreography Standards – The Case of REST vs. SOAP. *Decision Support Systems*, *40*(1).

Chapter 9
User Query Enhancement for Behavioral Targeting

Wei Xiong
Iona College, USA

Y. F. Brook Wu
New Jersey Institute of Technology, USA

ABSTRACT

Ad targeting has been receiving more and more attention in the online publishing world, where advertisers want their ads to be seen by potential consumers at the right time. This chapter aims to address the major challenges with user queries in the context of behavioral targeting advertising by proposing a user intent representation strategy and a query enhancement mechanism. The authors focus on investigating the intent based user classification performance and the effectiveness of user segmentation under a topic model that helps explore semantic relation between user queries in behavioral targeting. In addition, the authors propose an alternative to define user's search intent for the evaluation purpose, in the case that the dataset is sanitized.

INTRODUCTION

Online advertising started out as online banner ads back in 1994 and has turned into a multi-billion dollar market that continues growing. It has been the fastest growing adverting medium in history. There have been studies on ad targeting technologies which try to understand characteristics of online users and deliver them ads based on their interests. For example, the most basic targeting approach is to show ads based on the geographic information of the users, such as the physical location of the user. This approach is effective for advertisers who want to target a specific location, such as countries, cities or a radius around a location. One of the main reasons one may use geographic targeting is simply because one only offers products or services within specific areas. Geographic targeting also offers advertisers the ability to target their ads to users based on other parameters such as user connection speed, Internet Service Provider (ISP), domain name, and so on. For example, advertisers can deliver a competitive ad based on a user's domain name.

DOI: 10.4018/978-1-5225-2058-0.ch009

Similarly, demographic targeting approach targets ads to people based on the demographic information of the users, such as gender, income, age and more. For example, if you are a skateboard advertiser and know that skateboard users tend to be young males, you can set your campaign to show mostly to that audience. One of the advantages of demographic targeting is that advertisers can select a small amount of users based on demographics rather than displaying ads to all the users. However, this approach could also miss out potential buyers who do not fall into a specific demographic category. For example, a grandmother can also be a skateboard buyer if she wants to give a skateboard to her grandson as a gift.

Another three commonly used targeting methods are contextual targeting, keywords targeting, and retargeting. Contextual targeting is an advertising model where advertisements are targeted to the content of a webpage. In this model, the advertisement in a webpage is usually relevant to the content of that webpage. For instance, if a user is viewing a webpage pertaining to travel and that webpage uses contextual advertising, the user may see banner or pop-up ads for travel-related companies, such as flights dealers, hotels, and so on. Google AdSense was a major contextual advertising network and a large part of Google's profit is from its share of the contextual advertisements displayed on the websites running the AdSense program that searches for the relevant ads using Google's search algorithm. Contextual ads will be displayed based on the keywords after a contextual advertising system scans the text of a webpage.

On the other hand, keywords-targeted advertisements are displayed on the search results pages based on the keywords in the queries issued in search engines. Google AdWords is one of the most well-known forms of keywords targeting, where Google displays search ads based on the word(s) typed into its search box. One of the most widely used strategies is to bid on keywords by geography, allowing advertisers to maximize click-through-rate (CTR). For instance, one could adjust bids by geographic areas to get more exposure in areas that perform well. Furthermore, the keyword targeted campaigns are usually charged on a cost-per-click (CPC) basis, where advertisers are only charged when a user clicks on their ad and is taken to their landing page. The final CPC rate is calculated based on the advertiser's maximum CPC bid as well as the search engine's internal system of scoring keyword ads. Therefore, it is crucial to select accurate and appropriate keywords relevant to the product or service in the ad and set the maximum CPC bid (the most the advertiser is willing to pay per click).

Retargeting works by keeping track of users who visit a company's website and displaying ads from that company encouraging them to buy its products while they are visiting other sites online. The idea behind retargeting is that, only a small amount of users will convert on the first visit to a website. Retargeting was introduced in an effort to help advertisers allocate their advertising budget efficiently to their targeted audience and hence increase the effectiveness of online advertising. Yahoo! Retargeting, for example, is an online advertising platform that tracks users who have browsed a publisher's website before and tries to bring them back by displaying the ads the next time the user is on a Yahoo network. As a powerful and effective targeting strategy, retargeting focuses the advertising spending on users who are already familiar with the product or have recently shown interest. By displaying ads to the users multiple times after they leave the website, retargeting increases the chances that they will come back again.

Unlike contextual targeting and keywords targeting, behavioral targeting does not primarily rely on the contextual information. Instead, behavioral targeting helps advertisers reach the most relevant users by learning from user's online behavior, such as user's search queries and web browsing history. With the rapidly expanding breadth of Internet usage data collected by marketers, accurately predicting user's online intent underlying their search queries has played an important role in satisfying user's online experience. It helps advertisement campaign to target more relevant users, content publishers to recommend web content, search engines to return personalized results, and many other service providers to facilitate user's online experience. For instance, a user with a travel plan in his mind would have a higher probability of clicking a flight advertisement. Thus from a perspective of a flight advertiser, identifying users who are likely to travel could help target ads delivery and increase effectiveness. Similarly, if a content publisher knows a user's online intent, it can recommend relevant content to match user's interests.

Assume a user who issued queries such as "best carry-on luggage" and "foreign transaction fees". From the observation of these user queries, it can be inferred that this user is probably planning an overseas trip and may have the intent to purchase a flight. Thus, it is an opportunity both for advertisers to deliver flight advertisements, and also for other online service providers to offer travel related services.

This study is focused on capturing relevant users based on their online intents. The authors explore this problem in three major aspects, which can be summarized as follows:

- **Representing a User's Online Intent:** A user's online intent is modeled based on the user's online behavior, such as the search queries issued by the user or the web pages viewed by the user.
- **User Classification:** For advertisers who are interested in users who have a specific intent, a user can be classified as either having or not having this intent. Therefore, a good intent representation strategy should be able to effectively differentiate users based on their online intents.
- **User Clustering:** It would be also interesting to investigate how much intent-based user clustering could help behavioral targeting by grouping similar users into segments according to their online intent.

As a rich source of information on web searchers' behavior, query logs have been utilized by advertising companies to deliver personalized advertisements and leveraged by researchers to tackle other application problems, such as query suggestion. To carry out research on behavioral targeting, it is desirable to have golden standard datasets, which contain both query logs and ad click information. This type of datasets is used by advertising companies to train and test a model that predicts user's ad click behavior. However, they are not available in academic community, which makes conducting research in this area difficult.

The publicly available query logs are small, dated, and sanitized, since search engine companies are reluctant to release complete query log data. In the past decade, web search has grown at an unprecedented pace. Typical queries issued by users contain very few terms. In an empirical study (Jansen, Spink, & Saracevic, 2000), about 62% of all queries contain one or two terms, and fewer than 4% of the queries have more than six terms. On average, a query only contains 2.21 terms, which can carry only a small amount of information about the user. The tendency of users to use short and ambiguous queries makes it difficult to fully describe and distinguish a user's intent. For instance, the user intent behind query "Steve Jobs" will be represented as two terms in the bag of words model: "Steve" and "Jobs", along with their weights in the feature space, which could describe an intent of a user who is either interested in the person "Steve Jobs" or looking for a job.

Another important aspect of user's search query is that, the volume of queries is huge and follows the Zipf's law, where a small amount of queries appear very often while most queries appear only a few times. This makes the query feature space sparse and hence could undermine a classifier's performance in predicting future unseen data. For example, "laptops" and "cameras" are frequent queries and there are advertisers bidding ads on these queries. However, "T61" and "D60" are more specific queries with much fewer occurrences. Without knowing "T61" is a laptop model and "D60" is a camera model, these queries would not lead to more focused advertisements.

Overall, the intent-based user classification problem involves the following three challenges:

- **Lack of Golden Standard Datasets on Behavioral Targeting in Academia:** To evaluate performance on targeted advertising, such datasets are necessary. Also, the amount of training data is vital to any classification problems. Lack of enough training datasets could cause overfitting or high-bias when learning a classifier.
- **Short and Ambiguous Queries Making it Difficult to Describe and Distinguish a User's Intent:** In addition, the amount of queries issued by different users over a period of time greatly varies. Even less information can be captured from the users who issue only a couple of search queries in a given period of time, which makes the problem even more challenging.
- **Sparseness of Query Space:** While frequent queries usually can lead to targeted advertisement, those "tail" queries do not have enough statistical learning instances to "match" with advertisement.

The motivation of this study is to meet these challenges in Behavioral Targeting. In this chapter, the authors leverage user query log to enhance user's queries and hence help understand a user's search intent for better user classification and behavioral targeting effectiveness.

The main contributions of this study are as follows. First, the authors propose a query enhancement mechanism that augments the query by leveraging a user query log. This provides more information about the user's interests and hence reduces the ambiguity in the user's intent. It also helps tackle the feature sparseness problem. In the previous example, if the query "Steve Jobs" can be augmented by some related queries, such as "Apple", the user who issues query "Steve Jobs" is more likely to have the person name intent than the job intent. Similarly, query "D60" augmented with query "cameras" can obviously lead to more targeted advertisements. The empirical evaluation demonstrates that our methodology for query enhancement achieves greater improvement than baseline models in both intent-based user classification and user segmentation. Comparing with a classical clustering algorithm, K-means, the experimental results indicate that the proposed user segmentation strategy helps improve behavioral targeting effectiveness significantly by incorporating the query enhancement mechanism with a topic model. Last but not least, this chapter proposes alternatives to define user's search intent. The authors propose an approach that automatically labels a large amount of users in a click graph, which are then used in training intent-based user classifier.

BACKGROUND

With the creation of ever increasing volumes of digital data, the web search engines have become the most widely used tools for people to seek online information or service. The earlier studies on query logs date back to late 1990s mainly focused on investigating important details of user's queries, such as query length distribution and number of clicked URLs (Jansen et al., 2000; Spink, Ozmutlu, Ozmutlu, & Jansen, 2002). These studies provide important details of user's search behavior and have served as the foundation of later works on search query. Its related applications including query suggestion (Wen, Nie, & Zhang, 2001, 2002), and search results re-ranking (Joachims, Granka, Pan, Hembrooke, & Gay, 2005). However, the publicly available query log resources are fairly limited and dated.

Behavioral-Targeting

Behavioral-targeting (BT) learns from past user behavior to match best ads to users. Every time a user loads a page with a spot for advertisement, an auction is held for advertisers to bid for the opportunity to display their ads to this user. Advertisers make their bid decisions by predicting the user's interest. This process is very fast as the communication between advertisers and publisher takes place in only milliseconds while the page is loading.

During this process, there are two important datasets used to predict a user's interest, and a third dataset for the advertising bid request. The first dataset is the accumulated data about each user from their online search activities. This data includes cookie id, user's search term, clicked link, data and time, IP address and so on. The second data stream indicates date and time of user conversion activities. Depending on the type of the advertisement, a conversion could be a purchase, a credit card sign up, a click on an ad, etc. The third dataset, the bid request, contains data to allow many different companies to bid on an ad on an individual user's page view. This includes the topic of the page, the cookie id, the local time of the day, the web location (URL), and the size, type and location of the ad space.

Many commercial systems involving behavioral targeting have been developed. An empirical study conducted by Yan et al. (Yan et al., 2009) finds that user search behavior can be used to produce much better efficiency than user browsing behavior, when used as user representation strategies for BT. Another study (C. Wang, Zhang, Choi, & Eredita, 2002) points out that ads need to be relevant to user's interest in order to increase the probabilities of ad clicks.

Currently, BT advertising inventory comes in the form of some kind of demand-driven taxonomy, which consists of BT categories designed to capture a broad set of user interests. Chen et al. (Chen, Pavlov, & Canny, 2009) propose a Poisson model to estimate the click probability of a user, when shown a display advertisement in a BT category. In their work, ad clicks, page views and search queries are considered as three types of entities and a simple frequency-based feature selection method is adopted. Publicly available ontologies are also used to represent a user's interest. Wang et al. (X. J. Wang, Yu, Zhang, Cai, & Ma, 2009) build a hierarchical and efficient topic space based on ODP (Open Directory Project) ontology to match a user's photo tags with ads. The ads are represented in a topic space, and their topic distributions are matched with the target user interest.

Machine learning techniques have been leveraged in several prior works. Ranking SVM is applied in (Liu et al., 2010) to rank users according to their probability of interest in an advertisement. User's search query history and click history are used to create a user's profile. Similarly, Ratnaparkhi et al. (Ratnaparkhi, 1992) propose a model that attempts to estimate the probability that a user will click a given ad shown on a page. In their work, the feature space is extracted by combining user search queries, the ad, and the page on which this ad is shown. Lacerda et al. (Lacerda et al., 2006) also propose a framework for associating ads with web pages based on Genetic Programming (GP). Their experimental results indicate that GP is able to discover effective ranking functions for placing ads in relevant web pages.

User Segmentation

One of the crucial steps in Behavioral-targeting is to segment users according to their online interests or preferences. As a popular clustering algorithm, K-means (Kanungo et al., 2002), has been widely used to perform user segmentation in recent studies due to its quickness, good scalability and high efficiency in handling large datasets. Zheng et al. (Zheng, Xiong, Cui, Chen, & Han, 2012) apply K-means to cluster users by analyzing the characteristics of Web service and user's interests. The experimental results in their study indicate that they can effectively recommend web services to users by clustering users and establishing a recommendation service library. An empirical study conducted by Yan et al. (Yan et al., 2009) uses K-means for user segmentation and find that the user search behavior can be used to produce much better prediction accuracy than user browsing behavior, when used as user representation strategies for BT.

K-means based user segmentation also has been used to improve online recommendation systems by clustering users based on their historical data. Bouras et al. (Bouras & Tsogkas, 2011) incorporate an external knowledge source with K-means algorithm to cluster user's preferences and demonstrate its effectiveness on a recommendation engine. A similar work is found in (Xu & Liu, 2010) where a K-means based algorithm for mining user clusters is presented. In addition, K-means has also been applied in several studies on market segmentation (Kuo, An, Wang, & Chung, 2006; Sağlam, Salman, Sayın, & Türkay, 2006).

Although K-means has been widely applied in user segmentation, most previous studies fail to take semantics of user behaviors into consideration, which makes it very hard to correctly segment users who have the similar interest but no common queries. While the above works achieve desirable results in behavioral targeting, they all use different datasets to evaluate their approaches that are not publicly available. Therefore the authors are not able compare our approach directly with the above works. Instead, the authors propose a new evaluation setup which will be discussed in next section.

USER INTENT REPRESENTATION

Baseline Model

In order to differentiate users by their online intents, the intent representation should consider user's online behavior which can be characterized by their search queries and clicks on the search results. The queries issued by a user could contain hidden information about the user's intent. For example, a user's recent queries "map", "visa application" and "hotel reservation" have a strong indication that a user may also have an intention to purchase a flight ticket, even if the user did not explicitly issue queries like "cheap flight" or "airfares". Thus, a user's online intent can be built by considering all terms that appear in the user's queries.

Using Bag of Words (BOW) model (Salton & Buckley, 1988), users can be represented as a user-by-term matrix, where each row of the matrix is a user and each column of the matrix is a term. In this model, search queries are represented as a collection of terms that appear in the queries, without considering the order of terms. In this representation model, a user who issues query "new york weather" will have the same intent as the user who issues query "weather new york", because both of the users are represented as terms "new", "york", and "weather". Therefore, each distinct term can be treated as a feature while all distinct terms in user's queries make up the feature space.

In the baseline model, each term is weighted by the classical Term Frequency Inverse Document Frequency (TFIDF), which is the product of two statistics: term frequency and inverse document frequency. Let t be a term and d be a collection of queries from a user. In this case, the term frequency

$tf(t, d)$ is the number of occurrences of the term t in a user's query collection d, while the inverse document frequency is defined as follows:

$$idf(t, D) = \log \frac{|D|}{1 + |\{d \in D : t \in d\}|}$$

where $|D|$ is the total number of users, and $|\{d \in D : t \in d\}|$ is the number of users whose queries contain term t. Then the weight for each term can be calculated as:

$$tf * idf(t, d, D) = tf(t, d) \times idf(t, D)$$

Therefore in the user-by-term matrix $R^{d \times t}$ where d is the total number of users and t is the total number of terms that appear in user queries, a user's intent can be represented as a real valued vector. Clearly, the weight for a term increases when the term has a high frequency in a user's queries but decreases when it appears in too many users' queries.

Query Enhancement

In this section, the authors propose a mechanism that automatically augments queries by leveraging a user query log. The click graph (Craswell & Szummer, 2007), a bipartite graph between queries and URLs, has been used to describe the connection between queries and URLs, where edges connect a query with a clicked URL. Figure 1 is an example of a click graph with 3 queries and 4 URLs. One of the most useful features in the click graph is that, the edges of the graph carry some semantic relations between queries and URLs. For instance, "Steve Jobs" and "Apple" are co-clicked with URL "www.apple. com", and hence are related to each other. Clearly this graph can be employed to augment query "Steve

Figure 1. An example of click graph

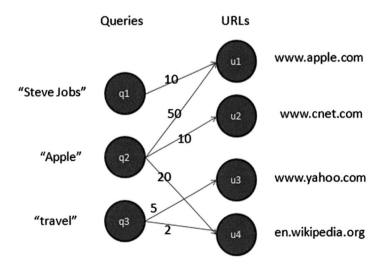

Jobs" with "Apple" to provide more information about the user's intent. Therefore, it is important that the authors represent queries in a way that the semantic relations between each query can be measured so that closely related queries can be captured.

Let $Q = \{q_1, q_2, \ldots, q_i\}$ be a set of i unique queries collected in a query log during a period of time. Let $U = \{u_1, u_2, \ldots, u_j\}$ be a set of j URLs clicked for these queries. For each edge (q_i, u_j), the authors assign the click frequency as its weight to measure how frequent u_j was clicked by the user who issued query q_i. Intuitively, this click frequency cf can be considered as the *Term Frequency* in the classical TF*IDF model, where each query is a "document" and each URL is a "term". Table 1 is an example of how click frequency data in Figure 1 is represented using a matrix.

Similarly, the concept of *inverse document frequency* can be borrowed to measure the *inverse query frequency*, where the discriminative capability of a URL should be inversely proportional to entropy. Let $|I|$ be the total number of queries in the query log, and the authors have the *inverse query frequency* for the URL u_j defined as:

$$iqf\left(u_j\right) = log \frac{|I|}{1 + \left|\{q \in Q : u_j \in q\}\right|}$$

where $\left|\{q \in Q : u_j \in q\}\right|$ is the number of queries that are associated with URL u_j. One of the important benefits of inverse query frequency, like inverse document frequency, is that it helps balance the bias of the clicks on those highly ranked URLs which usually tend to have more clicks (no matter whether those URLs are really relevant or not for that query).

To weight the edges in the click graph, a natural choice would be to incorporate the click frequency cf with inverse query frequency iqf in a similar TF*IDF model, which is defined as:

$$cf * iqf(q_i, u_j) = cf_{ij} \times iqf\left(u_j\right)$$

Therefore, each query q_i can be represented as a vector where the feature space consists of URLs, and the weight can be measured by $cf * iqf(q_i, u_j)$.

As mentioned previously, the goal of query enhancement is to augment the query with closely related or similar queries. This is especially important for the queries that have ambiguous meanings and for

Table 1. Click frequency matrix

	u_1	u_2	u_3	u_4
q_1	10	0	0	0
q_2	50	10	0	20
q_3	0	0	5	2

the users who only issued a few queries from which the user's intent can hardly be predicted due to the lack of information about the user.

To measure the similarity between queries, the authors adopt the cosine function between two query vectors. It is calculated as:

$$Cos(q_i, q_j) = \frac{\vec{qi} \cdot \vec{qj}}{\left\|\vec{q_i}\right\| \left\|\vec{q_j}\right\|}$$

where $\vec{q_i}$ indicates the vector of a query q_i.

After calculating the similarities between queries, for each query, the rest of the queries are ranked in the descending order of the similarities with the original query. The top k queries will be picked to augment the original query. Since the process can be executed offline with a large query log, the authors represent the user's intent by his/her issued queries along with the associated top k queries for each of the original query, and represent the terms in a BOW model. Table 2 illustrates an example of query enhancement results.

Labeling Users

Before the authors evaluate the impact of query enhancement on the user classification and user clustering, the authors need to label the positive users who have a specific online intent. The most straightforward way to identify the positive users is to see if the user has clicked a relevant ad. For instance, if a user clicks a flight ad, the user should be considered to have a travel intent. However, as discussed previously, such datasets are not publicly available in academia, which makes it difficult to evaluate our approach. Therefore, the authors attempt to find a reasonable alternative that defines a user's intent by utilizing external data which is not user log.

An important aspect of user's online behavior is that, users tend to only make clicks on URLs which are of interest to them. Therefore, it is reasonable to associate a user's online intent with the URLs clicked by that user. It is worth mentioning that a user may click multiple URLs during a period of time, and have multiple intents. This work aims to label the users by only considering one specific intent each time. However, it can be easily extended to other intents as explained later in this chapter.

Since the content of each URL can be described by different words or phrases, ideally the authors need each URL to be associated with a set of labels that cover the topics of the URL as comprehensive

Table 2. Example of query enhancement results

Query = microphone equipment
Stereo microphone
Recording karaoke
Audio gear
Used microphone
Digital recorder
Microphone ebay
Equalizer

as possible. For example, the URL "www.united.com" is tagged with phrases such as "airline", "airfare", "travel", "flight", among many others. Therefore, the authors adopt Delicious, a social bookmarking web service, as an external data source to identify the positive users and label them with a specific intent to build an evaluation dataset. It is one of the best researched folksonomy and each URL can be bookmarked and tagged by the entire community. When given a URL, it returns all the popular tags associated with that URL which allows us to match our targeted intent with those tags.

An advertisement displayed to the users contains the information about the product or service that the advertiser wants to promote, and it could reflect the user's interests if the user clicks the ad. In addition, the title of an advertisement always contains the keywords about the advertisement. Therefore, instead of arbitrarily defining an intent, the authors use the keywords in the title of an advertisement to represent a targeted online intent. For instance, keywords in the ad title "Cheap Flight Travel" can be used to label the positive users who have a travel intent and interested in purchasing cheap flight tickets. The pre-process of ads is as follows.

Step 1: Remove stop words from advertisement title and extract the keywords.

Step 2: Get tags for each clicked URL from Delicious dataset.

Step 3: Stem tags and keywords.

Step 4: Get the URLs whose tags cover all the keywords extracted from the ad title. If none of the URLs has the tags that cover all the keywords, get the URLs whose tags cover the most of the keywords, where at least half of the keywords in a title should be covered; otherwise this ad will not be included in our evaluation dataset.

Step 5: Label the users as positive who have clicked any URLs resulted from Step 4.

There are three major benefits of using Delicious as an alternative to label users. First, the tags associated with each URL are comprehensive, and can be added by any Delicious user. This is very important because the authors do not want to miss out any positive users. Secondly, the dataset in Delicious is large and updated every day. Almost all of the clicked URLs in the query log can be found in Delicious dataset. Finally, this approach does not need any manual effort while still creates reasonable training datasets for behavioral targeting research in academia. Table 3 demonstrates some of the URLs whose tags cover the keywords in the ad title.

Table 3. Examples of the URLs whose tags cover the keywords in the ad title "Cheap Flight Travel"

URLs	Tags
Kayak.co.uk	travel, flights, search, cheapflights, cheap, flight, comparison, airline, holiday, Tickets
travelzoo.com	travel, deals, airfare, flights, vacation, search, airline, shopping, cheap, shop
skyscanner.com	travel, flights, airfare, airlines, search, cheap, flight, airline, tickets, discount
jetblue.com	travel, airlines, flights, airline, airfare, usa, jetblue, cheap, inspiration, webdesign
airasia.com	travel, flights, asia, airlines, airline, thailand, malaysia, cheap, flight, lowcost
flycheapo.com	travel, airlines, lowcost, cheap, search, europe, airfare, airline, flight

USER CLASSIFICATION

The performance of user classification has a great impact on the effectiveness of behavioral targeting advertising as it only makes sense to deliver ads to those who have a matching intent. Ideally, an advertiser should be able to define an intent domain related to its product or service, and the user classifier automatically classifies a group of users based on this intent. Therefore, the user classifier discussed in this section makes binary decisions regarding whether a user has a particular intent which is indicated by the title of an advertisement. The authors evaluate our approach in three domains: Travel, Jobs, and Real estate, while our approach is general enough to be applied to other domains as well. Under each domain, the titles of the ads displayed on Google search are used as the specific intents to evaluate our approach.

Datasets

In this study, the authors used a subset of AOL query log to perform user classification. It is the most recent publicly available query log for the academic community that was released by AOL in 2006, which contains more than 30 million queries sampled in three months from over 650,000 users (Pass, Chowdhury, & Torgeson, 2006). The dataset includes AnonID, Query, QueryTime, ItemRank, and ClickURL. The detailed data format is summarized in Table 4.

In order to avoid noise, the users who have more than 1,000 clicks within one day are filtered out (they are most likely robots). In addition, stop words, punctuation marks and queries that appear less than 2 times are also removed. A quarter of the AOL dataset is taken to perform query enhancement, which contains 220,138 unique queries and 233,291 unique URLs. For the rest of the AOL dataset, 5,000 users who fulfill both of the following two conditions are randomly picked for each intent classification experiment:

1.   The users have issued queries in the first 7 days (01 March – 07 March).
2.   The users have clicked URLs after the first 7 days (08 March – 31 May).

The queries issued in the first 7 days are used to build the bag of words representation and the URLs clicked after the first 7 days along with the Delicious dataset are used to label the users for each intent. The reason is to use the user's queries in the first 7 days as user's historical online behavior to predict user's interest. After the preprocessing, 5,000 labeled users are collected and each of them is represented by the bag of words model as a baseline. To compare with the baseline, query enhancement is applied before building the bag of words model. The top *k* queries will be picked to augment the original query and in our experiments, *k* is set to be 10.

Table 4. Detailed dataset format

AnonID	An anonymous user ID number
Query	The query issued by the user
QueryTime	The time at which the query was submitted for search
ItemRank	The rank of the URL if clicked
ClickURL	Clicked URL
QueryTime	The time at which the query was submitted

Experiment Setup and Evaluation Metrics

For each user classification experiment, the authors aim to examine how our approach compared with the baseline model. After enhancing user's query, each user's intent is represented in a BOW model (as opposed to using user's raw queries in the baseline model). The logistic regression is adopted as the classifier and the users are classified based on the different online intents across three domains.

The evaluation metric used in our study is the positive precision. The authors evaluated the performance of the classification on each of testing datasets through filling the table as shown in Box 1.

Positive precision is defined as:

$$Positive\ precision = \frac{tp}{tp + fp}$$

The reason the authors concentrate on positive precision is that advertisers always want to deliver ads to those who have a high probability of having an intent related to the product.

Experimental Results

The amount of labeled instances (training data) is vital to any classification problems. In this experiment, Delicious dataset is used as an alternative to label users. The tags associated with each URL are comprehensive, and can be added by any Delicious user. This is very important because it is unwise to miss out any positive users. In addition, the proposed user labeling approach does not need any manual effort while still creates reasonable training datasets for behavioral targeting research in academia.

In this section, the authors present our experimental results and compare our approach with the baseline model for each of the specific intents across three domains. As discussed in the previous section, the title of the advertisement is used to indicate a specific online intent for the evaluation purpose. Specifically, the titles of the ads used in the experiments are listed in Table 5, Table 6 and Table 7. Table 8, Table 9 and Table 10 demonstrate the user classification results based on a 5-fold cross validation in three domains.

In all of the three domains, the performance of the proposed user classification compared to the baseline model is statistically significant at two-tailed p value < 0.05, using a paired t test. This suggests that, by incorporating the proposed query enhancement in user classification, the performance of intent-based user classification can be significantly improved. It is worth mentioning that the advertisement titles used in this experiment are all from real ads displayed in the search results on Google, and the experiment can be easily extended to other domains. After the advertiser decided the title of the ad he or she wants to display, the classifier can be trained offline and a new user can be classified as interested in the ad or not interested in the ad automatically. This improvement of user classification can greatly help advertisers deliver their ads to users who are likely to be interested in their ads, and hence click the ads.

Box 1.

	Labeled user class	
Predicted positive	*tp*	*fp*
Predicted negative	*fn*	*tn*

Table 5. Travel related ads title

1	Travelocity Travel Deals - Give Yourself A Break
2	Expedia Travel - Book a Hotel + Flight & Save More
3	Travelocity Travel Deals - Travelocity.com
4	Cheap Flight Travel
5	Buy Cheap Airline Tickets
6	Cheap Travel: 80% Off?
7	Priceline Travel Web Site
8	Hotwire® Flights For Less
9	Travel
10	Last Minute Travel
11	TripAdvisor Official Site

Table 6. Job related ads title

1	New Jersey Jobs - Your New Job is right Around the Corner
2	Find Jobs - Find Job Openings In Your Area
3	Find Jobs in Your Area - indeed.com
4	New Jersey Jobs (Hiring)
5	Local Jobs Hiring Now
6	CareerBuilder Job Search
7	10 Best Job Search Sites
8	2013 Jobs Hiring $25+/Hr

Table 7. Real estate related ads title

1	New Jersey Real Estate - remax.com
2	Real Estate - Weichert.com
3	Real Estate For Sale - Zillow.com
4	Coldwell Banker
5	Century 21 Official Site
6	RealEstate.com
7	HUD Homes low as $10,000
8	MLS.com -Search for homes
9	Real Estate in NJ

In the process of query enhancement, top k similar queries are added to the original query. Based on empirical results, k is set to be 10 in this experiment. In order to achieve optimal classification results, two factors need to be considered when determining k: the size of the datasets and the computing resources. In practice, additional empirical effort needs to be devoted in order to achieve optimal results.

USER SEGMENTATION

Publishers and other service providers always want to have their ads displayed to the most relevant users in sponsor search. From an online service provider's perspective, it could be extremely useful to identify users who have a high probability of clicking its ads and display them in the sponsor search results. Therefore, in this section our goal is to group the similar users into segments according to their online intent, and the authors look at the clustering results to see whether there are any user segments in which positive user rate (PUR) is significantly higher than before performing user segmentation.

Table 8. User classification results in Travel domain

Travel											
ads	1	2	3	4	5	6	7	8	9	10	11
Baseline	0.593	0.580	0.657	0.745	0.714	0.770	0.742	0.814	0.829	0.710	0.693
QueryEnhancement	0.637	0.631	0.710	0.793	0.778	0.825	0.790	0.878	0.860	0.762	0.746
Difference	0.044	0.051	0.053	0.048	0.064	0.055	0.048	0.064	0.031	0.052	0.053

Table 9. User classification results in Job domain

Job								
ads	1	2	3	4	5	6	7	8
Baseline	0.614	0.626	0.718	0.707	0.748	0.708	0.723	0.714
QueryEnhancement	0.662	0.680	0.749	0.772	0.809	0.741	0.779	0.786
Difference	0.048	0.054	0.031	0.065	0.061	0.033	0.056	0.072

Table 10. User classification results in Real estate domain

Real Estate									
ads	1	2	3	4	5	6	7	8	9
Baseline	0.731	0.695	0.634	0.710	0.689	0.758	0.713	0.680	0.736
QueryEnhancement	0.811	0.743	0.696	0.758	0.724	0.802	0.766	0.722	0.814
Difference	0.08	0.048	0.062	0.048	0.035	0.044	0.053	0.042	0.078

The authors use the query enhancement (QE) mechanism described earlier to augment user's queries. For each user, the authors represent a user's intent by the queries s/he issued and the augmented queries. Since topics derived from query space have close semantic relationship with queries issued by users, the authors represent each user's intent under an LDA model with topics being user segments. As discussed in earlier, K-means has been widely used in recent studies on user segmentation. It is also a fast clustering algorithm with good scalability and high efficiency. Therefore, the authors adopt K-means as a baseline to carry out experiments on user segmentation. We also examine if the proposed query enhancement (QE) mechanism can improve the performance of the baseline in the context of user segmentation for behavioral targeting.

Latent Dirichlet Allocation

Latent Dirichlet Allocation (LDA) is a generative probabilistic model for collections of documents, where it considers every document as a distribution over the topics in a corpus and every topic as a distribution over the words of the vocabulary. The assumption behind this is that all the samples are from Dirichlet distributions. Figure 2 is the graphical model representation of LDA, where M denotes the number of documents; N is the number of words in a document; θ_i is the topic distribution for document

I ; and z_{ij} indicates the topic for the *j*th word in document I , while α and β are the parameters. A more detailed elaboration can be found in (Blei, Ng, & Jordan, 2003). The key inferential problem in LDA is to find the posterior distribution of the hidden variables given a document:

$$P\left(\theta, z \mid w, \; \alpha, \; \beta\right) = \frac{p(.,z,w \mid \pm,^{2})}{p(w \mid \pm,^{2})}$$

As a topic model, LDA involves three levels where the topic node is sampled repeatedly within the document, and documents can be associated with multiple topics. This is similar to the fact that a user can have multiple intents, if the authors consider a user as a document and his or her intent as a topic.

Experiments

The authors used the same dataset as described in the previous section to perform user clustering for each of the intents across the three domains. Under each experiment, after computing all $P\left(t_{k} \mid u_{i}\right)$ (the probability a user u_{i} belongs to topic t_{k}) where k is the number of topics and i is number of users, the authors assign each user into the topic group that gives the highest probability.

The authors define positive user rate in segment *k* as:

$$PUR\left(S_{K}\right) = \frac{\#\ \text{of positive users in}\ \ S_{K}}{\#\ \text{of all users in}\ \ S_{K}}$$

while *PUR* over all users before segmentation as:

$$PUR = \frac{\#\ \text{of all positive users}}{\#\ \text{of all users}}$$

Figure 2. Graphical model representation of LDA

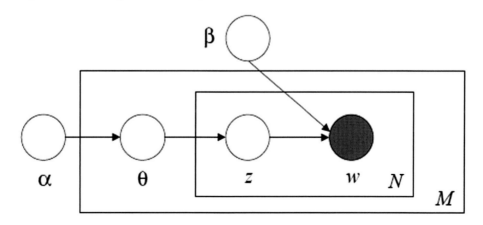

Because online service providers always aim to target the user segment with highest *PUR*, the authors choose the segment that has highest $PUR(S_k)$ when calculating the *PUR* improvement as:

$$\Delta(PUR) = \frac{PUR(S_k) - PUR}{PUR}$$

$PUR(S_k)$ is determined by the following two constrains:

1. **Maximum:** Choosing the segment that has the maximum *PUR*. This is reasonable since service providers always tend to recommend the user segment that has the highest ad click probability to advertiser for ads delivery.
2. **Majority:** The number of users in this segment cannot be less than average. This condition is also necessary, because it reduces some special situation. For example, some user segments may only have 1 user and he/she is a positive user. Obviously, this segment cannot be recommended to the advertiser even though it has the highest *PUR*.

Results

For each experiment the authors look at the PUR improvement under different number of segments using different user segmentation strategies. The experimental results are shown in Table 11, Table 12 and Table 13.

Table 11. PUR improvement of different user segmentation strategies in Travel domain

Travel												
ads	1	2	3	4	5	6	7	8	9	10	11	**Avg.**
5 Segments												
K-means	45.4%	50.8%	44.2%	51.4%	46.1%	42.9%	41.0%	43.2%	52.3%	48.9%	43.5%	**46.3%**
K-means+QE	49.7%	56.3%	52.1%	57.6%	53.5%	48.8%	50.6%	54.8%	60.5%	55.2%	51.7%	**53.7%**
LDA+QE	54.5%	60.3%	58.7%	68.0%	66.4%	61.2%	57.3%	64.0%	67.5%	62.0%	60.7%	**61.9%**
10 Segments												
K-means	57.7%	52.0%	53.7%	58.5%	54.9%	61.0%	50.3%	57.1%	56.6%	52.8%	51.2%	**55.1%**
K-means+QE	63.6%	58.3%	61.4%	65.6%	63.1%	66.2%	59.8%	64.9%	65.5%	62.5%	60.4%	**62.9%**
LDA+QE	76.1%	69.2%	74.0%	83.3%	81.5%	79.4%	74.4%	80.2%	73.9%	80.2%	77.4%	**77.2%**
20 Segments												
K-means	64.2%	71.2%	70.0%	74.8%	80.7%	74.5%	73.4%	79.4%	82.2%	72.8%	70.7%	**74.0%**
K-means+QE	73.0%	80.8%	77.2%	90.2%	89.9%	83.6%	88.4%	83.0%	91.5%	84.0%	79.5%	**83.8%**
LDA+QE	89.7%	93.6%	88.4%	102.9%	103.2%	98.0%	95.8%	95.3%	106.4%	98.1%	92.9%	**96.8%**
40 Segments												
K-means	92.6%	88.0%	87.8%	96.4%	95.5%	89.1%	87.7%	90.4%	94.1%	83.9%	98.8%	**91.3%**
K-means+QE	103.4%	94.7%	98.4%	112.4%	105.8%	97.6%	94.2%	101.6%	107.3%	95.2%	111.5%	**102.0%**
LDA+QE	114.9%	107.0%	120.5%	130.3%	127.8%	123.2%	108.6%	118.9%	122.4%	115.0%	126.4%	**119.6%**

Table 12. PUR improvement of different user segmentation strategies in Job domain

ads	1	2	3	4	5	6	7	8	Avg.
Job									
5 Segments									
K-means	42.6%	39.5%	45.2%	43.1%	37.7%	40.4%	42.3%	41.5%	**41.6%**
K-means+QE	50.5%	44.7%	51.6%	49.4%	47.6%	53.4%	55.1%	53.3%	**50.7%**
LDA+QE	54.2%	51.0%	60.2%	56.8%	59.0%	64.5%	61.2%	64.8%	**59.0%**
10 Segments									
K-means	47.2%	50.2%	62.3%	55.4%	57.9%	62.9%	52.7%	51.5%	**55.0%**
K-means+QE	56.0%	61.5%	67.4%	62.4%	63.0%	73.5%	64.7%	61.7%	**63.8%**
LDA+QE	67.8%	70.2%	75.0%	69.3%	76.1%	81.4%	72.5%	72.8%	**73.1%**
20 Segments									
K-means	63.3%	68.7%	74.2%	71.5%	67.7%	72.1%	70.9%	66.8%	**69.4%**
K-means+QE	78.5%	77.5%	80.5%	82.5%	78.9%	83.4%	84.8%	82.6%	**81.1%**
LDA+QE	92.0%	88.4%	91.6%	94.9%	99.2%	97.0%	94.4%	91.9%	**93.7%**
40 Segments									
K-means	85.8%	71.9%	92.4%	86.2%	89.5%	86.4%	90.6%	78.6%	**85.2%**
K-means+QE	97.5%	82.7%	104.5%	99.6%	102.4%	93.2%	107.5%	96.1%	**97.9%**
LDA+QE	114.4%	106.9%	112.5%	110.4%	115.8%	106.3%	120.6%	109.0%	**112.0%**

Table 13. PUR improvement of different user segmentation strategies in Real Estate domain

ads	1	2	3	4	5	6	7	8	9	Avg.
Real Estate										
5 Segments										
K-means	43.7%	42.8%	48.8%	44.9%	47.1%	42.1%	45.0%	47.3%	42.4%	**44.9%**
K-means+QE	51.8%	48.4%	54.3%	52.6%	52.9%	50.8%	55.3%	55.8%	53.1%	**52.8%**
LDA+QE	63.5%	59.8%	69.7%	65.2%	68.8%	70.4%	67.0%	71.6%	67.8%	**67.1%**
10 Segments										
K-means	50.3%	47.9%	57.4%	53.2%	56.9%	54.6%	52.5%	58.0%	55.6%	**54.0%**
K-means+QE	58.8%	54.4%	66.2%	60.6%	69.1%	65.9%	69.2%	70.5%	63.7%	**64.3%**
LDA+QE	71.3%	64.6%	81.0%	74.7%	84.5%	88.1%	78.1%	89.8%	85.2%	**79.7%**
20 Segments										
K-means	66.0%	70.6%	77.9%	71.8%	73.3%	72.8%	69.5%	79.7%	75.5%	**73.0%**
K-means+QE	75.1%	78.0%	85.6%	79.9%	82.0%	88.4%	84.2%	90.8%	87.5%	**83.5%**
LDA+QE	88.2%	87.3%	95.4%	86.6%	93.6%	103.2%	98.2%	108.5%	104.0%	**96.1%**
40 Segments										
K-means	80.9%	79.1%	86.1%	87.4%	83.5%	95.6%	84.8%	86.5%	91.2%	**86.1%**
K-means+QE	90.5%	87.0%	94.0%	103.5%	96.7%	112.2%	91.7%	108.3%	104.6%	**98.7%**
LDA+QE	108.0%	101.4%	116.6%	113.0%	104.0%	124.5%	105.5%	126.2%	117.7%	**113.0%**

In the above user segmentation experiments, the performance of the proposed LDA based user segmentation is compared with the performance of K-means based user segmentation to see whether the semantic approach improves performance of the traditional clustering algorithm. In order to examine the impact of the proposed query enhancement mechanism on user segmentation, the experiments also compare the performance of K-means based user segmentation with the performance of K-means based user segmentation with the proposed query enhancement mechanism. To investigate whether the proposed approach is domain-independent, experiments are carried out independently across three domains, and in each domain the averaged results of individual ads are taken as the final outcome.

Through user segmentation, it is clear that the behavioral targeted advertising can significantly improve the positive user rate, if the advertisements are delivered to the proper segments of users. The experimental results indicate that the proposed query enhancement mechanism can be used to improve the effectiveness of user segmentation, as the average PUR improvement rates under "K-means + QE" strategy are increased over simple K-means strategy in different number of segments across all three domains. The PUR improvement rate can be as high as 127.8% by using our user's intent representation technique with query enhancement mechanism under LDA model. By further analysis, the proposed "LDA + QE" strategy totally exceeds K-means and "K-means + QE". This fact proves that semantic approach is appropriate to be utilized in behavioral targeting and the results verify the correctness of the proposed strategy.

For user intent representation, LDA is adopted over other simple Dirichlet-multinomial clustering models. Unlike simple Dirichlet-multinomial clustering model, LDA involves three levels where the topic node is sampled repeatedly within the document, and documents can be associated with multiple topics. This is similar to the fact that a user can have multiple intents, if a user is considered as a document and his or her intent as a topic. Under the LDA model, the relationship between users and queries can be considered parallel to documents and words.

In the experiments of this study, each user is only allowed to belong to one user segment by assigning the user into the topic segment that gives the highest probability under the LDA model. Otherwise it is unfair to compare the proposed approach with K-means because K-means, as the baseline model, permits one user to belong to only one user segment. However, the number of users in the segment can be adjusted in practice by allowing a user to fall into multiple segments. This can be done by setting up a threshold and if the probability of a user belonging to a topic segment is equal to or greater than the threshold, the user is assigned to that segment.

It is also worth pointing out that the PUR improvement increases as the number of segments increases. However, it is not wise to increase the number of segments to extreme; otherwise some segment may only have a few users, which is not useful for advertiser to deliver ads, even though those users are positive users and might have the purchase intent. When the segment number approaches to infinity and every user belongs to a distinct segment, the PUR of all the segmentation approach will be the same. In addition, increasing the number of topics in LDA to extreme also may cause the over-fitting problem.

From an advertiser's perspective, even though PUR improvement increases as the number of segments increases, there should be a tradeoff between the PUR improvement and the number of segments, depending on various factors, such as the ways of pricing online advertising and the budget for the advertising campaigns.

CONCLUSION

This study introduces a user intent representation strategy and proposes a query enhancement mechanism by leveraging user query log. Unlike traditional user segmentation methods, which take little semantics of user behaviors into consideration, this study incorporates the query enhancement mechanism with a topic model to explore the relationships between users and their behaviors in order to segment users in a semantic manner. The proposed method can be used to improve the performance of both user classification and topic-based user segmentation in the context of online advertising, which could lead to more successful campaigns and better user satisfaction. The authors also proposed a method to address the problem of the lack of gold standard datasets available in this field in academia. It provides an opportunity for scholars who do not have access to the entire user online datasets (especially ad click data) to carry out the research in the area of online advertising. Furthermore, this approach does not need human effort and can be executed in a large scale.

It is worth pointing out that the proposed query enchantment mechanism needs a relatively large query log to obtain better results, especially when the authors do not have enough data about the users at the beginning. As a matter of fact, cold start is a widely known problem involved in data modeling. In addition, it is hard to predict the ordering of user's intents. For example, showing a flight advertisement after a user has already bought a flight ticket may not be useful. This is also the area that our future work will focus on.

Another limitation of this work involves the difficulties in predicting the sequence of user's intents by using external data source. The sequence of user's intents may involve user's offline activities. For example, showing a flight advertisement after a user has already bought a flight ticket by phone may not be useful. Similarly, a user clicking on an airline website may not be interested in purchasing a flight because the user may be just trying to check in online with a ticket bought long time ago.

In our future work, the authors plan to explore the problem further in two directions. First, as introduced in the previous section, the authors assume that advertisers provide us with the intent domains that they think related to their products or services. The authors will expand the provided intents by taking into consideration other semantic similar tags in Delicious dataset. By calculating tag-to-tag similarity, the authors will be able to find more tags that are closely related with the original intent, and thus to capture more potential relevant users. Second, the authors will investigate the impact of representing user's intent by historical queries over different time windows. For example, the authors will examine the differences in behavioral targeting effectiveness between using short term user queries and long term user queries.

REFERENCES

Blei, D. M., Ng, A. Y., & Jordan, M. I. (2003). Latent dirichlet allocation. *The Journal of Machine Learning Research, 3*, 993–1022.

Bouras, C., & Tsogkas, V. (2011). Clustering User Preferences Using W-kmeans.*2011 Seventh International Conference on Signal-Image Technology and Internet-Based Systems (SITIS)* (pp. 75–82). doi:10.1109/SITIS.2011.19

Chen, Y., Pavlov, D., & Canny, J. F. (2009). Large-scale behavioral targeting. *Proceedings of the 15th ACM SIGKDD international conference on Knowledge discovery and data mining* (pp. 209–218). Retrieved from http://cc.gatech.edu/~zha/CSE8801/ad/p209-chen.pdf

Craswell, N., & Szummer, M. (2007). Random walks on the click graph. *Proceedings of the 30th annual international ACM SIGIR conference on Research and development in information retrieval* (pp. 239–246). Retrieved from http://dl.acm.org/citation.cfm?id=1277784

Jansen, B. J., Spink, A., & Saracevic, T. (2000). Real life, real users, and real needs: A study and analysis of user queries on the web. *Information Processing & Management, 36*(2), 207–227. doi:10.1016/S0306-4573(99)00056-4

Joachims, T., Granka, L., Pan, B., Hembrooke, H., & Gay, G. (2005). Accurately interpreting clickthrough data as implicit feedback. *Proceedings of the 28th annual international ACM SIGIR conference on Research and development in information retrieval* (pp. 154–161). Retrieved from http://dl.acm.org/citation.cfm?id=1076063

Kanungo, T., Mount, D. M., Netanyahu, N. S., Piatko, C. D., Silverman, R., & Wu, A. Y. (2002). An efficient k-means clustering algorithm: Analysis and implementation. *Pattern Analysis and Machine Intelligence. IEEE Transactions on, 24*(7), 881–892.

Kuo, R. J., An, Y. L., Wang, H. S., & Chung, W. J. (2006). Integration of self-organizing feature maps neural network and genetic K-means algorithm for market segmentation. *Expert Systems with Applications, 30*(2), 313–324. doi:10.1016/j.eswa.2005.07.036

Lacerda, A., Cristo, M., Goncalves, M. A., Fan, W., Ziviani, N., & Ribeiro-Neto, B. (2006). Learning to advertise. *Proceedings of the 29th annual international ACM SIGIR conference on Research and development in information retrieval* (pp. 549–556). Retrieved from http://dl.acm.org/citation.cfm?id=1148265

Liu, N., Yan, J., Shen, D., Chen, D., Chen, Z., & Li, Y. (2010). Learning to rank audience for behavioral targeting. *Proceedings of the 33rd international ACM SIGIR conference on Research and development in information retrieval* (pp. 719–720). Retrieved from http://dl.acm.org/citation.cfm?id=1835582

Pass, G., Chowdhury, A., & Torgeson, C. (2006). A picture of search. *Proceedings of the 1st international conference on Scalable information systems* (p. 1). Retrieved from http://citeseerx.ist.psu.edu/viewdoc/download?doi=10.1.1.92.3074&rep=rep1&type=pdf

Ratnaparkhi, A. (1992). Finding predictive search queries for behavioral targeting. *Training, 10*(27,920,032,253), 27–920.

Sağlam, B., Salman, F. S., Sayın, S., & Türkay, M. (2006). A mixed-integer programming approach to the clustering problem with an application in customer segmentation. *European Journal of Operational Research, 173*(3), 866–879. doi:10.1016/j.ejor.2005.04.048

Salton, G., & Buckley, C. (1988). Term-weighting approaches in automatic text retrieval. *Information Processing & Management, 24*(5), 513–523. doi:10.1016/0306-4573(88)90021-0

Spink, A., Ozmutlu, S., Ozmutlu, H. C., & Jansen, B. J. (2002). US versus European Web searching trends (Vol. 36). ACM SIGIR Forum. Retrieved from http://dl.acm.org/citation.cfm?id=792555

Wang, C., Zhang, P., Choi, R., & Eredita, M. D. (2002). Understanding consumers attitude toward advertising. *Eighth Americas conference on information systems* (pp. 1143–1148). Retrieved from http://citeseerx.ist.psu.edu/viewdoc/download?doi=10.1.1.12.8755&rep=rep1&type=pdf

Wang, X. J., Yu, M., Zhang, L., Cai, R., & Ma, W. Y. (2009). Argo: intelligent advertising by mining a user's interest from his photo collections. *Proceedings of the Third International Workshop on Data Mining and Audience Intelligence for Advertising* (pp. 18–26). Retrieved from http://dl.acm.org/citation.cfm?id=1592752

Wen, J. R., Nie, J. Y., & Zhang, H. J. (2001). Clustering user queries of a search engine. *Proceedings of the 10th international conference on World Wide Web* (pp. 162–168). Retrieved from http://dl.acm.org/citation.cfm?id=371974

Wen, J. R., Nie, J. Y., & Zhang, H. J. (2002). Query clustering using user logs. *ACM Transactions on Information Systems*, *20*(1), 59–81. doi:10.1145/503104.503108

Xu, J., & Liu, H. (2010). Web user clustering analysis based on KMeans algorithm. *2010 International Conference on Information Networking and Automation (ICINA)* (Vol. 2, pp. V2–6–V2–9). doi:10.1109/ICINA.2010.5636772

Yan, J., Liu, N., Wang, G., Zhang, W., Jiang, Y., & Chen, Z. (2009). How much can behavioral targeting help online advertising? *Proceedings of the 18th international conference on World wide web* (pp. 261–270). Retrieved from http://dl.acm.org/citation.cfm?id=1526745

Zheng, K., Xiong, H., Cui, Y., Chen, J., & Han, L. (2012). User Clustering-Based Web Service Discovery. *2012 Sixth International Conference on Internet Computing for Science and Engineering (ICICSE)* (pp. 276–279). doi:10.1109/ICICSE.2012.40

Section 2

Chapter 10
A Generic Model of Ontology to Visualize Information Science Domain (OIS)

Ahlam F. Sawsaa
University of Huddersfield, UK & Benghazi University, Libya

Joan Lu
University of Huddersfield, UK

ABSTRACT

Ontology has been a subject of many studies carried out in artificial intelligence (AI) and information system communities. Ontology has become an important component of the semantic web, covering a variety of knowledge domains. Although building domain ontologies still remains a big challenge with regard to its designing and implementation, there are still many areas that need to create ontologies. Information Science (IS) is one of these areas that need a unified ontology model to facilitate information access among the heterogeneous data resources and share a common understanding of the domain knowledge. The objective of this study is to develop a generic model of ontology that serves as a foundation of knowledge modelling for applications and aggregation with other ontologies to facilitate information exchanging between different systems. This model will be a metadata for a knowledge base system to be used in different purposes of interest, such as education applications to support educational needs for teachers and students and information system developers, and enhancing the index tool in libraries to facilitate access to information collections. The findings of the research revealed that overall feedback from the IS community has been positive and that the model met the ontology quality criteria. It was appropriate to provide consistency and clear understanding of the subject area. OIS ontology unifies information science, which is composed of library science, computer science and archival science, by creating the theoretical base useful for further practical systems. Developing ontology of information science (OIS) is not an easy task, due to the complex nature of the field. It needs to be integrated with other ontologies such as social science, cognitive science, philosophy, law management and mathematics, to provide a basic knowledge for the semantic web and also to leverage information retrieval.

DOI: 10.4018/978-1-5225-2058-0.ch010

INTRODUCTION

Recently, the development of domain ontologies has become increasingly important for knowledge level interoperation and information integration. They provide functional features for AI and knowledge representation. Domain Ontology is a central foundation of growth for the semantic web that provides a general knowledge for correspondence and communication among heterogeneous systems. Particularly with a rise of ontology in the artificial intelligence (AI) domain, it can be seen as an almost inevitable development in computer science and AI in general.

Ontologies are useful for different applications to be able to share information between heterogeneous data resources. They are also essential for enabling knowledge-level interoperation of agents, when these agents are interacting to share a common interpretation of the vocabulary. Moreover, it is useful for human understanding and interaction to reach a consensus amongst a professional community.

Although there are a range of domain ontologies on the semantic web such as Gene Ontology (GeneOntology, 2009), Biological science ontology (Sabou 2005), CIDOC-CRM ontology of culture heritage documentation, FRBR in Bibliographic and NCI cancer ontology (Golbeck et al., 2008), there still exists a lack of domain ontologies, which has led to the loss of knowledge in specific domains. This is a significant problem for scholars and researchers who need to be able to access information within their interest area.

Ontology provides a vocabulary for metadata description with machine understandable terminology. Ontology provides a format for explaining and understanding terminology and the knowledge contained in a software system. By using shared concepts and terms in accordance with a specific approach, a lot of information remains in people's heads. It is discussed in chapter 2.

However, information science (IS) is a fast paced discipline and communication technology is rapidly increasing, so it is imperative to take advantage of this development. IS is a multidisciplinary field and it has gained the fundamental root of its theory from different related fields. The analysis includes the three branches of the field, which are; Library Science, Archival Science and Computer Science. Meanwhile it overlaps with other sciences, as stated in chapter 2, e.g., communication, cognitive science, philosophical science, management, social science and marketing. More precisely, the relationships between information and marketing can be subdivided into marketing information, marketing information services, marketing of library services. These kinds of relationships need logical ontology to clarify their relations and the science boundaries, amongst others. Therefore, Information Science still needs identity.

However, there is a lack of IS ontology representing the unified model that combines all concepts and their relationships. Moreover, IS as any domains which use the natural language. It contains a lot of jargon which needs to be in a formal language for programming or logic. Alternatively, integration of the computer with the internet has led to the emergence of new concepts in the field of IS such as, Electronic Library, Virtual Library, Library Without Walls, Digital Library and Information Management, as well as Nerve Centres. Even the information concept itself has strong and complex relations with other concepts, for example some people have defined it as fact, energy, data, and symbols. Also, it can be composed with other words such as; information age, information revaluation, information crisis, information explosion. However, there are 400 definitions for information in the literature (Yuexiao, 1988). It is hard to differentiate between these concepts. Even within the same field, there is still confusion over defining information - everyone defines it based on his background, for example librarians know it in term of facts, and data can be in containers such as journals, books and documents. The computer scientists conceive it as small units such as bits and bytes.

Consequently, modelling the IS domain necessarily assumes the need to represent the correct picture of the whole domain, and any changes in the domain will have to be added to keep the model up to date (Mommers, 2010, Yuexiao, 1988).

Our consideration is that in developing an ontology of Information science OIS to define its boundaries, and avoid ambiguous concepts.

Therefore, there is a lack of unified model of domain knowledge, because of the inconsistency in structure of domain which led to difficulty of using and sharing data in syntax and semantic level.

PROBLEM IDENTIFICATION

Information Science is seeking its identity and it is one of the many domains which use natural language including much jargon. Also, integration of the computer with the internet has led to emerging concepts in the field of IS such as, Electronic Library, Virtual Library, Library without walls, digital Library It is hard to differentiate between them.

Furthermore, its structure led to lack of a unified model of domain knowledge. This led to lack of a unified model of domain knowledge, and difficulty of using and sharing data at syntax and semantic levels. The OIS ontology provides a standard terminology and shared representation of domain concepts.

Therefore, the ontology of information science is missing in ontological engineering area. Our consideration is that developing ontology of Information science to define its boundaries, and to avoid the concepts ambiguous.

The research problem of the study was defined as the following:

Q: How an ontology of Information Science (OIS) model can be developed to visualise the IS domain, and how the model could capture and represent this knowledge?

To achieve the primary objective, the researcher asks questions to be answered through this study such as:

- What domain knowledge does the ontology represent?
- What is the level of knowledge that the ontology will represent?
- Which knowledge representation techniques and languages should be used?
- What are the relations that will be used to structure the knowledge, and which structure for the ontology will it have e.g. tree, graph, and its main components of ontology (e.g., classes, instances, relations, rules)?
- What is the value of tools such virtual community of practice ontocop? Could they be valuable in supporting the developing process?
- Does the developing process of the ontology follow designing criteria?
- Is the ontology evaluated based on specific criteria?

AIMS AND OBJECTIVES

The aim of this research is to develop a generic model of ontology that visualize domain knowledge of IS that serves as a foundation of knowledge modelling for applications and aggregation with other ontologies.

The visualisation stage provides an extensible and commonly understood semantic framework by describing the terminology of the domain. Achieving this aim in the current study will fulfill the following Objectives:

- Building a conceptual model for establishing a better analysis framework to understand, classify and compare various classes of Information Science.
- Providing a framework to make it possible to share a common understanding of Information Science by identifying the key objects of IS domain and relationships.

Providing a specification of information requirement for both developers and end users, to be used in different applications.

METHODOLOGY AND IMPLEMENTATION

The aim of this part is to investigate whether the results found in the literature study could be applied in practice by focusing on ontologies in a specific area. For this purpose, the virtual community of practice (Ontocop) was designed to visualise the area of Information Science (IS). Also, to involve other people as member of VCops by using some process of negotiation, to give us feedback on the ontology it is been developed. Additionally, they will help the researcher to assist and evaluate the ontology. There are many different methods for asking for feedback and analysis what the results are.

The literature review will be used in this research to address the research problem as identified by Saunders, et al (2000). It will be include the key of academic theories through the chosen area, and revealing that knowledge of your chosen area is new. Beside explain how the research relates to previous published research, to justify arguments by referencing prior works. Furthermore, enabling readers to find the original work you cite through apparent reference.

Regarding building the ontology, a methodology for building ontologies decides the main development stage and proposes guidelines for each stage dependent on use of the ontology. Many methodologies have been proposed since the 1990s to build ontologies. Each one has a different approach, such as Methontology, and SENSUS. Gòmez-Pérez et al. (2004) have made comparisons between these methods, and have pointed out that these methods have common development stages most of them have conceptualisation, requirements analysis, formalisation, implementation, maintaining and evaluating. Hence, there seems to be no general agreement on methodology to building and design ontology, due to the fact that it depends on its application and purpose of using it Noy and McGuinness (2009). To build a new ontology from scratch, or reuse another ontology, it should be built according to present needs and the purpose from it (Pinto and Martins 2001).

In this study, a new approach is proposed for designing a system to build ontology through sharing and reusing knowledge between members of communities of practice of Information Science (IS). The first step is building the ontology through the (VCops). The second step is building ontology of Information Science (OIS). In this sense our approach to visualise the knowledge of IS domain, will be as depicted in Chapter 3.

CONTRIBUTIONS

In this research the main contribution presented through this research is:

- Creating ontology of Information Science OIS model to unify IS knowledge. The OIS ontology is a general model for the domain, enabling the integration of a large amount of information resources. It designed to be flexible, reusable for other implementations, and compatible in knowledge base systems rather than imposing a specific solution.
- The model has fundamental roots in a framework based on analysis of the knowledge of IS domain; our framework is to identify the domain boundaries and relationships among them by providing IS taxonomy. Although there are many classification systems in the world none of them represent this in a formal way. In this study OIS taxonomy will be represented in OWL formal presentation; the taxonomy approach. The model has defined 706 concepts which will be widely used in Information Science applications. It provides the standard definitions for domain terms used in annotation databases for the domain terms, and avoids the consistency problems caused by various ontologies which will have the potential of development by different groups and institutions in the IS domain area.
- Design VCops (Ontocop) to support and assess the development process as specific virtual community of IS. The Ontocop consists of a number of experts in the subject area around the world. Their feedback and assessment improve the ontology development during the creating process.

The structured ontology was developed as a specific model of IS domain by following Methontology based on the IEEE standard (1996, 2006) for development software life cycle process. It mainly consists of the four main stages. The methodology and tools of design ontology was determined based on the experiments of Uschold and Grüninger M.(1996), Noy and McGuinness, (2001).

The designing evaluation tool is presented in chapter 4. The research tools adopted were;

1. Design a virtual community of practice (ontocop) evaluation ontology model.
2. The study used information extraction (IE) techniques to annotate the key entities of IS using JAPE grammar and General Architecture for Text Engineering (GATE) for data annotation; more details can be found in chapter 4.

The principle resources that have been used are domain experts through Ontocop, who were consulted to assess the ontology based on their experience and knowledge.

This research attempts to improve understanding of the distinctions among information science as a whole. Therefore, it is seeking to describe the constituents of the IS field, and ideally to put these into set theoretical foundations in chapter 3.

The research does not provide any a priori assumptions of using precise details about the IS domain, insofar as it is a generic model intended to provide a control vocabulary that can be applied for IS applications. It is important to note that the ontology model does not cover the range of individuals and extending relations. Nevertheless, it defines the concepts that serve as the foundation of IS, such as Actors, Methods, Domains, etc., which need to be extended in future use with corresponding ontologies.

OIS ontology is structured as a combination of domain and an upper ontology. The upper ontology contains a foundation of the ontology. It offers very general entities with subclasses, attributes, objects that give potential sources of integration with other ontologies. The IS domain has a strong relation with others.

The reason behind that, however, is that the domain ontology presents specific concepts of the domain in eclectic ways, which are often incompatible and incomplete. These kind of ontologies need to be merged and shared with other ontologies into more general representation. Also, it should be well-matched to the equivalent semantic area with corresponding ontology. Particularly in the IS domain, this consists of a complex combination. By using a common foundation, ontology provides basic elements for emerging domains ontologies automatically. The ontology model is a comprehensive scope covering three branches that are closely related to the domain; library science, archival science, and computer science.

The purpose of the OIS model is not to serve a broad spectrum of librarians, academic staff, publishers, information service providers only insofar it takes into account a variety of applications. Entities, relationships and attributes are the basic components of the model; these elements were derived from logical analysis of IS data.

Furthermore, the research describes the strategy and method developed to build the domain ontology of IS. It believes that this research offers significant advantages to modelling domain knowledge, in term of the contents of developing the IS ontology. This study created domain ontology and it is not considered task and application ontology. The main purpose of the OIS ontology is to provide a unified model of domain knowledge that supports knowledge sharing and the exchange of data among databases.

MOTIVATION OF STUDY

Ontology is not just identifying classes as entities and their relations and concept hierarchy but also specifying them by using specific ontology representation languages. OIS ontology seeks to provide a formal model of Information Science domain that is formulated in description logic. OIS ontology aims to represent domain knowledge to use independently of any application.

The motivation will be therefore at these possible levels:

- Ontologies represent knowledge about the real world. Nowadays, with growing attention to ontology, IS needs ontology. The problematic situation is identification of IS itself, especially the overlap between it and library science, computer science and archives science. On the other hand, there are many attempts to change the identity of the science to Knowledge science rather IS (Zins, 2007a). From this perspective we need a serious attempt to challenge the identity of IS through identification of its boundaries and relations with other fields, through this research, in chapter 2.
- Information Science just as any other scientific field requires a framework for organising its knowledge, especially with the fast speed of development disciplines. The terms data information and knowledge still have definition issues, although there have been many attempts to define and distinguish between them, precise definition is still problematic (Zins, 2007a, Wiederhold, 1986, Bubenko and Orci, 1989).
- Providing a consensual knowledge model of the IS field to be used by application ontologies. Hence, developing ontology enables the application to manage complex and disparate information. Also, changing the semantic web structure from surface composition to be captured in the application logic.

- Using a virtual community of practice as a way of sharing knowledge. Although there has been extensive discussion about the use of communities of practice in this way, no formal academic research has been identified relating specifically to the context of evaluating ontology via VCops in the Information Science domain.

CONCLUSION

In this chapter, introduce how to develop domain ontologies of Information Science (IS), and significance of visualizing the domain knowledge. The problem identified to fined solution of domain modelling by constructing a new model of Information Science ontology OIS. The OIS ontology is a generic model that contains only the key objects and associated attributes with relationships. An overview of the research approach is how structure of IS domain can lead to use and share data in syntax and semantic level. The Research aims and objectives are given. Finally the research outline is presented.

REFRENCES

Bubenko, J. A., & Orci, I. P. (1989). *Knowledge base management system Foundation of knowledge base management system*. New York: Springer,Verlag.

Geneontology. (2009). *Welcome to the Gene Ontology website!* Retrieved from http://www.geneontology.org/

Golbeck, J., Fragoso, G., Hartel, F., Hendler, J., Oberthaler, J., & Parsia, B. (2008). *The National Cancer Institute's Thesaurus and Ontology*. Retrieved from http://www.mindswap.org/papers/WebSemantics-NCI.pdf

Gòmez-Pérez, A., Fernandez-Lopez, M., & Corcho, O. (2004). *Ontological Engineering:with examples from the areas of knowledge management, e-commerce and the semantic web*. Springer.

Mommers, L. (2010). Ontologies in the Legal Domain. In Theory and Applications of Ontology: Philosophical Perspectives. London: Springer.

Noy, N. F., & Mcguinness, D. L. (2001). *Ontology Development 101: A Guide to Creating Your First Ontology*. Retrieved from http://liris.cnrs.fr/alain.mille/enseignements/Ecole_Centrale/What%20is%20an%20ontology%20and%20why%20we%20need%20it.htm

Pinto, H., & Martins, J. (2001). *A methodology for ontology integration*. International Conference on Knowledge CaptureK-CAP'01 Victoria, British Canada.

Sabou, M., Wore, C., Goble, C., & Mishne, G. (2005). Learning domain ontologies for web service descriptions; an experiment in bioinformatics. IEEE Computer Society.

Uschold, M., & Grüninger, M. (1996). Ontologies: Principles. *Methods and Applications Knowledge Engineering Review, 11*(02), 93–155. doi:10.1017/S0269888900007797

Wiederhold, G. (1986). *Knowledge Base Management System*. New York: Springer.

Yuexiao, Z. (1988). Definitions and Sciences of Information. *Information Processing & Management*, 24(4), 479–491. doi:10.1016/0306-4573(88)90050-7

Zins, C. (2007). Conceptions of, Information Science. *Journal of the American Society for Information Science and Technology*, 58(3), 335–350. doi:10.1002/asi.20507

Chapter 11
Research Background on Ontology

Ahlam F. Sawsaa
Benghazi University, Libya

Joan Lu
University of Huddersfield, UK

ABSTRACT

The literature review gives the background to the research process, which consisted of three main aspects to find out the theoretical background essential to this project. These aspects were: ontological engineering, Information Science, and Communities of Practice within knowledge management. The following sections provide an overview of key literature relevant to this project. Firstly, however, the background starts with some basic definitions to establish what is meant by ontology and what the significance of creating ontology is. The survey will come back to the three key aspects of this study and review literature on these; firstly, ontology.

ONTOLOGY OVERVIEW

Ontology plays an important role to use as a source of shared defined terms – for instance metadata – which can be used in a specific domain (Gaoyun et al., 2010). The concept of ontology became popular in the 1990s. Ontology's meaning can change according to the context of where it is used – for instance in philosophy, computers, linguistics, mathematics or social science. It is defined differently in work relating to computer science. Barry Smith (2003) said that ontology is a science of the existence of beings, and as such it has a relationship with computer and information science as a field.

Interest in the area of ontology in computer science has grown in recent years (Amira et al., 2007, Bhatt et al., 2009). In the early 1990s, ontology definitions as a term within computer science emerged. Computer science defined ontology based on knowledge systems (KMS) as a classification of knowledge (Guarino, 1997).

Ontology has a long history of development which predates computer science. This section will begin by reviewing the historical background of ontology, and the philosophical perspective will be introduced.

DOI: 10.4018/978-1-5225-2058-0.ch011

Then, moving forward to defining ontology based on comparing the original use with its current use in computer science will be combined, which will lead to a formal definition of an ontology that will be the basis for this research. Then, the research will move on to describe the development of ontology and share an explanation of the benefits of developing ontologies. It summarising approaches to modelling ontology with some examples of ontologies. Finally, we summarise some methodology, and explain the tools such as Protégé and the languages used for representing ontologies.

HISTORICAL AND PHILOSOPHICAL PERSECTIVE OF THE ONTOLOGY

To understand the ontological foundation for the ontology of Information Science it required reviewing diverse approaches to the notion of this concept. This section reviews some of the literature that is relevant to philosophical ontology. We explore some views from logicians that have influenced this project.

The ontology concept came from a branch of philosophy. Philosophers used ontology as a synonym of metaphysics - that means anything comes after the physical (Smith, 2003). Consequently, they defined it as a theory related to the study of relationships between beings (Webster's, 2010). More accurately, ontology is the study of things categories that may exist or already do exist in some domains (Sowa, 2000).

Back to the history from a philosophical perspective, Aristotle (384-322BC) invented ontology as a study of the ways that the universe is organised into categories. The category is the highest level of universal obtained from those domains; all other universals reorganised their hierarchies that need the top levels of categories, such as City, Man, and Organism. In (1200-1600) medieval scholars developed a common control vocabulary for talking about these universals in terms of sorts of reality. Descartes only initiated a movement of epistemology as a centre of philosophy rather than ontology or metaphysics until around (1960-61) by differentiating between mental and physical subspecies which had not been a problem for Aristotle. Brentano (1838-1917) denied the differences between philosophy and science; he said they are one and the same. Husserl (1859-1938) influenced by Brentano, invented formal ontology as a discipline distinct from formal logic. He showed how philosophy and science had become detached from the real life world or ordinary experience (Calero et al., 2006).

Philosophical ontology is a way of describing reality by providing a comprehensive classification of entities. That means organising all kinds of relations by classes or entities collectively (Merrill, 2011).

In general, methods of philosophical ontology are derived from philosophical methods. These methods include theory development, and testing and modifying them. Furthermore, these methods were similar to Aristotle's view.

Many philosophers had made distinctions between logic, computation models and ontology. Robert Poli (2003) has discriminated further between Husserlian formal ontology, descriptive and formalized ontologies. This distinction appeared from discussion of the main role of logic in these formalisms of ontology. Husserl's logical view had asserted that logic is an essential part of formal ontology (Poli, 2003). The group of AI has followed this theory where the formal ontology contained concepts, logical axioms, theorems and mereology. However, according to Tim Berners-Lee's semantic web tower, logic is the top layer above ontology vocabulary (Berners-Lee, 2001). More interestingly the technical and knowledge representation aspects have been using a robust concept of Web Ontology Language (OWL) as W3C recommendations are based on the description logic.

Recently, ontology has become associated with AI and information systems. AI logicists have focused attention on the knowledge-based craft. In 1980 McCarthy recognized the overlap between philosophical ontology and building logical theories of AI systems. McCarthy (1980) confirmed that developers of logic based on intelligent systems need to accumulate everything that exists to build the ontology.

Nirenburg and Raskin (2001) emphasize that ontological semantics is a theory of meaning in a Natural Language Process (NLP) that supports many applications such as information extracting and machine translation. Crucially, however, a good ontology requires choosing concepts that have to be covered and reasonably consistent. The ontology designers decide how to arrange and organise the concepts to be included (Nirenburg and Raskin, 2001, Nirenburg and Raskin, 2004).

In the interim, a similar view of overlap with philosophical ontology was proposed by Joan Sowa; ontology is to be considered as catalogue for possible global use that puts everything together and defines how it works (Sowa, 1984).

The AI community prefers to use the concept of ontology in knowledge engineering without much overlapping with the field of philosophical ontology. They work under the title of "ontology" that is related to logical semantics and logical theory.

Alexander et al., (1986) initially used the concept in the AI sense. This concept has been grown considerably in different fields of Database Management Systems (DBMS), knowledge engineering, domain modelling and conceptual modelling.

Definition of Ontology

Since the AI community discovered the power and knowledge within their systems, ontologies can refer to an engineering artefact to present a formal specification developed with AI, or an informal specification for human users. The AI community defined ontology as:

Ontology is a theory of what entities can exist in the mind of a knowledgeable agent. (Wielinga and Schreiber, 1993)

In 1993 Tom Gruber coined the concept Ontology in a sub-field of computer science. Gruber gave us the most widely-shared definition of ontology as a conceptual model:

An ontology is an explicit specification of conceptualisation. (Gruber, 1993a)

But his definition has many interpretations, which are that ontology can provide a specification of conceptualisation of generic notions such as space and time or domain application. A number of researchers in the computer science community have attempted to clarify and formalise the ontology definition further such as (Guarino, 1998).

Guarino and Giaretta (1995) highlighted the importance of terminological classification, to avoid misunderstandings over an ontology as a conceptual framework at knowledge level and an ontology as an artefact at symbol level, used for a specific purpose. The concept was further developed in 1999 when Welty and his colleagues described a range of information artefacts that had been classified as ontology (Welty et al., 1999).

Meadche (2002) defined ontology formally as containing classes, relations and axioms, whilst also allowing for lexical entities referring to multiple concepts and relationships (homonym). It also refers to the concepts and relations through several lexical entries (synonym). In 1993 Gruber defined ontology as:

An ontology is a specification of a conceptualization. (Gruber, 1993b)

His definition has been developed to be more accurate for defining ontology which is:

Formal explicit specification of shared conceptualization.

Ontology makes the term clearer and indicates in which context the term can be used. The definition consists mainly of:

- **A Formal:** Ontology should be machine readable and processed by AI systems. We do not need it to be a communication device between people and people, or even people and machine. Ontology should be formally defined as a formal language (Morbach et al., 2009).
- **Specification:** Means written specifications of language syntax to satisfy certain criteria such as precise, unambiguous, consistent, complete and implementation independent statements (Turner and T.L, 1994). It should offer a communication tool whereby users can share knowledge in consensual ways.
- **Shared:** Ontology represents consensual knowledge that, has been arranged and agreed on by group of people as result of social networks rather than an individual's view.
- **Conceptualisation:** This is an abstract model of a domain that is driven by user application, and represents concepts and relationships to be shared and reused. Conceptualisation is based on objects, concepts and other entities already in existence in the area of interest.

Based on this, ontology should be formally defined as being processed by a machine. The ontology is a specific type of information object or artifact. The way the ontology is constructed refers to classes, relations and their instances, all of which play explicitly specified roles in the conceptualisation. Otherwise, the backbone of the ontology consists of specification or generalisation hierarchy of concepts. However, Ontology is not software, though, so whilst it can be used by programs, it cannot run as a program

A far more interesting question is what information systems could learn from philosophical ontology. It is a shared belief that there is a similarity inherent in ontology from philosophical and applied scientific perspectives. Philosophical ontology is describing the real world as it exists, while computational ontology is describing the world as it should be (Kabilan, 2007).

ONTOLOGY THEORETIC

Category Theory

A number of thinkers and pioneers as Aristotle, Hartmann and Husserl (Bello, 2010, Hartmann, 1952), point out that ontology is adopted as a categorical framework that means it seeks for what is universal (Poli, 2010). Husserl's emphasis on the premise of the category theory could be reflected in many ways according to different viewpoints The precise meaning of ontology relies on the theory of category as a grounding in contemporary mathematics (Lawvere, 1969, Krötzsch et al., 2005, Johnson and Dampney, 2001, Awodey, 2006, Hu and Weng, 2010).

Table 1. Similarity between ontology and category theory

Similarity	Ontology	Category Theory
Classification	as Tree	grammars using tree or TAGS
Defining language	present language by defining term	Mathematical concepts
Node	Has node of tree	Has node of tree
relations	Interrelations	Close relations between formal linguistic presentation of domain & tree base representation.

Similarities in the relationship between category theory and ontological representation technique are summarised in Table 1.

However, categories appear in different ways such as taxonomy (is-a superclass, subclass), to group the domain in classical taxonomical categories according to Aristotle perspective. Recently Aristotle framework becomes matter particularly with time. Theories can help to define formal ontological properties that contribute to characterising the concepts. Husserl introduced the theory of Mereology as basic for formal ontology, and it is an alternative of set theory described by Tennant (2007).

Mereotopolgy Theory

Mereology is a formal theory concerned with wholes and parts structures (Husserl, 1970), whereas topology is a theory of wholeness that defines the relations connected to its properties, and how to be represent these components within the system (Varzi, 1996).

The basic metrological system is $M = (E, \leq)$ in which E is domain entities, and $\leq$ is binary relations. The $E, \leq$ binary relation is denoted; M can be considered as ground Mereology. The ground Mereology is the first order partial ordering theory as reflexive, antisymmetric, transitive relations; some relations can be axiomatised as follows:

$\forall x \ (x \leq x)$, (reflexive) (M1)

$\forall xy \ (x \leq y \wedge y \leq x \rightarrow x = y)$, (anti-symmetry) (M2)

$\forall x \ y \ z \ (x \leq y \wedge y \leq z \rightarrow \ \leq z)$, (transitivity). (M3)

More precisely, the general framework Mereology system is defined to the level of granularity and predicate:

$M(D) = (E, wh(x, l), P(x,y))$

Any domain is introduced M(D), and where/why(x, l) is the level of granularity and predicate, expressing that x is entity of the level of granularity L.

But with the weakness of this theory it requires more axioms to recomplete the functions (Varzi, 1996, Herre, 2010) The formal precise theory identifies and describes the classical first order logic using variables Y, X, Z etc. For the theory to be semantically and ontologically adequate it is required.

The axioms in Mereotopolgy are designed to serve a formal ontological system. The primitive relations of parthood or constituency are as follows: if says x is a part of y 'x P y' then y will be consisted with x's being identical to y:

x overlaps y xOy: $= \exists z\ (zPx \wedge zPy)$

x is discrete from y: xDy: $= xOy$

x is a point Pt (x): $= \forall y\ (yPx \rightarrow y = x)$

While, Boundaries defined as follows:

xBy: $= \forall z\ (zP\times \vee z\backslash sty)$

If X is tangent y then x T y:$= \exists z(zPx \vee zTy)$
If X cross y then xXy:$= xPy \wedge -xDy$ (Barry, 1996)
This research is based on (Herre, 2010)'s view about constricting a domain which is:

D=(obj(D), V(D), CP(D).

D is a domain that is determined by set of objects obj(D) connected to it. These objects rely on a set of views V(D), and a set of classification principles (CP) for objects obj(D). To make the components highly formal it is necessary to use categories and relations between them. In this case, the domain should be represent as:

Concepts (D) = Cat(D), Rel(D), Obj(D).

It is based on (Gurbe, 1993)'s approach of specification of conceptualization. The domain components are supported by relationships Rel(D), classification principle- taxonomy CP(D), additionally the concepts of the domain will be determined by adding axioms, these axioms are presented by interrelations between categories and its properties.

REFERCING AND MEANING IN THE ONTOLOGY

Human communication theory is expressed in a general communication context using the triangle of meaning. As depicted by Ogden et.al (1949) this contains three relationships between words, thoughts and things. This describes the real world interaction between thoughts (concepts), words (terms) and things (objects), as depicted in Figure 1.

The diagram shows the relationship between objects and concepts, and an indirect relationship between terms and objects, meaning there is no matching between words and things. In natural languages such as Spanish or English, each concept has a meaning. To explain further, a concept often carries more than one meaning, based on the knowledge background and historical structure in an individual's mind; for example, if someone talks about "AAAE5", the person listening to them won't understand them because

Figure 1. The meaning triangle

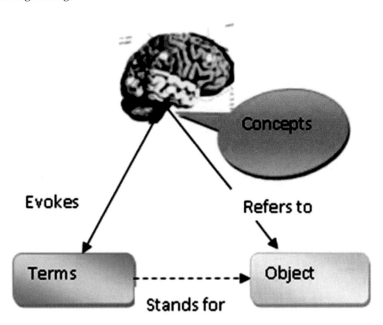

there's no matching image in his mind to interpret this or connect it to the real world. However, when the conversation is about a specific concept, for example "jaguar", everyone will interpret or imagine it, based on their background knowledge. One will think it is an expensive car that has an engine, four tyres and needs oil to move, and so on. The other thinks it is a big cat. In this way, one concept can have different meanings.

Concepts are a basic part of the proposition. They can express a certain meaning. The conceptual model helps to abstract models of parts of reality, by describing the key concepts and their relations.

More interesting than this, however, is what ontology can do in this case as a type of conceptual modelling method. Ontology attempts to represent the meaning of concepts, their properties, values and attributes. It provides a clear definition by stimulating a particular meaning, in this case that a jaguar is a big cat with four legs which lives in America. Ontology helps to avoid confusion and supports effective communication.

ONTOLOGY SPECTRUM

The first task in the ontology of IS is to control the vocabulary being used. The intention of ontology is to capture and reuse knowledge on a particular subject between software applications and groups of people (Gómez-Pérez et al., 2003). In reality, the nature of ontology has many aspects – some people consider it a thesaurus, some a data dictionary, and others a representation of concepts, classifications or taxonomy.

Thesaurus

However, the most popular way of controlling vocabulary is the thesaurus, which is a list of words grouped together, based on their meaning. Librarians in libraries and information centres use it as a tool to categorise information for the purpose of information retrieval. A thesaurus is similar to ontology in some aspects:

- Organizing terminologies in consistent ways.
- Using hierarchy structure as category and subcategory.
- Using terms in a particular domain.
- Providing information as synonym relation.

A thesaurus differs from ontology because a thesaurus provides ambiguity in relationships and offers alternative words and meanings. (Broader then BT, Narrow then NT, Related to RT). These relations are offered but they are unclear and aren't formally defined, unlike ontological relations. The relations should relate to a specific term rather than a range of terms and should also indicate that this term is a part of another term, e.g. (A) is subclass of (B) and (D) is a superclass of (A). Furthermore, the relationships in ontology indicate classes, subclasses, relations and properties, axioms. Ontology therefore provides far more than relationships. Relating to this Daconta (2003) pointed out other relations that had parallels with terms in the thesaurus, such as:

- **Equivalence:** If term (A) has a synonym then term (B) is equivalent.
- **Homographic:** When term (Y) is spelled as (F) but has different meaning.
- **Hierarchical**: The term could be narrower than and broader than, e.g.
  - If (A) is broader than (B); then (A) is superclass of (B).
  - If (C) is narrower than (D); then (C) is subclass of (D).

Figure 2. Relations between terms in Thesaurus

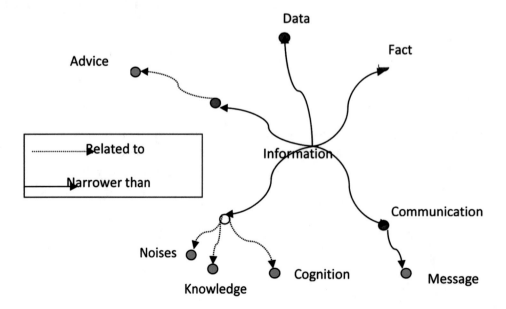

- **Associative:** This means that when (Z) is associated with (Y), there are non- specified relationships between the two terms (Daconta Michael C. et al., 2003). Figure 2 displays some of these relations.

Ontology's aim is different from that of a thesaurus. The former defines concepts in a structure by revealing the relationships between them, whilst a thesaurus merely illustrates the relations between terms, rather than presenting any defining terms. The thesaurus works to navigate between terms and for information retrieval. The thesaurus is weak in providing strong and rich relations amongst concepts, without taxonomy using narrow and broad relations.

It is more interesting, however, to use ontology in practical applications. This could be better than using a thesaurus, particularly when using searching and query processes for specific information. This is because ontology has machine-interpretable concept definitions, so it can infer precise concepts from information resources.

Taxonomy

Ontology is a table of categories. Each entity is tied and captured in some nodes in the form of the hierarchy tree, which basically lays Aristotle's roots of thinking on categories, as well as his medieval successors. Taxonomy classifies entities in a hierarchical configuration – this offers concepts and relations in a domain, which are labelled child and parent. For example, taxonomy supports users in searching and browsing online (Tsui et al., 2009). Figure 3 shows a simple example of categories.

For the sake of clarity, we can say that ontology is similar to taxonomy in its use of classes and subclasses, but ontology provides more conclusions than taxonomy, not just things and parts. It has Classes C, Individuals I, Relations R and Axioms AX, and is formulated by a formal modelling language L. Besides providing a semantic link between classes such as (is –a) relations and synonyms and antonyms.

Figure 3. Simple Taxonomy

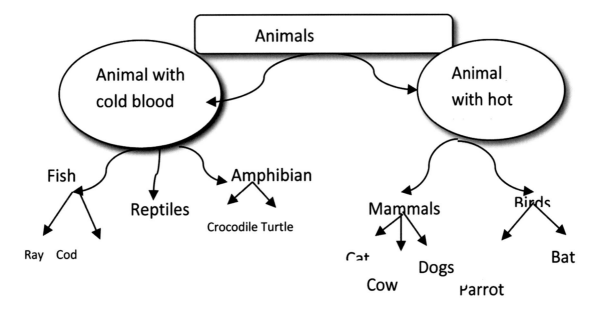

Figure 4. Spectrum of ontology
(Daconta et al., 2003)

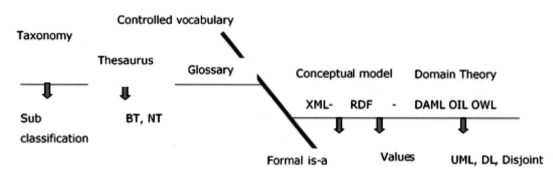

Furthermore, ontology could shift the semantic web from a weak to a strong tool for information retrieval. So before using ontology, the semantic web is based on a taxonomy, thesaurus and conceptual model. Taxonomy offers and supplies the main structure of information, with ontology adding details to it, whereas the semantic web is a machine that formulates data to enable computers' applications to understand it Daconta et al., (2003). For instance, Yahoo provides top-level taxonomy as a basic notion of generalisation and specification of concepts. Yet it does not provides Is-A relation.

However, the semantic web can infer any documents on the web, such as an XML document, XML taxonomy and XML ontology, but the differences appear here in information retrieval. The XML taxonomy gives mixed information from the web while the XML ontology gives information in more detail in a logical way Figure 4 illustrates the range of ontology.

Based on the above, the Table 2 therefore shows which differentiates ontology from similar concepts

To sum up, the synonym of taxonomy is a tree; things are arranged in a hierarchical structure as sub-type, super-type relations; a tiger is subtype of cats, for instance. Whereas, the synonym of ontology is model - that means a formal method for organising knowledge; by putting entities in categories and linking these categories with relations. E.g. ontology describes a tiger that has four legs and has a relation to Asia, the continent where it lives.

In the knowledge representation field, object-oriented software engineering and database development all employ ontology that is conceived as taxonomy. The Table 2 highlights the differences between ontology and taxonomy. Taxonomy has a hierarchy structure to arrange terms, classes and relations as 'child' and 'parent'. They cannot therefore present an explicit hierarchy – for instance, the taxonomy of data concept is a subclass of information, whilst in ontology a piece of data can be organised so it classes as information. Ontology could develop from taxonomy – from the knowledge of hierarchy structure, to the thesaurus, to a conceptual model written in unified modelling language (UML), and on to logical theory, arranging knowledge to be rich, complex, consistent and to have meaning.

APPROACHES FOR MODELLING ONTOLOGY

The approaches of software designing and developing - top-down, bottom up and middle-out - are well established in computer science.

Table 2. Differences between taxonomy and ontology

Element	Taxonomy	Thesaurus	Conceptual model	Semantic web	Ontology
Synonym	Tree	Control vocabulary	-	-	model
Presenting	Classification of concept, terms, things	List of words and synonyms organised in a specific order. Connecting the meaning of the term	a mental model about area of knowledge	Describing information on the www	Represents complex semantic of concepts & relations
structure	Hierarchy, tree	By standards of relationships as: Equivalence, Homographic, Hierarchical	Hierarchy in complicated way of knowledge	tree	Relationships between categories
Links of concept	Parent & child	BT, NT, RT relations	Entity, relationships, values, rules	Hierarchy	Classes, instances, relations, properties, constrains.
Based on	Glossary, Thesaurus	Glossary	Taxonomy	Taxonomy	Taxonomy
Purpose	Classify things	Conceptual navigation, research & information retrieval	Represents primary entities in a domain	Automation, integration, reuse information cross applications	To capture and represent the meaning of a domain
Retrieval information	Weak	Weak	Weak	Weak	Strong

Top-Down Approach

Emphasises the planning and complete understanding of domain modelling which starts with modelling concepts and relationships in every generic level of knowledge, to classifying into specific concepts. The IBM researchers Mills et al., (1995) initially promoted this approach. The main feature of top—down strategy is control over the level of details.

Bottom–Up Approach

In 1980 a bottom–up approach became popular when object oriented programming emerged. The strategy is identifying the specific concepts to be generalised into abstract concepts, to compose a whole system.

Prieto-Diaz (2003) used the literary warrant technique to categorise keyword and phrases to build the domain ontology automatically.

This approach is an insufficient strategy because it increases the risk of inconsistencies which require reworking and extra effort. (Sure et al., 2008)

Middle Out Approach

This approach is the most popular approach. It starts by reusing pre-existing knowledge to define the upper level of concepts, and sequencing of the upper level arises naturally.

Figure 6 shows an example of using the middle-out approach effectively. In the example of an animal, the concepts of mammal, reptile and bird are the most important for us. The higher level will be

Figure 5. Illustration of middle-out approach

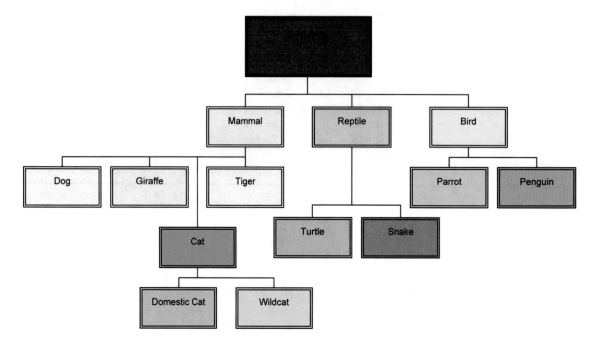

generated as seen in the example at the top, which is animal, and the bottom concepts for bird are parrot and penguin.

In the context of ontology development, a top down approach as Uschold & Gruninger (1996) argued results in a good control of the details. Though it starts at the top level of knowledge it involves some random concepts that are pre-determined at the high level, which leads to less stability in the ontology. A bottom-up approach, on the other hand, requires investing a high degree of effort, and it is hard to stop commonality among the terms. Hence, the risk of inconsistency will be increased during the developing process, therefore requiring more reworking.

Thus, the middle out approach according to Uschold & Gruninger (1996) identifies the most important concepts and the higher category rises naturally with more stability, with less overall effort and reworking. In this study we adopt and recommend the top-down, and bottom-up approaches in OIS ontology development.

STRUCTURE OF ONTOLOGY

Ontology structure has many definitions widely accepted, such as ISO standards 407 2009 of terminology work and principles and methods, and OKBC model (Chaudhri et al., 1998). Ontology structure is introduced in the literature as explicit sign level, based on semiotics, the study of signs. In semiotics theory there are three interlinked parts, namely:

- **Syntax:** The study of relations among signs.
- **Semantics:** Analysing the relationships between signs in reality.

- **Pragmatics:** Searching for how signs are used and analysing the relations between a specific agent and sign (Maedche, 2003). Links between different levels are shown in the triangle of meaning above.

However, construction ontology involves the concepts/classes to be put together with instances, relationships and attributes. So, ontology components are:

1. **Entities (Classes):** Things that can be clearly identified and that represent concepts.
2. **Instances (Individuals):** Are used to present elements in the ontology.
3. **Properties:** Are used to link relationships between instances or from instance to data value, such as has-A, Is-a, hasChild. They can be symmetric, transitive or functional. The standard ANSI/NISOZ39.19.2005(Standards, 2005) indicates the types of semantic relationships in the ontology that links between entities, namely;
   a. **Hierarchy Relation:** Type of superclass and subclass.
   b. **Equivalency Relation:** Is like synonym of terms
4. **Associative Relation:** Covers associations between concepts such as; cause / effect / accident / injury
5. **Restrictions:** Is information about entities. This information indicates how properties can be used by instances of a class, such as (someValuesFrom, allValuesFrom, cardinality restriction).
6. **Axioms:** Used to represent a sentence that is true. These are very useful to infer new knowledge.

Noy and McGuinness (2001) clarified that there is confusion when using classes and concepts. Classes are concepts and properties are slots. They give each class features and attributes. Additionally, the restrictions on properties are called fact or roles. Hence, the Reasoning task (classification, subsumption) is used to make sure this ontology is built for a specific purpose.

ONTOLOGY CATEGORIZATION

In general, ontologies are categorised from different approaches and have many classifications based on their structure. Ontologies are different from each other. Their different roles and features make them unique. The differences can be as follows:

Ontology scope and purpose: each ontology has a conceptual scope based on the description of its content, in specific domains such as biomedical-information science. This sort of ontology describes the key concepts and relationships.

Ontology describes levels of knowledge from simple lexicons through to taxonomy, where terms are hierarchically related to distinguish between properties.

Ontology has a historical part consisting of terminological and sectional components. The former is about the terms and structure of the ontology domain, while the latter is about populating the ontology with the instances that manifest the terminological definitions. Ontology can be built in different languages such as Open Knowledge Base Connectivity (OKBC), DAML+OIL, or Web Ontology Language (OWL) Dmterie and Verbeek (2008).

Generally speaking, types of ontology vary from heavyweight, lightweight, formal and informal, and upper or top ontology. The light weight ontology contains topic hierarchy and use is-, a relation to search the concepts on the web engine, while the heavy one includes ontologies that have very precise definitions of concepts, and have rigorous relationships between them. This kind of ontology is modelling the targeted conceptualisation of the world to guarantee the consistency. Another type of ontology is top-level or upper-level ontology; this has a level of category to describe general concepts and presents indications about the root concepts, linking them to existing ontology.

Philosophers have attempted to carry this out in their work, for example Guarino (1998) who divides the level of dependence of particular task into four parts. These parts provide structural design for domain ontology modelling. His proposal is influential in research methodology. His suggestion is dependent on identifying the main specific concepts required in application ontology, and then creating the domain and task ontologies which will be abstracted into top level ontology. These contain the general concepts to link with top level ontologies among different domains. His idea is suitable for designing ontology from scratch. However, we focus on Guarino's classification in more details. Guarino has classified the ontology based on their generality, Figure 6 illustrates ontology classification in more detail.

- **Top Level Ontology:** Alternatively, called top, generic or upper ontology represents general concepts independent of the domain, such as matter, kinds, even time and space. The most likely purpose is to unify criteria among different users.
- **Domain Ontology:** Describes concepts related to the generic domain such as biomedical, electronic engineering, information systems. Also, domain ontology specifies the domain concepts that are present in the generic model.
- **Task and Problem Solving Ontology:** Describes ontology relating to a specific task or problem
- **Application Ontology:** Describes concepts related to specific applications.

Figure 6. Guarino's proposal for ontology Modularization

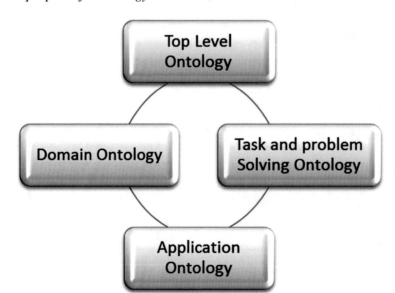

Broadly, Aristotle's ontology has ten categories including matter, relation, quantity, time, location, etc. Also, Sowa presents four categories; continuant, occurrent, concrete and abstract (Sowa, 2005). Some pioneers show negative attitudes to generic models of ontologies due to the fact that they believe there is on -independent use of ontology; on the other hand, some have justified using upper ontology as a good way to organize the domain knowledge. In this interim, Sowa (2000) has categorized ontology into:

Informal Ontology

Informal ontology could be specified by a catalogue of types - these are either undefined or defined only by statements in a natural language. It contains all the terminology of a domain, classifying the concepts and the relations. More precisely, informal ontology is specified by a collection of names for concepts and relation types organized in a partial ordering by the type-subtype relation.

Formal Ontology

Formal ontology is processed by machine and usually uses ontological languages to encode ontology, e.g. DAML+ OIL and OWL (Sowa, 2000).

Both formal and informal ontologies are fundamental components of knowledge about a domain.

Domain Ontology

The domain ontology is a specific area of knowledge, containing the main concepts and their relations. Gomez-Perez asserted that this kind of ontology has weaknesses including emerging upper-level ontology. It classifies its concepts according to different criteria, which leads to heterogeneity in knowledge. The domain ontology is the solution of specific concepts in each domain. e.g. medical, knowledge, economic, (Gòmez-Pérez et al., 2004, Sowa, 2012). To sum up, we compared between these approaches in Table 3.

RELATED RESEARCH

The number of studies on ontologies has been growing rapidly recently in the knowledge engineering area. Most of the studies in this area are focused on ontology construction. Gartner indicated that the semantic web integration will have a big impact on technologies in the next few years. Ontologies are used as a foundation to enable interoperability through the semantic web (Gartner, 2006). Bhatt provided an approach of sub-ontology extraction to fulfil users' needs based on unified medical language system (UMLS); he designed ontoMove to develop the semantic web. It used RDF, RDFs schema and OWL languages (Bhatt et al., 2009). OntoCAPE is large scale ontology for Chemical process to be used in the industrial field. His proposed ontoSpider which is a novel ontology extractor to extract ontology from HTML web. Nevertheless, the lexical semantic and natural languages have a negative effect on the result because the complicated knowledge and difference of outcome when a word or link is missing (Du et al., 2009).

Ontologies play a fundamental role in defining terms that can be used as metadata. Sabou's project is to develop ontology from OWL-s files in order to describe the web services (Sabou 2005), particularly in a specific domain such as biomedical ontologies - which play a fundamental role in accessing the

Table 3. Ontology categories

Approaches	Categorizations of Ontologies
Mizoguchi & colleagues 1995	• Content ontology • Communication ontology for sharing knowledge • Indexing ontology • Meta-ontology

Van Heijst & colleagues 1997	Classify ontologies into two diminutions:
	1. It has three categories:
	   o Terminological ontologies as lexicons.
	   o Information ontologies as database schemata
	   o Knowledge modelling
	2. It has four categories:
	   o Representation
	   o Generic
	   o Domain
	      Application ontology

Guarino 1998	Ontology is also categorised based on its level of dependency in a particular task: • Top level ontology • Domain ontology • Task ontology • Application ontology
Sowa 2000	1. Informal ontology 2. Formal ontology 3. Domain ontology

Lassila and McGuinness 2001	Based on the ontology needs and the richness of its structure
	    • Controlled vocabularies
	    • Glossaries
	    • Thesaurus
	    • Informal is-a relations.
	    • Formal is-a hierarchy
	    • Formal instance
	    • Frames, value restriction
	    • General logical constraints.

heterogeneous sources of medical information - and using and sharing patients' data. Many studies on developing domain ontology are proposed, for instance those mentioned below.

The Budgetary domain to analysis budget concepts of expenses followed Methontology; it was designed for the public sector to organise an organisation's knowledge (Brusa et al., 2006).

Domain ontology of e-learning in educational systems aims to describe the learning material (Gascueña et al., 2006, Hong-Yan et al., 2009).

Chi et al., (2006) study described a framework of ontological techniques for reusing and sharing knowledge in natural science museums. This study developed two ontologies of vascular plant and herbal drugs.

Elena (2006) study was about developing historical archive ontology where users are centre of the methodology for extracting the ontology. The ontology expanded mainly to these classes; time instants and time periods, and university things such as students and personnel.

Ontology of the legal domain in Spain was developed by domain experts. The study shows how domain experts can develop domain ontology by themselves, and how Methontology methods and WebODE software can help them (Corcho et al., 2002).

Cooking ontology is for the cooking domain; it described the building process that followed the Methontology. The results was four models, namely; utensils, food, recipes, and action (Batista et al., 2006).

Furthermore, Geoinformatics ontology was proposed as a domain ontology that consists of a semantic layer and a syntactic layer. The knowledge acquiring process was based on a corpus of multilingual dictionaries of the geographical information system GIS (Deliiska, 2007).

GALEN (Generalised Architecture for Languages Encyclopaedias and Nomenclatures) provides reusable terminology resources for clinical systems. It contains 25,000 concepts used to represent a complex structure that describes a medical procedure (Trombert-Paviot et al., 2002). Furthermore, commerce ontologies facilitate exchange of information between suppliers and customers and offer a framework to identify the services and products in the markets.

GENE ontology (GO) was developed by the National Human Genome Research Institute in 1998. It presents a control vocabulary of gene and gene products attributes. It contains (30,000) concepts and is organized as follows; cellular component, molecular function, and biological process. It is regularly updated and is available in several formats (Gasevic et al., 2006, GeneOntology, 2009, Jepsen, 2009).

Standardized Nomenclature for Medicine - clinical terminology (SNOMED) is an ontology containing health care terminology. It contains 350,000 terms that represent clinical meaning. Each concept has a number, ID and full specific name (FSN). SNOMED has the ability to automate functions related to medical record administration and facilitate data collection for research purposes (Jepsen, 2009).

Enterprise ontology is developed to define and arrange company knowledge. The knowledge is included in the processes, activities, strategies and organizations. TOVE (Toronto Virtual Enterprise) is developed in the Integration Laboratory at the University of Toronto. It provides a shared terminology to be understood and shared between commercial and public enterprise. TOVE was implemented in C++ and Prolog for axioms. It covers activities, time, parts and resources (Laboratory, 2011).

Economic ontology is constructed to define the economic domain from economic documents. It uses OntGen tool to semi-automatically construe ontology. The ontology is based on machine learning methods (Vogrincic & Bosnic, 2011).

The ontology of the International Council of Museums- Conceptual Reference Model (CIDOC-CRM) is intended to represent a formal structure to describe concepts with its definitions in the area of cultural heritage documentation. It encodes in RDFs to describe classes and properties. They had created their own properties because RDF does not support properties. Its classes and properties are defined by their initial codes such as E1 entity, P4 property (Group, 2008).

The concept model of Bibliographical records developed by IFLA is called Functional Requirements for Bibliographic Records (FRBR). It was created to develop an entity relationships model to view the bibliographic universe; it aimed to develop OCLC's catalogue and to be implemented in large catalogue databases. It includes four levels of representation; work, expression, item and manifestation (Tillett, 2004).

The ontology for cultural heritage resources was developed to facilitates access to collection of digital material. This study developed by library of the University of North Carolina by involving the social studies teachers in designing and evaluation the ontology. The study focused on modelling prototypes, and its scope covered the collection of Tobacco Bag Stringing (TBS). The TBS ontology is an indexing tool that supports semantic annotations of the TBS collection (Pattuelli, 2011). Table 4 summarises some of the domain ontologies.

In summary, comparison of these studies with this research will be original because:

In this study we consider the development of an ontology of Information science OIS for defining its boundaries and avoiding ambiguities in the concepts. Furthermore, the OIS ontology will be coded by OWL language. It will be metadata for knowledge base systems in a specific domain and improve

Table 4. Domain ontologies

Domain Ontologies	Aim	Concepts	Relations	Assertions
Open GALEN, 2002clinical medicine	supporting terminology services	25,000	594	216,000
SNOMED CT, 2004	Acquiring and capturing information to be shared and aggregated for health care information	350,00	50	1.5
UMLS semantic etwork,2004	Bio-medicine ontology to offer a consistent classification of the concepts	135	54	6,864
GENE ontology (GO) 1998	a control vocabulary of gene and gene products attributes	30,000	-	-
CIDO-CRM Conceptual Reference Model 2000	Cultural heritage documentation ontology	90	194	-
FRBR concept model for Bibliographic Records	Intended to develop relation model to bibliographic universe/	9	12	-

the retrieval information process on the World Wide Web in the domain of Information Science. This work has never previously been done.

Significantly, however, the domain ontologies contain concepts in a specific subject that provide control vocabulary to control the domain concepts and to construct the relationships between them in a consistent manner. In addition, domain ontologies offer clear boundaries and theories through these definitions. Consequently, domain ontology offers connections between the concepts and their meaning. In natural languages there are different meanings for one concept e.g., "Data". In a dictionary a user might find many definitions of it, whereas ontologies specifying a formal definition avoid vagueness and ambiguity, to be able to choose the accurate meaning. Looking at meaning of data in the Oxford Dictionary, for example, the user will discover many definitions. Ontologies therefore provide single definitions, as revealed in Figure 7.

On the other hand, the confusion between data and information terms is still a big problem, especially between the domain specialists and users of the libraries and information sciences community. Processing data both manually and by computer produces information. This outcome has a specific context and a high degree of reliability. The information has the effect of changing situations through its reception to become knowledge. Furthermore, information differs from data due to the fact that information provides opportunities to make decision after analysing the data. However, the data remains fuzzy and it cannot be used until it is fully processed to become information (Stonier, 1990).

Designing Criteria for Ontology

Gruber has proposed initial sets of designing criteria for ontologies. These designing criteria are as follows (Gruber, 1993, Burtonjones et al., 2005, Fluit et al., 2002):

1. **Clarity:** The ontology concepts should be defined in formal and complete mode, which can be defined according to specific purposes of the design. It helps the communication to be effective and efficient. Consequently, most of the definitions are derived from the social contexts; however, they should be independent of social contexts documented in natural language (NL).

Figure 7. An example of ontology role

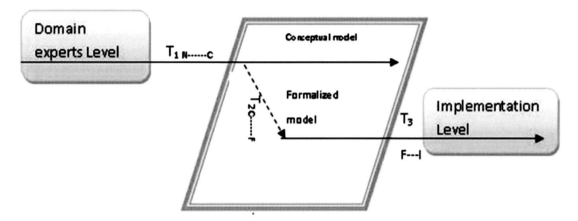

2. **Extendibility:** Designing ontologies is used for shared concepts. It should provide a conceptual foundation for a diversity of expected tasks whose outcome can be predicted.
3. **Coherence:** Is a vital criterion in evaluating ontologies for ensuring the consistency of concepts which are defined formally. It should permit inference that is consistent with logical definitions
4. **Encoding Bias:** It applies when a representation alternative has been made only for ease of implementation.
5. **Minimal Ontological Commitment:** Ontologies need a sufficient ontological commitment to maintain the predictable knowledge sharing tasks ahead.

As you can see the above criteria play a crucial role for designing and developing ontology. It is through defining the requirements for ontology artifact to ensure the ontology is correct, true, and consistent, that it can be evaluated.

ONTOLOGY EVALUATION APPROACHES

The evaluation is still a key problem in ontology development; formal ontologies need to be guided and evaluated and also require objective criteria. The predefined criteria help ontologists to evaluate ontologies. In the literature different approaches have been considered to evaluate ontologies (Brewster et al., 2004, Lozano-Tello and Gomez-Perez, 2004, Maedche and Staab, 2002b, Porzel and Malaka, 2004). Despite this, there is no preferred approach to ontology evaluation. The approach depends on the purpose and kind of ontology being developed. The evaluation process is necessary even when building an ontology for a particular domain from the beginning or modifying an existing one(Gòmez-Pérez et al., 2004, Cristani and Cuel, 2005) .

Additionally, evaluation is required to check the quality of the ontology during the engineering process to ensure it fulfils the requirements. Also, it is useful to be applied in applications. However, there are many approaches, as shown in Table 5. Some of them can be done through developing a process to fix errors early, which also ensures they contain the correct data and information to be selected by

Table 5. Approaches of ontology evaluation

References	Approaches
(Gòmez-Pérez et al., 2004)	-ontology verification - ontology validation

(Yao et al., 2005)	Ontology cohesion metrics:
	    − Number of Root Class: (NoR)
	    − Number of Leaf Classes: (NoL)
	    − Average Depth of Inheritance Tree of Leaf Nodes (ADIT-LN)

(Maedche and Staab, 2002a, Porzel and Malaka, 2004, Brewster et al., 2004, Lozano-Tello and Gomez-Perez, 2004)	Ontology evaluation can be classified into these categories: -Compressing with other ontologies(Golden-Standard) - Using ontology application to evaluate the results. - Compressing with source data of the domain Knowledge. - Assessment ontology by experts in the specific area based on predefined criteria.

(Vrandecic, 2010)	Ontology can be evaluated:
	    - By them selves
	    - With some context
	    - Within an application
	    - In the context of an application and task

the knowledge engineers and end users for applications. Ontology can be evaluated by comparing two ontologies, O1, and O2. Using specific tools that facilitate knowledge, engineers work to select the most suitable ontology for applications, such as Onto metric.

Gòmez-Pérez et al., (2004) indicates a different approach which involves dividing the ontology evaluation into ontology validation and ontology verification. The verification assesses the ontology to be built correctly and implements its definitions correctly. The validation indicates whether ontology definitions represent the real world or not, according to the purpose of its creation. Her emphasis on the aim of evaluating ontologies is to ensure whether the concepts are defined correctly or not. The verification of ontology relates to these criteria:

- **Consistency:** Which means the class will not obtain a contradictory conclusion, which is called Consistency error.
- **Completeness:** Is about in which level the ontology represents the real world. If it does not cover the whole domain, for instance, that is called Completeness error.

The Conciseness criteria are concerned with the consistency of all the information that is available in the ontology, which are called redundancy errors.

The validation approach is important to assess ontology quality. It can be performed automatically by the DL reasoner. The DL reasoner performs range of inference types, because most of the results are unpredictable, Baader and Nutt provide example of:

Child $\equiv$ ∩ Person $\exists$ hasParent. Mother ∩

$\exists$ hasParent.Father

Child $\subseteq$ 2 = hasChild

Child $\equiv$ Person ∩ $\exists$ hasParent.Mother ∩

∃ hasParent.Father ∩ 2= hasChild (Baader and Nutt, 2003)

To define format semantic of concepts, we suppose that child is person and has parent mother and father that mean child ≡ equivalent to a person.

Based on the validation approach the quality criteria are discussed. The domain experts can evaluate the ontologies according to quality criteria such as:

1. **Consistency:** Means there is no contradiction between the concepts of the ontology. So, inconsistency manifests itself by:
   a. Circularity.
   b. Disjoint partition error.
   c. Incorrect classification.
2. **Completeness:** Means how the ontology covers the ontology subjects. The incompleteness can be indicated by:
   a. Concepts are imprecisely defined.
   b. Missing some concepts.
   c. Some concepts are partially defined.
   d. Disjoin properties.
   e. Redundancy of classes, relationships, or instances.
      1. **Conciseness:** Means that needless information is present in the ontology.
      2. **Clarity:** Is how the ontology presents concepts in effective meaning.
      3. **Generality:** Is how the ontology will be used for a variety of purposes in the same domain.
      4. **Robustness:** Means how the ontology has the ability to support any future changes.
      5. **Semantic Data Richness:** Identify the richness and diversity of the ontology conceptualisation.
      6. **Subject Coverage:** Of a particular domain and its richness:
   a. Determine which Level the ontology will cover exact subject.

The OIS ontology evaluation will be based on Gòmez- Pérez' approach. The OIS ontology has been revised by domain experts filling out a quality evaluation report that consisted of several question related to the criteria.

However, it is clear that the domain's experts can assess ontology at various levels, such as; lexical, vocabulary, concept, data to ensure the ontology meets the scope and components required. The context application level is useful for evaluating ontology if it is a part of large ontology. Also, the Syntactic Structure/architecture/design is useful if the ontology is manually structured or if it needs a certain structure, whereas other approaches cannot cover this as well, for example, application based, data driven and level golden standard. Table 6 summarises these approaches.

Ontology Engineering Methodologies

Since ontology is the backbone of the semantic web and the semantic web is a conscious version of the WWW, methodologies support the crucial process of creating ontologies. Methodology offers guidelines for developing ontologies, choosing suitable techniques for each activity of the building process. Since the 1990s many methodologies have been proposed to build ontologies. Most of these have different

Table 6. An overview of levels of ontology evaluation

Evaluation levels	Approaches			
Complexity Level	Level Golden standard	Application based	Data driven	Assessment by humans
Data, Lexical, concept, vocabulary.	+	+	+	+
The hierarchal taxonomy	+	+	+	+
Other semantic relations	+	+	+	+
Context, application	+	+	+	+
Syntactic	+	-	-	+
Ontology designing, architecture, Structure.	-	-	-	+

approaches; some methods are designed for creating ontology from scratch and others reuse existing ontologies.

The ontology building process as widely known in the ontological engineering community is more of a craft than engineering activities. Furthermore, each method of creating ontology follows its own principle of activity and design even if it is not clear whether their contribution is successful or not. In fact, it is the absence of agreed guidelines and methodologies that hinders ontology development (Gasevic et al., 2006).

Methodology of developing ontology can be classified into three categories; the methodology approach for building ontology from scratch, for example Cyc methods were created in the 1990s by Lenat and Guha. In 1995 Uschold & King proposed developing ontology enterprise modelling (TOVE), followed by Grüninger & Fox's methods in 1995 in the same field of ontology enterprise. In 1996 Uschold and Grüninger proposed outlines of developing ontology. Methontology emerged in 1996, as one of the methods used to build ontology using tools such as OntoEdit and Protégé. It provides a general framework defining designing criteria for ontology criteria. (Noy and Musen, 2000, Sure et al., 2002, Pattuelli, 2011). In 1997 SENSUS methodology was extended to Methontology, which proposed creating SENSUS, a huge ontology. But it still represents methodology for creating ontologies from scratch. The next section presents and analyses some prominent methodologies against the IEEE 1074- 2006 standards for developing the software Life Cycle.

CYC Method

The Cyc method was created in the 1980s by Microelectronics and Computer Technology Corporation (MCC) (Lenat, 1990). Cyc encompasses a knowledge base of more than 1,000,000 hand defined assertions. Each assertion is presented in a Microtheory. The Microtheory organises the knowledge hierarchy to facilitate inferential focus and knowledge reuse. The Cyc knowledge is separated into collections of 164.000 concepts and 3,300,000 facts, in a specific area of knowledge. Cyc uses the Cyc language (CycL) for implementation. CycL is a hybrid language that combines predicate calculus with frames. (Curtis et al., 2005).

1. Lenat 1990, proposed three stages for the ontology design process, as follows:

2. Articles and pieces of knowledge could be manual coding. This stage of knowledge is acquired by hand since learning machines and natural language systems do not have a common specific knowledge, hence in search knowledge is acquired as follows:

3. The encoding of knowledge requires the knowledge that is already in books and articles. This is searching and representing the fundamental knowledge that is already assumed to belong to the readers.

4. The assessment and examination of the contents of articles that is incorrect. This examination is finding out where those articles are incorrect.

5. Question identification for users, to be able to answer their questions by reading the text.

6. The coding supported by using tools based on the knowledge stored in the Cyc Knowledge base.

Uschold and King Method

The first method of creating ontologies was presented by Uschold & King in 1995. It was extended in 1996 by Uschold & Gruninger. They point out this method is insufficient and the relationships are unspecified between the stages. As a result they proposed guidelines of ontology designing and developing. (Uschold and Grüninger M., 1996) The methodology is summarized as follows:

Stage 1: Identifying the purpose of creating the ontology, its scope and which domain it will cover, besides determining the users and developers.

Stage 2: Building the ontology: building the ontology starts with the following phases:
- **Ontology Capture:** This phase is capturing the knowledge of the ontology such as:
  - Identifying the domain concepts and relationships.
  - Generating accurate definitions for the concepts and relationships within the domain.
  - Identifying each term that indicates to identified concepts and its relationships for consensus on the concepts.
- **Coding:** Capturing the knowledge to represent it explicitly. Uschold & Gruninger recommend committing general terms to be used to specify the ontology, and choosing formal languages to write its codes.
- **Integrating Existing Ontologies:** Refers to using existing ontologies in capturing ontology or even in coding it.

Stage 3: Evaluating the ontology: Uschold & Gruninger assert that evaluation of the ontology is very important to be able to make a technical judgment.

Stage 4: Documentation: documenting the ontology process, which means guidelines are established (Fernández-López, 1999).

Gruninger and Fox Method

Gruninger & Fox (1995) provide a formal design approach for creating and evaluating ontology, compared with Uschold & Gruninger's methods. This method based on the first order logic and extensive ontology such as Toronto Virtual Enterprise (TOVE). TOVE is a set of ontologies for different features of the business projects. Gruninger & Fox's method consists of these steps:

1. **Identify Motivation Scenarios:** The motivated scenario is a problem that has not been addressed in existing ontology. These scenarios have a vital impact on guiding the ontology design and providing a possible solution to the problem. The provided solution offers informal semantics of the objects and their relationships.

2. **Elaborate Some Informal Competency Questions from the Specified Scenario:** The ontology represents these questions using formal terminology. The competency questions support the evaluation of ontological commitment for developing the ontology.

3. **Using a Formal Language to Specify the Ontology Terminology:** Using informal competency questions for the purpose of extracting ontology content and specifying terminology in a formal language. This means to formally represent the concepts, attributes and relationships through ontology language. Actually this step corresponds to the coding stage in Uschold & King's method, discussed previously.

4. Write formal competency questions to define the competency questions formally.

5. **Using the First Order Logic to Specify Axioms:** Gruninger & Fox (1992) declare that axioms should be specifying the definitions of concepts and constraints by using first order logic.

6. **Specification of Completeness Theorem:** The establishing of conditions characterises completeness of developing ontology, so defining the conditions under which solutions to the question are completed (Gòmez-Pérez et al., 2004).

SENSUS Methodology

The SENSUS methodology is designed to assist in the creation of new domain ontologies from a large ontology, to generate its skeleton (Swartout 1997). The main process in this ontology is linking domain concepts to the SENSUS ontology. The main processes of it are as follows:

- **Process 1 – Identifying the Seed Terms:** The key terms relevant to a specific domain are identified.
- **Process 2 – Linking the Seed Terms Manually to SENSUS:** Thereafter, the terms are linked by using OntoSarus to broaden the coverage of the ontology.
- **Process 3 – Adding Paths to the Roots:** Requires collecting all concepts to be linked to roots of SUESUS.
- **Process 4 – Adding New Domain Terms:** That have not yet been included which are relevant to the domain.
- **Process 5 – Adding Complete Sub Trees:** Sub trees should be added to the final ontology, if nodes of a sub tree are relevant. (Gòmez-Pérez et al., 2004)

Methontology

Methontology was developed at the Polytechnic University of Madrid in a Artificial Intelligence laboratory (Fernadez-Lopez et al., 1999). Methontology is used for creating ontologies from scratch or to reuse ontology. Its framework facilitates the construction of ontology at the knowledge levels. Fernandez (1997) proposed several steps that are similar to Gurninger and Fox (1995), and Uschold and Gruninger (1996). But it differs by emphasizing the evaluation and documentation steps. Furthermore, it supports the ontology life cycle based on evolving a prototype which makes changing and adding easier at each new phase, contrasting with others that support top down, middle out, or bottom-up approaches (Fernández-López et al., 1997).

Gòmez-Pérez, et al. (2004) indicates that the framework of methodology includes the following phases:

Phase 1 Specification: The ontology specification step starts with several activities, such as; identifying goals, scope, strategy and boundary. It must specify the purpose of building and designing the ontology, and its scope.

Within the specifications phase, questions should be answered about the main reason for developing ontology, as proposed by (Fernández-López et al., 1997) questions and answers (both formal and informal) are written down to establish the purpose and scope; these questions are similar to the competency questions recommended by Uschold & Gruninger (1996).

This phase aims to assemble the resources covering the ontology's objects, purposes, scope and granularity. This includes:

- **Knowledge Acquisition:** Building the conceptual model needs acquisition knowledge. It is an essential activity to start with because the concepts must be assessed to ensure their currency, which helps to reduce many errors in future stages.

    Phase 2 Conceptualisation: Provides a conceptual model in the ontology to be created, whose purpose is integrating the domain knowledge in a way that arranges and structures knowledge through the knowledge acquisition phase, which will impact on the rest of the ontology construction.

Following knowledge capture and acquisition, the knowledge needs to be conceptualised. The ontology's designer needs to use the conceptual model technique as proposed by (Gòmez-Pérez et al., 2004). The conceptual model contains tasks of knowledge construction in formal models.

Creating a conceptual model is to determine the ontology construction, also, to present the preliminary designing activity. Its intent is to organise the acquisition of domain knowledge. There is a very strong relationship between conceptual modelling and knowledge acquisition, as illustrated in Blum's model tree of fundamental software process. Figure 9 consists of three activities described as:

1. (T1: N _____ C) this is for the transfer of domain concepts to the conceptual model and describing users' needs.
2. (T2: C _____ F) transfers the conceptual model to a formal model that describes essential properties in the produced software.
3. (T3: F _____ I) transfers the formal model to software that is correct in respect of the formal model. (Blum, 1996).

The activity of building the conceptual model is as follows:

- Building Glossary of terms to identify which terms need to be included in the ontology; the glossary includes the term name, Synonym, Acronyms, and a description of it.
- Identify the binary relations between concepts of the ontology.

Figure 8. Conceptual modelling

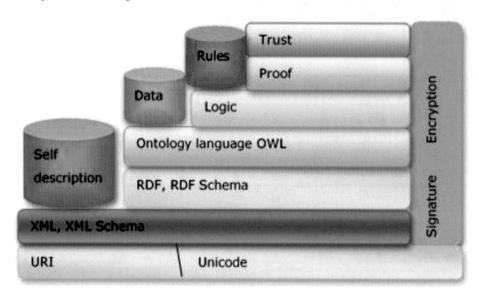

- Build concept classification.
- Build the data dictionary to identify the concepts with their meaning, instance, class attributes, and their relations.
- In the data dictionary the instances attribute should be described in more detail, and class attributes also needs to be described.
- Describe the formal axioms and the rules (Gòmez-Pérez et al., 2004). In Methontology the rule of conceptual modelling is introduced in ontology designing.

    Phase 3 Formalisation: Conceptual model needs to transform into a formal or semi-computable model. The formalisation of ontology needs to be represented by using representation languages.

    Phase 4 Integration: Methontology supports the integration of existing ontologies. Much research has been done in semantic integration ontology and ontology mapping such as (Noy, 2004).

    Phase 5 Coding: In this stage the computable model has been created in computational language to be machine readable.

    Phase 6 Evaluation: Gómez-Pérez (1995) emphasises the necessity of evaluating the ontology to guarantee that the information that is attached to each concept is completed and to ensure all descriptions and instance attributes are correctly defined, thus minimising errors. Furthermore, ensuring both the class attributes and instance attributes are consistent and makes sense with each concept.

    Step 7 Documentation: The documentation is a very important phase, which helps to facilitate the reusability of the ontology designed as with any software developing project.

    Step 8 Maintenance: Gómez-Pérez recommended that ontology needs to be updated and maintained once it is designed.

Table 7. implementation of Methontology

	Ontologies Developed With It	Applications Using It
Methontology	Chemical ontology(Fernández López et al., 1999)	Onto Agent (Arpirez et al., 1998)http://delicias.dia.fi.upm.es/OntoAgent.
	Environmental pollutants ontologies (Gòmez-Pérez and Rojas, 1999)	Chemical OntoAgent(Arpirez et al., 1998)
	The reference ontology(Arpirez et al., 1998)	Ontogeneration (Aguado et al., 1998)
	Knowledge acquisition ontology (KA)(Blazquez et al., 1998)	

Methontology has been adopted to develop ontologies and implemented in many applications such as a chemical ontology Fernández López et al. (1999), and legal ontology Corcho et al. (2002), as shown in Table 7

Ontology development is an area of knowledge engineering, whose purpose is to enable the control of knowledge within software applications and projects in a domain. Our approach visualises IS knowledge in this context.

Comparison of Methodology

Roughly speaking, the majority of methodologies are based on the experience of developing enterprise ontologies. These methods propose common development stages to ontology engineers. The main phases are: identifying the purpose, knowledge capture, codifying the concepts and their relations. There is no specific agreement on the best methodology for designing and building ontology, because decisions are based on application and purpose (Noy and McGuinness, 2001). Purpose and need must be the starting points for the construction of a new ontology or the reuse of an existing one. (Pinto and Martins, 2001).

The study conducts a contrasting of the previous methodologies based on ontology dependency level with respect to its application. According to these criteria methodologies could be categorised as:

- **Application Independent:** The ontology process is independent from users, such as Cyc, Methontology, and Uschold & King methodology.
- **Application Dependent:** Scenarios of ontologies are identified in a specification process.
- **Application Semi-Dependent:** This type of ontology is based on applications that use them, such as Gruninger & Fox, SENSUS methodology. (Fernandez-Lopez and Gomez-Perez, 2002).

Methods used for different ontology projects have been used as a way of justifying why Methontology was selected as a mature methodology.(Fernadez-Lopez and Gomez - Perez, 2002). "Methontology is a framework that enables the construction of ontologies at the knowledge level" (Calero et al., 2006 p.18). Methontology is the methodology of creating ontologies both from scratch or reusing an existing one. Its stages are conceptualisation, requirements analysis, formalisation, implementation, maintaining and evaluating. Methontology is involved in re-engineering methods for the purpose of creating a conceptual model. On one hand, re-engineering methods are considered an extension of the Methontology framework. On the other hand, Methontology emphasises the possibility of return to the previous activity if limitations are found later. SENSUS methodology does not evolve a life cycle model. There

Table 8. Comparison between methodologies

Ontology	Cyc	Uschold & King's	Gruninger & Fox's	SENSUS	ONION	Methontology
Purpose of designing	To capture what consensus knowledge that people have about the world	To provide guidelines for developing ontologies	To develop knowledge base system by using first logic order	Building the skeleton of domain ontology starting from huge one.	Integration of terminology in medical domain	Enabling the construction of ontology at the knowledge level
Advantage	Ability to use it for building Cyc knowledge base about the world	The methodology process clearly defines acquisition, coding, evaluation	It can be used as direct to convert informal scenarios in quantifiable models	Linking two independent developed ontologies	Integration many sub-domain ontologies in medicine domain. - has an ontology open to revisions without giving maintenance trouble. - support creating, integration, updating and maintenance ontology.	-It has its root in activities that identified in software development process & knowledge engineering methodologies – Live cycle based on prototype to enabling adding and moving terms. – possibility of return to any process to amending or modifying
Based on ontology	Yes	No	TOVO project of business process	Yes	Yes	Depends ontologuia
Tools	Cyc tools	Not – specific	Not – specific	OntoSaurus	Not – specific	Portage, WebODE, OntoEdit
Details of methodology	Little	Very little	Little	Little	Medium	A lot
Strategy of building application	Application-independent	Application-independent	Application-independent	Application-independent	Application- dependent	Application- independent
Strategy of identifying concepts	Not specified	Middle-out	Middle-out	Not specified	Not specified	Middle-out

is a similarity between constricting ontologies. In Uscholdard in Gòmez-Pérez and colleagues' method 1996, the first stage of building chemical ontology is to acquire knowledge while the second phase is building a requirements specification document. First stage in constructing chemical ontology is to gather knowledge, and then a requirements specification document must be built. A Cyc method was created in the 1980s; it does not code the contents of books and articles in its codification process, but instead looks at knowledge available to readers, and seeks to represent it. Languages such as ODE and WebODE both support Methontology. Table 8 summarises differences between methodologies.

Evaluation of Ontology Methodologies

Evaluation methodologies of building ontology are compliant with IEEE 1074–1995 standards. IEEE 1074–1995 describes the process of software development.

According to the IEEE definition, software is "computer programs, procedures, and possibly associated documentation and data pertaining to the operation of a computer system"; ontologies are part (sometimes only potentially) of software products. Therefore, ontologies should be developed according to the standards proposed for software generally, which should be adapted to the special characteristics of Ontologies. (Fernández-López, 1999p.4-2)

Fernandez Lopez (1999) points out the framework bases on IEEE 1074-1995 to evaluate different ontologies' development process, which is:

1. Project management process; includes the creation framework for ontology life cycle.
2. Ontology development process that is divided into three parts:
    a. Pre-development that is related to feasibility study.
    b. Development of the ontology designing and implementation.
3. Post-developing ontologies includes all operations, and maintaining processes.
4. Integral process means the completion of the project successfully. It starts with capturing knowledge, configuration, evaluation, and documentation (Fernadez-Lopez and Gomez-Perez, 2002, Hong-Yan et al., 2009). Table 9 summarises this analysis.

Generally speaking, "most of the methodologies focus on development activities, especially on the codification of the ontology, and they do not pay attention to other important aspects related to management. This is because ontological engineering is relatively new" (Fernadez-Lopez and Gomez-Perez, 2002). There are several methods for corporate Knowledge Management, to design and implement an intensive information system. Some of them focus on initial stages of developing a knowledge management application. Other methodologies support application scenarios.

Techniques Involved

Ontology is a key part of the semantic web for capturing knowledge and translating it into a machine-readable form. The web ontology language (OWL) formalises knowledge in a semantic framework (Horridge, 2009). When a new ontology is to be built, several questions must be asked: which tools are needed? Which language will be used in importing knowledge? This section explains the tools and

Table 9. Methodology standards

Methodology Standards		Cyc	Uschold and King	Grüninger and Fox	SENSUS	Methondology
Project management processes		No	No	No	No	partially
Project development-oriented processes	Predevelopment Processes	No	No	No	No	No
	Development process	No	Yes	Yes	Yes	Yes
	Post development processes	No	No	No	No	partially
Integral processes		partially	partially	partially	No	partially

No-not support / Yes-support/ partially support

Figure 9. Semantic web languages

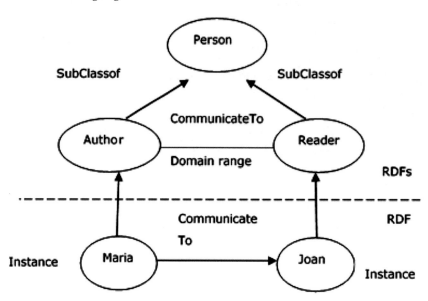

languages of ontology, to show their differences, similarities, and development, so we can determine which tool to implement.

Ontology Languages

There are several ontology languages discussed in literature, all of which have been created in order to represent knowledge and implementation of ontologies. These languages enable us to access web content and also present extra semantic information, so that it can be shared, processed and understood by computers as a way of exchanging and processing data rather than just presenting information.

Tim Berners-Lee's (2000) analysis supports the notion that more mark-up languages are needed for the web to be able to display information and resources. An ongoing effort is therefore taking place to represent logical knowledge in web language. Primary approaches work at Extensible Mark-up Language (XML) level, but different languages must be used to explain information in a logical way – for this, Resource Description Framework (RDF), (RDFs) schema level and ontology language (OWL) are used (Antoniou and Harmelen, 2004). Figure 9 is a widely-cited in the literature that shows some information about semantic web languages.

As well as being called semantic web languages, these are also called mark up languages. Semantic web technologies contain many layers, as asserted by the W3C Consortium, so these languages will require re-evaluation in future. Furthermore, these layers are built on the basic of URLs, and XML, XML schema, followed by RDF and RDFs. OWL and its rules sit at the top of the pyramid, created through logic, proof and trust. XML data can be defined as a nest of elements for building a data model. The model originates from the precursor of XML, called SGML. SGML is used as the mark up languages for describing text.

Resource Description Framework RDF, and RDFs

XML language has a standard syntax specifically for meta language, which allows user to mark up documents by using some tags. XML does not, however, provide any semantic meaning for data. There is, for instance, no meaning associated with nesting tags. Below is an example of a sentence written using XML, showing how tags are used:

```
Melvil Dewey is a developer of Dewey Decimal class (DDC)
```

Illustrating the sentence can be done in various ways, such as:

```
< developer name="Melvil Dewey">
<system> DDC</system>
</developer>
```

Or

```
<system name="DDC">
<developedby> Melvil Dewey</developedby>
    </system>
```

The above example shows nesting that provides the same information. It illustrates that there is no consistency to assigning meanings in tag nesting.

RDF language represents relationships between things. In RDF statements is an object, attribute, or value, for instance. Alexander Maedche is an author of an ontology learning publication, as shown in the example below:

RDF syntax is given in XML. When RDFs provide definitions, users are able to define terminology in schema language, as used in the RDF data model. As shown above, the relationships between objects can be shown as:

```
 Information retrieval is a subclass of information system
Classification schema is a subclass of classification
```

In this sentence DDC is a classification system. (subClassof) shows us that there is associated meaning, which allows us to illustrate why RDFs based on XML tags are important.

```
<Classification > DDC</classification>
<Developed by>Melvil Dewey</developed by>
<subject "Geography">
<content> 10 Categories</content>
</subject>
```

This illustration shows that this information makes the semantic model possible in a specific domain, but not in XML or RDF. If we use RDFs we get semantic data, which can be machine-processed.

Figure 10. Semantic net in RDF, RDFs

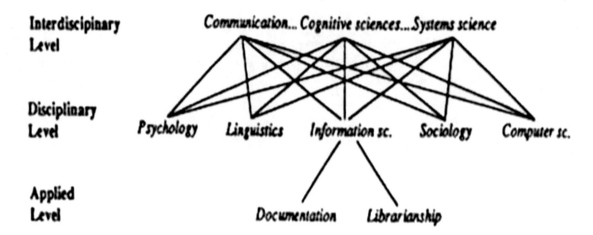

RDFs also organises vocabulary in hierarchical ways, for instance classes, sub-classesOf, properties, sub-propertiesOf, resources and domain – all arranged through using formal language. Figure 10 shows the semantic net using RDFs.

The XML schema describes how XML documents are constructed. In RDF sentences will always contain (object, attribute and value), called statements, as RDF is a data model showing relations between things.

Web Ontology Language (OWL)

This section explains the motivation behind choosing Web Ontology Language (OWL) as the language for building the OIS ontology research tool.

The designing of OWL is focused on representing information about objects, and in which way the objects are interrelated and organised within a specific category (Krivov et al., 2007a). OWL is derived from description logic that aimed to bring reasoning and expressive power to the semantic web. OWL sits on top of RDFs to describe classes and subclasses. It also provides definitions of vocabulary. OWL is a W3C standard; this is as important for building and developing ontologies as any other applications or tools that share information to make it readable and understandable. It is designed to be well-matched with existing web standards such as XML, RDF and DARPA Agent Mark-up Language (DAML); it has been built on DAML+OIL. It differs from RDF in machine interpretability, as it has a large vocabulary and a strong syntax.

Furthermore, it is uses a language construct called Restrictions class. Restrictions define members of a class by existing properties and classes. These restrictions are namely; owl: someValueFromand owl: allValueFrom, owl: hasValue (Allemang and Hendler, 2008)

OWL Layers

OWL is one of the knowledge representation languages. It has a history and evaluation affects its design, which comes in three layers (Horrocks et al., 2003). OWL is built on RDF schema (RDFs), to develop

Table 10. Comparison between semantic languages

Languages	contexts		Object class & properties		Inheritance / concept of inheritance	Property/ element Range	Property element domain	Property element cardinality restrictions	Basic data Type (T Type)			Enumeration of property value	Order data set	Bounded List	Transitive properties	Negation	Necessary & sufficient
	Depending	Type	Class	property					numerical	string	literals						
XML schema	☒	xmlns	☒	☒	☒	☒	☒	☒	☑	☑	☒	☒	Defult	☒	☒	☒	☒
RDF schema	☑	xml	☑	☒	☑	☑	☑	☒	☒	☒	☑	☒	<rdf:seq...> tag	☒	☒	☒	☒
OWL	☑	xml1+ rdfs	☑	☑	☑	☑	☑	☑	☑	☑	☑	☑	<owl:list>tag	☑	☑	☑	☑

ontologies. Its purpose is just like RDFs, to define ontologies in classes, properties and relations. Yet it describes relationships in more richness and capability. Liyang Yu (2011) defined OWL language:

OWL = RDF Schema + new constructs for better expressiveness.

1. **OWL Lite (Light):** Provides simple classification and enabling to defined ontology classes and properties but it is more expressive than RDFs.
2. **OWL DL (Description Logic):** Is more expressive than owl Lite - by allowing cardinality restrictions, DL enables creation of class expressions using Boolean combinatory such as, intersectionOf, UnionOf.
3. **OWL Full:** Gives clear expressiveness and the syntax is self modifying. which means it is free from RDFs(Jepsen, 2009).

Although there are some differences between OWL full and OWL DL, they use the same set of modelling constructs. OWL lite has limitations in cardinality restrictions and does not have any hasValue restriction. (Allemang and Hendler, 2008)

OWL Semantic

The semantic structure of OWL is designed to complete the description logic system. Both OWL Lite and DL have a clean DL semantic. DL language is built on two primal symbols; concepts and roles. The concepts are interpreted as unary predicate symbols. The roles are interpreted as binary predicate symbols which are used for expressing the relations between concepts. One type of concept is concept expression which is formed based on Boolean operations and role restrictions (Krivov et al., 2007a, Krivov et al., 2007b). OWL has many role restrictions, as shown in the example:

- *(∃P,C) ∃ hasChild, male* the written concept indicates that all individuals have at least one male child.
- *(∀P. C) ∀ hasChild. Female* the written concept indicates that all individuals whose children are all female.
- *(≥ nP) ≥ 2 hasChild* this concept is denotes to a set of individuals who have at least two children.

As Modelling motivates a logical definition of OWL, OWL statements are constructed on formal logic. The specific logical system of OWL is Description Logic (DL), which is a logic based knowledge representation formalism - it can be represented as statements in formal descriptions of class and individuals, and can make relations among them; for example, in this example the letter C refers to the concept (class). (C1⊆ C2) means concept C1 is a subclass of concept C2, and (C1 C2) man male the class man is equivalent to class male. Some of the OWL constructors are shown in Table 11. The DL system has different sets of class constructors and axioms for building complex classes and roles. OWL consists of classes and axioms that offer semantics by inferring information based on the explicit data. These axioms interpretation and facts are illustrated in Table 12.

The Table 13 compares the most relevant ontology languages, with the aim of illustrating differences and similarities between them. For each cell in the table we put symbolP, to indicate that this element supported in the language, while Θis used for "does not support it".

From the table we can reveal that there are some differences between traditional languages and ontology mark up languages. Also, some of them represent heavyweight and lightweight ontologies; the heavyweight ontology language represents formal axioms rules, functions and other components, while the lightweight ontology language represents concepts, concepts taxonomy and their relations. Obviously, the components of representation knowledge can be modelled in traditional language such as Ontolingua LOOM, and OCML. Most ontology languages permit representation of concepts and define them by their attributes except RDFs and SHOE. In fact, the disjoint, conjunction, and disjunction axiom is provided by most languages such as Ontologuia, OCML, IL, DAML+Oil and OWL. The binary relation between concepts can be represented in all languages, while hierarchy semantic relations cannot be represented in OKBC, FLogic, SHOW and XOL. Moreover, OWL has the ability to define restriction class. The anonymous classes can be defined based on the restrictions of the value for a specific property of the class.

Ontology Tools

The aim of using a tool for building ontologies is providing sustainability for the ontology life cycle and ontology reuse. Constructing ontology can be a very challenging task, made easier by using ontology tools. many of these tools were created in 1990s, supporting users by offering interfaces. Many have

Table 11. OWL constructors

Constructor	DL syntax	Example
intersectionOf	C1π....πCn	Human ∧ male
UnionOf	C1μ....μCn	Doctor ∨Lawyer
ComplementOf	-C	- male
OneOf	{X1........Xn}	{John, Mary}
toClass	∀P. C	∀ hasChild. female
hasClass	∃P,C	∃ hasChild, male
hasValue	∃P.{X}	∃ citizenOf.{USA}
Max Cardinality	≤ nP	≤1 hasChild
minCardinalityQ	≥ nP	≥ 2 hasChild.

appeared recently, with rise of the semantic web. Gòmez-Pérez, (2004) distinguishes between them by dividing them into groups, see Table 14. Some of these tools are presented below.

Ontologua Server

This was the first ontology tool developed at Stanford University in the Knowledge System Laboratory in the mid 1990s. Ontologua is an easy tool for developing, evaluating and maintaining ontologies. The ontology editor is the main application inside Ontologua server works with a form-based web interface (Farquhar et al., 1996). The Ontologua server enables access to an ontology library for the creation of new ontologies and even for modifying existing ontology. Interacting with the server could be in different ways:

- **Remote Application:** Ontology could be modified and browsed over the internet because it is stored at the server.
- Remote disseminated groups enable multiple users to work simultaneously on the ontology.
- Translating the ontology into specific format, to use in several applications such as, LOOM,CLIPS or Prolog.

Table 12. OWL axioms interpretation and fact

Axiom	DL syntax	Examples
subClassOf	*C1 C2*	Human ⊆ Animal
equivalentClass	C1≡ C2	Man ≡male
disjointWith	C1∩ C2	Female∩ male
sameIndividualAs	{x1} ≡(Alani et al.)	President Obama≡Barack Obama
SubPropertyOf	*P1 P2*	hasSon⊆ hasChild
equivalentProperty	P1≡P2	Price ≡Cost

Table 13. Comparison between ontology languages

Elements	Concept		Attribute				Instance			Axioms				Semantic Relations			
Languages	Definition	Name	Definition	Name	Basic Type	Instance Attribute	Name	Concept instance	Relation	Conjunction	Disjunction	Disjoint	Covering	Binary relation	n-ray	IS-a	Hierarchies
KIF	✓	✓	✓	✓	✓	✓	✓	✓	✓	✗	✓	✓	✓	✓	✓	✓	✓
Ontolingua	✓	✓	✓	✓	✓	✓	✓	✓	✓	✓	✓	✓	✓	✓	✓	✓	✓
LOOM	✓	✓	✓	✓	✓	✓	✓	✓	✓	✓	✓	✓	✗	✓	✓	✓	✓
OKBC	✓	✓	✓	✓	✓	✓	✓	✓	✓	✗	✗	✗	✗	✓	✗	✗	✗
OCML	✓	✓	✓	✓	✓	✓	✓	✓	✓	✓	✓	✓	✗	✓	✓	✗	✓
FLogic	✓	✓	✓	✓	✓	✓	✓	✗	✓	✗	✗	✗	✗	✓	✗	✗	✗
SHOE	✓	✓	✗	✓	✓	✓	✓	✗	✓	✗	✗	✗	✓	✓	✓	✗	✗
XOL	✓	✓	✓	✓	✓	✓	✓	✓	✓	✗	✗	✓	✗	✓	✗	✗	✗
RDFs	✓	✓	✗	✗	✓	✓	✓	✓	✓	✗	✗	✓	✓	✓	✗	✗	✓
OIL	✓	✓	✓	✓	✓	✓	✗	✓	✓	✓	✓	✓	✓	✓	✗	✗	✓
DAML+OIL	✓	✓	✓	✓	✓	✓	✓	✓	✓	✓	✓	✓	✗	✓	✗	✗	✓
OWL	✓	✓	✓	✓	✓	✓	✓	✓	✓	✓	✓	✓	✓	✓	✗	✗	✓

OntoSaurus

Table 14. Groups of ontologies tools

Ontology Tools	Purpose of using	Types
Ontology development	Building new ontology from scratch	Ontolingua Server, OntoSaurus, WebOnto, OilEd, Protégé, WebODE, OntoEdit, KAON
Ontology evaluation	Evaluating the content of ontology, to reduce problems	
Ontology merge and alignment	Solving problems that emerge from different ontologies in a specific domain	Protégé & Chimaera
Ontology – based annotation tools	Use for insert new instance and relations (semi-automatically)	GATE & Cmap
Ontology querying & inference engines	Using to implement ontology	____

OntoSaurus was created at the University of South Carolina in the Information Science Institution. It was implemented for browsing and editing on LOOM ontologies. Moreover, it consists of two modules; web browser and ontology server, to use the system of representing knowledge attached with LOOM language (Swartout 1997, Gòmez-Pérez et al., 2004)

WebOnto

WebOnto was developed to be a tool to edit and browse ontologies collaboratively, which supports cooperation ontology edition synchronously and asynchronously. It was designed at the Open University at the Knowledge Media Institute in 1997. It is an ontology editor using OCML language to represent expressions. WebOnto's editor is based on Java applets rather than HTML forms (Domingue, 1998).

OilEd

In 2001 OilEd was developed at the University of Manchester by Sean Bechhofer as an editor for developing ontologies using ontology interchange language (OIL). OilEd was adopted to export ontology in OWL or DAML +OIL format. It is a tool for helping users to model ontology, and checks its consistency using the reasoner Fast Classification of Terminologies (FaCT) (Bechhofer et al., 2001).

Cmap Tools

Concept Map (Cmap) was developed at Florida Institute of Technology and it is an application to encourage and facilitate collaboration between creation knowledge models. It also, allows members to modify and add to the knowledge model. Furthermore, users can edit and save the Cmaps automatically, updating the website without the need for any technical involvement.

Protégé

Protégé was developed at Stanford University by Stanford Medical Informatics. It is open source, and as an ontology editor, it provides a suite of tools to construct the domain model using various formats. Also, using plug-ins for adding further functions makes it flexible. These plug-ins such as importing and exporting ontology language (XML, OIL, FLogic) and a reasoner, for instance. The platform of Protégé supports two ways of modelling ontologies:

- Protégé frame editors, which enable users to create and populate ontology support by Open Knowledge Base Connectivity protocol (OKBC).
- Protégé OWL editor, which enables users to create and develop ontologies using web ontology language (protégé, 2011b, Noy and McGuinness, 2001).

Web Protégé

WebProtégé is a web interface which provides a flexible environment for experts to work collaboratively. It is a tool to develop ontologies processes and make the ontology accessible from any web browser.

There is a difference between WebProtégé and other tools such as Wikis. It supports OWL 2.0 which is compatible with Protégé 4 (Tudorache et al., 2011, Tania Tudorache et al., 2010).

General Architecture for Text Engineering (GATE)

In the field of language engineering GATE is one of the most used tools. It has plug-ins such as part of speech (POS) taggers, Named Entity Recognizers, and sentence splitters. Using natural language processing (NLP) includes information extracting tools.

GATE was developed by a team at the University of Sheffield in the early 1990s as a free open source tool. It runs on any platform and supports JAVA 5 .0. It has a user interface to enable user editing, visualisation and quick application development, and, in addition to ontology management, it supports manual annotation, semi-automatic and semantic (Moens, 2006).

The automatic and semi-automatic semantic annotation and manual annotation features help users to create own annotation; the GATE developer is used for extracting terms and concepts from specific texts for this purpose. It will be also speed up the ontology process of building a conceptual model as an ontology of IS. GATE supports many languages such as XHTML, XML, HTML, PDF, Emails., MS word, plain text, etc. (Cunningham and Tablan, 2000)

Comparison of Ontology Tools

These tools are compared using different criteria that are summarised in the above table. Clearly, it can help to provide interoperability solutions among tools and languages. Table 15 shows ontology tools that was researched and evaluated. These contain criteria of formal axiom languages which are the most functional features to be used when developing ontologies with them. Another criterion is architecture of ontology tools (client server, standalone). Concerning ease of use, Protégé and WebOnto offer graphical vision to present a data overview. The table shows that most tools are based on first order logic. The lexical capability of tools such as OntoSaurus and WebOnto does not support it, whereas Protégé provides query searching in the ontology. Overall, the most important tool selected is Protégé, which has many features such as; allowing representing class, partitions, relations, attributes and axioms. It has a graphical interface that makes it easy to use. It also supports several languages that can be exported in RDFs, XML, FLogic, Java and ClIPS. It is standalone, free, open source as well being built on a reasoner that helps to infer answers. Furthermore, it has extensible plug-ins, it is powerful and it has easy to use such as features as the DL query tab that allows ontology to be searched (Protégé, 2011a).

INFORMATION SCIENCE (IS)

Overview

Information science (IS) has a comprehensive history. It needs to determine the interdisciplinary relationships with other fields, to clarify the confusion surrounding its specialisation to identity and define its position among other sciences. IS acquires and collects, organises, retrieves the information resources that contain information held by libraries and information centres. IS faces a big problem of how to be

Table 15. Comparison between ontology tools

Ontology editor	Designed	base	Import from language	Export to language	Usage (web support)	View graphic text	Architecture	Lexical capability
Ontolingua server	1990	Ontolingua	KIF, CML, IDL	Export, KIF, LOOM, Epikit, IDL	Web accesses to services	NO	Client / server	Search for terms in loaded ontologies
ontosaurus	2002	LOOM	LOOM IDL onto C++ KIF: Loom	LOOM IDL onto C++ KIF: Loom	No HPPT Browser	Yes hierarchy	Client / server	NO
webonto	1997	OCML	OCML	RDF, export: R, DFs, GXL, Ontolingua, OIL	Web service deployment site	YES	Client / server	NO
oiled	2004	DAML+ OIL	RDFs, OIL, DAML+O IL, SHIQ	:RDFs, OIL, DAML+OIL, OWL	RDF URI's limited namespaces, limited XML schema; exportedHTML	YES	Standalove	synonyms
Cmap tools	2004	Java		None	url refrences	Yes	Standalone	Syntax, speil check, world net
protege	2000	OWL	Xmlrdfs, OWL, XMLS	XML, RDFs, OWL, XMLS, Flogic, Java	Refence ontologies by URL	Yes	Standalone	Query tab allows searching
ontogen	2007	Natural language			URL documents	Yes	Standalone	Querying for particular concepts

(Corcho et al, 2003)

defined. A number of researchers have dealt with its historical perspective, such as Buckland and Liu (1995), Cleverdon (1987), Shera and Cleveland (1977)Bourne (1980)Farkas-Conn (1990).

The IS is concerned with studying properties and behaviours of information, and creating, using, controlling the flow for it to be accessed and used. This includes processes of production and dissemination of information. Hence, IS is derived from mathematics and logic, linguistics, psychology, information technology, computer and operation research, communication and library science, for instance. It also has a strong relationship with social science and humanities. It provides a service to all members of the community through libraries and information centres. These libraries and documentation centres play an important role in collecting human intellectual heritage and preserving it for the benefit of future generations.

Definitions

The term IS began to be used in 1958 (Hanson, 1968), and developed over time. The first formal usage of the term of IS dates back to 1959, when it was presented by Moore School of Electrical Engineering at the University of Pennsylvania. But by 1962 in the USA this term was still not use in titles of books or even conferences held in that period. But the terms information retrieval and scientific information were used instead, and sometimes the term documentation was used to refer to any recorded information.

The first significant definition of IS was published in October 1962 at the Georgia Institute of Technology conference (USA):

Information Science is a science that investigates the properties and the behaviour of information, and the means of processing information for optimum accessibility and usability. The processes include the organization, dissemination, collection, storage, retrieval, interpretation and use of information. (Nicolae, 1961 p.1)

In spite of this the following early pioneers in the IS field, such as:

- Cyril Cleverdon.
- Robert Fairthorne.
- Derek De Solla.
- Eugene Garfield.
- Manfred Kochen.
- Frederick Wilfrid Lancaster.
- Brian Vickery.
- B. C. Brooke.

Were interested in finding a proper definition of IS as unitary discipline. There is a lack of unanimity on what constitutes IS.

Although using the same information technology in the document preparation process and providing information for users, however, the separation between concepts of libraries and information continued until the period after World War II in many countries. The impact of this separation can easily note from the title Library and information science.

Shera's (1983) theory indicates that library science is an alternative term for information science. He emphasises that information transmission by the library cannot be done without transfer of information itself. Also, he indicates that the concept of IS is derived from Shannon's theory of information. Information theory focused on the word information to coin the term; it can be quantified, analyzed, and coded. (CHEUNG et al., 1984)

The information quantity is entropy H indicates how easily message can be compressed whereas X can measure the information amount to get the communication rate. Also, Brookes defined aspects of the information science through the basic equation;

$$K(S) + I = K(S + S1) \text{ (Bawden,} \qquad 2011)$$

This equation clarifies in general the aspects of the IS science, which indicates the change in the cognitive structures $K(S)$ to a new case of the knowledge to become $K(S + S1)$ by adding more information (I) where (S) Q refers to the change in the situation.

Relationship of Information Science with Other Sciences

IS is a science without identity, due to the fact that it is intended to develop the foundations of the theory among other fields. It was a theoretical stalemate and the lack of scientific methodologies and philosophy led to a big problem, particularly when information scientists tried to establish the main basic areas of the science and identify its boundaries against other fields. The pioneers of information science emphasise that IS, as any natural science, has its basic roles and foundations (Machlup and Mansfield, 1983).

At that time IS began to establish IS theories, but most of them are relative to other fields, such as applications of computer technology in the fields of medicine and chemistry. It was a clear trend to attach it to communication science or to computer science as Informatics, although there were attempts to establish it as an independent science with its own identity and boundaries.

The main characters of IS are:

- The nature of IS is interdisciplinary and its relations with other fields are changing over time.
- IS is connected to information technology.

IS has deep human and social dimensions. In fact, information science consists of a set of sciences, such as:

- Library science, which concerns transferring information and recorded knowledge.
- Communication science, which deals with the principles, roles and theories governing the transfer of messages and signals.

If we study some of these fields to highlight the relations between them, we find that:

- Computer science plays a great role in information systems, in particular the processes that are related to storage and retrieval of information.
- Communication science has the role of transferring information by different methods.
- Psychology is related to the study of reading and using information. There is a lot of research in psychology-oriented studies relating to the process of storage, search and retrieval of information in the human memory, as illustrated in Figure 11.

Any self-discipline or field of knowledge is based primarily on the challenge of its relations with other disciplines, to find out the degree of overlap with them. However, IS has been affected by a large number of other disciplines which still need to be identified. Buckland said:

[we] should now make more of a distinction between the Information Science, or overlaps with, Library and Information Science and the formal, quantitative Information Science associated with cybernetics and general systems theory. (Zins, 2007a)

A lot of work has been done to organise knowledge of the IS field. Zins developed four articles from a critical Delphi study which used questionnaires to explore the foundation of Information Science. The international panel contained 57 leading scholars from 16 countries, representing important aspects of the field. This study has mapped 10 basic categories of information science: Foundations, Resources, Knowledge Workers, Contents, Applications, Operations and Processes, Technologies, Environments, Organizations, and Users. See Figure 12 (Zins, 2007d).

Figure 11. Information Science relations with other sciences
(Ingwersen, 1992 p.103)

Domain	Foci	Main Categories (1st division)	Sub-Categories (2nd division)	Sub-Categories*/Examples & Explanations** (3rd division)	Exemplary Fields
Meta-Knowledge	Knowledge on the field of IS itself	**1. Foundations**	**Theory**	**A. Conceptions** **B. Disciplines** (e.g., Anthropology (e.g., "culture"), Arts (e.g., "design"), Communication (e.g., "communication", "media", "message"), Computer science (e.g., "computer language"), Economics (e.g., "information economics"), Education (e.g., "learning"), Engineering (e.g., "information technology"), History (e.g., "primary source", "secondary sources", "tertiary source"), Law (e.g., "intellectual property", "copyright"), Linguistics (e.g., "language"), Philosophy (Epistemology (e.g. "knowledge"), Ethics (e.g., "information ethics", "professional ethics"), Political Science (e.g., "democracy"), Psychology (e.g., "cognition"), Research Methodology (e.g., "evaluation", "research", "research methodology"), Semiotics (e.g., "sign"), Sociology ("e.g., "society") **C. Theories**	Theory of IS
			Research	**A. Theoretical** **B. Empirical** **1. Quantitative** **2. Qualitative**	Research Methodology
			Education	academic education and to professional training: theoretical knowledge and practical knowledge.	LIS Education
			History	Historical accounts of the field.	History of IS
Subject-based knowledge	Knowledge on the explored phenomena (i.e., the mediating aspects & conditions of human knowledge)	**2. Resources**	**Issues**	quality information (resources), information (resources) quality	Information Quality Information Systems
			Types	Primary resources (i.e., the human originators), secondary resources, tertiary resources	
		Mediating factors – Who? – mediators – **3. Knowledge Workers**	**Issues**	**A. Personality traits** **B. Theoretical knowledge** **C. Applied knowledge and practice**	Information Ethics LIS Education
			Types	Taxonomies of professional workers by fields of expertise (e.g., medical informatics), and organizational sector (e.g., librarians, archivists)	
		Mediating factors – What? – matters – **4. Contents**	**Issues**	Content related issues (e.g., What is a subject?)	
			Types	Taxonomies of structures (e.g., knowledge maps, subject classifications schemes, thesauri), classification systems (e.g., LCC, DDC, UDC, CC, BC), subjects (i.e., Archeology, biology, Computer Science) and the like.	
		Mediating factors – Why? – Motives – **5. Applications**	**Issues**	Issues related to the development of application oriented systems.	
			Types	Taxonomy of applications (e.g., (information) searching, shopping, socialization and socializing).	
		Mediating factors – How? – methods – **6. Operations & Processes**	**Issues**	Issues related to the various operations and processes involved in mediating human knowledge.	
			Types	Taxonomy of operations and processes: documentation, representation, organization, processing, dissemination, publication, storage, manipulation, evaluation, measurement, searching, and retrieving knowledge.	
		Mediating factors – How? – means (media) – **7. Technologies**	**Issues**	Technological related issues (e.g., user-interface design).	
			Types	Taxonomy of knowledge technologies and media: electronic-based technologies (e.g., computer-based information systems, Internet), paper-based and printing-based technologies (e.g., books), communication-based technologies and media (e.g., cellular phones, MP3).	
		Mediating factors – Where and when? – milieus – **8. Environments**	**Issues**	Social issues (e.g., Information policy, information accessibility), including ethnic and cultural issues, professional issues related to the settings, as well as legal issues (e.g., Intellectual property, privacy), and ethical issues (e.g., privacy vs. public interests).	Information Ethics Social Informatics
			Types	**A. Ethnic & Cultural environments** **B. Settings** (e.g., Education, Health)	
		Mediating factors – Where and when? – milieus – **9. Organizations**	**Issues**	Issues related to the organizational settings (e.g., managing knowledge in business organizations)	
			Types	**A. Organizational Type:** **1. Governmental Sector** **2. Public sector** **3. Private sector** **B. Functional type** **1. Memory organizations** **2. Information services**	
		10. Users	**Issues**	User related issues (e.g., user information needs, user behavior, user search strategies)	User Studies Information Behavior
			Types	**A. Individuals** **B. Groups and Communities** **1. Gender-based** **2. Age-based** **3. Culture & ethnicity-based** **4. Need & interest based** (e.g., division by profession)	

* The words in **bold** are categories. ** The other terms are exemplary terms (entries).

Information Science Taxonomy

In the past, ever since people started to record and collect information, there has been an urgent need to organize this information. Recently there has been a growth in using computers and search engines to search for information, which requires organisation of the information. These demands increased particularly with growing knowledge in different fields, which causes the knowledge heterogeneity. The search engine is based on the traditional role of classification schemes to retrieve information.

Classification is recognised as an electronic information retrieval tool. Also, classification schemes have been used to arrange library items to be available for users to access these items physically. We

Figure 12. Knowledge map of Information Science
(Zins, 2007c)

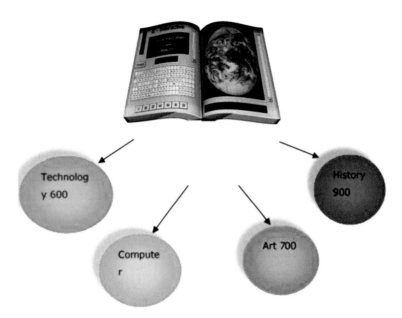

need to explore several classification methods including their disadvantages, to show the feasibility of our methodology.

In the history of classification systems there are several universal classification schemes such as Dewey Decimal Classification (DDC) which is still used in most libraries around the world - there are 200,000 libraries in 35 countries still using it as the main tool to physically arrange the resources. DDC divides knowledge into 10 categories, and each category is dividing into 10 sub-categories (OCLC, 2010).

In DDC structure there is a general class such as 000 - computer science, information and general works. This class is broad and is not limited to a specific work or discipline. However, this class deals with any subject under computers and information in general.

Within this specification 001 is knowledge, 002 any books in this area, 003 systems, 004 data processing and computer science and 005 computer programming and data. The DDC divisions are based on categorising the subjects for physically putting books on the shelves.

In this system computer science is compressed into the low-level class which has 001.64 numbers. On the other hand, in the 20th edition of Dewey classification, computer science is promoted into three levels of his divisions to be in 004 Data processing and computer science, and 006 special computer methods (Broughton, 1999).

Although, DDC is still widely used today, it makes communication poor. If you are looking for a book on human computer interaction, for instance, in Dewey classification you will find it under 004, which includes all computer science found under 004 in the section of general works. Computer human interaction is classified under 600: technology and applied science. 004.019 advances in human –computer interaction. Is another example for a book entitled 3D sound for virtual reality and multimedia.

The subjects of the book are virtual, human-computer interaction and computer processing, classified under 600 Technology, then under 621.3893. As a result users will miss a large section of information contained in different resources, which are physically classified under different numbers and locations.

The shortcomings of the DDC classification system are widely acknowledged amongst the scientific community.

Universal Decimal Classification (UDC)

The first edition was published in 1905. It is a system of library classification for information retrieval. UDC develops Dewey classification by adding auxiliary signs to the hierarchy division for Dewey, to specify a variety of special aspects of subject and the relationships between subjects. Additionally, it improves the process of information retrieval. The difference between UDC and DDC is that it facilitates the identification process on the substantive divisions, which reflect on the nature of classification and its motives as a tool of information retrieval (McIlwaine, 1997).

Library of Congress Classification (LCC)

LCC is developed by specialists in various sciences for special needs and purposes to arrange books in the congress Library. LCC divides subjects into broad divisions consisting of letters and numbers. An advantage of LCC classification is that it provides accurate details of many of the topics that are not available in other classifications because it covers various topics. Also, a disadvantage it has specifying books in the library rather than universally (Miksa, 1998).

Colon Classification Scheme (CCS)

This is also called Facet classification, which was developed by Ranganthan in 1933. Facet classification is an appropriate method for knowledge organising (Wang and Jhuo, 2009). Ranganthan pioneered an alternative dynamic and multidimensional view for universal knowledge organisation, by analysing and representing things in a scheme of classification.

Ranganathan's contribution was delivered in facet analysis. His approach was the creation of five categories, namely: personality, matter, energy, space and time. These are called PMEST.

These categories could analyse any component of any subject and his approach builds classes from the bottom up rather than the top down. Comparing with the earliest universal classification schemes, today CCS is not widely used. These categories as analytic synthetic analysis derive from two main processes, namely:

- **Analysis:** This means breaking down the subject into element concepts.
- **Synthetics:** Which is recombining these concepts into subject strings or a descriptor.

A far more interesting case, however, is that of Ranganthan, whose approach was more broad than Dewey's. He catalyzed that classification scheme for change; any item could be classified under five classes rather just one topic. He expressed the idea that any topic had various angles and it could seen from different perspectives.

For example, the book titled: A history of photograph and computer art. In Dewey classification this will be into 770 from Art division 700. According to Ranganthan classification, this subject is analysed from different angles, such as photography, electronic art and history. It could be under History 900, technology 600, computer 400 and Art 700 as illustrated in Figure 13.

Figure 13. Differences between Dewey & Ranganthan classification

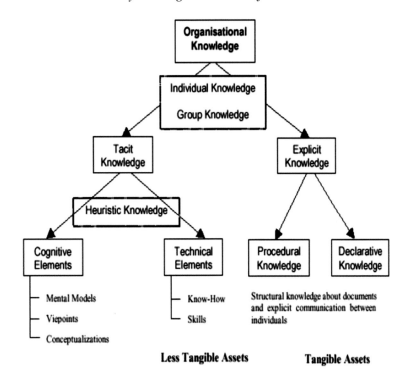

The Advantages of Facet Analysis System (FAS)

The Facet analysis system (FAS) is relevant to an electronic context. In fact, it provides flexible methods for organizing digital materials in the electronic environment.

A number of research studies have shown that classification information in a multidimensional hierarchy is more easily reached than a one-dimensional classification. The notation of a facet classification system may be useful for the researchers to compound concepts. The combination of analysis concepts can be extended to provide hierarchy structure.(Broughton, 2001)

For example: the heading of (Library) could be extended to offer the following list of headings:

- Library.
- Library – Academic.
- Library – Academic – University library.
- Library – Academic – College library.
- Library – Academic – Higher education institution.
- Library – Academic – Department library.
- Library – International.
- Library – Public.
- Library – School - Multimedia Centre.
- Library – School- Learning Centre.
- Library – School - Resource Centre.

- Library – School- Learning Resource Centre.
- Library – School - Audio-Visual Centre.
- Library – School- Library Media Centre.
- Library – School - Instructional Materials Centre.
- Library – School - Comprehensive Library.
- Library – School – service.
- Library – School – service – Loan.
- Library – School – service- Loan – Internal.
- Library – School – service- Loan – External.
- Library – Special.
- Library - Special – Scientific research centre.
- Library - Special – Library of institutions of commerce and industry.
- Library - Special – Library of organisations and non-profit organisations.
- Library - Special – specialized libraries in institutions.

The structure in this way could be predictable visible and logical to retrieve easily. A far more interesting case, however, is facet analysis principle, which offers a wide range of standard categories that could be extended to include additional properties of digital materials. Thus, the rule of combination in IS is more complex than in physical collections. However, FAS provides the ability to express a complex subject through electronic documents. It ensures the system syntax is managed in a consistent manner.

Classification Research Group (CRG)

In 1955 British experts were influenced by Ranganthan's approach and they pronounced that facet classification should be followed as the basic method for information retrieval by filling the gap between theory and practice. CRG adopted Ranganthan's theory in which they analysed the subject based on the five categories but they had extended it to a thirteen-faceted approach; things, kind, part, property, material, process, operation, agent, patient, product, by space and time. (McIiwaine and Broughton, 2000).

Broughton (2001) points out that the five categories could be extended as much as the subject's requirements and needs.

..... fundamental thirteen categories have been found to be sufficient for the analysis of vocabulary in almost all areas on knowledge. It is however quite likely that other general categories exist; it is certainly the case that there are some domain specific categories, such as those of form and genre in the field of literature. (Broughton, 2001. pp 79 - 80)

His suggestions had catalysed to create the facet classification that is needed. Also, Vickery's soil classification in 1960 has 18 eighteen categories. Broadly, there are many attempts at developing classification schemes after the (FAS) became more popular in the www for information retrieval.

Petersen (1994) created a small facet classification for the Art and Architecture Thesaurus (AAT) for the Getty Research Institute, as followed: Associated Concepts, Physical Attributes, Styles and Periods (as Space and Time), Agents (Organisations or People), Activities (Energy), Materials (Matter), and Objects (Personality).

Social care taxonomy is a hierarchy arrangement in free database that covers the material of social care; includes over 100,000 records such as documents of the government policy and research report. Yet this taxonomy is similar to the structure of a thesaurus, using terms like RT related to (NT) Narrow than (T) Top term, (GO) go term, (S) stop term and so on (SCIE, 2010). Also, mathematical science education is classified basic on dividing the subject into 9 categories - each category has many categories (MSEB, 2010).

Why Information Science Taxonomy

Taxonomy of Information science is providing a control vocabulary and hierarchical arrangement of IS topics for browsing, searching and indexing material on an IS subject. In contrast to this, the frame system and subsumption in OWL means necessary implication, so the hierarchy means that:

All Librarians is Employee

All Employees is person

Does it mean that Employees and users, are different, and can there be anything that is both Employee and users? We assume that they were different unless they had an explicit common child. Likewise, they are to be used as sharing terminology in an area to improve the exchange of information between professionals and organisations in the field of IS.

Taxonomy of IS allows the building of complex topic-based search string algorithms to find a word where one or many strings or patterns are found within a text. IS taxonomy is developed to covers a broad range of IS issues and is created to improve and enable browsing for research results in a database that amplifies in size.

KNOWLEDGE MANAGEMENT (KM) AND VIRTUAL COMMUNITIES OF PRACTICE (VCOPS)

Whilst a lot of literature covers the use of communities of practice as a part of knowledge management strategy, no formal academic research has been identified that relates specifically to the context of supporting ontology development via virtual communities of practice (VCops) in the Information Science domain. This section provides an overview of some perspectives from knowledge management (KM) and (VCops). It provides a background of the key literature relevant to this research, giving the reader a comprehensive overview. First, however, it starts with some basic definitions. The next section need to establish what is meant by data, information and knowledge.

The Main Components of Knowledge Management

This section will begin with discussion of the concepts of data, information, and knowledge that have been discussed in the literature. Many of the pioneers used these terms interchangeably (Huber and Daft, 1987). Davenport and Prusak (1998) emphasised the relationship between data, information and knowledge, but highlighted they are have different definitions. To define knowledge clearly should distinguish between these terms, because the fundamental problem behind the failure of defining knowledge management is lack of understanding of the meaning of knowledge itself. It is often confused with information and data (Senge, 2003).

Marco(2003) asserted that the former terms are central to knowledge management. However, misunderstanding and confusion between these terms can lead to a problem in information systems design and knowledge representation (Davenport, 1998). Hence, discussing them has important implications for developing ontology of information science.

DATA

Many researchers have defined data as the raw material of information, and it is a set of symbols which have not been interpreted. Davenport (2000) defined data as

a set of discrete, objective facts about events. (Davenport, 2000, p.2)

Furthermore, Dalkir (2005) provided a comprehensive definition of data which is

Data are necessary inputs into information and knowledge, and are defined as a series of observations, measurements, or facts in the form of numbers, words, sounds, and/or images. Data have no meaning, but provide the raw material from which information is produced. (Dalkir, 2005p. 430)

Information

Information is data which has been processed and organized to become a useful and meaningful. Thus, information describes particular conditions and situations.(Zins, 2007b, Feather and Sturges, 2003, Tuomi, 2000). Roberts (2000), briefly defined information as:

analyzed data – facts that have been organized in order to impart meaning. (Roberts, 2000 p. 335)

Knowledge

We assess and order information in order to turn it into knowledge that can be used appropriately (Feather and Sturges, 2003). This means knowledge is a combination of meanings, concepts, and beliefs composed in the human mind as we observe, assess and understand phenomena around us, whilst also solving complex problems. Knowledge is defined by Nonaka (1995) as,

A dynamic human process of justifying personal belief toward the truth. (Nonaka I., 1995, P58)

Knowledge is defined in Webster (2011) as certain and clear insight into something.

the fact or condition of knowing something with familiarity gained through experience or association. (Webster, 2011)

Furthermore, knowledge has four types:

- **Know- What:** Including knowledge of facts which are close to traditional knowledge such as doctors knowing medical facts.
- **Know- Why:** Including knowledge of the reasons that lie behind natural phenomena, and its ability to serve human beings and scientific and technological processes.
- **Know- Who:** This knowledge refers to the experience of doing and executing objects, whether these objects are individual management or operation of processes. This knowledge is usually owned by the company or institution.
- **Know- How:** The importance of this knowledge has increased as it improves business performance and most projects need this knowledge to speed up implementations and ensure success.

Learning how to gain these four types of knowledge ensures improvement in organisational performance. The Know-what and Know–why type of knowledge can be acquired from books, and databases; they can be accessed from different sources, but Know–how and know–who are only gained from practice and experience, which is important in learning and managing. (Polanyi, 1974).

It is widely agreed that data, which is simple facts, becomes information in a meaningful form. Subsequently, information becomes knowledge when people have the ability to add information and organise it in the right context.

Knowledge Management

Knowledge management has become a significant development over the last twenty years, capturing the attention of organizations (Davenport and Prusak, 1998).

Knowledge is an essential part of both the management process and the performance of organisations. There are innumerable books and articles on virtually every aspect of knowledge management (Leonard, 1995; Nonaka, 1991; Nonaka and Takeuchi, 1995; Stewart, 1997).

The subject area has attracted many perspectives (BSI, 2003; SAI, 2001; Polanyi, 1974).

Knowledge sharing between individuals, groups and organisations, using efficient tools of knowledge management systems technology (KMS) is a particularly interesting aspect (Davenport and Prusak, 1998; Wenger, 1998; Dixon, 2002; Nonaka and Konno, 1998; Wasko and Faraj, 2000). Knowledge can be shared and created in an organisation at individual or group levels. The author has selected the SECI model of knowledge creation, which places tacit knowledge at the heart of capturing and communicating knowledge. If we consider Nonaka's approach of tacit knowledge, and its transformation to explicit knowledge, his research considers knowledge as simply a presentation of real life, in a representational approach (Nonaka, 1991; Nonaka and Takeuchi, 1995), for which it is necessary to obtain a clear understanding of how knowledge sharing and creation work in practice. Despite numerous studies in the area, there is still only a small amount of attention paid to how knowledge is created, because knowledge is created by individuals and not by organisations – to do anything else is impossible..

The Ontological Diagram of Organisational Knowledge illustrates the fundamental elements of knowledge (Vasconcelos, J, Kimble, C., & Gouveia, F. R. (2000).

In fact, knowledge exists at two levels, which are individual and group, in both tacit and explicit forms. This dichotomy between explicit and tacit knowledge is vital, and is essential in understanding the challenges in the KM discipline. Tacit knowledge is known as individual knowledge that results from interaction between individuals or groups of people (Mohamed et al., 2006). On the other hand, explicit knowledge is viewed as being procedural or declarative knowledge (Anderson, 1983).

The procedural knowledge is describing the action for the subsequent step and responds the question of How? (Perez-Soltero et al., 2006p. 44)

The declarative knowledge is interrelated to the physical aspect of the knowledge and answers the questions of What- Who- Where- and When. It describes specific actions to perform certain tasks.

Human knowledge has previously been classified into many types of knowledge, for instance, explicit and tacit; hard and soft; implicit and formal (Nonaka, 1991; Kimble and Hildereth, 2005). However, knowledge takes many forms – it can be tacit or explicit, individual or collective knowledge. Social activity, discussion, and problem solving enables tacit knowledge to be converted to become numerical, linguistic and transmitted (Nonaka, 1991; Nonaka and Takeuchi, 1995; Rangachari, 2009).

Nonaka and Takeuchi (1995) defined explicit knowledge as:

Explicit knowledge can easily be processed by a computer, transmitted electronically, or stored in a data base", whereas, "tacit knowledge is not easily visible and expressible. (Nonaka and Takeuchi 1995: P.8, 9)

Nonaka and Takeuchi believe that tacit knowledge contains technical skills – informal, individual experience, beliefs, values that can be captured in the term 'know how'.

Nonaka & Konno (1998) Say that tacit knowledge is intertwined with the notion of creativity which consists of using digital and numerical language to express oneself and share thoughts. This connects with the second aspect of this research (Gourlay, 2002).

In the interim, "knowledge is unstructured and understood, but not clearly expressed as implicit knowledge. If knowledge is organized and easy to share it is called structured knowledge. To convert implicit knowledge into explicit knowledge, it must be extracted and formatted" (Power, 2000 p.9).

Ontology is intended to make tacit domain knowledge explicit and it has been widely applied in the context of knowledge representation (Berners-Lee et al., 2001). In this respect, we see that ontologies are a knowledge representation of specific domains. Thus, ontologies are a form of knowledge base comparative with meta-data, thesaurus, taxonomy and knowledge base, according to Victor Lombardi's definition (2003):

An Ontology populated with data. (Lombardi, 2003)

It focuses on the important aspect of this research, Knowledge Representation (KR). Thus, the scope of KR and its roles in AI can be explored, as well as the role of ontology in knowledge management as a whole.

Knowledge Engineering (KE)

Sowa (2000) defines Knowledge Engineering as "an application of logic and ontology to the task of building computable models of some domain for some purpose". (Sowa, 2000, p. 132) Knowledge Engineering is the process of creating an expert system that is a form of Artificial Intelligence system (AI). AI has a long history in dealing with knowledge from both practical and theoretical perspectives, which is a major requirement. Furthermore, knowledge engineering has a strong connection with conceptual analysis and formal ontology that can establish the foundations of the ontological engineering field (Guarino, 1997). In the meantime, ontological engineering is a subfield of knowledge engineering concerned with controlling explicit knowledge using software applications (Shadbolt and Milton, 1999).

Knowledge Engineering is composed of many principal stages, namely:

- Knowledge Acquisition is related to knowledge collection approaches and mechanisms.
- Knowledge Representation is related to the method of analysis and represents the gathered information.
- Knowledge Validation is related to validation of knowledge representation.
- Knowledge inference, explanation and justification are related to the model that has been identified to be explained and justified.

Ontology is an emerging meaning of knowledge representation. It can develop information management and organization in many applications. This research concentrates on knowledge representation as the focus of research on domain ontology representation, as ontology of Information Science OIS.

Knowledge Representation (KR)

Knowledge Representation looks at how to use symbols that represent a set of facts inside a knowledge domain, to facilitate inferring facts to create a new element of knowledge (Markman, 1999). Knowledge representation plays a crucial role in the AI field as described by (Davis et al., 1993), namely:

Role 1: Knowledge Representation is a surrogate.

In the real world things such as physical objects and relationships need to be represented in a model to describe them, to be stored in a computer which is essential for AI agents to be readable, understandable and computable. The symbols serve as surrogates for the external world. Inference in KR made by the artificial agents can make the model of the real world that is based on logical facts.

Role 2: Knowledge Representation is a set of ontological commitments.

Sowa (2000) indicates that ontological commitment is determined by a variety of variables in the knowledge representation. As ontology is a study of existence, so it determines whether or not the categories of things are existing. Then ontological commitment makes conscious choices about aspects and boundaries of the real world. Furthermore, ontology is an appropriate form of knowledge representation. Ontology can be represented by using specific languages such as Frame-Logic(F-Logic), Ontology Conceptual Modelling Language(OCML), Web Ontology Language(OWL); Davis and his colleagues point out that "the essential information is not the form of this language but the content, that is the set of concepts offered as a way of thinking about the world" (Davis et al., 1993p. 20).

Role 3: Knowledge Representation is a sub- theory of intelligent reasoning.

It is the key role in knowledge representation, especially for AI applications. This is often implicit, but is evident by studying its components:

(1) the representation's fundamental conception of intelligent inference, (2) the set of inferences that the representation sanctions, (3) the set of inferences that the representation recommends. (Davis et al., 1993p. 21)

Hence, ontology as defined inside the AI scope sticks to this role. This the reason behind choosing the formal logic based on the language rather than frame based language for knowledge representation.

Role 4: Knowledge Representation is a medium for efficient computation.

Knowledge should be encoded within the AI system to be processed by the computer efficiently. Any problem can be represented easily, yet solving it may need time and effort to compute. The design and use of knowledge representation languages has been influenced by the development of software and hardware theory.

Role 5: Knowledge Representation is a medium of human expression.

Finally, the main role of representation language facilitates communication between domain experts and knowledge engineers. The knowledge engineer writes the rules and definitions and the experts read them (Sowa, 2000).

In brief, knowledge representation means expressing things in the real world through the medium of communication and expression that informs the machine about the real world. It aims to facilitate efficient communication between humans and machines, and express things in the real world to be understandable for both. In the interim, ontology becomes inevitable.

Communities of Practice (Cops)

The Community of Practice (Cop) is not just a process of obtaining learning as social structure, but also a way of gathering knowledge that could be developed regarding Mayo's theory of human relations knowledge. It can be formed and shaped at team levels through negotiations, discussion and conversation. This study has adopted Mayo's theory, takes an approach regarding knowledge as a product of discussion and resulting social processes. (Mayo, 1975). Mizoguchi argues that ontology should be developed by many people or a community. This way supports the ontology construction by people with the same interest and subject area rather than knowledge engineers (Mizoguchi, 2003).

Cops is introduced by Lave and (Wenger, 1998) as a learning process within Legitimate Peripheral Participation (LPP). LPP, in his perspective, is an important aspect of effective social learning. LPP is based on the idea that members of the community with less experience will learn from social interaction with experts in a specific domain. This initial definition is related to the theory of situativity: situated learning in ethnographic study (Andrew et al., 2008).

Cops developed more extensively when it was redefined by(Wenger, 1998). It has been used in business environments, but could be used in knowledge management as a tool for successful knowledge sharing processes, as it has received a lot of interest from both scholars and participants in the knowledge management area. A Cop is defined as:

... group that coheres through mutual engagement on an indigenous (or appropriated) enterprise, creating a common repertoire. The tight knit nature of relation is created by sustained mutual engagement. (Cox, 2005 p. 531)

A system of relationships between people, activities, and the world; developing with time, and in relation to other tangential and overlapping communities of practice 'is an intrinsic condition of the existence of knowledge. (Roberts, 2006 p.624)

The above definitions refer to the idea of information exchange, knowledge and sharing concerns within groups of people.

Cops is not a formal structure for knowledge generation. The generation of knowledge accrues when people co-operate and communicate to seek resolutions of problems or to develop a new product. Many studies conducted show that the community of practice is the best and strongest way to unite a team (Nirenberg, 1995, Stewart, 1997).

Wenger (2008) declared that a Cop consists of a small group who participate in the community regularly with their own leadership. We cannot call any group of individuals working together a Cop unless the characteristics of Cops are present, which are: mutual engagement, learning or identity acquisition, a sense of joint enterprise, and a shared set of communal resources. Wenger stated that a Community of Practice requires individuals to do things together to create a source of learning and knowing. Also, they can bring benefits for learning and competency (Coakes and Clarke, 2008, Thrysoe et al., 2010).

Group members are more likely to share commonalities with volunteers than a group of employees at a company (Wenger 2002).

Cops have been investigated in knowledge management literature taking several approaches, which have highlighted several different sorts: e.g. physical Cops, social groups, network Cops, and online Cops, which might take names like: community of commitment (COC) community of interest (COI), network of practice (NOP), virtual cops, Networks Cop (Malhotra, 2002, Nolan et al., 2007).

Cops can take many forms, for instance study groups or informal discussion groups; many Cops also exist online (Murillo-othon., 2006, Noriko H., 2007, Porra and Parks, 2006). The rise of the internet as a communication tool has influenced the formation of Cops to a significant extent. Cops function as a mediated tool in computers to improve communication between people; these may take the form of websites, electronic bulletin boards, emails, blogs and forums. (Hildreth et al., 1998).

Wenger (2005) says that Cops are mediated by technology that has been developed by interaction, discussion, and the exchange of views in order to solve problems and generate artefacts (Wenger, 2005).

Furthermore, McDermott (1999) has indicated that are points to take into account when building communities, depending on the area of interest:

1. Gather as a group of specialists, using informal discussion to exchange knowledge.
2. Some communities make attempts to gather knowledge from group members.
3. Members of the group contact one another irregularly to exchange advice and solutions.
4. The use of information technology keeps members connected.
5. Members of the group identify themselves as a Community of practice.

6. Some communities attempt to capture knowledge from members.
7. Many communities are keeping people involved by using information technology (McDermott, 1999).

However, widespread development of the organisations, around the world led to challenges in accessing knowledge that resides in a specific context.

Virtual Communities of Practice (VCops)

Virtual communities have emerged from technological development. People are able to connect and share conversation, play games or build relationships, as well as sharing knowledge across the world (Jansen W 2002, Wenger 2002).

'Virtual community' was coined by J.C.R Licklider as computer network. This term can be used as:

- Group of people using computers as a social network to communicate.
- Online group using chat rooms and listing services and activities online (Gourlay, 2001).

A virtual community has been defined as:

A group that shares knowledge and meets through networks as internet, they are separated by time and place. (Catherine et al., 2000p. 229)

Are social aggregations that emerge from the net where enough people carrying on those public discussions long enough, with sufficient human feeling, form webs of personal relationships in cyberspace? (Gomez, 1998p.218)

Virtual teams are composed of geographically dispersed individuals who interact through interdependent tasks guided by a common purpose with links strengthened by web of communication technologies. (Panteli and Duncan, 2004p.424)

VCops are a crucial tool for knowledge acquisition. The reason behind that is tacit knowledge is embedded in people's minds and storytelling and conversation take place between experts when they talk about their experience to gain skills. Since the world become a small village and face-to face communication is limited to exchange ideas, and with the rise of websites on the internet, virtual communities have become an alternative to a physical community of practice with dispersed multinational organisations. (Araujo, 1998, Ardichvili et al., 2003).

There is no single agreement on what constitutes VCops of Practice, when looking at literature on the subject; this study defines some of the key features from the literature review; these features are:

1. The ability to meet in a virtual space and communicate via the Internet.
2. People who might never meet face-to-face are brought together by means of a technical platform.
3. VCops facilitate activities by using Information Technology (IT).
4. The existence of the virtual community can help to identify of an idea or task.
5. Groups can self-select.

6. That members' interests are usually related to a specific Knowledge Domain.
7. Community members can establish social relationship and a sense of belonging to the groups.
8. Building trust.

VCop is team of individuals who communicate and meet virtually; they are linked by a specific interest and social relationship. Their key tool is a technical infrastructure to enable knowledge exchange within virtual communities, and using it allows the transfer of tacit knowledge which is difficult to articulate.

Also, trust is a crucial feature of the success of VCops in bonding member together to develop the quality of conversation and discussion (Usoro, 2003, Fang and Chiu, 2010). In the meantime, distrust is a common element related to internet relationships - it really is a threat to the success of virtual communities(VCs), due to the fact that anonymity is easy; joining web groups and pretending to be a member of the community who has the same interest is easy, and even though people in Cops are connected to each other by their interest. they need trust to communicate efficiently (Leimeister et al., 2008, Schwen and Hara, 2003).

Recently, many VCs are based on social networks on the internet, for instance, YouTube, news groups, wiki, Facebook, Twitter and LinkedIn. All of them focus on working as virtual groups, whereas not all VCs are VCops; in the former, knowledge can be transferred from expert to inexpert, but later on knowledge can be exchanged between peers whether they are professionals or experts in a specific domain. (Lu and Yang, 2011). There are more than 800 million active users on Facebook (Facebook, 2011). Also professionals using Cops possess skills to codify tacit knowledge, which decreases vagueness in coding and analysis.

This research gives a clear explanation to distinguish between VCs and VCops; it also provides some empirical insights into the application of the concept of VCops (Lin et al., 2008, Dube et al., 2006, Llum et al., 2010). VCs are social aggregations that come from the internet, in which people can interact and exchange information.(Chan and Li, 2010)

In terms of classifying VCs many studies have been investigated. Herring, (2008) clustered VCs on the internet into five groups:

- Support groups like Health groups.
- Interest groups such as Soap opera fans.
- Task- related such groups as Cops.
- Groups based on geographical distances like community networks.
- Commercial groups such as product websites.

He point out that Cops are one of the type of VCs called Task-related groups, whereas Cops could be physical or virtual. (Herring, 2008).

Members of VCoPs should be professionals in a specific domain to ensure an accurate representational approach to knowledge sharing. Professionals should be those who hold knowledge in a particular domain, who have the ability to solve problems and who are committed to efficient working. This means VCops should be groups of experts who are able to represent the knowledge used in the knowledge base (KB). In real life there are many VCops in existence, for instance, VCops in the educational domain such as Tapped In htpp://www.tappedin.org.(TappedIn, 2010).

Not all VCs are VCops, as Zhang (2008) reminds us (Zhang and Watts, 2008) – many types of group work collaboratively. Roberts (2008) reviewed different types of collaborative working: task-based work, epistemic collaboration, professional practice, virtual collaboration. This study concentrates solely on professional practice in virtual collaborative environments in the IS domain. Our review of available literature highlighted several characteristics common to communities where knowledge is obtained, aggregated and dispersed by professionals. Opportunities to improve competency is vital in tacit and explicit knowledge sharing so that newcomers can move from peripheral participation to full involvement. Creativity is a way of connecting these various groups exchanging knowledge and facilitating interaction by using the same language; These people are specialists in its language (Roberts, 2008, Gervassis, 2004, Walsh and Crumbie, 2011).

According to Wenger's characterisation of Cops, there are many ways in which virtual professional Communities of Practice (VCops) are different from virtual communities. These characteristics include:

- Topics of discussion in VCops are driven by participants or users under control of a moderator.
- The moderator of a VCop plays an important role in keeping the discussion focussed on the main issues.
- Participants' activities develop through a website.
- Participants of VCops have shared norms and values.
- Mutual engagement: widely distributed user interactions.
- Communities: participants build strong personal relationships despite having no face-to-face contact.
- Learning or identity acquisition: members are valued by participants within the learning environment.
- Joint enterprise: members sustain focused negotiations.
- Shared repertoire and development of knowledge repository. These characteristics will be considered in designing the ontocop website.

Many studies and projects are relevant to this research, and are inspired by various perspectives to combine to form a new framework to create IS Ontology, these include previous work in the area of ontologies and communities of practice which are briefly presented and discussed. Several pieces of research have illustrated how ontology can serve as a symbolic tool within a community of practice (Domingue et al., 2001). Ankolekar, Sycara's work presents a semantic web system for open resources software communities relying on a specific ontology (Ankolekar et al., 2006). This study, which is titled "an ontology for supporting Cop" presents an ontology built from an analysis of information sources about eleven Cops available in Palette project. It is aimed both at modelling the members of the Cop and at annotating the Cop's knowledge resources (Tifous et al., 2007)

Ontocopi (2003) is a project based on a community of practice identified through ontology network analysis (ONA). Ontocopi used a spreading activation algorithm to crawl through the knowledge network to identify similar objects and the relations between them. This study does not follow standard methodology to integrate Ontocopi because the community of practice lacks establishing methodology. Ontocopi plugs-in protégé and uses AKT ontology which provides opportunities for users to select the class and the class instance display on the panel, and select the relation based on its importance. (O'Hara et al., 2002, Alani et al., 2003)

As you can see the author reviews the literature to discover the basic features of Cops, Vcos and VCops to explain our virtual community of professional practice. Table 16 summarises the differences between communities of practice.

Table 16. Comparison between communities of practice

Category	Traditional Cop	Virtual Cos	Virtual VCops
Communication via the internet	☒	☑	☑
Existence for an identification of an idea or task	☒	☑	☑
Existence according to a place based	☑	☒	☒
Norms	☑	☒	☑
Groups self-selected	☒	☑	☑
Groups emerge through task	☑	☒	☑
Leadership	☑	☒	☑
Boundaries	Evolving	Fluid	fluid
Transparency	Low	High	High
Knowledge Domain	Interest –related work	Interest –related knowledge	Interest –related knowledge
Trust	☑	☒	☑
Membership criteria	☑	☒	☑
Level of member participation	Limited	Widely	widely

CONCLUSION

This chapter investigated and discussed the related subjects to be considered as theoretical framework for this study in three sections. Ontology in philosophy is dealing with being or realty. It is logical semantic built on the theory of meaning, that mean ontology is an important part on semantic web. The ontology concept was discussed, and its development from the philosophical approach to the Computer science approach.

In addition, it conducted numerous comparisons between theories and methodologies of ontology building and designing. It also investigated designing criteria and the tools used for that purpose in order to stand on and follow the proper way in this study.

All of these issues were taken into consideration for design OIS ontology information.

In the second section were analyzed characteristics of information science which need to be considered as a science still needs identification and there are many problems need to be solved. Although, there are many studies have been done to identify this science. In addition, reviewing and analyzing classifications systems that used in library science such as UDC, LCC, CCS, and CRG to identify their advantages and disadvantages in order to find the appropriate classification, which is FAS classification system. The FAS is multidimensional hierarchy and more easily reached than a one-dimensional classification. The notation of FAS may be useful for the researchers to compound concepts.

While, in the final section has been dealt with knowledge management to identify the role of VCops. The VCops are teams of individuals who meet and communicate virtually with others; they are linked by a specific interest. VCops has an enormous affect in transferring tacit knowledge which is difficult to articulate. It support acquiring and representing domain knowledge and how they are employed for the purpose of this research.

Meanwhile, Ontological engineering is subfield of knowledge engineering concerned with controlling knowledge using software application, and how to systemizing knowledge to fill the semantic gap between metadata. It is a set of activities that concern the ontology development process, the ontology life cycle, as well as the methodologies, tools and languages required for building ontologies.

REFRENCES

Alexander, J. H., Freiling, M. J., Shulman, S. J., Staley, J. L., Rehfuss, S., & Messick, S. L. (1986). Knowledge Level Engineering: Ontological Analysis. In *Proceedings of ICSE 1991: The international Conference on Software Engineering*. ACM Press.

Allemang, D., & Hendler, J. (2008). *Semantic web for the working ontologist: Effective modeling in RDFs and OWL*. Elsevier.

Amin, A., & Roberts, J. (2008). Knowing in action: Beyond communities of practice. *Research Policy*, *37*(2), 353–369. doi:10.1016/j.respol.2007.11.003

Amira, T., Adil El, G., Rose, D.-K., Alain, G., & Christina, C., G & Raldine, V. (2007) An ontology for supporting communities of practice. *Proceedings of the 4th international conference on Knowledge capture*. Whistler, BC, Canada: ACM.

Anderson, J. R. (1983). A spreading activation theory of memory. *Journal of Verbal Learning and Verbal Behavior*, *22*(3), 261–295. doi:10.1016/S0022-5371(83)90201-3

Andrew, N., Tolson, D., & Ferguson, D. (2008). Building on Wenger: Communities of practice in nursing. *Nurse Education Today*, *28*(2), 246–252. doi:10.1016/j.nedt.2007.05.002 PMID:17599697

Antoniou, G., & Harmelen, F. V. (2004). *Semantic web primer*. Massachusetts Institute of Technology.

Araujo, L. (1998). Knowing and learning as networking. *Management Learning, 29*, 317-336.

Ardichvili, A., Page, V., & Wentling, T. (2003). Motivation and barriers to participation in virtual knowledge -sharing communities of practice. *Knowledge Management, 7*, 64-77.

Awodey, S. (2006). *Category Theory*. Oxford Science Publication. Retrieved from http://www.google.co.uk/#hl=en&q=on%20catego

Baader, F., & Nutt, W. (2003). *The description logic handbook: Theory, implementation, and application*. Cambridge University Press.

Barry, S. (1996). Mereotopology: A Theory of parts and boundaries. *Data & Knowledge Engineering*, *20*(3), 287–303. doi:10.1016/S0169-023X(96)00015-8

Batista, F., Pardal, J. P., Mamede, N. J., Vaz, P., & Ribeiro, R. D. (2006). *Ontology construction: cooking domain*. Retrieved from http://www.inesc-id.pt/pt/indicadores/Ficheiros/3615.pdf

Bawden, D. (2011). Brookes equation: The basis for a qualitative characterization of information behaviours. *Journal of Information Science*, *37*(1), 101–108. doi:10.1177/0165551510395351

Bechhofer, S., Horrocks, I., Goble, C., & Stevens, R. (2001). OilEd: A Reasonable Ontology Editor for the Semantic Web. In *Joint German/Austrian conference on Artificial Intelligence*. Berlin: Springer.

Bello, A. (2010). Ontology and Phenomenology. In Theory and Applications of Ontology: Philosophical Perspectives. London: Springer.

Berners-Lee, T., Hendler, J., & Lassila, O. (2001). The Semantic Web. *Scientific American, 284*(5), 34–43. doi:10.1038/scientificamerican0501-34 PMID:11396337

Bhatt, M., Rahayu, W., Soni, S. P., & Wouters, C. (2009). Ontology driven semantic profiling and retrieval in medical information systems. *Web Semantics: Science, Services, and Agents on the World Wide Web, 7*(4), 317–331. doi:10.1016/j.websem.2009.05.004

Blum, B. I. (1996). Beyond programming Oxford Unversity Press. New York: Academic Press.

Bourne, C. P. (1980). On-line systems: History, technology and economics. *Journal of the American Society for Information Science, 31*(3), 155–160. doi:10.1002/asi.4630310307

Brewster, C., Alani, H., Dasmahapatra, S., & Wilks, Y. (2004). *Data Driven Ontology Evaluation.* In International Conference on Language Resources and Evaluation, Lisbon, Portugal.

Broughton, V. (2001). Faceted classification as a basis for knowledge organization in a digital environment; the Bliss Bibliographic Classification as a model for vocabulary management and the creation of multidimensional knowledge structures. *New Review of Hypermedia and Multimedia, 7*(1), 67–102. doi:10.1080/13614560108914727

Brusa, G., Caliusco, M. L., & Chiotti, O. (2006). *A Process for Building a Domain Ontology: an Experience in Developing a Government Budgetary Ontology.* Conferences in Research and Practice in Information Technology,Hobart, Australia.

Buckland, M. K., & Liu, Z. (1995). History of information science. *Annual Review of Information Science & Technology*, 385–416.

Burtonjones, et al. (2005). A semiotic metrics suite for assessing the quality of ontologies. Data & Knowledge Engineering, 55, 84-102.

Calero, C., Ruiz, F., & Piattini, M. (2006). *Ontologies for software engineering and software technology.* Springer. doi:10.1007/3-540-34518-3

Catherine, C. M., Shipman, F. M., III, & Raymond, J. M. (2000). Making large-scale information resources serve communities of practice. *Journal of Management Information Systems, 11*, 65–86.

Chan, K. W., & Li, S. Y. (2010). Understanding consumer- to consumer interactions in virtual communities: The salience of reciprocity. *Journal of Business Research*, 1033-1040.

Chaudhri, V., Farquhar, A., Fikes, R., Karp, P., & Rice, J. (1998). OKBC: A programmatic foundation for knowledge base interoperability. In *Proceedings 15 th National conference on artificial Intelligence.*

Chi, Y.-L., Hsu, T.-Y., & Yang, W.-P. (2006). Ontological techniques for reuse and sharing knowledge in digital museums. *The Electronic Library, 24*(2), 147–159. doi:10.1108/02640470610660341

Cleverdon, C. (1987). Historical note: Perspectives. *Journal of the American Society for Information Science, 38*, 152–155.

Coakes, E., & Clarke, S. (2008). Boundaries in Communities.Encyclopedia of Communities of Practice in Information and Knowledge Management. Academic Press.

Corcho, O. (2002). *Building legal ontologies with METHONTOLOGY and WebODE*. Retrieved from http://academic.research.microsoft.com/Paper/1856108.aspx

Cox, A. (2005). What are communities of practice? A comparative review of four seminal works. *Journal of Information Science, 31*(6), 527–540. doi:10.1177/0165551505057016

Cunningham, H., Maynard, D., & Tablan, V. (2000). *JAPE: A Java Annotation Patterns Engine* (2nd ed.). Research Memorandum CS-00-10. Department of Computer Science, University of Sheffield.

Curtis, J., Matthews, G., & Baxter, D. (2005). *On the Effective Use of Cyc in a Question Answering System.IJCAI Workshop on Knowledge and Reasoning for Answering Questions*, Edinburgh, UK.

Dalkir, K. (2005). *KM in theory and practice*. Oxford, UK: Elsevier Butterworth-Heinemann.

Davenport, T., & Prusak, L. (2000). Working knowledge: How organisations manage what they know. Boston: Harvard Business School.

Davenport, T. H. (1998). *Some Principles of knowledge management*. Retrieved from http://www.strategy-business.com/article/8776?gko=f91a7

Davis, R., Shrobe, H., & Szolovits, P. (1993). What is a knowledge Representation? *AI Magazine, 14,* 17–33.

Deliiska, B. (2007). Thesaurus and Domain ontology of Gioinformatics. *Journal Compilation, 11,* 637–651.

Dmterie, J., & Verbeek, F. J. (2008). *Information visualisation from ontology*. Formal ontology in information systems Fifth international conference FOIS2008.

Domingue, J. (1998). *Tadzebao and Webonto: Discussing, Browsing and Editing ontologies on the web*. 11th knowledge Acquisition workshop (KAW98), Banff, Canada.

Domingue, J., Enrico, M., Buckingham, S. S., Maria, V.-V., Yannis, K., & Nick, F. (2001) Supporting ontology driven document enrichment within communities of practice.*Proceedings of the 1st international conference on Knowledge capture*. Victoria, British Columbia, Canada: ACM. doi:10.1145/500737.500746

Du, T. C., Li, F., & King, I. (2009). Managing knowledge on the Web - Extracting ontology from HTML Web. *Decision Support Systems, 47*(4), 319–331. doi:10.1016/j.dss.2009.02.011

Dube, L., Bourhis, A., & Jacob, R. (2006). Towards a Typology of virtual communities of practice. *Interdisciplinary Journal of Information, Knowledge and Management, 1,* 71-93.

Fang, Y.-H., & Chiu, C.-M. (2010). In justice we trust: Exploring knowledge-sharing continuance intentions in virtual communities of practice. *Computers in Human Behavior, 26*(2), 235–246. doi:10.1016/j.chb.2009.09.005

Farkas-Conn, I. (1990). *From documentation to information science: The beginning and early development of the American Documentation Institute American Society for Information Science*. New York: Greenwood.

Farquhar, A., Fikes, R., & Rice, J. (1996). *The Ontolingua Server: A Tool for Collaborative Ontology Construction.* 10th knowledge acquisition for knowledge-based systems workshop (KAW96), Banff, Canada.

Feather, J., & Sturges, P. (2003). International Encyclopedia of Information and Library Science (2nd ed.). New York, NY: Routledge.

Fernadez-Lopez, M. (1999). Building a chemical ontology using methontology and the ontology design environment. *IEEE Intelligent Systems & their Applications, 4*(1), 37–46. doi:10.1109/5254.747904

Fernadez-Lopez, M., & Gomez-Perez, A. (2002). Overview and analysis of methodologies for building ontologies. *The Knowledge Engineering Review, 17*(2), 129–156.

Fernández-López, M., Gómez-Pérez, A., & Juristo, N. (1997). Methontology: from ontological art towards ontological engineering. *Proceedings of the AAAI97 Spring Symposium Series on Ontological Engineering.*

Fernández-López, M. (1999). *Overview of methodologies for building ontologies.* In *Workshop Ontologies and Problem-Solving Methods: Lessons Learned and Future Trends de la conferencia International Joint Conference for Artificial Intelligence (IJCAI'99)*, Stockholm, Sweden.

Fluit, C., Sabou, M., & Harmelen, F. V. (2002). *Ontology-based Information Visualisation. In visualisation the semantic web.* Springer, Verlag.

Fox, M. S. (1992). The Tove project: Towards a common-sense model of the enterprise.Industrial and Engineering Applications of Artificial Intelligence and Expert Systems (pp. 25-34).

Gaoyun, J., Jianliang, W., & Shaohua, Y. (2010). *A method for consistent ocean ontology construction Industrial and Information Systems.* IIS.

Gartner, N. R. (2006). *Emerging Technologies Hype Cycle Highlights Key Technology Themes.* Academic Press.

Gomez, R. (1998). The nostalgia of virtual community: A study of computer- mediated communications use in Colombian non- governmental organisation. *Information Technology & People, 11*(3), 217–234. doi:10.1108/09593849810228020

Gómez-Pérez, Juristo, N., & Pazos, J. (1995). *Evaluation and Assessment of knowledge sharing Technology. Towards very large knowledge base.* Amsterdam: IOS.

Gómez-Pérez, A., Corcho, O., & Fernández-López, M. (2003). Methodologies, tools and languages for building ontologies. Where is their meeting point? *Data & Knowledge Engineering, 46*(1), 41–64. doi:10.1016/S0169-023X(02)00195-7

Gòmez-Pérez, A., Fernandez-Lopez, M., & Corcho, O. (2004). *Ontological Engineering:with examples from the areas of knowledge management,e-commerce and the semantic web.* Springer.

Gourlay, S. (2002). *Tacit knowledge or behaving?* European Conference on Organizational Knowledge, Athens, Greece.

Group, D. S. W. (2008). *The CIDOC Conceptual Reference Model.* Author.

Gruber, T. R. (1993). Toward principles for the design of ontologies used for knowledge sharing. In Formal ontology. Kluwer Academic Publishers.

Guarino, N. (1997). Understanding, building and using ontologies. *International Journal of Human-Computer Studies*, *46*(2-3), 293–310. doi:10.1006/ijhc.1996.0091

Guarino, N. (1998) Formal Ontology and Information Systems.*Proceedings of FOIS'98*. Trento, Italy: IOS Press.

Guarino, N., & Giaretta, P. (1995). Ontologies and Knowledge Bases: Towards a Terminological Clarification. Amsterdam: Academic Press.

Guruninger, M., & Fox, M. S. (1995). Methodology for the design and evaluation of ontologies. In *Workshop on Basic ontological issues in knowledge sharing*.

Hartmann, N. (1952). The new ways of ontology. Chicago: Academic Press.

Herre, H. (2010). The Ontology of Mereological Systems: A Logical Approach. In Theory and Applications of Ontology: Philosophical Perspectives. London: Springer.

Horridge, M., & Patel-Schneider, P. F. (2009). OWL 2 Web Ontology Language Manchester Syntax. Academic Press.

Horrocks, I., Patel-Schneider, P., & Van Harmelen, F. (2003). From SHIQ and RDF to OWL: The making of web ontology language. *Web Semantics: Science, Services, and Agents on the World Wide Web*, *1*(1), 7–26. doi:10.1016/j.websem.2003.07.001

Hu, L., & Weng, J. (2010). Geo-ontology integration Based on Category Theory. *International Conference on Computer Design and applications* (ICCDA2010).

Husserl, E. (1970). *Logical Investigations*. London: Routledge and Kegan Paul.

Ingwersen, P. (1992). Information and Information Science in context. *Libri*, *42*(2), 99–153. doi:10.1515/libr.1992.42.2.99

Jansen, W., & Steenbakkers, H. (2002). Knowledge management and virtual communities. In Knowledge mapping and management. IRM Press.

Jepsen, T. C. (2009). *Just what is an ontology*. IEEE Computer Society.

Kabilan, V. (2007). *Ontology for Information Systems (O4IS) Design Methodology: Conceptualizing, Designing and Representing Domain Ontologies. School of Information and Communication Technology, Department of Computer and Systems Sciences*. The Royal Institute of Technology.

Krivov, S., Villa, F., Williams, R., & Wu, X. (2007a). *On visualization of OWL ontologies*. Semantic Web Springer. doi:10.1007/978-0-387-48438-9_11

Krivov, S., Williams, R., & Villa, F. (2007b). GrOWL: A tool for visualization and editing of OWL ontologies. *Web Semantics: Science, Services, and Agents on the World Wide Web*, *5*(2), 54–57. doi:10.1016/j.websem.2007.03.005

Krötzsch, M., Hitzler, P., Ehrig, M., & Sure, Y. (2005). *Category theory in ontology research: Concrete gain from an abstract approach*. Karlsruhe, Germany: Institut AIFB, Universität Karlsruhe.

Lawvere, W. (1969). Adjointness in foundations. *Dialectica, 23*(3-4), 281–296. doi:10.1111/j.1746-8361.1969.tb01194.x

Leimeister, J., Schweizer, K., & Leimeister, S. (2008). Do virtual communities matter for the social support of patients? Antecedents and effects of virtual relationships in online communities. *Information Technology & People, 21*(4), 350–374. doi:10.1108/09593840810919671

Lenat, D., & Guha, R. (1990). *Building Large Knowledge-Based Systems: Representation and Inference in the Cyc Project*. Addison-Wesley.

Lin, F.-R., Lin, S.-C., & Huang, T.-P. (2008). Knowledge sharing and creation in a teachers professional virtual community. *Computers & Education, 50*(3), 742–756. doi:10.1016/j.compedu.2006.07.009

Lombardi, V. (2003). *Noise between stations meta data glossary*. Retrieved from http://www.noisebetweenstations.com/personal/essays/metadata_glossary/metadata_glossary.html

Lozano-Tello, A., & Gomez-Perez, A. (2004). ONTOMETRIC: A Method to Choose the Appropriate Ontology. *Journal of Database Management, 15*(2), 1–18. doi:10.4018/jdm.2004040101

Machlup, F., & Mansfield, U. (1983). *The Study of Information*. New York: Wiley.

Maedche, A. (2003). *Ontology learning for the semantic Web*. Kluwer Academic Publishers.

Maedche, A., & Staab, S. (2002a). Measuring Similarity between Ontologies. In *Proceedings of the 13th International Conference on Knowledge Engineering and Knowledge Management*. Springer-Verlag. doi:10.1007/3-540-45810-7_24

Maedche, A. D. (2002). *Ontology learning for the semantic web*. Kluwer Academic.

Maedche, E., & Staab, S. (2002b). Measuring Similarity between Ontologies. In *Proceedings of the European Conference on Knowledge Acquisition and Management* (EKAW).

Mccarthy, J. (1980). Circumscription- A form of Non-Monotonic Reasoning. *Artificial Intelligence, 5*(1-2), 27–39. doi:10.1016/0004-3702(80)90011-9

Mcdermott, R. (1999). *Nurturing three dimensional cops: How to get the most out of human networks*. Retrieved from http://home.att.net/~discon/KM/Dimensions.pdf

Mciiwaine, I., & Broughton, V. (2000). The classification Research Group: Then and now. *Knowledge Organization, 27*, 195–199.

Merrill, G. H. (2011). Ontology, ontologies, and science. Humanities. *Social Sciences and Law, 30*, 71–83.

Miksa, F. L. (1998). The DCC, the universe of knowledge, and the post- modern library. Albany, NY: Forest Press.

Mills, H., & Hevner, A. R. (1995). Box-structured requirements determination methods. Decision Support Systems, 13, 223-239.

Mizoguchi, R. (2003). Tutorial on ontological engineering. *New Generation Computing, 21*(4), 363–384. doi:10.1007/BF03037310

Moens, M.-F. (2006). *Information Extraction: Algorithms and prospects in a retrieval context.* Springer.

Mohamed, A. H., Lee, S. P., & Salim, S. S. (2006). Managing Evolution in Software-Engineering Knowledge Management Systems Digital. *Information & Management, 3,* 19–24.

Morbach, J., Wiesner, A., & Marquardt, W. (2009). OntoCAPEis a large–scale ontology for chemical process engineering. Engineering Applications of Artificial Intelligence. *Computers & Chemical Engineering, 20,* 147–161.

MSEB. (2010). *Mathematical Science Education Board.* Retrieved from http://www7.nationalacademies.org/mseb/

Murillo-Othon. (2006). *Searching for Virtual Communities of Practice in the discussion network.* Bradford.

Nicolae, D. (1961). *Information Science Syllabus and Teaching Practice within the Higher Education.* Georgia Institute of Technology.

Nirenburg, S., & Raskin, V. (2001). Ontological semantics, formal ontology and ambiguity. *Proceedings of FOIS.*

Nirenburg, S., & Raskin, V. (2004). *Ontological semantics.* Cambridge, MA: MIT Press.

Nonaka, I. (1995). *The knowledge creating company: how Japanese companies create the dynamics of innovation.* New York: Oxford University Press.

Nonaka, I., & Konno, N. (1998). The concept of Ba: Building a Foundation for Knowledge Creation. *California Management Review.*

Noy, N. F. (2004). Semantic Integration: A Survey Of Ontology-Based Approaches. *SIGMOD Record, 33*(4), 65–70. doi:10.1145/1041410.1041421

Noy, N. F., & Mcguinness, D. L. (2001). *Ontology Development 101: A Guide to Creating Your First Ontology.* Retrieved from http://liris.cnrs.fr/alain.mille/enseignements/Ecole_Centrale/What%20is%20an%20ontology%20and%20why%20we%20need%20it.htm

Noy, N. F., & Musen, M. A. (2000). *PROMPT: Algorithems and tools for automated ontology merging and alignment.* 17th National Conference on Artificial Intelligence (AAAI'00), Austin, TX.

O'Hara, K., Alani, H., & Shadbolt, N. (2002). ONTOCOPI: Methods and Tools for Identifying Communities of Practice. In *IFIP 17th World Computer Congress - TC12 Stream on Intelligent Information Processing.* Retrieved from http://eprints.ecs.soton.ac.uk/6521/

OCLC. (2010). *Dewey Decimal Classification (DDC) system.* Retrieved from http://www.oclc.org/dewey/versions/ddc22print/intro.pdf

Ogden, C. K., Richards, I. A., Malinowski, Bronislaw, & Corookshank, F. G. (1949). The meaning of meaning: a study of the influence of language upon thought and of the science of symbolism. London: Routledge & Kegan Paul.

Panteli, N., & Duncan, E. (2004). Trust and Temporary Virtual Teams: Alternative explanations dramaturgical relationships. *Information Technology & People, 17*(4), 423–441. doi:10.1108/09593840410570276

Pattuelli, M. C. (2011). Modeling a domain ontology for cultural heritage resources: A user-centered approach. *Journal of the American Society for Information Science and Technology, 62*(2), 314–342. doi:10.1002/asi.21453

Perez-Soltero, A., Sanchez-Schmitz, G., Barcelo-Valenzuela, M., Palma-Mendez, J. T., & Martin-Rubio, F. (2006). Ontologies as Strategy to Represent Knowledge Audit Outcomes. *International Journal of Technology Knowledge in Society, 2*, 43–53.

Petersen, T. (1994). *Art & architecture thesaurus.* New York: Oxford University Press. Retrieved fromhttp://www.getty.edu/research/tools/vocabularies/index.html

Pinto, H., & Martins, J. (2001). *A methodology for ontology integration.* International Conference on Knowledge CaptureK-CAP'01, Victoria, Canada.

Polanyi, M. (1974). *Personal knowledge: toward a past-critical philosophy.* Chicago: The University of Chicago Press.

Poli, R. (2010). Ontology: The Categorial Stance. In *Theory and Applications of Ontology: Philosophical Perspectives.* London: Springer.

Porra, J., & Parks, M. M. (2006). *Sustainable virtual communities: Suggestions from the colonial model.* Springer-Verlag.

Porzel, R., & Malaka, R. (2004). A Task-based Approach for Ontology Evaluation. In *Proc. of ECAI 2004 Workshop on Ontology Learning and Population.*

Power, D. J. (2000). *The decision support system glossary.* Retrieved fromhttp://dssresources.com/glossary/

Prieto-Diaz, R. (2003). A faceted approach to building ontologies Information Reuse and Integration IRI 2003.*IEEE International Conference.*

PROTÉGÉ. (2011a). *Welcome to Protégé.* Retrieved from http://protege.stanford.edu/doc/faq.html

PROTÉGÉ. (2011b). *What is protégé?* Retrieved from http://protege.stanford.edu/overview/

Ranganathan, S. R. (1962). *Elements of library classification New York.* Asia Publishing House.

Roberts, J. (2000). From know-how to show-how? Questioning the role of information and communications technologies in knowledge transfer. *Technology Analysis and Strategic Management, 12*(4), 429–443. doi:10.1080/713698499

Roberts, J. (2006). Limits to Communities of Practice. *Journal of Management Studies, 43*(3), 624–639. doi:10.1111/j.1467-6486.2006.00618.x

Sabou, M., Wore, C., Goble, C., & Mishne, G. (2005). Learning domain ontologies for web service descriptions; an experiment in bioinformatics. www2005, China, Japan.

Shadbolt, N., & Milton, N. (1999). From knowledge Engineering to knowledge management. *British Journal of Management, 10*(4), 309–322. doi:10.1111/1467-8551.00141

Shera, J. H. (1983). Librarianship and information science. In The Study of Information. New York: Wiley.

Shera, J. H., & Cleveland, D. (1977). The history and foundation of information science. *Annual Review of Information Science & Technology*, 250–275.

Smith, B. (2003). *Ontology and Information Systems*. Oxford Blackwell. Retrieved from http://ontology. buffalo.edu/ontology(PIC).pdf

Sowa, J. (2005). Distinction, combination, and constraints. *Proceeding of IJCAI-95 workshop on basic ontological issue in knowledge sharing.*

Sowa, J. F. (1984). *Conceptual Structures: Information Processing in Mind and Machine*. Addison-Wesley.

Sowa, J. F. (2000). *Knowledge Representation: Logical, Philosophical, and Computational Foundations.* Pacific Grove, CA: Brooks Cole Publishing Co.Retrieved fromhttp://www.jfsowa.com/krbook/

Stewart, T. (1997). *The invisible key to success*. Fortune.

Stonier, T. (1990). *Information and the internal structure of the universe: An exploration into information physics.* Springer. doi:10.1007/978-1-4471-3265-3

Sure, Y., Erdmann, M., Angele, J., Staab, S., Studer, R., & Wenke, D. (2002). *OntoEdite: collaborative ontology engineering for the semantic web.First International Semantic Web Conference (ISWC'02)*, Sardinia, Italy.

Sure, Y., Staab, S., & Suder, R. (2008). *Ontology Engineering Methodology*. Springer.

Swartout, B. E. A. (1997). Toward distributed use of large -scale ontologies.*AAAI Symposium on Ontology Engineering Stanford.*

TAPPEDIN. (2010). *Community of educational domain*. Retrieved from http://tappedin.org/tappedin/

Tennant, N. (2007). Parts, Classes and Parts of Classes: An Anti-Realist Reading of Lewisian Mereology. The SAC Conference on David Lewis's Contributions to Formal Philosophy, Copenhagen, Denmark.

Thrysoe, L., Hounsgaard, L., Dohn, N. B., & Wenger, L. (2010). Participating in a community of practice as a prerquisite for becoming a nurse- Trajectories as final year nursing students. *Nurse Education in Practice*, *10*(6), 361–366. doi:10.1016/j.nepr.2010.05.004 PMID:20937575

Tifous, A., Adil, E., & Rose, D. (2007). Ontology for supporting communities of practice. *Proceedings of the 4th International Conference on Knowledge Capture*. Retrieved from http://dl.acm.org/citation. cfm?id=1298415

Tillett, B. (2004). *FRBR: A Conceptual Model for the Bibliographic Universe*. Library of Congress Cataloging Distribution Service.

Trombert-Paviot, B., Rodrigues, J., Rogers, J., & Baud, R. (2002). GALEN: A Third Generation Terminology Tool to support multipurpose National Coding System for surgical procedures. *International Journal of Medical Informatics*, *58*, 71–85. PMID:10978911

Tsui, E., Wang, W. M., Cheung, C. F., & Lau, A. S. M. (2009). A concept-relationship acquisition and inference approach for hierarchical taxonomy construction from tags. *Information Processing & Management*, *46*(1), 44–57. doi:10.1016/j.ipm.2009.05.009

Tudorache, T. (2011). WebProtégé: A Collaborative Ontology Editor and Knowledge Acquisition Tool for the Web. *Semantic Web*, *11*, 154–165. PMID:23807872

Tuomi, I. (2000). Data is more than knowledge: Implications of the reversed knowledge hierarchy for knowledge management and organizational memory. *Journal of Management Information Systems*, *16*(3), 103–117. doi:10.1080/07421222.1999.11518258

Turner, J. G., & MacClusky, T. L. (1994). *The construction of formal specifications An introduction to the model- based and Algebraic Approaches*. McGraw-Hill.

Uschold, M., & Grüninger, M. (1996). ONTOLOGIES: Principles. *Methods and Applications Knowledge Engineering Review*, *11*(02), 93–155. doi:10.1017/S0269888900007797

Varzi, A. (1996). Parts, wholes, and part-whole relations: The prospects of Mereotopology. *Data & Knowledge Engineering*, *20*(3), 259–286. doi:10.1016/S0169-023X(96)00017-1

Vasconcelos, J., Kimble, C., & Gouveia, F. R. (2000). A design for a Group Memory system using Ontologies.*Proceedings of 5th UKAIS Conference*. McGraw Hill.

Vogrincic, S., & Bosnic, Z. (2011). Ontology- based multi-label classification of economic articles. *ComSIS*, *8*(1), 101–119. doi:10.2298/CSIS100420034V

Vrandecic, D. (2010). *Ontology Evaluation*. Academic Press.

Walsh, M., & Crumbie, A. (2011). Initial evaluation of Stilwell:A multimedia virtual community. *Nurse Education in Practice*, *11*(2), 136–140. doi:10.1016/j.nepr.2010.10.004 PMID:21071274

Wang, Y.-H., & Jhuo, P.-S. (2009). A Semantic Faceted Search with Rule-based Inference.*Proceedings of the International MultiConference of Engineers and Computer Scientists*.

Webster. (2011). *Definition of Knowledge*. Retrieved from http://www.merriam-webster.com/dictionary/knowledge?show=0&t=1316553888

Welty, C., Lehmann, F., Gruninger, G., & Uschold, M. (1999). *Ontologies: Expert Systems all over again?* In *The National Conference on Artificial Intelligence*, Austin, TX.

Wenger, E. (1998). *Communities of practice: Learning, Meaning, Identity*. Cambridge, UK: Cambridge University Press. doi:10.1017/CBO9780511803932

Wenger, R. M., & Snyder, W. (2002). Cultivating Communities of practice: A guide to managing knowledge. Harvard Business School Press.

Wielinga, B. J., & Schreiber, A. T. (1993). *Reusable and searchable knowledge bases: a European perspective*. First international conference on building and sharing of very large-scaled knowledge base, Tokyo, Japan.

Zhang, W., & Watts, S. (2008). Online communities as communities of practice: A case study. *Journal of Knowledge Management*, *12*(4), 55–71. doi:10.1108/13673270810884255

Zins, C. (2007a). Conceptions of, Information Science. *Journal of the American Society for Information Science and Technology*, *58*(3), 335–350. doi:10.1002/asi.20507

Chapter 12
Methodology of Creating Ontology of Information Science (OIS)

Ahlam F. Sawsaa
University of Huddersfield, UK & Benghazi University, Libya

Joan Lu
University of Huddersfield, UK

ABSTRACT

In the previous chapter we have discussed the main fields related to the research: ontological engineering, knowledge management, and Virtual communities of practice. As stated before, our concern is representing domain knowledge by creating OIS ontology. After reviewing the ontology literature to find an appropriate theoretical perspective focusing on the content-related variables for theoretical model construction, we found that theories can help to define formal ontological properties that contribute to characterising the concepts. Meanwhile, ontologists nowadays have a choice of formal frameworks which derive from formal logic, algebra, category theory, set theory and Mereotopology. However, to gain a better understand of OIS ontology development and its role in semantic web, the framework is established to describe the main theoretical base. The theoretical base of our framework is based on ontology theoretic.

THEORETICAL APPROACHES

Ontology theoretic is about concepts classification which based on faceted classification system, and ontology algebra which is based on Mereotopology theory.

Ontology is usually organized in taxonomy which contains a primitive model such as classes, relations, instances and axioms. This chapter presents the main theory of ontology developing from information science by organizing IS classification. To achieve the research objectives, which is based on category theory. The OIS ontology will defined as follows:

The Definition of OIS=

DOI: 10.4018/978-1-5225-2058-0.ch012

C: Is concepts of information science objects.

R: Is the relationship of the concepts.

A: Is the attributes of information science object.

X: Is axioms of the concepts.

I: Is instances.

Taxonomy of OIS Ontology Approach

In the ontological engineering area attention has been given to the content of information rather than just the formats and languages used to represent information. The research approach consisted of constructing the contents of OIS ontology based on faceted classification system as a solid theoretical and philosophical foundation. The approach emerged from both ideas:

First idea; Information science is multidisciplinary, as noted in the literature, it overlaps with other sciences, and it has been changed dramatically over time. This change needs logical ontology to clarify the science boundaries among others. Ontology of Information Science draws a number of disciplines in several sciences, including archive science, library science, and computer science as shown diagrammatically in Figure 1

The initial idea was to analyse each of these branches separately, based on the main categories of each one. It could be divided into two main parts; practical and theoretical, as illustrated in Figure 2

The practical part of library science is composing from collection, organisation, preservation, information retrieval, information service, for instance. Research in these fields includes a variety of specialised terminology. To get actionable results, some of the connections between different fields should be made in a systematic way. Yet the complexity of these fields makes it hard to track what of the information in each field is relevant to another field. For this purpose the modularisation is supposed to be contained in three single models: archive science, library science, computer science. Creating small ontologies for each with a specific domain (sub-ontology model) to be integrated has advantages and disadvantages, such as that the building process could be more flexible and manageable, and helps to increase efficient use of the ontology during its usage within the application, even minimising the needs of the whole ontology, in terms of being used when it is not necessary. Also, different domain views can be presented within single overall domain ontology to introduce clear and flexible design.

Figure 1 the main components of OIS ontology

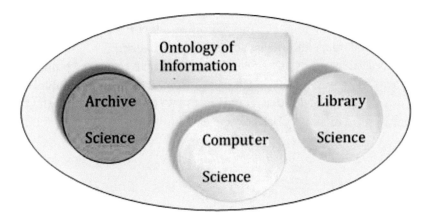

Figure 2 taxonomy of Library Science module

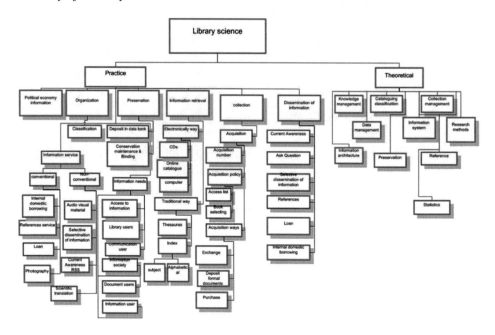

On the other hand, it is supposed to be partitioned into many separate modules, which require much more consideration. In this case, each aspect of ontology modelling should be designed independently from the perspective of usability, although it is difficult to make them completely independent. Yet it could be possible to determine that each module has different concepts and it is easy to define them. In the obvious example it is reasonably indubitable that the concept *information retrieval* would be defined in the computer science model.

In certain cases it is could be unclear as it can be under the *Library science* class or a subclass of the main functions of the library science module.

In this case, for clarity, there is a need to determine in which module it will be appropriate to define the concepts, e.g. if one thinks that information retrieval would be determined in the computer science module, so it is also quite possible to be defined in a different module. It is impossible to keep both of the modules with concepts that are incompatible unless the module supports their view when its relations are defended to avoid conflict.

But this view is limited and inflexible in creating many of the relations between these entities that are inconsistent with the notion of ontology. For this reason we adopt Facet Classification (FAS) to design taxonomy of IS to express domain knowledge accurately and readably.

Second idea; (IS) is a science as is any science. We must make clear the comprehensive concept of the word science itself, where the word science comes from, even what the nature of science is. The definition of the word science indicates that it contains every type of knowledge, theoretical and practical. For instance the Webster dictionary defines science as follows:

Knowledge attained through study or practice. (Webster,2011)

From this definition we can interpret the aim of science to be acquiring knowledge according to specific methods and techniques applied by scientists, controlled by law, regulations, and ethics. Operations and the outcome of the science are based on the studies and theories, applying methods and techniques processed by actors. So the study interprets this view to categorise the high level of the OIS ontology.

Based on this explanation the OIS ontology has been developed by identifying the entities representing the key objects to meet multiple requirements. This approach has been influenced by the Aristotelian perspective of categorising the higher levels of the universe.

The classification of OIS ontology is basically based on a faceted analytic-synthetic system (Ranganathan, 1962). As well as this, our approach is corresponding to Research group classification (CRG) which has extended these categories into 14 facets.

Based on above, we analyse IS as a domain split into 14 extensions; these categories are the upper level of classes of ontology that are as follows:

Actors, Method, Practice, Studies, Mediator, Kinds, Domains, Resources, Legislation, Philosophy & theories, Societal, Tool, Time, Space.

These classes are identified and structured in a hierarchy connected by relationships, and the taxonomy schema of the IS domain is shown in Appendix B.

The IS terms for this study were identified to provide clear definitions for classes that would be of interest to the domain users and developers. The associated attributes and characteristics of the objects with their relations were also identified.

Each entity has attributes and type of relations for operating between these entities. The study intends to provide a conceptual model to serve as a base for related specific relations and attributes. Furthermore, the research is focusing on analysis of IS data to define in a systematic way in which ways the information will be used.

The Methodology to be Adopted

The choice of method relies on the research motivations and aims, and analyses some development ontology methodologies and IEEE 1074-2006 standards for developing a software project life cycle process as criteria. This methodology uses an iterative approach, allowing us to create ontologies in an accurate manner for the Information Science domain. This research adopts the Methontology methodology to develop ontology of Information Science OIS.

Methontology is the most representative of methods. It also fared quite well against other methodologies in comparison.

Techniques and Tools to be Employed

Several questions need to be answered when building a new ontology, such as: Which tools do we need and which language should we use for implanting it? For this part we present tools and languages of ontology to understand the differences and similarities are between them, and to demonstrate their development through time.

The landscape of the study tools that support different stages of ontology creation and development comprises of:

- Knowledge management tool Community of practice (Ontocop). Tools such as this are used when feedback is needed.
  - General Architecture for Text Engineering (GATE).
  - Ontology language (Web Ontology Language (OWL)) for coding the ontology, which formalises knowledge in a semantic model.
  - Ontology editing (Protégé Editor) used to edit the ontology
  - Ontology publishing (WebProtégé) is an ontology library for ontology browsing, used when the stable version of the ontology was created to get feedback.

ESTABLISHING THE ONTOLOG MODEL

In general, creating ontology requires design to be applied through the development process. The designing process consists of the *conceptual aspect* and the *computational aspect*.

Conceptual Aspect

The principle in the conceptual aspect is to represent the domain clearly and accurately and to be easy for users to use. Ontology in conceptual aspect should be created based on:

- **Represent Accurately as Possible:** It is difficult to represent the whole domain in a complete and accurate manner. Describing the domain needs firstly full agreement between experts in the domain and knowledge engineers. Recognising this is crucial for capturing the knowledge, particularly when there is not full agreement, to avoid ambiguous concepts or when the concepts are equally valid for representing in the ontology. There is an important consideration over describing the concepts in a domain in detail, to ensure the concept is captured within the context of the domain. Also, some concepts are more important than other concepts.
- **Reusing the Ontology:** The domain ontology as reference for building other ontology should be designed to be reused; Whether the whole ontology or some element of it requires a hierarchical taxonomy to cover the domain and use inheritance when it is needed. The hierarchy taxonomy should not be deep, to facilitate use of concepts at the bottom to avoid conflict between the relations and between structures of ontology. These relations should be expressed within the domain correctly and accurately to describe the whole domain.

Computational Aspect

The computational aspect interprets the conceptual model by the machine, to be machine readable as accurately as possible. Ontologies are represented by the machine using OWL language, to describe it in a logical manner. Still there is debate whether or not OWL is expressive enough. On one hand, some people say OWL is not enough to represent the whole domain. On other hand, we believe that it is a more expressive language than other la languages due to the fact that it expresses difficult relations in logical description.

Introducing OIS Design Methodology

This section presents our proposed methodology for ontology conceptualisation, designing and development. The proposed approach is targeted to answering the aim of the research, namely how the OIS ontology has been created to model the domain knowledge and how the Ontocop community can assess the developing process. Methodology of creating OIS ontology mainly consists of two phases, namely:

- Designing ontology of Information Science model.
- Designing Ontocop website tool

Designing Ontology Model

The ontology moves slowly from knowledge level to implementation level to be machine understandable. Firstly, we begin by introducing a method for constructing OIS ontology, which comprises two stages; building the conceptual model and converting it to a logical model. Development of the OIS ontology starts from identifying the specific purpose and scope that is included in specification

Specifications

- **Identify Goals, Scope, Strategy and Boundary of the Domain:** To identify the domain interest to be captured and scope of the domain - this refers to the limitations or boundaries for constraining the conceptualisation of the domain. In this stage there are many questions that need to be answered as recommended by Uschold and Grüninger, which are similar to the competency questions. These questions put together the resources that cover the ontology's objects, purposes, scope and granularity
- What are the general characteristics of ontology of information science? To answer this question the content of the ontology should be described which include: taxonomic organisation, the kind of concepts it will cover at top-level division, internal structure of the concept.
- What is the scope of the domain - will it cover the general domain or be specific?
- What is the purpose of ontology of IS?
- Identify targeted users, applications and functional requirement.
- Choose knowledge acquisition method and tool
- Choose tool to create the ontology.
- Choose modelling approaches of ontology that will be used. In this stage, the designer should make decisions about how to start the analysis and design the domain ontology.
- Choose level of ontology representation; it is necessary to decide what level of ontology will be represented; informal or formal, which has been discussed
- To evaluate the OIS ontology, the consistency checking and domain experts evaluation suggested by (Guruninger and Fox, 1995) has been chosen.
- Using and maintaining the ontology - in this step we follow Methontology to model, develop, maintain and document the ontology. Ontologies need to be maintained particularly for adding new concepts to update them, removing redundant concepts.
- **Knowledge Acquisition:** In this study the acquisition method and tool for collecting domain knowledge have been chosen.

Conceptualisation

After gathering the knowledge it needs to be conceptualised. The activity of building the conceptual model is:

- Building Glossary of terms to identify which terms need to be included in the ontology; the glossary includes the term names, synonyms, acronyms, and descriptions of each term.
- Identify the binary relations between concepts of the ontology.
- Building concept classification.
- Building the data dictionary to identify the concepts with their meaning, instance, class attributes, and their relations.
- In the data dictionary the instances attributes should be described in more detail, and class attributes also need to be described.

Computational Model starts from:

- **Formalising Ontology:** By transferring the conceptual model into a formal model. Ontology needs to be coded using the chosen knowledge representation languages and tools, such as Protégé and OWL.
- **Evaluation:** Ontology needs to be assessed. So, its contents need to tested and verified to satisfy the real world that need to be modelled.
  - Documentation facilitates the reusability of the ontology design.
  - Refinement and maintenance: ontology never completes its need to be updated and maintained over time, as revealed by the development process in Figure 3.

Designing Ontocop Website Tool

The website designing stage requires us to ask many questions in order to start, to identify the aim and needs for the VCops before starting this stage – see Section 4.2.

- What I do need from the website?
- What technology do I need in the website to make it more attractive?
- How can I attract members of the community to make them come back?
- What are the needs of members in this community?

These questions would be helpful in clarifying what exactly should be the purpose and aims of the website.

CONCLUSION

In this chapter the theoretical foundation of developing domain ontologies was addressed. The theoretical base of the OIS emerged from analysing archive science, library science, and computer science. It resulted OIS ontology classification which basically based on a faceted analytic-synthetic system. Also,

Figure 3 Domain ontology of OIS developing process

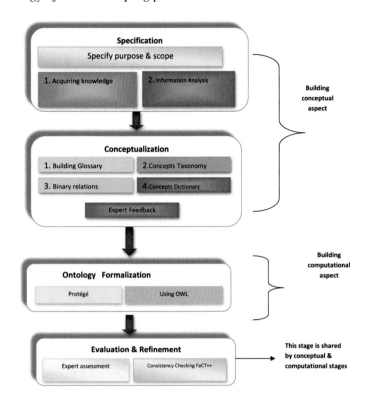

this approach is corresponded to CRG Research group classification which has extended these categories into 14 facets that will be formalized. Furthermore, methodology for ontology conceptualization, designing and development was proposed. The methodology mainly consists of two phases, namely: designing ontology of Information Science model and designing Ontocop website tool.

REFERENCES

Guruninger, M., & Fox, M. S. (1995). Methodology for the design and evaluation of ontologies. In *Workshop on Basic ontological issues in knowledge sharing*.

IEEE 1074-2006. (2006). *IEEE Standard for Developing a Software Project Life Cycle Process*. IEEE Computer Society.

PROTÉGÉ. (2011a). *Welcome to Protégé*. Retrieved from http://protege.stanford.edu/doc/faq.html

Uschold, M., & Grüninger, M. (1996). ONTOLOGIES: Principles, Methods and Applications. *The Knowledge Engineering Review, 11*(02), 93–155. doi:10.1017/S0269888900007797

Webster. (2011). *Definition of Knowledge*. Retrieved from http://www.merriam-webster.com/dictionary/knowledge?show=0&t=1316553888

Chapter 13
Modelling Design of OIS Ontology

Ahlam F. Sawsaa
University of Huddersfield, UK & Benghazi University, Libya

Joan Lu
University of Huddersfield, UK

ABSTRACT

This chapter presents the development of OIS ontology and the main elements that formalised in OWL-DL. The OIS ontology followed Methontology as a general framework of methodology. The main result will be introduced, namely, the modelling design of OIS ontology which follows the description of the activities involved in designing the OIS ontology model. The OIS ontology model identifies the terms and definitions in the IS domain. Also, designing the ontocop system and how it can be a useful platform for supporting and assessing the OIS ontology. It starts by introducing OIS designing methodology. At the end of this chapter we will discuss how this tool will help to develop the OIS ontology to be modelled in a comprehensive and consistent manner.

BUILDING CONCEOTUAL MODEL

1.1.1 Specifications

Ontology specification comprises of several activities. It needs to specify the goal of building and designing the ontology, and the scope of the domain that will be captured in the ontology, as well as whether it will be one domain or more than one domain. Identifying the scope indicates the level of detail that is required. This stage aims to put together the resources that cover the ontology's objects, purposes, scope and granularity. This activity includes:

DOI: 10.4018/978-1-5225-2058-0.ch013

1.1.1.1 Identifying the Purpose and the Scope

In software design methodology, the designer needs to establish the domain scope to be captured and described in the proposed ontology, even whether the domain is a single domain or a combination of domains. Prescribing the ontology is important in identifying the domain boundaries to be investigated. In the specification phase we answer questions about the main purpose for building the ontology: why is the ontology of information science (OIS) being built? What are its planned uses? Who are the end users? It is necessary to identify the boundaries of the domain that the ontology will cover.

The process in this stage is to start by identifying the domain ontology that the ontology will be used for and where it will be implemented, by identifying the main features to gain an understanding how the ontology is related to other domains. As shown in Table 1. In Figure 1 we illustrate the domain scope of the proposed ontology of IS.

1.1.1.2 Knowledge Acquisition

Building a conceptual model requires gaining knowledge that describes the domain. Knowledge needs to be elicited, analysed and interpreted, and transferred into a machine representation.

The purpose of knowledge acquisition is to capture the domain concepts of information science (IS) to be organized into a hierarchical structure-based ontology competence. Furthermore, identifying the main concepts and the necessary information to be described, and discerning the core relationships between these concepts.

Table 1. The scope of IS domain

Domain Ontology	Information Science
Date	2009- 2012
Built by	Research student at Informatics department in School of Computing and Engineering – University of Huddersfield.
Purposes	Providing consensual knowledge modeling of IS domain. It is to be accessible and usable by scholars and ultimately users of IS domain. The OIS ontology will be used when the information about the domain is required in technique, process, analysis. Also, it could be applied in other applications for shared knowledge as an index tool for supporting semantic web mark-up of IS knowledge.
Scope	The scope reflects the domain knowledge in semantic model. The OIS ontology is domain specific. It covers each of these branches; library science, computer science, archival science..
Level of formality	Formal ontology
Sources of knowledge	Ontocop experts' publications and domain publications in general. The following dictionaries: International Conference on Science Abstracting http://jpw.umdl.umich.edu/pubs/teixml-lc/sld003.htm http://www.thefreedictionary.com/administrative+data+processing http://www.fact-index.com/i/in/information_science_glossary_of_terms.html http://lu.com/odlis/index.cfm Dictionary of information and library management Stevenson, Janet., ebrary, Inc. London: A. & C. Black, 2006. electronic book http://site.ebrary.com/lib/uoh/docDetail. action?docID=10196635 Dictionary of ICT The Blackwell Encyclopaedic Dictionary

Figure 1. The main component of IS domain

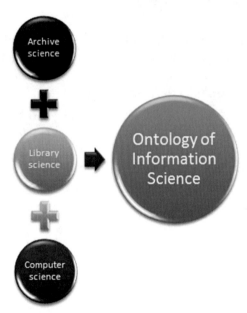

As knowledge representation is procedural it is difficult for people to develop ontology. The AI community approach tends to acquire knowledge as preliminary stage by domain experts before coding the knowledge. Our strategy in this study is performing the process manually and semi-automatically because of the large number of literary outputs in the field. The knowledge acquisition helps to frame the ontology structure and provides the main set of concepts. The terms of IS were aggregated through text analysis of domain documents. The concepts are identified either by pattern extraction or from the natural text of domain documentation.

A far more interesting case, however, is the engagement of domain experts in developing the process of the OIS ontology, which supports organising and structuring the domain knowledge. The experts have a deep understanding of the domain construction that offers a very strong foundation of the ontology. The knowledge organisation systems were consulted in the developing process mentioned in Table 1 above in the knowledge resources part.

The main technique used to analyse and annotate text was GATE. It starts by creating a list of terms in a Gazetteer list to match, and extracts relevant concepts from text to develop the conceptual model. Figure 2 shows a screenshot of the IS Gazetteer in GATE software.

This research presents the semi-automatic extraction method based on A Nearly New Information Extraction System (ANNE) by creating Java Annotation Patterns Engine (JAPE) grammars that help to extract concepts form different formats - XML, and HTML. The process followed the method presented in IEEE standards (1996) for developing software life cycle process as indicated in Sawsaa and Lu's paper (2011). The paper describes a method of annotation concepts of Information Science, to build domain ontology, using Natural Language programming NLP technology. We used our JAPE grammars (Java Annotation Patterns Engine) to support regular expression matching to annotate IS concepts by using GATE developer tool. This is for speed up the developing ontology process as time consuming and experts in the domain has many barriers as time and loads to do. The following JAPE rules have written to extract concepts.

Figure 2. Screenshot of IS Gazetteer

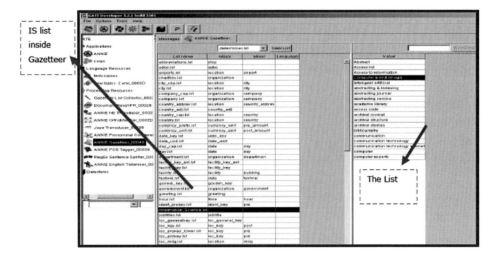

- **Phase 1:** Information.
- **Input:** Token Lookup.
- **Options:** Control = all.
- **Rule:** Concept1.

```
(
({Token.string == "information"})
{Token.string == "service"}
({Lookup.minorType == region}): reginName
): service
-->
: reginName.Location = {},
: Information service.concept = {}
```

The first entity detected is Information service {Type=Token, start=867, end= 837, id= 4210, majorType=concept} labelled as information service .concept.

- **Phase:** Two.
- **Input:** Lookup Token.
- **Options:** Control = all.
- **Rule:** Concept2.
- **Priority:** 20.

```
(
({Token.string == "information"})
{Token.string == "service"}
({Lookup. major Type == "concept"})
```

```
): information
-->
: Information. concept = {Rule=concept2}
```

For more precise details we apply regular expressions for matching strings of text, e.g

- **Phase:** Concept.
- **Input:** Lookup Token.
- **Options:** Control = appelt.
- **Rule:** Glossary.

```
(
({Token.string == "catalog?e"})
): concept
-->
:{} .concept= {Rule= "Glossary"}
```

The rule is specifying a string of the text {Token.string == } string matching to specify the attributes of the annotation by using operators as "==",which provide the whole string matching. Some of these regular expressions in the next example annotate concepts related to (abstract) meta-characters(dot, *, [ ], |),

```
{Token.string == "abstract(ing)"}
```

It may be abstract, abstracting, abstractor.

Also, if we want to annotate the acquisition concept followed by another word as:

```
{Token.string == "acquisition. number"}
```

It could be annotated thus:

```
Acquisition. police
Acquisition .service
{Token.string == "archival * "}
```

It will annotate archival library, archival journal, archival processing, archival software, and archival studies. All these rules are sorted in the INFCO. JAPE file .The result is as shown in Figure 3

Extraction of IS concepts by using JAPE grammar and Regular expression, based on the GATE developer for automated extracting of information, provides a significant output. The main idea of using JAPE and Regular Expression is to identify IS terminology as tokens, for example, Computing, Libraries and Information Technology, from a large text where terms are located. The term 'identification' relies on lookup from the Gazatteer list of IS which could match; for instance, it could be book art, book card, book guidance or book catalogue. Also, it will look up concepts such as computer application, computer science, computer experts, computer file, or computer image. The corpus was used to extract information science concepts contains 300 documents which were obtained. Therefore, the total document is

Figure 3. Annotations of IS terms

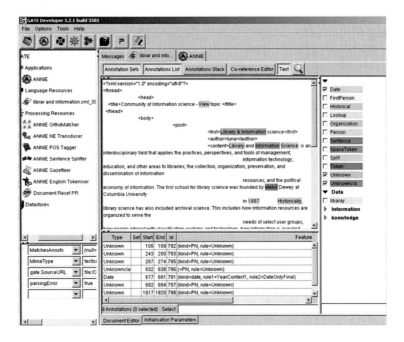

analysed by running the ANNIE application organised as document reset, Tokenizer, Sentence Splitter Gazetteer, POS tagger, JAPE transducer and Orthomatcher. In annotation the set appeared in the display panel and concepts are highlighted in the annotation default.

Figure 3 presents the results of annotating the IS concepts after running ANNIE and highlighting the matching concepts. The results show that our approach successfully annotates concepts. We recalled 541 of the *Knowledge* concept, 275 Information concepts and 35 of the *organisation* concept see Figure 4. Each annotation starts from a specific point and ends at a different point, based on how many tokens it has. The knowledge concept starts at point 557 and ends at 566, while the organization concept starts at 624 and ends at 636, with its features {major Type=concept}.

We conduct this experiment to achieve accuracy rates that are equal to the manual output by IS experts for the annotating concepts. Statistics of the corpus show pattern matching of IS concepts based on the lookup IS list 402, correct concepts and accuracy were generally higher, with partially correct 0 missing and false positives 0.

However, we use GATE due to its benefits as open source and it contains multi-language NLP models which can be reused for developing other resources.

The primary outcome of this stage is a glossary that contains the list of concepts relevant to domain knowledge. We will present it in the next section.

1.1.2 Conceptualisation of IS Entities Ontology

According to Methontology, conceptual models contain tasks for constructing information in a logical model. Conceptualisation starts when most of the knowledge has been acquired and it needs to be organised. Furthermore, when the conceptualisation is completed the ontology displays for the experts to evaluate it.

Figure 4. Annotation of IS concepts

Start	End	Key	Features	=?	Start	End	Response	Feature
557	566	knowledge	{majorType=concept, minorType=term}	=	557	566	knowledge	{majorType=concept, n
624	636	organization	{majorType=concept, minorType=term}	=	624	636	organization	{majorType=concept, n
751	760	knowledge	{majorType=concept, minorType=term}	=	751	760	knowledge	{majorType=concept, n
867	879	organization	{majorType=concept, minorType=term}	=	867	879	organization	{majorType=concept, n
896	905	knowledge	{majorType=concept, minorType=term}	=	896	905	knowledge	{majorType=concept, n
1023	1032	knowledge	{majorType=concept, minorType=term}	=	1023	1032	knowledge	{majorType=concept, n
1084	1096	organization	{majorType=concept, minorType=term}	=	1084	1096	organization	{majorType=concept, n
1151	1160	knowledge	{majorType=concept, minorType=term}	=	1151	1160	knowledge	{majorType=concept, n
1280	1289	knowledge	{majorType=concept, minorType=term}	=	1280	1289	knowledge	{majorType=concept, n
1323	1332	knowledge	{majorType=concept, minorType=term}	=	1323	1332	knowledge	{majorType=concept, n
1492	1501	knowledge	{majorType=concept, minorType=term}	=	1492	1501	knowledge	{majorType=concept, n
1876	1885	knowledge	{majorType=concept, minorType=term}	=	1876	1885	knowledge	{majorType=concept, n
1898	1910	organization	{majorType=concept, minorType=term}	=	1898	1910	organization	{majorType=concept, n

Figure 5. Result accuracy

			Recall	Precision	F-measure
Correct:	403				
Partially correct:	0	Strict:	1.00	1.00	1.00
Missing:	0	Lenient:	1.00	1.00	1.00
False positives:	0	Average:	1.00	1.00	1.00

Statistics | Adjudication

1.1.2.1 Identification of Concepts and Relations

This task starts with building glossary terms which emphasises the ontology components that are described above (Concepts, Relationships, Individuals, Attributes, Constants, Formal Axioms and Rules). These components build inside conceptualisation activity as illustrated in Figure 6.

1.1.2.2 Building Glossary of Terms of IS

The starting point in creating a glossary of IS is requiring the integration of all relevant terms in the field of IS. Building a conceptual model of ontology is creating the glossary of terms, which includes synonyms, acronyms and a simple description for each term included in the ontology. Table 2 shows a section of the glossary of terms of the IS entity ontology. Initially, the glossary contains 650 terms.

Figure 6. Conceptualisation activities

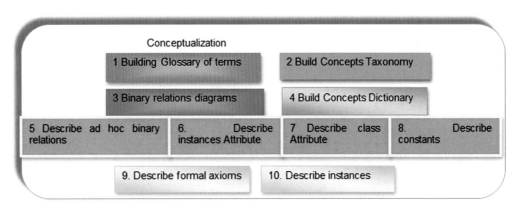

Table 2. Part of the glossary of terms of OIS ontology

Concept Name	Synonyms	Acronyms	Description	Type (Class, Instance)
Abstract	theoretical	-	Summarises ideas of the contents of document, and it is usually accompanied by description bibliography to enable access to the original document[1]	class
Artificial Intelligent	Thinking machines	AI	An area of computer science focusing on mimicking human ability. This device and its applications is used to make decisions	class
abstracting & indexing	-	-	Service provides bibliographic citation and abstract of the literature in a specific subject.	class
abstracting			Process of producing, extracts as much information from the document and expression. This process is complementary to the indexing	class
abstracting journal	Abstracts of articles	-	A journal that specialises in providing summary (is for journal)	subclass

1.1.2.3 Building Concepts Taxonomy

Building the concepts taxonomy starts when the glossary of IS contains a sizable number of domain terms. Natural language is used to define unambiguous and precise classes to be structured in semi-formal hierarchy, before creating a computational model of the ontology is really fundamental.

Building a concept taxonomy of the IS domain provides concepts, classifications and descriptions, to be described in a hierarchy. The concepts taxonomy follows ontology construction approaches to develop it. These methods are top-down and bottom-up, which allows identification of the first concept to control the level of details such as (Classes –Subclasses of – Partition-of). Methods of Information science architecture. The workflow of building OIS ontology is composed from creating taxonomy. Our approach of building OIS ontology is based on a combined method which is Top-Down.

To involve a better understanding of the IS domain, the study defines the high level structure of the ontology based on assumption or what could be postulated. It emerged as result of reinitialise 28 classification schema in Zins' work.

This process postulated and captured, based on Aristotle's view. The domain to identify key concepts based on FAS. The reason behind adopting Facet Classification (FAS) to design taxonomy of IS to express domain knowledge accurately and readably, as seen in Figure 7

Implementation starts with most general concepts in the domain such as: Information services, Users, Foundation.

Furthermore, the four taxonomic relations in Methontology are used, such as Subclass-Of, Exhaustive-Decomposition, Disjoint- Decomposition and Partition.

- This can be seen if class C1 is subclass of C2, and an instance of C1 is also an instance of class C1, then C2 is a subclass of class C1, e.g. a library user is a subclass of users, since every library user is users.
- The Exhaustive-Decomposition relation of the class C1 is a set of subclass of C2 that means they have common subclasses and instances e.g. if class American Library association and Canadian Library association are Exhaustive-Decomposition relations of the class Professional association that means these classes have common instances, such as that Library association is Canadian Library association and American Library association.
- If the class C1 is a set of subclass of C2 and there are no common instances between them, then the relation is disjoint-Decomposition e.g. the class funding agents and service provider disjoint–Decomposition of class institution because an institution can be a funding agent and service provider at the same time.
- The Partition relation can be depicted in this example. If a class C1 is a subset of C2 they do not have common instances but if C1 covers part of C2 then the relation is Partition. e.g. Class Library user and Researcher make a Partition relation of class Users because every user is either Library user or Researcher. Figure 8 outlines the taxonomy of OIS ontology.

Figure 7. Shows Top-Down method

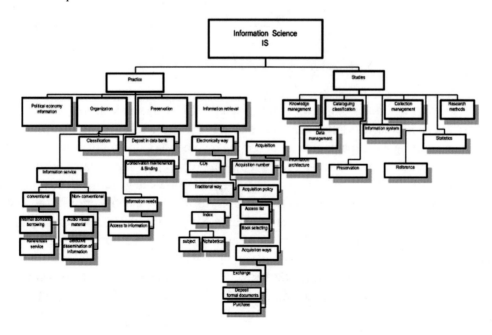

Figure 8. Concept Taxonomy of OIS ontology

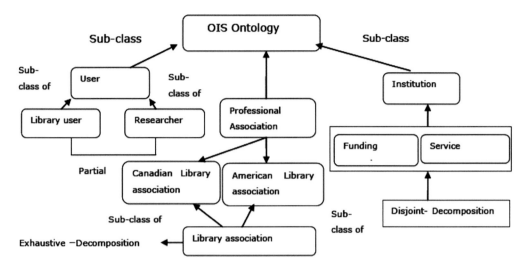

Bottom–Up Methods

This involves precise understanding of field details that help users to explore related content, as seen in Figure 9. In this process concepts are clustered and categorised, and informed manually. This approach is consistent with Prieto-Diaz's view. Our approach differs from his approach due to the fact that human thinking is still better than machine for clustering and representing concepts in a specific domain based on expertise.

Figure 9. Bottom–up methods

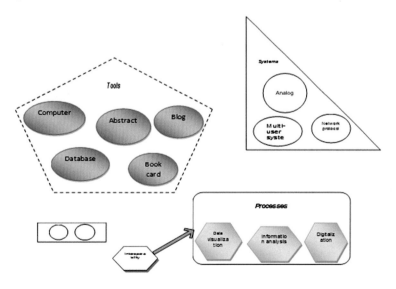

The Mechanism of Bottom–Up Method

Text annotating assists in creating a list of key words and concepts. Keywords and terms are extracted from the document of the IS domain. This list is the main input in clustering and grouping domain concepts. Annotating text processing is a mature technique which starts with document Reset, Tokenising process and annotated beads on the ANNIE Gazetteer using JAPE Transducer. The resulting key words are annotated in the editor. Additional details are contained in (Sawsaa and Lu, 2011) .

The concepts are clustered manually, based on grouping, and categorised similar concepts that are related to each other and have things in common under a common classes name, for instance, an operation in library science is collecting, classifying, and dissemination information. So, all of these concepts are clustered under operation or process, to identify facets.

This process provides initial clusters significant to the task of building the taxonomy of IS ontology concept clustering; the Bottom-Up approach provides initial groups of related terms. See Table 3.

Implementation of this approach reduces individuals and instances to general concepts, for example: information scientists, archivists, record managers, and librarians can be classified under the concept Information professional.

This approach was based on the idea of archival science as the base of information science, and library science builds on this approach. That IS and computer science emerged at the same time and they have complex relationships cannot be ignored. Each approach is classified on the view of researchers, and it will be reviewed by the members of the ontocop community to evaluate its accuracy and gain full agreement on the ontology's foundation.

1.1.2.4 Building ad Hoc Binary Relation

After building the concepts taxonomy the binary relations should be built. In this activity the binary relations aim to establish ad hoc relations between same or different concepts that already included in the concept dictionary. Figure 11 presents the ad hoc binary relations of OIS ontology with the relations Has-A, and Is-A and their inverse relations isPartOf, and haspartA; these relations connect between these classes Archival Science is part of Information Science in the OIS ontology. Before going further the ad hoc binary relations should be checked to ensure there are no errors, particularly if the domain and ranges axiom is applied.

Figure 10. Fragment of OIS Taxonomy

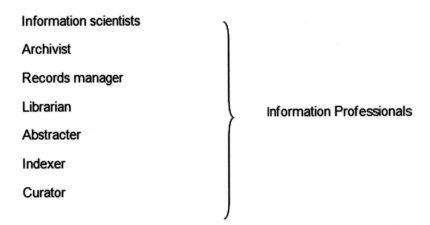

Table 3. Concepts clustering

Tool	Process	Location / Organization	Service	Resource	Media	Activates
A programing language	Abstracting	Academic library	Access service	Active database	Compact disc	Advertising
Abstract	Abstracting and indexing	Acquisition in archival	Abstract service	Active document	Digital image	Infomercial
Abstract journal	Abstracting service	Alxandrain library	Acquisition service	Archival copy	Digital video disc	
Access	Access charge	Architecture library	Archival reference service	Archival file	Disk	
Access code	Access control	Archival administration	Ask librarian	Archival journal	DVD	
Access point	Access to information	Archival library	Bibliographic service	Archive group	DVD-RAM	
Access policy	Administration data process	Biblotheca / historical library	Document delivery	Audio book	DVD-ROMDVD-RW	
Administration history	Algorithm design	Biblotheca alexandrina	Electronic document delivery	Audio newspaper	Floppy disc	
Alphabetization	Archival agreement	Collection archives	Electronic mail	Audiovisual materials	Random access memory	
Alphabetic subject catalogue	Alphabetization	College library	Electronic information retrieval	Book	Video	
Anglo-American ataloguing rules	Annotation	Depository	Financial service	Book	Video compact discs	
Aperture card	Annotation computing	Descriptive cataloging	Frequent ask question	Bulletins		
Appendix	Archival description	Document center	Information & referral	Children book		
Archival box	Archival practice	Government library	Information dissemination	Dictionary		
Archival database	Archival processing	Information center	Inter library loan	Dissertation		
Archival quality	Archival preservation	Institutional library	Internet service provider	Document		
Archival standard	Art	International library	Library information services	Documentary		
Archival teaching unit	Availability	Law library	Library statistics	Documentary drama		
Archival textile box	Batch	Library	Management information system	Electronic journal		
Archive policy	Batch process	Library media center	Non-conventional information services	Electronic book		
artificial diget	Bibliographic description	Library of congress	Online processing	Electronic collection		
Artificial classification	Biblogony	Library school	Q&A fact retrieval system	Electronic magazine		
Attachment	Bibliographic retrieval	Map library	Really simple syndication	Electronic newsletter		
Audiovisual	Browse	Mobile library	Reference service	Encyclopedia		
Authoatic abstract	Communication technology internet	Museum	Traditional information retrieval	Essay		
Author abstract	Clustering	National library	Traditional information service	Film		
Author bibliography	Collection management	Organization	Web-based service	Full text database		
Author catalogue	Classification	Picture library		General encyclopedia		
Author entry	Communication	Public archives		Gazette		

Box. 1.

Communication	Libraries
Telecommunication	Alexandrian library
Cable	Archival library
Wireless	Art library
Satellite	Academic library
Mobile devices	university library
Digital camera	college library
Fax machine	Department Library
Radio communication	University Library
Telemetric	Government library
Teletext	Library of Congress
Networks	Library media centre
Distributed networks	School Library Library media centre
Internet network	special library
Invisible Web	National library
web address	International library
Web- based service	Map library
Internet protocol	Architecture library
web server	Picture library
search engines	Public library
	Virtual library
	audiovisual library
	Mobile library
	Information centres
	Health information centre
	Military information centre
	International information centre

If the *Information* class has *Fact* as subclass, the relationship will be named Has-A, and the inverse relationship will be is- an elementOf

1.1.2.5 Build the Concept Dictionary

Ontology identifies relationships and instance attributes of each class. The classes should be defined in a dictionary that contains the domain concepts, such as concept name - class attribute - relations.

Figure 11. Ad hoc binary relations

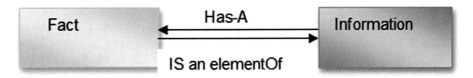

Table 4. Concepts dictionary

Concept Name	Instances	Class Attribute	Instance Attribute	Relations
Library	Public Library, National library, Law library digital library	Library type	Name, size, service, URL	Is part of, has relation with, subclassOf
Classification Rules	Anglo-American Cataloguing Rules	Rules name	standards	Is kind of
Tools	Digital Video Disc	-	size	Has A, Is A

1.1.2.6 Define Ad Hoc Binary Relation

This activity aims to explain the binary relationships in the classification tree. The binary relations are sorted in a table to specify each relation name, names of source and target concept, cardinality and inverse relationship for each ad hoc relationship to identify the correct binary relations. Table 5 presents section of the ad hoc binary relation of OIS ontology.

1.1.2.7 Define Instance Attributes

The main target of the instance attributes table is to describe them in more detail than are included in the concepts dictionary. The instance attribute is what has been defined in the concept yet it takes a value in this instance. The table includes the following fields; its name, the concept name that belongs to it, value type, value range (numerical value), and cardinality (max, min). Table 6 shows part of the instance attributes of OIS ontology.

Table 5. Part of the ad hoc binary relation of OIS ontology

Relation Name	Source Concept	Cardinality	Target Concepts	Inverse Relation
accessableBy	Library	N	User	ToAccess
employeeIn	Information Center	N	Staff	worksFor

Table 6. Part of instance attributes of OIS ontology

Instance Attributes Name	Concept Name	Value Type	Value Range	Cardinality
Bibliographic classification	Classification Schemes	String	-	(1,1)
American Library Association	Library association	String	-	(1,1)

1.1.2.8 Create Class Attributes Table

The aim of the class attributes table is to describe class attributes in more detail than is included in the concepts dictionary. The Ontologist should put this information in the class attributes table to include the following fields; name, defined concept name where the attribute is defined, value type, and cardinality (max, min). Table 7 shows part of the class attributes of OIS ontology.

1.1.2.9 Define Constants

In this activity the constants are specified by their names, describing natural language, value type, and value and measurement unit. The attributes can inferred based on constants. Table 8 illustrates a fragment of the constants of OIS ontology.

1.1.2.10 Define Formal Axiom

Identifying formal axioms is not an easy task, which requires a precise description. Methontology specifies the following information; Axiom name, description, expression, referred concepts, referred relations and variables.

1.1.2.11 Define Instances

Methontology proposes to identify the relevant instance that included in concept dictionary. The following information should define; instance name, concept name, attribute and values. As the OIS is a general model, individuals are not included now. But it provides some of them to explain the individual role in the model for future development, based on specific applications of use. The current version contains only 99 individuals. Table 9 illustrates some of them.

Table 7. A section of the instance attributes table of OIS ontology

Class Attributes Name	Defined Concept	Value Type	Cardinality	Value
Publication date	publication	integer	(1,2)	Date
Name of course	Education of computer science	String	(1,1)	string

Table 8. A section of constants table of OIS ontology

Class Attributes Name	Defined Concept	Value Type	Cardinality	Value
Academic staff education	Employee	Cardinal	Min 1 certificate	year
Publication date	Publication	Cardinal	2000	year

Table 9. The instance table of the OIS ontology

Instance Name	Concept Name	Attributes	Values
Dewey Decimal classification	Classification Schemes	Number of schedule	30
Digital Video Disk Read only	Compact Disk	Decimal	Max 8 GB

1.1.3 Conceptual Model of OIS Ontology

In this stage, a list of the core basic terms is elaborated according to the Methontology method. The outcome of conceptualisation is a conceptual model to visualise and express the theoretical construct that represents the IS domain. Conceptual models reflect on the computational model; it could be a communication device with experts in the domain. The conceptual model was developed using ArgoUML software. It shows the entity classes, attributes and their relationships in OIS ontology. We elaborate the main relationships among the defined classes.

The first entity, *Actors,* endeavours to cover all people and organizations that provide service to everyone who need information, to be used for different purposes, and represents relationships with other subclasses as depicted in Figure 12. The study assumes Actors is a person but it could be an individual or group. The individual, such as Researchers, Library users, can access Resources by Mediator such as Libraries, Information Centres etc.

Another example is the *Library* class related to the *Resources* class by hasA Book. The book is createdBy Author and hasA specific Location. The specific location determinedBy, or AccessedBy author Entry, Tilte Entry or Subject Entry. At the same time author Entry, Tilte Entry or Subject Entry part of

Figure 12. Part of conceptual model of OIS ontology

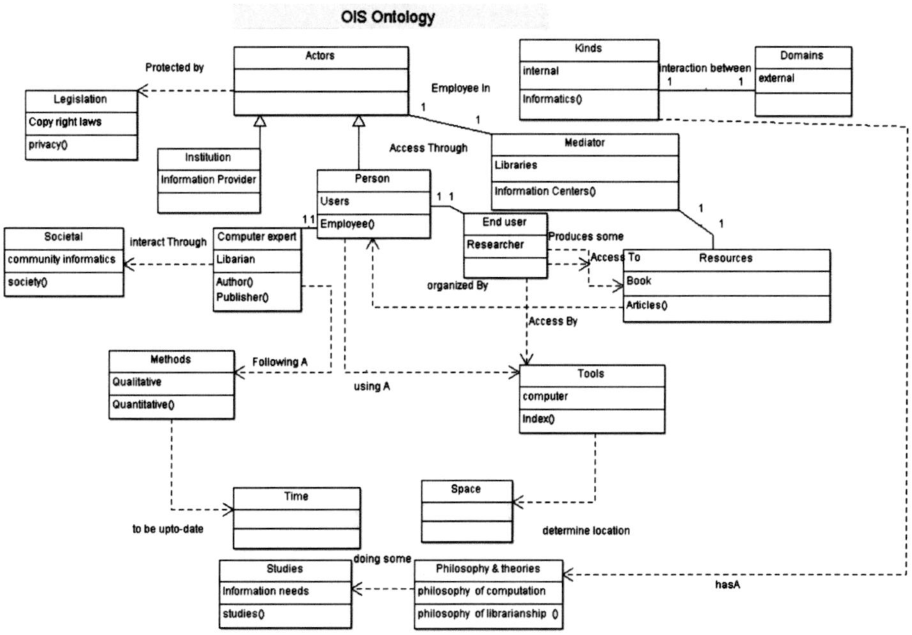

LibraryCatalogue. It could be a traditional catalogue or digital catalogue. Each user hasA access ID to access the Library Catalogue. This combination lets us express the relationship between these classes. Some of the results are not shown for the reason that the data is too big to present here.

1.2 BUILDING COMPUTATIONAL MODEL: FORMALIZATION

Conceptual model of the IS in natural language need to be modelled. The primary output of this stage is OIS ontology, which is structured in the appropriate ontology editor such as Protégé. The OIS ontology is structured in natural language to be suitable for data modelling and knowledge representation.

It indents for expression of unambiguous and complete specification of domain concepts with relations between them, and organises them in super-types and sub-types of hierarchy. Furthermore, ontology in Protégé can be exported to different formats such as RDF and XML, shows the ontology in OWL language.

OIS Ontology is Written by OWL

```
<rdf:RDF xmlns="http://www.semanticweb.org/ontologies/2011/1/Ontol-
ogy1298894565306.owl#"    xml:base="http://www.semanticweb.org/ontolo-
gies/2011/1/Ontology1298894565306.owl"
     xmlns:dc="http://purl.org/dc/elements/1.1/"
     xmlns:rdfs="http://www.w3.org/2000/01/rdf-schema#"
     xmlns:owl2xml="http://www.w3.org/2006/12/owl2-xml#"
     xmlns:owl="http://www.w3.org/2002/07/owl#"
     xmlns:xsd="http://www.w3.org/2001/XMLSchema#"
     xmlns:rdf="http://www.w3.org/1999/02/22-rdf-syntax-ns#"
     xmlns:Philosophy="&Ontology1298894565306;Philosophy&amp;"    xmlns:O
ntology1298894565306="http://www.semanticweb.org/ontologies/2011/1/Ontol-
ogy1298894565306.owl#">    <owl:Ontologyrdf:about="http://www.semanticweb.org/
ontologies/2011/1/Ontology1298894565306.owl#">
        <rdfs:comment>Information Science ontology that describes the domain
of IS.</rdfs:comment>
        <dc:creator xml:lang="en"
            >Ahlam Sawsaa 2011.</dc:creator>
     </owl:Ontology>
```

The OIS ontology allows the users to explore the ontology structure by browsing the upper level of the tree. The upper level provides a general understanding of the IS domain, whereas the deeper levels can be reached when they are navigated to through multiple levels of the tree.

The Upper-level of classes contains abstract entities created based on taxonomy of IS and the philosophical approach of science definition. The OIS model includes fourteen level of representation, which provides the foundation of knowledge framework for the OIS ontology. The OIS ontology root classes are: Actors, Method, Practice, Studies, Tools, Mediator, Kinds, Domains, Resources, Legislation, Philosophy & theories, Societal, Time, Space. The root classes are hierarchically specialized, each sub class is grouped under a main class, for instance "Education of Information Science", "Education of Computer

Figure 13. Upper-level of OIS ontology

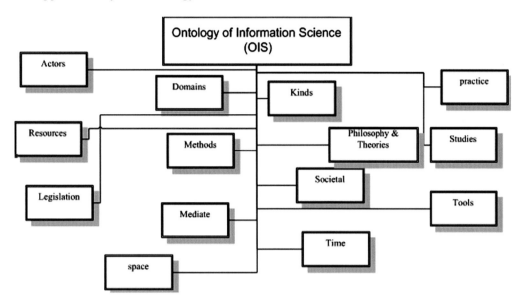

Science", "Education of Library Science", were grouped under the Education class, as shown in Figure 13. The OIS ontology structure is extendable and flexible.

The root class in OWL is thing (owl: Thing) which is the root of all classes such as Resources in RDF (rdfs: resources) The list below displays a simple hierarchy of the main classes of OIS ontology by owl; the upper-classes of our OIS ontology are as shown in List 2.

Upper-Classes of OIS Ontology

Furthermore, the current version is defined by a large number of classes 706 and consists of approximately 179 assertions, including more than 70 rules and relations, to determine the rich semantic expression capability of the language. The restrictions of classes are defined as Necessary conditions not Sufficient and Necessary conditions for the reason that class inference is not applied at instances levels. The classes' interrelations and characteristics defined through means of OWL property and ontological restriction are presented in the next subsections.

1.2.1 Actors

The *Actors* class is an abstract entity that describes a person or institution's act in the domain. The actor class is identified as the main components of OIS ontology. This upper category is important to stress the personal relationships and their roles in the IS field as human beings. In what concerns the Actors class, two main concepts were used to structure the information, as shown in Figure 14.

List 2.

```
<!-- http://www.semanticweb.org/ontologies/2011/1/Ontology1298894565306.
owl#Abstract -->    <owl:Class rdf:about="#Abstract">
      <rdfs:subClassOf rdf:resource="#Tools"/>
      <rdfs:comment >representation of the contents of document.</
rdfs:comment>
   </owl:Class>   http://www.semanticweb.org/ontologies/2011/1/Ontolo-
gy1298894565306.owl#AbstractJournal -->
   <owl:Class rdf:about="#AbstractJournal">
      <rdfs:subClassOf rdf:resource="#Abstract"/>
      <rdfs:comment >Summaries of the articles.</rdfs:comment>
   </owl:Class>       <http://www.semanticweb.org/ontologies/2011/1/Ontol-
ogy1298894565306.owl#Abstracting -->
   <owl:Class rdf:about="#Abstracting">
      <rdfs:subClassOf rdf:resource="#NonConventional"/>
      <rdfs:comment >Processing of creating extract as much information
from the document and expression. This process is complementary to the index-
ing.</rdfs:comment>
   </owl:Class>        <!-- http://www.semanticweb.org/ontologies/2011/1/On-
tology1298894565306.owl#AbstractingJournal -->
      </owl:Class>
```

1.2.1.1 Person

The person concept means who is doing activities in the domain, such as the person who works at libraries and information centres to provide service to users, as well as the users of the field. Person conceptualisation is a hierarchy with multiple inheritances of Actors concepts. It consists of two main areas;

Subclasses; *Employee and User*. The User class could be a Group or Individual. The Employee class
has sub-classes such as academic staff, archivist, author, Information specialist and librarian. These subclasses correspond to the main people they working at and beneficiary from the domain. Librarian can
be: ChildernLibrarian, LibraryDirector, LibrarianManager, SpecialLibrarian, or acadmicLibrarian, all of
these subclasses have relationships with the class StudiedLibrarianship by property hasA and studied In.
Another example, The Museologist annotation axiom is "specialist provides specific service in museums
and historical centres. Museologist is subclass of Employee, who WorksIn Museum, studied Museology.

Also, Library User: is a person who obtain the LibraryService Library User: is subclassOf AccessTo
∃ some Libraries ∩ and using ∀ only Libraries.The excerpt of Person and Employee class is illustrated
in Figure 45.

Figure 14. Main Actors class

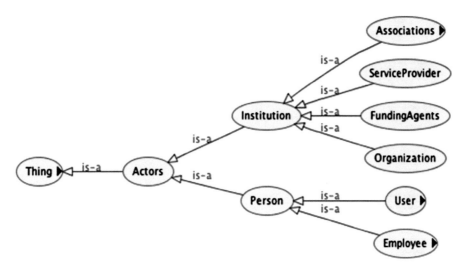

Figure 15. Person class

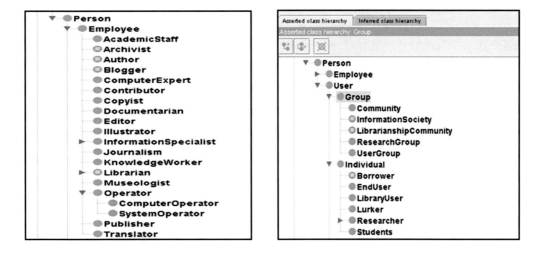

1.2.1.2 Institution

The Institution class structures knowledge about the main institution in the field of information science that provides information service to users, the institution class is specialised into four main subclasses such as:

- Association.
- Funding agents.
- Organization.
- Service providers; see Figure 16.

Figure 16. Institution Class

A relationship defied for Institution subclass is inspired in common IS organization and agents, for example:

- Institution is an Actor.
- Institution is not Person. So, it is not joint class Person.
- Associations is Subclass of Institution.
- Then, CollageLibrary Class is =equivalentTo Institution., which is provide serviceTo ∃ some Institution.

Also, FundingAgents and ServiceProvider are subclasses of Institution. The NetworkserviceProvider is type of ServiecProvider, it is annotation axiom is " a body that provides service to others such as, web service, internet access, mobile phone operator and web application hosting".

1.2.2 Domains

The Domains class is a meta-class about areas of knowledge that have interaction with information science and other sciences, such as Chemical domain, Geographical information science and Informatics. All the knowledge required about the relationship between Information Science and other sciences is structured under class domain, which will link with other ontologies of other domains, as illustrated in Figure 17.

Figure 17. Domains Class

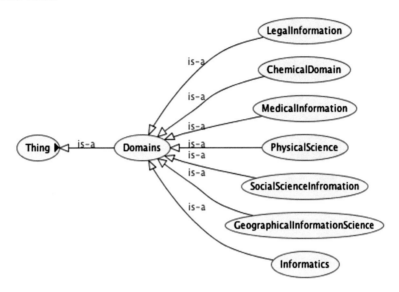

1.2.3 Kinds

The kinds class indicates the internal relationships between Information science with other sciences that have had a big effect on its structure, such as Archival science and Information architecture, Museology and computer science, as demonstrated in Figure 18.

1.2.4 Practice

The Practice class consists of (15) concepts for structuring information about the activities that actors do when they prepare information services. Figure 19 illustrates them in hierarchy:

Figure 18. Kinds class

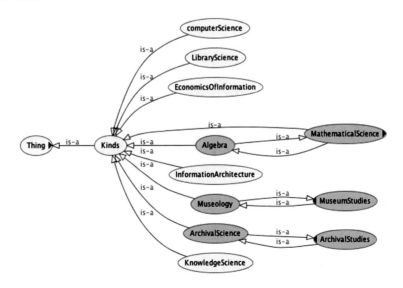

- Information service.
- Visualization.
- Acquisition.
- Evaluation.
- Preservation.
- Administration.
- Storage.
- Access.
- Transmission.
- Data process.
- Publication.
- Information process.
- Dissemination.
- Knowledge process.

1.2.4.1 Information Service

The Information Service sub-class defines the process of providing useful information for users. The information service is divided into two main parts:

- **Conventional:** The information structured under this class is about all the traditional services that Libraries and Information centres provide, such as; archival reference service, bibliographic service, classification, Loan, and subject analysis.
- **Non- Conventional:** The non-conventional structure is for information that is related to non-traditional services that can be provided to users, such as; Abstracting, Ask librarian, Cataloguing, and current Awareness. As shown in Figure 20

Figure 19. Practice concepts

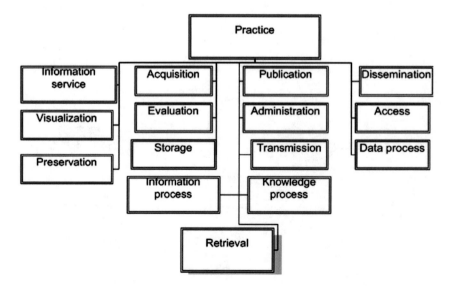

Figure 20. Information service class

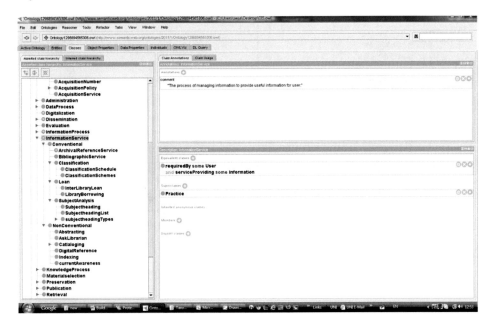

1.2.5 Studies

The studies class is structured around the information that related to applying methods to learning and understanding the subject in the IS domain. The major studies in the field can be archival studies, computer studies, librarianship, information economics studies, usability studies and user studies. The information economics studies class is described next.

1.2.5.1 Information Economics Studies

The information economics studies sub-class is about the theory in microeconomics that has developed simply because of the unique nature of information, and it has two subclasses, which are: Information economic and microeconomic, see Figure 21.

1.2.6 Mediator

This entity is a mediator between users and the actor who is provider of information services like libraries, information centres, archives, websites and museums. The Mediator class has 7 subclasses, as follows:

- Archives.
- Libraries.
- Centres media.
- Documentation centres.
- Information Centres.
- Museums.
- Websites.

Figure 21. Information Economics studies class

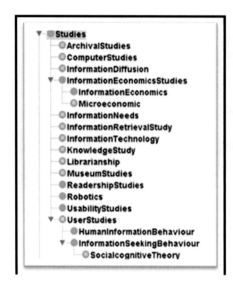 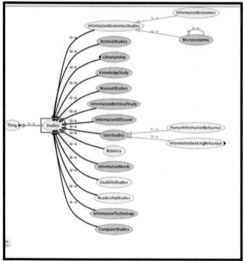

An archive is a place where a large number of historical documents are stored. It divided into 3 sub-classes, which are; digital, general and specialised archive. The Film archive came from specialised archive class, see Figure 22.

Libraries are places that contain collections of materials organised for usage. The libraries class has 15 subclasses based on its types, for instance academic, archival, art, audiovisual, bibliotheca, government, map, national, picture, school, special, virtual and library media centre.

Figure 22. Mediator class

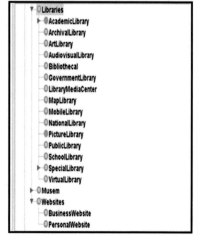 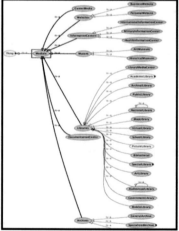

1.2.7 Methods

Method is a class about the methods to follow to do something systematically. It can be Quantitative or Qualitative. The Quantitative method was developed in natural science to study natural phenomena. The Quantitative class is divided mainly into five subclasses, namely; Analytic, Archival Methodology, Bibliometrics, statistical Bibliography and Webmetrics, see Figure 23.

1.2.8 Resources

Any field has its own information sources related to the field. The Recourses class consists of certain types of information sources which is divided into two main classes, as shown in Figure 24; *Documented, Non-documented.* The documented type is structured information that is recorded on specific container, such as; audio, visual, audiovisual and readable resources, while the 'non-documented' resources collect all kind of resources that differ from documented, like stories, informal information, genres, speeches, tacit knowledge and indigenous knowledge.

1.2.9 Tools

Information science uses certain tools that allow the circulation of information and help with the performance of work for each of the users and staff in the field. These tools are used: computers, systems, index, catalogue, communication, presentation tools and abstracts. The abstract is a very important tool for instance for the librarian and information scientist who work in libraries and information centres, as well as the users. It represents the contents of a document. The class abstract consists of; abstract journal, indicative abstract, evaluative abstract and descriptor.

Figure 23. Methods class

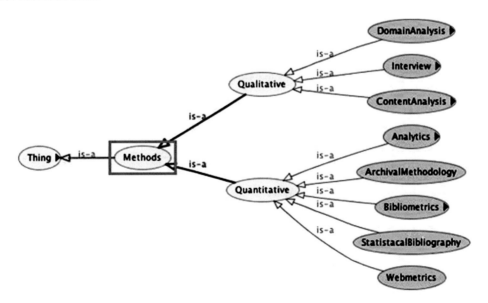

Figure 24. Resources class

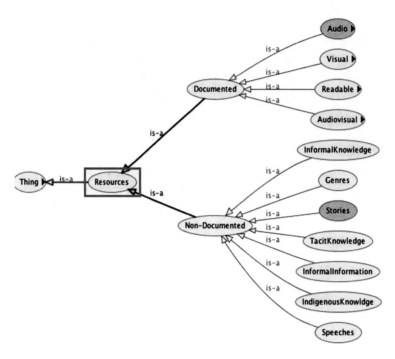

1.2.10 Philosophy and Theories

The class Philosophy and Theories structures information about the main theories and philosophies in the domain. It consists of two main sub-classes; philosophy and theories as illustrated in Figure 25.

Figure 25. Philosophy and theories class

1.2.11 Legislation

The class Legislation is related to the law. It consists of all the domain issues that require more control, such as accessibility, archival jurisdiction and standards, copyright, ComputerCrime or InternetCrime. InformationPolicy, and InformationEthics, The concept Accessibility is a hierarchy of related concepts like; AccessCharge, AccessCode, AccessControal, AsseccCopy, AccessPolicy. The sub-class AccessCode has a synonym which is IdentificationCode.

1.2.12 Societal

This structures the knowledge that is related to the social issues of the field, like Informatics communities, education, history, and industry. The information under the CommunityInformatic concept is defined as group of people who have the same interest in the information field. It is structured as follows;

- **InformationSociety:** Which is a society that relies on information by creating, sharing, using, distributing and integrating it.
- **InternetSociety:** This concept is defined as group of people developing and looking after the internet. That relates to the internet and it is a kind of organisation
- **LibraryCommunity:** This concept can be defined as group of people who have has interest in the Library field and are related only to it.

1.2.13 Time

The temporal dimension is important in recognising the temporal entities, particularly those that are related to historical periods, and to indicate dates of particular studies or researches. Ontology needs employees in the model to identify the present time and time length. The model represents temporal concepts and temporal properties which are required for Semantic Web applications. It needs to be defined at the present time in its current role by assuming some axioms for interval time. Time is a measurement rather than a representation. Instances of the time can be associated with an instance of an event rather than being made independently. In this study the OIS ontology does not present a temporal aspect, because it is a generic model and as such, it does not include any temporal contents.

1.2.14 Space

The geospatial dimension applies the ontology for applications. Space indicates the entities of places. It could be a word, more than word, city, or street for example; Paris, London. It is still a big challenge in the Ontology community to represent spatial concepts because they can be known by different names. This model does not represent geographic dimension as it provides basic knowledge.

A result, through the OIS ontology creating and modifying subclasses is possible to represent variations of axioms. Therefore, ontologies create links among data to be accessed, manipulated, reused, and readily accessible on the internet.

The OIS ontology is visualised by using OWLViz that integrates with the Protégé –OWL plug-in to enables class hierarchies in OIS ontology to be viewed. It also enables comparison between asserted and inferred models using the same colour schema for both primitive classes and defined classes. Besides this, it saves and loads graphs and settings in xml format, and provides the ability to hide and show individual slots as shown in Figure 26.

1.2.15 OIS Components

The main components of OIS ontology are:

1.2.15.1 Classes

Classes in OIS ontology (also called concepts) are a type of object in the real world, e.g. the class "Tools" models the class of all tools that are used in the domain to facilitate doing and providing services. Classes in OIS ontology are defined to be unique by their definitions. Classes have too many relationships to each other. The relation type indicates that a class has a relationship with other subclasses by specific relations like is-a and part of. If the class "Library" has is-a relationship to class "PublicLibrary", that means the class "PublicLibrary" is a subclass of the class "Library". Also, that means all instances of the class Libraries will be instance of the class "PublicLibrary".

Figure 26. Visualizing OIS by OWLViz

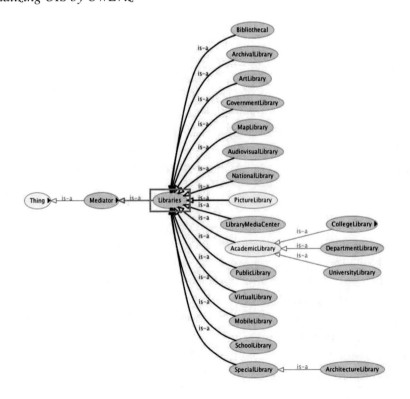

Classes can be subsumed in Protégé as each class is defined as an owl class that can be used to arrange many subclasses. e.g.

OIS- Library Owl: Class.
OIS- Acquisition Owl: Class.

In Additional, Abstracting is a subclass of Practices as shown in the OWL below:

```
<owl:Class rdf:about="#Abstracting">
        <rdfs: subClassOf rdf:practices="#NonConventional"/>
        <rdfs: commen >Processing of creating extract as much information from
the document and expression. This process is complementary to the indexing.</
rdfs:comment>
    </owl:Class>
```

All members of the subclass can be inferred to be members of its superclass.
Thing is a superclass of all classes. Things in Protégé as superclass subsume all other classes. e.g.

(Actors class)is subsumption of (person).
(Actors) is superclass of (person)
(Person) is subclass of (Actors)
Then, all members of (person) are also members of Actors.

Defining Classes of OIS In Owl

Owl uses many methods to define classes, as shown in Figure 27. Classes can be defined by using:

1. Restrictions.
2. Equivalent class.
3. Enumerating class
4. Disjoint classes

Owl Restrictions

The restrictions in owl are used to describe anonymous classes and define them by adding restriction on some properties. The restriction has two parts, namely:

- It is applied to the restructuration on a specific property such as *owl:onProperty* property.
- It is about what the constraint is in owl, such as *cardinality constraints*, to put constraints on the number of value properties, and *value constraints,* to put constrains on the range of property . Adding these constraints on a property means defining a class that satisfies a specific need (Yu, 2011).
- Value constraints.
- **OWL:** Some values from constriction.

Figure 27. Methods of defining class in OWL

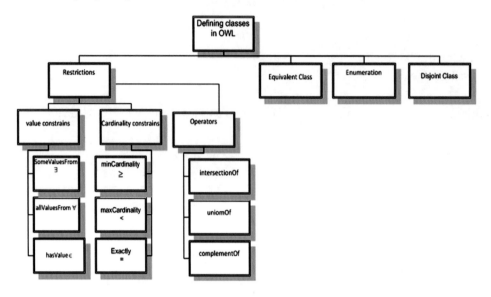

List 4 use owl:someValuesFrom to define Mobile library class.

```
<!-- http://www.semanticweb.org/ontologies/2011/1/Ontology1298894565306.
owl#MobileLibrary -->
    <owl:Class rdf:about="#MobileLibrary">
            <owl:Class>
                <owl:intersectionOf rdf:parseType="Collection">
                    <rdf:Description rdf:about="#Libraries"/>
                    <owl:Class>
                        <owl:intersectionOf rdf:parseType="Collection">
                            <owl:Restriction>
                                <owl:onProperty rdf:resource="#provideService
To"/
```

This restriction is used to ensure that *MobileLibrary* provides service to users using Van. We can make the restriction less by adding that it can be used by residential for example. The class called *MobileLibrary* is defined as a sub-class of *Libraries*, and it has a property called provideServiceTo. Furthermore, at least one value of provideServiceTO property is an instance of students. For expressing the idea, see List 4.

- **OWL:** allValuesFrom constriction.

This restriction is used to ensure that Mobile Library provides services only to students using only Van.. To express this idea, see the fragment from OIS ontology:

```
<!-- http://www.semanticweb.org/ontologies/2011/1/Ontology1298894565306.
owl#MobileLibrary -->
```

```
<owl:Class rdf:about="#MobileLibrary">
       <owl:Class>
           <owl:intersectionOf rdf:parseType="Collection">
               <rdf: Description rdf:about="#Libraries"/>
               <owl:Class>
                   <owl:intersectionOf rdf:parseType="Collection">
                       <owl:Restriction>
                           <owl: onProperty rdf:
resource="#provideServiceTo"/>
                           <owl:allValuesFrom rdf:resource="#Students"/>
                       </owl:Restriction>
                               </owl:Class>
```

- Cardinality Constraints.

Adding Cardinality constraints to anonymous class makes it defined for specific usage and makes the ontology more accurate. These cardinality constraints are; Max, Min, Exactly.

- Operator Restrictions (Boolean).

One of the enhancing powers of owl is using operator restrictions to define classes.

- **owl:intersectionOf (and):** If c1 is intersectionOf class C2,C3,C4,.... then C1 is subclass of each class C2,C3,C4.
- **owl:unionOf (or):** If C1 is UnionOf list of classes such as C2,C3,C4 then each class is subclass of C1
- **owl:ComplementOf (not):** If C1 is ComplementOf C2 then all the subclasses of C1 is disjoint with C2, see list 6.

Enumerating Class

</owl:Class> Classes can also be defined by enumerating their instances, identifying the equivalent classes and disjoint classes (Yu, 2011). The defining classes in Owl are shown diagrammatically in Figure 28; the class *AcademicLibrary* has been defined as the Type of libraries that support all research needs and provide services to some employees and users.

Disjoint Classes

Classes are designed using properties to make restrictions. For example, from a simple taxonomy of OIS ontology, the hierarchy means that

- "All computer expert is employee", that
- "All employee is person" or
- "All computer expert is person".

List 6 Definition of class Government Publication using owl:complementOf

```
<!-- http://www.semanticweb.org/ontologies/2011/1/Ontology1298894565306.
owl#GovernmentPublication -->
    <owl:Class rdf:about="#GovernmentPublication">
            <owl:Restriction>
                <owl:onProperty rdf:resource="#hasA"/>
                <owl:someValuesFrom rdf:resource="#GovernmentPublication"/>
            </owl:Restriction>
                <rdfs:subClassOf rdf:resource="#Documents"/>
        <rdfs:subClassOf>
            <owl:Class>
                <owl:complementOf rdf:resource="#Libraries"/>
            </owl:Class>
        </rdfs:subClassOf>
        <rdfs:comment
            >Publications issued by the government such as statistical re-
ports, survey and press releases.</rdfs:comment>
```

Figure 28. Defined class in owl

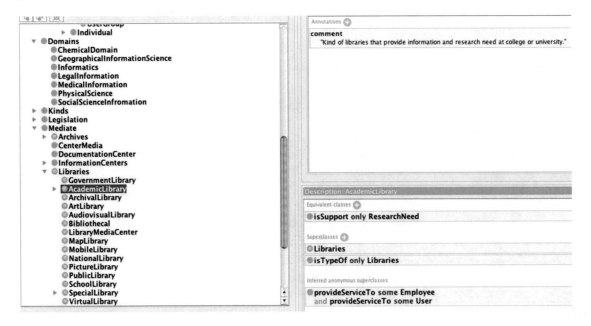

Does this mean that "employee" and "computer expert" are different? We can assume that both "employee" and "computer expert" are different, unless they have a common child. However, classes in OWL cannot overlap if the disjoint axioms are entered.

The main classes are primitive to describe the primitive domain, so they cannot be defined in the same way as actors, users, methods, practice. We assume that classes overlap. If we state that classes are not disjoint that means an individual cannot be in two classes at the same time. For instance

Women Owl- DisjointWith: Man
Fruit Owl- DisjointWith: Meat

From OIS ontology the classes of Practice disjoint with Class Actor as they have different individuals, as illustrated in Figure 29.

Together individuals cannot be joining, whereas, an individual could be in Actors and Domains at the same time.

Also, this kind of definition for concepts and relations provides powered ontology software that enables expression to interpret it correctly. In the meantime, OIS ontology is designed to be relatively small due to the fact that these concepts and assertions should be easy to apply and understand.

1.2.15.2 Axioms

Ontology has axioms which are basic statements; these axioms represent a basic knowledge, e.g. <owl:Class rdf:about="#Film">

```
        <rdfs:subClassOf rdf:resource="#Audiovisual"/> film class is a sub-
class of the Audiovisual class - it is an axiom.
```

1.2.15.3 Properties

In the OIS ontology relationships are called properties in OWL and some other description logic languages. The attributes are created in object properties - Owl: Object property - and data property view - Owl:Data Type property. The object property is the relationship between instances, whilst data property describes the relationships between instances and data values, which link an instance to RDF or to XML schema.

Figure 29. An example of disjoint class

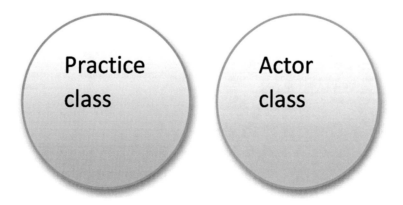

The data property is similar to the object property unless it can be just functional in characteristic, not inverse in description. The relations in object properties are shown in below and the graph 40.

```
<!-- http://www.semanticweb.org/ontologies/2011/1/Ontology1298894565306.
owl#hasA -->
    <owl:ObjectProperty rdf:about="#hasA">
        <rdf:type rdf:resource="&owl;InverseFunctionalProperty"/>
        <rdfs:domain rdf:resource="#Actors"/>
        <rdfs:range rdf:resource="#Associations"/>
    </owl:ObjectProperty>
```

There are two main groups of relations type in OIS ontology, which are:

- Relations between classes to describe type of relation links among two classes.
- Relations between individuals and general concepts in the ontology to describe type of relation links between classes and individuals.

The OIS ontology defines the relations types such as <Is-A> <is Part Of> <has A> between superclass and subclass. Is-A relation is represented in the class hierarchy that is called Generalisation, while *Part of* relations are called Aggregate. If A is a subclass of B, then every instance of A is also an instance of B.

For example, *CopyRightLaw* is a subclass of *Legislation* class. Other taxonomic relations are *<is Part Of> <has A> <kind Of>*. Table 10 illustrates types of relations between classes.

Figure 30. Object properties

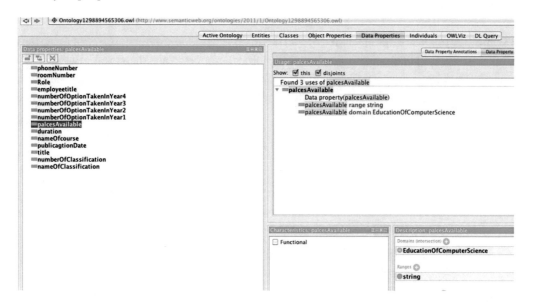

Table 10. Types of relations between terms

Term	Relations	Term
Information	Is a part of	Knowledge
Data	Is a piece of	Information
Organization	Is a part Of	Institution
Professional association	Works In	Institution
Canadian Library association	Is kind of	library associations

The properties have many features such as;

1. Inverse.
2. Symmetric.
3. Transitive.
4. Functional.
5. Inverse functional.

Inverse Property

In OWL this relation is relating between two properties explicitly in case these properties are the same. That means each object property has a corresponding inverse property as shown below, and Figure 31.

```
owl: inversOf
<owl:ObjectPr operty rdf:ID="hasAuthor">
  <owl: inverseOf rdf:resource="#hasBook"/>
</owl:ObjectProperty>
Symmetric Property
```

Figure 31. InversOf relation

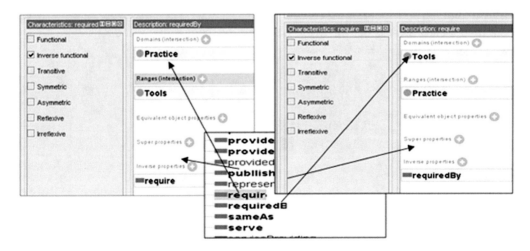

List 9.

```
<owl: Symmetric Property rdf:ID="EmpolyeeIn">
  <rdfs:domain rdf:resource="#Organization"/>
  <rdfs: range  rdf:resource="#Organization"/>
</owl: SymmetricProperty>
<owl:SymmetricProperty
    <owl:Class rdf:about="# isFriendOf">
  <rdfs:domain rdf:resource="#Editor"/>
   <rdfs:range rdf:resource="#Editor"/>
 </owl:SymmetricProperty>
```

It is just one facet of a single property to express memberships of a class. This relation could be: studiedIn; owl:inversOf; studiedBy. The symmetric property expresses the relationship between many classes, such as: If C1 connects to C2 by isfriendOf then C3 isfriendOf C1. For the example from OIS ontology see List 9.

Transitive Property

This property is representing certain part-whole relations between classes. If Ca is connected to Cb by property A, and Cb is connected to Cd by the same property then Ca is also connected to Cd by property A.

```
<!-- http://www.semanticweb.org/ontologies/2011/1/Ontology1298894565306.
owl#hasPolicy -->
    <owl:ObjectProperty rdf:about="#hasPolicy">
        <rdf:type rdf:resource="&owl;TransitiveProperty"/>
    </owl:ObjectProperty>
```

Functional Property

In owl, Functional Property is for property that has a single unambiguous value, i.e. for just one value that cannot be repeated. In mathematics, functional property provides one value to one or particular input. For example,

If y2 is a function, so there is one value for y, this means there is one value for y2.

Another way if y= x then y2 = x 2.

```
!-- http://www.semanticweb.org/ontologies/2011/1/Ontology1298894565306.
owl#isDescribeA -->
    <owl:ObjectProperty rdf:about="#isDescribeA">
        <rdf:type rdf:resource="&owl;FunctionalProperty"/>
    </owl:ObjectProperty>
```

Inverse Functional Property

This property describes relations between classes, e.g. if class C1 is connected to C2 by property a, then the inverse property a will connect C1 to C2.

```
<!-- http://www.semanticweb.org/ontologies/2011/1/Ontology1298894565306.
owl#isPolicyOf -->
   <owl:ObjectProperty rdf:about="#isPolicyOf">
       <rdf:type rdf:resource="&owl;TransitiveProperty"/>
       <owl:inverseOf rdf:resource="#hasPolicy"/>
   </owl:ObjectProperty>
```

Annotation Property

In Protégé OWL allows classes, individual (instance) and properties to be annotated. Annotations in OWL are to add a piece of information such as references or resources for example. OWL has many predefined annotation properties as restrictions to annotate class, individual and property; these annotation properties are namely, Owl: versionInof: which provides information about the ontology version, and Owl:priorVersion, which provides information about the prior ontology version.

Rdfs: comment: This is to add a comment on the class
Rdfs:lable, to offer alternative names of class or property
Rdfs:seeAlso, uses for references as URL (Horridge, 2011)

1.2.15.4 Individuals

Ontology Instances in Protégé are called individuals of classes that are created in the individuals view. Each instance can be described in the description tab as the Type and name of the same individual. The instance Institute of Electronical and Electronical engineering, is described under types as a computing standard and the same name is IEEE. This is shown in Figure 32.

Attribute is allocated in data property assertion, and the relations under the object property assertion. It can be seen from Figure 34. The class description appears on the description tap above Type; Library Science Courses, and the property assertions shows object property assertions and data property assertions. In this research the individual is not our concern. The research focuses on the classes and object properties only, providing this example to show how the OIS will work in further research, and how it will be useful in the Information science education process

1.2.16 Usage Class Tab

Protégé provides a great feature for checking the uses of classes and individuals in the ontology, for example the class *Website* has been used in the ontology eleven times, and to see how many relationships and axioms it has, see Figure 43. One of the usages in Analytics is equivalent class to measuring websites which recognise it as methods. The second one is Business website and Personal website, which are subclasses of Website.

Figure 32 Individuals of OIS ontology

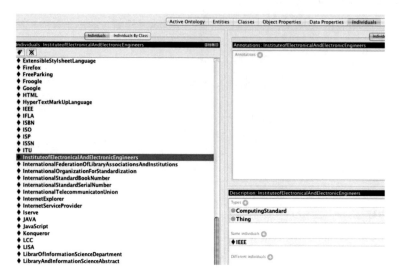

Figure 33. Properties assertions of OIS ontology

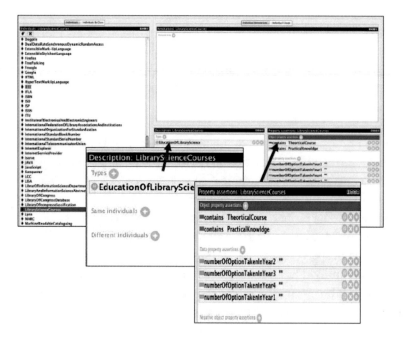

1.3 ONTOCOP: A SYSTEM OF VISUALISATION OF IS KNOWLEDGE

The Ontocop system is designed by the author of research to support group interaction; it allows communication through the community of Information Science IS to enable members to communicate and interact across diverse destinations. Ontocop is a tool to support the OIS ontology.

Figure 34. Usage class tap in protégé

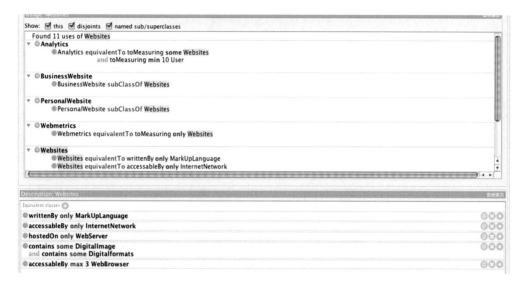

1.3.1 System Requirements

The system must be usable and sociable. Usability features include consistency between pages and words used in the website, such as title of pages and headings. There should be no difficulty for members in navigating easily and following links easily. The navigation bar is consistent throughout the website, and the main page has a common browser. If users have problems using other browsers, they can use Firefox or Internet Explorer.

To maintain the website's integrity, a registration policy for new members keeps information in the database and other sites under control. This has been introduced because this community exists purely for research purposes and is for information science domain experts only.

1.3.2 System Architecture

This section presents the architecture of Ontocop system in Figure 35. The architecture is organised into 5 layers, the first layer is the homepage, which contains the navigation icon to search on Google or on the website itself. The News layer provides recent news about the developing ontology. Tool layer consists of:

- **Events:** To display Events on the website, to organise the discussion topics to be realised for participation.
- **Forum:** For debate and discussion about Information Science topics, as well as Chat and E-conferencing online.

The Information layer explains and clarifies some information about the Ontocop and the reasons for supporting the ontology model, and shows frequently asked questions (FAQ), feedback, members' profiles, and contact details.

Figure 35. Website layout

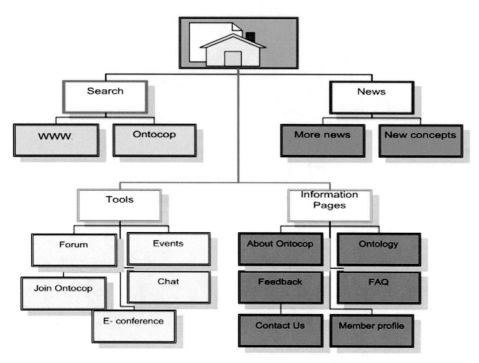

1.3.3 System Implementing

Ontocop was launched in November 2009, by inviting people to get involved. The online community was created, designed and moderated by a research student to support her research project. The website designer has chosen to use the chat room features provided free by the phpfree Chat Company and forum features provided free by phpBB3. The site also uses e-conference features. (Koch, 2000).

1.3.3.1 Technical Features

Ontocop is hosted by a server in Huddersfield which has proven suitable for this project and which has been developed in this research; the site has been tested on Microsoft Internet Explorer and Mozilla Firefox.

Most of the pages in Ontocop's original WebPages use the following mark-up languages: Hyper Text Mark-up Language (HTML) tag standards and Extensible Hypertext Mark up Language (XHTML). Cascading Style Sheets (CSS) have been used to maintain consistency of style, maintaining the website theme in the background, text, font, image and so on to provide an easy user interface. Also, PHP, JavaScript, and MySQL have also been used. The software has been successfully tested in the following hardware:

Microsoft Windows XP Professional version 2002, Service pack3.Computer intel (R) core (™) Duo CPU, E 7500@2.93 GHz, 2.96 GHz RAM Physical address.

- Microsoft Windows XP Professional version 2002,Service pack3.Computer intel (R) core (™) Duot CPU, E 7500@2.93 GHz, 2.96 GHz RAM

- Physical address. Toshiba personal Rating: 1.0 Windows Experience 2 Dou CPU. E 7400@2.80 GHz 2.80 GHz. Memory (RAM) 4.00 GB system type 32-bit operating system, Windows Vista Home Premium, 2007.

1.3.3.2 Aesthetic Features

Ontocop's format has been designed to be helpful for users.

A white background with some bright colours like blue and yellow makes for easy user experience and more proper for human interactions. Multiple colours and fonts have not been used. Yellow is used to draw the visitor's attention to the main menu and left menu, whilst magenta has been used for visited navigational links.

The main fonts used are the verdana, Arial, helvetica, and sans-serif family for the main body and headings. The graphics continue the website theme. Modifications of the main page work with the other pages such as ontology, contact us, FAQ pages, as well as the forum and chat features (Sawsaa and Lu, 2010).

1.3.4 System Developments

The core function of VCop is to generate ideas and elaborate tacit knowledge through problem solving and suggesting topics to be discussed. This knowledge could be stored in a multimedia database where it is easier to extract knowledge. Tacit knowledge is shared in VCops through technology using several tools. VCops requires resources to operate its functions, such as space for members' meetings, a database to store discussions, information ideas, ways to share tacit knowledge and also record activities. The designer decided to make the following resources available:

Members' meeting space: members of a community require a place to meet face to face or virtually; this space needs to be easy to access to enable members to interact and communicate asynchronously by leaving comments and ideas. The virtual space is provided online via software such as forums, online chat, virtual meeting rooms and e-conferencing. Figure 36 shows the Forum, which is an essential part of the website infrastructure. A professional community should be restricted by rules to follow such as having to register and sending ID and password for users. The access is just for the community members themselves Ontocop is accessible by these criteria.

By inviting people after activation of their account, pseudonyms are not permitted.

Obviously in a physical space members communicate face to face, but in the virtual community members can do this through technology, using e-conferencing and chat. Figure 37 shows a Chat page, which provides a communication space for online users to debate specific subject matter.

Figure 38 shows the Event Management calendar which is the record of the community's activities. The Community needs software to keep concepts to generate ideas for ongoing discussions. These general concepts help to suggest topics and future activity. As a calendar of events or activity it can be in electronic format to be updated frequently, and also as record of past events.

Figure 39 List of members of Ontocop: a community needs to identify its members. Physically members are identified by creating a list of members to clarify who the members of the community are. Members in ontocop have profiles kept verifiable via a record kept in the database. A member profile helps to create a social network by linking members with the same interest.

Figure 36. Ontocop Forum

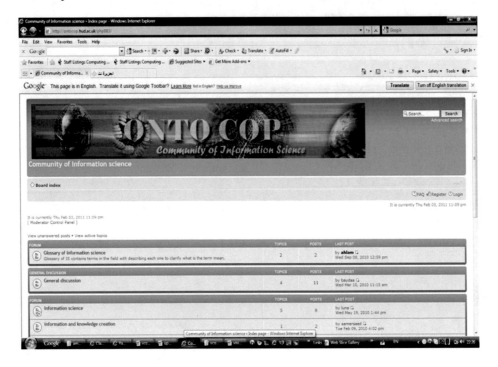

Figure 37. Ontocop chatting page

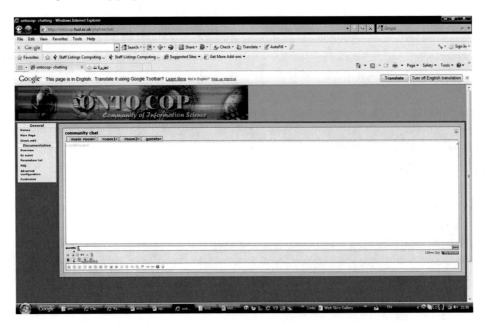

Figure 38. Ontocop chatting page

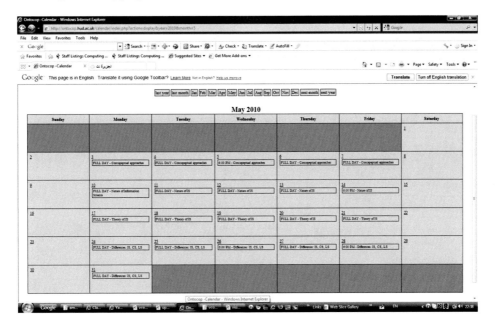

Figure 39. Ontocop Members list

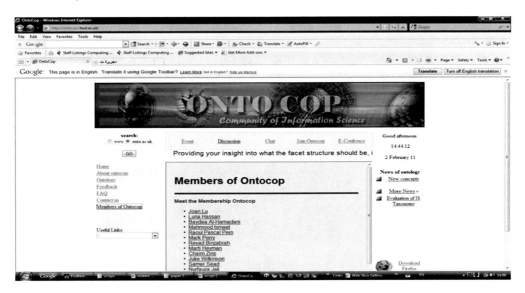

Members of the community can stay up-to-date with developments in building the ontology. See Figure 40.

Users can help to improve Ontocop by providing Feedback. See Figure 41.

Figure 42 shows the space for Questions and Answers and FAQ, which provide clarification about ambiguous areas within the community.

Figure 40. Ontology Page

Figure 41. Feedback Page

Figure 43 shows the Contact us page, which allows users to email the moderator to clarify issues or make contact. With regard to links to members of Ontocop, trust is as vital in the online community as in offline communities. The Ontocop can be accessible by using this link: http://ontocop.hud.ac.uk/

Figure 42. FQA Page

Figure 43. Contact Page

1.3.5 Description and Potentials of Ontocop Components

The process of invitation was started by sending emails after collecting information from different universities around the world. Then we repeated the process several times of inviting people to participate, http://ontocop.hud.ac.uk/.

The members at Ontocop have already collaborated for some time. Thirty 30 participants responded and they are active participants. The core group review events and topics to be discussed from the calendar http://ontocop.hud.ac.uk/.

Here we outline some critical points to measure the success of Ontocop at this stage based on specific criteria. As is widely known, creating a social network is a big challenge.

- **Trust:** Members need to know each other. Interview the potential members of Ontocop by arranging virtual meeting using chat tools, to allow them to introduce themselves and to get know existing members. Furthermore, create members' profile pages to display their information. Also, people need to know the reason for creating an online community and what the specific goal or target is.
- **Education:** Providing some information about the website to educate people first, due to the fact that people will not be involved till they do know how to contribute. Creating a section in the Home page is to cover simple guidelines; for these criteria e.g. "Getting Started", to explain the method of registration http://ontocop.hud.ac.uk/.
- **Guide and Template:** There is an assumption about people that they panic on an empty page. Examples have been prepared in the forum to make members participate effectively by writing down some definitions and argument issues and letting them follow the templates.
- **Refreshing:** To encourage the community in keeping the content up to date and interesting for everybody.
- **Easy Access:** Ontocop is not a commercial website that is easy to find, but it could be accessed by searching in search engines.
- **Authentic and Personal:** Present the developer of ontocop in the "About" page to help people to know the person behind Ontocop.
- The great challenge in this community is to know how it will develop over time. I will outline a potential future and some intentions for Ontocop:

Potential:

- At the beginning it is essential to find out who will participate in the community and be a member of it, to share common background and experience. This helps to make a new challenge easier.
- The initial stage started with inviting people to be the core group in Ontocop, which began as follows:
  - Gathering information about people working in IS field and add it to the database, to find out if potential members of Ontocop are interested in joining the project, and ensuring the database is ready at the moment of invitation. The total number of people is 1633 from 58 universities around the world. A part of collected data is indicated in http://ontocop.hud.ac.uk/.
  - Collecting data is requested: first name, last name, full address, email address, picture and their Webpages and interests. Thereafter, we send the invitation letter including the URL of the website. This stage helps to determine whether or not they are willing to share the community, by sending an email to set at ease starting. See http://ontocop.hud.ac.uk/.

CONCLUSION

Our consideration is that OIS ontology purpose is to use for a particular knowledge base, its important making a clear distinguishes between knowledge base and application ontology. OIS ontology is describes facts, assertions, and axioms to provide formal and reusable model. The core ontology has constraints between concepts to hold between the concepts. Also, to avoid unambiguous terms, these concepts and constraints were presented in the ontology model. The OIS ontology takes advantages of a formal semantic in OWL language to balance the domain requirements. The conceptualization in a specific domain could be represented, analysed and interpreted in different ways, that dependents on in which contexts and circumstances that created under it. Also, it is formalized based on whom doing it. Therefore, OIS ontology is made to utility the conceptualization to be reusable and sharable on specific context of ontological commitments that were made obviously. The development of OIS ontology that followed Methontology was presented. It starts by introducing OIS designing activities and the main result was introduced.

Furthermore, the modelling design of OIS ontology consisted of fourteen entities that abstract the main components of domain knowledge. The OIS ontology model identifies the terms and definitions in the IS domain. Finally, designing the ontocop system and how it can be a useful platform for supporting and assessing the OIS ontology to be in a comprehensive and consistent manner.

REFERENCES

Horridge, M. (2011). A Practical Guide To Building OWL Ontologies Using Protege 4 and CO-ODE Tools. The University Of Manchester.

Koch, M. (2000). Learning from civilization. *Line Zine*. Retrieved from http://linezine.com/3.1/features/mklic.htm

Sawsaa, A., & Lu, J. (2010). Ontocop: A virtual community of practice to create ontology of Information science.*International Conference on Internet Computing (ICOMP'10)*.

Sawsaa, A., & Lu, J. (2011) Extracting Information Science concepts based on Jape Regular Expression. In *The 2011 World Congress in Computer Science, Computer Engineering, and Applied Computing*. Las Vegas, NV: IEEE.

Yu, L. (2011). *A Developer's Guide to the Semantic Web*. Springer.

Zins, C. (2007a). Conceptions of, Information Science. *Journal of the American Society for Information Science and Technology*, 58(3), 335–350. doi:10.1002/asi.20507

Zins, C. (2007b). Conceptual Approaches for defining data, information, and knowledge. *Journal of the American Society for Information Science and Technology*, 58(4), 479–493. doi:10.1002/asi.20508

Zins, C. (2007c). Knowledge Map of Information Science. *Journal of the American Society for Information Science and Technology*, 58(4), 526–535. doi:10.1002/asi.20505

Zins, C. (2007d). Knowledge mapping: Of information science. *Journal of the American Society for Information Science and Technology*, 58(4), 526–535. doi:10.1002/asi.20505

Chapter 14
Findings for Ontology in IS and Discussion

Ahlam F. Sawsaa
University of Huddersfield, UK & Benghazi University, Libya

Joan Lu
University of Huddersfield, UK

ABSTRACT

Ontology development is meaningful and useful for both users and IR; therefore, it needs to be evaluated. In this chapter, we are going to test and evaluate the results produced in the research, which is the development of the OIS ontology life cycle. It describes the testing and validation which was applied to the whole model from the initial implementation to ensure consistency of modelled knowledge. The evaluation objective was to collect feedback on OIS ontology by using our evaluation system. The Ontocop system is a platform that has been implemented to get feedback from the IS community. The feedback is assessing and eliciting further details that support the ontology development. The evaluation and discussion will be at two levels based on Gòmez-Pérez's view.

1. EVALUATION OIS ONTOLOGY

1.1. Ontology Validation

The validation of the OIS ontology is conducted from two points to measure in which way the ontology has been written, and that the ontology syntax does not contain any errors and anomalies. Thus, we make certain of richness and complexity of syntactic issues of the ontology, not just correctness.

On the one hand, testing the modelled knowledge coherence by the FaCT++ reasoner which is an owl-Dl. in OWL semantic languages the OWL statements are constructed on formal logic to provide high expressive and automated reasoning. The reasoning aims to check the consistency of the ontology entities, relationships, and restrictions.

Significantly, the reasoner checks whether or not the statements and class definitions are consistent. Furthermore, FaCT++ was applied during the developing process of the ontology. With respect to

DOI: 10.4018/978-1-5225-2058-0.ch014

consistency checking of the OIS, the reasoner was used. It achieved this by using the FaCT++ plug-in that combines with Protégé 4.0.2.

This tool infers classification and class hierarchy in the ontology, which helps to correct any errors and inconsistence classes in ontology classification. In fact checking the consistency is necessary to find out if there are any contradictions; to ensure the modelling constructs are being used correctly, and avoid reaching any incorrect inferences.

In Protégé there are two structures of taxonomy; the computed method is called inferred hierarchy and the manual way is called asserted hierarchy. The main evidence of automatic computation of the ontology checking is revealed through appearance of the root of hierarchy (nothing) in red colour in the pane of the inferred hierarchy.

The FaCT++ reasoner shows errors in the classes that had been classified in a red colour. The changing of the OIS ontology model was driven by the discovery of errors during the implementation stage. The process of improving it considered its inadequate performance and improvement of the domain knowledge. The early tests around the reasoner highlighted many errors, some of which arose from adding more information to the model without revising the existing axioms. These errors have been eliminated. However, in practice the first round revealed some errors as shown in Table 1.

The table reveals that these classes were classified under different meta-classes, such as that *Analytics* is a sub-class of Actors while it should be a subclass of Quantitative class under Methods. Also, the classes ArchitecturLibrary, GovernmentLibrary and SpecialLibrary are classified under the different meta–classes Actors, Domain, and Space whereas they should classified under Libraries Class.

Figure 1 illustrates that some classes have circularity in the OIS after running the reasoner second time. These classes are: DataPrivacy, InformationPrivicy, CopyRight, IntellectualProperty, ComputerCrime, InternetCrime, FreeSpeech, FreedomExpression, IdenticationCode, AccessCode.

Figure 2 illustrates that the asserted and inferred hierarchies after running the FaCT++ reasoner are decreased. It can be seen that there is inconsistency in the class *GovernmentLibrary which* appears in red colour under *Domains* class; this means it should be under *Mediator* as sub-class of *Libraries*. Otherwise, after that the reasoner was run many times to ensure there is no difference between the inferred and asserted taxonomies and nothing appeared that indicates tasks to be completed and semantically validated.

This is also to ensure there are no confounding and contradictory concepts. Also, ensuring terms have consistency of meaning with clarity. Ontology should provide mapping according to the meaning

Table 1. Inconsistence classes

First Round of Running Fact++ Reasoned		Second Round	
Class	**Inconsistence Class**	**Class**	**Inconsistence Class**
Actors	Analytics ArchitectureLibrary Dissemination	Legislation	DataPrivcy, InformationPrivicy
Domain	ElectronicDocumetDelivery GovernmentLibrary InformationDiffusion		CopyRight, IntellectualProperty
Practice	ReallSimpleSyndication		ComputerCriem,InternetCrime.
Resource	SelectiveDisseminationOfInformation		FreeSpeech, FreedomExpression
Space	SpecialLibrary		IdenticationCod,AccessCode

Figure 1. Circular classes

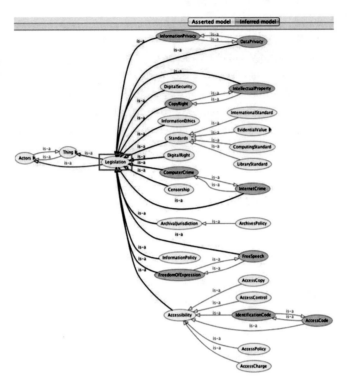

Figure 2. Inferred class hierarchy

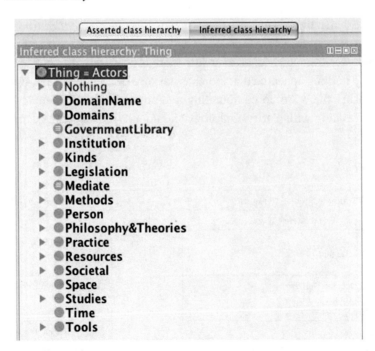

Figure 3. Part of OIS ontology verification results

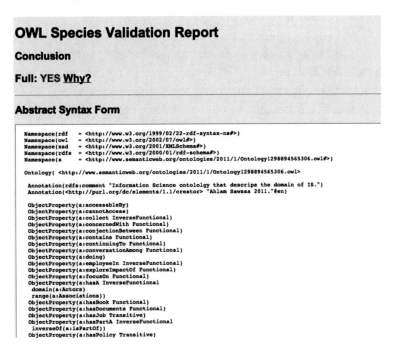

of its contents. However, the consistency and the syntax of the generated OWL file can be verified by using an OWL ontology validator. The OIS ontology was verified by using OWL validation as well, for more testing and validation. Once the ontology was uploaded to the validator, the abstract syntax –Full OWL - form says Yes: Why, this means the ontology has succeeded and the results are good. Figure 3 shows a segment of the verification results.

However, after testing and validating the OIS ontology it was introduced to the domain experts to be evaluated.

1.2 Ontology Verification

The ontology was evaluated by IS experts. They identified some classes needing to extended and divided further, and added or deleted some layers from the ontology. The next section, the user case scenario, describes the whole process of ontology verification.

1.3 Use case Scenario of Evaluation

Using the user case scenario provides the main components of ontology evaluation.

1.   The developer creates the first version of the OIS ontology in Protégé. During the development the ontology is assisted from ontocop members at the conceptualisation stage to ensure the conceptual model is built correctly.

2.   The developer displays the taxonomy of OIS on ontocop to be accessible and viewed. The members have been notified to provide their insights in order to configure the classification of the IS domain and change some parts of the ontology taxonomy. See Figure 4 (http://ontocop.hud.ac.uk/).

3.   The developer publishes the ontology version on WebProtégé; at the same time another copy is displayed on ontocop in OWL formats. The developer keeps the original copy of the current work to continue working to make edits when the others access the ontology. The OIS ontology is displayed on WebProtégé that can be accessible through Ontology page in Ontocop, as shown in Figure 5.

4.   Before asking the members to answer the questions on the OIS ontology and sending feedback, some details are displayed on ontocop to give them an overview. It provides how they can search on it, as shown in Figure 6.

5.   The evaluators were asked to complete a web-based survey to evaluate the OIS with indications as to the level of satisfaction, based on the criteria. Also, they were asked to answer the following questions as shown in Table 2, to obtain information about their impressions of developing the OIS ontology.

6.   The members' access the ontology by using a direct link in WebProtégé to navigate around the taxonomy tree and look at metadata and properties that are provided. They provide some notes to OIS and make comments on some classes and add suggestions to add new concepts.

7.   The developer is notified through an email and the ontocop database. The editing on ontology takes place based on their comments.

8.   The developer publishes the new version of the ontology in WebProtégé, and members are notified when the new version is published.

Figure 4. Evaluation of IS taxonomy

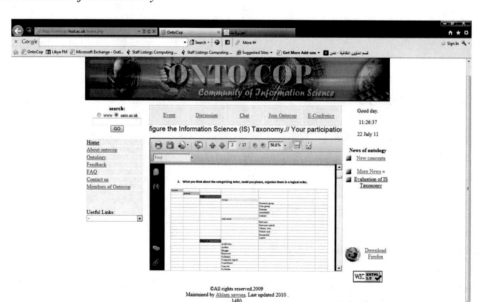

Figure 5. Snapshot of OIS ontology on WebProtégé

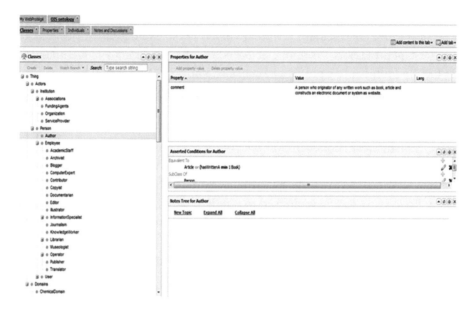

Figure 6 OIS documentation

Table 2. The questions in OIS ontology survey

Q1.	What do you like about the ontology?
Q2.	What do you think needs to be improved?
Q3.	What would you like to add or change at any part of the domain knowledge?
Q4.	Do you think it is a completed ontology?
Q5.	Do you think the ontology has a clean taxonomical structure?
Q6.	Do you think the ontology is mappable to some specific upper ontology?

Participants

The members 30 of Information specialists were involved in the evaluation. We asked 30 Information Specialists: 12 Assistant professors, 2 senior Lecturers,5 professors, 2 knowledge management consultants, 3 adjunct faculty professors, 1 professor Emeritus, and 5 PhD Informatics students.

1.4 Results of Evaluation

The OIS ontology evaluation was obtained over two months. The survey answers were received through following the link on Ontocop. We asked 30 participants, and 25 of them responded. The gathered data analysed after a fair period of the publishing the ontology on WebProtégé to understand the comments participants made. Discussion results were used to obtain research findings that aided us in addressing research questions. In the survey it was very important to capture the participants' satisfaction about the ontology based on predefined criteria.

The first part of the survey asked about the experts' level of satisfaction, based on predefined criteria. The first criterion was ontology consistency. 64% of respondents indicated level 3 of satisfaction, and others expressed levels 2 and 4 by 20%, 12% respectively, see Figure 7.

The second criterion was consistency of is-a and part-of –relationships. 14 of the participants indicated their satisfaction with the consistency of ontology relations at Level 3, 56% while 6 of them 24% pointed to level 2. Figure 8 illustrates this.

For the third criterion the majority of participants identified level 3 to indicate their level of satisfaction to assess completeness of OIS ontology which is 48%, in comparison with level 1 and 5. Figure 5-9 shows the percentage of completeness of the ontology.

The fourth criterion was clarity of OIS ontology. The vast majority of participants found that the OIS ontology is clear. Due to the fact that they were familiar with the most of the ontology concepts. Only one that criticised "Thing" asked why it was the first class. This was a little confusing because

Figure 7. Ontology consistency

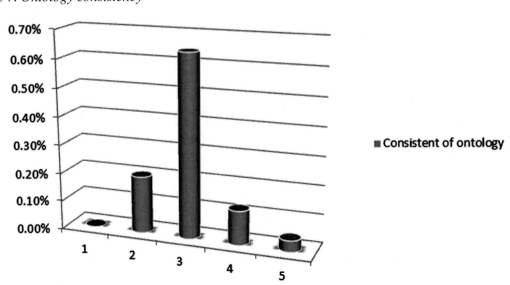

Figure 8. Consistency of is-a and part-of –relationships

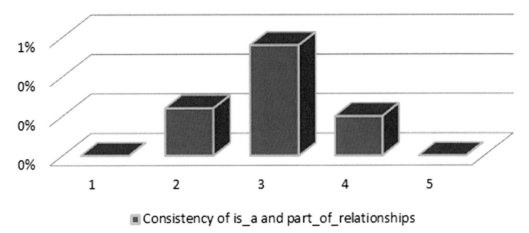

■ Consistency of is_a and part_of_relationships

Figure 9. Completeness of ontology

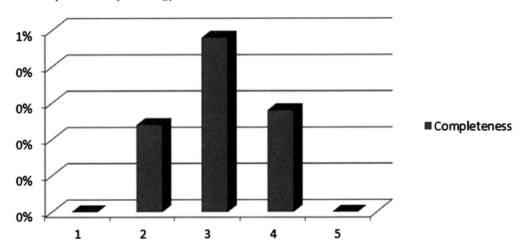

■ Completeness

Thing is OWL root. However, participants selected both Level 3 and 4 by 40% to identify the level of clarity, while level 2 was chosen by only 20% from the participants. Figure 5-10 shows the participants' satisfaction levels.

The fifth criterion was ontology generality. 88% of participants are satisfied with the Generality criterion of ontology which they indicated by selecting level 3 or 4. Whereas about 12% of participants selected level 2 to point out that they were unsatisfied with the ontology components to cover the whole domain Figure 11 shows the results.

The sixth criterion was semantic data richness of the ontology. The results indicated that 12 participants - about 48% - say their satisfaction is at level 3, while 24% identified level 4, but 28% pointed to level 2 because the ontology does not contain instances at this stage. Figure 12 illustrates this.

The second part of the survey contains six open questions – as stated in Table 2 - to ask participants whether the construction approach of the OIS ontology was right and the possibility of improving it, or changing some parts of the domain knowledge.

Figure 10. Clarity of OIS ontology

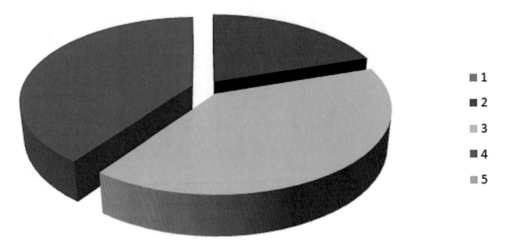

Figure 11. Ontology generality

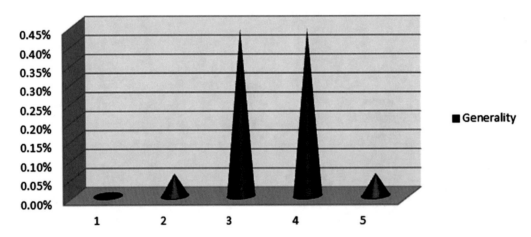

Figure 12. Semantic data richness of the ontology

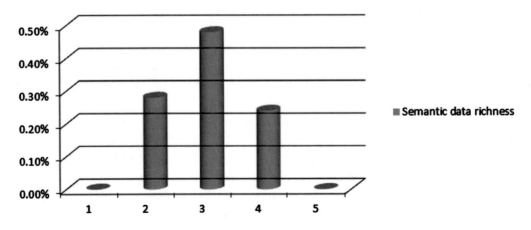

The first question asked participants what they liked about the ontology. The responses were primarily positive. Most of the responses indicated what they like as whole model and some of them indicated some parts, e.g., one respondent indicated that "she likes [the] inclusion of Standards as a Class".

The second question was asked about whether the ontology needs to be improved. Fifteen out of twenty five responded "yes", it needs some improvements, e.g. one respondent indicated that the subclasses "Evidential Value" and Historical Value" of Standards, and that Value should be in separate classes. Others suggest changing the class "Person" to "People" and "Organization" rather than "Institution" because organization is more general than institution.

The third question asked participants if they would like to add and change any classes in the model. Some responses suggested a number of concepts to be added, e.g., Bibliometrics, scientometrics, and infometrics as subclasses to the Methods class. Also, adding Mathematics, Engineering, Natural science, Chemistry, and Physics to the Domain class. However, one respondent raised an interesting point about the "Author" class; She pointed out that not all "Author" are employee, she said they can be employed or independent, so it needs to be listed directly under "Person". Another suggestion was related to adding facts such as -Mandate, to include accountability, institutional memory, research, and support of human rights, and -Sector to include government, corporate, religious, and academic

The fourth question was asked to point out whether the model covers the domain knowledge. Eighteen out of twenty five answered with a clear "yes" and three of the rest answered I do not know, while six did not answer, i.e., "It seems to cover all the classes I would expect for this domain".

The fifth question asked was about the taxonomy structure of the ontology. Some of the respondents felt that some of the hierarchical relationships could be enhanced or improved, e.g, "Indexer" is not restricted to working at libraries only, he or she could work at publishing companies such as Cengage learning, or resources aggregators for example.

The sixth question was asked about whether the model can be mapped with other specific models or not as a general model according to their theory. Sixteen out of twenty five answered "yes" it could be mappable. Others answered "do not know". Most of the participants indicated to some concepts that could be linked with other ontology for integration of sub-domain ontologies, e.g, People, Methods, Practice, Studies in order of these concepts are general and available in all domains.

The final question was about the general assessment of the model - whether they satisfied or not with the whole model. Twenty of the respondents were positive - "agree" - on the ontology structure. They point this out "Given that no ontology is ever finished" but it is valuable.

In general, the comments of participants were positive on the ontology structure, and overall they agreed with and liked the concepts that were used, see Figure 13.

2. RESULTS OF ONTOCOP SYSTEM

The core group are professionals who are involved in Library & Information Studies- computer science departments at universities around the world, from different geographic locations, from different universities, and different languages. So the English language is not the native language for many of them, as illustrated in Figure 14. On the other hand, it is important to make members feel that they are participating at a voluntary level and that their participation will keep them up-to-date in their field.

To take Ontocop a step forward, the research outlines some actions that have been taken.

Figure 13. The General assessment on OIS ontology

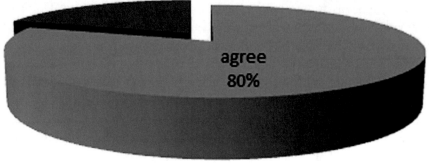

Figure 14. Participants of Ontocop

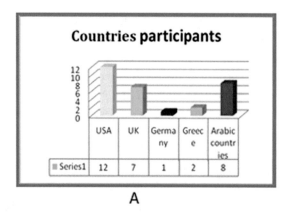

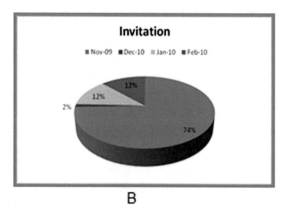

A

B

Launch the Ontocop With a Grand Kick-Off

Send 1633 emails in November and December 2009 respectively. At the beginning only 15 people responded offering their support - see some response emails as indicated in http://ontocop.hud.ac.uk/ - while 112 emails had failed through a mistake in the mailing address and the rest did not respond. By January and February 2010 the number had increased to 30 active participants. Overall, most of the emails sent were in November 2009 - about 74% - while approximately 12% were sent in January and February 2010.

The result of potential participations on this project is derived from Piwiki, the website analysis tool. Piwiki provides details on Ontocop website visitors. Using this tool helps to assess how and when users have been visiting the website. Visitors started visiting the community and participating in Jan 2010, and the number increased in Feb, Mar, and April respectively, as illustrated in Figure 15.

Analysing these results even from this fairly small period, we discovered many interesting points:

1. Users found collaboration in developing the OIS ontology is useful and interesting and involved active discussion.

Figure 15. Visitors of Ontocop

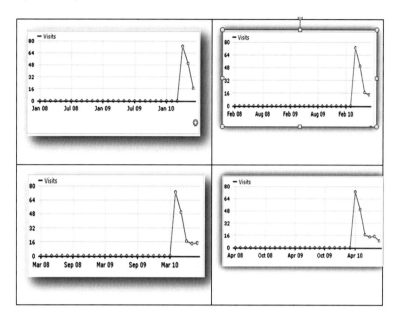

2. Participants were new to the system and some of them had difficulties with basic usability issues. We have addressed this by providing explanations to help them.
3. Participants at the beginning did not understand aspects of the tool functionality.
4. Language barriers affected their communication.

3. DISCUSSION AND ANALYSIS

Returning to the research questions that we introduced, the results of our evaluation attempt to answer these questions to address research objectives; these objectives were fulfilled by assessment of the ontology by domain experts.

Regarding the first question was answered by revealing that the OIS ontology was developed to visualise the domain knowledge. It described the process of developing in a practical way. The workflows of the developing process differ from ontology to ontology. The answer to this question is positive through the results of evaluation, where the participants considered it to be clear and comprehensive. The completeness is verified by checking the OIS ontology has fulfilled the objectives, which have been defined as;

- **Domain Interest:** The OIS was modelled for the IS domain knowledge
- **Ontology Purpose:** Creating this ontology for providing a domain model to be used as knowledge base. OIS ontology is providing a formal representation of the domain concepts and describing the relationships between them.

For the question of the knowledge that represent by the ontology, the OIS ontology represents the IS domain knowledge - its scope covers the tree branches which are; library science, archival science, and computer science. By describing the domain's content, the ontology's construction considered the users by answering these questions: who are the users of the OIS? What are the problems it attempts to solve? What could we do with the OIS ontology? For instance the users of OIS are domain experts and ordinary users - it helps users to search and studying the relations in the domain's content as mentioned. It can be used for database components to be integrated with other components such as lexical resource and supporting analysis of natural languages.

The third and fourth questions were answered by analysing different ontology methods and determining the ones that are most efficient in constructing ontology. The OIS Ontology expresses the domain conceptualization at formal level. It represents IS concepts by formal language using OWL 2 which gives a clear expressiveness and the semantic syntax, and was coded by using ontology editor Protégé and WebProtégé.

The question of the ontology relationships that have been used, in the OIS ontology two types of relationships were implemented, as contained below;

- Relations between classes to describe type of relations links among two classes.
- Relations between individuals and general concepts in the ontology to describe type of relations links between classes and individuals.

The relations definition between concepts needs to be more flexible for extra modifications in the future and for introducing new domain specifications.

The ontology is structured in the taxonomy tree and visualisation is complete by OWLVis plug-in in protégé.

Regarding the value of using tool such Ontocop system this study indicated that Examining Winger's communities of practice theory, particularly his constructs of common engagement and sharing community memory, a community of practice consists of the domain, practice and community. Through a process of negotiation of meaning, learning takes place within identity formation. Because of the importance and value of tacit knowledge, many developers of knowledge-based systems are spending significant time in obtaining information from experts, which is considered as a tacit knowledge, and making it accessible and machine-readable. On the basis of Winger's theory some specific requirements for the visualisation approach were conducted.

Collaboration with experts helps to overcome inconsistencies in the building process. Although there is a difference in views about classifying the knowledge according to their subject background, but it increases the richness of the ontology. The Ontocop community supports the developing process at different stages to validate the ontology construction. During this study they know about the ontology in its early stages to be familiar with it.

The final answer to these research questions is an implementation of OIS ontology. The OIS ontology was designed based on specific criteria meet the requirements. Also, in chapter 2, we have reviewed different evaluation approaches. The produced model was evaluated based on specific criteria.

The OIS was structured as a generic model to visualise the IS domain by unifying the domain knowledge to model the real world. The implementation acts as an example of how the actual research problem can be solved. Overall, the process of creating the OIS ontology was successful and the work proceeded without any significant problems.

In comparing with the related work in the area such as Zins' work (2007). it has clarified the relationships between concepts in the field, but there are many concepts still to be explored; for instance, in researching this study, a range of subdivisions have been uncovered so the study does not reflect the most current knowledge. One of the reactions to Zins' knowledge map is about the validation of its findings, as the participators provide assumptions about the domain as it is now. As we know, the IS field is a fast paced discipline.

Furthermore, Anthony Debons (one of the evaluator in Zin's study) indicates the diversity of IS and its language, which need to be agreed between the information scientists by creating lexicon to rely on during the work. In this study scientists have provided 57 definitions of Data, Information and Knowledge using different terminology; they used same terms that describe different meanings. Consequently, terms can be misleading and need to be clarified to get consensual meaning.

Overall, the nature of IS domain is less structured such as legal or social domains, which posed major challenges to the ontology development. Furthermore, the lack of domain ontology in this area made necessary to develop OIS ontology from scratch, although, there are ontologies that related to this area such as CIDOC-CRM which is focused on cultural heritage documentation, and FRBR to develop relational model of OCLC's catalogue, and ontology of cultural heritage resources is focused on modelling prototypes collection of Tobacco Bag Stringing (TBS). They considered specific division of the domain, while OIS ontology is more general focuses to develop knowledge base for the whole domain, is not considered any specific ontology for Library, museum or archive. It is as basic for the IS domain that facilitates creating or developing further domain ontologies for specific applications, such as archival collections, or library collections.

The research finding were encouraging about the potential of OIS ontology to benefit IS studies for instance. The evaluation outcomes provide an approach led to strengthen modelling results and receiving suggestions on how to improve it.

The produced model of OIS ontology was assessed in this study. The results of the OIS ontology evaluation revealed that the OIS ontology model can offer adequate functionality to meet user's requirements on supplementary information modelling. Furthermore it can help to build semantic capturing with objects designed to support semantic sharing between other disciplines. We have found the results to be satisfactory and the model is valid.

The evaluation results are reflected in the ontology; we made approximately 35 changes to the OIS ontology. Most of the changing was on the class based on the Domains Object class, with 19 classes entered, which were:

- **Natural Science:**
  - Astronomy,
  - Biology,
  - Chemistry,
  - Physic, and
  - **Earth Science:**
    - Atmospheric Science, and
    - Oceanography.
- **Social Science:**
  - Anthropology,
  - Economics,
  - Geography,
  - Political Science,
  - Psychology,

- ◦ Art, and
- ◦ Humanities.
- **Applied Science:**
  - ◦ Engineering, and
  - ◦ Medicine and Biology.

The participants were asked to indicate to their level of satisfaction on the ontology in general and the quality of term definitions, as illustrated in Figure 16.

The chart shows the satisfaction levels of the experts with the OIS ontology. The consistency of the ontology and relationships were satisfied. It is notable that the respondents expressed their level of satisfaction by choosing level three which is the middle level of evaluation, while, the same level decreased to 10% on semantic data richness criterion. The consistency of the ontology was remarked upon by 60% in comparison with the generality and clarity which are 44% and 48% respectively, as illustrated in Figure 17 and Table 3

It is notable that the OIS ontology was evaluated at levels 2, 3, and 4. Meanwhile, participants did not indicate level 1 and 5 which means the ontology is neither negative nor completely sufficient. The choosing of middle levels revealed evidence that the ontology met the designing criteria and it is an appropriate model. The findings of the evaluation stage provided a rich source of data that has been considered in refining the current model.

Figure 16. Satisfaction levels with the OIS ontology

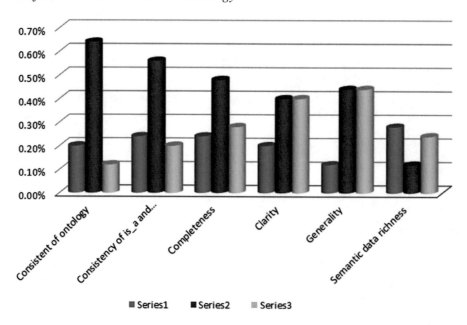

Figure 17. Evaluation criteria at level 3

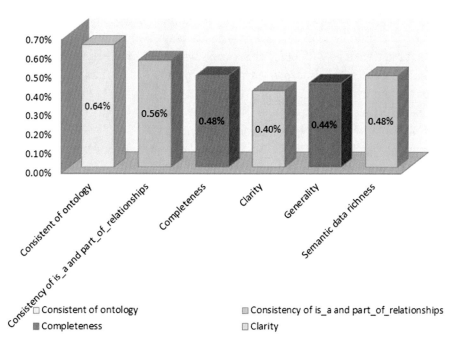

Table 3. Level 3 of satisfaction on ontology based on specific criteria

Criteria	Percentage
Consistent of ontology	0.64%
Consistency of is_a and part_of_relationships	0.56%
Completeness	0. 48%
Clarity	0.40%
Generality	0.44%
Semantic data richness	0.48%

The Analysis of the results points to many interesting issues: firstly:

- The evaluation of ontology model is not a communal practice in knowledge engineering, also it is uncommon when conducted from VCops. Furthermore, the main challenge in this part of the study was related to designing issue such designing and evaluation criteria. It is usual to evaluate ontology using systems performance or testing formal quality of ontology.
- Collaboration on such a virtual community of practice is interesting; some of the participants found the idea of using VCop valuable, it can be used to develop any universal software collaboratively.
- Respondents were new to using the ontology in WebProtégé software. So some of them had difficulties in accessing the ontology. Some of these difficulties were caused by using different internet browsers.

- The WebProtégé tool made the access to OIS ontology easier to browse and navigate through the ontology components, with concerns arising in online discussions about how to navigate and browse at the same time in quick and easy ways. Through WebProtégé, users can search on concepts and their relationships with other classes and where they were used. For example, the result of searching on the concept Information provides 64 result that indicate uses of this concept through the ontology such as:
  - Information Broker.
  - Health Information Center Infromation Transfer.
  - InformationS earch.
  - Information Centres.
  - General Information.
  - Library Of Information Department.
  - Information Management System.
  - Information Seeking Behaviour.
  - Information Retrieval System.

Overall, the aim of this study was visualise the IS domain by providing the framework to share a common understanding of Information science, and the ultimate aim was creating ontology model of IS.

Figure 18. Searching on WebProtégé

Figure 19. Ontology matrices

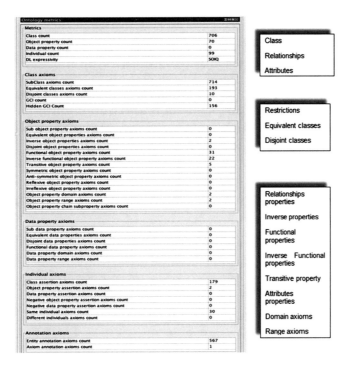

4. REVISED OIS MODEL

The OIS was changed after some comments had been gathered. The comments were made on the classification to enrich the ontology such as:

- Domains need to include arts, humanities
- Divide the science in the Domains into natural science, applied science and social science to add more subclasses under each one.
- Add Mandate as it has subclasses such as; accountability, institutional memory, research and support of human rights.

The final version of the OIS ontology has 706 classes, 70 object properties, 99) individuals. We can see this from the ontology matrices and ontology Figure 19.

REFERNCES

Gómez-Pérez, Juristo, N., & Pazos, J. (1995). *Evaluation and assessment of knowledge sharing Technology. Towards very large knowledge base.* Amsterdam: IOS.

Zins, C. (2007a). Conceptions of, Information Science. *Journal of the American Society for Information Science and Technology, 58*(3), 335–350. doi:10.1002/asi.20507

Zins, C. (2007b). Conceptual Approaches for defining data, information, and knowledge. *Journal of the American Society for Information Science and Technology, 58*(4), 479–493. doi:10.1002/asi.20508

Zins, C. (2007c). Knowledge Map of Information Science. *Journal of the American Society for Information Science and Technology, 58*(4), 526–535. doi:10.1002/asi.20505

Zins, C. (2007d). Knowledge mapping: Of information science. *Journal of the American Society for Information Science and Technology, 58*(4), 526–535. doi:10.1002/asi.20505

Chapter 15
Final Remarks for the Investigation in Ontology in IS and Possible Future Directions

Ahlam F. Sawsaa
University of Huddersfield, UK & Benghazi University, Libya

Joan Lu
University of Huddersfield, UK

ABSTRACT

This study is concluded in this chapter. The research problem and questions derived from it are answered. In addition, the achievements and the limitations of this study are discussed. The research started with identifying the problem. To achieve these objectives, the OIS was designed and developed. Feedback and evaluation from the domain's experts has led to constant improvement in the ontology's development. The current version of the OIS ontology is presented in this research. At the end of this chapter, possible research leads for the future are suggested. The study aimed at the creation of OIS ontology of Information Science domain to visualise its knowledge, in order to be integrated with other ontologies to be applied for a specific application. The resulting ontology covers three main areas of domain knowledge: library science, archival science and computing science. The vocabularies of these branches are formalised in class hierarchy with relations which are interconnecting concepts from all these areas, in order to define a sufficient model of the Information Science domain.

1. CONTRIBUTIONS

The main contributions in this study are presented in Figure 1, which are:

1. Designing ontology of Information Science (OIS): is presented to design OIS domain ontology to visualize a specific area. The OIS contains 706 concepts. These concepts identified to provide clear definitions for classes that would be interest to the domain users and developers. Also, identify the associated attributes and characteristics of the objects with their relations. Each entity has attributes

DOI: 10.4018/978-1-5225-2058-0.ch015

Figure 1. Architecture of system design approach

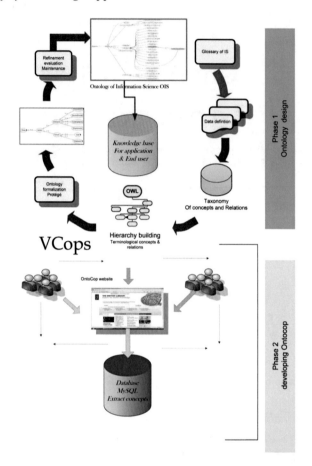

and type of relations for operating between these entities. The study intent to provide conceptual model serve as base to related specific relations and attributes. Furthermore, the research is focusing on analysis IS data to be defined in a systematic way in which way that how the information can be used.

2. A new strategy of conceptual representation of the domain knowledge that supported by both human and machine.

3. Developing IS taxonomy which is a novel methods to classify the domain knowledge. It describes the main concepts in a hierarchy tree. Our approach is overlapping on shortcomings of the classification systems that are widely acknowledged amongst the scientific community based on (FAS) and reinitialized previous classification schemas.

4. Designing Ontocop system a novel method presented to support the developing process as specific virtual community of IS.

1. ACHIEVEMENTS

The main achievement of this study is the creating a new model of OIS ontology. The OIS ontology was implemented in the process of the life cycle of ontology development, which was strongly influenced by Methontology. The creation process divided mainly into four processes: specification, conceptualisation, formalisation, and evaluation. The evaluation was essential to gather results on the produced model. The information resources were acquired manually and semi-automatically from domain's publications, books and dictionaries, where the text analysis and annotation techniques have been used. Conceptualisation essentially relied on the identification of concepts and groups of concepts and in building specific classification trees. The knowledge model was then formalised using Protégé, and WebProtégé to use the OIS ontology; it was also used to generate the ontology code automatically. Another relevant issue was using a standard evaluation methodology to check if the ontology satisfied needs.

The OIS is a data model representing set of concepts and sets of relations that connect the concepts; each instance is restricted by some axioms.

This model aimed to provide a shared terminology among agents and specialists in the domain and to define the meaning of all concepts in an accurate manner.

Identifying a research problem and justifying its need for a solution, required devoting an artefact as a solution. The research problem of the study was defined. The research problem was solved by answering the research.

The problems that were considered were:

- The IS domain was too broad for the specific time of the study.
- Since the beginning of the 1990s ontologies have been developed without clear guidance for developers. Nevertheless, some design criteria, principles, methods and methodologies must be followed.
- Despite some problems we have faced, the OIS ontology has reached a usable state. The concepts of the domain were structured and documented. The ontology is currently published in WebProtégé, since that work will be used for an application of IS domain to be used in specific purposes. At the end of this study, the implemented approach was evaluated.

2. FUTURE WORK

For reusing, sharing, and maintenance of the OIS ontology, there are future issues that relate to our ontology that need to be considered. In the OIS module there is always space for improvement. Ontologies are changing over time, due to changes in the domain and conceptualisation, so its structure should be extensible and flexible:

- It has the potential to be a collective knowledge base for the information science domain.
- Improve it by adding new or missing concepts and adding new classifications based on different criteria and perspectives.
- Most Information Science concepts were considered. Another, more interesting, possibility would be to link this general model with other science that is related to the domain.

- The OIS ontology is a key piece in the future development of Informatics applications such as Geographical information system, Management Information systems, and decision support systems.
- Translate ontology into another language, Spanish and Arabic for example. Once the ontology has been conceptualized, all the terms can be translated into another language using Multilanguage thesaurus and electronic dictionary.
- The main purpose of the OIS ontology is supporting knowledge sharing and exchange of data among databases as a generic model e.g. Actors, Domains, Kinds, Practice and so on. This ontology can be extended to create instances to general classes such as Author name.

The subclass author can be defined as follows: author: (author, name) the author is a subclass of person that indicates to any author must be a person (person, author) and each author has associated name and has some document, at least one book or article.

This ontology can be used by knowledge engineers or domain analysts. It requires search modules to provide a basic mechanism for searching. The OIS ontology uses natural language or keywords. Also, it provides advance research to retrieve specific knowledge that users are seeking for, see Figure 2

The search module is to facilitate:

- Reuse of the ontology components by equipping the application to deal with certain ontologies.
- Sharing knowledge that is contained in the repository.
- Helps users to retrieve any subsection of the OIS ontology for use in applications.

OIS can be used in many applications that range from knowledge base systems to information systems, for instance in information retrieval.

Figure 2. Interface of OIS ontology searching

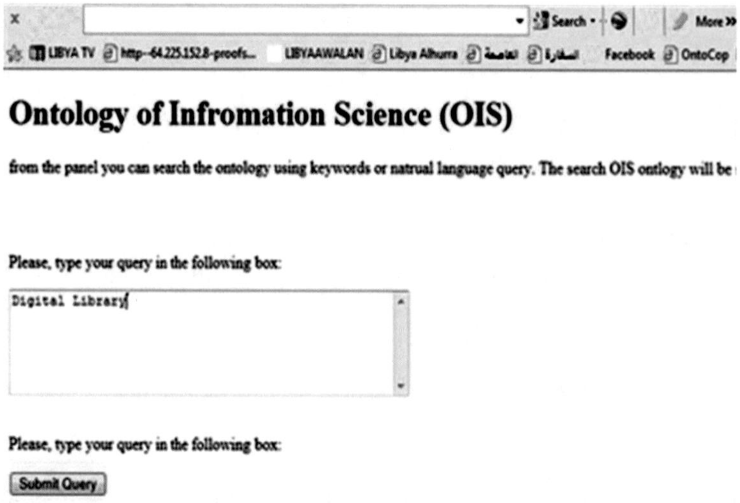

The OIS ontology is a domain ontology that will be used as a foundation for task ontologies, which provides a defined vocabulary to data ontology and database. The task ontology provides vocabulary for applications, whereas application ontology is designed for solving specific problems, which are accessed by the application, by implementing the semantics in sets of axioms to enable OIS ontology to deduce the answers of questions about the IS domain automatically. The relationship between these ontologies is shown diagrammatically in Figure 3.

The model of OIS is possible using application ontology. The appropriate use of OIS ontology is in Information science education; it helps teachers and students to obtain more details about their courses. It can provide outlines and summaries of topics that are covered in the courses. Also, it can answer questions such as:

- What are the courses in the domain?
- How many courses are in the domain?
- How many places are available to each course?
- How many students are studying each year?

Figure 3. Relationships between ontologies

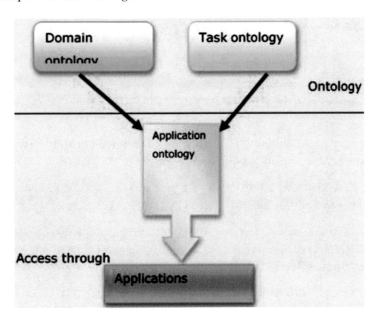

Compilation of References

10181-1, I.-T. R. X. I. I. (1996). *Information technology — Security Frameworks in Open Systems: Overview*. Author.

10181-1, I.-T. X. I. (1996). *Information technology — Security Frameworks in Open Systems: Overview*. Author.

Abiteboul, S. (1996). *Querying Semi-Structured Data*. Stanford InfoLab.

Abiteboul, S. (1999). Data on the Web: From Relations to Semi structured Data and XML. Morgan Kaufmann.

Abiteboul, S. (1993). Querying and updating the file. In *Proceedings of 19th International Conference on Very Large Databases*.

Abiteboul, S. (1997). Queries and Computation on the Web.*International Conference on Database Theory ICDT*. doi:10.1007/3-540-62222-5_50

Abiteboul, S. (1997). Querying Semi Structured Data. In *Proceedings of International Conference on Database Theory ICDT*. doi:10.1007/3-540-62222-5_33

Abiteboul, S. (1997). The Lorel Query Language for Semistrucutred data. *International Journal on Digital Libraries*, *1*(1), 68–88.

Abiteboul, S. (2001). Semistructured Data: from Practice to Theory. In *Proceedings of the 16th Annual IEEE Symposium on Logic in Computer Science LICS*. IEEE Computer Society. doi:10.1109/LICS.2001.932513

Abiteboul, S., Segoufin, L., & Vianu, V. (2006). Representing and querying XML with incomplete information. *ACM Transactions on Database Systems*, *31*(1), 208–254. doi:10.1145/1132863.1132869

Additional Protocol to the Convention on Cybercrime. (2003). *Concerning the criminalisation of acts of a racist and xenophobic nature committed through computer systems*. Council of Europe. Retrieved July 19, 2013, from http://conventions.coe.int/Treaty/en/ Treaties/Word/189.doc

Adeel, M., & Iqbal, A. (2004). TCP Congestion Window Optimization for CDMA2000 Packet Data Networks. *International Conference on Information Technology (ITNG'07)*. doi:10.1109/ITNG.2007.190

Aggarwal, C. C., & Yu, P. S. (2009). A survey of uncertain data algorithms and applications. *IEEE Transactions on Knowledge and Data Engineering*, *21*(5), 609–623. doi:10.1109/TKDE.2008.190

Agrawal, R., Gehrke, J., Gunopulos, D., & Raghavan, P. (1998). Automatic subspace clustering of high dimensional data for data mining applications. ACM.

Agrawal, R., Imieliński, T., & Swami, A. N. (1993). Mining association rules between sets of items in large databases. In P. Buneman, & S. Jajodia (Eds.), *Proceedings of the 1993 ACM SIGMOD International Conference on Management of Data* (pp. 207-216). New York: ACM. doi:10.1145/170035.170072

Agrawal, R., & Srikank, R. (1994). Fast algorithms for mining association rules in large databases. In J.B. Bocca, M. Jarke, & C. Zaniolo (Eds.), *Proceedings of the 20th International Conference on Very Large Data Bases* (pp. 487-499). San Francisco, CA: Morgan Kaufmann.

Ahlberg, C. (1996). Spotfire: An information exploration environment. *SIGMOD Record*, *25*(4), 25–29. doi:10.1145/245882.245893

Ahmed, A. U., Ahmed, C. F., Samiullah, M., Adnan, N., & Leung, C. K.-S. (2016). Mining interesting patterns from uncertain databases. *Information Sciences*, *354*, 60–85. doi:10.1016/j.ins.2016.03.007

Ajit, S., & Deepak, G. (2011). Implementation and Performance Analysis of Exponential Tree Sorting. International Journal of Computer Applications, 24(3), 34-38.

Akdeniz, Y. (2004). Who watches the Watchmen? The role of filtering software in Internet content regulation. In C. Moller & A. Amouroux (Eds.), *The Media Freedom Internet Cookbook* (pp. 101–121). Vienna: Academic Press.

Akinyemi, F. A. (2010). Conceptual Poverty Mapping Data Model. *Transactions in GIS*, *14*, 85–100. doi:10.1111/j.1467-9671.2010.01207.x

Akoglu, L., Chau, D. H., Kang, U., Koutra, D., & Faloutsos, C. (2012). OPAvion: mining and visualization in large graphs. In K.S. Candan, Y. Chen, R.T. Snodgrass, L. Gravano, & A. Fuxman (Eds.), *Proceedings of the 2012 ACM SIGMOD International Conference on Management of Data* (pp.717-720). New York: ACM. doi:10.1145/2213836.2213941

Aldana, W. A. (2000). *A Brief History of Data Mining*. Academic Press.

Alencar, A. B., de Oliveira, M. C. F., & Paulovich, F. V. (2012). Seeing beyond reading: A survey on visual text analytics. *WIREs Data Mining and Knowledge Discovery*, *2*(6), 476–492. doi:10.1002/widm.1071

Alexa. (2011). Top sites in Thailand. *Alexa*. Retrieved July 21, 2013, from http://www.alexa.com/topsites/countries/

Alexander, J. H., Freiling, M. J., Shulman, S. J., Staley, J. L., Rehfuss, S., & Messick, S. L. (1986). Knowledge Level Engineering: Ontological Analysis. In *Proceedings of ICSE 1991: The international Conference on Software Engineering*. ACM Press.

Alhoniemi, E., Himberg, J., Hollm´en, J., Laine, S., PasiLehtim¨aki, Raivio, K., . . . Vesanto, J. (2002). *SOM in data mining*. Academic Press.

Allemang, D., & Hendler, J. (2008). *Semantic web for the working ontologist: Effective modeling in RDFs and OWL*. Elsevier.

Al-Noukari, M., & Al-Hussan, W. (2008). *Using Data Mining Techniques for Predicting Future Car market Demand; DCX Case Study*. Paper presented at the Information and Communication Technologies: From Theory to Applications, 2008. ICTTA 2008. 3rd International Conference on. doi:10.1109/ICTTA.2008.4530367

Al-Rajab, M. M., & Lu, J. (2016). A study on the most common algorithms implemented for cancer gene search and classifications. *International Journal of Data Mining and Bioinformatics*, *14*(2), 159–176. doi:10.1504/IJDMB.2016.074685

Al-Wasil, F. (2006). Query Translation for Distributed Heterogeneous Structured and Semi structured Databases.*British National Conference on Databases BNCOD*. doi:10.1007/11788911_6

Al-Wasil, F. (2006a). Establishing an XML metadata knowledge base to assist integration of structured and semi-structured databases. In *Proceedings of the 17th Australasian Database Conference*.

Amer-Yahia, S. (2002). A Mapping Schema and Interface for XML Stores. In *Proceedings of the 4th international Workshop on Web information and Data Management WIDM*. doi:10.1145/584931.584937

Amin, A., & Roberts, J. (2008). Knowing in action: Beyond communities of practice. *Research Policy, 37*(2), 353–369. doi:10.1016/j.respol.2007.11.003

Amira, T., Adil El, G., Rose, D.-K., Alain, G., & Christina, C., G & Raldine, V. (2007) An ontology for supporting communities of practice. *Proceedings of the 4th international conference on Knowledge capture*. Whistler, BC, Canada: ACM.

Anderson, N., & Hong, J. (2013). Visually extracting data records from query result pages. In Y. Ishikawa, J. Li, W. Wang, R. Zhang, & W. Zhang (Eds.), *Proceedings of the 15th Asia-Pacific Web Conference* (LNCS), (vol. 7808, pp. 392-403). Heidelberg, Germany: Springer. doi:10.1007/978-3-642-37401-2_40

Anderson, J. R. (1983). A spreading activation theory of memory. *Journal of Verbal Learning and Verbal Behavior, 22*(3), 261–295. doi:10.1016/S0022-5371(83)90201-3

Andrew, N., Tolson, D., & Ferguson, D. (2008). Building on Wenger: Communities of practice in nursing. *Nurse Education Today, 28*(2), 246–252. doi:10.1016/j.nedt.2007.05.002 PMID:17599697

Ankerst, M., Elsen, C., Ester, M., & Kriegel, H.-P. (1999). Visual classification: an interactive approach to decision tree construction. In U. Fayyad, S. Chaudhuri, & D. Madigan (Eds.), *Proceedings of the Fifth ACM SIGKDD International Conference on Knowledge Discovery and Data Mining* (pp. 392-396). New York: ACM. doi:10.1145/312129.312298

Antoniou, G., & Harmelen, F. V. (2004). *Semantic web primer*. Massachusetts Institute of Technology.

Araujo, L. (1998). Knowing and learning as networking. *Management Learning, 29*, 317-336.

Ardagna, C., Damiani E., Vimercati, S., & Samarati, P. (2007). *Security, Privacy, and Trust in Modern Data Management Data-Centric Systems and Applications*. DOI: 10.1007/978-3-540-69861-6_6

Ardichvili, A., Page, V., & Wentling, T. (2003). Motivation and barriers to participation in virtual knowledge -sharing communities of practice. *Knowledge Management, 7*, 64-77.

Arnab, A., & Hutchion, A. (2005). *Requirement analysis of enterprise DRM systems*. Academic Press.

Arnold, J. (2010). *Why businesses need to think differently about cloud communications*. Academic Press.

Article 19. (2005). Freedom of expression and the media in Thailand. *Article 19*. Retrieved July 22, 2013, from http://www.article19.org/data/files/pdfs/publications/thailand-baseline-study.pdf

Article 19. (2009). Impact of defamation law on freedom of expression in Thailand. *Article 19*. Retrieved July 24, 2013, from http://www.article19.org/data/files/pdfs/analysis/thailand-impact-of-defamation-law-on-freedom-of-expression.pdf

Article 19. (2011). Article 19's Submission to the UN Universal Periodic Review: Kingdom of Thailand. *Article 19*. Retrieved June 29, 2013, from http://www.refworld.org/docid/4d8073465b9.html

Arya, S., Mount, D. M., Netanyahu, N., Silverman, R., & Wu, A. Y. (1994, January). An optimal algorithm for approximate nearest neighbor searching in fixed dimensions. In *Proc. 5th ACM-SIAM Sympos. Discrete Algorithms* (pp. 573-582).

Asaeedi, S., Didehvar, F., & Mohades, A. (2013). *Alpha-Concave Hull, a Generalization of Convex Hull*. arXiv preprint arXiv:1309.7829

Ashby, W. R. (1956). *An Introduction to Cybernetics*. Chapman and Hall.

Atay, M. (2004). Mapping XML data to relational data: A DOM-based approach. In *8th IASTED International Conference on Internet and Multimedia Systems and Applications*.

Atay, M., Chebotko, A., Liu, D., Lu, S., & Fotouhi, F. (2007). Efficient schema based XML-to-Relational data mapping. *Information Systems*, *32*(3), 458–476. doi:10.1016/j.is.2005.12.008

Awodey, S. (2006). *Category Theory*. Oxford Science Publication. Retrieved from http://www.google.co.uk/#hl=en&q=on%20catego

Baader, F., & Nutt, W. (2003). *The description logic handbook: Theory, implementation, and application*. Cambridge University Press.

Baeza-Yates, R., & Ribeiro-Neto, B. (1999). *Modern information retrieval*. Reading, MA: Addison Wesley Longman.

Balmin, A., & Papakonstantinou, Y. (2005). Storing and Querying XML data using demoralized relational databases. *The VLDB Journal*, *14*(1), 30–49. doi:10.1007/s00778-003-0113-1

Bangkok Post. (2009, January 6). Web censoring needs a debate. *Bangkok Post*. Retrieved June 23, 2013, from http://www.bangkokpost.com/opinion/opinion/9202/

Barbosa, D. (2001). ToX: The Toronto XML Engine. In *Proceedings of the Workshop on Information Integration on the Web*.

Barre, P., Paasch, C., & Bonaventure, O. (2011). *MultiPath TCP: From Theory to Practice*. IFIP Networking.

Barre, R., Greenhalgh, P., & Handley, W. (2011). Improving datacenter performance and robustness with multipath TCP. *Proceedings of the ACM SIGCOMM 2011 Conference*.

Barry, S. (1996). Mereotopology: A Theory of parts and boundaries. *Data & Knowledge Engineering*, *20*(3), 287–303. doi:10.1016/S0169-023X(96)00015-8

Bartel, M., Boyer, J., Fox, B., LaMacchia, B., & Simon, E. (2002). *XML-Signature Syntax and Processing*. W3C Recommendation.

Bartel, M., Boyer, J., Fox, B., LaMacchia, B., & Simon, E. (2008). XML signature syntax and processing (2nd ed.). Academic Press.

Batista, F., Pardal, J. P., Mamede, N. J., Vaz, P., & Ribeiro, R. D. (2006). *Ontology construction: cooking domain*. Retrieved from http://www.inesc-id.pt/pt/indicadores/Ficheiros/3615.pdf

Baum, M., & Hanebeck, U. D. (2010, September). Tracking a minimum bounding rectangle based on extreme value theory. In *Multisensor Fusion and Integration for Intelligent Systems (MFI), 2010 IEEE Conference on* (pp. 56-61). IEEE. doi:10.1109/MFI.2010.5604456

Bawden, D. (2011). Brookes equation: The basis for a qualitative characterization of information behaviours. *Journal of Information Science*, *37*(1), 101–108. doi:10.1177/0165551510395351

Becerra-Fernandez, I., Zanakis, S. H., & Walczak, S. (2002). Knowledge discovery techniques for predicting country investment risk. *Computers & Industrial Engineering*, *43*(4), 787–800. doi:10.1016/S0360-8352(02)00140-7

Bechhofer, S., Horrocks, I., Goble, C., & Stevens, R. (2001). OilEd: A Reasonable Ontology Editor for the Semantic Web. In *Joint German/Austrian conference on Artificial Intelligence*. Berlin: Springer.

Belciu, A. V., & Olaru, S. (2011). *Optimizing spatial databases*. Available at SSRN 1800758

Bellinger, G., Castro, D., & Mills, A. (2010). *Data*. Information, Knowledge, and Wisdom.

Bellman, R. E. (1957). *Dynamic programming*. Princeton, NJ: Princeton University Press.

Bello, A. (2010). Ontology and Phenomenology. In Theory and Applications of Ontology: Philosophical Perspectives. London: Springer.

Berchtold, S., & Keim, D. A. (1996). The X-tree: An Index Structure for High-Dimensional Data. *Proceedings of the 22nd VLDB Conference*.

Berchtold, S., Bohm, C., Keim, D., & Kriegel H.-P. (1997). A cost model for nearest neighbor search in high-dimensional data space. In *Proceedings of the 16th Symposium on Principles of Database Systems* (PODS).

Berchtold, S., Keim, D. A., & Kriegel, H. P. (2001). An index structure for high-dimensional data. Readings in multimedia computing and networking.

Berchtold, S., Jagadish, H. V., & Ross, K. A. (1998). Independence diagrams: a technique for visual data mining. In R. Agrawal, P.E. Stolorz, & G. Piatetsky-Shapiro (Eds.), *Proceedings of the Fourth International Conference on Knowledge Discovery and Data Mining* (pp. 139-143). Menlo Park, CA: AAAI Press.

Berkhin, P. (2006). *A Survey of Clustering Data Mining Techniques*. Academic Press.

Berners-Lee, T., Hendler, J., & Lassila, O. (2001, May). The Semantic Web. *Scientific American*, *284*(5), 34–43. doi:10.1038/scientificamerican0501-34 PMID:11323639

Beyer, K., Goldstein, J., Ramakrishnan, R., & Shaft, U. (1999). When is Nearest Neighbors Meaningful?*Proc. of the Int. Conf. Database Theorie*, (pp. 217-235).

Bhatt, M., Rahayu, W., Soni, S. P., & Wouters, C. (2009). Ontology driven semantic profiling and retrieval in medical information systems. *Web Semantics: Science, Services, and Agents on the World Wide Web*, *7*(4), 317–331. doi:10.1016/j.websem.2009.05.004

Biddle, P., England, P., Peinado, M., & Willman, B. (n.d.). *The darknet and the future of content distribution*. Retrieved from http://msl1.mit.edu/ESD10/docs/darknet5.pdf

Birman, K., Hillman, R., & Pleisch, S. (2005). Building network-centri military applications over service oriented architecture. *SPIE Defence and Security Symposium*, Orlando, FL.

Blahut, R. (2004). *Algebraic Codes for Data Transmission*. Cambridge University Press.

Blair, D. (2001). *Re: attribute encryption (from XML encryption mailing list)*. Academic Press.

Blanchard, J., Guillet, F., & Briand, H. (2007). Interactive visual exploration of association rules with rule-focusing methodology. *Knowledge and Information Systems*, *13*(1), 43–75. doi:10.1007/s10115-006-0046-2

Blei, D. M., Ng, A. Y., & Jordan, M. I. (2003). Latent dirichlet allocation. *The Journal of Machine Learning Research*, *3*, 993–1022.

Blum, B. I. (1996). Beyond programming Oxford Unversity Press. New York: Academic Press.

Böhm, C., Berchtold, S., & Keim, D. A. (2001). Searching in high-dimensional spaces: Index structures for improving the performance of multimedia databases. *ACM Computing Surveys*, *33*(3), 322–373. doi:10.1145/502807.502809

Bolstad, P. (2002). GIS Fundamentals: A First Text on GIS. Eider Press.

Bonchi, F. (2009). Constraint-based pattern discovery. In J. Wang (Ed.), *Encyclopedia of data warehousing and mining* (2nd ed.; pp. 313–319). Hershey, PA: IGI Global. doi:10.4018/978-1-60566-010-3.ch050

Bothorel, G., Serrurier, M., & Hurter, C. (2013). Visualization of frequent itemsets with nested circular layout and bundling algorithm. In G. Bebis, R. Boyle, B. Parvin, D. Koracin, B. Li, F. Porikli, V. Zordan, J. Klosowski, S. Coquillart, X. Luo, M. Chen, & D. Gotz (Eds.), *Proceedings of the 9th International Symposium on Visual Computing* (LNCS), (vol. 8034, pp. 396-405). Heidelberg, Germany: Springer. doi:10.1007/978-3-642-41939-3_38

Bouras, C., & Tsogkas, V. (2011). Clustering User Preferences Using W-kmeans.*2011 Seventh International Conference on Signal-Image Technology and Internet-Based Systems (SITIS)* (pp. 75–82). doi:10.1109/SITIS.2011.19

Bourne, M. (2015). *Applications of integration*. Retrieved from http://www.intmath.com/applications-integration/5-centroid-area.php

Bourne, C. P. (1980). On-line systems: History, technology and economics. *Journal of the American Society for Information Science*, *31*(3), 155–160. doi:10.1002/asi.4630310307

Boyer, J. (2001). *Canonical XML Version 1.0*. RFC Editor.

Boyer, J., Eastlake, D. E., & Reagle, J. (2002). *Exclusive XML Canonicalization, Version 1.0*. Retrieved from http://www.w3.org/TR/2002/REC-xml-exc-c14n-20020718/

Boyer, J., Hughes, M., & Reagle, J. (2003). *XML-Signature XPath Filter 2.0*. RFC Editor.

Brank, J., Grobelnik, M., Milic-Frayling, N., & Mladenic, D. (2003). *Training text classifiers with SVM on very few positive examples*. Academic Press.

Bray, T., Paoli, J., Sperberg-McQueen, C. M., Maler, E., & Yergeau, F. (2008). *Extensible Markup Language (XML) 1.0* (5th ed.). Retrieved from http://www.w3.org/TR/REC-xml/

Bray, T., Paoli, J., Sperberg-McQueen, C. M., Maler, E., & Yergeau, F. (2007). *Extensible Markup Language (XML) 1.0* (4th ed.). Academic Press.

Brewster, C., Alani, H., Dasmahapatra, S., & Wilks, Y. (2004). *Data Driven Ontology Evaluation*. In International Conference on Language Resources and Evaluation, Lisbon, Portugal.

Bridges, S. M., & Vaughn, R. B. (2001). *Fuzzy Data Mining And Genetic Algorithms Applied To Intrusion Detection*. Paper presented at the 23rd National Information Systems Security Conference.

Broughton, V. (2001). Faceted classification as a basis for knowledge organization in a digital environment; the Bliss Bibliographic Classification as a model for vocabulary management and the creation of multidimensional knowledge structures. *New Review of Hypermedia and Multimedia*, *7*(1), 67–102. doi:10.1080/13614560108914727

Brusa, G., Caliusco, M. L., & Chiotti, O. (2006). *A Process for Building a Domain Ontology: an Experience in Developing a Government Budgetary Ontology*. Conferences in Research and Practice in Information Technology,Hobart, Australia.

Bryant, D., Atallah, J., & Stytz, R. (2004). A survey of Anti-Tamper technologies CrossTalk. *The Journal of Defense Software Engineering*, *17*(11), 12–16. Retrieved from http://www.arxan.com/ATknowledgePortal/pdfs/Crosstalk-Article-A-Surve-ofAntiTamper-Technologies.pdf

Bubenko, J. A., & Orci, I. P. (1989). *Knowledge base management system Foundation of knowledge base management system*. New York: Springer,Verlag.

Buckland, M. K., & Liu, Z. (1995). History of information science. *Annual Review of Information Science & Technology*, 385–416.

Buneman, P., Choi, B., Fan, W., Mann, R., & Hutchison, R. (2005). Vectorizing and Querying Large XML Repositories. Academic Press.

Buneman, P. (1996). A query language and optimization techniques for unstructured data. In *Proceedings of ACMSIG-MOD International Conference on Management of Data*. doi:10.1145/233269.233368

Buneman, P. (1997). Adding Structure to unstructured data. In *Proceeding of the international conference on Database Theory* (pp. 336–350). Springer Verlag.

Buneman, P., Fernandez, M., & Suciu, D. (2000). UnQL: A query language and algebra for semi structured data based on structural recursion. *The VLDB Journal, 9*(1), 76. doi:10.1007/s007780050084

Bunyavejchewin, P. (2010). Internet politics: Internet as a political tool in Thailand. *Canadian Social Science, 6*(3), 67–72.

Burtonjones, et al. (2005). A semiotic metrics suite for assessing the quality of ontologies. Data & Knowledge Engineering, 55, 84-102.

Bushell-Embling, D. (2010). Malaysia's pricey leased lines. *Telecom Asia, 21.*

Bustamante, F., Eisenhauer, G., Schwan, K., & Widener, P. (2000). Efficient wire formats for high performance computing. In *Proceedings of the ACM/IEEE 2000 Conference on Supercomputing*. doi:10.1109/SC.2000.10046

Büttcher, S., Clarke, C. L. A., & Cormack, G. V. (2010). *Information retrieval: Implementing and evaluating search engines*. Cambridge, MA: MIT Press.

Calero, C., Ruiz, F., & Piattini, M. (2006). *Ontologies for software engineering and software technology*. Springer. doi:10.1007/3-540-34518-3

Candan, K. S., & Sapino, M. L. (2010). *Data management for multimedia retrieval*. Cambridge University Press. doi:10.1017/CBO9780511781636

Cantor, S., Kemp, J., Philpott, R., & Maler, E. (2005). *Assertions and Protocols for the OASIS Security Assertion Markup Language (SAML) v2.0*. Academic Press.

Catherine, C. M., Shipman, F. M., III, & Raymond, J. M. (2000). Making large-scale information resources serve communities of practice. *Journal of Management Information Systems, 11*, 65–86.

Cattell, R. (2000). *The Object Data Standard ODMG 3.0*. Morgan Kaufmann.

Cazals, F., Emiris, I. Z., Chazal, F., Gärtner, B., Lammersen, C., Giesen, J., & Rote, G. (2013). *D2. 1: Handling High-Dimensional Data*. Computational Geometric Learning (CGL) Technical Report No.: CGL-TR-01.

CDT. (2012). *Shielding the messengers: CDT travels to Thailand to argue against intermediary liability*. Center for Democracy & Technology (CDT). Retrieved July 19, 2013, from https://www.cdt.org/blogs/ kevin-bankston/0504shielding-messengers-cdt-travels-thailand-argue- against-intermediary-liabil

Cendrowska, J. (1987). PRISM: An algorithm for inducing modular rules. *International Journal of Man-Machine Studies, 27*(4), 349–370. doi:10.1016/S0020-7373(87)80003-2

Census. (2011). *Wards in Yorkshire and the Humber*. Available at http://ukdataexplorer.com/census/yorkshireandtheh umber/#KS206EW0007

Chamberlin, D. (2000). *An XML Query Language for Heterogeneous Data Sources*. International Workshop on the Web and Databases (WebDB'2000), Dallas, TX.

Chan, K. W., & Li, S. Y. (2010). Understanding consumer- to consumer interactions in virtual communities: The salience of reciprocity. *Journal of Business Research*, 1033-1040.

Chaparro, B., Baker, J. R., Shaikh, A. D., Hull, S., & Brady, L. (2004, July). *Reading Online Text: A Comparison of Four White Space Layouts. Usability News, 6*(2). Retrieved from The Psychology Department of Wichita State University: http://psychology.wichita.edu/surl/usabilitynews/62/whitespace.htm

Chaudhri, V., Farquhar, A., Fikes, R., Karp, P., & Rice, J. (1998). OKBC: A programmatic foundation for knowledge base interoperability. In *Proceedings 15 th National conference on artificial Intelligence.*

Chaudhuri, S., Chen, Z., Shim, K., & Wu, Y. (2005). Storing XML (with XSD) in SQL Databases: Interplay of Logical and Physical Designs. *IEEE Transactions on Knowledge and Data Engineering, 17*(12), 1595–1609. doi:10.1109/TKDE.2005.204

Chawathe, S. (1994). The TSIMMIS Project: "Integration of Heterogeneous Information Sources". In *Proceedings of 10th Meeting of the Information Processing Society Conference.*

Chen, J., Hu, C., & Ji, Z. (2011). Self-Tuning Random Early Detection Algorithm to Improve Performance of Network Transmission. *Educational Researcher, 39*(7), 515 – 524.

Chen, Y., Pavlov, D., & Canny, J. F. (2009). Large-scale behavioral targeting. *Proceedings of the 15th ACM SIGKDD international conference on Knowledge discovery and data mining* (pp. 209–218). Retrieved from http://cc.gatech.edu/~zha/CSE8801/ad/p209-chen.pdf

Cheng, H., & Han, J. (2009). Frequent itemsets and association rules. In L. Liu & M. T. Özsu (Eds.), *Encyclopedia of database systems* (pp. 1184–1187). New York: Springer.

Chen, L., & Brown, S. D. (2014). Use of a tree-structured hierarchical model for estimation of location and uncertainty in multivariate spatial data. *Journal of Chemometrics, 28*(6), 523–538. doi:10.1002/cem.2611

Chhabra, S., Siefkes, C., Assis, F., & Yerazunis, W. S. (2004, September). Combining winnow and orthogonal sparse bigrams for incremental spam filtering. In *European Conference on Principles of Data Mining and Knowledge Discovery* (pp. 410-421). Springer Berlin Heidelberg.

Chi, Y.-L., Hsu, T.-Y., & Yang, W.-P. (2006). Ontological techniques for reuse and sharing knowledge in digital museums. *The Electronic Library, 24*(2), 147–159. doi:10.1108/02640470610660341

Christophides, V. (1994). From structured documents to novel query facilities. *SIGMOD Record, 23*(2), 313 – 324.

Cios, K. J., Pedrycz, W., Swiniarski, R., & Kurgan, L. A. (2007). *Data Mining- A knowledge discovery approach.* Academic Press.

Clark, J. (2001). *TREX - Tree Regular Expressions for XML.* Academic Press.

Cleverdon, C. (1987). Historical note: Perspectives. *Journal of the American Society for Information Science, 38*, 152–155.

Coakes, E., & Clarke, S. (2008). Boundaries in Communities.Encyclopedia of Communities of Practice in Information and Knowledge Management. Academic Press.

Cohen, W. W. (1995). Fast Effective Rule Induction In *Proceedings of the Twelfth International Conference on Machine Learning* (pp. 115-123): Morgan Kaufmann.

Corbin, J., & Strauss, A. (2008). *Basics of qualitative research: techniques and procedures for developing grounded theory* (3rd ed.). London: Sage Publications. doi:10.4135/9781452230153

Corcho, O. (2002). *Building legal ontologies with METHONTOLOGY and WebODE*. Retrieved from http://academic. research.microsoft.com/Paper/1856108.aspx

Corley, C., Mihalcea, R., & Strapparava, C. (2006). Corpus-based and Knowledge based Measures of Text similarity. *AAAI'06: Proceedings of the 21st national conference on Artificial intelligence*. AAAI Press.

Cox, A. (2005). What are communities of practice? A comparative review of four seminal works. *Journal of Information Science, 31*(6), 527–540. doi:10.1177/0165551505057016

Cox, E. (2001a). Fuzzy logic and the measures of certainty in eCommerce expert systems. *PC AI, 15*(3), 16–22.

Cox, E. (2001b). *Fuzzy Logic and the Measures of Certainty in eCommerce Expert Systems*. Scianta Intelligence.

Craswell, N., & Szummer, M. (2007). Random walks on the click graph. *Proceedings of the 30th annual international ACM SIGIR conference on Research and development in information retrieval* (pp. 239–246). Retrieved from http:// dl.acm.org/citation.cfm?id=1277784

Cunningham, H., Maynard, D., & Tablan, V. (2000). *JAPE: A Java Annotation Patterns Engine* (2nd ed.). Research Memorandum CS-00-10. Department of Computer Science, University of Sheffield.

Curtis, J., Matthews, G., & Baxter, D. (2005). *On the Effective Use of Cyc in a Question Answering System.IJCAI Workshop on Knowledge and Reasoning for Answering Questions*, Edinburgh, UK.

Cuzzocrea, A., Jiang, F., Leung, C.K., Liu, D., Peddle, A., & Tanbeer, S.K. (2015). Mining popular patterns: a novel mining problem and its application to static transactional databases and dynamic data streams. *LNCS Transactions on Large-Scale Data- and Knowledge-Centered Systems (TLDKS) XXI* (LNCS), (vol. 9260, pp. 115-139). Springer. doi:10.1007/978-3-662-47804-2_6

Cuzzocrea, A., Lee, W., & Leung, C. K.-S. (2015). High-recall information retrieval from linked big data. In S.I. Ahamed, C.K. Chang, W. Chu, I. Crnkovic, P.-A. Hsiung, G. Huang, & J. Yang (Eds.), *Proceedings of the 39th IEEE International Computer Software and Applications Conference* (Vol. 2, pp. 712-717). Los Alamitos, CA: IEEE Computer Society. doi:10.1109/COMPSAC.2015.152

Cuzzocrea, A., Leung, C. K., & MacKinnon, R. K. (2014). Mining constrained frequent itemsets from distributed uncertain data. *Future Generation Computer Systems, 37*, 117–126. doi:10.1016/j.future.2013.10.026

Dalkir, K. (2005). *KM in theory and practice*. Oxford, UK: Elsevier Butterworth-Heinemann.

Danilova, N., & Stupples, D. (2012). Application of Natural Language Processing to Web-based Intelligence Information Acquisition. *EISIC2012 Proceedings*. Odense, Denmark: IEEE Computer Society.

Davenport, T. H. (1998). *Some Principles of knowledge management*. Retrieved from http://www.strategy-business.com/ article/8776?gko=f91a7

Davenport, T., & Prusak, L. (2000). Working knowledge: How organisations manage what they know. Boston: Harvard Business School.

Davis, D., & Parashar, M. (2002). Latency performance of SOAP implementations. In *Proceedings of the 2nd IEEE/ ACM International Symposium on Cluster Computing and the Grid*. doi:10.1109/CCGRID.2002.1017169

Davis, R., Shrobe, H., & Szolovits, P. (1993). What is a knowledge Representation? *AI Magazine, 14*, 17–33.

Deering, S., & Hinden, R. (1998). *Internet Protocol, Version 6 (IPv6) Specification, Internet Engineering Task Force*. RFC 2460.

Deibert, R. J. (2009). The geopolitics of Internet control: Censorship, sovereignty, and cyberspace. In A. Cbadwick & P. N. Howard (Eds.), *The Routledge Handbook of Internet Politics* (pp. 323–336). New York: Routledge.

Delavari, N., & Beikzadeh, M. R. (2004). *A new model for using data mining in higher educational system*. Academic Press.

Delavari, N., Beikzadeh, M. R., & Amnuaisuk, S. (2005). *Application of enhanced analysis model for data mining processes in higher educational system*. Academic Press.

Deliiska, B. (2007). Thesaurus and Domain ontology of Gioinformatics. *Journal Compilation, 11*, 637–651.

Dempster, A. P. (1968). A generalization of the Bayesian inference. *Journal of the Royal Statistical Society. Series A (General), 30*, 205–447.

Denoyer, L., & Gallinari, P. (2004). Bayesian network model for semi-structured document classification. *Information Processing & Management, 40*(5), 807–827. doi:10.1016/j.ipm.2004.04.009

Dietrich, C. J., Rossow, C., & Pohlmann, N. (2013). Exploiting visual appearance to cluster and detect rogue software. In S.Y. Shin, & J.C. Maldonado (Eds.), *Proceedings of the 28th Annual ACM Symposium on Applied Computing* (pp. 1776-1783). New York: ACM. doi:10.1145/2480362.2480697

Diffie, W., & Hellman, M. E. (1976). New directions in cryptography. *Information Theory. IEEE Transactions on, 22*(6), 644–654. doi:10.1109/tit.1976.1055638

Ding, Y. (2007). *Handling complex, high dimensional data for classification and clustering*. University of Mississippi.

Dmterie, J., & Verbeek, F. J. (2008). *Information visualisation from ontology*. Formal ontology in information systems Fifth international conference FOIS2008.

Domingue, J. (1998). *Tadzebao and Webonto: Discussing, Browsing and Editing ontologies on the web*. 11th knowledge Acquisition workshop (KAW98), Banff, Canada.

Domingue, J., Enrico, M., Buckingham, S. S., Maria, V.-V., Yannis, K., & Nick, F. (2001) Supporting ontology driven document enrichment within communities of practice.*Proceedings of the 1st international conference on Knowledge capture*. Victoria, British Columbia, Canada: ACM. doi:10.1145/500737.500746

Douglas, C. (1995). Internetworking with TCP/IP, Volume 1: Principles, Protocols, and Architecture. Prentice Hall.

Douglas, C. (2006). *Internetworking with TCP/IP: Principles, Protocols, and Architecture (5ʰ Ed.)*. Prentice Hall.

Dröge, G. & Schek. (1993). Query-Adaptive Data Space Partitioning Using Variable-Size Storage Clusters.*Proc. 3rd Intl. Symposium on Large Spatial Databases*.

Drucker, H., Wu, D., & Vapnik, V. N. (1999). Support vector machines for spam categorization. *IEEE Transactions on Neural Networks, 10*(5), 1048–1054. doi:10.1109/72.788645 PMID:18252607

Dube, L., Bourhis, A., & Jacob, R. (2006). Towards a Typology of virtual communities of practice. *Interdisciplinary Journal of Information, Knowledge and Management, 1*, 71-93.

Duftler, C., Khalaf, M., Nagy, R., Mukhi, W., & Weerawarana, S. (2002). Unraveling the web services web: An introduction to SOAP, WSDL, UDDI. *IEEE Internet Computing, 6*(2), 86–93. doi:10.1109/4236.991449

Du, T. C., Li, F., & King, I. (2009). Managing knowledge on the Web - Extracting ontology from HTML Web. *Decision Support Systems, 47*(4), 319–331. doi:10.1016/j.dss.2009.02.011

Dziczkowski, G., & Wegrzyn-Wolska, K. (2008, December). An autonomous system designed for automatic detection and rating of film reviews. In *Proceedings of the 2008 IEEE/WIC/ACM International Conference on Web Intelligence and Intelligent Agent Technology* (pp. 847-850). IEEE Computer Society. doi:10.1109/WIIAT.2008.262

E, S., & B, L. (2000). *XML encryption strawman proposal.* Retrieved from http://lists.w3.org/Archives/Public/xml-encryption/2000Aug/0001.html

Eastlake, D., & Reagle, J. (2002). *XML Encryption Syntax and Processing.* Academic Press.

Eberly, D. (2015). *Minimum-Area Rectangle Containing a Set of Points.* Geometric Tools, LLC. Retrieved from http://www.geometrictools.com/

Ed, S. (2000). *XML Encryption: Issues Regarding Attribute Values and Referenced.* Retrieved from http://www.w3.org/Encryption/2001/Minutes/0103-Boston/simon-attribute-encryption.html

Ed, S. (2001). *Re: attribute encryption, schema validation, role of XSLT, scope of XML encryption document (from XML encryption mailing list).* Academic Press.

Efunda. (2016). *Solids: Centre of Mass.* Available at http://www.efunda.com/math/solids/CenterOfMass.cfm

Emina, S., Liu, R., & Spasojevic, P. (2004). *Hybrid ARQ with Random Transmission Assignments.* Retrieved from http://ect.bell-labs.com/who/emina/papers/hatc.pdf

Ernest, R., & Djaoen, S. (2015). *Introduction to SQL Server Spatial Data.* Retrieved from https://www.simple-talk.com/sql/t-sql-programming/introduction-to-sql-server-spatial-data

Ester, M., Kriegel, H. P., & Sander, J. (1997). Spatial data mining: A database approach. In *Advances in spatial databases* (pp. 47–66). Springer Berlin Heidelberg. doi:10.1007/3-540-63238-7_24

Ester, M., Kriegel, H. P., & Sander, J. (1999). *Knowledge discovery in spatial databases.* Springer Berlin Heidelberg.

Fallside, D. (2001). *XML schema part 0: primer.* W3C Recommendation.

Fallside, D. C., & Walmsley, P. (2004). XML Schema Part 0: Primer Second Edition. W3C Recommendation.

Famili, F. (2009). *Knowledge discovery and management in life sciences: Impacts and challenges.* Paper presented at the Data Mining and Optimization, 2009. DMO '09. 2nd Conference on.

Fan, W., Chan, C., & Garofalakis, M. (2004). Secure XML querying with security views. In *Proceedings of the 2004 ACM SIGMOD international conference on Management of data.* doi:10.1145/1007568.1007634

Fangjun, W. (2010). *Apply Data Mining to Students' Choosing Teachers Under Complete Credit Hour.* Paper presented at the Education Technology and Computer Science (ETCS), 2010 Second International Workshop on.

Fang, Y.-H., & Chiu, C.-M. (2010). In justice we trust: Exploring knowledge-sharing continuance intentions in virtual communities of practice. *Computers in Human Behavior, 26*(2), 235–246. doi:10.1016/j.chb.2009.09.005

Fariha, A., Ahmed, C. F., Leung, C. K.-S., Samiullah, M., Pervin, S., & Cao, L. (2015). A new framework for mining frequent interaction patterns from meeting databases. *Engineering Applications of Artificial Intelligence, 45*, 103–118. doi:10.1016/j.engappai.2015.06.019

Faris, R., & Villeneuve, N. (2008). Measuring global Internet filtering. In R. J. Deibert, J. G. Palfrey, R. Rohozinski, & J. Zittrain (Eds.), *Access Denied: The Practice and Policy of Global Internet Filtering* (pp. 5–27). Cambridge, MA: MIT Press.

Farkas-Conn, I. (1990). *From documentation to information science: The beginning and early development of the American Documentation Institute American Society for Information Science.* New York: Greenwood.

Farkas-Conn, I. S. (1990). *From documentation to information science: The beginnings and early development of the American Documentation Institute.* Westport, CT: Greenwood Press.

Farquhar, A., Fikes, R., & Rice, J. (1996). *The Ontolingua Server: A Tool for Collaborative Ontology Construction.* 10th knowledge acquisition for knowledge-based systems workshop (KAW96), Banff, Canada.

Fayyad, U. M., & Uthurusamy, R. (1996). *Data mining and knowledge discovery in databases.* Academic Press.

Feather, J., & Sturges, P. (2003). International Encyclopedia of Information and Library Science (2nd ed.). New York, NY: Routledge.

Fellbaum, C. (1998). *WordNet: An Electronic Lexical Database.* Cambridge, MA: The MIT Press.

Felten, W., & Halderman, A. (2006). *digital rights management, spyware, and security.* Los Alamitos, CA: IEEE Comput.Soc.

Fernadez-Lopez, M. (1999). Building a chemical ontology using methontology and the ontology design environment. *IEEE Intelligent Systems & their Applications, 4*(1), 37–46. doi:10.1109/5254.747904

Fernadez-Lopez, M., & Gomez-Perez, A. (2002). Overview and analysis of methodologies for building ontologies. *The Knowledge Engineering Review, 17*(2), 129–156.

Fernández-López, M., Gómez-Pérez, A., & Juristo, N. (1997). Methontology: from ontological art towards ontological engineering. *Proceedings of the AAAI97 Spring Symposium Series on Ontological Engineering.*

Fernández-López, M. (1999). *Overview of methodologies for building ontologies.* In *Workshop Ontologies and Problem-Solving Methods: Lessons Learned and Future Trends de la conferencia International Joint Conference for Artificial Intelligence (IJCAI'99)*, Stockholm, Sweden.

Fernando, G. (2009). On the implementation of TCP urgent data. *73rd IETF meeting Gregorio J. URI Templates.* Retrieved from http://bitworking.org/projects/ URI-Templates/

Fielding, R. (2007). A little REST and Relaxation. *The International Conference on Java Technology (JAZOON07)*, Zurich, Switzerland

Firth, J. (1957). A Synopsis of Linguistic Theory, 1930-55. *Studies in Linguistic Analysis, 1952*(59), 168-205.

FIX Protocol Ltd. (n.d.). *FIXML: A markup language for the FIX application message layer. Version 4.4.* Retrieved from http://www.fixprotocol.org/specifications/fix4.4fixml

FIX Protocol Ltd. (n.d.). *The Financial Information Exchange Protocol (FIX), version 5.0.* Retrieved from http://www.fixprotocol.org/specifications/FIX.5.0SP2

FIXML. (n.d.). *FpML Overview of the schema FIXML 4.4.* Retrieved from http://www.fixprotocol.org/specifications/fix4.4fixml

Fluit, C., Sabou, M., & Harmelen, F. V. (2002). *Ontology-based Information Visualisation. In visualisation the semantic web.* Springer, Verlag.

Fortin, M. J., & Dale, M. R. (2009). Spatial autocorrelation in ecological studies: A legacy of solutions and myths. *Geographical Analysis, 41*(4), 392–397. doi:10.1111/j.1538-4632.2009.00766.x

Fox, C. J. (1990). A Stop List for General Text. *ACM Special Interest Group on Information Retrieval Forum, 24*, 19-35.

Fox, M. S. (1992). The Tove project: Towards a common-sense model of the enterprise.Industrial and Engineering Applications of Artificial Intelligence and Expert Systems (pp. 25-34).

Frawley, W. J., Piatetsky-Shapiro, G., & Matheus, C. J. (1991). Knowledge discovery in databases: an overview. In G. Piatetsky-Shapiro & W. J. Frawley (Eds.), *Knowledge discovery in databases* (pp. 1–30). Cambridge, MA: The MIT Press.

Freedom House. (2009). Freedom on the Net: A global assessment of Internet and digital media. *Freedom House.* Retrieved June 30,2013, from http://www.freedomhouse.org/uploads/specialreports/NetFreedom2009/FreedomOn-TheNet_FullReport.pdf

Freeman, H., & Shapira, R. (1975). Determining the minimum-area encasing rectangle for an arbitrary closed curve. *Communications of the ACM, 18*(7), 409–413. doi:10.1145/360881.360919

Fuhr, N., & Weikum, G. (2002). Classification and Intelligent Search on Information in XML. *Bulletin of the IEEE Technical Committee on Data Engineering, 25*, 51–58.

Gaber, M. M., Zaslavsky, A., & Krishnaswamy, S. (2005). Mining data streams: A review. *SIGMOD Record, 34*(2), 18–26. doi:10.1145/1083784.1083789

GADM. (2009). *Global Administrative Areas: Boundaries without limit.* Available at http://www.gadm.org/download

Galindo, J. (2008). *Handbook of Research on Fuzzy Information Processing in Databases.* IGI Global. doi:10.4018/978-1-59904-853-6

Gamess, E., & Suro, R. (2011). An upper bound model for TCP and UDP throughput in IPv4 and IPv6. *Internet Technology and Applications (iTAP),2011 International Conference.*

Ganguly, A. R., & Steinhaeuser, K. (2008). Data mining for climate change and impacts. In ICDM Workshops. doi:10.1109/ICDMW.2008.30

Gaoyun, J., Jianliang, W., & Shaohua, Y. (2010). *A method for consistent ocean ontology construction Industrial and Information Systems.* IIS.

Gartner, N. R. (2006). *Emerging Technologies Hype Cycle Highlights Key Technology Themes.* Academic Press.

Garvin, P. L. (1963). *Natural language and the computer.* New York: McGraw-Hill.

Gauch, S., Madrid, J. M., Induri, S., Ravindran, D., & Chadlavada, S. (2004). *KeyConcept: A Conceptual Search Engine.* University of Kansas.

Gaurav, A., & Alhajj, R. (2006). *Incorporating fuzziness in XML and mapping fuzzy relational data into fuzzy XML.* Paper presented at the 2006 ACM symposium on Applied computing, Dijon, France. doi:10.1145/1141277.1141386

Geneontology. (2009). *Welcome to the Gene Ontology website!* Retrieved from http://www.geneontology.org/

Geuer-Pollmann, C. (2002). *XML pool encryption.* Paper presented at the 2002 ACM workshop on XML security, Fairfax, VA. doi:10.1145/764792.764794

Ghanbari, M. (2007). *Visualization Overview.* Paper presented at the System Theory, 2007. SSST '07. Thirty-Ninth Southeastern Symposium on.

Giao, B. C., & Anh, D. T. (2015). Improving Sort-Tile-Recusive algorithm for R-tree packing in indexing time series. In *Computing & Communication Technologies-Research, Innovation, and Vision for the Future (RIVF), 2015 IEEE RIVF International Conference on* (pp. 117-122). IEEE.

Godik, S., & Moses, T. (2002). *XACML 1.0 - The OASIS extensible Access Control Markup Language (XACML)*. Retrieved from http://www.oasis-open.org/committees/xacml/

Godik, S., & Moses, T. (2003). *eXtensible Access Control Markup Language (XACML) Version 1.0*. Retrieved from http://www.oasis-open.org/committees/xacml/repository/

Golbeck, J., Fragoso, G., Hartel, F., Hendler, J., Oberthaler, J., & Parsia, B. (2008). *The National Cancer Institute's Thesaurus and Ontology*. Retrieved from http://www.mindswap.org/papers/WebSemantics-NCI.pdf

Gómez-Pérez, Juristo, N., & Pazos, J. (1995). *Evaluation and assessment of knowledge sharing Technology. Towards very large knowledge base*. Amsterdam: IOS.

Gómez-Pérez, Juristo, N., & Pazos, J. (1995). *Evaluation and Assessment of knowledge sharing Technology. Towards very large knowledge base*. Amsterdam: IOS.

Gómez-Pérez, A., Corcho, O., & Fernández-López, M. (2003). Methodologies, tools and languages for building ontologies. Where is their meeting point? *Data & Knowledge Engineering, 46*(1), 41–64. doi:10.1016/S0169-023X(02)00195-7

Gòmez-Pérez, A., Fernandez-Lopez, M., & Corcho, O. (2004). *Ontological Engineering:with examples from the areas of knowledge management, e-commerce and the semantic web*. Springer.

Gòmez-Pérez, A., Fernandez-Lopez, M., & Corcho, O. (2004). *Ontological Engineering:with examples from the areas of knowledge management,e-commerce and the semantic web*. Springer.

Gomez, R. (1998). The nostalgia of virtual community: A study of computer- mediated communications use in Colombian non- governmental organisation. *Information Technology & People, 11*(3), 217–234. doi:10.1108/09593849810228020

Gourlay, S. (2002). *Tacit knowledge or behaving?* European Conference on Organizational Knowledge, Athens, Greece.

Grinstein, G., Plaisant, C., Laskowski, S., O'Connell, T., Scholtz, J., & Whiting, M. (2008). VAST 2008 Challenge: introducing mini-challenges. In D. Ebert, & T. Ertl (Eds.), *Proceedings of the 2008 IEEE Symposium on Visual Analytics Science and Technology* (pp. 195-196). Piscataway, NJ: IEEE. doi:10.1109/VAST.2008.4677383

Group, D. S. W. (2008). *The CIDOC Conceptual Reference Model*. Author.

Gruber, T. R. (1993). Toward principles for the design of ontologies used for knowledge sharing. In Formal ontology. Kluwer Academic Publishers.

Guarino, N., & Giaretta, P. (1995). Ontologies and Knowledge Bases: Towards a Terminological Clarification. Amsterdam: Academic Press.

Guarino, N. (1997). Understanding, building and using ontologies. *International Journal of Human-Computer Studies, 46*(2-3), 293–310. doi:10.1006/ijhc.1996.0091

Guarino, N. (1998) Formal Ontology and Information Systems.*Proceedings of FOIS'98*. Trento, Italy: IOS Press.

Guo, G., Wang, H., Bell, D., Bi, Y., & Greer, K. (2006). Using kNN model for automatic text categorization. *Soft Computing, 10*(5), 423–430. doi:10.1007/s00500-005-0503-y

Guruler, H., Istanbullu, A., & Karahasan, M. (2010). A new student performance analysing system using knowledge discovery in higher educational databases. *Computers & Education, 55*(1), 247–254. doi:10.1016/j.compedu.2010.01.010

Guruninger, M., & Fox, M. S. (1995). Methodology for the design and evaluation of ontologies. In *Workshop on Basic ontological issues in knowledge sharing*.

Güting, R. H. (1994). An introduction to spatial database systems. *The VLDB Journal—The International Journal on Very Large Data Bases, 3*(4), 357-399.

Güting, R. H., & Schneider, M. (1993). Realms: A foundation for spatial data types in database systems. In Advances in Spatial Databases (pp. 14-35). Springer Berlin Heidelberg. doi:10.1007/3-540-56869-7_2

Hallam-Baker, P., & Mysore, S. H. (2005). *XML Key Management Specification (XKMS 2.0)*. Retrieved June, 2010, from http://www.w3.org/TR/xkms2/

Hamou, R. M., Amine, A., Lokbani, A. C., & Simonet, M. (2012). *Visualization and clustering by 3D cellular automata: Application to unstructured data*. arXiv preprint arXiv:1211.5766.

Hamou, R. M., Lehireche, A., Lokbani, A. C., & Rahmani, M. (2010b, October). Text clustering by 2D cellular automata based on the N-grams. In *Cryptography and Network Security, Data Mining and Knowledge Discovery, E-Commerce & Its Applications and Embedded Systems (CDEE), 2010 First ACIS International Symposium on* (pp. 271-277). IEEE.

Hamou, R. M., Amine, A., & Lokbani, A. C. (2013a). Study of Sensitive Parameters of PSO Application to Clustering of Texts. *International Journal of Applied Evolutionary Computation, 4*(2), 41–55. doi:10.4018/jaec.2013040104

Hamou, R. M., Amine, A., Rahmouni, A., Lokbani, A. C., & Simonet, M. (2013b). Modeling of Inclusion by Genetic Algorithms: Application to the Beta-Cyclodextrin and Triphenylphosphine. *International Journal of Chemoinformatics and Chemical Engineering, 3*(1), 19–36. doi:10.4018/ijcce.2013010103

Hamou, R. M., Lehireche, A., Lokbani, A. C., & Rahmani, M. (2010a). Representation of textual documents by the approach wordnet and n-grams for the unsupervised classification (clustering) with 2D cellular automata: A comparative study. *Computer and Information Science, 3*(3), 240–255.

Han, J., & Cercone, N. (2000). AViz: A visualization system for discovering numeric association rules. In T. Terano, H. Liu, & A.L.P. Chen (Eds.), *Proceedings of the Fourth Pacific-Asia Conference on Knowledge Discovery and Data Mining* (LNAI), (vol. 1805, pp. 269-280). Heidelberg, Germany: Springer. doi:10.1007/3-540-45571-X_33

Hanbury, A., Kazai, G., Rauber, A., & Fuhr, N. (Eds.). (2015). *Proceedings of the advances in information retrieval, 37th European conference on IR research*. Vienna, Austria: Springer.

Han, J., Cheng, H., Xin, D., & Yan, X. (2007). Frequent pattern mining: Current status and future directions. *Data Mining and Knowledge Discovery, 15*(1), 55–86. doi:10.1007/s10618-006-0059-1

Harms, J., & Holte, R. (2005). Impact of Lossy Links on Performance of Multihop WirelessNetworks. In *Proceedings of the 14th International Conference on Computer Communications and Networks* (pp. 303 - 308). Retrieved from http://www.gont.com.ar/talks/hacklu2009/fgont-hacklu2009-tcp-security.pdf

Hartmann, N. (1952). The new ways of ontology. Chicago: Academic Press.

Head, J. (2009, March 6). Police arrest Thai website editor. *BBC News*. Retrieved June 21,2013, from http://news.bbc.co.uk/mobile/i/bbc_news/asia_pacific/792/79281/story7928159.shtml

Hégaret, P. L., Whitmer, R., & Wood, L. (2005). *Document Object Model (DOM)*. Retrieved from http://www.w3.org/DOM/

Heimerl, F., Han, Q., Koch, S., & Ertl, T. (2016). CiteRivers: Visual analytics of citation patterns. *IEEE Transactions on Visualization and Computer Graphics, 22*(1), 190–199. doi:10.1109/TVCG.2015.2467621 PMID:26529699

Herre, H. (2010). The Ontology of Mereological Systems: A Logical Approach. In Theory and Applications of Ontology: Philosophical Perspectives. London: Springer.

Herrera, F., Herrera-Viedma, E., & Verdegay, J. L. (1996). Direct approach processes in group decision making using linguistic OWA operators. *Fuzzy Sets and Systems*, *79*(2), 175–190. doi:10.1016/0165-0114(95)00162-X

Herrera-Viedma, E., Peis, E., Morales-del-Castillo, J. M., Alonso, S., & Anaya, K. (2007). A fuzzy linguistic model to evaluate the quality of Web sites that store XML documents. *International Journal of Approximate Reasoning*, *46*(1), 226–253. doi:10.1016/j.ijar.2006.12.010

Hilderman, R. J., Liangchun, L., & Hamilton, H. J. (1997). *Data visualization in the DB-Discover system*. Paper presented at the Tools with Artificial Intelligence, 1997. Proceedings., Ninth IEEE International Conference on.

Himberg, J. (1999). *SOM based cluster visualization and its application for false coloring*. Academic Press.

Hinneburg, A., Aggarwal, C. C., & Keim, D. A. (2000). What is the nearest neighbor in high dimensional spaces? In *26th Internat. Conference on Very Large Databases* (pp. 506-515).

Holmes, G., Donkin, A., & Witten, I. H. (1994). *Weka: A machine learning workbench*. Academic Press.

Horridge, M. (2011). A Practical Guide To Building OWL Ontologies Using Protege 4 and CO-ODE Tools. The University Of Manchester.

Horridge, M., & Patel-Schneider, P. F. (2009). OWL 2 Web Ontology Language Manchester Syntax. Academic Press.

Horrocks, I., Patel-Schneider, P., & Van Harmelen, F. (2003). From SHIQ and RDF to OWL: The making of web ontology language. *Web Semantics: Science, Services, and Agents on the World Wide Web*, *1*(1), 7–26. doi:10.1016/j.websem.2003.07.001

Hu, L., & Weng, J. (2010). Geo-ontology integration Based on Category Theory. *International Conference on Computer Design and applications* (ICCDA2010).

Hughes, J., Cantor, S., Hodges, J., Hirsch, F., Mishra, P., Philpott, R., & Maler, E. (2005). *Profiles for the OASIS Security Assertion Markup Language (SAML) V2.0*. Academic Press.

Hunter, D., Cagle, K., Dix, C., & Cable, D. (2001). *Beginning XML* (2nd ed.). Wrox Press.

Husserl, E. (1970). *Logical Investigations*. London: Routledge and Kegan Paul.

Huutunen, S., Vihavainen, A., Du, M., & Yangarber, R. (2012). *Predicting Relevance of Event Extraction for the End User. In Multi-source, Multilingual Information Extraction and Summarization* (pp. 163–176). Berlin, Germany: Springer.

IEEE 1074-2006. (2006). *IEEE Standard for Developing a Software Project Life Cycle Process*. IEEE Computer Society.

IEEE. (1990). IEEE Standard Glossary of Software Engineering Terminology. *IEEE Std 610.12-1990*, 1-84. doi: 10.1109/ieeestd.1990.101064

iLaw. (2010). Situational report on control and censorship of online media, through the use of laws and the imposition of Thai state policies. *iLaw*. Retrieved June 27,2013, from http://www.scribd.com/doc/44962197/Situational-Report-on-Control-and-Censorship-of-Online-Media-through-the-Use-of-Laws-and-the-Imposition-of-Thai-State-Polocies

Imamura, T., Dillaway, B., & Simon, E. (2002). *XML Encryption Syntax and Processing*. Academic Press.

Ingwersen, P. (1992). Information and Information Science in context. *Libri*, *42*(2), 99–153. doi:10.1515/libr.1992.42.2.99

International Business Machines. (1996). IBM Intelligent Miner User's Guide, Version 1 Release 1, SH12-6213-00 edition. Author.

Ioannidis, S., Keromytis, D., Bellovin, M., & Smith, M. (2000). Implementing a Distributed Firewall. In *Proceedings of Computer and Communications Security* (pp. 190–199). CCS.

ISO/IEC11770. (n.d.). *Information technology — Security techniques — Key management*. ISO.

ISO/IEC9798-1. (1997). *Information technology — Security techniques — Entity authentication — Part 1: General*. ISO.

ISO10181-1, I.-T. X. (n.d.). *Information technology — Security Frameworks in Open Systems: Overview*. ISO.

JAB. (2013). *Jordan Ahli Bank*. Retrieved from http://www.ahli.com/

Jacobi, J. (2011). Optimize Your Router for VoIP and Video Streams. *PC World, 29*(3).

Jacobs, P. S. (1992). *Text-based intelligent systems: Current research and practice in information extraction and retrieval*. Hoboken, NJ: Lawrence Erlbaum Associates.

Jagadish, H. V., Ooi, B. C., Vu, Q. H., Zhang, R., & Zhou, A. (2006). Vbi-tree: A peer-to-peer framework for supporting multi-dimensional indexing schemes. In *Data Engineering, 2006. ICDE'06.Proceedings of the 22nd International Conference on* (pp. 34-34). IEEE. doi:10.1109/ICDE.2006.169

Jain, A. K., Murty, M. N., & Flynn, P. J. (1999). Data clustering: A review. *ACM Computing Surveys, 31*(3), 264–323. doi:10.1145/331499.331504

Jansen, W., & Steenbakkers, H. (2002). Knowledge management and virtual communities. In Knowledge mapping and management. IRM Press.

Jansen, B. J., Spink, A., & Saracevic, T. (2000). Real life, real users, and real needs: A study and analysis of user queries on the web. *Information Processing & Management, 36*(2), 207–227. doi:10.1016/S0306-4573(99)00056-4

Jelliffe, R. (2006). *Resource Directory (RDDL) for Schematron 1.5*. Retrieved June 2010, from http://xml.ascc.net/schematron/

Jepsen, T. C. (2009). *Just what is an ontology*. IEEE Computer Society.

Jerrett, M., Burnett, R., Willis, A., Krewski, D., Goldberg, M., DeLuca, P., & Finkelstein, N. (2003). Spatial Analysis of the Air Pollution Mortality Relationship in the Context of Ecologic Confounders. *Journal of Toxicology and Environmental Health. Part A., 66*(16-19), 1735–1778. doi:10.1080/15287390306438 PMID:12959842

Jiang, F., & Leung, C. K.-S. (2015). A data analytic algorithm for managing, querying, and processing uncertain big data in cloud environments. *Algorithms, 8*(4), 1175–1194. doi:10.3390/a8041175

Jiawei-Han, M. K. (2001). *Data Mining: Concepts and Techniques*. Morgan Kaufmann Publishers.

Joachims, T., Granka, L., Pan, B., Hembrooke, H., & Gay, G. (2005). Accurately interpreting clickthrough data as implicit feedback. *Proceedings of the 28th annual international ACM SIGIR conference on Research and development in information retrieval* (pp. 154–161). Retrieved from http://dl.acm.org/citation.cfm?id=1076063

Joseph, R. (2001). *XML Encryption Requirements*. Retrieved November, 2011, from http://www.w3.org/TR/xml-encryption-req

Kabilan, V. (2007). *Ontology for Information Systems (O4IS) Design Methodology: Conceptualizing, Designing and Representing Domain Ontologies. School of Information and Communication Technology, Department of Computer and Systems Sciences.* The Royal Institute of Technology.

Kanungo, T., Mount, D. M., Netanyahu, N. S., Piatko, C. D., Silverman, R., & Wu, A. Y. (2002). An efficient k-means clustering algorithm: Analysis and implementation. *Pattern Analysis and Machine Intelligence. IEEE Transactions on, 24*(7), 881–892.

Katayama, N., & Satoh, S. (2002). Experimental evaluation of disk based data structures for nearest neighbour searching. *AMS DIMACS Series, 59*, 87.

Keim, D. A., Mansmann, F., Schneidewind, J., & Ziegler, H. (2006). Challenges in visual data analysis. In E. Banissi, R.A. Burkhard, A. Ursyn, J.J. Zhang, M. Bannatyne, C. Maple, A.J. Cowell, G.Y. Tian, & M. Hou (Eds.), *Proceedings of the 10th IEEE International Conference on Information Visualisation* (pp. 9-16). Los Alamitos, CA: IEEE Computer Society. doi:10.1109/IV.2006.31

Keim, D. A., Mansmann, F., Schneidewind, J., Thomas, J., & Ziegler, H. (2008). Visual analytics: scope and challenges. In S.J. Simoff, M.H. Böhlen, & A. Mazeika (Eds.), Visual Data Mining: Theory, Techniques and Tools for Visual Analytics (LNCS), (vol. 4404, pp. 76-90). Heidelberg, Germany: Springer. doi:10.1007/978-3-540-71080-6_6

Keim, D. A., & Kriegel, H.-P. (1996). Visualization techniques for mining large databases: A comparison. *IEEE Transactions on Knowledge and Data Engineering, 8*(6), 923–938. doi:10.1109/69.553159

Keim, D. A., Mansmann, F., Stoffel, A., & Ziegler, H. (2009a). Visual analytics. In L. Liu & M. T. Özsu (Eds.), *Encyclopedia of database systems* (pp. 3341–3346). New York: Springer.

Keim, D. A., Mansmann, F., & Thomas, J. (2009b). Visual analytics: How much visualization and how much analytics? *SIGKDD Explorations, 11*(2), 5–8. doi:10.1145/1809400.1809403

Keim, D. A., Qu, H., & Ma, K.-L. (2013). Big-data visualization. *IEEE Computer Graphics and Applications, 33*(4), 20–21. doi:10.1109/MCG.2013.54 PMID:24921095

Kenneth, P., Chen, B., Hopkinson, K., Thomas, R., Thorp, J., Renesse, R., & Vogels, W. (2005). Overcoming Communications Challenges in Software for Monitoring and Controlling Power Systems. *International Conference on Data Engineering.* ICDE.

Kent, C., & Mogul, J. (1995). Fragmentation Considered Harmful. *ACM SIGCOMM Computer Communication Review, 25.*

Kim, S. (2002). A Data Model and Algebra for Document-Centric XML Document. *Information Networking, Wireless Communications Technologies and Network Applications,International Conference.* doi:10.1007/3-540-45801-8_67

King, S. (2003). Threats and Solutions to Web Services Security. *Network Security, 2003*(9), 8–11. doi:10.1016/S1353-4858(03)00907-3

Klang, M. (2006). Social informatics: An information soceity for all? IFIP International Federation for Information Processing, 223, 185-194.

Klarlund, N., Møller, A., & Schwartzbach, M. I. (2000). *DSD: A Schema Language for XML.* Paper presented at the Workshop on Formal Methods in Software Practice, Portland, OR. Retrieved from http://www.brics.dk/DSD/dsd.html

Kleinsteuber, H. J. (2004). The Internet between regulation and governance. In C. Moller & A. Amouroux (Eds.), *The Media Freedom Internet Cookbook* (pp. 61–75). Vienna: Academic Press.

Klir, G. J., & Yuan, B. (1995). *Fuzzy sets and fuzzy logic: theory and applications.* Prentice-Hall, Inc.

Koch, M. (2000). Learning from civilization. *Line Zine*. Retrieved from http://linezine.com/3.1/features/mklic.htm

Kohloff, C., & Steele, R. (2003). *Evaluating SOAP for High Performance Business Applications: Real-Time Trading Systems*. Retrieved from http://www2003.org/cdrom/papers/alternate/P872/p872\kohl

Koren, Y., & Harel, D. (2003). A two-way visualization method for clustered data. In L. Getoor, T.E. Senator, P. Domingos, & C. Faloutsos (Eds.), *Proceedings of the Ninth ACM SIGKDD International Conference on Knowledge Discovery and Data Mining* (pp. 589-594). New York: ACM. doi:10.1145/956750.956824

Koua, E. L. (2005). *Using self-organizing maps for information visualization and knowledge discovery in complex geospatial datasets*. Seminar on Data and Information Management SS 2005 2D, 3D and High-dimensional Data and Information Visualization.

Kouiroukidis, N., & Evangelidis, G. (2011). The effects of dimensionality curse in high dimensional knn search. In *Informatics (PCI), 2011 15th Panhellenic Conference on* (pp. 41-45). IEEE. doi:10.1109/PCI.2011.45

Krivov, S., Villa, F., Williams, R., & Wu, X. (2007a). *On visualization of OWL ontologies*. Semantic Web Springer. doi:10.1007/978-0-387-48438-9_11

Krivov, S., Williams, R., & Villa, F. (2007b). GrOWL: A tool for visualization and editing of OWL ontologies. *Web Semantics: Science, Services, and Agents on the World Wide Web, 5*(2), 54–57. doi:10.1016/j.websem.2007.03.005

Krötzsch, M., Hitzler, P., Ehrig, M., & Sure, Y. (2005). *Category theory in ontology research: Concrete gain from an abstract approach*. Karlsruhe, Germany: Institut AIFB, Universität Karlsruhe.

Kudrass, T. (2002). Management of XML Documents in Object- Relational Databases. In. Lecture Notes in Computer Science: Vol. 2490. *EDBT2002 workshops* (pp. 210–227). Springer-Verlag. doi:10.1007/3-540-36128-6_12

Kumar, A., Kumar, S., & Saxena, S. (2012). An efficient approach for incremental association rule mining through histogram matching technique. *International Journal of Information Retrieval Research, 2*(2), 29–42. doi:10.4018/ijirr.2012040103

Kuo, R. J., An, Y. L., Wang, H. S., & Chung, W. J. (2006). Integration of self-organizing feature maps neural network and genetic K-means algorithm for market segmentation. *Expert Systems with Applications, 30*(2), 313–324. doi:10.1016/j.eswa.2005.07.036

Kurose, F., & Ross, W. (2010). *Computer Networking: A Top-Down Approach* (5th ed.). Boston, MA: Pearson Education.

Kushilevitz, E., Ostrovsky, R., & Rabani, Y. (2000). Efficient search for approximate nearest neighbor in high dimensional spaces. *SIAM Journal on Computing, 30*(2), 457–474. doi:10.1137/S0097539798347177

Lacerda, A., Cristo, M., Goncalves, M. A., Fan, W., Ziviani, N., & Ribeiro-Neto, B. (2006). Learning to advertise. *Proceedings of the 29th annual international ACM SIGIR conference on Research and development in information retrieval* (pp. 549–556). Retrieved from http://dl.acm.org/citation.cfm?id=1148265

Lakshmanan, L. V. S., Leung, C. K.-S., & Ng, R. T. (2003). Efficient dynamic mining of constrained frequent sets. *ACM Transactions on Database Systems, 28*(4), 337–389. doi:10.1145/958942.958944

Lam, S. B. (2007). *Data mining with clustering and classification*. Academic Press.

Larose. (2005). Discovering knowledge in data. Academic Press.

Lau, H., Ng, W., Yang, Y., & Cheng, J. (2006). An efficient Approach to Support Querying Secure Outsourced XML Information. In *Proceedings of the 18th international conference on Advanced Information Systems Engineering*. Springer-Verlag.

Lawvere, W. (1969). Adjointness in foundations. *Dialectica, 23*(3-4), 281–296. doi:10.1111/j.1746-8361.1969.tb01194.x

Lee, J., & Fanjiang, Y.-y. (2003). Modeling imprecise requirements with XML. *Information and Software Technology, 45*(7), 445–460. doi:10.1016/S0950-5849(03)00015-6

Legendre, P. (1993). Spatial autocorrelation: Trouble or new paradigm? *Ecology, 74*(6), 1659–1673. doi:10.2307/1939924

Legendre, P., & Fortin, M. J. (1989). Spatial pattern and ecological analysis. *Vegetatio, 80*(2), 107–138. doi:10.1007/BF00048036

Lehmann, J., Schüppel, J., & Auer, S. (2007). Discovering Unknown Connections - the DBpedia Relationship Finder. CSSWeb'07 Proceedings.

Leimeister, J., Schweizer, K., & Leimeister, S. (2008). Do virtual communities matter for the social support of patients? Antecedents and effects of virtual relationships in online communities. *Information Technology & People, 21*(4), 350–374. doi:10.1108/09593840810919671

Lenat, D., & Guha, R. (1990). *Building Large Knowledge-Based Systems: Representation and Inference in the Cyc Project*. Addison-Wesley.

Leonov, A., & Khusnutdinov, R. R. (2004). Construction of an Optimal Relational Schema for Storing XML Documents in an RDBMS without Using DTD/XML Schema. *Programming and Computer Software, 30*(6), 323–336. doi:10.1023/B:PACS.0000049510.04348.ee

Lessig, L. (1999). *Codes and other laws of cyberspace*. New York: Perseus Book.

Leung, C. K.-S., & Carmichael, C. L. (2011). iVAS: An interactive visual analytics system for frequent set mining. In Q. Zhang, R. Segall, & M. Cao (Eds.), Visual analytics and interactive technologies: Data text, and web mining (pp. 213-231). Hershey, PA: IGI Global. doi:10.4018/978-1-60960-102-7.ch013

Leung, C. K.-S., & Jiang, F. (2012). RadialViz: An orientation-free frequent pattern visualizer. In P.-N. Tan, S. Chawla, C.K. Ho, & J. Bailey (Eds.), *Proceedings of 16th Pacific-Asia Conference on Knowledge Discovery and Data Mining* (LNAI), (vol. 7302, pp. 322-334). Heidelberg, Germany: Springer. doi:10.1007/978-3-642-30220-6_27

Leung, C. K.-S., & Jiang, F. (2015) Big data analytics of social networks for the discovery of "following" patterns. In S. Madria & T. Hara (Eds.), *Proceedings of 17th International Conference on Big Data Analytics and Knowledge Discovery* (LNCS), (vol. 9263, pp. 123-135). Heidelberg, Germany: Springer. doi:10.1007/978-3-319-22729-0_10

Leung, C. K.-S., & Tanbeer, S. K. (2013). PUF-tree: a compact tree structure for frequent pattern mining of uncertain data. In J. Pei, V.S. Tseng, L. Cao, H. Motoda, & G. Xu (Eds.), *Proceedings of the 17th Pacific-Asia Conference on Knowledge Discovery and Data Mining* (LNAI), (vol. 7818, pp. 13-25). Heidelberg, Germany: Springer. doi:10.1007/978-3-642-37453-1_2

Leung, C. K.-S., Irani, P. P., & Carmichael, C. L. (2008a). FIsViz: a frequent itemset visualizer. In T. Washio, E. Suzuki, K.M. Ting, & A. Inokuchi (Eds.), *Proceedings of the 12th Pacific-Asia Conference on Knowledge Discovery and Data Mining* (LNAI), (vol. 5012, pp. 644-652). Heidelberg, Germany: Springer. doi:10.1007/978-3-540-68125-0_60

Leung, C. K.-S., Irani, P. P., & Carmichael, C. L. (2008b). WiFIsViz: effective visualization of frequent itemsets. In F. Giannotti, D. Gunopulos, F. Turini, C. Zaniolo, N. Ramakrishnan, & X. Wu (Eds.), *Proceedings of the Eighth IEEE International Conference on Data Mining* (pp. 875-880). Los Alamitos, CA: IEEE Computer Society. doi:10.1109/ICDM.2008.93

Leung, C. K.-S., Mateo, M. A. F., & Brajczuk, D. A. (2008c). A tree-based approach for frequent pattern mining from uncertain data. In T. Washio, E. Suzuki, K.M. Ting, & A. Inokuchi (Eds.), *Proceedings of the 12th Pacific-Asia Conference on Knowledge Discovery and Data Mining (LNAI 5012,* pp. 653-661). Heidelberg, Germany: Springer. doi:10.1007/978-3-540-68125-0_61

Leung, C.K.-S., Cuzzocrea, A., & Jiang, F. (2013a). Discovering frequent patterns from uncertain data streams with time-fading and landmark models. *LNCS Transactions on Large-Scale Data- and Knowledge-Centered Systems, 8,* 174-196. doi:10.1007/978-3-642-37574-3_8

Leung, C. K.-S. (2009). Constraint-based association rule mining. In J. Wang (Ed.), *Encyclopedia of data warehousing and mining* (2nd ed.; pp. 307–312). Hershey, PA: IGI Global. doi:10.4018/978-1-60566-010-3.ch049

Leung, C. K.-S. (2014). Big data mining and analytics. In J. Wang (Ed.), *Encyclopedia of data business analytics and optimization.* Hershey, PA: IGI Global. doi:10.4018/978-1-4666-5202-6.ch030

Leung, C. K.-S., & Carmichael, C. L. (2009). FpViz: A visualizer for frequent pattern mining. In K. Puolamäki (Ed.), *Proceedings of the ACM SIGKDD Workshop on Visual Analytics and Knowledge Discovery: Integrating Automated Analysis with Interactive Exploration* (pp. 30-39). New York: ACM. doi:10.1145/1562849.1562853

Leung, C. K.-S., Jiang, F., & Irani, P. P. (2011). FpMapViz: a space-filling visualization for frequent patterns. In M. Spiliopoulou, H. Wang, D.J. Cook, J. Pei, W. Wang, O.R. Zaïane, & X. Wu (Eds.), *Workshop Proceedings of 2011 IEEE 11th International Conference on Data Mining* (pp. 804-811). Los Alamitos, CA: IEEE Computer Society. doi:10.1109/ICDMW.2011.86

Leung, C. K.-S., Jiang, F., Pazdor, A. G. M., & Peddle, A. M. (2016a). Parallel social network mining for interesting following patterns. *Concurrency and Computation, 28*(15), 3994–4012. doi:10.1002/cpe.3773

Leung, C. K.-S., Jiang, F., Sun, L., & Wang, Y. (2012). A constrained frequent pattern mining system for handling aggregate constraints. In B.C. Desai, J. Pokorný, & J. Bernardino (Eds.), *Proceedings of the 16th International Database Engineering & Applications Symposium* (pp. 14-23). New York: ACM. doi:10.1145/2351476.2351479

Leung, C. K.-S., Khan, Q. I., Li, Z., & Hoque, T. (2007). CanTree: A canonical-order tree for incremental frequent-pattern mining. *Knowledge and Information Systems, 11*(3), 287–311. doi:10.1007/s10115-006-0032-8

Leung, C. K.-S., MacKinnon, R. K., & Tanbeer, S. K. (2014). Fast algorithms for frequent itemset mining from uncertain data. In R. Kumar, H. Toivonen, J. Pei, J.Z. Huang, & X. Wu (Eds.), *Proceedings of the 14th IEEE International Conference on Data Mining* (pp. 893-898). Los Alamitos, CA: IEEE Computer Society. doi:10.1109/ICDM.2014.146

Leung, C. K.-S., Medina, I. J. M., & Tanbeer, S. K. (2013b). Analyzing social networks to mine important friends. In G. Xu & L. Li (Eds.), *Social media mining and social network analysis: Emerging research* (pp. 90–104). Hershey, PA: IGI Global. doi:10.4018/978-1-4666-2806-9.ch006

Leung, C. K.-S., Tanbeer, S. K., & Cameron, J. J. (2014). Interactive discovery of influential friends from social networks. *Social Network Analysis and Mining, 4*(1), 154. doi:10.1007/s13278-014-0154-z

Leung, C. K.-S., Tanbeer, S. K., Cuzzocrea, A., Braun, P., & MacKinnon, R. K. (2016b). Interactive mining of diverse social entities. *International Journal of Knowledge-based and Intelligent Engineering Systems, 20*(2), 97–111. doi:10.3233/KES-160332

Lifshits, Y., & Zhang, S. (2009). Combinatorial algorithms for nearest neighbors, near-duplicates and small-world design. In *Proc. SODA.* doi:10.1137/1.9781611973068.36

Lin, F.-R., Lin, S.-C., & Huang, T.-P. (2008). Knowledge sharing and creation in a teachers professional virtual community. *Computers & Education*, *50*(3), 742–756. doi:10.1016/j.compedu.2006.07.009

Liu, B., Hsu, W., & Ma, Y. (1998). Integrating Classification and Association Rule Mining. Academic Press.

Liu, G., Suchitra, A., Zhang, H., Feng, M., Ng, S.-K., & Wong, L. (2013). AssocExplorer: an association rule visualization system for exploratory data analysis. In Q. Yang, D. Agarwal, & J. Pei (Eds.), *Proceedings of the 18th ACM SIGKDD International Conference on Knowledge Discovery and Data Mining* (pp. 1536-1539). New York: ACM Press. doi:10.1145/2339530.2339774

Liu, N., Yan, J., Shen, D., Chen, D., Chen, Z., & Li, Y. (2010). Learning to rank audience for behavioral targeting. *Proceedings of the 33rd international ACM SIGIR conference on Research and development in information retrieval* (pp. 719–720). Retrieved from http://dl.acm.org/citation.cfm?id=1835582

Liu, B. (2009). Classification by association rule analysis. In L. Liu & M. T. Özsu (Eds.), *Encyclopedia of database systems* (pp. 335–340). New York: Springer.

Lombardi, V. (2003). *Noise between stations meta data glossary*. Retrieved from http://www.noisebetweenstations.com/personal/essays/metadata_glossary/metadata_glossary.html

Lozano-Tello, A., & Gomez-Perez, A. (2004). ONTOMETRIC: A Method to Choose the Appropriate Ontology. *Journal of Database Management*, *15*(2), 1–18. doi:10.4018/jdm.2004040101

Luhn, H. (1958). The Automatic Creation of Literature Abstracts. *IBM Journal*, 159-165.

Lukasiewicz, T., & Straccia, U. (2008). Managing uncertainty and vagueness in description logics for the Semantic Web. *Web Semantics: Science, Services, and Agents on the World Wide Web*, *6*(4), 291–308. doi:10.1016/j.websem.2008.04.001

Lungu, I., & Velicanu, A. (2009). Spatial Database Technology Used In Developing Geographic Information Systems. *The 9th International Conference on Informatics in Economy – Education, Research & Business Technologies*. Academy of Economic Studies, Bucharest.

Macan-Markar, M. (2009, March 8). Media-Thailand: Police target websites unflattering to royalty. *IPS*. Retrieved July 1, 2013, from http://www.ipsnews.net/news.asp?idnews=46023

Machlup, F., & Mansfield, U. (1983). *The Study of Information*. New York: Wiley.

MacKinnon, R. (2009). Chinas censorship 2.0: How companies censor bloggers. *First Monday*, *14*(2), 2089. doi:10.5210/fm.v14i2.2378

MacQueen, J. (1967, June). Some methods for classification and analysis of multivariate observations. In *Proceedings of the fifth Berkeley symposium on mathematical statistics and probability* (*Vol. 1*, No. 14, pp. 281-297). Academic Press.

Maedche, A. (2003). *Ontology learning for the semantic Web*. Kluwer Academic Publishers.

Maedche, A. D. (2002). *Ontology learning for the semantic web*. Kluwer Academic.

Maedche, A., & Staab, S. (2002a). Measuring Similarity between Ontologies. In *Proceedings of the 13th International Conference on Knowledge Engineering and Knowledge Management*. Springer-Verlag. doi:10.1007/3-540-45810-7_24

Maedche, E., & Staab, S. (2002b). Measuring Similarity between Ontologies. In *Proceedings of the European Conference on Knowledge Acquisition and Management* (EKAW).

Mahant, N. (2004). Risk Assessment is Fuzzy Business—Fuzzy Logic Provides the Way to Assess Off-site Risk from Industrial Installations. Bechtel, Australia. *Risk (Concord, NH)*.

Makoto, M. (2002). *RELAX (Regular Language description for XML)*. Retrieved June 2010, from http://www.xml.gr.jp/relax/

Makoto, M., Walsh, N., & McRae, M. (2001). *TREX and RELAX Unified as RELAX NG, a Lightweight XML Language Validation Specification*. Academic Press.

Mamdani, E. H., & Assilian, S. (1975). An experiment in linguistic synthesis with a fuzzy logic controller. *International Journal of Man-Machine Studies*, *7*(1), 1–13. doi:10.1016/S0020-7373(75)80002-2

Mamoulis, N. (2012). *Spatial data management* (1st ed.). Morgan & Claypool Publishers.

Mannila, H. (1996). *Data mining: machine learning, statistics, and databases*. Paper presented at the Scientific and Statistical Database Systems, 1996. Proceedings., Eighth International Conference on.

Manning, C. D., Raghavan, P., & Schütze, H. (2008). *Introduction to information retrieval*. Cambridge, UK: Cambridge University Press.

Marsden, C. (2004). Co- and self-regulation in European media and Internet sectors: The results of Oxford university's study. In C. Moller & A. Amouroux (Eds.), The Media Freedom Internet Cookbook (pp. 76–100). Vienna: Academic Press. Retrieved from www.selfregulation.info

Martin, G., Dimitris, A., & Roland, W. (1998). Cost-efficient network synthesis from leased lines. *Annals of Operations Research, 76*, 1-20.

Martin, P., & Turner, B. (1986). Grounded Theory and Organizational Research. *The Journal of Applied Behavioral Science, 22*(2), 141–157. doi:10.1177/002188638602200207

Maruyama, H., & Imamura, T. (2000). *Element-Wise XML Encryption*. Retrieved February 2008, from http://lists.w3.org/Archives/Public/xml-encryption/2000Apr/att-0005/01-xmlenc

Ma, Z. M., & Yan, L. (2007). Fuzzy XML data modeling with the UML and relational data models. *Data & Knowledge Engineering, 63*(3), 972–996. doi:10.1016/j.datak.2007.06.003

Mazurczyk, W., & Szczypiorski, K. (2009). *Cryptography and Security*. Retrieved from http://arxiv.org/abs/1006.0495

McCallum, A., & Nigam, K. (1998). *A comparison of event models for Naive Bayes text classification*. Academic Press.

McCallum, A., Nigam, K., & Ungar, L. H. (2000, August). Efficient clustering of high-dimensional data sets with application to reference matching. In *Proceedings of the sixth ACM SIGKDD international conference on Knowledge discovery and data mining* (pp. 169-178). ACM. doi:10.1145/347090.347123

Mccarthy, J. (1980). Circumscription- A form of Non-Monotonic Reasoning. *Artificial Intelligence, 5*(1-2), 27–39. doi:10.1016/0004-3702(80)90011-9

Mcdermott, R. (1999). *Nurturing three dimensional cops: How to get the most out of human networks*. Retrieved from http://home.att.net/~discon/KM/Dimensions.pdf

McHugh, J., & Widom, J. (1999). Query Optimization for XML. In *Proceedings 25th International Conference on Very Large Databases*. Morgan Kaufmann.

Mciiwaine, I., & Broughton, V. (2000). The classification Research Group: Then and now. *Knowledge Organization, 27*, 195–199.

Mclaughlin, B., & Edelson, J. (2006). *Java and XML* (3rd ed.). O'Reilly.

Megan Meier Cyberbullying Prevention Act (2009). H.R. 1966, 111th Congress.

Meng, Z., & Lu, J. (2013). Integrating technical advance in mobile devices to enhance the information retrieval in mobile learning. *International Journal of Information Retrieval Research*, *3*(3), 1–25. doi:10.4018/ijirr.2013070101

Merrill, G. H. (2011). Ontology, ontologies, and science. Humanities. *Social Sciences and Law*, *30*, 71–83.

Mierle, K., K., L., Roweis, S., & Wilson, G. (2005). *Mining student CVS repositories for performance indicators*. Academic Press.

Miklau, G. (2006). *The XML data repository*. Retrieved from http://www.cs.washington.edu/research/xmldatasets/

Miksa, F. L. (1998). The DCC, the universe of knowledge, and the post- modern library. Albany, NY: Forest Press.

Mills, H., & Hevner, A. R. (1995). Box-structured requirements determination methods.Decision Support Systems, *13*, 223-239.

Mitchell, T. M. (1997). *Machine Learning*. Academic Press.

Mizoguchi, R. (2003). Tutorial on ontological engineering. *New Generation Computing*, *21*(4), 363–384. doi:10.1007/BF03037310

Moens, M.-F. (2006). *Information Extraction: Algorithms and prospects in a retrieval context*. Springer.

Mohamed, A. H., Lee, S. P., & Salim, S. S. (2006). Managing Evolution in Software-Engineering Knowledge Management Systems Digital. *Information & Management*, *3*, 19–24.

Mohammad, S. (2008). *Measuring Semantic Distance Using Distributional Profiles of Concepts*. Toronto, Canada: University of Toronto.

Mohammad, S., & Hirst, G. (2006). *Measuring semantic distance, using distributional profiles of concepts*. New York: Association for Computational Linguistics.

Moller, A. (2005, December). *Document Structure Description 2.0*. Academic Press.

Möller, B., & Löf, S. (2009). *A Management Overview of the HLA Evolved Web Service API*. Retrieved from http://www.pitch.se/images/06f-siw-024.pdf

Mommers, L. (2010). Ontologies in the Legal Domain. In Theory and Applications of Ontology: Philosophical Perspectives. London: Springer.

Morbach, J., Wiesner, A., & Marquardt, W. (2009). OntoCAPEis a large–scale ontology for chemical process engineering. Engineering Applications of Artificial Intelligence. *Computers & Chemical Engineering*, *20*, 147–161.

Mosley, R. C. (2010). *Handling High Dimensional Variables*. Pinnacle Actuarial Resources, Inc.

MSEB. (2010). *Mathematical Science Education Board*. Retrieved from http://www7.nationalacademies.org/mseb/

Muller, E., Gunnemann, S., Assent, & Seidl, T. (2009). Evaluating Clustering in Subspace Projections of High Dimensional Data. *VLDB '09*. Lyon, France: VLDB Endowment.

Munzer, T., Kong, Q., Ng, R. T., Lee, J., Klawe, J., Radulovic, D., & Leung, C. K.-S. (2005). *Visual mining of power sets with large alphabets (Tech. rep. UBC CS TR-2005-25)*. Vancouver, BC, Canada: The University of British Columbia.

Murillo-Othon. (2006). *Searching for Virtual Communities of Practice in the discussion network*. Bradford.

Murphy, D., & Heffernan, D. (2003). *Assembly Automation*. Academic Press.

Ng, H. T., Goh, W. B., & Low, K. L. (1997). Feature selection, perceptron learning, and a usability case study for text categorization. *SIGIR Forum, 31*(SI), 67-73. doi:10.1145/278459.258537

Nicolae, D. (1961). *Information Science Syllabus and Teaching Practice within the Higher Education.* Georgia Institute of Technology.

Nielsen Norman Group. (2006, April 17). *F-Shaped Pattern For Reading Web Content.* Retrieved from Nielsen Norman Group: http://www.nngroup.com/articles/f-shaped-pattern-reading-Web-content/

Nielsen Norman Group. (2008, May 6). *How Little Do Users Read?* Retrieved from Nielsen Norman Group: http://www.nngroup.com/articles/how-little-do-users-read/

Nierman, A., & Jagadish, H. V. (2002). ProTDB: Probabilistic data in XML. In *Proceedings of the 28th VLDB Conference* (pp. 646-657). Springer.

Nirenburg, S., & Raskin, V. (2001). Ontological semantics, formal ontology and ambiguity. *Proceedings of FOIS.*

Nirenburg, S., & Raskin, V. (2004). *Ontological semantics.* Cambridge, MA: MIT Press.

Nonaka, I. (1995). *The knowledge creating company: how Japanese companies create the dynamics of innovation.* New York: Oxford University Press.

Nonaka, I., & Konno, N. (1998). The concept of Ba: Building a Foundation for Knowledge Creation. *California Management Review.*

Novak, L., & Zamulin, A. (2005). Algebraic Semantics of XML Schema. *LNCS, 3631,* 209–222.

Noy, N. F., & Mcguinness, D. L. (2001). *Ontology Development 101: A Guide to Creating Your First Ontology.* Retrieved from http://liris.cnrs.fr/alain.mille/enseignements/Ecole_Centrale/What%20is%20an%20ontology%20and%20why%20we%20need%20it.htm

Noy, N. F., & Musen, M. A. (2000). *PROMPT: Algorithems and tools for automated ontology merging and alignment.* 17th National Conference on Artificial Intelligence (AAAI'00), Austin, TX.

Noy, N. F. (2004). Semantic Integration: A Survey Of Ontology-Based Approaches. *SIGMOD Record, 33*(4), 65–70. doi:10.1145/1041410.1041421

O'Hara, K., Alani, H., & Shadbolt, N. (2002). ONTOCOPI: Methods and Tools for Identifying Communities of Practice. In *IFIP 17th World Computer Congress - TC12 Stream on Intelligent Information Processing.* Retrieved from http://eprints.ecs.soton.ac.uk/6521/

OASIS. S. S. T. C. o. (2002). *Oasis security services (saml).* Retrieved October 2010, from http://www.oasis-open.org/committees/security/

OCLC. (2010). *Dewey Decimal Classification (DDC) system.* Retrieved from http://www.oclc.org/dewey/versions/ddc22print/intro.pdf

Ogden, C. K., Richards, I. A., Malinowski, Bronislaw, & Corookshank, F. G. (1949). The meaning of meaning: a study of the influence of language upon thought and of the science of symbolism. London: Routledge & Kegan Paul.

Olovsson, T., & John, W. (2008). Detection of malicious traffic on back-bone links via packet header analysis. *Campus-Wide Information Systems, 25*(5), 342 – 358.

O'Neill, M. (2003). Web Services Security. McGraw-Hill Osborne Media.

Ong, C. S. (2000). *Knowledge discovery in databases: An information retrieval perspective.* Academic Press.

OpenNet Initiative. (n.d.). *About filtering.* Retrieved June 15,2013, from http://opennet.net/about-filtering

Ortega, F. B. (2008). *Managing Vagueness in Ontologies* (PhD Dissertation). University of Granada, Spain.

Paithankar, R., & Tidke, B. (2015). *A H-K Clustering Algorithm for High Dimensional Data Using Ensemble Learning.* arXiv preprint arXiv:1501.02431

Panteli, N., & Duncan, E. (2004). Trust and Temporary Virtual Teams: Alternative explanations dramaturgical relationships. *Information Technology & People, 17*(4), 423–441. doi:10.1108/09593840410570276

Papadias, D., Zhang, J., Mamoulis, N., & Tao, Y. (2003). Query processing in spatial network databases. In *Proceedings of the 29th international conference on Very large data bases* (vol. 29, pp. 802-813). VLDB Endowment.

Parsons, L., Haque, E., & Liu, H. (2004). Subspace clustering for high dimensional data: A review. *ACM SIGKDD Explorations Newsletter, 6*(1), 90–105. doi:10.1145/1007730.1007731

Pasquier, N., Bastide, Y., Taouil, R., & Lakhal, L. (1999). Discovering frequent closed itemsets for association rules. In C. Beeri & P. Buneman (Eds.), *Proceedings of the Seventh International Conference on Database Theory* (LNCS), (vol. 1540, pp. 398-416). Heidelberg, Germany: Springer. doi:10.1007/3-540-49257-7_25

Pass, G., Chowdhury, A., & Torgeson, C. (2006). A picture of search. *Proceedings of the 1st international conference on Scalable information systems* (p. 1). Retrieved from http://citeseerx.ist.psu.edu/viewdoc/download?doi=10.1.1.92.3074&rep=rep1&type=pdf

Patel, P., & Garg, D. (2012). *Comparison of Advance Tree Data Structures.* arXiv preprint arXiv:1209.6495.

Pattuelli, M. C. (2011). Modeling a domain ontology for cultural heritage resources: A user-centered approach. *Journal of the American Society for Information Science and Technology, 62*(2), 314–342. doi:10.1002/asi.21453

Paul, E. B. (2008). Point access method. In *Dictionary of Algorithms and Data Structures.* Available from: http://www.nist.gov/dads/HTML/pointAccessMethod.html

Pautasso, C., Zimmermann, O., & Leymann, F. (2008). RESTful Web Services vs. Big Web Services: Making the Right Architectural Decision. *17th International World Wide Web Conference,*Beijing, China. doi:10.1145/1367497.1367606

Pazzani, M. J. (2000). Knowledge discovery from data? *Intelligent Systems and their Applications, IEEE, 15*(2), 10-12.

Pei, J., Han, J., Mortazavi-Asl, B., & Zhu, H. (2000). Mining access patterns efficiently from web logs. In T. Terano, H. Liu, & A.L.P. Chen (Eds.), *Proceedings of the Fourth Pacific-Asia Conference on Knowledge Discovery and Data Mining* (LNAI), (vol. 1805, pp. 396-407). Heidelberg, Germany: Springer. doi:10.1007/3-540-45571-X_47

Perez, A., Zarate, V., Montes, A., & Garcia, C. (2006). Quality of Service Analysis of IPSec VPNs for Voice and Video Traffic. *Telecommunications, 2006. AICT-ICIW '06.International Conference on Internet and Web Applications and Services/Advanced International Conference.* doi:10.1109/AICT-ICIW.2006.157

Perez-Soltero, A., Sanchez-Schmitz, G., Barcelo-Valenzuela, M., Palma-Mendez, J. T., & Martin-Rubio, F. (2006). Ontologies as Strategy to Represent Knowledge Audit Outcomes. *International Journal of Technology Knowledge in Society, 2*, 43–53.

Petersen, T. (1994). *Art & architecture thesaurus.* New York: Oxford University Press. Retrieved fromhttp://www.getty.edu/research/tools/vocabularies/index.html

Peterson, L., & Davie, B. (2000). Computer Networks: A Systems Approach. Morgan Kaufmann.

Petrovic, D., Roy, R., & Petrovic, R. (1999). Supply chain modelling using fuzzy sets. *International Journal of Production Economics*, *59*(1–3), 443–453. doi:10.1016/S0925-5273(98)00109-1

Phillip, M. H.-B., & Ford, W. (2001). *XML Key Management Specification (XKMS)*. Retrieved from http://www10.org/cdrom/posters/1129.pdf

Pinto, H., & Martins, J. (2001). *A methodology for ontology integration*. International Conference on Knowledge CaptureK-CAP'01 Victoria, British Canada.

Pinto, H., & Martins, J. (2001). *A methodology for ontology integration*. International Conference on Knowledge CaptureK-CAP'01, Victoria, Canada.

Polanyi, M. (1974). *Personal knowledge: toward a past-critical philosophy*. Chicago: The University of Chicago Press.

Poli, R. (2010). Ontology: The Categorial Stance. In *Theory and Applications of Ontology: Philosophical Perspectives*. London: Springer.

Popoviciu, C., Levy-Abegnoli, E., & Grossetete, P. (2006). *Deploying IPv6 networks* (1st ed.). Cisco Press.

Porra, J., & Parks, M. M. (2006). *Sustainable virtual communities: Suggestions from the colonial model*. Springer-Verlag.

Porzel, R., & Malaka, R. (2004). A Task-based Approach for Ontology Evaluation. In *Proc. of ECAI 2004 Workshop on Ontology Learning and Population*.

Power, D. J. (2000). *The decision support system glossary*. Retrieved from http://dssresources.com/glossary/

Pressman, R. (2009). Software Engineering: A Practitioner's Approach (7th ed.). McGraw-Hill.

Prieto-Diaz, R. (2003). A faceted approach to building ontologies Information Reuse and Integration IRI 2003. *IEEE International Conference*.

PROTÉGÉ. (2011a). *Welcome to Protégé*. Retrieved from http://protege.stanford.edu/doc/faq.html

PROTÉGÉ. (2011b). *What is protégé?* Retrieved from http://protege.stanford.edu/overview/

Qi, Y. (2013). Text mining in bioinformatics: Research and application. *International Journal of Information Retrieval Research*, *3*(2), 30–39. doi:10.4018/ijirr.2013040102

Quinlan, J. R. (1979). *Discovering rules from large collections of examples: a case study*. Academic Press.

Quinlan, J. R. (1998). *Data Mining Tools see5 and c5*. Academic Press.

Quinlan, J. R. (1986). Induction of Decision Trees. *Machine Learning*, *1*(1), 81–106. doi:10.1007/BF00116251

Quinlan, J. R. (1996). Improved Use of Continuous Attributes in C4.5. *Journal of Artificial Intelligence Research*, *4*, 77–90.

Rabhi, F., & Benatallah, B. (2002). An integrated service architecture for managing capital market systems. *IEEE Network*, *16*(1), 15–19. doi:10.1109/65.980540

Ramakrishnan, R., & Gehrke, J. (2003). *Database management systems* (3rd ed.). New York: McGraw-Hill.

Ranganathan, S. R. (1962). *Elements of library classification New York*. Asia Publishing House.

Ratnaparkhi, A. (1992). Finding predictive search queries for behavioral targeting. *Training, 10*(27,920,032,253), 27–920.

Ray, E. T. (2003). *Learning XML - creating self-describing data: cover schemas* (2nd ed.). O'Reilly.

Reporters Without Borders. (2005, September 6). Information supplied by Yahoo! Helped journalist Shi Tao get 10 years in prison. *Reporter Without Borders*. Retrieved June 17,2013, from http://www.rsf.org/article.php3?id_article=14884

RFC 2460. (1998). *Internet Protocol, Version 6 (IPv6) Specification*. Author.

Rigaux, P., Scholl, M., & Voisard, A. (2003). Spatial Databases with Application to GIS. *SIGMOD Record, 32*(4), 111.

Rittinghouse, J., & Ransome, J. (2009). *Cloud Computing: Implementation, Management, and Security*. doi:10.1201/9781439806814

Rivest, R. L., Shamir, A., & Adleman, L. (1978). A method for obtaining digital signatures and public-key cryptosystems. *Communications of the ACM, 21*(2), 120–126. doi:10.1145/359340.359342

Rizzolo, F., & Mendelzon, A. (2001). *Indexing XML Data with ToXin*. WebDB.

Roberts, J. (2000). From know-how to show-how? Questioning the role of information and communications technologies in knowledge transfer. *Technology Analysis and Strategic Management, 12*(4), 429–443. doi:10.1080/713698499

Roberts, J. (2006). Limits to Communities of Practice. *Journal of Management Studies, 43*(3), 624–639. doi:10.1111/j.1467-6486.2006.00618.x

Robie, J. (1998). *XML Query Language (XQL) online*. Available from http://www.w3.org/TandS/QL/QL98/pp/xql.html

Rosario, R. (2001). *Secure XML An Overview of XML Encryption*. Academic Press.

Rosasco, N., & Larochelle, D. (2003). *How and Why More Secure Technologies Succeed in Legacy Markets: Lessons from the Success of SSH*. Dept. of Computer Science, Univ. of Virginia. Retrieved from http://www.cs.virginia.edu/~drl7x/sshVsTelnetWeb3.pdf

Rossi, J. P., & Quénéhervé, P. (1998). Relating species density to environmental variables in presence of spatial autocorrelation: A study case on soil nematodes distribution. *Ecography, 21*(2), 117–123. doi:10.1111/j.1600-0587.1998.tb00665.x

Rubenstein, H., & Goodenough, J. (1965, October). Contextual Correlates of Synonymy. *Communications of the ACM, 8*(10), 627–633. doi:10.1145/365628.365657

Rumsfeld, D. (2002). *News Transcript: DoD News Briefing*. Washington, DC: U.S. Department of Defence.

Sabou, M., Wore, C., Goble, C., & Mishne, G. (2005). Learning domain ontologies for web service descriptions; an experiment in bioinformatics. IEEE Computer Society.

Sabou, M., Wore, C., Goble, C., & Mishne, G. (2005). Learning domain ontologies for web service descriptions; an experiment in bioinformatics. www2005, China, Japan.

Sağlam, B., Salman, F. S., Sayın, S., & Türkay, M. (2006). A mixed-integer programming approach to the clustering problem with an application in customer segmentation. *European Journal of Operational Research, 173*(3), 866–879. doi:10.1016/j.ejor.2005.04.048

Sahami, M., Dumais, S., Heckerman, D., & Horvitz, E. (1998, July). A Bayesian approach to filtering junk e-mail. In *Learning for Text Categorization:Papers from the 1998 workshop* (Vol. 62, pp. 98-105). Academic Press.

Salazar, A., Gosalbez, J., Bosch, I., Miralles, R., & Vergara, L. (2004). *A case study of knowledge discovery on academic achievement, student desertion and student retention*. Paper presented at the Information Technology: Research and Education, 2004. ITRE 2004. 2nd International Conference on.

Salton, G., & Buckley, C. (1988). Term-weighting approaches in automatic text retrieval. *Information Processing & Management, 24*(5), 513–523. doi:10.1016/0306-4573(88)90021-0

Samet, H. (2010, December). Sorting in space: multidimensional, spatial, and metric data structures for computer graphics applications. In ACM SIGGRAPH ASIA 2010 Courses (p. 3). ACM. doi:10.1145/1900520.1900523

Samet, H. (1995). *Spatial data structures, Modern database systems: the object model, interoperability, and beyond.* New York, NY: ACM Press/Addison-Wesley Publishing Co.

Samet, H. (2006). *Foundations of Multidimensional and Metric Data Structures*. Morgan Kaufmann.

Samet, H. (2009). Sorting spatial data by spatial occupancy. In *GeoSpatial Visual Analytics* (pp. 31–43). Springer Netherlands.

Samson, G. L., Lu, J., Wang, L., & Wilson, D. (2013). An approach for mining complex spatial dataset. *Proceeding of Int'l Conference on Information and Knowledge Engineering.* Retrieved from http://worldcompproceedings.com/proc/proc2013/ike/IKE_Papers.pdf

Samson, G. L., Lu, J., & Showole, A. A. (2014). Mining Complex Spatial Patterns: Issues and Techniques. *Journal of Information & Knowledge Management, 13*(02), 1450019. doi:10.1142/S0219649214500191

Saraee, M. H., & Theodoulidis, B. (1995). *Knowledge discovery in temporal databases.* Paper presented at the Knowledge Discovery in Databases, IEE Colloquium on (Digest No. 1995/021 (A)).

Sawsaa, A., & Lu, J. (2011) Extracting Information Science concepts based on Jape Regular Expression. In *The 2011 World Congress in Computer Science, Computer Engineering, and Applied Computing.* Las Vegas, NV: IEEE.

Sawsaa, A., & Lu, J. (2010). Ontocop: A virtual community of practice to create ontology of Information science.*International Conference on Internet Computing (ICOMP'10).*

Schaffer, D. (2011). Network security in the Automation world. *InTech, 58*(2).

Schneider, M. (1997). Spatial Data Types for Database Systems - Finite Resolution Geometry for Geographic information systems. *LNCS, 1288.*

Schneider, M. (1999). Spatial Data Types: Conceptual Foundation for the Design and Implementation of Spatial Database Systems and GIS. In *Proceedings of 6th International Symposium on Spatial Databases.*

Schreck, T., Bernard, J., Tekušová, T., & Kohlhammer, J. (2008). Visual cluster analysis of trajectory data with interactive Kohonen Maps. In D. Ebert, & T. Ertl (Eds.), *Proceedings of the 2008 IEEE Symposium on Visual Analytics Science and Technology* (pp. 3-10). Piscataway, NJ: IEEE. doi:10.1109/VAST.2008.4677350

Schreck, T., & Keim, D. (2013). Visual analysis of social media data. *IEEE Computer, 46*(5), 68–75. doi:10.1109/MC.2012.430

Sedova, M., Jaroszewski, L., & Godzik, A. (2016). Protael: Protein data visualization library for the web. *Bioinformatics (Oxford, England), 32*(4), 602–604. doi:10.1093/bioinformatics/btv605 PMID:26515826

Serrão, C., Dias, M., & Delgado, J. (2006). *Bringing DRM Interoperability to Digital Content Rendering Applications.* DOI: 10.1007/1-4020-5261-8_50

Shadbolt, N., & Milton, N. (1999). From knowledge Engineering to knowledge management. *British Journal of Management, 10*(4), 309–322. doi:10.1111/1467-8551.00141

Shafer, G. (1976). *A Mathematical Theory of Evidence.* Princeton, NJ: Princeton University Press.

Shannon, C. E. (1948). A note on the concept of entropy. *The Bell System Technical Journal, 27,* 379–423. doi:10.1002/j.1538-7305.1948.tb01338.x

Shekhar, S., & Chawla, S. (2003). Spatial databases: A tour. Upper Saddle River, NJ: Prentice Hall.

Shekhar, S., Chawla, S., Ravada, S., Fetterer, A., Liu, X., & Lu, C. (1999). Spatial Databases - Accomplishments and Research Needs. *IEEE Transactions on Knowledge and Data Engineering, 11*(1), 45–55. doi:10.1109/69.755614

Shekhar, S., Evans, M. R., Kang, J. M., & Mohan, P. (2011). Identifying patterns in spatial information: A survey of methods. *Wiley Interdisciplinary Reviews: Data Mining and Knowledge Discovery, 1*(3), 193–214.

Shera, J. H. (1983). Librarianship and information science. In The Study of Information. New York: Wiley.

Shera, J. H., & Cleveland, D. (1977). The history and foundation of information science. *Annual Review of Information Science & Technology*, 250–275.

Shiau, W., Li, Y., Chao, H., & Hsu, P. (2006). Evaluating IPv6 on a large-scale network. *Computer Communications, 29*(16), 3113–21.

Shneiderman, B. (1996). The eyes have it: A task by data type taxonomy for information visualizations. In *Proceedings of the 1996 IEEE Symposium on Visual Languages* (pp. 336-343). Los Alamitos, CA: IEEE Computer Society. doi:10.1109/VL.1996.545307

Siau, K., Nah, F. F.-H., Mennecke, B. E., & Schiller, S. Z. (2010). Co-creation and collaboration in a virtual world: A 3D visualization design project in second life. *Journal of Database Management, 21*(4), 1–13. doi:10.4018/jdm.2010100101

Singh, S. P., & Singh, P. (2014). Modelling a Geo-Spatial Database for Managing Travelers 'demand. *International Journal of Database Management Systems, 6*(2), 3–47. doi:10.5121/ijdms.2014.6203

Siraj, F., & Abdoulha, M. A. (2009). *Uncovering Hidden Information Within University's Student Enrollment Data Using Data Mining*. Paper presented at the Modelling & Simulation, 2009. AMS '09. Third Asia International Conference on. doi:10.1109/AMS.2009.117

Smets, P. (1996). *Imperfect Information: Imprecision and Uncertainty*. Uncertainty Management in Information Systems.

Smith, B. (2003). *Ontology and Information Systems*. Oxford Blackwell. Retrieved from http://ontology.buffalo.edu/ontology(PIC).pdf

Sowa, J. (2005). Distinction, combination, and constraints. *Proceeding of IJCAI-95 workshop on basic ontological issue in knowledge sharing*.

Sowa, J. F. (1984). *Conceptual Structures: Information Processing in Mind and Machine*. Addison-Wesley.

Sowa, J. F. (2000). *Knowledge Representation: Logical, Philosophical, and Computational Foundations*. Pacific Grove, CA: Brooks Cole Publishing Co.Retrieved fromhttp://www.jfsowa.com/krbook/

Spink, A., Ozmutlu, S., Ozmutlu, H. C., & Jansen, B. J. (2002). US versus European Web searching trends (Vol. 36). ACM SIGIR Forum. Retrieved from http://dl.acm.org/citation.cfm?id=792555

Staken, K. (2001). *Introduction to Native XML Database*. Available from: http://www.xml.com/lpt/a/2001/10/31/nativexmldb.html

Stanton, R. (2005). Securing VPNs: comparing SSL and IPsec. *Computer Fraud & Security*, (9), 17-19.

Steinbach, M., Ertöz, L., & Kumar, V. (2004). The challenges of clustering high dimensional data. In *New directions in statistical physics* (pp. 273–309). Springer Berlin Heidelberg. doi:10.1007/978-3-662-08968-2_16

Steve, W. (2001). *Re: attribute encryption (from XML encryption mailing list)*. Academic Press.

Stewart, T. (1997). *The invisible key to success*. Fortune.

Stolte, C., Tang, D., & Hanrahan, P. (2002). Query, analysis, and visualization of hierarchically structured data using Polaris. In D. Hand, D. Keim, & R. Ng (Eds.), *Proceedings of the Eighth ACM SIGKDD International Conference on Knowledge Discovery and Data Mining* (pp. 112-122). New York: ACM. doi:10.1145/775047.775064

Stonebraker, M., Rowe, L. A., Lindsay, B. G., Gray, J., Carey, M. J., Brodie, M. L., & Beech, D. et al. (1990). Third-generation database system manifesto. *SIGMOD Record, 19*(3), 31–44. doi:10.1145/101077.390001

Stonier, T. (1990). *Information and the internal structure of the universe: An exploration into information physics*. Springer. doi:10.1007/978-1-4471-3265-3

Sugeno, M. (1985). An introductory survey of fuzzy control. *Information Sciences, 36*(1-2), 59–83. doi:10.1016/0020-0255(85)90026-X

Sure, Y., Erdmann, M., Angele, J., Staab, S., Studer, R., & Wenke, D. (2002). *OntoEdite: collaborative ontology engineering for the semantic web.First International Semantic Web Conference (ISWC'02)*, Sardinia, Italy.

Sure, Y., Staab, S., & Suder, R. (2008). *Ontology Engineering Methodology*. Springer.

Swartout, B. E. A. (1997). Toward distributed use of large -scale ontologies.*AAAI Symposium on Ontology Engineering Stanford*.

Takeshi, I., & Hiroshi, M. (2000). *Specification of element-wise XML encryption*. Retrieved from http://lists.w3.org/Archives/Public/xml-encryption/2000Aug/att-0005/01-xmlenc-spec.html

Tan, S. (2006). Introduction to Data Mining. Academic Press.

TAPPEDIN. (2010). *Community of educational domain*. Retrieved from http://tappedin.org/tappedin/

Tennant, N. (2007). Parts, Classes and Parts of Classes: An Anti-Realist Reading of Lewisian Mereology. The SAC Conference on David Lewis's Contributions to Formal Philosophy, Copenhagen, Denmark.

Thomas, J. J., & Cook, K. A. (Eds.). (2005). *Illuminating the path: the research and development agenda for visual analytics*. Los Alamitos, CA: IEEE Computer Society.

Thornycroft, P. (2010). *Moving communications into the cloud*. Retrieved from http://agentsandbrokers.phoneplusmag.com/articles/moving-communications-into-thecloud.html

Thrysoe, L., Hounsgaard, L., Dohn, N. B., & Wenger, L. (2010). Participating in a community of practice as a prerquisite for becoming a nurse- Trajectories as final year nursing students. *Nurse Education in Practice, 10*(6), 361–366. doi:10.1016/j.nepr.2010.05.004 PMID:20937575

Tifous, A., Adil, E., & Rose, D. (2007). Ontology for supporting communities of practice. *Proceedings of the 4th International Conference on Knowledge Capture*. Retrieved from http://dl.acm.org/citation.cfm?id=1298415

Tillett, B. (2004). *FRBR: A Conceptual Model for the Bibliographic Universe*. Library of Congress Cataloging Distribution Service.

Tong, Y., Chen, L., & Ding, B. (2012). Discovering threshold-based frequent closed itemsets over probabilistic data. In A. Kementsietsidis, M. Antonio, & V. Salles (Eds.), *Proceedings of the IEEE 28th International Conference on Data Engineering* (pp. 270-281). Los Alamitos, CA: IEEE Computer Society. doi:10.1109/ICDE.2012.51

Torisawa, K., De Saeger, S., Kazama, J., Sumida, A., Noguchi, D., Kakizawa, Y., & Yamada, I. et al. (2010). Organizing the Webs Information Explosion to Discover Unknown Unknowns. *New Generation Computing*, *28*(3), 217–236. doi:10.1007/s00354-009-0087-7

Trombert-Paviot, B., Rodrigues, J., Rogers, J., & Baud, R. (2002). GALEN: A Third Generation Terminology Tool to support multipurpose National Coding System for surgical procedures. *International Journal of Medical Informatics*, *58*, 71–85. PMID:10978911

Tsai, P. S. M., & Chen, C.-M. (2001). Discovering knowledge from large databases using prestored information. *Information Systems*, *26*(1), 1–14. doi:10.1016/S0306-4379(01)00006-0

Tseng, C., Khamisy, W., & Vu, T. (2005). Universal fuzzy system representation with XML. *Computer Standards & Interfaces*, *28*(2), 218–230. doi:10.1016/j.csi.2004.11.005

Tsui, E., Wang, W. M., Cheung, C. F., & Lau, A. S. M. (2009). A concept-relationship acquisition and inference approach for hierarchical taxonomy construction from tags. *Information Processing & Management*, *46*(1), 44–57. doi:10.1016/j.ipm.2009.05.009

Tudorache, T. (2011). WebProtégé: A Collaborative Ontology Editor and Knowledge Acquisition Tool for the Web. *Semantic Web*, *11*, 154–165. PMID:23807872

Tuomi, I. (2000). Data is more than knowledge: Implications of the reversed knowledge hierarchy for knowledge management and organizational memory. *Journal of Management Information Systems*, *16*(3), 103–117. doi:10.1080/0742 1222.1999.11518258

Turner, J. G., & MacClusky, T. L. (1994). *The construction of formal specifications An introduction to the model- based and Algebraic Approaches*. McGraw-Hill.

Turowski, K., & Weng, U. (2002). Representing and processing fuzzy information — an XML-based approach. *Knowledge-Based Systems*, *15*(1–2), 67–75. doi:10.1016/S0950-7051(01)00122-8

Uschold, M., & Grüninger, M. (1996). Ontologies: Principles. *Methods and Applications Knowledge Engineering Review*, *11*(02), 93–155. doi:10.1017/S0269888900007797

Van Rijsbergen, C. J. (1979). *Information Retrieval*. London: Butterworths.

Van Rijsbergen, C. J. (1992). Probabilistic retrieval revisited. *The Computer Journal*, *35*(3), 291–298. doi:10.1093/comjnl/35.3.291

Varzi, A. (1996). Parts, wholes, and part-whole relations: The prospects of Mereotopology. *Data & Knowledge Engineering*, *20*(3), 259–286. doi:10.1016/S0169-023X(96)00017-1

Vasconcelos, J., Kimble, C., & Gouveia, F. R. (2000). A design for a Group Memory system using Ontologies. *Proceedings of 5th UKAIS Conference*. McGraw Hill.

Velicanu, A., & Olaru, S. (2010). Optimizing Spatial Databases. *Informatica Economica*, *14*(2), 61–71.

Vembu, S., & Baumann, S. (2004). A Self-Organizing Map Based Knowledge Discovery for Music Recommendation Systems. *Computer Music Modeling and Retrieval Second International Symposium, CMMR 2004*.

Venus, S., & Akbari, A. H. A. (2008). *Mining of statistical data of one university to discover successful students*. Academic Press.

Verleysen, M., & François, D. (2005, June). The curse of dimensionality in data mining and time series prediction. In *International Work-Conference on Artificial Neural Networks* (pp. 758–770). Springer Berlin Heidelberg. doi:10.1007/11494669_93

Vesanto, J., & Alhoniemi, E. (2000). Clustering of the Self-Organizing Map. *IEEE Transactions on Neural Networks,* 11. PMID:18249787

Vesanto, J., Himberg, J., Alhoniemi, E., & Parhankangas, J. (1999). Self-organizing map in Matlab: the SOM Toolbox. *Proceedings of the Matlab DSP Conference 1999.*

Violleau, T. (2001). *Java Technology and XML.* Academic Press.

Vogrincic, S., & Bosnic, Z. (2011). Ontology- based multi-label classification of economic articles. *ComSIS, 8*(1), 101–119. doi:10.2298/CSIS100420034V

Vrandecic, D. (2010). *Ontology Evaluation.* Academic Press.

W3C, Boyer, J., Eastlake, D. E., & Reagle, J. (2002). *Exclusive XML Canonicalization, Version 1.0.* Retrieved April 2011, from http://www.w3.org/TR/2002/REC-xml-exc-c14n-20020718/

W3C. (1998). *Extensible Markup Language.* Retrieved October 2009, from http://www.w3.org/TR/1998/REC-xml-19980210

W3C. (2001). *XML Encryption Syntax and Processing.* W3C.

Walsh, M., & Crumbie, A. (2011). Initial evaluation of Stilwell:A multimedia virtual community. *Nurse Education in Practice, 11*(2), 136–140. doi:10.1016/j.nepr.2010.10.004 PMID:21071274

Wang, C., Zhang, P., Choi, R., & Eredita, M. D. (2002). Understanding consumers attitude toward advertising. *Eighth Americas conference on information systems* (pp. 1143–1148). Retrieved from http://citeseerx.ist.psu.edu/viewdoc/download?doi=10.1.1.12.8755&rep=rep1&type=pdf

Wang, X. J., Yu, M., Zhang, L., Cai, R., & Ma, W. Y. (2009). Argo: intelligent advertising by mining a user's interest from his photo collections. *Proceedings of the Third International Workshop on Data Mining and Audience Intelligence for Advertising* (pp. 18–26). Retrieved from http://dl.acm.org/citation.cfm?id=1592752

Wang, Y.-H., & Jhuo, P.-S. (2009). A Semantic Faceted Search with Rule-based Inference.*Proceedings of the International MultiConference of Engineers and Computer Scientists.*

Webster. (2011). *Definition of Knowledge.* Retrieved from http://www.merriam-webster.com/dictionary/knowledge?show=0&t=1316553888

Weckert, J. (2000). What is so bad about Internet content regulation? *Ethics and Information Technology, 2*(2), 105–111. doi:10.1023/A:1010077520614

Weerasinghe, D., Elmufti, K., Rajarajan, M., & Rakocevic, V. (2006). *XML Security based Access Control for Healthcare Information in Mobile Environment.* Paper presented at the Pervasive Health Conference and Workshops.

Weinberg, J. (2010). *2G Applications, An emerging media channel in developing nations.* Retrieved from http://nydigitallab.ogilvy.com/2010/05/19/2g-applications-an-emerging-media-channelin-developing-nations/

Weinberger, K. Q., & Saul, L. K. (2004). Unsupervised learning of image manifolds by semidefinite programming. In *Proceedings of the IEEE Conference on Computer Vision and Pattern Recognition (CVPR-04).*

Welty, C., Lehmann, F., Gruninger, G., & Uschold, M. (1999). *Ontologies: Expert Systems all over again?* In *The National Conference on Artificial Intelligence*, Austin, TX.

Wen, J. R., Nie, J. Y., & Zhang, H. J. (2001). Clustering user queries of a search engine. *Proceedings of the 10th international conference on World Wide Web* (pp. 162–168). Retrieved from http://dl.acm.org/citation.cfm?id=371974

Wenger, R. M., & Snyder, W. (2002). Cultivating Communities of practice: A guide to managing knowledge. Harvard Business School Press.

Wenger, E. (1998). *Communities of practice: Learning, Meaning, Identity.* Cambridge, UK: Cambridge University Press. doi:10.1017/CBO9780511803932

Wen, J. R., Nie, J. Y., & Zhang, H. J. (2002). Query clustering using user logs. *ACM Transactions on Information Systems*, *20*(1), 59–81. doi:10.1145/503104.503108

Whitemore, J. (2009). *Unified communications for the enterprise: hosted VoIP or cloud communications.* Retrieved from http://www.westipc.com/blog/2009/06/04/hosted-voip-or-cloud-communications/

Wiederhold, G. (1986). *Knowledge Base Management System.* New York: Springer.

Wielinga, B. J., & Schreiber, A. T. (1993). *Reusable and searchable knowledge bases: a European perspective.* First international conference on building and sharing of very large-scaled knowledge base, Tokyo, Japan.

Wilkinson, P. (2005). Construction Collaboration Technologies: The Extranet Evolution. Academic Press.

Williams, I. (2009). *Beginning XSLT and XPath: Transforming XML Documents and Data.* Wrox Press.

Witten, I. H., & Frank, E. (2005a). *Data Mining: Practical Machine Learning Tools and Techniques.* Academic Press.

Witten, I. H., & Frank, E. (2005b). Data Mining: Practical machine learning tools and techniques (2nd ed.). Academic Press.

Xu, J., & Liu, H. (2010). Web user clustering analysis based on KMeans algorithm. *2010 International Conference on Information Networking and Automation (ICINA)* (Vol. 2, pp. V2–6–V2–9). doi:10.1109/ICINA.2010.5636772

Yager, R. R. (2000). Targeted e-commerce marketing using fuzzy intelligent agents. *Intelligent Systems and their Applications, IEEE, 15*(6), 42-45. doi: 10.1109/5254.895859

Yager, R. R. (1988). On ordered weighted averaging aggregation operators in multicriteria decisionmaking. *Systems, Man and Cybernetics. IEEE Transactions on, 18*(1), 183–190. doi:10.1109/21.87068

Yager, R. R., & Pasi, G. (2001). Product category description for web-shopping in e-commerce. *International Journal of Intelligent Systems, 16*(8), 1009–1021. doi:10.1002/int.1046

Yan, J., Liu, N., Wang, G., Zhang, W., Jiang, Y., & Chen, Z. (2009). How much can behavioral targeting help online advertising? *Proceedings of the 18th international conference on World wide web* (pp. 261–270). Retrieved from http://dl.acm.org/citation.cfm?id=1526745

Yang, Y., & Chute, C. G. (1993). *An application of least squares fit mapping to text information retrieval.* Paper presented at the 16th annual international ACM SIGIR conference on Research and development in information retrieval, Pittsburgh, PA. doi:10.1145/160688.160738

Yang, Y., & Liu, X. (1999). *A re-examination of text categorization methods.* Paper presented at the 22nd annual international ACM SIGIR conference on Research and development in information retrieval, Berkeley, CA.

Yang, L. (2005). Pruning and visualizing generalized association rules in parallel coordinates. *IEEE Transactions on Knowledge and Data Engineering, 17*(1), 60–70. doi:10.1109/TKDE.2005.14

Yang, L. (2009). Visual association rules. In L. Liu & M. T. Özsu (Eds.), *Encyclopedia of Database Systems* (pp. 3346–3352). New York: Springer.

Yghini, M., Akbari, A., & Sharifi, M. (2008). *Mining on students and discovering groups of students those are available from the data and their relations.* Academic Press.

Yu, L. (2011). *A Developer's Guide to the Semantic Web.* Springer.

Yuexiao, Z. (1988). Definitions and Sciences of Information. *Information Processing & Management, 24*(4), 479–491. doi:10.1016/0306-4573(88)90050-7

Yu, J., & Liu, C. (2006). Performance Analysis of Mobile VPN Architecture. *4th Annual Conference on Telecommunications, and Information Technology,* Las Vegas

Zadeh, L. A. (1984). Making computers think like people: The term `fuzzy thinkingÂ¿ is pejorative when applied to humans, but fuzzy logic is an asset to machines in applications from expert systems to process control. *Spectrum, IEEE, 21*(8), 26-32. doi: 10.1109/mspec.1984.6370431

Zadeh, L. A. (1965). Fuzzy Sets. *Information and Control, 8*(3), 338–353. doi:10.1016/S0019-9958(65)90241-X

Zaki, M. J., & Aggarwal, C. C. (2003). *XRules: an effective structural classifier for XML data.* Paper presented at the ninth ACM SIGKDD international conference on Knowledge discovery and data mining, Washington, DC. doi:10.1145/956750.956787

Zaki, M. J., & Hsiao, C.-J. (2005). Efficient algorithms for mining closed itemsets and their lattice structure. *IEEE Transactions on Knowledge and Data Engineering, 17*(4), 462–478. doi:10.1109/TKDE.2005.60

Zanakis, S. H., & Becerra-Fernandez, I. (2005). Competitiveness of nations: A knowledge discovery examination. *European Journal of Operational Research, 166*(1), 185–211. doi:10.1016/j.ejor.2004.03.028

Zernik, U. (1991). *Lexical acquisition: Exploiting on-line resources to build a lexicon.* Hoboken, NJ: Lawrence Erlbaum Associates.

Zhang, F., Ma, Z. M., & Yan, L. (2013). Construction of fuzzy ontologies from fuzzy XML models. *Knowledge-Based Systems, 42*(0), 20–39. doi:10.1016/j.knosys.2012.12.015

Zhang, L., Stoffel, A., Behrisch, M., Mittelstädt, S., Schreck, T., Pompl, R., & Keim, D. et al. (2013). Visual analytics for the big data era - a comparative review of state-of-the-art commercial systems. In G. Santucci, & M. Ward (Eds.), *Proceedings of the 2012 IEEE Conference on Visual Analytics Science and Technology* (pp.173-182). Los Alamitos, CA: IEEE Computer Society.

Zhang, W., & Watts, S. (2008). Online communities as communities of practice: A case study. *Journal of Knowledge Management, 12*(4), 55–71. doi:10.1108/13673270810884255

Zheng, K., Xiong, H., Cui, Y., Chen, J., & Han, L. (2012). User Clustering-Based Web Service Discovery.*2012 Sixth International Conference on Internet Computing for Science and Engineering (ICICSE)* (pp. 276–279). doi:10.1109/ICICSE.2012.40

Zhu, X., Huang, Z., & Wu, X. (2013). Multi-view visual classification via a mixed-norm regularizer. In J. Pei, V.S. Tseng, L. Cao, H. Motoda, & G. Xu (Eds.), *Proceedings of the 17th Pacific-Asia Conference on Knowledge Discovery and Data Mining* (LNAI), (vol. 7818, pp. 520-531). Heidelberg, Germany: Springer. doi:10.1007/978-3-642-37453-1_43

Zins, C. (2007). Conceptions of, Information Science. *Journal of the American Society for Information Science and Technology*, *58*(3), 335–350. doi:10.1002/asi.20507

Zins, C. (2007b). Conceptual Approaches for defining data, information, and knowledge. *Journal of the American Society for Information Science and Technology*, *58*(4), 479–493. doi:10.1002/asi.20508

Zins, C. (2007c). Knowledge Map of Information Science. *Journal of the American Society for Information Science and Technology*, *58*(4), 526–535. doi:10.1002/asi.20505

Zuckerman, E. (2009). Intermediary censorship. In R. J. Deibert, J. G. Palfrey, R. Rohozinski, & J. Zittrain (Eds.), *Access Controlled: The Shaping of Power, Rights, and Rule in Cyberspace* (pp. 71–85). Cambridge, MA: MIT Press.

Zuleita, H., Lau, V., & Cheng, R. (2009). Cross-Layer Design of FDD-OFDM Systems based on ACK/NAK Feedbacks. *Information Theory. IEEE Transactions on*, *55*(10), 4568–4584.

Zur-Muehlen, M., Nickerson, J., & Swenson, K. (2005). Developing Web Services Choreography Standards – The Case of REST vs. SOAP. *Decision Support Systems*, *40*(1).

About the Contributors

Joan Lu is Professor in Informatics in the University of Huddersfield. She has been working in the areas of XML database, information retrieval research, mobile computing, Internet computing, mobile learning, etc. Her research projects have been collaborated with several EU, UK and other international institutions and industrial partners. The research work has been published into public domain together with a number of researchers in the academic world. She is also a member of British Computer Society, and Fellow of Higher Education Academy, UK.

Qiang Xu is a Senior lecturer at the School of Computing and Engineering in The University of Huddersfield, UK. His research activities cover computational modeling. Previously, Dr Xu was Senior Lecturer in the School of Science and Engineering at Teesside University from 2006 to 2013. In this role, Dr Xu supervised a number of PhD research projects and completed over 15 consultancy and grant applications. Dr Xu was Visiting Professor at the Northwest Polytechnic University, China from 2007 to 2012 and co-editor of two conference proceedings, key note speakers, regular reviewer for several internal journals (reviewed over 70 papers), and several internal conference committee member; and has published more than 70 papers. Dr Xu's research work has been cited worldwide by researchers in 8 nations including China, the USA, UK, Germany, Poland, India, Iran, and Russia.

* * *

Abdelmalek Amine received an engineering degree in Computer Science, a Magister diploma in Computational Science and PhD from Djillali Liabes University in collaboration with Joseph Fourier University of Grenoble. His research interests include data mining, text mining, ontology, classification, clustering, neural networks, and biomimetic optimization methods. He participates in the program committees of several international conferences and on the editorial boards of international journals. Prof. Amine is the head of GeCoDe-knowledge management and complex data-laboratory at UTM University of Saida, Algeria; he also collaborates with the "knowledge base and database" team of TIMC laboratory at Joseph Fourier University of Grenoble.

Faisal Ammari is an expert in XML security in bank industry with extensive working experience.

Christopher L. Carmichael received his B.C.Sc. (Hons.) and M.Sc. degrees, both from University of Manitoba, Canada, under the academic supervision of Prof. Carson K. Leung. Before that, Carmichael earned his diploma in mechanical engineering technology from Red River College, Canada, and spent a long career in designing and programming commercial control systems for building heating/air conditioning ventilation systems. Carmichael is currently conducting research in the areas of data mining, data visualization, and visual analytics, as well as prototyping private P2P network systems for audio, video, email and webpages with use of low-powered computers like Raspberry Pi.

Reda Mohamed Hamou received an engineering degree in computer Science from the Computer Science department of Djillali Liabes University of Sidi-Belabbes-Algeria and PhD (Artificial intelligence) from the same University. He has several publications in the field of BioInspired and Metaheuristic. His research interests include Data Mining, Text Mining, Classification, Clustering, computational intelligence, neural networks, evolutionary computation and Biomimetic optimization method. He is a head of research team in GecoDe laboratory. Dr. Hamou is an associate professor in technology faculty in UTMS University of Saida-Algeria.

Hosein Jafarkarimi earned PhD in Information Systems in 2015 and his Msc in information teknology management from Universiti Teknologi Malaysia in 2011. He is now a lecturer in IAU Iran and also works in Tehran Internet Center as R&D expert. His field of interests include computer ethics, behavioral studies and data mining.

Patrick Johnstone received his B.Sc. degree—with major in computer science—from the University of Manitoba, Canada. During his study, Johnstone acquired research experience in the areas of data mining and visual analytics under the academic supervision of Prof. Carson K. Leung. Since graduation, Johnstone has been working as a software developer focused on distributed computing and system integration for a company offering software solutions for to the telecommunication sector. Recently, he has moved to a new role as a technical business analyst focused on in-depth analysis and system design in the same company in Winnipeg, Canada.

Carson K. Leung received his B.Sc. (Hons.), M.Sc., and Ph.D. degrees all from the University of British Columbia, Vancouver, Canada. He is currently a Professor at the University of Manitoba, Canada. He has contributed more than 150 refereed publications on the topics of big data analytics, databases, data mining, information retrieval, social network analysis, as well as visual analytics---including papers in ACM Transactions on Database Systems (TODS), Future Generation Computer Systems (FGCS), Journal of Organizational Computing and Electronic Commerce, Social Network Analysis and Mining, World Wide Web Journal (WWW), IEEE International Conference on Data Engineering (ICDE), IEEE International Conference on Data Mining (ICDM), the SCA 2012 Best Paper on social computing and its applications, the IEEE/ACM ASONAM-FAB 2016 Best Paper on foundations and applications of big data analytics, as well as five book chapters and encyclopedia entries for IGI Global.

Hee Jee Mei is a senior lecturer at the Faculty of Education, Universiti Teknologi Malaysia which is located at the southern part of Peninsular Malaysia. She has been serving the university since year 1998. She received her Ph.D from Deakin University, Australia, majoring in Online, Flexible and Distance Education. She has been teaching courses such as Educational Research Methodology, Assessment and Evaluation, Pedagogy, and Curriculum Development. Her research interested is in e-learning and online assessment.

Usman M. Mistura has B.Tech in Mathematics and Computer Science from Federal University of Technology Minna,in Niger State, Nigeria and M.sc in Computer Science from Ahmadu Bello University Zaria, Nigeria. She is currently teaching in Computer Science department, University of Abuja, Nigeria.

Baramee Navanopparatskul was born in January 1977. He received his Bachelor's degree in Environmental Engineering at King Mongkut's University of Technology Thonburi in 1997. He then pursued his study and graduated in Master's degree in Environmental Management at Illinois Institute of Technology, Chicago, USA, in 2000. Currently, he works as a news anchor at Channel 3 and as managing director at Suki Media Services Co., Ltd.

Yousef Rabadi is researcher in distributed systems with several years working experience in both industry and academic world.

Rananand, Pirongrong Ramasoota, PhD, is currently Head of the Department of Journalism and Information, at the Faculty of Communication Arts, Chulalongkorn University. She is also Director of the Media Policy Center (MPC) which is a collaborative project between the Faculty of Communication Arts and the National Telecommunications Commission (NTC) of Thailand. She has actively participated in several advocacy endeavors related to media reform, including being commissioner in the reading of the country's first Public Television law, and consistently organizing seminars about media policy and regulation. She received her PhD in communication studies from Simon Fraser University in Vancouver, Canada, where she received the Canadian International. Development Agency (CIDA) scholarship. She was also one of the principal researchers in the famous Media Reform research project, funded by the Thailand Research Fund (TRF). Her research interests include media policy and regulation, social implications of ICTs, and media and democratization.

Robab Saadatdoost received the B.E. degree in Software engineering from the University of Kharazmi, Iran, in 2005, the Master degree in Information Technology Management from Universiti Teknologi Malaysia in 2011 and the PhD degree in Information Systems in Universiti Teknologi Malaysia in 2016. She is lecturer in Parand University. Her current research interests include educational technologies, Cloud Computing, Qualitative researches and Data Mining / Knowledge discovery process. She was the recipient of the Malaysia International Scholarship (MIS) in 2011.

Grace L. Samson received a Bachelor of Science degree in Computer science in 2004 from the University of Abuja, Nigeria, an MSC in Computer Science and informatics in 2013 from the University of Huddersfield, UK, and she is currently a Doctoral research student in the Department of Computer Science and informatics, University of Huddersfield, which she joined in 2015. She has worked as a research and teaching staff at the Department of Computer Science, University of Abuja, Nigeria.

Ahlam Sawsaa She received her PhD from University of Huddersfield 2013, and B.s and M.S degree from Benghazi university in Library and Information Science. She is serving as lecture in the Department of Library and Information Science at Benghazi University, and supervisor of many projects of graduate degrees. She is author of a book and more than seven international publication, reviewer in international conferences and journals. She is interested in Ontologies and semantic.

Alex Tze Hiang Sim received his PhD degree from Monash University, Australia. He was working as a business & program analyst for six years after graduated from his first degree. He was then attached to the Department of Information Systems at Universiti Teknologi Malaysia (UTM) as a senior lecturer. He has been teaching courses such as Data Mining, Research Methods, and Databases. His research interest is in Data Mining and its applications. He has supervised more than twenty international PhD and master students. He is currently a member of AIS, IEEE and ACM.

Sukree Sinthupinyo, PhD, is currently a Assistant Professor at the Department of Computer Engineering, Chulalongkorn University. He is an expert in big data and artificial intelligence. He is also a team leader of student to compete in International Olympiad of Informatics for several years.

David Stupples's current role is Director of Electronic Warfare Systems Research at City, University of London with particular interest in electronic intelligence (ELINT). His focus is in data fusion for activity-based intelligence and sense-making within 'big data' collected from electromagnetic spectrum sensors. David's early career work was undertaken at Royal Signals and Radar Establishment (RSRE) Malvern in the UK, Hughes Aircraft Corporation in California and GCHQ, and involved Intelligence Surveillance & Reconnaissance (ISR) systems.

Brook Wu is an Associate Professor and currently Chair of the Informatics Department in the Ying Wu College of Computing at New Jersey Institute of Technology. She a Ph.D. in Information Science in 2001 from State University of New York at Albany. Her current research interests include: text mining, information extraction, knowledge organization, information retrieval, and natural language processing.

Roy Ruokun Xing received his B.Sc. degree—with major in computer science specialized in human-computer interaction (HCI)—from the University of Manitoba, Canada. During his study, Xing acquired research experience in the areas of data mining and visual analytics under the academic supervision of Prof. Carson K. Leung. Currently, Xing is working as a software developer in oil and gas industry in Calgary, Canada. Xing is interested in the software and database development, with a focus on user interface and database structure design.

Wei Xiong is an assistant professor of Information Systems in the School of Business at Iona College. His research interests include data mining and its business applications. He holds a Ph.D. and an M.S. in Information Systems from New Jersey Institute of Technology.

David Sonny Hung-Cheung Yuen received his B.Sc. degree with a major in computer science specialized in databases, human-computer interaction (HCI) and software engineering from the University of Manitoba, Canada. During his study, Yuen acquired research experience in the areas of data mining and visual analytics under the academic supervision of Prof. Carson K. Leung. Currently, Yuen is working for IBM Canada Ltd in Toronto, Canada.

Index

Stay Current on the Latest Emerging Research Developments

Become an IGI Global Reviewer for Authored Book Projects

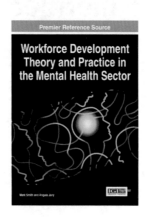

The overall success of an authored book project is dependent on quality and timely reviews.

In this competitive age of scholarly publishing, constructive and timely feedback significantly decreases the turnaround time of manuscripts from submission to acceptance, allowing the publication and discovery of progressive research at a much more expeditious rate. Several IGI Global authored book projects are currently seeking highly qualified experts in the field to fill vacancies on their respective editorial review boards:

Applications may be sent to:
development@igi-global.com

Applicants must have a doctorate (or an equivalent degree) as well as publishing and reviewing experience. Reviewers are asked to write reviews in a timely, collegial, and constructive manner. All reviewers will begin their role on an ad-hoc basis for a period of one year, and upon successful completion of this term can be considered for full editorial review board status, with the potential for a subsequent promotion to Associate Editor.

If you have a colleague that may be interested in this opportunity, we encourage you to share this information with them.

Information Resources Management Association

Become an IRMA Member

Members of the **Information Resources Management Association (IRMA)** understand the importance of community within their field of study. The Information Resources Management Association is an ideal venue through which professionals, students, and academicians can convene and share the latest industry innovations and scholarly research that is changing the field of information science and technology. Become a member today and enjoy the benefits of membership as well as the opportunity to collaborate and network with fellow experts in the field.

IRMA Membership Benefits:

- **One FREE Journal Subscription**

- **30% Off Additional Journal Subscriptions**

- **20% Off Book Purchases**

- Updates on the latest events and research on Information Resources Management through the IRMA-L listserv.

- Updates on new open access and downloadable content added to Research IRM.

- A copy of the Information Technology Management Newsletter twice a year.

- A certificate of membership.

IRMA Membership $195

Scan code or visit **irma-international.org** and begin by selecting your free journal subscription.

Membership is good for one full year.

Printed in the United States
By Bookmasters